Juvenile Delinquency

MACMILLAN CRIMINAL JUSTICE SERIES

Allen/Simonsen: *Corrections in America,* 4th ed.

Bartollas/with Jaeger: *American Criminal Justice*

Binder/Geis/Bruce: *Juvenile Delinquency*

Bottom/Kostanoski: *Security and Loss Control*

Bowker: *Women and Crime in America*

Brantingham/Brantingham: *Patterns in Crime*

Chambliss: *Criminal Law in Action*

Chambliss: *Exploring Criminology*

Chambliss: *Harry King: A Professional Thief's Journey*

Conklin: *Criminology,* 2nd ed.

Hagan: *Research Methods in Criminal Justice and Criminology*

Hudzik/Cordner/Edwards: *Planning in Criminal Justice Organizations and Systems*

McCaghy: *Crime in America,* 2nd ed.

Pursley: *Introduction to Criminal Justice,* 4th ed.

Radelet: *Police and the Community,* 4th ed.

Simonsen/Gordon: *Juvenile Justice in America,* 2nd ed.

Smykla: *Community-Based Corrections: Principles and Practices*

Smykla: *Probation and Parole*

Swanson/Territo/Taylor: *Police Administration,* 2nd ed.

Juvenile Delinquency

Historical, Cultural, Legal Perspectives

Arnold Binder
University of California, Irvine

Gilbert Geis
University of California, Irvine

Dickson Bruce
University of California, Irvine

Macmillan Publishing Company
NEW YORK

Collier Macmillan Publishers
LONDON

Copyright © 1988, Macmillan Publishing Company,
a division of Macmillan, Inc.

PRINTED IN THE UNITED STATES OF AMERICA

Macmillan Publishing Company
866 Third Avenue, New York, New York 10022

Collier Macmillan Canada, Inc.

LIBRARY OF CONGRESS CATALOGING-IN-PUBLICATION DATA

Binder, Arnold.
　Juvenile delinquency.

　Includes index.
　1. Juvenile delinquency.　2. Juvenile delinquency—
United States.　I. Geis, Gilbert.　II. Bruce, Dickson D.,
1946–　　　III. Title.
HV9069.B59　1988　　　364.3′6′0973　　　87-21975.
ISBN 0-02-309871-6

Printing: 1 2 3 4 5 6 7　　Year: 8 9 0 1 2 3 4

Picture research by Yvonne R. Freund

ISBN　0-02-309871-6

This book is dedicated to three groups of people,
critical elements in our respective lives:
Ginny, Jeff, and Jenni; Robley and the kids;
and Mary and Emily.

Preface

Juvenile Delinquency: Historical, Cultural, Legal Perspectives was written as the next step in an evolutionary process that has produced increasingly excellent textbooks on juvenile delinquency over the past two decades. The incremental improvement shown in our book includes:

- General comprehensiveness.
- Inclusion of the most recent empirical results and theoretical thinking.
- Treatment of juvenile delinquency as a social phenomenon that is in constant interaction with juvenile delinquency as a legal creation.
- Placement of the issues of delinquency and juvenile justice in an historical context that is fully developed up to the current era with the degree of accuracy one expects in a history text.
- Incorporation of the latest possible statutory enactments and case law decisions.
- And a writing style aimed at keeping students interested in the material presented.

To help in achieving those ends, the book has been rewritten several times over a four-year period while being used, in photocopy form, as the text in a high-enrollment course on juvenile delinquency at the University of California, Irvine.

We believe that the comprehensiveness of the book (including several topics not found in comparable texts) allows the instructor, as it has allowed us, to handle the course in other than traditional lecture style. Some lecturing is clearly necessary to clarify points, to expand the discussions in areas where the teacher is especially knowledgeable, and to discuss issues that are not covered despite the book's comprehensiveness, but, in general, those should not be extremely time-consuming considering the number of class hours available during a quarter or semester. We propose that the instructor allow the students to use the text as the source of almost all relevant information such that the class, no matter the size, may be used as a forum for: discussions generated by students' reactions to their developing knowledge in a genuinely engrossing field; presentations of invited guests who are professionals in the juvenile justice system or experts in a relevant field; and for currently available films and videotapes of high quality (several of these are discussed in the accompanying Instructor's Manual).

The book is divided into five parts. *Part I* provides the foundations for the central themes of the book by elucidating the meaning of the concept "juvenile delinquency," by indicating how delinquency is evaluated and related to socio-demographic variables, and by showing the development of notions regarding childhood and adolescence in Western civilization. *Part II* contains the theories, presented over the years, that explain delinquency and related phenomena, and details how such theories often collide with popular explanations. *Part III* traces the methods used in the attempts at social control of delinquency in the United States from the period shortly after independence. Emphasis is on current law and the modes of implementation. The methods of control in several other countries are covered too. *Part IV* focuses on the community as a resource in the treatment of delinquency and on certain of its institutions that are thought to be influential in stimulating or abetting delinquency. Finally, *Part V* is devoted to such special issues as female delinquency, significant problem areas in youthful offending, and future directions in three broad spheres of concern.

The book is well suited for a course that is a semester in length, but can be adapted easily for a quarter course, if the instructor so desires, by omitting certain of the chapters that are not critical in the development of the central themes. Chapters 13, 16, and 17 are such examples.

Finally, we would like to express our appreciation to several people. Dear to our collective hearts is Carol W. Wyatt. As friend, confidante, and master at word processing, she simultaneously made our lives more pleasant and mastered an overwhelmingly difficult task efficiently and gracefully. Many thanks to Carol and also to the following reviewers who evaluated an early version of the book: Donna Hale, Edward S. Ryan of *Mansfield University,* and William Selke of *Indiana University.* Their painstaking, effective, insightful reviews were critical in motivating and guiding a major revision — a revision which, we believe, has improved the book enormously.

A.B.
G.G.
D.B.

Contents

PART II   THEORIES AND THEIR USES

Chapter 3   Delinquency Theory: Present Considerations and Early Formulations

Chapter 4   Constitutional, Psychiatric, and Psychological Theories

PART V   SPECIAL ISSUES

PART I

Introduction to the Issues

CHAPTER 1

Defining Juvenile Delinquency and Determining Its Extent

© Dan Cabe, Photo Researchers

Every culture has a broad set of regulations and expectations that define proper behavior for children. These regulations and expectations take such forms as codes, laws, and rules and are conveyed to children either explicitly or by implication, as when they are told that certain behavior is "good" while other behavior is "bad." Supplementing the broad set of regulations and expectations of the general culture are the regulations and expectations of its various subcultures. Thus, in the United States we have general laws regarding school attendance and working conditions for children. But each school district and each school in a given district has regulations that apply to children within its domain. And the pattern extends down to one of the smallest subunits in our culture, the family, in which there are such rules as that one does not stay out past a certain hour without parental consent or that one does not hit a brother or sister.

The layers of regulations and expectations have evolved in their respective domains to serve many purposes. Some are aimed at preventing a child from directly hurting himself or herself or someone else; others are aimed at preventing damage to or loss of property; others are oriented toward inculcating habits and patterns of behavior that prepare a child for a style of life in the mode of those in authority; others attempt to make the child-rearing process as minimally disruptive to the social or family system as possible; and still others are aimed at controlling or inhibiting behavior that people in authority find annoying or personally offensive.

Associated with many of the regulations and expectations are sanctions or consequences that will, or may, result if behavior deviates significantly from prescribed paths. To illustrate at the family level, a youngster may be deprived of his allowance for the week if he strikes his sister, or a youngster may be sent to her room if she uses an obscenity at the dinner table. At another cultural level, an adolescent may be suspended from school if he or she has deliberately smashed a window or insulted a teacher.

At the general cultural level, we have developed complex systems to deal with the large array of children who show significant behavioral aberrations. Two prominent systems are the mental health system and the juvenile justice system. Generally speaking, the mental health system handles youngsters who show such disturbances as excessive anxiety or a fear of riding in a car, disturbances that are assumed to result from "illness of the mind." And the juvenile justice system primarily handles youngsters who violate laws designed to protect the personal and property rights of others. A child who assaults another person or who steals is, thus, a candidate for the juvenile justice system.

That there may be ambiguity as to which system is appropriate in a given instance is illustrated in the following news item from the *Los Angeles Times* (Part I, p. 8, February 16, 1985):

> A 15-year-old boy who was determined to be rid of his braces pulled a gun on an orthodontist and told him to remove them, the doctor said Friday.
> Police said the youth entered a dentist's office in Grosse Pointe Woods armed with a .45-caliber automatic pistol and asked to see a dentist to have his braces removed.
> The dentist refused because the boy did not have proof of parental permission, so the boy cocked the pistol and aimed it at the doctor, who immediately took the boy to a dental chair while a nurse called police.

Youngsters are introduced to some of the sanctions associated with the juvenile justice system.

When the police arrived, one officer spoke to the boy, and when he turned to look, the other officers rushed him. In the ensuing scuffle, the boy allegedly fired one shot that hit the floor, then grabbed an officer's pistol, causing another shot to be fired into the floor.

Jack Patterson, Grosse Pointe Woods director of public safety, said the boy spent a few hours at a psychiatric center after the Feb. 8 incident.

There were no further media reports about this episode, so we do not know whether the boy was found to be without need for further mental health care or whether he will continue to receive treatment. It is obvious that the boy might have been dealt with as a juvenile delinquent who had committed a serious offense, especially if the dentist had insisted. It should also be noted that the boy is not identified in the newspaper story, whereas an adult involved in a similar incident probably would have been.

In the United States a book devoted to the topic *juvenile delinquency* is generally considered to encompass youngsters who show behavioral patterning that could activate the juvenile justice system. That, of course, includes assault and stealing, but it also includes various other behaviors that are not as obviously appropriate possible triggers for intervention by that system. For example, children who are truant or who run away from home or who disobey their parents are candidates for intervention by the juvenile justice system as a result of fortuitous historical development of the system. It would seem at least arguable that the mental health system is more appropriate for truants or runaways or ungovernable children than the juvenile justice system.

The Meaning and Extent of Delinquency _____

What Is a "Juvenile Delinquent?"

In the preceding section, it was pointed out that a book on juvenile delinquency covers youngsters who behave in a fashion that can produce a reaction by the juvenile justice system. But that does not define the concept *juvenile delinquent*. As it turns out, the task of defining the phrase is vastly more difficult than it may seem on the surface.

Legal Codes. In exploring that issue, let us initially turn to the manner in which delinquency has been specified in legal statutes—the ultimate basis for all other formulations about the concept. In the process, we will use examples from the analysis of state statutes reported by Hutzler and Sestak in 1977. One must realize that statutes, particularly those dealing with crime and delinquency, change constantly, so that some of the examples presented below may no longer exist in code books. But the purpose of the illustrations is to demonstrate the diversity of definitions for delinquent behavior, not to present a summary of current statutes. Indeed, presenting current information regarding delinquency statutes in a book of this sort is like trying to reach a destination by going half the remaining distance on each move.

As a first example, a statute from Montana given by Hutzler and Sestak (1977:41) specifies:

> "Delinquent youth" means a youth: (a) who has committed an offense which, if committed by an adult, would constitute a criminal offense; (b) who, having been placed on probation as a delinquent youth or a youth in need of supervision, violates any condition of his probation.

On the other hand, a statute from Mississippi specifies (1977:40,41):

> "Delinquent child" is synonymous with the meaning of, what is commonly called a juvenile offender, and means any child not less than ten (10) years of age whose occupation, behavior, environment or associations are injurious to his welfare or the welfare of other children; or who deserts his home; or who is habitually disobedient to or beyond the control of his parents, guardian or custodian; or who being required to attend school willfully violates rules thereof, or willfully absents himself therefrom; or who violates any state law or municipal ordinance; or who, by reason of being habitually wayward or habitually disobedient, becomes an incorrigible or uncontrollable child; or who so deports himself as to injure or endanger the morals or health of himself or any other person.

The first level of difficulty in defining a juvenile delinquent becomes apparent in comparing the statutes. The Montana statute defines a "deliquent youth" as one who has either committed a crime or violated probation, while the Mississippi statute includes under "delinquent child" a youth (ten years of age or older) who is "habitually disobedient," whose "associations are injurious to his welfare or to the welfare of other children," and even who "deports himself" in a manner that may endanger public morals. Thus, a youngster who could be considered "delinquent" under the Mississippi code might not be so regarded under the Montana one.

Other state codes define a "delinquent child" in terms of such behavior as the following (1977:30,49,53):

> begs or solicits alms or money in public places [South Carolina]
> habitually uses obscene or profane language [South Carolina]
> associates with immoral or vicious persons [West Virginia]
> has engaged in indecent or immoral conduct [Connecticut]

And consider further a statute like that of Indiana, presented in Hutzler and Sestak (1977:34), which specifies a "delinquent child" as one "who commits an act which, if committed by an adult, would be a crime, except . . . murder," or the statutes of states like California, Missouri, and Nebraska, which only specify the jurisdiction of the juvenile court and do not use the word *delinquent* in any form. For example, the Missouri statute is as follows (1977:41):

> Except as otherwise provided herein, the juvenile court shall have exclusive original jurisdiction in proceedings: . . .
> (2) Involving any child who is alleged to have violated a state law or municipal ordinance, or any person who is alleged to have violated a state law or municipal ordinance prior to attaining the age of seventeen years, in which cases jurisdiction may be taken by the court of the circuit in which the child or person resides or may be found or in which the violation is alleged to have occurred.

Thus, under the code of Indiana a sixteen-year-old violent rapist would be "delinquent," as would a youngster who deliberately tried to shoot someone but missed, while a sixteen-year-old murderer would be regarded as an adult offender. And in California, Missouri, and Nebraska the codes provide no legal basis for designating a youngster delinquent. In California, a youth who commits a criminal act is simply specified as a 602 (a section of the state Welfare and Institutions Code) offender.

The Delinquent Act. Beyond the difficulties of defining *juvenile delinquent* that stem from the various idiosyncrasies of legal codes, there are complications associated with the meaning given to a behavioral act by social reaction to that act. Suppose, for example, two boys commit identical criminal acts, but only one of them is arrested and later adjudicated a delinquent under the relevant state statute, and perhaps sent to an institution. One might feel comfortable in calling that boy a juvenile delinquent. But what about the boy who was never arrested? He committed a criminal act identical to that of the adjudicated boy and may not have been taken into custody for entirely fortuitous reasons — perhaps for no reason other than that an absence of witnesses or a busy caseload kept the police from a thorough investigation in his case.

Are detection, arrest, adjudication (conviction), and confinement necessary to define a delinquent? If that were the case, only a very small proportion of youngsters who commit criminal offenses would be designated juvenile delinquents. And the problem is essentially the same if only detection, arrest, and adjudication are necessary for the definition.

The issue was faced by Wolfgang, Figlio, and Sellin (1972) in their longitudinal study of boys born in 1945 who lived in the city of Philadelphia from their tenth to their eighteenth birthdays. The goals of the investigation were to determine the age when delinquency started, its progression or cessation, and the relationship of the delinquent behavior to various personal and social characteristics of the delinquents. Comparison of the characteristics of delinquents with boys who never behaved in a delinquent manner was also important for the study. To accomplish those ends, it was necessary to define or identify the delinquents so that they could be studied and compared with the remaining group of nondelinquents. The investigators considered defining delinquents as youngsters who had been adjudicated (found guilty) by a court but rejected that approach because (1972:14)

> we would have had to ignore police data except when they applied to boys whose involvement in delinquent events was subsequently affirmed by a court decision, which in nearly all cases would have been handed down by a judge of the juvenile court. Another consequence of using such official judicial decisions for defining the delinquents in the cohort would necessarily have been the inclusion of all other boys, with no matter how many police contacts, among our nondelinquents.

In addition, they argued (1972:15):

> it is generally admitted today that to limit oneself to court-determined delinquency would result in a highly biased view of the problem. Juveniles brought into court are a selected group: boys, Negroes, older children, those with many previous arrests, those from high-rate delinquency areas, and those who have committed serious offenses dominate. The very young, the petty offender, and children from advantaged homes are underrepresented in the court group.

They consequently settled on identifying delinquents on the basis of police contact. Using police records, they argued, "we are closer in time to the offender's specific conduct and are not disturbed by the series of often unpredictable administrative decisions which intervene between the discovery of any given offender and his ultimate disposition by a court" (1972:15).

Wolfgang, Figlio, and Sellin were, of course, well aware that a vast array of juvenile offenses never come to the attention of the police and that arrests (and official records) do not follow in many cases when they do come to their attention. They take the following position on that point (1972:17):

> When one relies on police data for a study of delinquency, one realizes, therefore, that the delinquencies charged to boys apprehended by the police represent only the visible illegal conduct, that the total record of their delinquencies during their juvenile years contains only their officially recorded misbehaviors, and that an unknown number of illegal acts which they may have committed have escaped official notice. At present, we have no satisfactory way of estimating this number with confidence. Our research is based, then, on the officially recorded delinquencies of the cohort. We have been compelled to adopt this policy, fully conscious of the fact that its effect on the findings of our research is not calculable. We do know

that there are differences in the willingness of victims to bring an offender to public notice, depending on the social class of the offender, the degree of tolerance toward delinquent conduct in different areas and social groups in a community and toward different kinds of delinquency, the relative strength of the victim's belief in the ability or desire of the police to find the offender, etc. If, for instance, a delinquent's family indemnifies the victim for his loss of property and as a result the offense is not reported, a juvenile from a wealthy family would not have as full an official record of delinquency as one from a poor family, who lacks this means of covering up his misconduct. On the other hand, if poor people have less confidence in the police than have the middle and upper classes, they will fail to report offenses that would be reported by the well to do. We can only point to the existence of differential reporting of delinquency and admit that we cannot estimate its effect on our research.

In attempting to answer the question that opened this discussion, we can state that the expression *juvenile delinquent* is not definable in a formal way that carries widespread meaning. But clearly that does not rule out defining a delinquent, for a particular study or for a particular theoretical reason, as one who has been sent to a juvenile institution or as one who has been adjudicated or as one who has been arrested. Moreover, the use of the expression conveys enough information to make it useful in general communication. Thus, if a person states that he or she is taking a course in juvenile delinquency or that a group of boys is "a bunch of juvenile delinquents," one knows reasonably well the meaning being communicated. Trouble arises only when greater specificity is required or demanded.

What Is the Extent of Offending by Juveniles?

The Difficulties of Assessment. As we have seen in the preceding discussion of state statutes, offenses by youngsters include not only such crimes as murder, rape, and robbery but also such phenomena as truancy, ungovernability, and disobedience. These latter offenses are called *status offenses* because they are unique to the status of being a minor. That is, an adult could not be arrested for the offense of truancy no matter how many classes were missed, nor could an adult be charged with ungovernability or disobedience no matter how he or she behaved toward a parent, a teacher, or even a spouse.

In other terms, the justice system is an appropriate response mechanism when there is criminal behavior on the part of adults. But the justice system may be activated for minors not only when there is criminal behavior but also when there is a status offense such as truancy, ungovernability, or disobedience.

Returning to state statutes for the moment, it is important to point out that some list status offenses along with criminal offenses in the specification of "delinquency," as in the case of Mississippi, while others use separate categories for criminal and status offenses. In many of these latter cases, a youngster who commits a status offense is designated by expressions like "child in need of supervision" (frequently abbreviated as CHINS or CINS), "person in need of supervision" (frequently abbreviated as PINS), or "youth in need of supervision."

Montana is a state that separately specifies criminal and status offenses — its statute specifying a "delinquent youth" was given above. The code defines a status offender as follows (Hutzler and Sestak, 1977:41,42):

> "Youth in need of supervision" means a youth who commits an offense prohibited by law which, if committed by an adult, would not constitute a criminal offense, including but not limited to a youth who:
>
> **(a)** violates any Montana municipal or state law regarding use of alcoholic beverages by minors; or
> **(b)** habitually disobeys the reasonable and lawful demands of his parents or guardian, or is ungovernable and beyond their control; or
> **(c)** being subject to compulsory school attendance is habitually truant from school; or
> **(d)** has committed any of the acts of a delinquent youth but whom the youth court in its discretion chooses to regard as a youth in need of supervision.

Louisiana distinguishes between a "delinquent child" and a "child in need of supervision" as follows (1977:38):

> "Delinquent act" means an act designated a crime under the statutes or ordinances of this state, or of another state if the act occurred in another state, or under federal law.
> "Delinquent child" means a child who has committed a delinquent act and is in need of care or rehabilitation.
> "Child in need of supervision" means a child who:
>
> **(a)** being subject to compulsory school attendance, is habitually truant from school; or
> **(b)** habitually disobeys the reasonable and lawful demands of his parents, tutor, or other custodian, and is ungovernable and beyond their control; or
> **(c)** has committed an offense not classified as criminal or one applicable only to children; and
> **(d)** in any of the foregoing, is in need of care or rehabilitation.

As a final example of state statutes that separately classify "delinquents" and status offenders, we have the following from New York (1977:45):

> "Juvenile delinquent." A person over seven and less than sixteen years of age who does any act which, if done by an adult, would constitute a crime.
> "Person in need of supervision." A male less than sixteen years of age and a female less than eighteen years of age who does not attend school in accord with the provisions of part one of article sixty-five of the education law or who is incorrigible, ungovernable or habitually disobedient and beyond the lawful control of parent or other lawful authority.

Those states that do not use the term *delinquent* in their statutes, as is the case for California, Missouri, and Nebraska, among others, specify jurisdiction of the juvenile court separately for criminal-type offenders and status offenders. Thus, in Missouri, the counterpart for status offenders of the statute given above for violators of criminal laws is as follows (1977:41):

Except as otherwise provided herein, the juvenile court shall have exclusive original jurisdiction in proceedings: . . .

(1) Involving any child who may be a resident of or found within the county and who is alleged to be in need of care and treatment because: . . .
  (c) the behavior, environment or associations of the child are injurious to his welfare or to the welfare of others.

In California, where a youngster who commits a criminal act is called a 602 offender in accordance with the number of the defining section of the state code, a status offender is called a 601 offender. In both cases, the code states that a minor who behaves in a certain way — violating a criminal law in the case of Section 602 and acting in an unacceptable manner like not attending school in the case of Section 601 — falls within the jurisdiction of the juvenile court.

Official Data. Trying to deal with the issue of the extent of juvenile offending seems bewildering, given that statutory offenses for youngsters encompass the range from serious crimes to such peccadilloes as disobeying parents or sipping an alcoholic beverage. But order can be achieved by various simplifying paths. For one, it is possible to focus solely on the classifications used in such official records as those reported in the *Uniform Crime Reports (UCR)*, a document published annually by the Federal Bureau of Investigation (FBI). Data in *UCR* include numbers of offenses known to the police, numbers of offenses cleared by arrest, and characteristics of arrested people. Other major sources of crime data are the reports of state bureaus or divisions of criminal statistics. For example, the Bureau of Criminal Statistics and Special Services of California publishes statewide data in *Crime and Delinquency in California* and data on a county-by-county basis in a *Criminal Justice Profile* series. One can use a county profile to determine the number of juvenile arrests within each city of that county for various felonies, for misdemeanors, and for status offenses.

Beyond those major sources of official data, records are maintained by such public entities as county governments, city governments, police departments, probation departments, and courts. A prime illustration of the use of this type of source is the research of Wolfgang, Figlio, and Sellin (1972), which was discussed earlier in the chapter. Those investigators used the records of the Philadelphia Police Department to determine which youngsters in their pool had official contacts with the police (and who were, accordingly, designated delinquent).

But the existence of official records depends upon the process whereby some person reports an event to an official who enters it on an appropriate form or in a computer memory. Clearly, there is no entry in official records when a police officer disregards an alcoholic violation on the part of a minor, or when a youngster steals candy from a supermarket and the loss is never discovered, or when a woman is raped and does not report the incident.

Self-report Data. An attempt is made to obtain information about offenses that never make official records by the method of self-report. Self-reports were introduced as a systematic approach to measuring delinquency by Short

An arrest that will lead to an entry in the *UCR*.

and Nye in 1957 following preliminary work by Porterfield (1946), Wallerstein and Wyle (1947), and Murphy, Shirley, and Witmer (1946). In the method of self-report, youngsters of the general population are interviewed or administered a questionnaire that contains specific items about offenses they may have previously committed. The usual setting for sampling and interviewing or administering the questionnaire is the school.

The self-report approach was widely used over the years following 1957 and in that process became firmly established for measuring and evaluating delinquency. Particularly prominent in advancement of the technique is the work of Erickson and Empey (1963), Empey and Erickson (1966), Gold (1966), Hirschi (1969), Gold (1970), Hindelang (1971), Elliott and Voss (1974), Tittle, Villemez, and Smith (1978), and Hindelang, Hirschi, and Weis (1981).

The method of self-report depends upon two characteristics of the reporting youngsters that may or may not actually exist: good memory and reasonable honesty in responding to the items. One might expect some reluctance on the part of people to report their involvement in offenses, particularly if those offenses are serious crimes.

Victim Data. Another method of measuring crime is worthy of mention, although its implications for assessing delinquency are limited. The method consists of determining the characteristics of crimes from the victims of those crimes. A high level of sophistication in the overall approach has been achieved in the National Crime Survey, sponsored by the Bureau of Justice Statistics and conducted by the U.S. Census Bureau. In the survey, people, selected randomly, are asked if they have recently been victims of crime and, if they answer affirmatively, are asked questions about various characteristics of themselves, the crimes, and the offenders, including the perceived ages of the offenders.

As in the case of the self-report approach, success with this method depends upon both accurate memory and a willingness to respond.

Measurement Results: The Extent of Juvenile Delinquency and Its Distribution over Social Groups _____

One obvious goal in the measuring of delinquency is to determine its rate of occurrence, overall and by specific offenses. But another goal, one that has important practical and theoretical implications, is to determine the relative contributions of various social groups to the total figures. Both goals will be pursued in the following sections.

The Complications

As one might expect, the picture one gets of delinquency and its distributions is a function of the measurement method one uses. To illustrate, if official data such as *UCR* are used in the evaluation of delinquency, one is likely to infer that criminal behavior is concentrated among young males of low socioeconomic status living in cities and that there is particularly heavy concentration among blacks and Latinos. On the other hand, the use of self-report data is associated with the inference that criminal offending is so widespread throughout the population that it is artificial to associate it primarily with certain socioeconomic or racial or ethnic groups living in urban areas.

It is important to note that a given theory is often a direct function of the data source used, accepted, selected, or preferred by the theorizer. For example, Shaw and McKay (1942) used police, court, and correctional records in their study of delinquency in Chicago over the period 1900–1940. And their resulting theory is that the path toward juvenile delinquency starts with urban deterioration and proceeds as follows: urban deterioration produces socially disorganized communities that lack control over children; the lack of social control encourages the formation of street gangs, which in turn develop and transmit delinquent behavioral patterns. Minority-group involvement is high, not for any biological or genetic reasons but because minority-group members tend to be poor and live in inner (deteriorating) cities.

In contrast, Hirschi (1969) depended very heavily on self-report data in the formulation of his *social bond* theory, a theory based on universal human characteristics rather than such factors as socioeconomic status, race, and area of residence. According to Hirschi, the tendency toward delinquent behavior is a component of human nature and is held in check by various processes of social control. Thus, given delinquent behavior, one infers that there is a problem in such areas as emotional attachment to parents, involvement in school, and commitment to the values enunciated by parents, schools, and other social institutions.

In measuring delinquency using official or self-report data, it is important to keep in mind the different statistical bases for the data. Official records such as *UCR* report rate in terms of number of arrests (or other official contacts) per population grouping. As an example, there might be 13.6 arrests per 100,000 boys between the ages of ten and twelve for a certain offense. That figure, 13.6, is called the arrest *incidence* for boys in that age group and can be compared with the arrest incidences of other age groups for that offense.

In contrast, self-report data typically report the number of individuals in a given category who committed a given offense (or set of offenses). For example, 550 boys in the ten-to-twelve range may have been asked whether they had committed a certain offense, and 275 of them admitted that they had. In the literature, the resulting proportion of .50 (275/550) is called the *prevalence* of that offense among ten- to twelve-year-old boys. Incidence measures count each crime or official act as a unit (e.g., an arrest) and ignore the number of distinct offenders involved. Prevalence measures, on the other hand, count a person as a unit if he or she participated in the action of concern, regardless of the number of such participations. The action could be an official one like an arrest, the commission of a law violation, or admitting to the commission of a law violation. In the example of 13.6 per 100,000 ten- to twelve-year-olds, the 13.6 includes multiple arrests for some but does not tell us how many different boys were involved in the arrests. On the other hand, the figure .50 (275/550) tells us that half of the boys admitted to the criminal behavior but gives us no indication of how many times the crime occurred among members of that age group — a boy is counted once whether he committed the crime once, ten times, or a hundred times.

Official Statistics — Uniform Crime Reports

Sources and Types of Data. *UCR* depends on the voluntary monthly reporting of about 16,000 law enforcement agencies throughout the country. The information goes to the FBI either directly from an agency or through an intermediary at the state level. Many of the state-level programs, like that mentioned for California above in the context of types of official record, have reporting requirements that exceed those of the FBI in scope of data collected.

Primary emphasis for *UCR* is upon crimes that compose the Crime Index; they are also referred to as Index or Part I crimes. These are murder and nonnegligent manslaughter, forcible rape, robbery, aggravated assault, burglary, larceny-theft, motor vehicle theft, and arson.

The number of "actual offenses known" (from sources that are primarily citizen complaints and observations by officers) are crimes reported, whether or not arrests or prosecutions follow the knowledge. A given complaint of a crime to a police agency, it should be noted, is eliminated from the count if the police find the complaint unfounded or false. A central part of the monthly submission is the number of Part I offenses cleared by arrest for adults and for youngsters below the age of eighteen.

Secondarily, the *UCR* program collects data on persons arrested for all crimes except traffic violations, including age, sex, race, and ethnic origin. For purposes of computing crime rates for the United States and various geographic entities, the most recent population estimates from the Bureau of the Census are used.

Results by Age and Sex. Table 1.1 shows numbers of arrests in 1984 for Index crimes by age and sex groupings. In addition, a summary is provided for

TABLE 1.1   Arrests for Index Crimes (Estimated base population 203,035,000)

Total Offense Charged	All Ages	Youths Under 10	Youths Aged 10–17	Boys Aged 10–17	Girls Aged 10–17
Murder and nonnegligent manslaughter	15,777	3	1,308	1,186	122
Forcible rape	31,934	85	4,745	4,655	90
Robbery	120,501	255	29,899	27,860	2,039
Aggravated assault	263,120	824	35,433	29,892	5,541
Burglary	381,875	4,304	140,950	130,888	10,062
Larceny-theft	1,179,066	15,604	370,613	268,443	102,170
Motor vehicle theft	115,621	247	43,699	38,785	4,914
Arson	16,777	1,236	5,670	5,085	585
SUMMARY					
Crime Index total	2,124,671	22,558	632,317	506,794	125,523
percent		1.1	29.8	23.8	5.9
Violent crime	431,332	1,167	71,385	63,593	7,792
percent		0.3	16.6	14.7	1.8
Property crime	1,693,339	21,391	560,932	443,201	117,731
percent		1.3	33.1	26.1	6.9

Source: UCR (1985:174, 176, 178, 180)

the Crime Index as a whole and for its two components: violent crime (consisting of murder/nonnegligent manslaughter, forcible rape, robbery, and aggravated assault) and property crime (consisting of burglary, larceny-theft, motor vehicle theft, and arson). The summary shows both arrest total for each age-sex category and the percentage of arrests that the total represents.

Note first that youths under the age of ten were arrested for only 1.1 per cent of all Index crimes. Thus, it seems reasonable to disregard that age group in further discussions of youth crime. Accordingly, the remaining three columns in the table use the age grouping ten to seventeen.

As may be seen in the table, 29.8 per cent of all arrests for Index crimes were juveniles between the ages of ten and seventeen. Similarly, 16.6 per cent of the arrests for violent crimes and 33.1 per cent for property crimes in 1984 were juveniles aged ten to seventeen. And those figures become more dramatic when they are compared with the percentage of the relevant population aged ten to seventeen in that year — 12.6 per cent. In short, 12.6 per cent of the population were the arrestees in 29.8 per cent of the Index crimes, 16.6 per cent of violent crimes, and 33.1 per cent of property crimes.

Heaviest involvement by youths aged ten to seventeen was in burglary and motor vehicle theft, with respective percentages of 36.9 and 37.7; only somewhat below that was their percentage involvement in larceny-theft, 31.4.

Perhaps the most striking aspect of the table is the boy-to-girl ratio in numbers of arrests. For Index crimes as a whole, boys were arrested at a 4.0 ratio over girls; for violent crimes the ratio is 8.2 to 1, and for property crimes 3.8 to 1. Boys aged ten to seventeen constituted 23.8 per cent of all Index crime arrests, 14.7 per cent of violent crime arrests, and 26.1 per cent of property crime arrests even though they accounted for only 6.5 per cent of the base population.

Therefore, we can conclude from the *UCR* data shown in Table 1.1 that youths are arrested for serious crimes far out of proportion to their percentage in the population and that boys are arrested for those crimes at an overwhelmingly higher rate than are girls. In fact, about 80 per cent of the arrests of youths for serious crimes are boys and almost 90 per cent of the arrests of youths for violent serious crimes are boys.

Figure 1.1 presents a graphic summary of the effects of age and sex on arrest rate for violent crime in the year 1983. The highest arrest rate for violent crime is among males eighteen years of age. The actual figure for eighteen-year-old males is 1,231 arrests per 100,000 people in that group. Females that age were arrested at the much lower rate of 119 per 100,000, producing a ratio of more than 10 arrests of males for every arrest of a female. For seventeen- and sixteen-year-old males, the respective figures of 1,196 per 100,000 and 1,037 per 100,000 are not much lower than the 1,231 for eighteen-year-old males. For those lower ages, too, the male-to-female ratio of arrests for violent crimes is about 10 to 1. Notice, too, how rapidly the graph for males drops from its peak on both sides. Younger boys and older men have relatively low arrest rates.

Results by Race and Ethnicity. Let us now turn to another aspect of *UCR* — arrests by racial and ethnic groupings. Numbers and percentages of

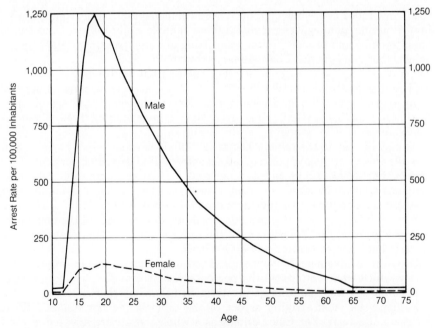

Figure 1-1 Age-Specific Violent Crime Arrest Rates, 1983
(*UCR*, 1984:346)

arrests for youths under eighteen are shown in Table 1.2 by racial groups and in Table 1.3 for Hispanics and non-Hispanics. Notice in Table 1.2 that of the 72,251 arrests of youths for violent crimes, 37,843 or 52.4 per cent, were black youths. Similarly, 28.6 per cent of the arrests of the young for Index crimes and 25.7 per cent of the arrests for property crimes were blacks.

For comparison, U.S. Census figures (1980) estimate the percentage of blacks under eighteen in the total population at 4 and the percentage of blacks under eighteen in the population of youths under eighteen at 15.

It should be pointed out that the numbers in Table 1.2 differ slightly from sums that may be obtained in Table 1.1 because a very few agencies did not report racial characteristics to the FBI, producing tiny decreases in arrest figures and estimated base population — the base population is 203,035,000 in Table 1.1 and 202,277,000 in Table 1.2. There is a greater loss in Table 1.3 showing arrests by ethnic origin.

In Table 1.3, we see that of the total arrests for Index crimes of youths under 18, 11.3 per cent were Hispanic. Similarly, 14.5 per cent of youths arrested for violent crimes and 11.0 per cent of youths arrested for property crimes were Hispanic. Census figures (1980) estimate the percentage of Hispanic youths among all youths under eighteen at 5.

Results by Population Concentration. Table 1.4 shows numbers of arrests and rates of arrest per 100,000 inhabitants for cities, suburban areas, and rural areas, over major categories of population density. In the case of the Crime Index total, the arrest rate is 1,241.7 per 100,000 in cities, 723.8 in suburban counties, and 470.6 in rural counties. Moreover, the rate decreases consistently over the six groupings of cities by population size, from 1,526.0 for Group I cities (each having a population of 250,000 or more) to 873.6 for Group VI cities (each having a population under 10,000). Similar patterns hold separately for violent crime and property crime rates.

Although the data in the table are for total arrests over all ages, it is reasonable to assume that the trends would be similar if only arrests of juveniles were considered. And the trends show clearly that the rate of arrests for serious crimes is a function of population density, with overwhelming concentration of serious crime in the bigger cities.

The Broad Picture. In overall summary of the evidence that comes from official recording of arrests for Index crimes, younger males, particularly if they are black or Hispanic, contribute to the numbers far beyond what is expected on the basis of numbers in the population. And arrests are predominantly phenomena of the cities, particularly the large cities.

Although *UCR* was used to establish those results, the conclusions would be essentially the same no matter what the source of arrest data.

It is hardly surprising, then, that theorists who have relied primarily on official data have developed theories that have explanatory constructs based on the struggles of inner-city boys, like the gang theories of Cohen (1955) and of Cloward and Ohlin (1960), the deterioration of neighborhoods (Shaw and McKay, 1942), or the organizational patterns of lower-class, urban cultures (Miller, 1958).

TABLE 1.2 Numbers and Percentages of Arrest by Race—Youths Under 18

Offense Charged	Number of Arrests					Percent Distribution				
	Total	White	Black	American Indian or Alaskan Native	Asian or Pacific Islander	Total	White	Black	American Indian or Alaskan Native	Asian or Pacific Islander
Murder and nonnegligent manslaughter ..	1,305	629	661	3	12	100.0	48.2	50.7	.2	.9
Forcible rape.	4,755	2,296	2,406	32	21	100.0	48.3	50.6	.7	.4
Robbery	30,032	9,638	20,060	87	247	100.0	32.1	66.8	.3	.8
Aggravated assault	36,159	20,895	14,716	303	245	100.0	57.8	40.7	.8	.7
Burglary.	144,807	109,861	32,582	1,140	1,224	100.0	75.9	22.5	.8	.8
Larceny-theft.	385,786	273,127	103,126	4,467	5,066	100.0	70.8	26.7	1.2	1.3
Motor vehicle theft	43,620	30,120	12,601	465	434	100.0	69.1	28.9	1.1	1.0
Arson	6,896	5,841	937	72	46	100.0	84.7	13.6	1.0	.7
Violent crime	72,251	33,458	37,843	425	525	100.0	46.3	52.4	.6	.7
Property crime	581,109	418,949	149,246	6,144	6,770	100.0	72.1	25.7	1.1	1.2
Crime Index total	653,360	452,407	187,089	6,569	7,295	100.0	69.2	28.6	1.0	1.1

Source: UCR (1985:183)

18

TABLE 1.3 Numbers and Percentages of Arrest, Hispanic Versus Non-Hispanic Youths Under 18

Offense Charged	Number of Arrests			Percent Distribution		
	Total	Hispanic	Non-Hispanic	Total	Hispanic	Non-Hispanic
Murder and nonnegligent manslaughter.	1,144	246	898	100.0	21.5	78.5
Forcible rape	3,981	376	3,605	100.0	9.4	90.6
Robbery	25,505	3,893	21,612	100.0	15.3	84.7
Aggravated assault	30,215	4,289	25,926	100.0	14.2	85.8
Burglary	126,353	16,648	109,705	100.0	13.2	86.8
Larceny-theft	341,982	34,212	307,770	100.0	10.0	90.0
Motor vehicle theft	38,651	4,867	33,784	100.0	12.6	87.4
Arson	6,281	569	5,712	100.0	9.1	90.9
Violent crime.	60,845	8,804	52,041	100.0	14.5	85.5
Property crime	513,267	56,296	456,971	100.0	11.0	89.0
Crime Index total	574,112	65,100	509,012	100.0	11.3	88.7

Source: UCR (1985:186)

TABLE 1.4 Numbers and Rates of Arrest Over Cities and Counties

Offense Charged	Total (11,249 agencies; 203,035,000)	Cities							Counties	
		Total cities; (7,682 cities; population 138,717,000)	Group I (55 cities, 250,000 and over; population 38,292,000)	Group II (120 cities, 100,000 to 249,999; population 17,375,000)	Group III (279 cities, 50,000 to 99,999; population 19,176,000)	Group IV (601 cities, 25,000 to 49,999; population 20,888,000)	Group V (1,481 cities, 10,000 to 24,999; population 23,370,000)	Group VI (5,146 cities under 10,000; population 19,616,000)	Suburban counties (1,107 agencies; population 39,328,000)	Rural counties (2,460 agencies; population 24,989,000)
Murder and nonnegligent manslaughter	15,777	11,504	6,907	1,512	955	849	693	588	2,783	1,490
Rate	7.8	8.3	18.0	8.7	5.0	4.1	3.0	3.0	7.1	6.0
Forcible rape	31,934	24,093	11,545	3,295	2,898	2,520	2,104	1,731	5,238	2,603
Rate	15.7	17.4	30.1	19.0	15.1	12.1	9.0	8.8	13.3	10.4
Robbery	120,501	103,755	62,119	13,925	10,717	8,146	5,816	3,032	14,038	2,708
Rate	59.3	74.8	162.2	80.1	55.9	39.0	24.9	15.5	35.7	10.8
Aggravated assault	263,120	197,884	83,630	28,736	23,244	22,296	20,340	19,638	43,262	21,974
Rate	129.6	142.7	218.4	165.4	121.2	106.7	87.0	100.1	110.0	87.9
Burglary	381,875	283,797	93,185	43,491	40,581	39,096	37,016	30,428	64,559	33,519
Rate	188.1	204.6	243.4	250.3	211.6	187.2	158.4	155.1	164.2	134.1
Larceny-theft	1,179,066	999,185	281,417	150,376	145,891	160,724	155,149	105,628	133,934	45,947
Rate	580.7	720.3	734.9	865.5	760.8	769.5	663.9	538.5	340.6	183.9
Motor vehicle theft	115,621	89,643	41,755	10,641	10,442	9,147	8,951	8,707	18,074	7,904
Rate	56.9	64.6	109.0	61.2	54.5	43.8	38.3	44.4	46.0	31.6
Arson	16,777	12,532	3,794	1,756	1,713	1,849	1,807	1,613	2,780	1,465
Rate	8.3	9.0	9.9	10.1	8.9	8.9	7.7	8.2	7.1	5.9
Violent crime	431,332	337,236	164,201	47,468	37,814	33,811	28,953	24,989	65,321	28,775
Rate	212.4	243.1	428.8	273.2	197.2	161.9	123.9	127.4	166.1	115.1
Property crime	1,693,339	1,385,157	420,151	206,264	198,627	210,816	202,923	146,376	219,347	88,835
Rate	834.0	998.5	1,097.2	1,187.1	1,035.8	1,009.3	868.3	746.2	557.7	355.5
Crime Index total	2,124,671	1,722,393	584,352	253,732	236,441	244,627	231,876	171,365	284,668	117,610
Rate	1,046.5	1,241.7	1,526.0	1,460.3	1,233.0	1,171.1	992.2	873.6	723.8	470.6

A given rate is number of arrests per 100,000 inhabitants.

Source: UCR (1985:166)

Self-report Data — The Seattle Youth Study

Principal Features of the Study. The study reported by Hindelang, Hirschi, and Weis (1981) was based on data collected in the city of Seattle during the academic year 1978–1979. Their self-report instrument consisted of sixty-nine items grouped into five categories for purposes of analysis: official contacts with the juvenile justice system, serious crimes, general delinquency, drug offenses, and school and family offenses. The full list of items may be seen in Table 1.5. Three major scales were derived on the basis of the two types of questions in which the items were embedded. There was a "Yes" or "No" response to the question "Have you ever . . . ?", and the score was the total number of "Yeses," or equivalently, the percentage of respondents who said "Yes." The question "How many times in the past year?" led to two scores: one based on the actual frequency reported and the other based on the assignment of a 1 if the frequency reported was one or more and a 0 otherwise.

But the investigators, almost without exception, used only the first scale throughout their report. Their explanation is as follows (1981:217):

> Our tendency throughout this monograph has been to rely on "ever variety" scoring procedures for all of our delinquency measures. This tendency does not stem from a priori theoretical consideration or from failure to examine alternative procedures. It stems instead from the simple fact that ever variety scales generally outperform scales with restricted content and time frames.

The investigators obtained their sample of participants from three distinct populations: (a) students enrolled in Seattle public schools who had never been arrested or referred to the juvenile court, (b) youths with a record of Seattle police contact, and (c) youths who had been referred to the Seattle juvenile court. A stratified sampling approach was used within each of the populations to assure that there was appropriate representation by race, sex, and socioeconomic status (SES).

In order to test for the effects of mode of administration, the instrument was administered in four ways: anonymous questionnaire, nonanonymous questionnaire, anonymous interview, and nonanonymous interview. The various ways permitted determining whether youngsters were more honest in answering the items when they were not identified, as well as the relative efficacy of oral and paper-and-pencil approaches to the questioning.

Interestingly, data from the study indicate that results of self-report approaches are independent of manner of administration, questionnaire or interview, and of whether the process is or is not anonymous. All methods of administration produced equally high reliability and validity measures.

The Prevalence of Violating. Earlier research using the self-report method had established that juvenile law violation is more prevalent than official data or general observation would lead one to expect. In their pioneering work, Short and Nye reported that delinquent behavior was "extensive" among the high school students they studied (1958:297). And a short while later, in the report of a study that compared delinquent and "nondelinquent" (in the sense of never having been caught) boys, Erickson and Empey (1963:458) stated,

TABLE 1.5   Percent Responding "Yes" to Question "Have You Ever . . . ?" on Seattle Survey Instrument

	White Males	Black Males	White Females	Black Females
Official Contact Index				
1. Been questioned as a suspect by the police about some crime	35.2	38.6	11.4	10.9
2. Been held by the police or court until you could be released into the custody of your parents or guardians	16.8	21.2	5.4	9.8
3. Been placed on probation by a juvenile court judge	8.7	18.8	2.1	9.3
4. Been caught shoplifting by the clerk or owner of a store	32.8	29.3	23.8	23.8
5. Been sentenced to a reformatory, training school, or some other institution by a judge	2.4	2.3	0.3	1.0
Serious Crime Index				
6. Sold something you had stolen yourself	18.4	19.5	3.6	3.0
7. Broken into a house, store, school or other building and taken money, stereo equipment, guns, or something else you wanted	16.8	12.9	4.9	4.3
8. Broken into a locked car to get something from it	16.5	11.6	1.7	0.9
9. Taken hubcaps, wheels, the battery, or some other expensive part of a car without the owner's permission	16.3	12.4	1.0	0.0
10. Taken gasoline from a car without the owner's permission	14.4	8.0	3.0	0.0
11. Taken things worth between $10 and $50 from a store without paying for them	13.5	14.2	14.2	15.2
12. Threatened to beat someone up if they didn't give you money or something else you wanted	12.8	17.8	4.0	10.0
13. Carried a razor, switchblade, or gun with the intention of using it in a fight	12.7	17.5	1.1	11.6
14. Pulled a knife, gun, or some other weapon on someone just to let them know you meant business	12.6	17.1	3.1	9.5
15. Beat someone up so badly they probably needed a doctor	10.2	15.4	3.1	8.9
16. Taken a car belonging to someone you didn't know for a ride without the owner's permission	9.7	7.3	0.8	1.7
17. Taken a tape deck or a CB radio from a car	9.0	6.7	0.1	0.6
18. Broken into a house, store, school, or other building with the intention of breaking things up or causing other damage	7.3	3.6	2.1	3.4
19. Taken things of large value (worth more than $50) from a store without paying for them	5.2	5.6	1.4	3.7

**TABLE 1.5   Percent Responding "Yes" to Question "Have You Ever . . . ?"
on Seattle Survey Instrument** *(continued)*

	White Males	Black Males	White Females	Black Females
20. Tried to get away from a police officer by fighting or struggling	4.9	4.5	0.6	0.4
21. Used physical force (like twisting an arm or choking) to get money from another person	4.1	7.9	0.7	5.3
22. Used a club, knife, or gun to get something from someone	3.7	7.1	1.0	3.0
23. Taken things from a wallet or purse (or the whole wallet or purse) while the owner wasn't around or wasn't looking	17.4	19.4	11.9	17.3
24. Hit a teacher or some other school official	11.6	17.1	3.2	12.6
25. Taken a bicycle belonging to someone you didn't know with no intention of returning it	11.0	16.0	1.8	0.7
26. Tried to pass a check by signing someone else's name	3.0	3.9	1.8	0.6
27. Intentionally started a building on fire	2.4	2.4	0.0	1.7
28. Grabbed a purse from someone and run with it	0.5	1.9	0.0	1.0
29. Forced another person to have sex relations with you when they did not want to	0.5	1.0	1.0	0.0
Delinquency Index				
30. Taken little things (worth less than $2) from a store without paying for them	62.8	52.4	55.8	37.2
31. Broken the windows of an empty house or other unoccupied building	48.6	58.0	11.0	16.6
32. Let the air out of car or truck tires	40.7	35.1	12.8	7.5
33. Used a slug or fake money in a candy, coke, coin or stamp machine	39.7	35.7	12.8	9.8
34. Fired a BB gun at some other person, at passing cars, or at windows of buildings	34.9	39.7	7.0	7.3
35. Taken things you weren't supposed to take from a desk or locker at school	31.6	40.0	15.0	24.4
36. Bought something you knew had been stolen	31.1	35.2	5.1	14.7
37. Broken the windows of a school building	29.0	30.0	10.0	9.2
38. Taken material or equipment from a construction site	26.0	11.9	4.6	6.1
39. Refused to tell the police or some other official what you knew about a crime	22.5	30.8	10.7	15.2
40. Purposely broken a car window	16.4	17.8	2.8	4.3
41. Picked a fight with someone you didn't know just for the hell of it	15.2	15.4	4.1	11.6
42. Helped break up chairs, tables, desks, or other furniture in a school, church, or other public building	10.6	6.5	1.7	0.6
43. Jumped or helped jump somebody and then beat them up	8.9	23.4	2.1	18.4

(continued)

**TABLE 1.5 Percent Responding "Yes" to Question "Have You Ever . . . ?"
on Seattle Survey Instrument** *(continued)*

	White Males	Black Males	White Females	Black Females
44. Slashed the seats in a bus, a movie house, or some other place	8.5	11.3	1.8	5.2
45. Punctured or slashed the tires of a car	7.9	6.8	0.4	1.3
46. Destroyed things at a construction site	13.0	8.4	1.8	1.7
47. Destroyed mailboxes	12.3	1.9	0.9	0.0
48. Kept money for yourself that you collected for a team, a charity (like the March of Dimes), or someone else's paper route	11.6	11.8	15.2	13.1
49. Driven away from the scene of an accident that you were involved in without identifying yourself	10.8	7.6	6.2	1.3
50. Taken mail from someone else's mailbox and opened it	10.1	10.1	5.1	3.6
51. Broken into a parking meter or the coin box of a pay phone	3.6	5.4	0.2	2.0
Drug Index				
52. Drunk beer or wine	93.1	85.0	93.0	73.7
53. Drunk whiskey, gin, vodka or other "hard" liquor	79.4	61.1	80.4	62.2
54. Smoked marijuana (grass, pot)	75.3	70.9	71.6	74.6
55. Gone to school when you were drunk or high on some drugs	54.2	46.6	43.2	34.6
56. Pretended to be older than you were to buy beer and cigarettes	42.9	37.6	38.9	22.5
57. Sold illegal drugs such as heroin, marijuana, LSD, or cocaine	41.5	31.3	13.2	15.5
58. Driven a car when you were drunk or high on some drugs	36.6	29.6	27.2	13.6
59. Taken barbiturates (downers) or methedrine (speed or other uppers) without a prescription	22.4	8.0	21.9	9.9
60. Used cocaine	21.6	18.8	15.7	12.1
61. Taken angel dust, LSD, or mescaline	16.9	9.6	14.7	7.0
62. Used heroin (smack)	0.8	0.6	0.8	1.0
School and Family Offenses Index				
63. Been sent out of a classroom	73.2	71.1	39.3	57.4
64. Stayed away from school when your parents thought you were there	60.0	60.2	59.3	55.4
65. Gone out at night when your parents told you that you couldn't go	51.2	39.6	32.1	22.5
66. Been suspended or expelled from school	38.0	64.6	15.0	51.3
67. Cursed or threatened an adult in a loud and mean way just to let them know who was boss	34.7	33.7	23.1	19.6
68. Run away from home and stayed overnight	16.5	13.6	16.0	19.8
69. Hit one of your parents	13.4	4.4	10.9	9.6

Source: Hindelang, Hirschi, and Weis (1981:223–226).

"The number of violations which respondents admitted having committed was tremendous." To illustrate, 92 per cent of the nondelinquents admitted minor thefts, 66 per cent "destroying property," and 32 per cent "breaking and entering." In terms of an overall figure based on interviews of a probability sample of boys and girls in the age range thirteen to sixteen, Williams and Gold (1972:213) state, "Eighty-eight percent of the teenagers in the sample confessed to committing at least one chargeable offense in the three years prior to their interview." They add, interestingly, "It is clear that, if the authorities were omniscient and technically zealous, a large majority of American 13- to 16-year olds would be labeled juvenile delinquents." Actually, less than 3 per cent of the reported offenses were detected by the police, and only 9 per cent of the youths had any contact with the police in the three years preceding the survey.

Similar indications of the prevalence of law-violating behavior have been reported by Murphy, Shirley, and Witmer (1946), Gold (1970), and Ageton and Elliot (1978).

The results of the Seattle study are in general accord with the conclusion that delinquent behavior is more widespread than assumed, although Hindelang, Hirschi, and Weis (1981:218) deny any implication that "everybody does it."

Results by Sex and Race. Table 1.5 contains the percentage of youngsters in the Seattle study, by sex and race, who indicated committing a certain type of behavior by responding affirmatively to the question "Have you ever . . . ?" The highest percentages are in the Drug Index with, among white youngsters, over 90 per cent admitting to the consumption of beer or wine, about 80 per cent the drinking of hard liquor, and over 70 per cent the smoking of marijuana.

As the previous discussion in this chapter shows, there are substantial differences in arrest rates over years of age and between the sexes. Significant age and sex differentials are also found with self-report data, but the sizes of the differences are much smaller than with official data. Early findings regarding age and sex effects may be found in Hirschi (1969), Gold (1970), Hindelang (1971), Williams and Gold (1972), Gold and Reimer (1974), Elliott and Voss (1974), and Ageton and Elliott (1978).

The Seattle data were analyzed in terms of sex differences, but not on the basis of age. The investigators used the ratio of proportion of males admitting the offense to proportion of females admitting the offense — called a sex ratio — to gauge sex differences. To illustrate, if .75 of the males admitted to a certain offense, as did .25 of the females, the sex ratio would be .75/.25 or 3.00. Similarly, if .45 of the males and .45 of the females admitted to an offense, the ratio would be .45/.45 = 1.00. The obtained sex ratios varied widely over the sixty-nine self-report items. Table 1.6 shows several of the items with a high sex ratio and several with a low ratio.

It is clear that boys heavily predominate over girls in the more serious, more destructive offenses, while there is little difference in the status offenses of truancy, running away, and using "hard" liquor; in the use of certain types of drugs; and in minor shoplifting. Girls clearly predominate in keeping collections for charities and other uses for themselves.

As we have seen above, official data like those in *UCR* show considerable racial differences. Early self-report studies (e.g., Gold, 1966; Hirschi, 1969;

TABLE 1.6 Offenses with High Sex Ratios and Offenses with Low Sex Ratios Controlling for Race

Total Offense	Population	White	Black
Taken hubcaps, wheels, the battery, or some other expensive part of a car without the owner's permission	18.80	1.55	12.42*
Destroyed mailboxes	10.01*	12.30*	1.89*
Broken into a locked car to get something from it	9.97	9.55	11.65*
Taken a car belonging to someone you didn't know for a ride without the owner's permission	9.10	9.71*	4.36
Taken a tape deck or CB radio from a car	8.48	8.98*	6.70*
Taken a bicycle belonging to someone you didn't know with no intention of returning it	7.92	6.23	16.01*
Destroyed things at a construction site	6.79	7.25	4.98
Drunk beer or wine	1.03	1.00	1.15
Stayed away from school when your parents thought you were there	1.03	1.01	1.09
Taken barbiturates (downers) or methedrine (speed or uppers) without a prescription	1.00	1.02	.81
Drunk whiskey, gin, vodka, or other "hard" liquor	.99	.99	.98
Run away from home and stayed overnight	.94	1.03	.69
Taken things worth between $10 and $50 from a store without paying for them	.94	.95	.93
Kept money for yourself that you collected for a team, a charity (like the March of Dimes), or someone else's paper route	.79	.76	.90

*Female per cent less than 1, male per cent shown.
Source: Hindelang, Hirschi, and Weis (1981).

Gould, 1969; Williams and Gold, 1972; Gold and Reimer, 1974; Elliott and Voss, 1974) found very little difference between black and white youngsters in the prevalence of law-violating behavior. Hindelang, Hirschi, and Weis (1981) constructed a table showing the black-to-white crime ratios from a number of studies based on official data. Using that table, they comment (1981:159):

> As is evident, in all comparisons available, the black rate of delinquency is equal to or greater than the white rate. Although there is considerable variation in ratios, apparently depending on the sample and on seriousness of offense or extent of official processing, there can be no doubt that marked differences in rates are to be expected in official data, with ratios in the 2–4 range common among boys and no ratio smaller than 3 in samples restricted to girls.

Hindelang, Hirschi, and Weis (1981:159) then go on to point out:

> In sharp contrast to these findings are black-to-white ratios in published studies based on self-reported delinquency. . . . The range of ratios in self-report samples restricted to a single sex (males, .8 to 1.3; females, .9 to 1.7) *does not overlap* with the range of ratios found in official data similarly restricted to single-sex groups (except in the Palmore and Hammond, 1964 study which yielded an official ratio of 1.2). The *very strong* relation between race and delinquency in official data is not

present in these self-report data. In fact, the self-report relation would have to be characterized as *weak* or *very weak*, with a mean black-to-white ratio of less than 1.1:1 expected on the basis of previous research.

Given that official data show black youths are arrested at a considerably higher rate than white youths, while self-report studies indicate little difference in law-violating behavior, one can appreciate the context for comments like the following (Quinney, 1970:129, 130):

> *The Racial Context of Arrest.* Considerable evidence suggests that the police have long had differential arrest policies in regard to race. It is apparent that police have tended to arrest Negroes on slight evidence in comparison to the amount of evidence required to arrest whites. Furthermore, Negroes have been exposed more than others to the misuses of police power.
>
> Selective enforcement according to racial factors results in part from long-held prejudices of individual policemen. But also important is the fact that the Negro tends to fit the stereotype that police have of the criminal. Through the use of certain cues, a probabilistic model of law violation, and their past experiences, the police are more likely to arrest the Negro than the white man in a similar offense situation.

In 1980, Elliott and Ageton raised several objections to the procedures used in the earlier self-report studies and described a new (self-report) approach that

Drawing by D. Reilly; © 1986 The New Yorker Magazine, Inc.

Discrimination takes many different forms.

overcame those claimed inadequacies. The new approach was based on a longitudinal study of delinquent behavior called the National Youth Survey (NYS). The NYS used a national sample of eleven- to seventeen-year-old youths that reflected principal characteristics of the broader youth population. Respondents were asked to indicate the number of times (over a year's period) that they committed each offense — thus, the investigations had both incidence and prevalence measures of delinquent acts. Unlike the preceding self-report studies, that of Elliott and Ageton (1980) found significant race differences: the black-to-white ratio for total offenses (corrected for sample sizes) was over 1.5 to 1, and for predatory crime it was over 2.0 to 1. The differences seemed primarily due to the large number of property crimes reported by blacks.

More recently, Huizinga and Elliott (1985) have analyzed NYS data for years 1976 to 1980 (the longitudinal survey is carried out on an annual basis) and came up with a conclusion at variance with the one based on the 1976 data. They looked at prevalence data, at incidence data, and at the numbers of youths in each racial group who committed offenses of a general sort and Index crimes at a high frequency and found, except for the year 1976, no consistent pattern differentiating racial groups. They conclude (1985:13), "Overall, these findings suggest that there are few if any substantial and consistent differences between the delinquency involvement of different racial groups."

Hindelang, Hirschi, and Weis (1981) computed the black-to-white ratio from each of the sixty-nine items in the Seattle survey (in the manner shown in Table 1.6 for sex ratios). There was just not much difference in the percentages of whites and blacks admitting offenses, leading the investigators to comment (1981:165, 169):

> Consistent with virtually all previous research, the overall impression from [the table showing black-to-white ratios for the sixty-nine items] is that blacks are only slightly more delinquent than whites, somewhat more so among females than among males. Overall, the black-to-white ratio in the Seattle data does not exceed the ratio of 1.1:1 mentioned earlier as the best guess of the ratio.

Moreover, conjecturing that the "abundance of trivial items" may have depressed the "relationship between race and self-report delinquency" (1981:169), the investigators computed ratios for a group of seventeen serious items. The resulting ratios remained small: total sample 1.16, male 1.08, female 1.37.

Finally, Hindelang, Hirschi, and Weis (1981) had access to the official records of the Seattle Police Department and of the local juvenile court and used that information to find a "strong tendency of black male official delinquents to underreport substantially the offenses in the official record" (1981:180). They illustrate the process as follows (1981:171):

> For example, the Seattle police or court records list four offenses in the vehicle theft category: auto theft, take motor vehicle without permission, take and ride or joyride, and ride in a stolen vehicle. Respondents were classified as reporting such an offense if they responded positively to the item "have you ever taken a car belonging to someone you didn't know for a ride without the owner's permission."
>
> . . . 19% of the white males with an official record of this type did not respond positively to the self-report auto theft item; among similarly situated black males

the rate of nonreporting was 57%. For serious offenses as a whole (burglary, robbery, vehicle theft, person offense, and weapons offense) the white [male] nonreporting rate was 20% compared to the rate of 57% among black [males].

On the basis of that type of evidence, they conclude, despite their negative findings using the ratios, that "there are true black/white differences in offending behavior" (1981:130) as indicated by official measures and by Elliott and Ageton (1980). It should perhaps be mentioned in passing that Elliott (1982) has raised questions about the analysis and interpretation of the data indicating underreporting by blacks. Accordingly, he has recommended replication of the effort before there is extrapolation of the conclusions to black youths in general.

Results by Socioeconomic Status. As the final possible correlate of delinquency, we consider socioeconomic status (SES). Although *UCR* does not report the SES of those arrested, it does have indirect information indicating higher crime among those in lower SESs. That is, we have seen that *UCR* shows arrests as predominantly phenomena of large cities and a strikingly disproportionate involvement of minority youths in serious crime.

Where SES data are available in official records, a negative correlation between SES and amount of crime involvement is invariably found.

The task force report of the President's Commission on Law Enforcement and Administration of Justice, arguing on the basis of official crime statistics for slum improvement, states emphatically (1967:42):

> Delinquency in the slums . . . is a disproportionately high percentage of all delinquency and includes a disproportionately high number of dangerous acts. . . . And besides delinquency rates, the other familiar signs of trouble — truancy, high unemployment, mental disorder, infant mortality, tuberculosis, families on relief — are all highest in the inner city.

And, in their study of a birth cohort in Philadelphia, based on official police data, Wolfgang et al. (1972) found that race and SES "were most strongly related to the offender-nonoffender classification" (1972:245) after examining the relationship of delinquency and those background variables as well as such others as type of school, residential and school moves, and IQ. More specifically, they found the rate of offending for lower-SES boys to be 548 per 1,000 subjects and the comparable rate for higher-SES boys 140 per 1,000 subjects — that is, a ratio of nearly four to one (1972:72, 73).

In contrast, as in the case of race, the earlier self-report studies found little or no difference in delinquent behavior due to SES. These results may be seen in Nye and Short, 1957; Empey and Erickson, 1966; Hirschi, 1969; Williams and Gold, 1972; Gold and Reimer, 1974; Elliott and Voss, 1974). As can be imagined, the markedly variant results between official and self-report data regarding the delinquency-SES relationship led to vigorous debate in the literature.

For example, Wheeler (1967) argued that an arrest must be considered a "three-way interaction between an offender, victims or citizens, and official agents" (1967:318) and thus reflects the police system and particular officers as well as the characteristics of the offender. That is in accord with the arguments of Turk (1969) and Quinney (1970) to the effect that police are biased against people of low SES and are more likely to intervene with arrest in their crimes (and thus elevate their contributions to official statistics).

On the other hand, Reiss (1975) has argued for the preferability of official over self-report measures of delinquency because "the methodological and technical foundations of . . . [self-report] studies do not invite confidence in the conclusions" (1975:214). And Nettler (1974) has argued, "Confessional data are at least as weak as the official statistics they are supposed to improve upon" (1974:36). He also states, "an evaluation of these unofficial ways of counting crime does not fulfill the promise that they would provide a better enumeration of offensive activity" (1974:96).

A review of the literature on the issue of delinquency and SES by Tittle, Villemez, and Smith (1978), following earlier research by Tittle and Villemez (1977), concluded that there is a tendency toward disproportionality of delinquency among low-SES youths but that overall differences over classes are slight. Moreover, they found an interesting historical trend in the studies of delinquency-SES relationships in that the early studies of all types were likely to find a relationship between SES and delinquency, whereas more recent studies were not. They summarize their findings as follows (1978:643):

> The overall results show only a slight negative relationship between class and criminality, with self-report studies reflecting lower association than official statistics studies. Moreover, analysis demonstrates a clear historical decline in magnitude of association to the point where both self-report and official statistics studies done in the current decade find no class variation.

Braithwaite (1981) has vigorously objected to the position of Tittle and his colleagues (as well as to the thoroughness of their research). In an introductory statement, Braithwaite (1981:37) amusingly points to the generally accepted higher risks of being mugged or raped in lower-class neighborhoods and states, "Perhaps Tittle et al. take their own findings seriously and adopt no extra precautions when moving about the slums of the world's great cities than they do when walking in the middle class areas of such cities." The conclusion that he reached on the basis of what he regards as a very comprehensive survey of the relevant literature (1981:49) is that "lower class people do commit those direct interpersonal types of crime which are normally handled by the police at a higher rate than middle class people."

Elliott and Ageton (1980) used the method discussed above in the context of race differences to examine the effects of SES. Their approach, you may recall, was developed to overcome inadequacies claimed to exist in earlier self-report studies; it used incidence rather than prevalence rates. In the category "predatory crimes against persons," lower-class youths reported on average four times as many offenses as did middle-class youths and one and one-half times as many as working-class youths. While there were substantial numerical differences over the three classes in average "predatory crimes against property," the differences were not statistically significant. On total offenses, there was a significant difference between lower-SES and both working- and middle-class youths, but there was no difference between the latter two groups.

For the Seattle study, Hindelang, Hirschi, and Weis (1981) brought SES into the picture in two ways. First, white males were sampled on the basis of median income of their residential areas. Second, an additional SES indicator was developed on the basis of the report of each respondent regarding the occupation of the primary family wage earner. The results are summarized as follows (1981:194):

> In the Seattle data the low-SES to high-SES official offense *incidence* ratio among white males is 1.2:1 when SES is measured by the median income of the census tract in which the respondent resides and 1.3:1 when SES is measured by the occupation of the principal wage earner (as reported by the respondent). The *prevalence* ratio of official delinquency by the census tract measure is 1.3:1. . . . by the occupation measure it is 1.1:1. These differences are, by all measures, small.

Moreover, when correlational measures of association were used between delinquency indexes and SES, the resulting table of correlations showed (1981:196) "that by neither measure of social class and by no measure of delinquency is there even a moderate relation between the two."

The most recent and perhaps most convincing evidence on the relationship between SES and delinquency may be found in the report of Elliott and Huizinga (1983). These investigators used three sets of self-report scales and derived both incidence and frequency measures. The scales included those which were specific to a type of offense, those which included more general classes of behavior, and those which encompassed a broad, heterogeneous grouping of offenses. An example of the most specific is Felony Assault, which included aggravated assault, sexual assault, and gang fights. An example of the middle category of specificity is Crimes Against Persons, which included the items under Felony Assault as well as "hit teacher, parent, or students" and "strong-armed students, teachers, or other." Finally, the most general scales included School Delinquency, Index Offenses, and General Delinquency.

They found that middle-class youths, girls as well as boys, are less likely to commit serious offenses than working- and lower-class youths and that when middle-class youths do commit serious offenses, they do so less frequently than youths in the two lower SES categories. In the study, moreover, sizable differences were found between the groupings for prevalence as well as incidence measures of serious offenses.

In the words of Elliott and Huizinga (1983:165), "When the focus is shifted from serious offenses to delinquent acts in general, there are few significant class differences in the proportions of youth reporting one or more delinquent acts." But working- and lower-class males do commit substantially more general acts of delinquency than do middle-class youths (that is, there is a higher incidence among the lower-SES boys); on the other hand, "there is no consistent pattern of class differences in female incidence rates" (1983:165).

As in all previous studies, females in all classes had lower rates of offending than working- and lower-class males without a clear pattern of differences over classes.

Because there is an obvious relationship between race and SES and because blacks generally show more involvement in serious crime, Elliott and Huizinga controlled for the possible effect of race by repeating their analyses for whites only. They report (1983:165), "With few exceptions, the same pattern of class differences was found."

The Broad Picture. What does the pattern of results for self-report studies tell us about the extent and nature of juvenile offending? In truth, the pattern tells us much about the evolutionary measurement processes, a little about the people who produce and interpret the results, and perhaps a bit about the law-violating tendency of youths as a whole and of subgroups of these youths.

We are inclined to agree with Elliott and Ageton (1980) and with Hindelang, Hirschi, and Weis (1981) in their arguments that *actual differences in occurrence of serious criminal acts are reflected in official statistics, although the picture is certainly not as dramatic as those data make it seem.*

Elliott and Ageton (1980:107) state:

> The consistent findings of earlier self-report studies have led many sociologists and criminologists to the conclusion that race and class differences in arrests are primarily the result of processing biases and have little or no basis in behavior. . . . The findings from the 1977 National Youth Survey suggest some behavioral basis for the observed class and race differences in official processing. In this sense, the National Youth Survey data are more consistent with official arrest data than are data from most prior self-report studies [that is, measures that ask "Have you ever . . . ?" types of questions].
>
> Further, these findings provide some insight into the mechanisms whereby official actions produce exaggerated race and class (as well as age and sex) differences in delinquent behavior when compared with self-reported differences in normal adolescent populations. On both logical and empirical grounds, it seems reasonable to argue that the more frequent and serious offenders are more likely to be arrested, and that the youth population represented in official police statistics is not a representative sample of all youth.
>
> Self-report studies are capturing a broader range of persons and levels of involvement in delinquent behavior than are official arrest statistics. Virtually all youth report some delinquent activity on self-report measures, but for the vast majority the offenses are neither very frequent nor very serious. Police contacts, on the other hand, are most likely to concern youth who are involved in either very serious or very frequent delinquent acts. Police contacts with youth thus involve a more restricted segment of the general youth population.
>
> The findings discussed previously indicate that race and class differences are more extreme at the high end of the frequency continuum, that part of the delinquency continuum where police contacts are more likely.

And Hindelang, Hirschi, and Weis (1981:218, 219) state:

> The best measures of delinquency appear to be those that consider a wide range of delinquent acts committed over a long span of time. This fact suggests to us that the phenomenon of delinquency is more stable than is often assumed. There appear to be enduring qualities of persons or conditions that affect the likelihood of delinquent acts over a variety of situations. This, of course, does not mean that situational determinants of delinquency are unimportant and can be ignored. It does mean that situational theories that exclude consideration of the properties of

individuals on the grounds that all such properties are irrelevant to delinquency are based on an assumption contrary to fact.

The success of ever variety measures [that is, measures that ask "Have you ever . . . ?" types of questions] also suggests to us that the phenomenon of delinquency is more general than is often assumed. The fact is that the vast majority of delinquent acts are positively correlated with each other. The unpalatability of this fact is well-known. It is often said to be a false fact responsible for misuse of state power by the juvenile court and other excessively moral persons and institutions. In our view, this test of fact is quite simply illegitimate because it introduces considerations outside the bounds of etiological research.

Whatever the specific measure of self-report delinquency, considerable variation across individuals is evident. The idea that "everybody does it" or that "it" is equally distributed among all segments of the population is simply not true. The basic results of self-report procedures do not support social constructionist explanations of delinquency, nor do they support the idea that the juvenile justice system is inherently unjust and discriminatory because any differential treatment of individuals must be based on considerations other than the delinquent behavior of the child. By the traditional standards of positivistic social science, delinquency exists and may be reliably distinguished from the social reaction to it.

Reconciliation between that picture of delinquency and one based on the early results of self-report studies indicating that delinquent behavior is equally characteristic of all segments of our culture is nicely provided in the following summary of the results of Elliott and Huizinga (1983:174):

> The fact that most prior self-report findings on the relationship between class and delinquency have relied on prevalence measures involving an unrepresentative set of offenses in summary scales could easily account for their failure to observe significant class differences in delinquency. The NYS data also revealed no significant class differences in prevalence on nonserious or global measures of delinquency. Had earlier studies used incidence measures (that is, response sets that permitted the calculation of incidence estimates) or developed a serious offense prevalence scale with a representative set of serious offenses, they might well have found significant class differences.

Criminal Victimization — the National Crime Survey (NCS)

Principal Features of the Survey. In 1967, the President's Commission on Law Enforcement and Administration of Justice issued its report, in which the following can be found (1967:20, 21):

> Although the police statistics indicate a lot of crime today, they do not begin to indicate the full amount. Crimes reported directly to prosecutors usually do not show up in the police statistics. Citizens often do not report crimes to the police. Some crimes reported to the police never get into the statistical system. Since better crime prevention and control programs depend upon a full and accurate knowledge about the amount and kinds of crime, the Commission initiated the first national survey ever made of crime victimization. The National Opinion Research Center of the University of Chicago surveyed 10,000 households, asking whether the person questioned, or any member of his or her household, had been a victim of crime during the past year, whether the crime had been reported and, if not, the reasons for not reporting.

That initial crime victimization survey indicated that actual crime was several times that indicated in *UCR*. For example, the rate of violent crime reported in the survey was almost twice that reported in *UCR*, and the rate of property crime more than twice as high.

Beginning in 1973, a program called the National Crime Survey (NCS) was established to collect victimization data. The NCS was originally developed within an agency called the Law Enforcement Assistance Administration and was transferred to the Bureau of Justice Statistics (of the U.S. Department of Justice) when it was established in 1980. The actual interviewing process is conducted by the U.S. Census Bureau.

Six crimes are measured in the NCS: rape, robbery, assault, household burglary, personal and household larceny, and motor vehicle theft. Clearly there is close similarity to the Index crimes of *UCR*, and even closer than appearance, given that the direct victims of murder and manslaughter cannot be interviewed. In the process, there are interviews of over 130,000 randomly sampled people in households throughout the country. The interviews are conducted semiannually. Each person selected in a sample is asked a series of screening questions at the start of an interview to determine whether he or she has been a victim of a crime during the preceding six-month period. If the person responds affirmatively to one or more of the screening questions, thus indicating that he or she has been a crime victim, the interviewer asks questions regarding characteristics of the victim, the crime itself, and the offender, where relevant. Details include age, race, and sex of the victim; place and time of occurrence of the crime; extent of injury or economic loss; relationship between victim and offender, if any; and perceptions regarding the offender on the part of the victim.

It is the last item that is used to obtain estimates of juvenile offense rates. Given the difficulty of age discrimination, especially in the context of occurrence of a crime, it is obvious that the victimization survey cannot be regarded as a powerful contributor to the measurement of juvenile delinquency.

A full description of the NCS method may be found in *An Introduction to the National Crime Survey*, published by the Bureau of Justice Statistics in 1977. A summary of the approaches to crime measurement by both *UCR* and NCS is contained in *Measuring Crime*, published in 1981 by the same agency. Finally, that bureau puts out periodic bulletins and technical reports that summarize victimization data—examples are the technical report *Criminal Victimization in the U.S., 1970–80 Changes, 1973–80 Trends* and the bulletin *Criminal Victimization 1985*.

Offender Characteristics. Figure 1.2, taken from the National Crime Survey Report (1983:11), shows several characteristics of offenders as perceived by the victims of violent crime. The summaries are presented separately for crimes where there was a single offender and where there were multiple offenders. For crimes with a single offender, about 30 per cent of the offenders appeared to be between twelve and twenty years of age; for crimes with multiple offenders, all were twelve to twenty in 40 per cent of the cases.

The figure also contains information on perceived sex and race. The vast majority of offenders in violent crimes are perceived to be males in cases of a single offender and of multiple offenders. Black participation in crimes reported by victims is much higher proportionately where there were multiple offenders.

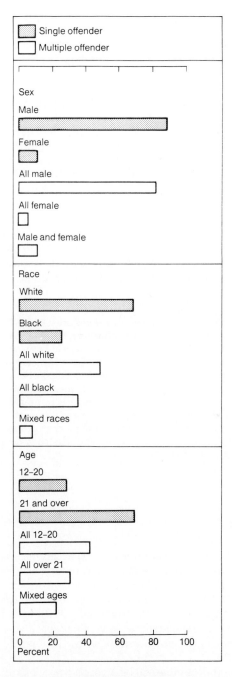

Figure 1-2 Percent Distribution of Violent Crimes, by Perceived Characteristics of Single and Multiple Offenders, 1981 (National Crime Survey Report, 1983:11).

Table 1.7 contains more specific information relating perceived age of offender to type of crime for the year 1981. While Census figures for 1980 indicate that about 10 per cent of the population was between the ages of twelve and seventeen, they were perceived as the offenders in 16.1 per cent of violent crimes in 1981.

Table 1.8 adds the dimension of age of victim to crime categories. It is abundantly clear that the victims of juvenile criminal violence are predominantly other juveniles. To illustrate, 44.3 per cent of the offenders in assaults against victims in the age range twelve to nineteen were perceived as youngsters between twelve and seventeen. At the other extreme, only 4.4 per cent of the offenders in assaults against victims above sixty-five were perceived as youngsters between twelve and seventeen. And the pattern for adult victims is closer to the figure for over sixty-five than for the young victims.

Clearly, the crime victimization survey cannot be considered a major contributor to knowledge of the offending characteristics of youngsters. But it does provide information not available elsewhere, like victim-offender age relationships, differential characteristics of single- and multiple-offender crimes, and the perceptions of victims. Although interesting in its own right, the last of these produces difficulties in interpreting actual criminal involvement. In the words of the NCS Report (1983:11):

> As with most NCS information, offender attributes are based solely on the victim's perceptions and ability to recall the crime. However, because the events often were stressful experiences, resulting in confusion or physical harm to the victim, it was likely that data concerning offender characteristics were more subject than other survey findings to distortion arising from erroneous responses. Many of the crimes probably occurred under somewhat vague circumstances, especially those at night. Furthermore, it is possible that victim preconceptions, or prejudices, at times may have influenced the attribution of offender characteristics. If victims tended to misidentify a particular trait (or a set of them) more than others, bias would have been introduced into the findings, and no method has been developed for determining the existence and effect of such bias.

Summary

In every society, there are regulations and expectations regarding acceptable and unacceptable behavior that are aimed at protecting people and property and at minimizing disruptions to social processes. To encourage conformity, sanctions may be imposed if there is significant deviation from the standards set by the regulations and expectations. Behavior that is thought to be particularly harmful or disruptive is regulated by laws that specify sanctioning by the criminal justice system, in the case of adults, or by the juvenile justice system, in the case of children.

A juvenile delinquent is assumed to be a youth who violates one of those laws (called criminal laws) and becomes subject to sanctioning by the juvenile justice system. But the task of defining the concept *juvenile delinquent* is difficult for two major reasons: first, a youth who may be a juvenile delinquent in one state

TABLE 1.7 Percent Distribution of Single-Offender Victimizations, by Type of Crime and Perceived Age of Offender

			Perceived Age of Offender					
			12–20					
Type of Crime	Total	Under 12	Total	12–14	15–17	18–20	21 and Over	Not Known and Not Available
Crimes of violence (4,457,000)	100.0	0.5	29.4	4.3	11.8	13.3	67.9	2.3
Rape (144,000)	100.0	a0.0	18.1	a1.0	a8.0	a9.0	80.1	a1.9
Robbery (624,000)	100.0	a0.2	34.5	2.9	14.0	17.6	60.5	4.8
Robbery with injury (189,000)	100.0	a0.0	27.6	1.4	13.2	12.9	66.8	a5.6
Robbery without injury (435,000)	100.0	a0.3	37.5	3.6	14.3	19.6	57.8	4.4
Assault (3,689,000)	100.0	0.6	28.9	4.6	11.6	12.7	68.6	1.9
Aggravated assault (1,220,000)	100.0	a0.4	25.3	3.7	9.3	12.2	71.8	2.5
Simple assault (2,469,000)	100.0	0.7	30.7	5.0	12.8	12.9	67.0	1.6

Detail may not add to total shown because of rounding. Number of victimizations shown in parentheses.
aEstimate, based on zero or on about 10 or fewer sample cases, is statistically unreliable.

Source: National Crime Survey Report, 1983:47

TABLE 1.8 Percent Distribution of Single-Offender Victimizations, by Type of Crime, Age of Victims, and Perceived Age of Offender

Type of Crime and Age of Victims	Total	Perceived Age of Offender						
			12–20					
		Under 12	*Total*	*12–14*	*15–17*	*18–20*	*21 and Over*	*Not Known and Not Available*
Crimes of violence[a]								
12–19 (1,233,000)	100.0	[b]1.1	61.9	12.2	30.3	19.3	35.4	1.7
20–34 (2,255,000)	100.0	[b]0.1	16.6	1.1	4.3	11.2	81.2	2.0
35–49 (608,000)	100.0	[b]0.5	18.6	[b]0.9	6.9	10.8	78.9	[b]2.0
50–64 (245,000)	100.0	[b]0.7	15.9	[b]3.0	4.1	8.8	77.9	[b]5.6
65 and over (117,000)	100.0	[b]1.1	17.0	[b]2.5	3.5	[b]11.0	74.6	[b]7.3
Robbery								
12–19 (156,000)	100.0	[b]0.0	59.7	[b]8.8	29.5	21.4	38.5	[b]1.8
20–34 (271,000)	100.0	[b]0.0	24.8	[b]1.1	9.1	14.6	70.8	[b]4.4
35–49 (92,000)	100.0	[b]0.0	30.2	[b]0.0	[b]10.1	20.0	66.8	[b]3.0
50–64 (53,000)	100.0	[b]0.0	[b]23.5	[b]0.0	[b]8.1	[b]15.4	64.3	[b]12.2
65 and over (51,000)	100.0	[b]2.6	[b]28.3	[b]2.6	[b]5.6	[b]20.0	57.8	[b]11.4
Assault								
12–19 (1,034,000)	100.0	[b]1.3	63.8	13.1	31.2	19.6	33.1	1.8
20–34 (1,902,000)	100.0	[b]0.2	15.2	1.1	3.5	10.6	82.9	1.7
35–49 (503,000)	100.0	[b]0.6	17.0	[b]1.1	6.5	9.4	80.8	[b]1.6
50–64 (184,000)	100.0	[b]0.9	14.2	[b]4.0	[b]3.1	[b]7.1	81.0	[b]3.9
65 and over (65,000)	100.0	[b]0.0	[b]8.7	[b]2.4	[b]2.0	[b]4.3	87.2	[b]4.2

Detail may not add to total shown because of rounding. Number of victimizations shown in parentheses.
[a]Includes data on rape, not shown separately.
[b]Estimate, based on zero or on about 10 or fewer sample cases, is statistically unreliable.

Source: National Crime Survey Report, 1983:48

may not be one in another state because of a differing set of laws; second, most violations of laws by youths are never detected, and few of those detected make it through the court procedures that establish the equivalent of guilt. To illustrate the difficulty, a youth may have been adjudicated a delinquent in Mississippi for behavior that is not even a violation of law in Montana. Moreover, if one defines *juvenile delinquent* on the basis of detection and arrest and several gang members commit an offense for which only one is caught, that gang member alone would be a delinquent even though others may have participated fully in the criminal act.

Children are, of course, subject to the same criminal laws that adults must obey. In addition, there are laws that are applicable only to the behavior of children. Among these are laws that mandate school attendance, obedience to parents, and compliance with curfews. Since offenses of the latter type can be committed only by those who have the status of children, they are called *status offenses.*

There are three principal ways to measure the extent of juvenile offending: using official data, using self-report data, and using information from the victims of crime. The central source for official data is the *Uniform Crime Reports (UCR)*, which contains tabulations of offenses reported to police departments and characteristics (age, sex, race, etc.) of people who have been arrested. The picture one gets from *UCR* is that the heaviest contributors to serious crime are minority boys in later adolescence who live in geographical areas of high population density.

Rate of activity in *UCR* is given in terms of number of arrests per unit of population, as, for example, 13.6 arrests per 100,000 boys between the ages of ten and twelve for a certain offense. The figure 13.6 is an *incidence* measure — it is a function of arrest counts where a given individual who is arrested more than once contributes accordingly to the total. On the other hand, self-report results typically use *prevalence* measures. When a youth responds "Yes" to a question asking whether he or she has ever committed a certain offense, there is only one entry in the total used to determine rate no matter how many times the offense was committed. The rate in prevalence form is, thus, of the form .5; that is, one half of those asked whether they had committed a certain offense admitted to doing so.

The picture one gets from the use of the self-report technique is that offending is more widespread than one assumes on the basis of *UCR* data, although boys do indicate many more of the serious, more destructive offenses than girls. Some studies have shown racial differences in self-reported crime of a magnitude comparable to those obtained from *UCR* data, but the vast majority of studies have shown little or no difference. The discrepancies may be explained at least in part by the differences between incidence and prevalence, by the observation in one study that black youths understate their involvement in crime on self-report instruments, or by arrest data reflecting more serious criminal offending than the types of questions predominating on self-report questionnaires. On the issue of socioeconomic status (SES) and delinquency, there is evidence from self-report studies indicating greater and more serious offending rates at the lowest SES levels but no pattern when comparison is over all SES levels.

Finally, victimization data on a nationwide basis come from the National

Crime Survey (NCS). The results indicate that youths are perceived as committing offenses by victims at a rate about 1.5 times their population proportion and that youths are more likely to commit offenses in groups. Moreover, black participation in criminal events appears to be much higher when there are multiple offenders. However, the results of victimization surveys must be used with great caution because they are dependent on the observations of people under stress who most often have little time for careful scrutiny.

References

Ageton, Suzanne S., and Elliott Delbert S. 1978. *The Incidence of Delinquent Behavior in a National Probability Sample of Adolescents.* Boulder, Colo.: Behavioral Research Institute.

Braithwaite, John. 1981. The Myth of Social Class and Criminality Reconsidered. *American Sociological Review* 46:36–57.

Bureau of Justice Statistics, U.S. Department of Justice. 1977. *An Introduction to the National Crime Survey.* SE-VAD-4-1977. Washington, D.C.: U.S. Department of Justice.

———. 1981. *Measuring Crime.* February Bulletin, Washington, D.C.

———. 1982. *Criminal Victimization in the U.S., 1979–80 Changes, 1973–80 Trends.* July Technical Report, Washington, D.C.

———. 1985. *Criminal Victimization 1985.* June Bulletin, Washington, D.C.

Cloward, Richard A., and Ohlin, Lloyd E. 1960. *Delinquency and Opportunity: A Theory of Delinquent Gangs.* New York: Free Press.

Cohen, Albert K. 1955. *Delinquent Boys: The Culture of the Gang.* New York: Free Press.

Elliott Delbert S. 1982. Review of *Measuring Delinquency*, by Michael J. Hindelang, Travis Hirschi, and Joseph G. Weis. *Criminology* 20:527–537.

———, and Ageton, Suzanne S. 1980. Reconciling Race and Class Differences in Self-reported and Official Estimates of Delinquency. *American Sociological Review* 45:95–110.

———, and Huizinga, David. 1983. Social Class and Delinquent Behavior in a National Youth Panel. *Criminology* 21:149–177.

———, and Voss, Harwin L. 1974. *Delinquency and Dropout.* Lexington, Mass., D. C. Heath.

Empey, LaMar T., and Erickson, Maynard L. 1966. Hidden Delinquency and Social Status. *Social Forces* 44:546–554.

Erickson, Maynard L., and Empey, LaMar. 1963. Court Records, Undetected Delinquency, and Decision-making. *Journal of Criminal Law, Criminology and Police Science* 54:456–469.

Gold, Martin. 1966. Undetected Delinquent Behavior. *Journal of Research in Crime and Delinquency* 3:27–46.

———. 1970 *Delinquent Behavior in an American City.* Belmont, Calif.: Brooks/Cole.

———, and Reimer, Donald J. 1974. Changing Pattern of Delinquent Behavior Among Americans 13–16 Years Old: 1967–72. *Crime and Delinquency Literature*, 7: 483–517.

Gould, Leroy C. 1969. Who Defines Delinquency: A Comparison of Self-reported and Officially-reported Indices of Delinquency for Three Racial Groups. *Social Problems* 16:325–336.

Hindelang, Michael J. 1971. Age, Sex, and the Versatility of Delinquent Involvements. *Social Problems* 18:522–535.

——, Hirschi, Travis, and Weis, Joseph G. 1981. *Measuring Delinquency.* Beverly Hills, Calif.: Sage.

Hirschi, Travis. 1969. *Causes of Delinquency* Berkeley, Calif.: Univ. of California Press.

Huizinga, David, and Elliott, Delbert S. 1985. *Juvenile Offenders Prevalence, Offender Incidence and Arrest Rates by Race.* Boulder, Colo.: Institute of Behavioral Science.

Hutzler, John L., and Sestak, Regina M. 1977. *Juvenile Court Jurisdiction over Children's Conduct: A Statutes Analysis.* Pittsburgh, Penn.: National Center for Juvenile Justice.

Miller, Walter B. 1958. Lower-class Culture as a Generating Milieu of Gang Delinquency. *Journal of Social Issues* 14:5–19.

Murphy, Fred J., Shirley, Mary M., and Witmer, Helen L. 1946. The Incidence of Hidden Delinquency. *American Journal of Orthopsychiatry* 16:686–695.

National Crime Survey Report. 1983. *Criminal Victimization in the United States, 1981.* Washington, D.C.: U.S. Department of Justice, Bureau of Justice Statistics.

Nettler, Gwynn. 1974. *Explaining Crime.* New York: McGraw-Hill.

Nye, F. Ivan, and Short, James F., Jr. 1957. Scaling Delinquent Behavior. *American Sociological Review* 22:326–331.

Porterfield, Austin L. 1946. *Youth in Trouble.* Fort· Worth, Tex.: Leo Potishman Foundation.

President's Commission on Law Enforcement and Administration of Justice. 1967. Task Force Report: *Juvenile Delinquency and Youth Crime.* Washington, D.C.: U.S. Government Printing Office.

Quinney, Richard. 1970. *The Social Reality of Crime.* Boston: Little, Brown.

Reiss, Albert J. 1975. Inappropriate Theories and Inadequate Methods as Policy Plagues: Self-reported Delinquency and the Law. In *Social Policy and Sociology*, edited by Nicholas J. Demerath III, Otto Larsen, and Karl F. Schuessler. New York: Academic Press.

Shaw, Clifford R., and McKay, Henry D. 1942. *Juvenile Delinquency and Urban Areas.* Chicago: Univ. of Chicago Press.

Short, James F., and Nye, F. Ivan. 1957. Reported Behavior as a Criterion of Deviant Behavior. *Social Problems* 5:207–213.

——. 1958. Extent of Unrecorded Juvenile Delinquency: Tentative Conclusions. *Journal of Criminal Law and Criminology* 49:296–302.

Tittle, Charles R., and Villemez, Wayne J. 1977. Social Class and Criminality. *Social Forces* 56:474–502.

——, and Smith, Douglas A. 1978. The Myth of Social Class and Criminality: An Empirical Assessment of the Empirical Evidence. *American Sociological Review* 43:643–656.

Turk, Austin. 1969. *Criminality and the Legal Order.* Chicago: Rand McNally.

Wallerstein, James S., and Wyle, Clement J. 1947. Our Law-abiding Lawbreakers. *Probation* 25:107–112.

Wheeler, Stanton. 1967. Criminal Statistics: A Reformulation of the Problem. *Journal of Criminal Law, Criminology and Police Science* 58:317–329.

Williams, Jay R., and Gold, Martin. 1972. From Delinquent Behavior to Official Delinquency. *Social Problems* 20:209–229.

Wolfgang, Marvin, Figlio, Robert M., and Sellin, Thorsten. 1972. *Delinquency in a Birth Cohort.* Chicago: Univ. of Chicago Press.

Children and Their Offenses in History

We have seen that the meaning and character of juvenile delinquency in our society are quite complex. One reason for this is that the very concepts of childhood and youth—basic to a notion of juvenile delinquency—are themselves complex. These concepts have changed significantly over time, and the changes have had much to do with the way people understand and respond to juvenile delinquency. Indeed, they have had much to do with the very idea that there is such a thing as juvenile delinquency.

Youth, as a stage of life, has not been universally recognized in human communities. People in different times and places have had ideas about childhood and youth very different from those current today. These differing ideas have had great implications for the ways in which young people have been brought up, as well as for the ways in which juveniles who commit crimes have been treated. In this chapter, we will look at the background and development of modern attitudes toward children, focusing our attention on the history of childhood and youth in Western civilization and at the relationship of ideas about childhood to an evolving understanding of juvenile delinquency.

Overview

If one may speak of an overall tendency in Western history, it would be toward an increasing "child-centeredness" in family and social life. By this is meant several things. First, family life has become increasingly oriented toward child rearing as its primary function. For much of our history, the family was mainly an economic unit. Roles within the family were understood in terms of the economic mission. In recent centuries, there has been a tendency to elevate the domestic, emotional focus of the family and, particularly since the early nineteenth century, to understand that focus in terms of the effort to raise children properly and even happily. Second, this child-centeredness has also meant an increasing stress on the distinctiveness of childhood. Although people have always acknowledged that adults and children are different, recent centuries have seen an increasing conviction in Western society that there are distinctive characteristics and needs associated with childhood as such that child-rearing practices must address. Concomitant with this has been an effort to investigate children in order to identify those characteristics as fully as possible. Finally, recent times have seen an increasing value placed on childhood and youth as in themselves good. This in itself has had much to do with the emergence of a concept of juvenile delinquency, a concept that can be dated to the period around 1800. It has also had much to do with the complexity of even contemporary approaches to delinquency. But, again, our modern child-centeredness was not always a part of Western society.

The Ancient and Medieval Worlds

In ancient and medieval times, little distinction was made between juveniles and adults in criminal justice systems. Although we shall discuss this in more detail in Chapter 7, we may note at this time that during the ancient and

The history of Western society over the past few centuries has shown an increasing tendency toward "child-centeredness" in family life.

medieval periods, there were no special codes defining anything like "juvenile delinquency," nor were there specific laws aimed at juveniles like those modern American codes which identify "status offenses" for which young people may be adjudged delinquent. Children were subject to the same criminal codes as were adults. The only real concession to childhood in society's response to criminal violations was a general recognition that children below a certain age—often the age of seven—should not be held responsible for their actions. The idea that youthful lawbreaking represented a distinctive social problem, the very basis of those issues discussed in Chapter 1, had no place in ancient or medieval social thought. This was in keeping with a world view that gave very little place to a notion of childhood as such.

Ancient Rome. Although we are limited by the availability of evidence in what we can know about attitudes toward children in ancient and medieval times, it is clear that there was little of our modern child-centeredness in those times. The differences between this early era and our own appear especially striking in regard to the position of the child under Roman law, that body of laws and practices which developed in Rome from the earliest days of the city, founded about 753 B.C., and continued into the Christian era, a body of laws that served as the basis of many of the legal systems in the Western world. Under Roman law, the most salient characteristic of the child was its membership in a family, and fundamental to that characteristic was its subjection to *patria potestas* — essentially, the power of the father over his family for as long as he lived. For much of Roman history, the father had the power of life or death over his children — even his grown children — although he might be punished if he exercised it arbitrarily. This meant that he could expose any infants — literally, leave them out and unattended to die — or could kill any older children or sell them into slavery (Watson, 1970).

It would be easy, as Rawson (1986) reminds us, to overemphasize the role of the *pater familias* and the practical significance of *patria potestas* in Roman family life. Formally, the father's power was virtually unlimited, and, as Rawson states, there is no evidence that he was expected to consult with other family members in making decisions. Practically, however, adult offspring at least seem to have had some freedom even while their father lived. And, in any case, in those days of lower life expectancy, many fathers did not live long after their children reached adulthood. Nevertheless, *patria potestas* was real and points to the undeniable focus of familial ideals in ancient Rome.

Toward the end of the fourth century, there emerged a clear trend toward the diminishing of paternal power under Roman law and in Roman ideas. In A.D. 374, exposure of infants was forbidden, for example. In the writings of such fathers of the Christian church as Tertullian (c. 160–230), Ambrose (340?–397), Augustine (354–430), and Salvian (fifth century), moreover, *patria potestas* was undermined by the development of the ideal of *paterna pietas* (fatherly love) (Mounteer, 1984:255). Nevertheless, *patria potestas* remained an important element in Roman law even to the time of Justinian, the great codifier of that law in the sixth century (Jolowicz, 1957).

Although the principle of *patria potestas* seems to have been distinctively Roman, a similar attitude toward the child as such seems to have prevailed in other societies from ancient times into Europe's Christian era. DeMause (1975) has shown that the practice of exposing infants was common throughout the ancient world, not only in Rome but in Greece as well, and that in many ancient societies, including those of the Celts, Gauls, Scandinavians, Egyptians, and Israelites, the practice of child sacrifice was well known. Such notions and practices remained widespread in Europe well into the medieval period and, in regard to infanticide, even beyond.

DeMause and others have emphasized the way in which such practices point to a conscious brutality toward children in the past. This may have been the case, but no less significantly, those practices and laws also indicate how society placed adult needs and concerns over those of the child. The ancient and early medieval world was preeminently an adult world, and children entered it on, indeed owed their very lives to, the sufferance of adults. Hence, it was quite legitimate to people in those times that children should be used to further economic and social ends, and in ways that are shocking to us today. Adult society and not the child was at the center of public concern.

Medieval Society. The Middle Ages saw a gradual lessening of the more brutal treatment of the child, mainly as a result of the influence of Christianity in the West. Church leaders pioneered the development of ideals of fatherly love. Moreover, believing that every individual was possessed of an immortal soul, early Christians began to develop a sense of childhood as a crucially formative stage of life at which the individual was particularly in need of — and able to profit from — religious and moral training (McLaughlin, 1975).

However, if much of the old brutality began to soften, there was still, in important ways, an indifference to childhood and children that remained throughout the Middle Ages and into the Renaissance. According to the pioneering historian of childhood Philippe Ariès, "In medieval society the idea of childhood did not exist; this is not to suggest that children were neglected, forsaken or despised. The idea of childhood is not to be confused with affection for children: it corresponds to an awareness of the particular nature of childhood, that particular nature which distinguishes the child from the adult, even the young adult. In medieval society this awareness was lacking" (1962:128). Ariès has often been accused of exaggerating this point, but he has adduced much evidence to show us what medieval society must have been like in this regard. What that society lacked, above all, were institutions especially oriented toward the child. For example, children learned their place in the society not by attending schools specially designed to fit their capacities and needs but by mixing in the adult world. They shared in the same pastimes, performed the same sorts of tasks, and otherwise learned to become adults by being around and interacting with adults. There was no sense that society had to address the child; rather, the child had to learn to be a part of the society.

The Emergence of Childhood

The Early Modern Era

In the sixteenth and seventeenth centuries, this lack of orientation toward childhood began to show signs of change. To be sure, notions of childhood were still very different from those of our own time, as adults showed great ambivalence about childhood and children. In 1642, the English philosopher Thomas Hobbes (in Marvick, 1975:259) summarized that ambivalence in this description of children:

> Unless you give children all they ask for, they are peevish and cry, aye, and strike their parents sometimes, and all this they have from nature. Yet they are free from guilt, neither may we properly call them wicked . . . because wanting the free use of reason they are exempted from all duty.

Hobbes did not see children as especially pleasant to have around, and he was not alone.

The sixteenth and seventeenth centuries did not constitute a remarkably sentimental age. Hunt has shown how, even in marriage, notions of romantic love were not entirely approved and how, at least among the elite, "marriage was more a contract, negotiated by two families, than an agreement between the bride and groom" (1970:58). Families had to be concerned with each other's social standing, with the property that would change hands as a result of the marriage — with, that is to say, the material interests of those involved in the arrangement. Love was definitely to be secondary. As Hunt cites the French writer Henri de Campion on marriages, "Those which are made for love are nearly always condemned with justice" (1970:59).

Such a lack of sentimentality was also maintained in the attitudes of parents toward their children. Hunt points out that parents were not always "over-joyed" by the conception and birth of a child and that abortion and infanticide continued to be practiced with some frequency even at this period (1970:81). Such attitudes were also manifested in several practical ways in the raising of young children, and of older ones as well.

Most revealing, perhaps, was the common practice among well-to-do parents of removing young children from contact, in some cases almost at the moment of birth. Among the greatest families of France, infants were placed in separate households — often with large staffs and with a governess to preside over their care. Henri IV was given over only moments after his birth. In other households, much of the early care was entrusted to a nurse, who not only cared for but even breastfed the infant — along with her own.

In part, such apparent indifference toward their children may have had to do not only with parents' belief about the nature of the child but also with the very high level of infant mortality at the time. Philippe Ariès suggests, "People could not allow themselves to become too attached to something that was regarded as a probable loss," and he cites the case of one harried seventeenth-century mother of five "little brats" who was calmed by being told, "Before they are old enough to bother you, you will have lost half of them, or perhaps all of them" (1962:38). But, whatever the cause, the child was not placed at the center of most families during this period.

And yet it would be wrong to portray only the bleaker side of children's lives during this period, for it was also a period of some change in ideas about childhood, especially among the more prosperous strata of society. As a result, thinking about child rearing was changing as well (Muncie, 1984). According to Ariès, people were becoming increasingly aware of what was believed to be the "special nature" of the child. In the Middle Ages, for example, children were portrayed pictorially simply as little adults, dressed much the same as their elders and displaying the same attitudes. In the sixteenth and seventeenth centuries, children were portrayed as more "childlike," and they were also dressed in ways intended to denote their distinctive stages of life. Whereas, in the past, parents had approached the problem of training their children simply through letting them participate in adult life, they were, beginning in the sixteenth century, increasingly concerned with the proper discipline of their children through methods addressed peculiarly to the needs of the child. There were developing, in other words, both an awareness of and an interest in children as such (see, e.g., Ariès, 1962).

The developments that Ariès describes, though he focuses mainly on France, were widespread in Europe. One manifestation of this may be found, for example, in the growing tendency of mothers to nurse their own infants rather than giving them over to a wet nurse, as they had typically done in the past (Hunt, 1970; Illick, 1975). Moreover, much of the hostility toward infants, in particular, seemed to be abating. A seventeenth-century English clergyman, Ralph Josselin, captured the new mood when he wrote in his diary that he valued his children "above gold and jewels" (Macfarlane, 1970:82). This new attitude was shown, finally, in the development of a genre of literature about children. For example, the first English book on pediatrics was published in 1545 (Tucker, 1975), anticipating a flow of books devoted strictly to the problems — medical or moral — peculiar to children, a flow that has continued to our own time.

These changes were not so extensive as to bring about major developments in the treatment of young offenders, although the sixteenth century did produce some of the most important legal precedents for state intervention in family life. We shall observe these in Chapter 7. For now, it is enough to note that the early modern period was most important as a transitional age in which one may see early forms of an appreciation for childhood and family life, an appreciation that has blossomed in recent centuries.

Colonial America

Interestingly, one of the first clear indications of the strength and meaning of these emerging notions of childhood and family life appeared in the English colonies of North America in New England, where, under the influence of Puritanism, there existed a great deal of concern and awareness about children and, more specifically, child rearing. The Puritans' views about childhood were not the same as those of contemporary Americans. Nevertheless, an examination of their ideas provides an essential background for understanding subsequent developments in our society's conceptions of childhood.

From the time of colonization into the late 1700s, the family was the center of activity in Puritan New England, and child rearing was a central activity in the family. The Puritan concern for the child had important religious roots. The Puritan was, above all, concerned about the salvation of souls — in the present and the hereafter — and this concern extended to the souls of others. But Puritanism gave a special twist to this concern for, as strict Calvinists, the early New England settlers believed that all humans, including children, were innately sinful and given to evil. To be sure, children were deeply loved, but this in itself increased the parents' concern for their salvation. Because children were born, in the words of the great Puritan minister Cotton Mather, "defiled, depraved, horribly polluted, with *original sin,* and fearfully perishing under the wrath and curse of God" (1690:117), they had to be taught as soon as possible to seek their salvation.

Such teaching was often quite frightening. Cotton Mather's father, Increase (I. Mather, 1678:22), declared to the children in his congregation in 1678:

> If you seek God in earnest, he will be found of you, but if you forsake him . . . better you had never been born: you will be left without excuse before the Lord, terrible witnesses shall rise up against you at the last day. Your godly Parents will testifie against you before the Son of God at that day: And the

Ministers of Christ will also be called in as witnesses against you for your condemnation, if you die in your sins.

Puritan parents would have to work hard in order to help their children avoid such a horrible fate.

Within the Puritan family, effort at proper child rearing involved inducing a proper combination of fear and love in the child toward its parents, for, as one Puritan minister declared, "we easily obey them whom we reverence" (in Morgan, 1966:107). Thus, for Puritans, a crucial task to be undertaken was the breaking of the child's will and enforcing its subordination to the instruction of the parents. In the words of John Robinson, a Massachusetts minister (in Demos, 1970:134–135):

> There is in all children . . . a stubbornness, and stoutness of mind arising from the natural pride, which must, in the first place, be broken and beaten down; that so the foundation of their education being laid in humility and tractableness, other virtues may, in their time, be built thereon. . . . For the beating, and keeping down of this stubbornness parents must provide carefully . . . that the children's wills and wilfulness be restrained and repressed, and that, in time; lest sooner than they imagine, the tender sprigs grow to that stiffness, that they will rather break than bow. Children should not know if it could be kept from them, that they have a will of their own, but in their parents' keeping; neither should these words be heard from them, save by way of consent, "I will" or "I will not."

And for Robinson and others, the point at which one began to break the will was probably somewhere between the ages of one and two, though the job would extend over many years in the young person's life.

Techniques for breaking the will were various. If children were believed to be wicked, they were not usually incorrigible and could be taught those good habits which would restrain the will. Admonishment was, of course, part of the routine, as was the occasional use of the rod. "Better Whipt, than Damn'd," Cotton Mather declared, although the rod was to be used with moderation and reluctance. Finally, and, perhaps most importantly, Puritans believed it to be absolutely essential that children not be spoiled or indulged by their parents or by any other adults. To indulge the child was to allow it to give free rein to impulse and to its own desires, and these impulses and desires were, again, born out of a corrupt nature. Constant vigilance and care would train the child into a virtuous adult; to be what Increase Mather called "sinfully indulgent" toward one's children could bring nothing but sorrow to parents and child alike (I. Mather, 1679:17).

Still, Morgan (1966:103, 105) has observed, if most Puritans agreed with Mather's epigram about whipping, most also agreed that "it was still better to be persuaded than whipped" and saw education rather than corporal punishment as the best approach to teaching self-restraint. The Puritans devoted great care and attention to educating their children in the proper attitudes. Children were exposed to religion at the earliest possible age, and Puritans designed special catechisms intended to instill piety in young minds.

Puritan teachings were encapsulated—and, indeed, spread far beyond the boundaries of New England—in the first and most widely influential early American schoolbook, the noted *New England Primer,* which was intended to

Culver Pictures, Inc.

Dunking stools were used as punishment in the America of the Puritans.

teach reading and piety at one and the same time. It has been estimated that over six million copies of the primer were printed in the years between 1680 and 1830, and the book was used not only in North America but in England and Scotland as well (Lystad, 1980). For children who read it, it offered lessons quite consistent with the religious and family orientations of Puritan society. Thus, for example, it contained lessons and scriptures reinforcing Puritan ideas, including such biblical passages as a verse from Ephesians urging, "Children obey your Parents in the Lord for this is right," or, more ominously, one from Proverbs that warned, "Whoso curseth his Father or his Mother, his Lamp shall be put out in obscure Darkness." And the primer's version of the alphabet has virtually entered American folklore, with such couplets as "In *Adam's* fall, / We sinned all" or "The idle *Fool* / is whipt at school" (*New England Primer,* 1735 ed.:no pp.) Even in the teaching of syllabification, the primer sought to focus on those words — and virtues — associated with self-restraint and a concentration on the child's own depravity and need for salvation.

Indeed, it might be suggested that the Puritans, with their strong sense of family hierarchy and their strong belief in discipline and obedience, may have legislated the first American "status offense," incorrigibility. In seventeenth-century Massachusetts, the following law was on the books (in Bremner et al., 1970:I, 38):

> If a man have a stubborn or rebellious son of sufficient years of understanding, *viz.* sixteen, which will not obey the voice of his father or the voice of his mother, and that when they have chastened him will not harken unto them, then shall his father and mother, being his natural parents, lay hold on him and bring him to the magistrate assembled in Court, and testify to them by sufficient evidence that this their son is stubborn and rebellious and will not obey their voice and chastisement, but lives in sundry notorious crime. Such a son shall be put to death.

Puritan youths were given good reason to obey the Fifth Commandment. Fortunately, however, there is no indication that such a sentence was ever carried out.

But the real importance of the Puritans lay not in their potentially drastic approach to incorrigibility but, rather, in their great self-consciousness about childhood and family life and in the great clarity with which they expressed their ideas. Certainly, many parents of this era clung to older values and attitudes. Thus, such a late-seventeenth- and early-eighteenth-century Virginia aristocrat as William Byrd of Westover continued to show the same indifference to his children that one may see in families of earlier generations (Zuckerman, 1979). But the Puritans gave voice to trends emerging throughout Western civilization in the years prior to the modern era, trends that were also found elsewhere in the American colonies (Walzer, 1975). An understanding of their thought provides a background for understanding more recent conceptions of childhood and family and of juvenile delinquency as well.

Apprenticeship and Youth

In the midst of these changing ideas of childhood and family, however, one institution remained that had important ties to the past and played a major role in the lives of young people, particularly for those whom we would now call "adolescents" — children in their teens or, perhaps, a bit younger. Throughout the period we have been examining, the major practice involved a continuation of the tradition of "putting out" children as apprentices, in which they went to live in another household in order to learn a trade. Apprenticeship, which may be traced back to ancient times, became quite systematized in Europe prior to the Industrial Revolution. In general, under apprenticeship, young men and women bound themselves to masters for a set period of years, during which they would work for their masters and learn their trades. In return, the masters were expected to provide their apprentices with food, shelter, and clothing. Indeed, in almost every way the apprentice was to become a member of the master's household.

Apprenticeship up to the eighteenth century was considered a part of the normal upbringing of a child. Even among aristocrats, it was common to send one's children to the home of another aristocrat in order to train them in good manners, while the children of the lesser classes were sent out to learn specific trades: those of the middling sorts might be apprenticed to a merchant, while those of the laboring classes would generally be sent out to learn a skilled trade (Tucker, 1975). The children of the fairly well-to-do seventeenth-century English clergyman Ralph Josselin were not unusual: all left home between the ages of ten and fifteen, some to be educated, but others to take positions in other households as servants or apprentices. Their places in the Josselin household were taken by others from outside the family (Macfarlane, 1970). And this was common practice. The age could vary, but usually by the time of puberty, and in some cases much before — historian Peter Laslett (1965) reports that poorer children were put out between the ages of ten and twelve, some as early as eight or nine — children left their own families and spent much of what we would term "adolescence" under the care of others.

The Puritans, for all their incipient child-centeredness, did not challenge the practice of apprenticeship. Indeed, they assigned it great importance as a safeguard against parental overindulgence and gave it an honored role in the proper upbringing of children. In New England, boys and girls were usually apprenticed between the ages of ten and fourteen (Morgan, 1966). Youngsters in the other colonies seem to have been apprenticed at about the same time in their lives, although, in eighteenth-century Virginia and Maryland, fourteen or fifteen was the more usual age (D. B. Smith, 1980). American apprenticeship even in Puritan New England seems to have differed from its European background in only a few significant ways. In England, apprenticeship had been intended mainly to control competition among the trades, a purpose largely irrelevant in a colonial setting of chronic labor shortages. In addition, the fixed seven-year term observed in England was not so important in the colonies, where, in fact, terms of service varied greatly. Finally, unlike England, the American colonies frequently required masters to provide for the education of their apprentices in reading and writing (Bremner et al., 1970).

The apprentice's life was not always an easy one. Though a youth, he or she was still expected to work, and to work hard. Moreover, historians have shown that apprentices were often quite harshly treated and subjected to brutal physical punishments: Steven R. Smith (1973) gives an account of a seventeenth-century female apprentice in London who, for disobedience, was stripped, hung by her thumbs, and given twenty-one lashes and another of a boy who was beaten, had salt put into his wounds, and was held naked next to a fire. Even without such patent cruelty, the apprentice's life could be a frustrating one, as was noted by colonial America's most famous apprentice, Benjamin Franklin. Bound out to his own brother — a printer — at the age of twelve, Franklin frequently found himself in disputes with his kinsman-master and often received beatings as a result. "Thinking my apprenticeship very tedious," he wrote, "I was continually wishing for some opportunity of shortening it" (1961:33), which he ultimately did by leaving his home in Boston and making his way to Philadelphia.

Beginning in the eighteenth century, the significance of apprenticeship started to decline, as more and more young people came to be kept at home for longer periods of time, and by the nineteenth century, as we shall see, the practice was clearly on the way out. Still, for much of the modern era, apprenticeship was an important state in the life of almost every child.

The Revolution of Sentiment in the Nineteenth Century: Toward the Child-Centered Family _____

The kinds of forces that contributed to the dying out of apprenticeship represented a nineteenth-century flowering of the family-centeredness and child-centeredness that had begun to emerge during the sixteenth through eighteenth centuries. The early years of the nineteenth century saw a revolution in sentiment that has continued to have implications for the way we understand childhood and youth today.

Modes of Child Rearing in Early-Nineteenth-Century America

At around the close of the eighteenth and the opening of the nineteenth century, ideas about child rearing were in a state of flux. Indeed, for America, Greven has argued that there were actually three major and distinctive approaches to bringing up and governing children: the evangelical, the moderate, and the genteel. The evangelical mode looked back to Puritanism, but it had also been powerfully encouraged by the great religious revivals sweeping America in the mid-1700s and in the early years of the nineteenth century. According to Greven (1977), the key aim in evangelical households was to teach children to love and fear their parents and God, and, accordingly, such families tended to be quite authoritarian, with the father at the top. Like the Puritans, these evangelicals feared indulgence and recognized that the only way to give their children true discipline was by first breaking their wills. Not surprisingly, they made use of corporal punishment but, believing self-discipline to be the highest achievement, generally saw the need to use the rod as a symbol of discipline's failure and as a measure of the last resort.

Moderates, by contrast, sought more to bend than to break the will and emphasized the pliability of the child's nature. Children were seen as a source of pleasure, and good behavior given as a product of affection instead of fear — or awe — was to be the main goal in moderate disciplinary practice. Evangelical parents often seemed to be at war with their children, so frequently did they talk about the need to conquer young willfulness. Moderate parents, on the other hand, tended to stress the modeling process that they felt was taking place. Like the evangelicals, to be sure, moderates stressed the importance of obedience and the need for self-discipline; unlike the evangelicals, however, they were convinced that virtue could be obtained through the careful inculcation of good habits and the consistent maintaining of love and domestic affection.

The genteel mode, confined largely to a portion of the American upper class, was in some ways a throwback in that much of the work of child raising was done by others: nurses, governesses, or, in the Southern states, slaves. Nevertheless, it differed from older modes in its extraordinary emphasis on domesticity and intimacy. Love and reverence were to bind family members together, and the family was seen as set apart, a place of refuge in which love and tranquility contrasted with the harshness of society at large. Children in such families tended to be indulged — none of the evangelical fears of indulgence were found here — and, indeed, the fact that much of the real work of child rearing was given over to others meant that parents could avoid many of the unpleasant duties of disciplining their children. Thus, domestic ties would at least appear to be unmarred by confrontation.

In the emphasis on domestic ties found especially in moderate and genteel homes, one sees what became the main theme running through ideas about family life and childhood in the nineteenth century manifested in several ways. In marriage, for example, love came to play a far more important role in the choice of a partner than it did for earlier generations. As Shorter (1975:79) puts it, young people at the end of the eighteenth century "began to court those whom they liked rather than those whom their parents thought best." In addition, as Shorter also points out, the family of this period was showing increasing awareness of itself as an emotional unit. Romantic love united husband and wife; maternal and paternal love united parents and children. And above all, the domestic circle's role as a refuge from a difficult world became increasingly stressed. One French observer, quoted by Shorter (1975:229, 230), noted in the 1820s that "family fathers" were far less frequently in cafés and other public places than they had been in previous times and explained, "The family father, obliged to occupy himself with difficult business problems during the day, can relax only when he goes home. Everyone crowds around him. He beams at the children's games; he prides himself on knowing them well and their accomplishments delight him. Family evenings together are for him a time of the purest and most complete happiness." Similar attitudes were also found in the United States. When a young North Carolinian wrote in a letter in 1845, "the intercourse of friends and relations should not be regulated by those circumscribed and often times contracted views that may, perhaps, with great propriety, influence our connection with the mass of acquaintances" (in Bruce, 1979:51), he was expressing a similar sharp distinction between the family and the outside world that Shorter found in France, though he was willing to broaden the circle to include, at least, friends.

New Ideas of Child Rearing. But the emphasis on domesticity was to be felt no less clearly in the triumph of those attitudes toward child rearing that Greven has termed "moderate." Because the family was to be a place of peace and order, a haven from an outside world of turmoil, neither evangelical warfare nor the genteel use of others could have been an appropriate model for bringing up children properly. Thus, during the first half of the nineteenth century, ideas about child rearing tended more and more in a "moderate" direction.

The historian Bernard Wishy (1968) has done the fullest analysis of this tendency in nineteenth-century American notions about child rearing and children. As he indicates, throughout the years from 1800 to the coming of the Civil War, men and women were reevaluating the nature of the child, rejecting ideas like those of "infant depravity" and the view that "the child's potentialities were limited by innate sinfulness" (1968:23). Although the creation of obedient, dutiful children remained an important goal, parents were increasingly urged to cease their warfare against their children's wills and, rather than subduing their children's nature, to draw on the natural character of the child, on an innate goodness, in order to achieve the desired effects.

There were many survivors of the older evangelical school. Indeed, much of the literature on child rearing produced in the first half of the nineteenth century grew out of the controversy between those who continued to believe the breaking of the child's will to be the central parental task and those who urged the encouragement of naturalness in the child (Kiefer, 1948). And many parents resorted to rather spectacular means to achieve the older goal of breaking the will: Robert Sunley (1955) cites the example of one mother, in 1834, whose daughter of only sixteen months refused to say "dear mama" upon her father's command. According to Sunley, the little girl was left alone in a room for ten minutes, screaming all the while, and then commanded again. When she refused, she was whipped and asked again. This ordeal was kept up for four hours, until the child finally obeyed. Such an approach was, however, gradually losing favor with many Americans.

The Ideas of Horace Bushnell. The new way of child rearing was to avoid the more repressive and authoritarian measures of family government that had been widely accepted in the past. Perhaps the most influential statement of these developing approaches was put forth in the major book on child rearing published in mid-nineteenth-century America, Horace Bushnell's *Christian Nurture*. Bushnell, a Congregationalist minister, sought to set forth in a logical, systematic way the proper principles for bringing up children. In doing so, he stressed the significance of the family as a distinctive group, held together by the ties of love and affection — it had to have what he called an "organic unity," and its strength was to be such that a consciousness of family membership and a mutual affection pervaded every element of every family member's life (1947:77).

From this point of view, Bushnell rejected much in family practice that had been derived from the Puritan and evangelical traditions. Above all, he asserted the importance of recognizing and appreciating the essential character of the child. The child was not a depraved creature whose every instinct had to be thwarted by an authoritarian parent. Rather, there was much good in the child, and the true task of the parent was to take that child's nature as it existed and to mold it into the proper form. Bushnell (1947:208) rejected the breaking of the will as a proper parental goal:

> [The child's] willfulness, or obstinacy, is not so purely bad, or evil, as it seems. It is partly his feeling of himself and you, in which he is getting hold of the conditions of authority and feeling out his limitations. No, this breaking of a child's will to which many well-meaning parents set themselves, with such instant, almost passionate resolution, is the way they take to make him a coward, or a thief, or a hypocrite, or a mean spirited and driveling sycophant — nothing in fact is more dreadful to thought than this breaking of a will, when it breaks, as it often does, the personality itself, and all highest, noblest firmness of manhood. The true problem is different; it is not to break, but to bend rather, to draw the will down, or away from self-assertion toward self-devotion, to teach it the way of submitting to wise limitations, and raise it into the great and glorious liberties of a state of loyalty to God.

Children were still to be obedient, but they were to be so because they wanted to be, not because they were forced to behave. And, indeed, Bushnell thoroughly rejected authoritarianism in the household. Those parents who, as he put it, "only storm about their house with heathenish ferocity" were hardly acting properly in the performance of parental duties. "It is frightful to think," he wrote, "how they batter and bruise the delicate, tender souls of their children, extinguishing in them what they ought to cultivate" (1947:44). In the place of such a harsh family government, Bushnell urged an atmosphere of "order, and quiet, and happy rule" (1947:278), firm, to be sure, but based on love and gentleness.

Gone were the days when a Cotton Mather would advise parents to "Look to it that you keep up a *Fear* of you, in the hearts of your children, and make them tremble to *Refuse* any fit thing that you shall *Enjoyn* upon them" (1690:118–119). Now parents were encouraged to approach their children in a manner that would "inspire them with reverence and love" (Whitlock, 1813:2), for love, it was believed, was better than terror at bringing about obedience. Indeed, it was thought, a mutual love between parents and child was the only proper motivation to right action on the child's part. In one rather fanciful little dialogue written in 1826, young Eliza argued that her mother should let her attend a party because she had been a good girl and done her schoolwork well, but her mother replied (Mother and Eliza, 1826:60–61):

> You speak of going to the party as a reward for getting good lessons — you are too old, my dear, and have learned, I trust, too well the nature of your duty to think of doing it solely for a reward. Let your first thought always be, that you do your duty because it is right; that is, because it is the will and pleasure of your heavenly father that you should do it; next you should do your duty for the sake of the approbation of your earthly parents; and then you will be rewarded by the pleasure you feel in the approbation of your consciousness.

In the words of an 1831 writer, if parents "managed" their children correctly, "they will do your requirements for you, because they love you" (Management of Children, 1831:240).

The Celebration of Childhood. With this new sense of the relationship between parents and child also came a new sense of the child as such. Bushnell captured much of this in his work on child rearing. In keeping with his disapproval of authoritarian family life, Bushnell (1947:254) urged parents not to place too many prohibitions on their youngsters, because, as he wrote, "the whole enjoyment, use, benefit, of life is quite used up by the prohibitions." Beyond that, however, Bushnell also noted the positive character of much that was in the child. Thus, unlike many of his predecessors, he would not equate play with idleness and try to repress the playfulness of the child. "Having set the young of all the animal races a playing, and made their beginning an age of frisking life and joyous gambol," he argued (1947:291), "it would be singular if God had made the young of humanity an exception." And, he made clear, play was important not for any lessons children might learn from their games but simply because it was play — an expression of the nature of the child. He was even willing to accept a bit of mischief now and again, as a product of "exuberant life and playfulness," as something to be corrected but not something to be dwelt upon or treated with undue severity (1947:262).

Thus, such a writer as Bushnell sought to build a scheme for child rearing that was based on encouraging and shaping the child's natural propensities rather than on destroying them. This point of view was manifested in many ways during the period. In children's books, for example, the change was unmistakable. We have already seen the heavy religious and moralistic content of the *New England Primer,* perhaps the most significant book for children in colonial America. Other children's books from the period maintained the same focus. In addition, most books meant for children dealt mainly with adult characters. Children were, after all, to be guided and controlled by adults, suppressing all their more childish impulses. Best, then, that children read about adults (Lystad, 1980).

In the years up to the Civil War, although children's books remained didactic —indeed, remained overwhelmingly religious — new trends began to appear. After about 1836, for example, an increasing portion of the books featured characters their audience's own age and focused specifically on the needs of young people (Lystad, 1980). No less significantly, there was an increase in the publication of books intended solely for amusement. Books of play and adventure began to appear with some frequency, as did collections of nonsense rhymes. The change even appeared in schoolbooks. Thus, while the most significant such book of the period, *McGuffey's Reader,* continued to seek to instill piety and virtue in the young scholars of the day — teaching articulation, for instance, by forcing students to repeat such lines as "Folly is never pleased with itself" or "Habitual evils change not on a sudden" (McGuffey, 1879:26–27) — its selections were not so unrelievedly moralistic as those of the earlier *New England Primer.* Students might be forced to read such selections as poems on "Work" or essays on "Respect for the Sabbath Rewarded," but they also found selections from Shakespeare or the life of William Tell, not to mention Charles Lamb's delightful "Dissertation on Roast Pig."

Gone, then, was the fear of childish impulses, and in its place was a sense that the basis for a proper upbringing lay in the children themselves. Here was a major revolution in notions of childhood and child rearing, one that had important implications for family and society in the Western world. Western families, including those in the United States, were becoming fully centered on the child.

The Birth of Juvenile Delinquency as a Concept

Concepts of Childhood and Juvenile Crime in a Changing America

The changes taking place in the first half of the nineteenth century were significant, but they were not spread uniformly in American society. Instead, they were closely tied to other changes in American life, particularly to the emergence of an American middle class. The United States, while overwhelmingly an agricultural nation during this period, was developing an important urban, industrial, and commercial cohort and, with it, a class of managerial and professional people who had great influence over the nation's social and cultural life. Educated, affluent, and Protestant, these were the people among whom ideas like Bushnell's had the greatest popularity. Indeed, as McDannell (1986) has shown, child-centeredness, in particular, penetrated Roman Catholic homes and domestic literature far more slowly than it did those of the Protestant middle class. It penetrated working-class life more slowly still. These class and religious biases were important for several reasons, but none was more significant than the creation of a concept of juvenile delinquency — of juvenile offending as something entirely different from adult crime.

These early formulations about delinquency, we must note, should not be viewed as systematic theories of delinquency. Such theories did not begin to develop until the late nineteenth century. Then American and other scholars of delinquency began to create explanations of delinquency that sought to meet the criteria of theory building we shall discuss in Chapter 3.

Rather, the concept of juvenile delinquency, as it developed in early-nineteenth-century America, was mainly a product of emerging concepts of childhood and family life. The notion, so long established, that children and adults should stand identically before the law was anathema to those who celebrated childhood's special nature and who had turned from punishment to nurture in their ideas about child rearing. We shall see the institutional and legal implications of this shift in Chapter 7. But for now we can stress that with the emergence of a belief in the distinctive nature of the child there also arose a belief that the juvenile offender was something more than simply a young criminal.

The concept of juvenile delinquency was also a product, however, of the middle-class, Protestant character of those who formulated the changing ideals of family life and childhood, because these were the men and women who did most to develop an American response to delinquency. As many historians have argued, these middle-class Protestant Americans confronted a world that was, from their point of view, increasingly troublesome — troublesome as a burgeoning democracy, troublesome as a society with an increasingly visible urban working class, and troublesome as an increasingly plural society, especially one with a growing immigrant population. This led to special anxiety about those children who appeared not to conform to developing middle-class ideas of childhood and family life.

The Stimulus of Urbanization

Urbanization was the catalyst for mobilizing middle-class concerns and for the creation of a concept of delinquency. After the American Revolution, many American cities began to grow at often remarkable rates. New York, for example, had been a city of only about 12,000 at the close of the revolution in 1783 but by 1790 had grown to 33,131. By 1825, only thirty-five years later, the city's population had reached over 166,000. The growth rate during that period was an astonishing 548.9 per cent (Mohl, 1971). Other cities did not match New York's rate of growth as it became, during this period, the nation's leading metropolis, but they, too, grew quickly, drawing population from the rural areas of the nation and from abroad.

And yet, almost every historian agrees, the cities themselves were horribly unprepared for such growth. Municipal services were slow to expand to reach all the newcomers, leading to difficulties in sanitation, water supply, and public health. Additional problems were created by the fact that many of those who arrived to populate America's cities brought little with them. Most, especially those from abroad, arrived virtually penniless and, given conditions of ocean travel, arrived in poor health as well. There is even some evidence that paupers were unloaded on America by European cities, which, in return for the emigration, paid their passage here (Bremner, 1956). The result was the presence in the cities of a sizable underclass of the permanently poor: men, women, and children with little hope of betterment who congregated in filthy and crowded slums. To their presence and to the urban environment itself many Americans ascribed the growing problem of juvenile delinquency during the first half of the nineteenth century. Put simply, many middle-class Americans believed that juvenile delinquency occurred because the family life of the urban slum was too far from the emerging middle-class ideal.

As we have seen, men and women of the nineteenth century were developing strong ideas about the family — about its importance as a domestic unit and, too, about the need for children to receive virtually ceaseless love and guidance from their parents. Looking at the families of the poor, they felt that such a proper family unit was seldom present or possible. Strongly moralistic, affluent Americans of the early nineteenth century tended to ascribe the cause of poverty to the way the poor lived: men and women were poor because they drank too much, or were lazy, or were improvident, or were extravagant (Mohl, 1971).

From such homes, they believed, came children who were likely to become juvenile delinquents. An 1832 Boston writer made this case clearly. Writing about "the offspring of poor persons . . . between seven and sixteen years of age," he noted rather typically for his day that those years represented "the spring of life, during which the twig may be bent in any way." And then he summed up the dangers facing children raised in urban poverty (House of Reformation, 1832:382):

> Many of them have no parents, and a great many might better be orphans, than be under the jurisdiction of those they have. Some see no examples at home but of vice; others are abandoned to their own evil guidance, but by far the greater number are made candidates for the penitentiary by parental indulgence.

The last group of parents consisted of those who gave their children no standards or discipline at all. Letting their children make their own way, such unsatisfactory parents were likely to produce delinquents.

Poverty was not, however, thought to be the only cause of delinquency. Other factors also operated to make the bad situation of poverty worse. Believing that many of America's immigrants came from the lowest classes in Europe, some Americans argued that children had arrived in this country already prone to delinquency. In the words of a New England minister (Waterston, 1852:402), "The emigration that is sweeping in is made up in no small degree of a class addicted to beggary and profligacy. Search out their homes, and if you find cheerlessness and discomfort, ignorance and wretchedness, there you will see children ripening daily into habits of evil and driven into sin as by dire necessity." Other observers noted the temptations of city life as such: "The low theatres and brilliantly lighted saloons," as one noted, tempted eager and immature youngsters to break the law (Rockwell, 1867:336).

Environment, Moral Deficiency, and the Urban Poor: An Early Concept

Here we see emerging a quite influential concept of juvenile delinquency. From this point of view, delinquency was for the most part the product of environment and, most especially, of the difficulty of maintaining a proper family environment in a setting of urban poverty. It was, moreover, chiefly a moral problem. Poverty originated in the deficient moral stature of the adult poor; it was perpetuated by the inability of the poor to give their children a proper upbringing. The English educator Mary Carpenter (1853:162), who had great influence on American thinking, wrote that delinquents came from families "where vicious indulgence, the gratification of the lowest animal tastes, hardened the heart against all good and holy influences, — stifled the voice of conscience, — deadened all natural affections." This meant that the proper relationship between parent and child, based on reverence and love, simply had not existed for delinquents; hence, they fell into crime. This same point was made, in slightly different terms, by the frequent characterization of delinquents as "precocious," by which it was meant that such children were — or at least tried to be — adults before their time and failed to recognize their own need to depend upon and follow the guidance of loving adults. An English reformer referred to juvenile delinquents as "stunted little men" (in Gillis, 1974:138).

Again, such difficulties were understood to be chiefly a fact of life for the urban poor. Although the children of other families might be tempted to do wrong, the problem was of a different order because, for such children, as Carpenter put it (1853:5, 6), "parental love shelters like a guardian angel tender childhood, defending it from physical want, from spiritual danger." The children of the urban poor were, by contrast, "moral orphans."

Perhaps it was because of this faith in affluent and rural families that juvenile delinquency was not seen as affecting them. Indeed, it must not be thought that the children of the slums were the only ones to engage in what would today be generally considered questionable if not criminal behavior. Violence, for example, was widespread among young men throughout the United States in the years prior to the Civil War, and at several levels. At one was the interpersonal violence of the brawl or, especially in the South, of the duel. In such places as South Carolina or New Orleans, duels — to the death — were not uncommon even between teenagers and might well take place under parental surveillance (Wyatt-Brown, 1982). On university campuses, violence was common, whether in the form of fist and knife fights or the more punctilious duel (Kett, 1977). And campus riots were widespread. At Brown, students stoned the president's home almost nightly in the 1820s. Harvard saw riots in 1766, 1805, and 1823 (Kett, 1977). At Columbia College, South Carolina, a major riot broke out when members of the junior class refused to attend prayer and recitations. And it is not to be thought that these student riots were tame affairs: a professor at the University of Virginia, perhaps the most eminent legal scholar in the state, was shot to death by a student when he interfered with a student riot on that campus (Bruce, 1979).

In rural areas, juvenile misbehavior was also fairly common. Children were pretty much left on their own, and there was certainly no great concern over, for example, fighting and what were called "pranks." "Backwoods boys," according to one who looked back on such a past, "were brought up to the trade of 'knock down, and drag out,'" and, indeed, the boy who would not fight was often covered with shame, even by his own parents (Bruce, 1979:96–97). Some rural customs would have been particularly shocking to the urban reformers of the early nineteenth century had they occurred among urban, poor children. The widespread "turnout" was one of these. When the students in a rural school felt the need for a holiday, or when they found the schoolmaster too overbearing, they might well take matters into their own hands by seizing the teacher bodily and forcing him out of the school. It may have been an effective way to get a holiday, but the "turnout" hardly represented the end of loving obedience prized in the child.

And yet, though some outside observers — British travelers, for example — might criticize the excessive "precocity" of middle-class and elite American children (Rapson, 1965) or find a lack of proper intimacy in rural, especially frontier families (Bartlett, 1974), the sense that such families had severe short-comings was never strongly expressed. Indeed, the general reaction to the violence and pranks, if it were not downright approval, was usually summed up by the cliché that, after all, "boys will be boys." Letting off a little youthful steam was thought to be a good thing; in general, one could feel secure that children and youths from favored backgrounds would ultimately outgrow what was widely accepted as normal youthful folly.

So, again, juvenile delinquency was consistently treated during this period as a problem of urban life and, more particularly, as a problem posed by the moral deficiencies in children of the urban poor. There can be little doubt that this bias on the part of reformers narrowed their perceptions of the problem and their approaches to its solution. Nevertheless, it was a bias that was rarely questioned until the late years of the nineteenth century. Indeed, perceptive students will note that it is a bias that, some would say, continues to inform much in the American juvenile justice system, as we discussed in Chapter 1, as well as in the theories of some contemporary scholars of delinquency, theories that we shall discuss in Chapters 3 – 6. And, as we shall see in Chapter 7, it was a guiding influence on Americans' earliest institutional approaches to the problems of delinquency, as well.

In summary, then, emerging concepts of childhood interacted with changing social and historical conditions to produce the first clear-cut notions of juvenile delinquency. Those emerging concepts of childhood were strong, normative, and closely tied to class and even ethnic biases. But they form a backdrop against which much subsequent American thinking about delinquency must be understood.

Adolescence: A Critical Stage in Human Development

Toward the close of the nineteenth century, basic ideas of childhood and delinquency were elaborated in ways that also have had continuing importance. Chiefly, during the latter 1800s, men and women from a variety of backgrounds began to take a less moralistic, more "scientific" approach to delinquency. They came to view delinquency not so much as a matter of moral deficiency but rather as a product of inherent problems in the maturation of the child, problems that could be exacerbated by environmental factors. A major key to this shifting view was the identification of adolescence as a distinctive phase in the process of child development.

If we look back to the time prior to the Industrial Revolution, we can see that in keeping with the general indifference to childhood, there was also little clarity about the importance of the various ages through which children passed. There were certain broad stages of life through which everyone traveled — childhood, youth, adulthood, old age — but people were vague about the ages to which those corresponded. This was shown, for example, in the medieval school. Young people tended to start school at differing ages, and classes contained students ranging from very young children to adults. As Ariès (1962) points out, the concept of a connection between age and studies was wholly foreign to the Middle Ages. By the end of the Middle Ages, however, changes had started to occur, and certainly by the seventeenth century, as distinctive concepts of childhood were beginning to appear, something like a regular school cycle had begun to emerge, with students taking a regular course of study commencing at about age eight, perhaps a little later, and progressing according to a fairly well defined sequence of subjects. By the eighteenth century, it was generally recognized that there had to be a close relationship among age, capacity, and school class, a recognition well in line with the general appreciation of the particularity of the child's world when contrasted with that of the adult.

In America, with the increasing valuation on childhood, although one can find a certain slackness in the language of age up to the early nineteenth century and the continuing combination of rather large age spans into single classrooms, the growing awareness of the meaning of different ages was visible. Schultz (1973), in a history of the early public schools of Boston, has shown how, beginning in the early 1820s, students of about the same age and level of progress were grouped together, a practice that many felt had practical as well as educational benefits. This practice was reinforced, beginning at about the middle of the nineteenth century, by the introduction of graded reading textbooks that sought to match reading level to the student's age (Calhoun, 1973). There was an awareness of what one 1830 writer saw as the need to "suit the instruction to the intellectual advancement of the pupil; to adapt the nourishment supplied, to the progressive state of the mind" (Books for Children, 1830:34–35).

The Prolongation of Childhood

But perhaps the most important development along these lines was what some scholars have referred to as the "prolongation of childhood," a development that became fully noticeable in the nineteenth century. As we have already seen, it was quite common, through the eighteenth century, for children to leave the household somewhere between the ages of ten and fourteen — and, in some cases, even as early as seven. This was a practice that began to disappear with the coming of the nineteenth century. Among affluent families, apprenticeship may have declined because the educational requirements of an industrial, commercial economy had little to do with traditional forms of learning a trade. Among working-class Americans, industrialization and the demand for wage labor made apprenticeship obsolete. But the result was that children began to live in their parents' households until a somewhat more advanced age. Ryan (1981), examining a community in New York, discovered that between 1790 and 1820, the age of seventeen was far more common than a younger one for a youngster to begin learning a trade (1981:57), and this does not seem to have been greatly different from practices in other parts of the country. The chief result was that young people were remaining in a state of dependence, or at least of semidependence, for longer than they had before (see Smith-Rosenberg, 1985).

Beginning about the mid-nineteenth century, according to Gillis (1974:99), "the consuming concern that had previously been reserved for the very young child appears to have been extended to older youth as well." Thrust out in the past, older youth—those from about fourteen to twenty—were coming to be seen as still part of the emotional complex we have seen that the family had become. To be sure, many youngsters of that age group were still sent away. Poorer youths might be put to work; those from the upper and middle classes, sent to boarding schools. But the relationship to the family had become qualitatively more complex, even for those sent away to schools. No longer were they believed to be out of the family and in the world by themselves. Now they remained closely tied to their own homes, living there or, if away at school, dependent on their parents for support. Those who worked did so to contribute to the family income, not to support their own independent lives. And, as Zelizer (1985:3) has shown, even this role for young people was increasingly frowned upon as the nineteenth century drew to a close, when Americans came to create the ideal she has instructively described as the "economically 'worthless' but emotionally 'priceless' child." Thus the late nineteenth century actually saw the passage of the first "child-labor laws," legislation designed to regulate the employment of youngsters in various jobs. Here, then, was a very new way of life for youth, one that developed fully over the course of the nineteenth century.

Katz (1987) has portrayed this process very well in his social history of nineteenth-century Hamilton, Ontario, Canada. Looking at the years between 1851 and 1871, he shows that the proportion of young men in the age range fifteen to nineteen who lived at home with their parents rose dramatically, from less than half in 1851 to over three quarters two decades later (1975:260). Other historians have made similar findings. Glasco (1977), in a study of Buffalo, New York, as it was in 1855, found that nineteen was the usual age for native-born young men to leave home, and that the same was true of Irish-born males as well—although he did note the survival of the apprenticeship tradition among that city's other major ethnic group, the Germans. Nevertheless, the implications were clear. Dependency was being prolonged for young people of the nineteenth century.

In this period, then, social forces and social ideas were rapidly in the process of identifying and defining a new "stage of life," what we have come to call "adolescence" (Bakan, 1971:979–981). To be sure, the people of the nineteenth century were not the first to notice the importance of the years between puberty and adulthood in an individual's life. The Puritans, for example, had identified the teens as crucial years for the inculcation of piety and had believed, too, that they were years in which an individual's life was marked by distinctive tendencies (Beales, 1975). And the word *adolescence* itself predates the nineteenth century: the *Oxford English Dictionary* records its use from as early as the late fourteenth century to describe the ages between fourteen and twenty-one. Moreover, historians have shown the presence of a peculiar "age consciousness" among teenage apprentices in sixteenth- and seventeenth-century Europe and in colonial America (see, e.g., N. Z. Davis, 1971; S. R. Smith, 1973; Thompson, 1984). But the nineteenth century, given its stress on the family and as a result of a prolongation of childhood which grew out of practical causes, focused on adolescence in ways that were very significant.

G. Stanley Hall and the Psychology of Adolescence

For much of the nineteenth century, adolescence was understood to be a time when the more "ardent passions" began to rise in young people. It was almost inevitable that, once morality began to focus on the family and, too, once the older youths began to remain within the family, attention should be centered on them. Thus, although much of the early child-rearing literature, which began to appear in great volume in the United States after about 1825, dealt mainly with children under thirteen, there also began to appear at about the same time a spate of books for "youth," addressing moral problems, especially those associated with growing strivings for independence and maturity (Demos and Demos, 1969). The task these books sought to fulfill was important. As one authority of the time noted, adolescence was an age at which "Desires before tame, now became almost resistless" and when, for girls, "maiden coyness, a modest bashfulness, a sweet smile, a sentimental reverie, a queenly grace of motion" began to mark "every look, lisp, and act" (in Kett, 1977:134). All of this had to be kept under control.

The result was that adolescence was identified not simply as a distinct stage of life but as one that was both particularly dangerous to and crucial for the formation of character. It remained for this point of view to be put in a systematic form by one of the most significant pioneer psychologists in nineteenth-century America, G. Stanley Hall. Although Hall did not publish his encylopedic *Adolescence: Its Psychology and Its Relations to Physiology, Anthropology, Sociology, Sex, Crime, Religion and Education* until 1904, the impact of his studies began to be felt as early as the 1880s, and his achievement was peculiarly important not only for bringing the new science of psychology to bear on the study of adolescence but also for summarizing and reshaping many of the popular ideas about youth that had been developing during the 1880s (Demos and Demos, 1969).

For Hall, adolescence was an especially difficult stage of life, mainly because it marked a period in which the individual was neither fully child nor fully adult. Moreover, Hall felt that the psychological costs of being in such a condition could be quite large. "The child from nine to twelve," he wrote, "is well adjusted to his environment and proportionately developed. . . . At dawning adolescence this old unity and harmony with nature is broken up; the child is driven from his paradise and must enter upon a long viaticum of ascent, must conquer a higher kingdom of man for himself" (1904:II, 71). "This long pilgrimage of the soul" (1904:II, 73) would be marked by many psychological difficulties, among them a love of "intense states of mind" and powerful and sudden "shifts of mood" (1904:II, 73, 75–76), and by moral difficulties as well. Adolescents were often overaggressive in asserting their individuality, willful, and given to folly, not to mention prone to envy and overeager for independence.

But, if adolescence were a particularly difficult stage of life, it was also, for Hall, a critical one, as youth was "the most plastic stage of both temperament and character" (1904:II, 364). Hence, he saw a special need for parental and social concern to be addressed to adolescent youth, to ensure that young people of this age should follow proper paths of life. As he wrote in the preface to his great study, his chief desire was to "help the young to exploit aright all the possibilities of the years from fourteen to twenty-four and to safeguard them

against . . . insidious dangers" (1904:I, xix), dangers to which youths were
especially subject.

The Influence of Hall. Many of Hall's ideas were adopted and put into
practice by those who, early in the twentieth century, felt a special need to
shape the lives of adolescents in proper ways. He was particularly influential,
for example, with those "boys-workers" whose efforts have been thoroughly
documented by such historians as Kett and Macleod. The "boys-workers"
hoped to create organizations that would shelter adolescents from the
difficulties — and temptations — of public life, while also bringing some degree
of order to what they felt was a notably unstable stage of life. Thus, by combining military and civic educational elements with an emphasis on physical activities, they sought to tame what was not quite civilized in the adolescent breast.
In Britain, one of the leaders in such "boys-work" was General Robert Baden-
Powell, whose Boy Scouts would be established in the United States in 1910.
Marked by rigid organization and a focus on physical toughness, the Boy Scouts
were established by leaders who looked directly to Hall's writings for inspira-
tion, both for understanding the apparent problems of adolescents and for
formulating answers to those problems (Kett, 1977; Macleod, 1983).

Thus, with the emphasis on adolescence in the latter years of the nineteenth
century, there arose the view that while youth, like childhood, could be fulfilling
and rewarding, it could also be quite trying. Indeed, whereas earlier authorities
had asserted that "the most critical, and, at the same time, the most precious
portion of life is comprised within the period measured by the first ten years"
(Primary Schools, 1864:85–86), with Hall and others of this later period, the
adolescent years were said to constitute the period of greatest plasticity and,
therefore, greatest danger. Such a view was to have great significance in American attitudes toward the young: just as childhood had been prolonged in quite
practical terms by the development of a concept of adolescence, so, too, had a
sense of the child's moral vulnerability been prolonged to include the much later
years of teenage life.

Adolescence and Delinquency: Early Ideas

Such a view of adolescence also had great influence on thinking about juvenile delinquency. Although, as we shall see, explanations of delinquency drawing on problems of immigration and urbanization remained alive throughout
the nineteenth century — and down to our own time — many scholars toward
the close of the nineteenth century turned to psychological explanations that
saw adolescence itself as a major cause of delinquent tendencies and
characteristics.

The most systematic analysis of the relationship between adolescence and
delinquency during this period was carried out, not surprisingly, by G. Stanley
Hall himself. Hall might, in fact, be considered the first real American psychological *theorist* of delinquency. Hall's understanding of juvenile crime was complex. His thinking was grounded to some extent in the work of such hereditarian
criminologists as Cesare Lombroso — whose ideas are discussed in detail in
Chapters 3 and 4 — and he wrote, at one place, "Juvenile criminals, as a class,

are inferior in body and mind to normal children" (1904:I, 401). However, the main thrust of Hall's analysis was to point up ways in which delinquency was closely related to the properties of adolescence as such. As he wrote, "Adolescence is the best key to the nature of crime. It is essentially antisocial, selfishness, refusing to submit to the laws of altruism" (1904:I, 405). Being a good citizen was not easy for the adolescent; turning to crime was not unnatural.

Hall identified several adolescent characteristics that might lead easily to delinquency. He wrote, for example, of "a chronic illusion of youth that gives 'elsewhere' a special charm" and that, if not controlled, "must lead to vagrancy" (1904:I, 349). He noted, too, that "all boys develop a greatly increased propensity to fight at puberty" as well as an unexplainable readiness to feel violent anger (1904:I, 356). Adolescents, too, are peculiarly susceptible to envy and

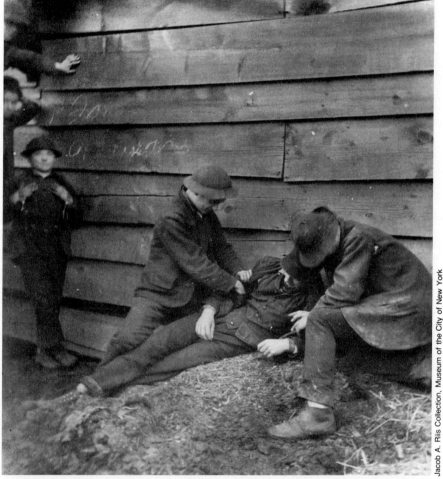

Jacob A. Riis Collection, Museum of the City of New York

Young offenders "rolling a drunk" — a widespread form of delinquency early in the twentieth century.

jealousy, and many juvenile crimes arise from such feelings. Hall's message was, then, that adolescence is a stage in which every youngster has antisocial tendencies; those whose tendencies are not controlled can easily slip into criminality.

One important implication of this view was to redefine juvenile crime in terms of the stages of life. As we saw earlier, juvenile delinquents were often described by nineteenth-century men and women as "precocious," as too adult for their ages. Hall and others in the latter part of the century tended to focus more on the immaturity of the delinquent, on the youthful offender's not having developed sufficiently mature restraint over his own natural tendencies. A contemporary of Hall's, M. P. E. Groszmann (1899:521), wrote, "it is probably due to some form of arrested development during the pubertal age, or to some unchecked impulses to realize in action the demoniac promptings of adolescent fancy, that we have so large a percentage of criminals of pubescent age." Such a shift in perspective was important, because it emphasized the extension of dependency into the years that were now labeled "adolescence." It made the delinquent seem to be much more of a child.

Environmentalism, Adolescence, and Delinquency in Turn-of-the-Century Thought

One result of this connection between adolescence and delinquency was not only to make the delinquent more of a child but also further to "decriminalize" the concept of delinquency itself. In the view of many, the delinquent was not a criminal but was, rather, a victim of his or her own natural—and not wholly controllable—impulses. And, in keeping with more traditional ideas, this was especially the case for those young people whose fall into delinquency had been encouraged by the problems of urban life. Such a view of delinquency was especially notable in the thinking of Jacob Riis, a leading social reformer of the turn of the century.

For Riis, juvenile delinquents were preeminently the victims of the inability of cities to supply needed services, particularly schooling, in urban slum neighborhoods. Citing one New York district in which over 1,500 youngsters were turned away from public schools solely because there was no room for them, Riis noted that those children had "practically been referred to the street for such education as they could pick up there" (1894:110). Such children would quickly progress from being truants by circumstance to being truants by choice. From there, it was but a short step to petty crimes and delinquency. Immigration and poverty were not themselves a problem; the failure of institutions to respond to immigration and poverty was at the root of delinquency in American cities. Riis even tied this social view of delinquency in with concepts of adolescence. Thus, one may note his discussion of the urban gang as an organization that "responds to a real need of the [boy's] nature. The distinguishing character of the American city boy is his genius for organization. . . . Unbridled, allowed to run riot, it results in the gang" (1892:215). No lover of gangs, Riis nevertheless believed that they were a natural direction in which youthful tendencies could go. Environmentalism thus went hand in hand with the discovery of adolescence to create a view of delinquency not as a moral deficiency in the delinquent but, instead, as a symptom of society's failure to deal adequately with a significant and difficult portion of the population.

Riis's perspective was not the only one current at the turn of the century. Many traditionalists continued to decry the moral failings of delinquent youngsters. Other thinkers — inspired by the work of the Italian criminologist Cesare Lombroso (see Chapters 3 and 4) — did influential studies of hereditarian factors in delinquency. But there is no doubt that views such as those of Riis dominated American ideas about delinquency during the period. These views stressed the dangers of the urban environment, the special problems raised by adolescence as a stage of life, and the character of the delinquent as a victim of society rather than a moral reprobate. They were views that served as the foundation for such an institution as the juvenile court, which we have briefly noted in Chapter 1 and which we shall discuss in more detail later. Hence, they provided major premises that have characterized American juvenile justice down to our own time.

The Twentieth Century

Indeed, much that we have seen in this chapter continues to guide our own era. For one thing, the appreciation for the distinctive nature of childhood and adolescence that we have traced has remained strong. As we noted at the opening of the chapter, this appreciation has led not only to certain ideas about how children should be treated but also to dedicated efforts to investigate child and adolescent development in order to identify their characteristics as fully as possible. This is not the place in which to survey the vast body of literature these efforts have produced. Here we will offer only an overview of twentieth-century ideas, stressing those which have had the greatest influence on American culture and society, and on American concepts of juvenile delinquency.

Child Rearing and Friendship: A Twentieth-Century Theme

In regard to child rearing, American thought has generally built on nineteenth-century ideals of encouraging "natural affection" by urging the development of relationships between parents and children modeled on companionship, even friendship. Martha Wolfenstein, looking at the child-rearing literature of the 1940s and 1950s, characterized this tendency in twentieth-century child-rearing ideas with the term "fun morality," by which she intended to stress the extent to which parents and children, like good friends, were supposed to enjoy each other's company by having fun together. According to Wolfenstein, even as recently as the second decade of the twentieth century, playing with a child, even with a baby, was thought to produce "unwholesome pleasure" and other ill effects. As one authority asserted in 1914, a few minutes' play "may result in nervous disturbance of the baby and upset his regular habits" (Wolfenstein, 1955: 172). By the 1940s, however, it was asserted, "Play and singing make both mother and baby enjoy the routine of life," and mothers and fathers alike were being encouraged to play with their children (1955:172). As Wolfenstein (1955:170) observes:

The opposition between the pleasant and the good is deeply grounded in older American morals. . . . There are strong doubts as to whether what is enjoyable is not wicked or deleterious. In recent years, however, there has been a marked effort to overcome this dichotomy, to say that what is pleasant is also good for you. The writers on childraising reflect the changing ideas on this issue.

Getting along with each other thus becomes a central goal for parents and their children.

The child-rearing literature examined by Wolfenstein was not the only way in which such attitudes were encouraged. Marchand (1985:230, 231), in a recent study of advertising from the 1920s and 1930s — a crucial period for the development of advertising techniques and influence — has shown how many ads "reflected and endorsed" what he describes as "more democratic, child-centered family relations," especially for their middle-class American audience. General Mills, in selling Wheaties, for example, argued that forcing children to eat what they did not want could turn "high spirited youngsters" into recalcitrant, possibly "perverse" creatures. Cream of Wheat even urged mothers to "make a game of important habits," proclaiming in one ad that such an approach was "full of fun but scientific, too."

The Thought of Dr. Benjamin Spock

One sees an especially influential statement of these democratic ideas in the most important popular American work on child rearing published since World War II, Dr. Benjamin Spock's (1957) *Common Sense Book of Baby and Child Care.* Spock's views on child rearing have often been exaggerated by commentators on American culture; he has frequently been described as a champion of excessive permissiveness in the raising of children. In fact, like earlier figures, Spock places great stress on bringing up obedient and mannerly young people and at several points notes that parents, to be successful, must be firm in responding to misbehavior, even in the very young. Nevertheless, in his emphasis on tailoring child rearing to the individual child, Spock took the trends we have been discussing in significant directions.

No one can read Spock's child-rearing manual without being impressed by his sense of how greatly children can differ from one another. Recognizing that individual children develop at different rates, he argues that different children (and different parents, for that matter) require different methods of disciplining. The good parent, he asserts, must make "allowances" for each child's "individuality," developing methods accordingly (1957:49). In this, Spock argues far differently from those in earlier generations who believed that rigid routines and set methods would do the best for any child and who took, therefore, a virtually mechanical approach to child development.

No less crucial is the absence of moralism in Spock's manual. To be sure, Spock has assigned great importance to raising children with principles — and his own life has testified to his moral concerns — but his treatment and interpretation of many issues of child rearing is far more pragmatic than moralistic. One may see an illustration of this by comparing Spock with the earlier figures in regard to a very common childhood foible, lying. The Puritan Increase Mather (1679:109) once addressed young people on lying in this way: "Art thou a lying Child? Then the Devil is thy Father, and except thou repent of this sin, and beware of it for the time to come, when once thy Soul is out of thy body, it must come into that Lake which burneth with fire and brimstone which is the second Death." In the nineteenth century, with its great emphasis on family ties, lying was seen as not uncommon but as a danger still to a family life based on mutual affection—an affection built, in part, on trust. Thus, parents were urged to guard against lying by their children, chiefly to maintain a proper family relation (Bushnell, 1947). Spock (1957:363) also sees lying as not uncommon but notes that, in some jams, "the only tactful way out is a small lie, and this is no cause for alarm." Asserting that "a child isn't naturally deceitful," Spock sees the lie as, above all, a symptom of stress, as a clue to what the child is worried about in life. Thus the moralism and piousness of past generations has been removed from thinking about the child and its place taken, here, by a greater concern for "adjustment."

And, indeed, in this concern for adjustment is to be found a central focus in Spock's child-rearing method: parents and children are supposed to be happy. The point is made in an early discussion of parental strictness. Spock (1957:48) does not argue that parents should not be strict, but his approval of strictness is couched in interesting terms:

> Moderate strictness—in the sense of requiring good manners, prompt obedience, orderliness—is not harmful to children so long as the parents are basically kind and so long as the children are growing up happy and friendly.

And here, indeed, was a key. For Spock, childhood should be pleasurable. Good behavior—from the parents' point of view—should never be achieved at the cost of happiness and friendliness in the child.

Thus, the child that Spock (1957:388) holds up as ideal—and it is an ideal he applies to young people well into adolescence—is one who is sociable and popular:

> How happily a person gets along as an adult in his job, in his family and social life, depends a great deal on how he got along with other children when he was young. If parents give a child high standards and high ideals at home, these form part of his character and show up in the long run, even though he goes through a period of bad English and rough manner in the middle period of childhood. But if parents are unhappy about the neighborhood they live in and the companions their child has, give him a feeling that he is different from the others, discourage him from making friends, the child may grow up unable to mix with any group or to make a happy life. Then his high standards won't be of any use to the world or to himself.

Sociability is a guiding principle in Spock's view of the goals of a proper upbringing.

The Weakening of the Family and the Twentieth-Century Child

Spock has been, however, only the most noted of those theorists for whom the stress in individuality and sociability and the rejection of moralism have been of central concern in post–World War II America. This point of view has dominated thought on child rearing, at least at the level at which child-rearing theories reach the general public. The upshot of this has been a progressive lessening of the role of the family itself in bringing up children.

The process does not date exactly from the work of Spock and his contemporaries. Lasch (1979) has traced it to the late nineteenth century, with the rise of the "helping professions" — especially in areas such as psychology and social work — which argued that bringing up children was a complex matter, one that required the guidance of those with expertise in the field. The thrust of the argument was to undermine the role of the family in child rearing. Indeed, even going back to those days, there were some who argued that giving the family too great a role in child rearing — and especially, placing too much stress on those values of love and affection so prized by preceding generations — was positively dangerous. This tendency, as Lasch has shown, has continued unabated up to the present time. In the words of one authority he quotes (Lasch, 1977:105):

> Today it requires more than mere enveloping love to prepare a person for a specifically challenging world. The child must learn practical social techniques of affiliating himself to others outside the family, neighborhood, and parish.

To be sure, the parent has not been wholly excluded from the process of child rearing. Indeed, the contemporary literature places great stress on "parenting" as an activity and emphasizes, in particular, the value of the time that parents and children spend together. However, in line with developments that have been taking place for about the last four decades, a model for parent-child relationships based on friendship rather than on either authority or a smothering affection has come to be seen as the ideal one, most in keeping with the bringing up of sociable, well-rounded individuals.

Recent Views of Adolescence

The kinds of developments that have affected child rearing generally have had special force insofar as adolescents are concerned. Adolescence has retained a crucial place in thinking about childhood down to the present time. There remains a strong belief in the formative significance of the adolescent years. But, at the same time, approaches to adolescence have undergone significant changes in the post – World War II period.

One of these has been the increasing stress on questions of individuality and identity, a stress consistent with the recognition of the individuality of the child. This has had great impact on the understanding of adolescence itself, particularly through the influential work of Erik H. Erikson. Erikson (1963), a psychoanalyst who has spent many years studying human development, has argued that adolescence is, preeminently, a time of identity confusion and crisis, as the youngster searches for both a sense of self and a legitimate social role. Much contemporary thought about how to deal with adolescence resembles Erikson's in stressing the importance of identity questions to adolescent life.

One may see this, for example, in the extremely popular works of the psychologist Haim Ginott. Seeking to guide parents in their relationships with their teenage children, Ginott (1969) advised modes of behavior that were clearly based on such notions as working with the natural character of the youngster and appreciating the youngster's individuality. Thus, he urged parents to respect the teenager's privacy and to accept "restlessness and discontent" as a natural part of teenage life. He urged, too, avoiding those actions which appeared to stress the youngster's dependent status and proximity to childhood. Identity was a basic issue for adolescents, and, like those who provided advice in regard to younger children, Ginott argued that it was very easy for parental guidance to send the wrong messages and to distort the natural development of the older child.

The focus on identity has also led to a considerable broadening of the category of adolescence itself. In Hall's time, and for some time thereafter, adolescence was pretty much identified with the onset of puberty. The biological changes of puberty, it was believed, helped to explain the psychological and emotional changes identified with adolescence as a stage of life. More recent scholars have emphasized, however, that much that has been observed about adolescence cannot be closely correlated with physiology. Traits associated with adolescence occur, in some youngsters, well before puberty; in others, well after. As a result, recent students have extended the age of adolescence downward to about eleven years old and have considered that adolescence continues in most individuals to about age nineteen. This is because, they argue, the kinds of identity concerns associated with adolescence tend to appear during those years.

Interestingly, the expansion of adolescence one finds in the works of students of human development is also a phenomenon of recent American society as well. On the one hand, since the 1940s, the age of adolescence has declined. During the 1930s and 1940s, children below fourteen or fifteen tended to be set apart, in many ways, from their older contemporaries. By the 1950s, subteenagers and teenagers had come to follow the same fashions, to pursue the same idols. Younger children, during that decade, began to participate in what had been considered adolescent activities. As a social category, then, adolescence has taken on greater importance for understanding an ever larger portion of a child's life.

But perhaps the most notable development in regard to adolescence in recent years has been the way in which the general weakening of the role of the family in child rearing has affected adolescent socialization. As Edward Shorter puts it, "adolescent children have begun to manifest a massive uninterest in their parent's values. . . . Now the peer group is again taking up the task of adolescent socialization: and as the children move through puberty, parental thoughts about good and bad, right and wrong, and which way is up are becoming ever more irrelevant to them" (1975:270–271). Peers rather than adults are setting the standards and defining the rules for contemporary adolescents.

Youth Culture

This has led at least some scholars, notably Coleman (1961), to argue that adolescents have, in recent years, sought to differentiate themselves from adults, to create a subculture separate from the adult world. Other scholars disagree that youths have created anything like a subculture, but most agree, at least, with the implication of Shorter's words in the preceding paragraph, that the alienation of adolescents from adult institutions and adult role models has been marked. This alienation has been expressed in everything from music to styles of dress to language.

Perhaps what the late twentieth century is witnessing is, above all, what might be termed a "crisis in dependency," in which young people are no longer subject to the same dependent roles and definitions that, since at least the early nineteenth century, have constituted the essence of childhood and, since the late nineteenth century, the essence of youth, as well. Thus, at the same time that there has been a notable alienation of young people from adult institutions and authority, there has not been an alienation from adulthood as such. Indeed, many of the obviously "youth-oriented" features of adolescent life in earlier years have recently been deemphasized as, concerned with sociability, young people have sought to become adept at what used to be adult social skills. Thus, many youth-oriented organizations such as the Boy Scouts have experienced severe declines in membership during this period, as young people are far more interested in developing techniques useful to the adult world. The new style, Kett (1977:268) has aptly put it, sanctions "dancing and tennis rather than knot tying and Indian lore." Perhaps it is an overstatement to argue, as has one historian, that adolescence is currently *losing* its status as a separate stage of life (Gillis, 1974). But there can be little doubt that trends in ideas about child rearing have powerfully influenced both conceptions of adolescence and adolescent life itself.

Twentieth-Century Conceptions of Delinquency: An Overview

Recent Popular Conceptions of Delinquency

The impact of twentieth-century developments in thinking about childhood, adolescence, and juvenile delinquency will be discussed in detail in the chapters that follow. For now, however, we should note that the impact has been great. Just as in earlier times concepts of childhood and youth fit closely with prevailing concepts of juvenile delinquency, so have they continued to inform such concepts in the twentieth century.

One sees this fit most clearly in those theories and conceptions which stress environmental causes for delinquency. Both have been extremely powerful at the popular level, as outlined in Chapter 3. Such conceptions, as we shall see, have stressed a range of familiar causal factors, including lack of job opportunities and lack of alternative routes for satisfaction as well as getting in with the "wrong kind of kids," ideas found in nineteenth-century thinking, too.

But no less important are what are clearly "subcultural" popular explanations for delinquency, seeing delinquency as a manifestation of a powerful, deviant youth culture, something well in keeping with the ideas of Coleman and others. Popular ideas have also adopted an almost Eriksonian image of the delinquent as the product of a misguided but otherwise normal effort to create a satisfying identity (Gilbert, 1986).

These conceptions have received strong support from the popular media, most notably from films. Film historians Mark McGee and R. J. Robertson (1982) have traced the "JD film," as a genre, back to the early 1920s. As they have shown, the earliest typical Hollywood portrayals of delinquents inevitably stressed environmental sources as the bases for juvenile crime—whether the source identified was the slum life portrayed in such early films as the "Dead End Kids" movies of the 1930s or the apparently violent mixture of adolescence and early rock-and-roll dramatized in *Blackboard Jungle* (1955). Beginning in the 1950s, however, JD films increasingly focused on the danger (and dangerous attractiveness) of a youth culture in which delinquency was not an aberration but a variant form. Certainly one may see this in such genuine classics as *The Wild One* (1954), and *Rebel Without a Cause* (1955), as well as in a host of lesser imitators made throughout the 1950s and 1960s. Moreover, there was a tendency in the best of the films to portray the delinquent hero as vulnerable and misunderstood, but certainly not bad—as a figure for whom delinquency was part of a search for self. The tendency remains alive in the delinquent, or near delinquent, characters in more recent "brat-pack" movies such as *The Breakfast Club* (1984).

As Gilbert (1986) has shown, these cinematic portrayals had their counterparts in other media treatments of delinquency and even helped to create—or at least to reinforce—what might be described as a delinquency scare in the mid-1950s. We shall have more to say of this in Chapter 8.

Concepts of Childhood, Popular Thought, and Delinquency Theory

The kinds of views of childhood and delinquency we have been reviewing here have not had an inevitable influence on delinquency theory—although, as we shall see in Chapters 6–11, their impact on social policy has been enormous. As we shall note in Chapters 3 and 4, especially, delinquency theory has its own intellectual tradition and has developed in some ways quite independent of concepts of childhood and youth. This is notably true of the hereditarian and "constitutional" arguments that may be traced to the early criminological theories of Cesare Lombroso. In the case of other theories, however, the connections between theory and concepts of childhood are strong, if not always obvious. In these theories, conceptions of childhood and youth enter as dominant assumptions upon which theorizing is based. This is especially so after about 1920, when, as we shall see, the most influential theories of delinquency took shape.

Of special importance in many of the theories we are about to review in detail in the next four chapters has been the great importance given to the role of peers in what might be called the socialization of delinquent values and delinquent behavior. Although, as we shall see in Chapter 5, especially, social scientists have hotly debated whether delinquency rests on a distinctive, deviant set of values, the debate itself—and the terms in which it has been conducted—has reflected the great significance given to peers in the understanding of the socialization of adolescents. And, as we shall see in Chapter 14, that same assumption has informed some of the most innovative approaches to the treatment of delinquency over the last thirty years. Students will notice this and other connections as, in the next four chapters, we explore various formal theories of delinquency in some detail. But for now we may note that such connections help to stress, at one level at least, how important the social-histor-

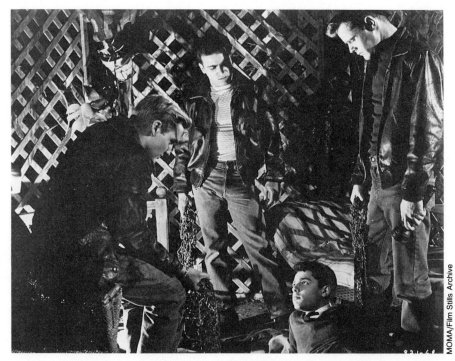

MOMA/Film Stills Archive

Portrayal of delinquency in the film *Rebel Without a Cause.*

ical construction of childhood has been to the understanding of juvenile delinquency.

Summary

The ideas about delinquency that have developed in American society are firmly based in ideas about childhood and youth, as such. These latter ideas themselves have a long and complex history. And it is possible to date to the early nineteenth century the belief that juvenile delinquency represents a distinctive category of unacceptable behavior.

Much of Western history shows a gross indifference to childhood. Adult society formed the focus of social concern; children were expected to find their way in the adult world. Only in the early modern era, beginning in about the sixteenth and seventeenth centuries, did adults begin to reveal a sense that there was something distinctive and special about children and that society had a duty to respond to the special needs of the child.

During the time of English colonization in America, these ideas were given significant shape by the American Puritans, who gave much thought to proper modes of child rearing. Although they did not take a clearly positive view of childhood, their great concern for salvation led them to stress the vulnerability of children and youth and the need for special care in the formation of character in the child. Their methods may appear foreign to us today, but their concern for the child clearly anticipated the child-centered focus of family life that came down to the twentieth century.

The nineteenth century was marked by a revolution in sentiment that promoted more positive views of childhood, especially among the middle class. Many Americans began to emphasize not only the child's vulnerability and malleability but also the basic goodness of children, a goodness that had to be encouraged by the family and by the environment.

This revolution in sentiment had much to do with the emergence of a clearcut concept of delinquency. When middle-class reformers, in particular, compared the needs of childhood with the conditions under which urban children had to mature, they saw clear reasons why such children could become delinquent. Here was an important step in the development of the idea of juvenile delinquency. It would serve as the basis for later, essentially environmentalist approaches to explaining juvenile crime.

But there have been other important developments as well. With the prolongation of childhood and the creation of a concept of adolescence — also datable to the nineteenth century — distinctly psychological approaches to the understanding of childhood and youth have become significant, as has a focus on older youngsters.

In addition, twentieth-century America has witnessed what many scholars consider a significant weakening of the family, both in terms of child-rearing practices and in terms of socialization. Increasingly, many experts agree, children and young people look more to their peers than to their parents as they seek to become a part of the larger society.

These developments, too, have had an impact on the way many Americans think about delinquency. Theories and popular conceptions stressing not only environmental factors but the apparently inevitable problems of "adjustment" have come to play an important role in the understanding of juvenile delinquency. So, too, have subcultural theories that view delinquency as an aspect of a "youth culture" that sets itself apart from the adult world. The theoretical ideas about juvenile delinquency that have emerged from such conditions will be the subject of the next four chapters.

References

Ariès, Philippe. 1962. *Centuries of Childhood: A Social History of Family Life.* Translated by Robert Baldick. New York: Vintage.

Bakan, David. 1971. Adolescence in America from Idea to Social Fact. *Daedalus* 100:979–995.

Bartlett, Richard A. 1974. *The New Country: A Social History of the American Frontier, 1776–1890.* New York: Oxford Univ. Press.

Beales, Ross W., Jr. 1975. In Search of the Historical Child: Miniature Adulthood and Youth in Colonial New England. *American Quarterly* 27:379–398.

Books for Children. 1830. *Christian Examiner* 8:22–35.

Bremner, Robert H. 1956. *From the Depths: The Discovery of Poverty in the United States.* New York: New York University Press.

————, ed. 1970. *Children and Youth in America: A Documentary History.* 3 vols. Cambridge, Mass.: Harvard Univ. Press.

Bruce, Dickson D., Jr. 1979. *Violence and Culture in the Antebellum South.* Austin, Tex.: Univ. of Texas Press.

Bushnell, Horace. 1947. *Christian Nurture.* New Haven: Yale Univ. Press.

Calhoun, Daniel. 1973. *The Intelligence of a People.* Princeton, N.J.: Princeton Univ. Press.

Carpenter, Mary. 1853. *Juvenile Delinquents: Their Condition and Treatment.* Rept. Montclair, N.J.: Patterson Smith, 1970.

Coleman, James S. 1961. *The Adolescent Society: The Social Life of the Teenager and Its Impact on Education.* Rept. Westport, Conn.: Greenwood Press, 1981.

Davis, Glenn. 1976. *Childhood and History in America.* New York: Psychohistory Press.

Davis, Natalie Z. 1971. The Reasons of Misrule: Youth Groups and Charivaris in Sixteenth Century France. *Past and Present* 50:41–75.

de Mause, Lloyd. 1975. The Evolution of Childhood. In *The History of Childhood*, edited by Lloyd de Mause, 1–73. New York: Harper Torchbooks.

Demos, John. 1970. *A Little Commonwealth: Family Life in Plymouth Colony.* New York: Oxford Univ. Press.

————, and Demos, Virginia. 1969. Adolescence in Historical Perspective. *Journal of Marriage and the Family* 31:632–638.

Erikson, Erik H. 1963. *Childhood and Society.* 2nd ed., revised and enlarged. New York: W. W. Norton.

Franklin, Benjamin. 1961. *The Autobiography and Other Writings.* Edited by L. Jesse Lemisch. New York: Signet Books.

Gilbert, James. 1986. *A Cycle of Outrage: America's Reaction to the Juvenile Delinquent in the 1950s.* New York: Oxford Univ. Press.

Gillis, John R. 1974. *Youth and History: Tradition and Change in European Age Relations, 1770–Present.* New York: Academic Press.

Ginott, Haim G. 1969. *Between Parent and Teenager.* New York: Macmillan.

Glasco, Laurence A. 1977. The Life Cycles and Household Structure of American Ethnic Groups: Irish, Germans, and Native-born Whites in Buffalo, New York, 1855. In *Family and Kin in Urban Communities, 1700–1930*, edited by Tamara K. Hareven, 122–143. New York: Franklin Watts.

Greven, Philip J., Jr. 1977. *The Protestant Temperament: Patterns of Child-Rearing, Religious Experience, and the Self in Early America.* New York: Knopf.

Groszman, M. P. E. 1899. Criminality in Children. *Arena* 22:509–525, 644–652.

Hall, G. Stanley, 1904. *Adolescence: Its Psychology and Its Relations to Physiology, Anthropology, Sociology, Sex, Crime, Religion and Education.* 2 vols. New York: Appleton.

Hawes, Joseph N. 1971. *Children in Urban Society: Juvenile Delinquency in Nineteenth-Century America.* New York: Oxford Univ. Press.

House of Reformation, The. 1832. *New England Magazine* 3:382–390.

Hunt, David. 1970. *Parents and Children in History: The Psychology of Family Life in Early Modern France.* New York: Basic Books.

Illick, Joseph. 1975. Child-Rearing in Seventeenth-Century England and America. In *The History of Childhood*, edited by Lloyd de Mause, 303–305. New York: Harper Torchbooks.

Jolowicz, H. F. 1957. *Roman Foundations of Modern Law.* London: Oxford Univ. Press.

Katz, Michael B. 1975. *The People of Hamilton, Canada West: Family and Class in a Mid-Nineteenth-Century City.* Cambridge, Mass.: Harvard Univ. Press.

Kett, Joseph F. 1977. *Rites of Passage: Adolescence in America, 1790 to the Present.* New York: Basic Books.

Kiefer, Monica. 1948. *American Children Through Their Books, 1700–1835.* Philadelphia: Univ. of Pennsylvania Press.

Lasch, Christopher. 1977. *Haven in a Heartless World: The Family Besieged.* New York: Basic Books.

———. 1979. *The Culture of Narcissism: American Life in an Age of Diminishing Expectations.* New York: Warner.

Laslett, Peter. 1965. *The World We Have Lost.* New York: Scribner's.

Lystad, Mary. 1980. *From Dr. Mather to Dr. Seuss: 200 Years of American Books for Children.* Boston: G. K. Hall.

McDannell, Colleen. 1986. *The Christian Home in Victorian America, 1840–1900.* Bloomington, Ind.: Indiana Univ. Press.

Macfarlane, Alan. 1970. *The Family Life of Ralph Josselin, a Seventeenth-Century Clergyman: An Essay in Historical Anthropology.* Cambridge: Cambridge Univ. Press.

McGee, Mark Thomas, and Robertson, R. J. 1982. *The J.D. Films: Juvenile Delinquency in the Movies.* Jefferson, N.C.: McFarland.

McGuffey, William Holmes. 1879. *McGuffey's Fifth Eclectic Reader.* Rept. New York: Signet Books, 1962.

McLaughlin, Mary Martin. 1975. Survivors and Surrogates: Children and Parents from the Ninth to the Thirteenth Centuries. In *The History of Childhood*, edited by Lloyd de Mause, 101–181. New York: Harper Torchbooks.

Macleod, David I. 1983. *Building Character in the American Boy: The Boy Scouts, YMCA, and Their Forerunners, 1870–1920.* Madison, Wisc.: Univ. of Wisconsin Press.

Management of Children. 1831. *Godey's Lady's Book* 2:240.

Marchand, Roland. 1985. *Advertising the American Dream: Making Way for Modernity, 1920–1940.* Berkeley, Calif.: Univ. of California Press.

Marvick, Elizabeth Wirth. 1975. Nature Versus Nurture: Patterns and Trends in Seventeenth-Century French Child-Rearing. In *The History of Childhood*, edited by Lloyd de Mause, 259–301. New York: Harper Torchbooks.

Mather, Cotton. 1690. *Addresses to Old Men, and Young Men, and Little Children.* Boston: Printed by R. Pierce.

Mather, Increase. 1678. *Pray for the Rising Generation.* Cambridge: Printed by Samuel Green.

———. 1679. *A Call from Heaven.* Boston.

Mennel, Robert M., 1973. *Thorns and Thistles: Juvenile Delinquents in the United States, 1825–1940.* Hanover, N.H.: Univ. Press of New England.

Mohl, Raymond A. 1971. *Poverty in New York, 1783–1825.* New York: Oxford Univ. Press.

Morgan, Edmund S. 1966. *The Puritan Family: Religion and Domestic Relations in Seventeenth-Century New England.* Rev. ed. New York: Harper and Row.

Mother and Eliza. 1826. *Juvenile Miscellany* 1, no. 2:57–61.

Mounteer, Carl A. 1984. Beginners on the Forum: Roman Adolescence and Youth, 200 B.C. to A.D. 100. *Journal of Psychohistory* 12:251–258.

Muncie, John. 1984. *"The Trouble with Kids Today": Youth and Crime in Post-War Britain.* London: Hutchinson.

Primary Schools. 1864. *American Educational Monthly* 1:85, 86.

Rapson, Richard L. 1965. The American Child As Seen by British Travelers, 1845–1935. *American Quarterly* 17:520–534.

Rawson, Beryl. 1986. The Roman Family. In *The Family in Ancient Rome: New Perspectives*, edited by Beryl Rawson, 1–57. Ithaca, N.Y.: Cornell Univ. Press.

Riis, Jacob A. 1892. *The Children of the Poor.* Rept. New York: Garrett Press, 1970.

———. 1894. The Making of Thieves in New York. *Century* 49 (n.s. 27):109–116.

Rockwell, Mrs. S. N. 1867. Facts and Thoughts About Reform Schools. *American Educational Monthly* 4:257–261, 295–298, 335–339, 375–378, 415–418.

Ryan, Mary P. 1981. *Cradle of the Middle Class: The Family in Oneida County, New York, 1790–1825.* Cambridge: Cambridge Univ. Press.

Schultz, Stanley K. 1973. *The Culture Factory: Boston Public Schools, 1789–1860.* New York: Oxford Univ. Press.

Shorter, Edward. 1975. *The Making of the Modern Family.* New York: Basic Books.

Smith, Daniel Blake. 1980. *Inside the Great House: Planter Family Life in Eighteenth-Century Chesapeake Society.* Ithaca, N.Y.: Cornell Univ. Press.

Smith, Steven R. 1973. The London Apprentices as Seventeenth-Century Adolescents. *Past and Present* 61:149–161.

Smith-Rosenberg, Carroll. 1985. *Disorderly Conduct: Visions of Gender in Victorian America.* New York: Knopf.

Spock, Benjamin. 1957. *The Common Sense Book of Baby and Child Care.* Rev. ed. New York: Duell, Sloan and Pearce.

Sunley, Robert. 1955. Early Nineteenth-Century American Literature on Child Rearing. In *Childhood in Contemporary Cultures,* edited by Margaret Mead and Martha Wolfenstein, 150–167. Chicago: Univ. of Chicago Press.

Thompson, Roger. 1984. Adolescent Culture in Colonial Massachusetts. *Journal of Family History* 9:127–144.

Tucker, M. J. 1975. The Child as Beginning and End: Fifteenth and Sixteenth Century English Childhood. In *The History of Childhood,* edited by Lloyd de Mause, 229–257. New York: Harper Torchbooks.

Walzer, John F. 1975. A Period of Ambivalence: Eighteenth-Century American Childhood. In *The History of Childhood,* edited by Lloyd de Mause, 351–382. New York: Harper Torchbooks.

Waterston, Robert C. 1852. Juvenile Depravity and Reformatory Schools. *Christian Examiner* 52:391–405.

Watson, Alan. 1970. *The Law of the Ancient Romans.* Dallas, Tex.: Southern Methodist Univ. Press.

Whitlock, Henry. 1813. The Editor's Address to Parents. *Youth's Repository of Christian Knowledge* 1:1–5.

Wishy, Bernard W. 1968. *The Child and the Republic: The Dawn of Modern American Child Nurture.* Philadelphia: Univ. of Pennsylvania Press.

Wolfenstein, Martha. 1955. Fun Morality: An Analysis of Recent American Child-Training Literature. In *Childhood in Contemporary Cultures,* edited by Margaret Mead and Martha Wolfenstein, 168–178. Chicago: Univ. of Chicago Press.

Wyatt-Brown, Bertram. 1982. *Southern Honor: Ethics and Behavior in the Old South.* New York: Oxford Univ. Press.

Zelizer, Viviana A. 1985. *Pricing the Priceless Child: The Changing Social Value of Children.* New York: Basic Books.

Zuckerman, Michael. 1979. William Byrd's Family. *Perspectives in American History* 12:255–311.

PART **II**

Theories and Their Uses

CHAPTER 3

Delinquency Theory: Present Considerations and Early Formulations

Courtesy Phil Coale, Tallahassee Democrat

It is essential to set into place a few basic ideas before reviewing the considerable array of past and present theories that attempt to explain the phenomena of juvenile delinquency. It is crucial to appreciate, as discussed in Chapter 1, that it is not possible to define the concept "juvenile delinquency" in a formal way, although it may be anchored and bounded by state laws that vary strikingly in their behavioral components. Therefore, it seems at times feckless, almost futile, to attempt to locate a theoretical explanation for an undefined concept that encompasses matters as diverse as murder, arson, shoplifting, possession of a dangerous drug, vandalism, rape, and incorrigibility, among many other acts. The only element that such things seem to have in common is that they have been outlawed, and that state-sanctioned punishment can be levied against persons within certain age brackets who are caught and successfully prosecuted for having committed such acts. Robert Rice (1956:10) has underlined the complexity of trying to locate a formula that provides helpful understanding of such a variety of behaviors by pointing out that matters defined as "juvenile delinquency have about as much in common as the words quail, deliquescence, pique, and kumquat — all of which can be said to be similar because each contains the letter 'q.'"

Only if the existence of the laws against delinquent behavior and the consequences of their violation were the essential ingredients in the occurrence of the delinquent acts would we be able to fasten upon a common factor that could tie together the diverse behaviors and permit a comprehensive explanation of their genesis. Sometimes, indeed, the law does appear to play a particularly prominent role in the elicitation of delinquent acts. Note, for instance, the observation of a heroin addict who insists that it is the illegal status of hard drug use that makes it so attractive to him:

> if narcotics was easy to come by, there wouldn't be half as many addicts. To take narcotics right now, it is cloak-and-dagger, it's spy work, it's something out of television, believe me. You have to walk the street, you have to secure a pusher, you have to locate the money to buy these narcotics, you have to check in dark hallways, on roofs, go through cellars, all this running about, all the time, keeping one eye out for the police. . . . This is an adventure for a young man. And when you finally get your narcotics back to your pad where you can use it, you say to yourself: Man, I did it, I beat the fuzz. I made the scene. (Larner, 1964:100)

Similarly, another delinquent (Rosenberg and Silverstein, 1969:151) reports that the appeal of what he is involved in lies in skirting danger, courting trouble, "feeling good inside" when he has had a close call after a caper: "Watching a guy get mad and letting him chase you. That's what I like," this delinquent insists.

In this sense, it might be argued that the truest cause of delinquency is the existence of laws defining it. Sometimes, either out of whimsy or because they are intellectually misguided, scholars have taken such a position. Abolish the laws, they proclaim, and we will have solved the problem of delinquency. It is true that such a step would cure the society of a phenomenon that bears the name of delinquency, but it is patently obvious that virtually all — and very likely more — of the same kinds of acts will persist and will continue to harm their victims and, at times, their perpetrators as well. Laws ought to be scrutinized and refashioned when they are found to be out of tune with just principles or to be counterproductive, but laws do not cause delinquency, except for those relatively rare persons who get particular satisfaction out of doing the legally forbidden. Laws only specify delinquent acts. Indeed, for many youths — probably most — the existence of laws against delinquent behavior probably is of rather little importance in determining how they act. Other considerations — personal anger, gang codes, temptation, and training, for instance — probably take precedence over the legal codes in determining how youngsters will behave. In some instances, delinquents will be found who are surprised that what they have done constitutes a legal violation; in such cases, it cannot in any way be claimed that the law conditioned their behavior. And, similarly, all of us organize our actions in many regards without particular attention to laws; for example, few of us would murder whether or not it was against the law, and many of us would react violently to a person who had maimed someone close to us, whatever the law stated.

A good illustration of the relative insignificance of law in inhibiting a young woman from beginning to obtain material things in exchange for sexual activity is found in a court psychiatrist's appraisal of her situation:

> If she has not already been getting clothes, etc. through her sexual life I expect that she will soon begin doing so. To be quite frank, I am not half so disturbed about this as I am about her realistic approach to the problem. She knows that she stammers, she knows that she is poor, she guesses that she is illegitimate, she knows that she is dumb, and in a rather cold way she looked me in the eye and asked whether I wouldn't do the same thing. (Rumney and Murphy, 1952:33–34)

At the same time, the law sets forth in a formal manner a roster of forbidden acts and thereby adds a moral dimension to such acts. Though the physiological consequences of usage may be equally harmful, it is very different to sell cigarettes and to sell marijuana. Vicious gossip may be more injurious than a simple assault, but the legal status of the first (within certain limits) and the illegality of the second cause them to have different meanings for most of us. In the Bible, Paul noted, "where there is no law there is no transgression" (Romans, 4:15) and that the laws brought him knowledge of sin (Romans 3:20). This anticipates later American scholarship: Michael and Adler (1933:5) note, for instance, "The criminal law is the formal cause of crime. That does not mean that the law produces the behavior which it prohibits. It means only that the criminal law gives behavior its quality of criminality."

It is important, when examining theories regarding juvenile delinquency, to appreciate that the behaviors encompassed under the label of "juvenile delinquency" inevitably lead many persons to search for theoretical propositions that will explain them all rather than for more modest formulations that might explain those which have significant similarities (Witmer and Kotinsky, 1956). It seems much more reasonable to subdivide the behaviors into analytically similar kinds of acts — say those involving aggression — and then to attempt to account theoretically for these homogeneous subgroups of actions. As we will learn in this and the following chapters, some theories do exactly that, while others, though they account for only some forms of delinquency, pretend that they are addressing all of the various manifestations of the phenomenon. Sociologists, for instance, possess a rich theoretical tradition aimed at providing understanding of the behavior of juvenile gangs. Investigations of gangs fit nicely with the long-standing sociological concern with interaction among groups of persons in bounded social settings such as slums. But theories of gang behavior, however sophisticated they are, will not carry us too far toward understanding a lone twelve-year-old arsonist who has no friends and who, after a brain scan test, is found to have a lesion of a kind that impairs social judgment. Psychologists, for their part, might be able to offer theories that help us to account for the behavior of certain kinds of individuals, but their work often proves to be insensitive to things such as social values that serve to define how a given personality will respond to a particular situation.

Mead's (1972) anthropological studies are particularly informative in regard to the shortcomings of inquiries confined to a particular personality without cognizance of the social setting in which the person operates. She points out, as an illustration, that the Arapesh disapproved of and downgraded human traits that we would find admirable. In Arapesh culture, for instance, it was not individual aggression that was looked down on but rather behavior that "roused anger and violence in another person." Thus, if a young man or woman, on the basis of the most decent motives, refused to do or tell something and thereby elicited a violent response from an adult, the young person would be viewed as the malefactor. Similarly, teasing that produces an angry response is regarded as unacceptable behavior. Traits that would be apt to lead to successful adjustment in our society are seen as deviant in Arapesh society — and undoubtedly prove to be disabling and to push toward delinquency.

> There were individuals among the Arapesh who were capable of good, clear thinking and some of the little boys did a fine job on the "ball and field" test of the Stanford-Binet intelligence test. These were, however, deviant individuals who had difficulty in dealing with the soft, uncertain outlines of the culture, in which no one did skilled work. (1972:198)

In short, as a concept in search of theoretical integrity, the construct "juvenile delinquency" leaves a great deal — indeed, an enormous amount — to be desired from a scientific viewpoint. Among other things, it is anchored in law and not behavior, it is inconstant in the sense that today's forbidden act can be tomorrow's permissible behavior, and it is restricted to an age span that varies from place to place and rests upon an arguable proposition — that there is something significantly different about youth crime in contrast to illegal acts committed by adults (see Chapter 2).

Theory Defined and Defended _____

Does all this mean that it is largely — or totally — a waste of time and intellectual energy to attempt to formulate theories that address the factual chaos that becomes characteristic of any body of information that is not transformed into some kind of systematic order? The answer inheres in the wording of the foregoing question: it is absolutely essential to try, however ineptly we do so, to organize the information that we possess in regard to delinquency in order to come to understand it better, to perceive meaningful regularities, and to be able to predict on the basis of our theoretical constructs the likely outcome in terms of delinquent behavior of differing social arrangements and personal conditions. It is not necessary, of course, to have a powerful theoretical understanding of the roots of delinquency in order to deal effectively with its manifestation: as pragmatists are fond of pointing out, quinine was employed as a treatment for malaria for centuries before physicians came to appreciate the crucial role of the anopheles mosquito in transmitting the disease.

Pragmatics notwithstanding, though, sound theory offers a much better likelihood of satisfactory interventions than a hit-or-miss or intuitive method for dealing with social issues such as delinquency. It is the extraordinary difficulty associated with formulating decent theoretical statements about delinquency that has led some writers, such as Bowman, seemingly to throw up their hands and virtually abandon the quest. Bowman (1960:12), for instance, writes:

> So far as the delinquent acts of single individuals or gangs are concerned, without considerable insight into all the factors involved all anyone can say is: there is convincing evidence that some young people are showing tragic compulsion to violate the rules of the game laid down by the powers that be. It may be that the rules are unworkable for them; it may be that the authority figures — parents, teachers, bosses, police — are imposing the rules in a bungling fashion; it may be that a variety of possibilities should be accorded within the rules of the game; it may be that society is making inadequate provision in all its institutions of the means to make social individuals of its children.

The Bowman quotation above is instructive beyond its pretense that we remain almost totally in the dark in regard to satisfactory explanations of delinquency. Actually, Bowman is pushing toward a theory, while rather disingenuously proclaiming that too little is known to support any definite interpretations. His entire quotation, if read carefully, can be seen to endorse the idea that delinquency is produced and can be best dealt with by social arrangements and rearrangements, a matter supported by the title of his book, *Youth and Delinquency in an Inadequate Society.* He is in pursuit of a theoretical viewpoint and merely stops short of trying to establish with more precision those things which he believes are fundamental to our understanding of delinquency, a matter that must be addressed if we are to have sophisticated theoretical postulations.

The President's Commission on Law Enforcement and Administration of Justice (1967:1–2) took an even more eclectic approach to causal explanations that might help to explain crime and juvenile delinquency. Each single illegal act, it maintained, "is a response to a specific situation by a person with an infinitely complicated psychological and emotional makeup who is subject to infinitely complicated external pressures." The causes of illegal behavior, the commission's report noted, "are numerous and mysterious and intertwined."

Obviously, both the President's Commission and Bowman are being notably sensitive to the dictum that "the history of social theory is too largely a record of generalizations wrung from insufficient facts" (Cairns, 1935:20). They may indeed agree with the caustic comment of consumer advocate Ralph Nader, who much prefers action to speculation, and who writes about "the leisure of the theory class" (McCarry, 1972:216), a play upon the title of Thorstein Veblen's classic study of conspicuous consumption, *The Theory of the Leisure Class* (1912).

Nonetheless, Nader's view notwithstanding, and despite the reservations of the President's Commission about the feasibility of the task, there has been compelling and continuous interest within the field of juvenile delinquency in the pursuit of theory. "The supreme goal of all theory," Einstein (1933:10–11) has written, "is to make the irreducible basic elements as simple and as few as possible without having to surrender the adequate representation of a single datum of experience." Einstein accomplished this feat—called parsimonious explanation—for the phenomenon of relativity by representing its essential traits in his famous formula $e = mc^2$. It seems impossible that juvenile delinquency ever will be able to be conceptualized in so elegant a manner; indeed, even for physical phenomena, causality can never be a precisely accurate statement of exactly what occurs: "Causal hypotheses," as Bunge (1959:337–338) has noted, "are no more (and no less) than rough, approximate, one-sided reconstructions."

A particular difficulty with theories lies in their ability at times to induce intellectual myopia, a blindness to information that does not fit in with the prevalent theoretical framework. A striking illustration of such a process can be found in the realm of ancient medicine:

> Galen was an energetic experimenter, but his method was faulty in that he insisted on having a theory for every phenomenon, whether or not it had any basis in fact. His superficial theories displaced the less showy and more laborious methods of Hippocrates, which were based upon direct observations and logical interpretation. Galen developed an elaborate theory of disease and its treatment based on the prevalent metaphysical conceptions of the nature of the body. According to this theory, the body, like the universe, was composed of four elements—fire, air, water, and earth. These elements represented the qualities of the body: fire was hot, air was dry, water was wet, and earth was cold. (Haggard, 1929:339–340)

A famous scientist once remarked that nothing is more tragic than the murder of a grand theory by a little fact. But he hastened to add that nothing proved more surprising than the way in which a theory will continue to survive long after its brains have been knocked out (Thomas, 1960). But the pursuit of sound theory, as we shall see, has a strong appeal. William James (1907:55–58) has outlined the character and value of theory in words that ought to be kept in mind as we review and critique diverse propositions in this and the following three chapters:

> Investigators have become accustomed to the notion that no theory is absolutely a transcript of reality but that any one of them may from some point of view be useful. Their great use is to summarize old facts and lead to new ones. They are only a man-made language, a conceptual shorthand . . . in which we write our reports of nature; and languages, as is well known, tolerate much choice of expression and many dialects.

Broken Homes and Delinquency

That so many different theories of juvenile delinquency exist—and persist—tells us a great deal about the problems connected with providing satisfactory theoretical interpretation of the behaviors grouped under that classification: so many exceptions to any proffered theoretical approach are apt to be located that efforts often are turned toward formulating a new — and possibly a better — theory.

Take, by way of illustration, the popular belief that "broken homes" — that is, families in which one parent is absent — "cause" juvenile delinquency. A few decades ago, when divorce was less common than it is today, emphasis on the terrible effects for children of rent families was much more popular. Delinquency would be reduced, it was said, only if mothers and fathers could be persuaded to remain together as a family unit, if only "for the sake of the children."

There most assuredly was a certain plausibility involved in the idea that broken homes, per se, produce delinquent children and wayward adolescents. For one thing, children of divorced parents almost invariably lived with the mother, and she was seen as having less control and authority, particularly over her sons, than would have been exerted had the father remained in the home. Also, a split family usually had to reduce its standard of living, creating the kinds of impoverishment that tend to be associated with delinquent behavior.

There are, however, innumerable and blatant inadequacies in the theoretical proposition that "broken homes cause delinquency." First, there has been a dramatic increase in the percentage of broken homes, well ahead of the escalating rate of delinquency. Second, it is obvious that millions of youngsters have been raised in homes that are broken by divorce or separation without having embarked upon delinquent careers or acts of delinquency other than the peccadilloes that are engaged in by almost every youngster. Finally, two basic facts collide head-on with the causative allegation focusing on broken homes: one, just as many girls as boys are the products of broken homes, and two, significantly fewer girls than boys engage in delinquent acts. Obviously, it is something other than or in addition to broken homes that can efficiently explain the genesis and the nature of delinquency.

Numerous studies have sought to pinpoint more precisely the aspects of broken homes that might be destructive. They have focused on the age of the children when the parents separated, the sex of each sibling, how many children there are and their age differences, remarriage and dating patterns of the parents, and similar matters. Weaver (1959:79), a British researcher, for instance, maintained that the intelligence of a child is an important mediator of the effect of a broken home: the more intelligent the child, he suggests, the better that child is able to cope with home inadequacies. An obvious difficulty with the broken-homes theory is that it does not specify what it is about the situation that may make it destructive of the behavior of the young persons resident in it. In this regard, not unexpectedly, Ivan Nye (1958) has found little relationship between delinquency and a home in which the parents had separated. What he did find was a significant association between the happiness and marital adjustment of the person parenting the youngster and delinquent behavior. It is apparent that many other matters feed into the effect, if any, of a broken home (Wells and Rankin, 1985; 1986): the outcome assuredly is apt to differ if a divorced woman marries a wealthy second husband who adores her and her infant child, or if a ghetto divorcee is forced onto welfare in order to care for two junior high school boys.

All told, the broken-homes theory provides, at best, some clues to the kind of family disturbances that might be related to delinquency under certain circumstances for certain kinds of people to whom other things might happen. It is by no means a powerful or a persuasive theoretical statement. It fails to meet satisfactorily any of the three attributes of a causal explanation as these attributes have been set forth by Kelly (1967): (1) *distinctiveness*—the degree to which the effect (delinquency) occurs primarily in the presence of one causal candidate (broken homes) and not in the presence of others; (2) *consistency*—the degree to which the effect is observed reliably when a particular causal candidate is present; and (3) *consensus*—the degree to which people other than the target actors show the effect.

Causation

It is important at this point to examine briefly the concept of cause. It should be understood, for instance, that a theory placing emphasis on broken homes cannot be discarded only on the ground that a single exception can be found to the postulated cause, or even because there are quite a few exceptions. We downgrade the theory primarily because it is so loose and omits so many fundamentally important qualifications and because it explains so little and deflects attention from what could prove to be more meaningful precedent and correlative factors associated with delinquent behavior.

Notably in the social sciences and especially in regard to such legally defined and variegated acts as those labeled juvenile delinquency, theory commonly falls far short of a perfect alignment between a stipulated causal factor and an invariant outcome. But in a good causal postulation, the gaps and irregularities are susceptible to empirical inquiry, and the direction of such inquiry can be efficiently determined from the theoretical statement. "What we call a cause typically is, and is recognized as being, only a partial cause," John Mackie (1980:xi) has noted. The stated cause, Mackie observes, is what makes the difference. John Stuart Mill (1843) suggested that instead of *cause* we ought to employ the term *condition*. In a famous dictum, Mill (1843:215) noted: "Nothing can better show the absence of any scientific ground for the distinction between the cause of a phenomenon and its condition than the capricious manner in which we select among the conditions that which we denominate the cause." More simply put, Mill is saying that when there are many circumstances playing into the production of a phenomenon such as delinquency, interpreters often select as "the cause" the one that best fits with their personal or political biases and preferences.

Suppose, during an intense storm, lightning strikes a barn and the barn catches fire. We would ordinarily say that the fire was "caused" by the lightning. Similarly, if a police officer shoots and kills a juvenile who was brandishing a rifle, we say that the youngster's death was "caused" by the officer's bullet. We could maintain, of course, that the "real" cause was that the juvenile had been given the rifle by his father for Christmas or that his irrational behavior related to a neurosis diagnosed by the school psychologist.

But the bullet and lightning examples convey our general understanding that

A caused B if the occurrence of A led to the occurrence of B and that if A had not occurred B would not have happened. In addition to the time sequencing, we use the term *cause* only when we have some idea or explanation of why the occurrence of A leads to the occurrence of B (Binder and Geis, 1983:214). However, philosophical analyses of the meaning of cause raise a good number of complications. Persons of the stature of David Hume, Bertrand Russell, and Karl Popper have been writing on the subject for hundreds of years. Yet in a general survey of "The Concept of Cause" in 1979, we find the following statement: "The epistemology of causation . . . is at present in a . . . state of near chaos. . . . We are far from satisfied with our treatment of it here and find in it no completely satisfying resolution of the major problems of causality" (Cook and Campbell, 1979:10).

If, then, students have difficulty in grasping satisfactorily the complex issue of causation, they may at least take satisfaction in the fact that their frustration is fully shared by some of the best minds of our and earlier times. For present purposes, the warnings noted in the foregoing paragraphs and recourse to the dictionary definition should suffice. *Webster's Seventh New Collegiate Dictionary* defines *cause* as "something that occasions or effects a result; a person or thing that is the occasion of an action or state, esp.: an agent that brings something about." This is how we will use *cause* in our review of theories of delinquency.

On Theoretical Thinking

We have noted that the aim of theories in regard to juvenile delinquency is to provide a better understanding of the behavior in question by showing how it is the product of particular conditions and particular processes. Once these matters are thoroughly understood, it is reasoned, then the behavior can be more effectively predicted and dealt with. Remember our point that quinine proved an effective *curative* for malaria long before the cause of the disease was discovered; but also appreciate that only when the role of the anopheles mosquito was discovered did it become possible to take effective *preventive* measures to control the spread and onset of malaria. If delinquency itself were a bodily disorder, means to prevent it could be sought by keeping the germ from the body, by inoculation, or by proper treatment of those who had caught and might convey the disease. But the cause of delinquency is more complicated than the cause of most physical disorders, and that has led to the production of a large number of theories, all competing for attention and endorsement. That competition will be resolved only when there is agreement that one or another theory offers the best insight into delinquency. This is the definition of truth: "the opinion which is fated to be agreed to by all who investigate" (Hartshorne and Weiss, 1934:408).

At this moment, we appear to be a very long way from the production of such a theory — and perhaps its quest will prove to be a hopeless task. But there is no question that the attempt is worthwhile. A sophisticated theory can organize an enormous amount of isolated information and scattered facts into coherent and impressively informative shapes. Consider, for instance, the theory of gravity, which is able to provide a single explanation for such varied knowledge as the movement of tides, the erect posture of trees, and the difficulty of writing on the ceiling with a ballpoint pen (Hirschi, 1973:165). A primitive person or a child might say that a stone dropped because it "wanted to." A profound thinker in Aristotle's time probably would have said that the stone dropped because it had the property of gravity. But after Newton propounded his theory, we could declare that the stone dropped because it existed in a field of forces of which the most relevant were the mass of the stone, the earth's gravitational pull, and the relative insubstantiality of the intervening medium, in this case air (Nisbett and Ross, 1980:205). The theory of gravity allows understanding of the extraordinary demands upon the human body, when standing erect, for blood circulation and explains why some quadrupeds not adapted to the upright position may be killed simply by suspending them vertically (Engel, 1962:28). Equally impressive are Darwin's theory of natural selection (the survival of the fittest) and a vast array of explanatory schemes in the natural sciences. Human behavior, however, seems more unresponsive to laws that can readily be reduced to theoretical shorthand. Besides, as we will point out in the section following, unlike the physical sciences, social science suffers from commentary by those outside its professional bounds who nonetheless remain quite convinced that they thoroughly understand the forces at work to produce any human act.

Popular Ideas on Delinquency Causation

The General Nature of Popular Ideas

Richard Nisbett and Lee Ross (1980:119) have pointed out that many theories, particularly in the realm of human conduct, represent no more than flimsy makeshift views, uncritically passed from one person to another. They note in this regard:

> many causal theories originate not from summaries of scientific theories or informed expert opinion, or from close and systematic observation, or even from reasoned armchair analysis, but rather originate from much more haphazard and uncertain sources. Many causal theories seem to have come from maxims, parables, myths, fables, epigrams, allegories, well-known songs or novels, and anecdotes about famous people or personal acquaintances.

The same writers note that many popular ideas contradict each other but that such logical inconsistency seems to have no effect on support for the views. Thus, for instance, some people are told that "absence makes the heart grow fonder" while others are equally seriously forewarned that "out of sight, out of mind." Others are told that "a penny saved is a penny earned," advice contradicted by the idea that you've got to spend money to make money.

Though most people will grant that they do not quite understand the principles that underlie space flight, much less why a television set does what it does, they often are convinced that they intuitively know why kids get into trouble. More than three hundred years ago, Michael Dalton (1677:413) tried to pinpoint for English justices of the peace those things which they ought to make note of in regard to wrongdoers brought before them. The justices were amateurs, country gentlemen holding part-time positions and in need of orientation. Dalton's ten points are repeated virtually word for word today in popular portraits of signs of delinquency. Attention should be paid, said Dalton, to these matters in determining likely guilt or innocence:

1. His parents, if they are wicked, and given to the same kind of fault.
2. His education, whether brought idly or in an honest occupation.
3. His ability of body, that is, if strong and swift, or weak or sickly, not likely to do the act.
4. His nature, if civil or haughty, witty and subtle, a quarreler, pilferer, or bloody-minded.
5. His means, if he have where to live or not.
6. His trade; for if a man liveth idly or vagrant it is good cause to arrest him upon suspicion, if there have been any felony committed.
7. His company, if ruffians, suspected persons, or his being in company with any of the offenders.
8. His course of life, that is, if a common ale-house haunter, or riotous in diet, play, or apparel.
9. Whether he be of evil fame or report.
10. Whether he hath committed the like offense before.

This list could readily be applied to early explanations of juvenile delinquency as they took shape after about 1800 and indicates how little change there has been in popular thought about the causes of crime and deliquency since Dalton wrote. Yet, at the same time, Dalton recommends that a suspected murderer be made to touch the dead body of the victim, because he believed, as did most of the people of the time, that God would cause the body to begin to bleed when the perpetrator made contact with it. Science has laid to rest such folklore, but no comparable progress has as yet been made toward more rigorous formulations about delinquency, in part, of course, because there are grains of truth in popular beliefs, and in part also because persons tend to be resistant to contradictions or refinements of things that they are quite certain "they just know" are true.

More recently, a study by two English research workers found that both in the United States and in the United Kingdom a majority of people thought that delinquency primarily was due to the lack of parental discipline. Older persons more than younger ones also believed that the decline of religion was a major contributor to ensuant delinquent behavior (Banks, Maloney, and Willcock, 1975). Another British study scrutinized the views of 300 persons of diverse backgrounds, asking them to evaluate thirty commonly offered explanations for delinquency and to rate each on a seven-point scale for importance. The results showed that a person's political beliefs were particularly related to that person's explanation of delinquency. Conservatives tended to explain delinquency primarily in terms of failure in social and moral education, while liberals tended to blame the injustices of society. Women more than men placed the onus for delinquency on home upbringing and faulty parental practices. Most prominent in the responses were these three items: (1) "There exist no job opportunities and high unemployment"; (2) "They live in areas of high delinquency"; (3) "There are inadequate recreational and leisure activities" (Furnham and Henderson, 1983). Despite their apparent validity, such explanations are far too simple to provide much insight. Unemployment is a social evil on its merits, but most studies suggest that it is at best poorly related to juvenile delinquency. Adults may commit more crime in periods of unemployment, but the fact that so many adults are out of work allows them more time to supervise their children. In addition, high employment means extra spending money for many adolescents, and such money can provide them with independence from parental care and with the wherewithal to get into trouble (Cullen, Larson, and Mathers, 1985). Youthful income, for instance, can finance the purchase of an automobile, and, as Jackson Toby (1985:303) has pointed out: "In the age of the automobile, an adolescent's home may be the place where he sleeps and little else." A car, Toby observes, is a notably "effective instrument for escaping the eyes of adults." Without work and concomitant income, some youths have much less freedom and therefore do not get into trouble. Taken as a whole, the relationship between factors such as unemployment and delinquency can be seen to be quite complex (Wilson and Cook, 1985).

It will be noted as we proceed with our inventory of theories that at times behavioral scientists have themselves focused upon and elaborated popular beliefs when they have constructed their theoretical system for interpreting delinquency. Some agreement between popular views and academic positions probably is essential if politicians are to be persuaded to appropriate funds for programs seeking to control delinquency, but the aim of theory must remain truth, and not necessarily a formula for action.

The Case of the Subway Vigilante

A particularly striking illustration of lay attribution of causation for delinquent behavior recently arose in what became known as the Case of the Subway Vigilante (Rubin, 1986). Bernhard H. Goetz, a thirty-seven-year-old electronics engineer living in New York City, was riding on the subway early in the afternoon on the Saturday before Christmas of 1984. Goetz had been attacked on the subway four years earlier and carried an unlicensed gun because, he said, he feared another attack. This time, four youths approached him and asked him for the time, then for a match, and, finally, for $5. Goetz responded by pulling out a .38-caliber handgun and firing at them several times, wounding each of the youths. Later the young men were discovered to have screwdrivers in their pockets, which presumably they might have used as weapons, though, as the story that follows indicates, they apparently intended to employ the screwdrivers to rob slot machines.

Public support for Goetz's action was very strong, though some persons condemned it as unconscionable, saying that the use of a gun to deal with panhandling and the seemingly remote possibility of violence was a form of vigilantism, much like imposing the death penalty on a wrongdoer for a minor offense and without recourse to due process of law. But a newspaper poll found that 49 per cent of New Yorkers approved Goetz's actions compared to 32 per cent who disapproved. Seventeen per cent believed he should be awarded a medal for shooting the four teenagers; 58 per cent disagreed with the charge of attempted murder filed against Goetz; 75 per cent thought he had acted in self-defense. Goetz's lawyer told a congressional hearing that his client was not a vigilante: "A vigilante gets a gun and goes out hunting like a rabbit hunter."

Riders on a West Side IRT subway train—the line where the Goetz shootings took place.

Goetz, the lawyer claimed, was "an ordinary, average American citizen, well-spoken, well-educated; a shy person, a sincere person." Chicago newspaper columnist Mike Royko, who a few months previously had himself been the victim of an armed robbery by "a couple of young men seeking to increase their net worth" illustrated the kind of support that Goetz's act elicited. "I'm glad that Goetz shot them," Royko wrote in his nationally syndicated column. "I don't care what his motives were or whether he has all his marbles. The punks looked for trouble, and they found it. Case closed." At first, the New York grand jury indicted Goetz only for illegal possession of a weapon. Later, the revelation that Goetz admitted firing a bullet into one of his victims with the words "You don't look so bad. Here's another" influenced a second impaneled jury to return indictments for both attempted murder and assault. Subsequently, one of Goetz's victims was arrested on the charge of raping a woman and stealing her earrings and three rings. Another was convicted for robbery, and a third entered a drug treatment program on conditional discharge after stealing $14 in quarters from a video game in a bar.

Of particular interest to us are the explanatory ideas for his behavior offered by the mother of one of the youths. Her son was the most seriously injured: he was in a coma with a severe brain injury when she was interviewed, and later he would be confined to a wheelchair for life and have the mental capacity of an eight-year-old. In the following story by Esther B. Fein, which appeared in the *New York Times* (January 12, 1985), we have placed in italic type some of the

The apparent position of many people in the United States.

causal items stressed by the mother as well as one (the absence of "constructive outlets for their energy") offered by the newspaper reporter:

. . . VICTIM'S MOTHER: WORRY AND SELF-DOUBT

When Darrel Cabey was arrested for armed robbery and possession of a weapon last October, his first serious offense, he called his mother from the police station and asked her to post bail.

Mrs. Cabey was reluctant then to put up the money. "I thought if he had to stay in jail, *he would choose his friends more carefully,*" she said.

Mrs. Cabey said she doubts even more now whether she did the right thing by letting relatives persuade her to bail Darrel out. He is in a coma now and paralyzed from the waist down, one of four teen-agers who were shot last month by Bernhard Hugo Goetz after they asked him for $5.

"I was really mad when he called," said Mrs. Cabey, whose son's robbery case is pending. "But everyone was saying, 'He's a good boy, don't be so hard.'"

There were signs that Darrel was heading for trouble, Mrs. Cabey said, signs that are familiar to people from the Claremont Village neighborhood in the South Bronx, where the four teen-agers live.

"He was *staying outside a lot, and I didn't know what he was doing,"* said Mrs. Cabey, a food-services worker who has five other children. "Knowing *the situation out there and the area* around here, I just should have known."

The concrete buildings of Claremont Village are on litter-choked lots, covering block after block of the South Bronx. About 13,500 people live in the city housing complex, and more than half are under 21.

Teen-agers who grow up there have *few constructive outlets for their energy,* said many people who live there. Many youngsters, they said, revert to petty crime — shoplifting, breaking into vending machines and video games.

It is not the only pattern, people are quick to point out. There are also honor students who win scholarships and talented athletes. Mostly, though, there are average teenagers with less than average opportunities.

"Kids who live here are under *a lot of peer pressure,"* said Mrs. Cabey. "I tried to talk to him, I told him, 'You have two strikes against you, *you're black and you're poor,* so you better get back to studying.' I told him there's more to life than hanging out in the streets. If only he had used *a little common sense."*

Mrs. Cabey said she did not know if her son, who is 19 years old, was friends with the three other teen-agers who were together on the IRT No. 2 subway on the afternoon of Dec. 22.

Friendship is a loose term in the projects, said some teen-agers who live there. Friend, they said, covers people who hang out together, play basketball together and people who head downtown to break into video games together.

"When I was 15, 16," said James Knight, 21, who used to live in Claremont Village, "there were four or five guys and we'd ride down to the city and jigger with videos. One guy was Roy and I never knew his last name, and Jones, I never knew his first name, and I haven't seem them for two years now. So is that a friend?"

The police and people in the neighborhood seem to agree that the four teen-agers had set out that Saturday to vandalize machines. Three of them had screwdrivers in their jackets.

"Screwdrivers? You only do that when you're going to bust machines," said a man named Ike, who refused to give his last name.

But sometime after the four got on the train, one or more of them decided to rob someone. In doing so, one crime analyst said, they crossed a very wide threshold.

"It is much riskier to try to accost a person," said Michael Smith, director of the Vera Institute of Justice, a crime research organization. "It's fairly common knowledge that getting hurt is a risk when engaging in that conduct. Burglary is not as risky. Breaking into a video machine you get the same instant cash as mugging without the risk."

Teenagers in the Claremont project talked knowledgeably and easily about the risk and sentences for various crimes. "Most guys just hit videos, because they're easy and it won't be so bad, like mugging, if they get caught," said Junior Mendez, a 17-year-old who lives in Claremont Village. "But it's bad to bust machines around here or, say, up in Harlem, because the owners go after you. Downtown they just call the cops."

Mr. Smith said that most teen-agers tended to commit crimes within a mile of their homes, mostly out of a feeling of territorial security.

Mrs. Cabey said that she encouraged her six children to entertain themselves at home, but she never allowed them to have friends visit because she was afraid they would later return to rob the apartment.

She said she was also careful about what she would allow her children to display outside the home. She said she never bought them expensive jackets or bicycles or radios because, she said, "lots of kids have been killed for a 10-speed bike."

Mrs. Cabey said it was difficult to instill values in her children in a neighborhood where wrongdoing and lawbreaking abound. *It was easier,* she said, *when Darrel was young and his father, Raymond Eugene Cabey, was alive.*

The family lived in Far Rockaway, Queens, then, but in 1973 Mr. Cabey was crushed to death by a car while trying to wrest his taxi from a thief. A year later, the family moved to Claremont.

"Everyone said *the change was too much,*" said Mrs. Cabey.

Darrel dropped out of high school when he was a junior, she said, adding, "I knew by the different things he was doing that something would be up."

But she said he remained a polite and affable young man, and she did not realize the extent of his *predilection for trouble.* It is difficult, she said, to control *a teen-ager who "wanted to be a man too fast."*

Friends and relatives have given her strength, said Mrs. Cabey, even as she and the families of the other three teen-agers have received letters condemning the youths and applauding Mr. Goetz. Some of the letters are from people who have been victims of crime. Some are very cruel.

"Drop Dead," was written in a greeting card that someone sent to Darrel Cabey.

"I'm not angry," said Mrs. Cabey, who presses the letters between pages of a Bible. "A lot of people have been victims and are boiled up to the boiling point. I am hurt, though, that people would take the time to be so mean. Time is so precious these days."

We see here a potpourri of explanatory ideas, each individually seemingly sensible, and all of them collectively forming a portrait that coincides generally with popular notions about some of the dynamics of delinquent behavior. We should keep these ideas in mind as we examine the more elaborate formulations of academic scholars and see how their theories line up with the interpretations of persons directly affected by the behavior.

After a seven-week trial in 1987, Goetz was acquitted of twelve of the thirteen counts in the indictment. Conviction was only for illegal possession of a weapon. The defense's position was that Goetz had entertained a justifiable belief that he was in danger when he had shot; that what he had done constituted self-defense. Members of the jury, questioned after the trial, said that the defense theory had not been overcome beyond the reasonable doubt required for criminal conviction. Goetz's statement that he had returned to fire at one of the youths a second time was dismissed by his own lawyer as a "fantasy." At the time he made the statement, the lawyer insisted, Goetz was "a traumatized, sick, psychologically upset individual." Ballistics and eye-witness evidence supported the lawyer's position, suggesting that Goetz had fired all the shots in one savage burst and that the victims had all been standing when they were shot.

Darrel Cabey was judged incompetent to testify because of his mental condition following his shooting. So as not to prejudice the jury, it was told only that Cabey was "unavailable." Another victim of Goetz, serving eight and one-half to twenty-five years for a rooftop rape, flew into a rage when cross-examined, hurling obscenities at the judge and defense attorney. This outburst led to eleven charges of contempt of court that added six months to his prison sentence. More important, courtroom observers thought that the young man had frightened the jury, thus lending credibility to Goetz' position. Goetz had said that the four youths had surrounded him: "They wanted to play with me. You know, it's kind of like a cat plays with a mouse."

As we begin our review of theories of juvenile delinquency, we also should bear in mind Donald Shoemaker's (1984:255) summary appraisal of them:

> The explanations of delinquency vary widely in substance and empirical verification. Certainly, no one theory can be used to explain all delinquency, or even certain types of delinquency. Furthermore, there is no unifying trait that can be used to connect the diverse and often competing theories. Each explanation has its own strengths and weaknesses, and some theories are, overall, more persuasive than others.

The Pioneers and Their Legacy

An Overview

There are two matters that are of particular significance to us as we enter into our review of theorists of importance to our understanding of juvenile delinquency. The first is clarity; the second is criticality. Richard Feynman, a theoretical physicist who won the Nobel Prize for his work, provides perceptive observations on both of these matters. First, he tells of attending a conference in which persons from various disciplines discussed their ideas. One paper that was read contained a sentence that went something like this: "The individual member of the social community often receives his information via visual, symbolic channels." Feynman (1985:281) puzzled his way through this verbiage and finally concluded that what the social scientist was trying to say was: "People read." The tendency of theorists to employ language in ways that camouflage and distort common understanding sometimes seems to be an occupational disease or, at least, a requirement that they believe they must meet if they intend to be taken seriously. Fancy language can never compensate for sloppy thought; we will try to reduce some of the theoretical statements to words that express their essential meaning without distorting their ingredients.

Second, Feynman emphasizes that theorists often become so attached to their own views that they develop a defensiveness about them; that is, they resist with all their ability ideas that might disprove what they have maintained. He says that, contrary to this, a good theorist ought to be especially diligent in seeking all possible criticisms of his or her own position and subjecting it to the best possible logical scrutiny. Feynman (1985:341) notes:

> Details that could throw doubt upon your interpretation must be given, if you know them. You must do the best you can—if you know anything at all wrong, or possibly wrong—to explain it. If you make a theory, for example, and advertise it, or put it out, then you must also put down all the facts that disagree with it. There is also a more subtle problem. When you have put a lot of ideas together to make an elaborate theory, you want to make sure, when explaining what it fits, that those things it fits are not just the things that gave you the idea for the new theory; but that the finished theory makes something else come out right, in addition.

Few theorists of juvenile delinquency meet the criteria set forth above. They sometimes tend, in fact, to be painfully adept at ignoring or hiding contradictory evidence. Unfortunately for them, however, there are others alert to pounce upon a vulnerable theory and to point out its real or imagined shortcomings. It is this critical literature that we will combine with our expositions of the theoretical statements to provide a full portrait of the ideas.

Two major theoretical schools of an earlier period serve to offer an understanding of the intellectual structure upon which most later ideas were constructed. The first is the *classical* or *utilitarian* school of thought, represented by an Englishman, Jeremy Bentham, and an Italian, Cesare Beccaria. It assumed that human beings exercise rational free will and voluntarily choose between good and evil after calculating the costs and benefits of alternative actions. The school is a precursor of lines of thought that focus on human interaction as the genesis of delinquent behavior. The second theoretical current is that dominated by Cesare Lombroso, an Italian physician, who located the causes of lawbreaking within the biological traits of the offender. It essentially is deterministic, insisting that persons with certain biological deficiencies inevitably are foreordained to criminal acts. This school has been known as the *positivistic* because of its attempt to relate certain conditions to certain behaviors in a scientific manner.

Both the classical and the positivistic theories focused almost exclusively upon adult crime, largely because, as our earlier historical review has demonstrated, the concept of juvenile delinquency had not yet been clearly differentiated. And, as we have noted, formal theories specifically focusing on juvenile delinquency did not begin to take shape until the close of the nineteenth century. Still, these early formulations provide an essential background for later theories of juvenile delinquency and juvenile justice, which seek to reconcile concepts of childhood and youth with those of crime and punishment, and to the intellectual tradition of which more contemporary theories of delinquency are a part.

The Classical School: Utilitarianism

The utilitarian school was based fundamentally upon the commonsense, but nonetheless profound, idea that the aim of all laws against crime and delinquency must be to promote "the greatest happiness for the greatest number of persons." This was to be accomplished through the employment of a yardstick by which actions could be evaluated. The yardstick involved the concepts of "pleasure" and "pain." All human beings, it is said, are self-interested creatures who seek pleasure and can be deterred from such a quest only by anticipation and infliction of pain, expressed by means of sanctions and punishments.

Jeremy Bentham. The leading proponent of utilitarianism in the English-speaking world was Jeremy Bentham (1748–1832), though many of his premises were derived from the Italian, Beccaria, who will be considered next. Bentham assuredly was an odd human being. Indeed, his body can be viewed today by any curious passerby because, in accord with his will, it was mummified and sits staring benignly at persons coming into University College, London. Since he was a man of exceptional intellect, Bentham reasoned, his remains ought to be publicly exhibited to inspire future generations of thinkers.

The mummified body of Jeremy Bentham resides at University College, London.

He called the body an "autoicon" and decreed that it should be seated in a favorite chair of his in his own clothes "in the attitude in which I am sitting when in thought." He also insisted on being placed at the table from time to time during meetings. Bentham has colorfully and not inaptly been described as possessing the "incredible egotism of a superb megalomaniac" (Volk, 1976:698). A lifelong bachelor, he spent virtually his entire existence writing in a pinched hand reams of manuscript putting forth programs for the reform of English criminal law. "He shrank from the world in which he was easily browbeaten to the study in which he could reign supreme," it has been said of Bentham (Stephen, 1900:I,175). Many of his papers, deposited in the British Museum and University College, are still unread today; one scholar has insisted, after tackling some of them, that "a complete examination would take a lifetime longer than Bentham's, since I am convinced that it would take more time to read what he wrote than it took him to write it!" (Steintrager, 1977:7).

Outstanding theorists often tend to be eccentric: it takes a distinctive kind of human being truly to see things differently from the rest of us and to dedicate himself or herself to enlightening us about new ways of looking at reality. Bentham deeply believed that he had the answer to total reform of the law, which at the time was both chaotic and mercilessly brutal. As late as 1833, for instance, a boy of nine was hanged for stealing (O'Donnell, 1950:15). The law was so barbarous that juries often would declare an offender innocent rather than permit him or her to undergo the harsh punishment mandated by law for what was deemed to be a minor offense (see Chapter 7). Bentham tried to introduce some logic into the process of determining how serious an offense might be, and he insisted stoutly that certain behaviors that harm no one but their perpetrators ought to be eliminated from the law. Punishment, he said, should not be an act of anger, resentment, or vengeance. There should be no punishment when (1) such punishment is groundless, because consent has been given or the evil is compensated for by the attendant good; (2) the punishment has no effect, as when the offender is an infant, is insane, or performed the act involuntarily; or (3) the punishment is unprofitable because the resultant evil exceeds that of the offense. In the last case, for instance, Bentham would not prosecute the son of an ambassador from a foreign country for a trivial shoplifting offense if such a prosecution would be likely to cause strained relations between the country and that of the ambassador (Geis, 1960:62).

Though he was largely in favor of fixed sentences so that potential offenders could readily calculate the pain that would attach to their behavior, Bentham (1838:I, 516) equivocated to the point of permitting some sentencing flexibility based on the belief that different sentences carried different meanings for different persons:

> There may, however, often arise, either with regard to the offenses themselves, or the person of the delinquent, unforeseen and particular circumstances, which would be productive of great inconveniences, if the law were altogether inflexible. It is therefore proper to allow a certain latitude to the judge, not of increasing, but of diminishing a punishment, in those cases in which it may be fairly presumed that one individual is less dangerous, or more responsible than another. The same nominal punishment is not always the same real punishment — some individuals, by reason of their education, family connections, and condition in the world, presenting if we may so speak, a greater surface for punishment to act upon.

There are many difficulties with utilitarianism, but its strengths should not be overlooked because of its shortcomings. It insists that laws ought to be examined in rational terms and an attempt made to determine how well they contribute to the general health and integrity of the society. Certainly such a principle must lie at the core of the scrutiny that has been given over recent years to the statutes outlawing possession and use of marijuana — and the striking changes that have taken place in such laws since the conclusion of the Second World War. Bentham also favored restitution by an offender directly to the victim, rather than the payment of a fine to the state. His utilitarianism sees human beings as making rational choices through the exercise of free will. Unfortunately, there is voluminous evidence that persons do not always act rationally: for one thing, they do not possess sufficient information to evaluate their own best interests; for another, even with adequate information, they are not able to look satisfactorily into the future to determine what will or will not make them happy. Besides, it is quite impossible to predict accurately the odds on a particular outcome. A potential delinquent might well know that a given theft will secure for him, say, 50 units of pleasure (however such pleasure might be measured) and that apprehension and a likely six-month stay in a juvenile institution will cause him 250 units of pain. Obviously, then, he ought not to undertake the theft — but this equation is relevant only if he is going to be caught and brought before the authorities. How does he determine accurately the chances that this will happen in regard to the particular theft being contemplated?

Besides, one person's pleasure is another's pain. Wits often point out that the wisdom of "Do unto others what you would have them do unto you" will not work very well with masochists, since by definition they enjoy pain. In the realm of crime and delinquency, it might be argued that a major good (pleasure) of some delinquency is to get caught and thereby obtain attention, to develop the "rep" so highly prized by some gang members. Jacob (1978:584), writing to this point, has observed that before we can proceed very far with analyses based on Bentham's ideas, we must figure out how different people perceive things: "A night in jail is abhorrent to some," Jacob notes, "a lark to others."

Bentham undoubtedly was correct when he harangued against the inefficacy of certain punishments; after all, extracting and burning the bowels of a traitor after he has been hanged but is still conscious seems rather beyond the point of necessity. Bentham attempted to find a simple formula by which to order human behavior. The true complexity of such behavior, however, has resulted in his theories' becoming primarily reminders of some things that ought to be taken into account in lawmaking and in punishment: the impact of the acts on human happiness and questions about the necessity for certain laws. Wesley Mitchell (1918:183), an eminent economist, wisely summarized the failings of Bentham's ideas on human motivation by noting that "the real reason we find his concept artificial is that we have another stock of ideas about behavior with which Bentham's views are incompatible." On the other side, John Stuart Mill (1859:I, 339), a disciple of Bentham, captured the essence of Bentham's theoretical contribution when he wrote, "It was not his opinions, but his method, that constituted the novelty and the value of what he did." That method was the method of evaluating costs and consequences and attempting in a systematic and humanistic manner to understand and direct human behavior (Rosenblum, 1978:10). This was truly, as Mill states, "a value beyond all price" (Mill, 1859:I, 339; see also Rosen, 1982).

Bentham's theoretical ideas were neither unique nor altogether original with him. The principle of striving for the greatest happiness for the greatest number had been enunciated by several thinkers in ancient times (Shackleton, 1972) and had been discussed at length by Frances Hutcheson, an English moral philosopher, early in the eighteenth century: "That action is best," Hutcheson (1738:181) wrote, "which procures the greatest happiness for the greatest number, and that worse, which, in like manner, occasions misery." But for Bentham, the primary source for this and many other ideas of criminal law reform had been in the work of an Italian, Cesare Beccaria (1738–1794), scion of an aristocratic family living in Milan.

Cesare Beccaria. Beccaria's *Dei delitti delle pene* (On Crimes and Punishments), published in 1764, when its author was only twenty-six years old, foretells Bentham's subsequent utilitarian schemes. It inveighs against capital punishment and the torturing of criminal suspects. It also calls for a rational relationship between the seriousness of a criminal act and the penalty that should be assessed for its commission. In particular, Beccaria stressed the importance of speed and certainty if a punishment was to be effective, a theme

The rack, a French instrument of torture, was one of the means of obtaining confessions to which Beccaria objected.

that continues to preoccupy contemporary scholars who are attempting to separate and determine the relative importance of these two considerations in deterring adult and juvenile lawbreaking (Gibbs, 1975; Nagel, 1982). Such "hints" from Beccaria, as Bentham called them (Hart, 1982:40), provided guidance and momentum for Bentham's own work, which came to overshadow the transient though momentarily great stir created by Beccaria's short treatise. Indeed, Jenkins (1984) has insisted that the enormous attention accorded to Beccaria's contribution in its time by persons such as John Adams in America and Voltaire in France lay in the fact that it was essentially a conservative rather than a radical statement. It was clearly evident when Beccaria wrote, Jenkins maintains, that the administration of criminal justice was a shambles, long overdue for overhaul. What Beccaria offered was a formula that supported amendments to the existing approach but did not challenge authority. That is, both Beccaria and, later, Bentham placed the blame for crime on the irrationality of the codes in their failure to curb the hedonistic, self-interested behavior of human beings. They did not castigate the unequal distribution of wealth or any other social conditions that might contribute to crime.

Why Delinquency?: Contemporary Utilitarianism. That the viewpoints of Bentham and Beccaria have immediate relevance to current theories of juvenile delinquency can be seen from the work of a Canadian, Maurice Cusson, who employs a traditional utilitarian approach as he attempts to answer the question: Why delinquency? Cusson (1983:14) calls his theory *strategic analysis,* and it represents an updating and extension of the Benthamite position:

> The fundamental hypothesis that strategic analysis leads to is that when someone means to commit a crime, he tends to choose the option that, considering his

opportunities, will have the greatest advantage at the least cost. Strategic analysis sees delinquent behavior as result-oriented, with its own rationality, taking into account the opportunities offered the actor and the behavior of his adversaries.

Unlike Bentham and Beccaria, Cusson (1983:21) grants that human beings have but limited options — "the person does not always have clear objectives; situations limit choice, and information is lacking":

> Our friends, our enemies, our personal abilities, the material means at our disposal, the circumstances, the opportunities offered us, our social milieu all limit us not only in the choice of the means to use but also in the choice of goals. There are projects that it is realistic to undertake, others that it is not. Goals are not purely intellectual choices; more often than not external circumstances make us decide what goals are worthwhile.

It is the aim or goal of delinquent activity that most concerns Cusson, and he provides an elaborate inventory of such goals, including as major headings *action* (to expend energy and have the sensation of living intensely), *appropriation* (to profit from another person's property), *aggression* (to kill, injure, or make another person suffer), and *domination* (to gain supremacy over someone). Delinquency thus becomes a way to achieve objectives that are vital to most human beings; it is "a means of feeling the intoxicating pleasure of intense activity; it brings riches that are otherwise inaccessible; it is a reaction for survival in the face of danger; it permits self-assertion" (1983:161–162). Delinquency, Cusson maintains, is an answer to what humans have always looked for: pleasure, wealth, security, power, and glory.

The merit of Cusson's theorizing is that it brings an understanding of delinquency more in line than is usual with attempts to comprehend the roots of all human activity, of which delinquent behavior is but one aspect. But Cusson's work, while testifying to the continuing vitality of utilitarian postulates, is more of a classificatory than an explanatory scheme. It is notable that he largely ignores discussion of countermeasures to reduce delinquency, being content to repeat Wilson's (1975:56) statement that no better answer than that of the utilitarians has yet to surface:

> The policy analyst is led to assume that the criminal acts as if crime were the product of free choice among competing opportunities and constraints. The radical individualism of Bentham and Beccaria may be scientifically questionable but prudentially necessary.

The Positivistic School

The sharp distinctions between the classical school of criminology and the positivistic school have been clearly drawn by Ray Jeffery (1960:366) in the following terms:

> The Classical School defined crime in legal terms; the Positive School rejected a legal definition of crime. The Classical School focused attention on crime as a legal entity; the Positive School focused attention on the act as a psychological entity. The Classical School emphasized free will; the Positive School emphasized deter-

minism. The Classical School theorized that punishment had a deterrent effect; the Positive said that punishment should be replaced by a scientific treatment of criminals calculated to protect society.

Cesare Lombroso. The positivists — under the pioneering intellectual leadership of Cesare Lombroso (1835–1909), a physician and psychiatrist and professor of forensic medicine at the University of Turin for a considerable period of his career — are generally credited with being the first to regard criminal behavior within a modern scientific context. Lombroso, it has been noted (Mannheim, 1955:70–71), "saved criminal science from the shackles of merely academic abstractions and fertilized it with the rich treasures of the natural sciences." The classical school, the same writer observes, "contented itself with endless theoretical arguments and tried by means of sterile conceptions to fix the penalty which was supposed to 'fit the crime.'"

In 1876, when the first edition of Lombroso's treatise on crime, *L'uomo delinquente* (*The Criminal Man*) was published, it drew upon major aspects of the nineteenth-century scientific revolution in biology and physics. The primary intellectual climate of the day had been supplied by the work of Charles Darwin, who had rudely shaken theological presuppositions. As Joseph Wood Krutch (1953:147) has put the matter, prior to this time man might aspire to be one of the angels; now he became a higher form of ape. Darwin's theory of evolution was an instrument not only to examine the modification of the species but also to look into all phases of human behavior. In keeping with the evolutionary doctrine, Lombroso thought that he could identify physical characteristics of offenders in the form of facial, cephalic, and bodily anomalies (referred to subsequently as the "Lombrosian stigmata"), suggesting that criminals were an "atavistic" form of human being. By atavistic he meant that criminals were a reversion to a primitive or subhuman type, characterized physically by a variety of inferior morphological traits reminiscent of apes and lower primates, occurring in more simian fossil men and to some extent preserved in what Lombroso called modern "savages," that is, members of preliterate tribes (Wolfgang, 1960:183). Criminals "talk differently from us because they do not feel in the same way; they talk like savages because they are veritable savages in the midst of this brilliant European civilization," Lombroso (1905:I, 497) noted.

Corresponding to the lawbreakers' physical characteristics of inadequacy were retarded psychological features, which Lombroso believed rendered such individuals incapable of adapting to more highly advanced social orders and were crucial in bringing about criminal behavior. These physically retarded types constituted for Lombroso "born criminals," individuals destined by their deficient heredity inevitably to enter into criminal activity. Lombroso granted, however, that not all criminals were "born." He felt that more than half were either insane or *criminaloid,* that is, individuals who by physical and psychological constitution were predisposed toward crime in the face of certain eliciting circumstances. The criminality of this group would result only if its members were confronted with environmental conditions capable of inciting such behavior. Comparable to the medical concept of diathesis — a predisposition toward a given disease with no certainty that the disease will result — this aspect of Lombroso's thinking raises a number of issues pertinent to contemporary social-psychological thinking about such things as "dangerousness." In the wake of Lombroso, the German criminologist Hentig (1948:450), in his emphasis on the doctrine of "temptation" as a causal factor in delinquency and crime, stresses that there is always a vulnerable group in every society. And the psychiatrist Bovet (1951:20), in a study of juvenile delinquency, refers to youths who are vulnerable but not yet delinquents as the "reserve troops of delinquency."

A quotation from Lombroso's (1911:xiv) opening speech at the Sixth Congress of Criminal Anthropology indicates the initial stage of the development of his ideas:

> In 1870 I was carrying out for several months researches in the prisons and asylums of Pavia upon cadavers and living persons in order to determine upon substantial differences between the insane and criminals, without succeeding very well. At last I found in the skull of a brigand a very long series of atavistic anomalies, above all an enormous middle occipital fossa [a hollow in the back part of the head] and a hypertrophy [morbid enlargement] of the vermis [the connecting mass between the two hemispheres of the brain] analogous to those that are found in inferior vertebrates. At the sight of these strange anomalies the problem of nature and of the origin of the criminal seemed to be resolved; the characteristics of primitive men and of inferior animals must be reproduced in our times. Many facts seemed to confirm this hypothesis, above all the psychology of the criminal; the frequency of tattooing and of professional slang; the passions as much more fleeting as they are more violent, above all that of vengeance; the lack of foresight which resembles courage and courage which alternates with cowardice, and idleness which alternates with the passion for play and activity.

In later editions of Lombroso's work, his view of the causes of crime were successively tempered to take into account a wide range of contributory environmental conditions. Certainly his more comprehensive views, removed from the restricted biological perspective with which he has been identified, indicate that Lombroso drew closer to modern ideas as his career matured. Among other items Lombroso examined were climate and rainfall, marriage customs, banking practices and religious beliefs. But at the heart of all this was a commitment to a rigid determinism that saw offenders as a class apart, almost predestined to their behavior. "All great criminals have given proof of their perversity in their youth, especially at the age of puberty and even before," Lombroso (1911:78) wrote, cataloging the sins of some notorious European malefactors:

> At 7 Dombey was already a thief, and added sacrilege to his theft at 12. At 3 Crocco tore out the feathers of living birds; Lasagne cut out the tongues of cattle at 11; at the same age Cartouche stole from his schoolmates; while Mme. Lafargue, as a child of 10, strangled fowls. Feuerbach tells of a parricide who had taken great delight as a child in making hens jump about after he had put out their eyes.

Determinism and Free Will. That Lombroso formulated a deterministic approach to the understanding of lawbreaking certainly placed the inquiry much more firmly in the mainstream of science. Science assumes that there are, overwhelmingly if not totally, regularities in the world that could be predicted

invariantly if we but knew enough about what causes what. A statement of the
deterministic position has been provided by William James (1909:150):

> It professes that those parts of the universe already laid down absolutely appoint
> and decree what other parts shall be. The future has no ambiguous possibilities
> hidden in its womb. . . . Any other future complement than the one fixed from
> eternity is impossible. The whole is in each and every part, and welds with the rest
> into an absolute unity, an iron block, in which there can be no equivocation.

Free will is the alternative position: "When I am said to have done something
of my own free will it is implied that I could have acted otherwise," notes the
philosopher A. J. Ayer (1982:15). The debate over free will and determinism,
though, is not notably germane for an accurate understanding of delinquency.
For one thing, most of us assume that we have free will — the choice to do as we
please — and we all know that nonetheless our choice obviously is limited in
endless ways: by what and who we are, among other things: a one-legged man is
not free to run a four-minute mile. Science presumes that what we choose is
sufficiently predetermined to make prediction possible, at least in terms of
statistical likelihood. And even the vaunted free will position of the classical
school has a large ingredient of determinism, since Bentham and Beccaria both
assumed that sufficiently severe penalties would "cause" persons to act in
law-abiding ways; whether they did so because they chose that path or whether
they were determined into the behavior by the penalty (which itself was predetermined) seems a matter largely beside the point.

Evaluation of Lombroso's Work. Nonetheless, the early hard-shelled
biological views of Lombroso have sometimes been regarded with greater intellectual tolerance than they merit. That Lombroso scorned the armchair and
employed the laboratory for his work is no cause for endorsement, unless it can
be upheld that poor science is by definition inevitably superior to first-rate
philosophy. Lombroso's caricatured and anecdotal case histories of prostitutes
("a demi-type . . . her ears stand out, she has big jaws, and cheek bones, and
very black hair, besides other anomalies, such as gigantic canine teeth and
dwarf incisors"), and his torturing of logic, such as an attempt to relate the
fatness of prostitutes, which "strikes those who look at them en masse," to the
obesity of Hottentots and then to relate both of these to a theory of atavism
(Lombroso and Ferrero, 1895:113–114) represents a dolorous twisting of the
scientific approach. The most on-target criticism of Lombroso remains that of
the French anthropologist Paul Topinard, who lived between 1830 and 1911 and
who gave criminology its name: when he was shown a collection of Lombroso's
pictures of allegedly atavistic criminals, he remarked wryly that the pictures
looked no different from those of his own friends (Tarde, 1912:220). Similarly,
the preeminent Canadian physician Sir William Osler (1882:146) experimentally rebutted the accuracy of Lombroso's ideas about the distinctiveness of the
brains of offenders. The law, Osler noted, should not allow "every rascal to
plead faulty gray-matter in extenuation of some crime."

It took many decades, unfortunately, before the main body of criminological
thought accepted the validity of Topinard's and Osler's perceptive criticisms of
Lombroso's theoretical stance. And yet there remains a germ of importance in

the Lombroso approach; otherwise we would not have tarried so long to set it forth here. Biological conditions clearly do play some part, and perhaps sometimes a very prominent part, in conditioning delinquency. In the next chapter, we will discuss recent theories, much more sophisticated than Lombroso's, which have sought to untangle the relationship between inherited traits and delinquency. It need only be noted here that there is no doubt that what you are, what you look like, and how you behave will influence in meaningful ways how you are seen by those around you. And how you are perceived and how you are treated inevitably will come to influence how you behave, whether in a delinquent or in a nondelinquent fashion. Unattractive people, for instance, have been found to be less well liked than attractive ones; their work is more likely to be judged inferior; they are more likely to be blamed for their transgressions; and those transgressions are more likely to be seen as indicative of a chronically antisocial character, a process that could indeed push them more readily into delinquency.

Summary

Theoretical interpretations of the genesis and the correlates of juvenile delinquency abound, often appearing something like a sailor's ditty bag, a container full of things rather haphazardly thrown together. A considerable part of the problem inheres in the fact that the concept of "juvenile delinquency" itself embraces a varied array of behaviors, some of them aggressive acts, others passive, some done alone, others carried out in small or large groups. It is extremely difficult to locate an explanatory schema that will provide understanding of matters as different as running away from home or incorrigibility (itself hardly a clear-cut behavioral entity) and cold-blooded murder. Theorists often settle for explanatory outlines that concentrate on some of the major kinds of delinquent acts and ignore the more unusual acts. They also focus on why youngsters get into trouble with the law — regardless of what kind of trouble it may be — and do not attempt any particular explanation of why the trouble takes the form that it does. In this regard, the theories try to differentiate conformity to law from illegal behavior — or at least to differentiate persons who get caught from those who do not.

Theories of delinquency often collide with popular explanations. Most persons suspect that they understand quite well why youngsters misbehave. They have friends, brothers or sisters, or children who provide them with what they regard as telling insight into the roots of "good" and "bad" behavior. Mothers and fathers readily proclaim that a child of theirs who is in trouble was "difficult" almost from the moment of birth. Sometimes, in fact, they will explain that identical twins — one in trouble, the other doing well — showed at any early age the proclivities that are now more manifest. One mother, in fact, explained the problems of a twin child in trouble with the law by the fact that he was born after his brother, that she had not expected to have twins, and that she resented the extra child. Confronted with the fact that she had never been told which of the two brothers had arrived first, she was momentarily nonplussed but then returned to the same "explanation," merely adding that she somehow "knew" which of the two had been born after the other.

Two major theoretical explanations marked the early days of attempts to explain juvenile delinquency and adult crime. Both are hardy survivors and still exert a strong influence on the content and direction of current thought. The classical school, represented by Jeremy Bentham and Cesare Beccaria and based on armchair philosophizing, maintained that offenders rationally calculate the gains and losses likely to ensue from delinquency. If the penalties exceed possible gains, then the behavior will not be undertaken. The classical school argued that all that was required to deter delinquency was a penalty slightly in excess of the likely gain from the behavior. The second theoretical school—the positivistic—founded by Cesare Lombroso, pushed the study of illegal behavior in the direction of empirical inquiry and experimental investigation. Its primary aim was to find distinctive traits that differentiated the law-abiding from the delinquent.

Revival of interest in classical criminology, according to Leon Sheleff, is based on a growing current "disillusionment . . . about the capacity to fully understand the etiology of crime" (1981:3). "A return to the classical writers," Sheleff further notes, "does not necessarily mean a return to all the ideas espoused by them. Debate over these ideas rages today no less than when they were first propounded as innovative ideas almost two centuries ago" (1981:3). Sheleff explains the renewed vitality of classical thought in the following terms:

> As positivistic criminology—whether Lombrosian biology, Freudian psychology, or Durkheimian sociology—seems to have reached an impasse and despite all the accumulation of knowledge and all the practical experimentation, the crime rate continues to rise, so the basic framework (if not the specific proposals) of Beccaria's and Bentham's ideas is slowly infiltrating back into criminological studies. Practitioners of the sociology of law are urging vigorously that there can be no understanding of crime without a prior investigation of the criminal-law system, with a special emphasis on the manner in which laws are passed and the political interests involved. . . . The whole process of social control through the criminal-law system is also being subjected to intense scrutiny. (1981:6)

Classical criminology, Sheleff argues, saw the criminal law and judicial practices to be of pivotal importance in determining the nature of society, the quality of its life, the essence of its morality. "This is why classical criminology should not be seen as some quaint and antiquated relic from the past but as possessed of vitality and significance for today" (Sheleff, 1981:12).

Positivism—the use of scientific inquiry to reach an understanding of delinquency—flourished from the time of Lombroso forward but has been under serious challenge in recent years, though it continues to dominate theoretical work. For one thing, early positivism was pessimistic about the likelihood of reformation by delinquents, since inherent traits were believed to have propelled them toward lawbreaking. Positivism's rationale for punishment, one that has taken hold today, was primarily to protect society, not to alter the offender. The achievements of positivism's progenitor have been summarized by Fishman (1981:7):

For many, the mere mention of Lombroso's name will be sufficient reason to ridicule, but the fact is that Lombroso did not represent a passing episode, and his contribution goes far beyond his substantive writings. His most important contribution was in the methodological-epistemological realm. The example set by his work, regardless of how incompetent it may be by present-day scientific research criteria, paved the way for future generations of criminologists, who, although they undoubtedly improved upon his research methods and explanatory variables, have not really altered Lombroso's essential paradigm for studying crime.

References

Agnew, Robert. 1984. Appearance and Delinquency. *Criminology* 22:421–440.

Ayer, Alfred, J. 1982. *Freedom and Necessity*. In *Free Will*, edited by Gary Watson, 15–23. Oxford: Oxford Univ. Press.

Banks, C., Maloney, E., and Willcock, H. D. 1975. Public Attitudes to Crime and the Penal System. *British Journal of Criminology* 15:228–240.

Beccaria, Cesare. 1963. *On Crimes and Punishments* [1764]. Translated by Henry Paolucci. Indianapolis: Bobbs-Merrill.

Bentham, Jeremy. 1838–1843. *The Works of Jeremy Bentham*. Edited by John Bowring. Edinburgh: Tait.

Binder, Arnold, and Geis, Gilbert. 1983. *Methods of Research in Criminology and Criminal Justice*. New York: McGraw-Hill.

Bovet, Lucien. 1951. *Psychiatric Aspects of Juvenile Delinquency*. Geneva: World Health Organization.

Bowman, LeRoy. 1960. *Youth and Delinquency in an Inadequate Society*. New York: League for Industrial Democracy.

Bunge, Mario A. 1959. *Causality: The Place of Causal Principles in Modern Science*. Cambridge, Mass.: Harvard Univ. Press.

Cairns, Huntington. 1935. *Law and the Social Sciences*. New York: Harcourt, Brace.

Cook, Thomas D., and Campbell, Donald T. 1979. *Quasi-Experimentation: Design and Analysis Issues for Field Settings*. Chicago: Rand McNally.

Cullen, Francis T., Larson, Martha Todd, and Mathers, Richard A. 1985. Having Money and Delinquent Involvement: The Neglect of Power in Delinqency Theory. *Criminal Justice and Behavior* 12:171–192.

Cusson, Maurice. 1983. *Why Delinquency?* Translated by Dorothy R. Crelinsten. Toronto: Univ. of Toronto Press.

Dalton, Michael. 1677. *The Countrey Justice*. London: T. Roycroft and W. Rawlins.

Einstein, Albert. 1933. *On the Method of Theoretical Physics*. New York: Oxford Univ. Press.

Engel, George L. 1962. *Fainting*. 2nd ed. Springfield, Ill.: Thomas.

Feynman, Richard. 1985. *"Surely You're Joking, Mr. Feynman!": Adventures of a Curious Character*. New York: W. W. Norton.

Fishman, Gideon. 1981. Positivism and Neo-Lombrosianism. In *The Mad, the Bad, and the Different: Essays in Honor of Simon Dinitz*, edited by Israel L. Barak-Glantz and C. Ronald Huff, 15–23. Lexington, Mass.: Lexington Books.

Furnham, Adrian, and Henderson, Monika. 1983. Lay Theories of Delinquency. *European Journal of Social Psychology* 13:107–120.

Geis, Gilbert. 1960. Jeremy Bentham. In *Pioneers in Criminology*, edited by Hermann Mannheim, 51–67. London: Stevens.

Gibbs, Jack P. 1975. *Crime, Punishment, and Deterrence.* New York: Elsevier.

Haggard, Howard W. 1929. *Devils, Drugs, and Doctors: The Story of the Science of Healing from Medicine-Man to Doctor.* New York: Blue Ribbon Books.

Hart, H. L. A. 1982. *Essays on Bentham: Studies in Jurisprudence and Political Theory.* Oxford: Clarendon Press.

Hartshorne, Charles, and Weiss, Paul S., eds. 1934. *The Collected Papers of Charles S. Peirce.* Cambridge, Mass.: Harvard Univ. Press.

Hentig, Hans von. 1948. *The Criminal and His Victim.* New Haven, Conn.: Yale Univ. Press.

Hirschi, Travis. 1973. Procedural Rules and the Study of Deviant Behavior. *Social Problems* 21:159–173.

Hutcheson, Frances. 1738. *An Inquiry into the Original of Our Ideas of Beauty and Virtue.* 4th ed. London: D. Midwinter.

Jacob, Herbert. 1978. Rationality and Criminality. *Social Science Quarterly* 59:584–585.

James, William. 1907. *Pragmatism: A New Name for Some Old Ways of Thinking.* New York: Longmans, Green.

———. 1909. *The Will to Believe and Other Essays in Popular Philosophy.* New York: Longmans, Green.

Jeffery, C. Ray. 1960. The Historical Development of Criminology. In *Pioneers in Criminology,* edited by Hermann Mannheim, 364–394. London: Stevens.

Jenkins, Philip. 1984. Varieties of Enlightenment Criminology: Beccaria, Godwin, de Sade. *British Journal of Criminology* 24:112–130.

Kelley, Harold H. 1967. Attribution Theory in Social Psychology. In *Nebraska Symposium on Motivation,* vol. 15; edited by David Levine, 192–238. Lincoln: Univ. of Nebraska Press.

Krutch, Joseph Wood. 1953. *The Measure of Man.* Indianapolis, Ind.: Bobbs-Merrill.

Larner, Jeremy, ed. 1964. *The Addict in the Street.* New York: Grove Press.

Lombroso, Cesare. 1905. *L'Homme criminel: Étude anthropologique et médicolégale.* Translated by G. Regnier and M. A. Bornet. Paris: F. Alcan.

———. 1911. *Crime: Its Causes and Consequences.* Translated by Henry P. Horton. Boston: Little, Brown.

———, and Ferrero, William. 1895. *The Female Offender.* New York: Appleton.

McCarry, Charles. 1972. *Citizen Nader.* New York: Saturday Review Press.

Mackie, John L. 1980. *The Cement of the Universe: A Survey of Causation.* Oxford: Clarendon Press.

Mannheim, Hermann. 1955. Lombroso and His Place in Modern Criminology. In *Group Problems in Crime and Punishment,* by Hermann Mannheim, 69–84. London: Routledge and Kegan Paul.

Mead, Margaret. 1972. *Blackberry Winter: My Earliest Years.* New York: Morrow.

Michael, Jerome, and Adler, Mortimer J. 1933. *Crime, Law, and Social Science.* New York: Harcourt, Brace.

Mill, John Stuart. 1843. *A System of Logic.* London: Longmans, Green.

———. 1859. Bentham. In *Dissertations and Discussions: Political, Philosophical, and Historical,* 330–392. London: J. W. Parker.

Mitchell, Wesley C. 1918. Bentham's Felicific Calculus. *Political Science Quarterly* 33:161–183.

Nagel, Stuart S. 1982. Tradeoffs in Crime Reduction Among Certainty, Severity, and Crime Benefits. *Rutgers Law Review* 35:101–131.

Nisbett, Richard, and Ross, Lee. 1980. *Human Inference: Strategies and Shortcomings of Human Judgment.* Englewood Cliffs, N.J.: Prentice-Hall.

Nye, F. Ivan. 1958. *Family Relationships and Delinquency.* New York: Wiley.

O'Donnell, Bernard. 1950. *The Old Bailey and Its Trials.* London: Clerke and Cockeran.

Osler, William. 1882. On the Brains of Criminals. *Canada Medical and Surgical Journal* 10:385–398.

President's Commission on Law Enforcement and Administration of Justice. 1967. *The Challenge of Crime in a Free Society.* Washington, D.C.: U.S. Government Printing Office.

Rice, Robert. 1956. *The Business of Crime.* New York: Farrar, Straus and Cudahy.

Rosen, Frederick, 1982. Jeremy Bentham: Recent Interpretations. *Political Studies* 30:575–581.

Rosenberg, Bernard, and Silverstein, Harry. 1969. *The Varieties of Delinquent Experience.* Waltham, Mass.: Blaisdell.

Rosenblum, Nancy L. 1978. *Bentham's Theory of the Modern State.* Cambridge, Mass.: Harvard Univ. Press.

Rubin, Lillian B. 1986. *Quiet Rage: Bernie Goetz in a Time of Madness.* New York: Farrar, Straus and Giroux.

Rumney, Jay, and Murphy, Joseph P. 1952. *Probation and Social Adjustment.* New Brunswick, N.J.: Rutgers Univ. Press.

Shackleton, Robert. 1972. The Greatest Happiness of the Greatest Number: The History of Bentham's Phrase. In *Studies on Voltaire and the Eighteenth Century,* edited by Theodore Besterman. Banbury, Oxfordshire: Voltaire Foundation.

Sheleff, Leon Shaskolsky. 1981. The Relevance of Classical Criminology Today. In *The Mad, the Bad, and the Different: Essays in Honor of Simon Dinitz,* edited by Israel L. Barak-Glantz and C. Ronald Huff, 3–13. Lexington, Mass.: Lexington Books.

Shoemaker, Donald J. 1984. *Theories of Delinquency: An Examination of Explanations of Delinquent Behavior.* New York: Oxford Univ. Press.

Steintrager, James. 1977. *Bentham.* London: George Allen and Unwin.

Stephen, Leslie. 1900. *The English Utilitarians.* New York: Putnam.

Tarde, Gabriel. 1912. *Penal Philosophy.* Translated by Rapalje Howell. Boston: Little, Brown.

Thomas, Helen. 1960. *Felix Frankfurter: Scholar on the Bench.* Baltimore: Johns Hopkins Univ. Press.

Toby, Jackson. 1985. Affluence and Adolescent Crime. In *Delinquency, Crime, and Social Process,* edited by Donald R. Cressey and David A. Ward, 285–311. New York: Harper and Row.

Volk, Charles R. 1976. Jeremy Bentham — Priest or Prophet of Criminal Law Reform? *University of Pittsburgh Law Review* 17:697–711.

Weaver, Anthony. 1959. *They Steal for Love.* New York: International Universities Press.

Wells, L. Edward, and Rankin, Joseph H. 1985. Broken Homes and Juvenile Delinquency: An Empirical Review. *Criminal Justice Abstracts* 17:249–273.

———. 1986. The Broken Homes Model of Delinquency: Analytic Issues. *Journal of Research in Crime and Delinquency* 23:68–93.

Wilson, James Q. 1975. *Thinking About Crime.* New York: Basic Books.

———, and Cook, Philip J. 1985. Unemployment and Crime: What Is the Connection? *The Public Interest* 79:3–8.

Witmer, Helen L., and Kotinsky, Ruth, eds. 1956. *New Perspectives for Research on Juvenile Delinquency.* Washington, D.C.: U.S. Government Printing Office.

Wolfgang, Marvin E. 1960. Cesare Lombroso. In *Pioneers in Criminology,* edited by Hermann Mannheim, 168–227. London: Stevens.

CHAPTER 4

Constitutional, Psychiatric, and Psychological Theories

© Allen Green, Visual Departures

The early theories of Cesare Lombroso represent an extreme point on the continuum of explanations of juvenile delinquency. In Lombroso's first writings, heredity inexorably played itself out as destiny; for him, the delinquent was there at birth, just waiting to appear after the passage of time. At the other extreme of the continuum are theories that regard human beings as *tabulae rasae,* totally blank sheets waiting only for social experience to determine how they will behave and what will become of them. Both sets of ideas about delinquency — those exclusively stressing heredity and those solely emphasizing environment — are far-fetched and lopsided. It is the interplay of what we are with what happens to us that will condition what we do — or what we choose to do — and will decree whether we perform certain acts that may fall into the realm of juvenile delinquency.

At the same time, it must be appreciated that the blend of experience and heredity that relates to human behavior can be unevenly mixed. Clearly, in some cases hereditary factors appear to play a particularly prominent part in the behavior; in others, environmental influences seem to dominate the causal interpretation. Take, for instance, the disease of encephalitis, whose name literally means "brain inflammation." During the years from 1916 to 1926, epidemics of encephalitis arose throughout the world. Sufferers experienced sleepiness, difficulties in swallowing, strabismus (a visual disorder marked by an inability to direct both eyes to the same object), and bizarre changes in personality. About half of those who got the disease died; the remainder tended to suffer from "marked mental changes" (Duvoisin, 1984:12).

A case history is supplied by Pfeiffer (1965:116–117):

> an epidemic of encephalitis broke out among horses in southeastern Massachusetts and three weeks later the malady spread to human beings. The list of Boston patients included a 10-year-old boy, a model child with an I.Q. of 145. He continued to be well-behaved and obtained his usual good marks until more than a year after passing through the crisis of the disease, when he began getting restless and noisy. He struck his mother, gouged holes in the walls with his pocket knife and had screaming temper tantrums followed by fits of remorse. In this case there was no question about the most likely cause. The boy's symptoms were brought under control with benzedrine and have not flared up again. (See also Bond and Appel, 1931)

Obviously, if a young person were behaving perfectly normally, even in an exemplary way, and after a bout of encephalitis got into constant difficulty with the juvenile authorities because of brawling aggressiveness, it might reasonably be argued that the disease's onset was the major cause of the delinquent behavior. Self-evident cases of heredity playing the preeminent role are less readily pinpointed, but it certainly is conceivable that some persons are born with brain conditions that, while they don't doom them to delinquency, can play a major role in the path toward such behavior.

There is no obvious framework into which we may set the various kinds of theories we will be reviewing here. It is possible, of course, to consider them chronologically, but that would result in an awkward back-and-forth shifting between very different kinds of ideas. Our task of arrangement would be much simpler if theories of delinquency had progressed along a path from simple and crude statements to more sophisticated and refined formulations, with each new

© Leonard Freed, Magnum

Constitutional, psychiatric, and psychological theories explain this result on the basis of aberrations in the individual.

theory building upon and further explicating its predecessors. But this is not what has happened. While some theories can with ease be clustered into categories, many abruptly strike out into wholly new and previously unexplored intellectual territory, ignoring what has gone before or casting it aside as irrelevant. Therefore, of necessity, our review here will have at times to explore one particular pathway and then abruptly turn to another. What we examine first and what last cannot be dictated by common agreement about priorities and superiorities. Advocates of many of the diverse theoretical positions we will unfold continue today to maintain that interpretations other than theirs are wrong-headed, dead-end ideas at best. Freudians, for instance, pay little heed to Marxists, and Marxists ignore social interactionists except occasionally to deplore their inability to understand truth even though (the Marxists say) it has been persuasively set before them.

For our purposes, we will employ a format that mixes chronological and subject-matter considerations. Formulations that appeared earliest will tend to be considered first, but we will carry some of them forward in order to offer an overview of the developmental pattern of the original position.

Constitutional Theorists and Theories

Charles Goring (1870–1919)

The heritage of Cesare Lombroso continues to occupy a distinctive niche in the pantheon of juvenile delinquency theory, as shown in Chapter 3. There undoubtedly is something especially attractive about the position that there can be found a constellation of biological factors that, once determined, can be linked to behavioral outcomes. Animals, following inherited instincts, do exactly what we know they will do when they swim upstream to spawn, fly north or south with the seasons, and build their nests in an invariant manner. Some persons are certain that humans do the same, and they keep seeking to locate these predetermined patterns. Another appeal of constitutional theory may be that it allows its adherents to establish themselves as a breed apart — and above. We know of no theorists who located physical traits that they themselves possessed as determinative of wrongdoing.

The most obvious flaw in Lombroso's work was that it failed to use a control group. Control groups typically are constituted of persons similar to those being studied except in terms of the item under inquiry. That is, a group of persons with the same background except for their criminality would constitute a control group for a study of criminal offenders. Lombroso, it will be remembered, claimed that delinquents possessed various "atavistic" characteristics — sloping foreheads, for instance. If a group of noncriminals, otherwise of similar age and equivalent background (that is, a control group), was found to have different forehead forms, Lombroso could well be said to be on to something. Unfortunately, this was a scientific strategy that he never utilized.

An Englishman, Charles Goring, is generally regarded as the prime debunker of Lombroso, though he merely refined rather than rebutted the Italian theorist's position. Goring, a physician in the English prisons, examined some 3,000 prisoners in terms of forty-three traits. He stated flatly that on the basis of his work it could be said that

> Criminality is not a morbid state akin to a physical disease which can be diagnosed and established by pure observation. As individuals, criminals possess no characteristics, physical or mental, which are not shared by all people. (Goring, 1913:7)

Goring criticized Lombroso for what he believed was his failure to take account of information that did not fit his theoretical presuppositions. He called his own theory *criminal diathesis* — a formulation that insisted that, at least for some persons, delinquency is the inevitable product of inborn inadequacy. Criminal diathesis, Goring (1913:26) said, was

> a constitutional proclivity, either mental, moral, or physical, present to some degree in all individuals, but so potent in some, as to determine for them, eventually, the fate of imprisonment.

Precisely how a general constitutional "moral" deficiency is transmitted biologically remains unstated, and assuredly, given, among other things, the great variation in moral codes throughout the world, such an idea appears highly dubious. It might also be noted, in regard to moral sentiments, that researchers have found prison inmates likely to provide stronger support to conventional morality than the average citizen (Adorno et al., 1950). Goring's theme, like so much early and primitive theorizing, is beyond science because, as it is stated, it cannot be tested. If, instead, he had maintained that all persons born with spinal ganglia of a certain length and with a certain level of intelligence "eventually" would be imprisoned, we might well try to determine the accuracy of such a position. But in what manner and when do we measure "constitutional moral proclivities," and how can we be assured that what we have measured, even if we can determine it, was not the product of experience? Studies of twins, as we shall see, have attempted to overcome some of these difficulties, but they do not truly address the core of Goring's problem because he states his view in so unscientific and imprecise a way.

Goring, though he took giant steps beyond Lombroso, also failed to use an adequate control group for his work (Driver, 1960). His noncriminals came from such diverse (and hardly comparable) groups as Cambridge, Oxford, and Aberdeen university students; University of London professors; mental hospital patients; German army recruits; and members of the British Royal Engineers. Interestingly enough, as Tannenbaum (1938) has observed, there were greater differences between men from one university and those from another than between the university students and the prisoners studied.

Earnest A. Hooton (1887–1954)

The next major figure in the debate on constitutional correlates of delinquency, Earnest Hooton, was responsible for a revival of doctrinaire Lombrosian theory. Hooton was a preeminent physical anthropologist at Harvard University, and his status and position made it particularly likely that his excursion into criminology, late in his career, would be attended to. Like Bentham, Hooton had his eccentricities. He would, for instance, include poems and couplets as footnotes at various points in erudite (and rather tedious) tomes that he wrote regarding the physical attributes of mankind. Though he had written these himself in moments of whimsy, he would say that he had found this or that of the ditties in a washroom or on the campus quad and that it had undoubtedly been written and discarded by one of the building's janitors. Hooton was a witty, engaging classroom lecturer (Shapiro, 1981) and wrote a variety of books for the popular market with titles such as *Apes, Men, and Morons; Why Men Behave Like Apes and Vice Versa;* and *"Young Man, You Are Normal."* There even was an apocryphal story that he had seriously considered naming his male child Newton; thus it would have been Newton Hooton.

Hooton's study of crime and delinquency represented an attempt to refute Goring and ultimately to identify morphological characteristics that were significantly linked with various types of criminal behavior. To this end, he examined 14,873 male convicts in prisons in ten states, using 107 different measurements. Hooton took issue in his work with Lombroso, noting that his presentation of data was "faulty in method" and "partisan in spirit" (1939:13), and adding:

> One of the greatest defects of Lombrosian presentation of criminal anthropological data is the sensational anecdotal method which is utilized to clinch arguments. Individual case descriptions are still spread over the pages of most works on criminology.

And with Goring he took issue in the following way:

> certain adverse and even harsh criticism [must be] expressed here. . . . The most serious charge is that he allowed his work to be influenced by a violent prejudice

against Lombroso and all his theories. . . . It must be asserted here that Goring, persistently, although probably unconsciously, used his statistical genius to twist the results of his investigation so that they would conform to his bias. (Hooton, 1939:18–19)

Having administered such strong rebukes to the works of his predecessors, it might be presumed that Hooton would now embark on a research program marked by immaculate procedures and sophisticated interpretations. Such was far from the case; Hooton's elaborate, time-consuming, energetic effort to find physical traits that marked criminals appears puzzling, almost quixotic. As Shapiro (1981:434) notes, when the results appeared in 1939, the work "was bitterly criticized." Shapiro, a protegé of Hooton, nonetheless, almost half a century after it was published, still calls Hooton's *The American Criminal* "a major work with many insights which may eventually be more fully appreciated." That judgment seems highly doubtful.

Hooton's (1939:309) major conclusion was forcefully stated:

Criminals are organically inferior. Crime is the resultant of the impact of environment upon low grade human organisms. It follows that the elimination of crime can be effected only by the extirpation of the physically, mentally, and morally unfit, or by their complete segregation in a socially aseptic environment.

There is something ominous and chilling in a prescription such as this, especially when we now can look back on the awful attempt by the Nazis to segregate and eliminate those they deemed to be "unfit" (see Moran, 1980). By no means could Hooton's findings, even presuming that they were accurate and meaningful — a very arguable assumption — be made to support so grim a policy recommendation. Nor is it likely that he would have been so remorsefully punitive had his study included white-collar criminals, such as income tax violators and corporate officials convicted of illegal dumping of toxic wastes or of antitrust violations.

What did Hooton's meticulous regimen of measurement disclose? Among other things, he found that "criminals are inferior to civilians in nearly all their bodily measurements" (1939:299) and that such things as "low foreheads, high pinched nasal roots, nasal bridges and tips varying to both extremes of breadth and narrowness, excess of nasal deflections, compressed faces and narrow jaws, fit well into the picture of general constitutional inferiority" (1939:306). Such inferiority was said to be due to heredity and not to situation or circumstances.

Criticisms of Hooton's work abound. For one thing, he was studying convicts, persons who represent the failures of crime and delinquency and not necessarily the most heinous or most dangerous depredators. For another — and extremely important — thing, Hooton's control group, those persons to whom he compared the prison inmates, was hardly, if at all, any better than that of Goring's. Its 3,203 members included (1) firemen in Nashville, (2) hospital outpatients, (3) patrons of a Massachusetts bathing beach, and (4) members of a militia company. Obviously, persons in the last group were apt to be in unusually good physical shape, and certainly there is every likelihood that those of us who elect to allow our physiques to be viewed publicly on a beach are overrepresented by physically prepossessing types. Hooton's findings might be regarded much more seriously had his control group consisted of law-abiding persons from the same social environments as those of the convicts. It is no excuse to state that it is virtually impossible and that the cost would be prohibitive to try to form a satisfactory control group in so demanding a study. If the study design is not scientifically satisfactory, the results will be highly suspect. It is often better that such work not be done at all than that it be done poorly. It seems unconscionable to call for such draconian measures against human beings on the basis of a study so flawed in its methods.

Other reservations about Hooton's work have been cataloged by Vold and Bernard (1979:61–65). They note that Hooton was guilty of circular reasoning: he assumed that the traits that he declared to be characteristic of criminals were marks of inferiority, while he defined such inferiority on the basis of his subjects' criminality. And, like Goring, Hooton often found (and ignored) differences between inmate groups at the various sites in which he worked that were much greater than those between the inmates and persons in the groups to which they were being compared.

Sheldon Glueck (1896–1980), Eleanor Glueck (1898–1972), and William H. Sheldon (1898–1977)

The Approach of the Gluecks. The work of Sheldon and Eleanor Glueck, like that of Hooton, was done at Harvard University, and it was heavily funded by private research organizations. The Gluecks' approach was fundamentally eclectic — they were interested in studying anything they could think of that might have a relationship to delinquency. Among the items the Gluecks emphasized were physical traits, though they also focused on numerous social correlates of delinquency.

Unlike Hooton, the Gluecks exerted a very strong influence on the study of crime, and especially that of juvenile delinquency. But it was an unusual kind of influence. Sheldon Glueck was based at the Harvard Law School, where he held the Roscoe Pound Chair. His teaching primarily was in the field of criminal law, so that his research on delinquency represented a trek into an area far afield from his academic training and responsibilities. His wife was a trained social worker. Few law students and faculty at the Harvard Law School cared a whit about the monumental research program that the Gluecks carried out; it had nothing to do with passing a bar examination. Social scientists, with a few exceptions, tended to scorn the Gluecks, to regard them as rather inept and amateurish intruders into a field that they were ill prepared professionally to comprehend. Their books were reviewed in social science journals with biting criticism and condescension. At the same time, the Gluecks were lionized overseas, where the study of delinquency was not dominated by sociologists but largely fell within the domain of lawyers and doctors. In addition, the Gluecks' affiliation with the Harvard Law School almost guaranteed that they would be accorded the kind of respectful attention and consideration by the public and the political establishment in the United States that they were denied by specialists in delinquency.

It is not easy to summarize briefly the corpus of the Gluecks' contribution: a chronological bibliography listing 258 items that they had written during forty years of work can be found in an appendix to one of their last books (Glueck and

Glueck, 1974:347–364). Essentially, the Gluecks sought to locate for a variety of personal and social circumstances those items which differentiated delinquents from nondelinquents. Their study group comprised 500 delinquent boys who were matched with 500 nondelinquent boys in regard to age, general intelligence, ethnicity, and the type of neighborhood in which they lived. For this study population, the Gluecks examined church attendance, school performance, recreational activities, home life, work habits and skills, economic status of the home, leisure-time companions, movie and burlesque show attendance, ambitions, and experience with criminal justice authorities and agencies, among other matters. Using an approach established by William Sheldon, they also scrutinized the physical attributes of the delinquents and nondelinquents. The Gluecks' eclecticism can be seen in the following observation:

> the enigmatic question of whether one factor or another "causes" delinquency" is . . . an unsound one; for, given certain surrounding conditions, internal or external, various combinations of biologic or social factors referred to by criminologists in the past can precipitate antisocial behavior. A *variety* of causal syndromes can bring about the very same criminalistic behavior. In one case certain biological ones predominate, in another certain sociocultural ones, in the sense that they apparently contribute the most *weight* in the combination of internal and external forces that culminates in antisocial behavior. (Glueck and Glueck, 1965:257)

Critiques of the Gluecks' Work. Had they confined themselves to such a general conclusion and to recital of their findings, the Gluecks might better have avoided the slings and arrows of their critics. But they also were interested in social reform, in the prevention and control of juvenile delinquency; and in this part of their work they sailed into largely uncharted and dangerous waters —where, to keep the metaphor going, they strayed too far from shore, got in too deep, and then ran aground. One of the Glueck's major proposals was that there ought to be a program of early intervention to head off future delinquent behavior:

> The selection of potential delinquents at the time of school entrance or soon thereafter would make possible the application of treatment measures that would be truly crime preventive. To wait for the certain manifestation of delinquency before applying therapy is to close the barn door after the horse has been stolen. Reliance on symptomatic behavior to select pre-delinquents is also a dubious procedure. (Glueck and Glueck, 1950:257)

The "prediction table" constructed by the Gluecks took into account "the practical matter of ease or difficulty of gathering the data by those who would be charged with the task" (1950:259). The five factors selected to predict delinquency were (1) discipline of boy by father (with categories of overstrict or erratic, lax, and firm but kindly); (2) supervision of boy by mother (unsuitable, fair, suitable); (3) affection of father for boy (indifferent or hostile, warm— including overprotective); (4) affection of mother for boy (same subgroups as for the father); and (5) cohesiveness of family (unintegrated, some elements of cohesion, and cohesive). One may note in the Gluecks' five factors the emphasis on that "friendly" relationship between parent and child that dominated child-rearing literature during the period in which they were writing.

Numerical ratings were to be given for each of these items on the basis of a formula established by the Gluecks. The total number of possible points ran from a low of 116.7 to a high of 414, with higher scores representing the greater likelihood of subsequent delinquent behavior. If a youth at age six had a score between 300 and 349, for instance, the Gluecks maintained—on the basis of their research—that he would have an 86 per cent chance of becoming a juvenile delinquent. A score in the range of 150 to 199 carried a 15.7 per cent prospect of delinquency. It was said that trained caseworkers could readily gather and interpret the materials required to predict a delinquent outcome. What the Gluecks had in mind is this:

> School systems will not be able and ready to use these predictive instrumentalities on all children. It is suggested that a beginning might be made in cases in which maladaptive behavior is already present and school authorities wish to determine whether or not the boy in question is really a potential delinquent. In an enlightened educational system, the school could function as the litmus paper of personality maladaptation, reflecting the acid test of the child's success or failure in his first attempts to cope with the problem of life posed by a restrictive, impersonal society and code. In such a system the best psychiatric, psychological, social, medical, and other facilities would be forced to cope with problems of personality distortion and maladaptive behavior at a critical point in the development of the child. (1950:269; see also Glueck and Glueck, 1952; 1968)

Only a few other researchers (e.g., Craig and Glick, 1963; Trevvett, 1965) have made an attempt to validate and employ the prediction tests put forward by the Gluecks. These studies indicate some success in pinpointing potential delinquents. Others have taken issue with specific conclusions of the Gluecks. One study, for instance (McCord, McCord, and Zola, 1959:78), found no evidence that "consistently punitive discipline" was associated with delinquency, despite the conventional wisdom. In fact, the fourteen children in the study who had been severely but consistently treated by their parents had the *lowest* rate of crime. Consistency of treatment was deemed to be much more important than the nature of the treatment (see also Peterson and Becker, 1965). Agnew (1983:234), following up on the McCord, McCord, and Zola findings, discovered that "when parents make inconsistent demands on their children, the use of physical punishment promotes delinquency" but that "when parents make consistent demands, physical punishment does not promote delinquency and may even reduce it."

The Gluecks' work has been subjected to further criticisms in two major regards. In particular, it is viewed as atheoretical, that is, as lacking any guiding principle but instead built on examination of a congeries of factors selected for scrutiny largely because their determination was somewhat plausible and possible. In many respects, the things studied seemed to reflect the Gluecks' own somewhat moralistic preconceptions of what might be important. The Gluecks had a streak of puritanism that seems to mark their scholarly work; in its obituary of Sheldon Glueck, for instance, *The New York Times* (March 13, 1980) notes that in their later years the Gluecks "expressed concern about 'wholesale permissiveness, bordering on license' within the ranks of society."

Criticism also has concentrated on the idea of intervening early in a youngster's school career on the basis of what at best is a statistical likelihood that he or she might be headed for a delinquent career. Under such an approach, numerous "false positives"—persons not truly destined for delinquency—would invariably have their lives disrupted. The danger exists that, as one of the nation's leading newspapers pointed out editorially, "the findings will be misapplied" (*New York Times,* September 26, 1972). In addition, there is no guarantee that an intervention would prove useful or successful. Some persons, as we shall note later, maintain that the process of officially labeling a six-year-old a "predelinquent" makes it more likely than otherwise that the youngster actually will come to embark on a delinquent career.

Methodologists have also faulted the Gluecks on the design of their study and the construction of their prediction table. Cavan (1969:97) suggests that the nondelinquents constituting the control groups were not truly matched but rather were youngsters who were "overly conforming," and Toby (1965), among many others, has challenged the statistical interpretations used by the Gluecks. Typical of the reservations expressed about the Gluecks' work are those of Tappan (1949:137):

> The difficulties in appraising or comparing adequate or defective discipline are apparent; differences in the families of delinquents and nondelinquents will often reflect variations in nationality, cultural, and social-class variables in the groups more than anything else. The adequacy and effort of disciplinary methods can be interpreted only in relation to total family situation. . . . It seems probable that disciplinary practices are "defective" by the standards of good mental hygiene in a great proportion of the homes of all social classes, although the techniques of family control vary a great deal. It is not sound to impute poor discipline only to lower socioeconomic groups.

Sheldon's Approach. One of the prominent measures that the Gluecks employed in attempting to distinguish delinquents from nondelinquents—and the reason we are considering their work in this section of the chapter—was a theoretical descendant of the Lombroso and Hooton tradition. They incorporated into their work the ideas of Sheldon, who had formulated a theory of somatotypes, or body types. Sheldon designated three major body structures: the endomorphic (fat), the ectomorphic (thin), and the mesomorphic (muscular, active), with many intermediate shapes between these distinctive forms. Each body type was said to correspond to a kind of temperament. Endomorphs were declared to be relaxed and gluttonous, to love comfort and to crave affection. This was because, of the three types, they had the greatest amount of body exposure to the sensory stimuli of the outer world. Mesomorphs were said to be vigorous and active, and the ectomorphs to be inhibited, self-conscious, and marked by feelings of inadequacy (Sheldon et al., 1949). Later researchers have criticized Sheldon's formulation on conceptual, methodological, and statistical grounds (e.g., Humphreys, 1957; Ekman, 1951). For instance, they note that Sheldon and his co-workers themselves rated both the body type and the personality: it has been thoroughly demonstrated experimentally (Lerner, 1969; Janssen and Whiting, 1984) that particular types of body builds are stereotypically associated with particular behaviors and that persons unconsciously "see" personality when they are confronted with an individual who has a certain body structure.

Sheldon's application of his ideas to the field of juvenile delinquency claimed to identify a physically aberrant group, its inferiority the product of heredity (Sheldon, Hartl, and McDermott, 1949). Sheldon had been appointed clinical director of the Hayden Goodwill Inn School for Boys in Dorchester, Massachusetts. In that role, he examined 200 young boys who were resident in the facility because of various behaviors—some serious, many not notably serious (e.g., runaways). Three decades later, a number of Sheldon's earlier colleagues sought to determine how his ideas had stood up in terms of the subsequent careers of the study sample. Forty-six of the 200 boys were dead, and eight could not be located and were presumed no longer to be living. For the remainder, the authors report that "of all the [original] findings, the one that has stood up the most consistently is the association of mesomorphic body build with delinquency" (Hartl, Monnelly, and Elderkin, 1982:538; see also Gibbens, 1963; Cortes and Gatti, 1972). There is something monumentally ironic in the fact that the most persistent of Sheldon's findings describes a mesomorphic build— the athletic body structure most valued by Americans—as having the strongest relationship to delinquency, given the fact that Sheldon advocated measures that would inhibit the breeding of his "hereditary" delinquents.

Criticisms of Sheldon's Work.   Edwin H. Sutherland, the leading figure in sociological studies of crime, whose differential association theory will be discussed in Chapter 6, was pitiless in his condemnation of Sheldon's work. Sheldon, Sutherland said (1956:280), "declares dogmatically that [his] is the only way to study personality and behavior and insists that it is the Messiah for a world rushing into social chaos." Sutherland believed that Sheldon's work was "useless" as a demonstration of the value of constitutional psychology in action and that this "should have been obvious from the previous failure of analogous studies" (1956:288–289). Sutherland also maintained that "Sheldon's most general conclusion, which he expresses with something approaching religious hysteria, affirms the necessity of selective breeding," but such a conclusion Sutherland found "completely unrelated to his data" (1956:286). More particularly, Sutherland (1956:289) itemized the following deficiencies in Sheldon's work:

> [His] definition of delinquency cannot be used in empirical research; his selection of cases prevents him from generalizing about any given population; his method of scoring delinquency is subjective and unreliable; his varieties of delinquent youth are meaningless, because no one of his varieties differs from any other somatotypal or psychiatric indexes; his findings on these indexes have no evaluative significance; and his argument for selective breeding is based on preconceptions, not on the data of his study.

Having savaged virtually all aspects of Sheldon's contribution, Sutherland went on to note that indeed he found the case studies included in the Sheldon book interesting—a kind of back-handed compliment that accentuated the ferocity of his critical observations. It must be noted, though, that the accuracy of Sutherland's critique (and it is an accurate appraisal) in no way demonstrates that constitutional factors are not related to delinquency but only points out that Sheldon had been scientifically inept in his attempt to prove such a thesis.

The Gluecks' Adaptation of Sheldon's Work. In their work with Sheldon's body types, the Gluecks found that 11.8 per cent of their 500 delinquents were endomorphs, as were 15.0 per cent of the nondelinquents. For mesomorphs the percentages were 60.1 for the delinquents and 30.7 for the nondelinquents, while 14.4 per cent of the delinquents were ectomorphs and 39.6 of the nondelinquents. No dominant body type was found in 14 per cent of the sample (Glueck and Glueck, 1965).

Judgments in the Glueck study on body type were rendered by two physical anthropologists, first on the basis of commingled pictures of both nondelinquents and delinquents and second by comparing a delinquent with his nondelinquent match. That mesomorphs so disproportionately dominated the ranks of delinquency has been regarded as testimony to the importance of a good body build to cope with the rigors of the delinquent life. Put another way, it can be argued that physically inadequate persons are well advised to avoid delinquency; they are apt to fare poorly in violent gang encounters and to lack the strength and the stamina helpful for stealing and other gang activities. Persons with less adequate body makeups might well retreat to the library or to other settings where they will be less vulnerable to being hurt and in this process of retreat avoid becoming delinquents.

On face at least, the Glueck-Sheldon data on body type make some sense, but they fit awkwardly at best with the array of other measurements — such as family atmosphere and parental discipline — that were employed in the attempt to predict delinquency. The measurement of body type is rather crude, and it is not unlikely, for instance, that with passing years persons will change from one category to another. The tie between body type and personality also seems primitive. In all, Sheldon's theories and the Gluecks' adoption of them appear to represent a detour off the main road to the discovery of the roots of delinquent behavior.

Chromosomal Theories: The XYY Type

The idea that delinquents have some genetic traits that distinguish them from nondelinquents did not die out in the wake of the antagonism and indifference to the physiological positions of Lombroso and his followers. For a time, for instance, the belief flourished that there existed a distinctive chromosomal pattern that predisposed some males to low intelligence and to aggressive behavior and, because of this, to crime and delinquency. Normally, individuals possess twenty-three pairs of chromosomes that determine their inherited traits, such as gender. Females have an XX chromosomal combination, males an XY. But in some instances — the best estimate is for 1 person in 236 (Dorus et al., 1976) — male infants are born with an extra Y chromosome, sometimes known as the forty-seventh chromosome. These XYY persons, first recognized in 1961 (Sandberg et al., 1961), have been alleged to be destined to engage in acts of violence to a much greater extent than their XY fellows.

This propensity was initially supported by research with killifish. Killifish with an XYY makeup were said to act as "supermales," winning female favor about 88 per cent more often than their competition and acting unduly aggressive. Australian and Scottish studies also indicated that persons with XYY chromosomes constituted a disproportionate element in hospitals for the criminally insane. Defense lawyers were quick to seize upon such arguments to attempt to avoid punishment for clients alleged not to be responsible for their delinquent behavior because of abnormal chromosome patterns (Price and Whatmore, 1963; Jacobs, Brunton, and Melville, 1965; Montagu, 1968).

Subsequent investigations began to pick away at the alleged linkage between XYY chromosome structure and delinquency. A 1972 Canadian research probe reported only one of sixty-five prison inmates to have an XYY configuration. Nor did this person display traits, such as aggressiveness, said to be manifested by XYYs (Joneja, Travill, and Scott, 1972). A year later, an Australian report concluded on the basis of prisoner research that XYY abnormalities did not correlate significantly with aggressive behavior as measured by the crime of murder (Bartholemew and Sutherland, 1973). A sophisticated overview a few years later took the position that the studies to date were inconclusive at best, though XYY males did appear to demonstrate *better* institutional behavior and adjustment than XY males (Shah, 1967; see also Borgaonkar and Shah, 1974). Another wrinkle was added to this line of work by a subsequent report that XYYs showed no particular pattern of delinquency but that persons with any kind of chromosomal abnormality were likely to engage in more deviant behavior than so-called normals (Meyer-Bahlburg, 1974).

In the most sophisticated test to date of a number of aspects of the XYY syndrome, Theilgaard (1984) took as her study cohort the 31,438 males born in Copenhagen in Denmark between the first day of 1944 and the last day of 1947. She drew a sample of the tallest 15 per cent, since the extra chromosomal pattern tends to be located within this group. Of the 4,591 persons who eventually could be examined, 12 were identified as XYYs and 16 as XXY. Members of the latter group possess what is known as Klinefelter's syndrome (Klinefelter, Reifenstein, and Albright, 1941) and are alleged, in contrast to XYYs, to be "feminized." Theilgaard used as her contrast group 52 male XYs. She concluded that the XXYs and XYYs were "more alike than different" (1984:106), showing a wide spectrum of intelligence scores and no evidence of variations in cognitive styles. The XXYs were more rigid in their thinking than the XYYs, but this difference was only "slight." In short, she concluded that "the degree and nature of the disparities between the two karytypic anomalies are not so essential as to warrant the description 'distinctive psychological anomalies'" (1984:106). The XYYs did not appear to be in any greater danger of committing criminal offenses than XY men of a similar background. Summarizing her work, Theilgaard (1984:108) made this eminently sensible observation:

> As in all human beings, the XYYs and XXYs are the result of an interplay of genetic, environmental and psychological processes. It follows that there is no ground for anticipating that a person with a certain cytogenic status will demonstrate a preordained, inflexible and irremediable personality or pathology.

Intelligence and Delinquency

The search for a biological Holy Grail that would serve to provide quick and rather easy enlightenment about the roots of delinquency has hardly been confined to those traits detailed in the foregoing pages. Virtually every other possible characteristic of humans has at some time or other found a person who was ready to insist that in its dysfunction lay the key to understanding delinquency. In this section, we will briefly examine a handful of such ideas through the years to provide a final taste of this genre of theoretical work.

Shortly after the turn of the century, defective intelligence was heralded as the prime cause of delinquent behavior. This idea went hand in hand with a strong social movement calling for eugenic measures to improve the human breed, in the manner in which better horses and livestock are produced by mating those with desired traits and controlling the fertility of those with unwanted characteristics. Henry H. Goddard (1866–1957), superintendent of a school for mental defectives, wrote two major books — *The Kallikak Family* (1912) and *The Criminal Imbecile* (1915) — in which he argued that feeblemindedness is inherited and that it leads those who suffer from it to become juvenile delinquents and criminals because they cannot adequately comprehend the law's imperatives. Goddard campaigned against unrestricted immigration, alleging that certain nationality groups had unusually high proportions of feebleminded persons (Gelb, 1986). The term *moron*, a harsh new word, was invented by Goddard as the translation of Alfred Binet's French *debiles*, literally meaning "weak ones" (Fancher, 1985:107). A case history used by Goddard (1915:65–93) demonstrates his thinking:

> Fred Tronson . . . lived in Portland, Oregon for two years and in that time he held seven different positions as an elevator man. He met and became infatuated with Emma Ulrich, a stenographer. . . . He asked her to marry him, but she refused. Later he was arrested for threatening her and was ordered to leave town. . . . On November 16, he waited for her outside of her home with two loaded revolvers. When she stepped off the streetcar, he again asked her to marry him. She became frightened and ran toward her home. . . . He followed her into her own house and there shot her down. He was convicted in 15 minutes. He was examined by two alienists [psychologists] and pronounced sane, but of low mentality. Binet tests showed him to have a mentality of nine years. . . .
>
> When his confession was read to the jury, Tronson leaned over and asked a clergyman on the jury, "Well, what do you think of it?" When the verdict was given, he did not understand what it meant, and asked to be told. His only remark was that he didn't think there was much of a crowd out for the trial. . . .
>
> This man had been an imbecile at least since he was 12 years of age, and he could have been cared for, and thus this atrocious murder prevented. There are hundreds of just such persons, now in their youth, who are potential criminals. . . . Many of them will repeat the career of Tronson. . . . Shall we learn the lesson and take care of the other Fred Tronsons who are now in our public schools and on our streets?

The difficulty with Goddard's position is that it does not stand up under empirical scrutiny. Mentally defective persons as a group commit no more and by some studies even fewer crimes than persons with average and higher intelligence. And this finding would be even more telling if white-collar offenses such as embezzlement, which require training and intelligence, were considered. Mentally defective persons tend to lack the aggressive initiative often associated with crimes of violence, and they are apt to escape behavior conflicts, which can lie at the core of delinquency. And rather than committing crimes because of a failure to understand the law, the mentally defective often lack the intelligence to plan and coordinate illegal actions. Studies have continually demonstrated that groups such as army recruits and prisoners test out at much the same level; intelligence and delinquency do not notably go together. This becomes especially significant when we realize that defective intelligence often means that the person will escape some of the constraints of socialization and may experience frustration in such institutions as the schools.

Epilepsy and Delinquency

Epilepsy is another condition often tied to delinquency. The typical seizures of the uncontrolled disorder led it to be labeled the "sacred disease" in ancient Greece because of the seemingly awesome nature of the clonic fits that mark it. Most epilepsy is idiopathic, that is, neither preceded nor caused by any other known disease, and the disease is not hereditary. It has been said to be related to delinquency because persons with epilepsy were deemed to be marked by moodiness, egocentricity, and a lack of adaptability. These traits, however, even presuming they are diagnostically accurate (and they appear not to be), could more reasonably be regarded as a consequence of social responses to the epileptic rather than to the disorder itself. At any rate, Anderson (1936) several decades ago put an end to the theorizing about epilepsy and crime in a research report that noted that 254 of 100,000 prisoners had the disorder, compared to 210 of 100,000 persons outside the prisons. The difference was not statistically significant, indicating that epilepsy and lawbreaking were not likely to be related. Similarly, Hsu and his colleagues (1985) found no difference in the prevalence of electroencephalograph (EEG) brain abnormalities between delinquents and nondelinquents, belying experimentally the alleged relationship between psychomotor epilepsy and delinquency, especially violent delinquent acts.

A sample of similar kinds of theoretical efforts would include the following. Researchers have maintained that left-handed persons were overrepresented among juvenile delinquents. It was argued (Fitzhugh, 1973; Flor-Henry, 1978) that left-handedness was associated with aggressiveness and psychopathy because of dysfunction of the left hemisphere of the brain. A later investigation, however, showed that, if anything, left-handed offenders were less violent than right-handed ones and that this conclusion held up across sex and ethnic groups (Andrew, 1980). Similarly, a study indicated that plasma testosterone levels, another trait sometimes said to be linked to delinquency, did not differ between aggressive and nonaggressive individuals and were not correlated with hostility or anxiety. Those inmates who had committed particularly violent crimes did, however, show notably high testosterone levels, suggesting that for a limited population this line of inquiry remains worthy of further pursuit (Kreuz and Rose, 1972).

Recent Biosocial Theorizing

The biosocial theories commanding the greatest amount of attention at the moment are those of Sarnoff Mednick. Unlike his predecessors in this line of research, Mednick has astutely incorporated his work among that of the social scientists, who make up by far the largest segment of scholars dealing with problems of juvenile delinquency. He often publishes in criminological journals and attends national professional conferences on the subject. Thus, his research cannot be ignored in the way that the efforts of the Gluecks, Hooton, and Sheldon were bypassed.

Marvin E. Wolfgang, one of the intellectual leaders of work on crime and delinquency, has pointed out that the studies of Mednick and his various collaborators are "not a revival of Lombroso, Hooton . . . or Sheldon." Wolfgang finds them "new and exciting, buttressed by control groups and experimental analyses" (Wolfgang, 1977:v). In the biosocial realm, Mednick has concluded that electrodermal responses may well provide a predictive precursor of delinquent behavior. He followed 313 Danish youths who had been intensively examined in 1962 and found that 36 came to have "serious disagreement with the law." These men demonstrated electrodermal responses significantly slower than those of members of the control group. This rate is regarded as an indication of inadequate autonomic nervous system functioning. Mednick suggests that the trait is transmitted by heredity, so that it might well be "a characteristic a criminal father could pass to a biological son, which (given the proper environmental circumstances) could increase the probability of the child failing to learn adequately to inhibit asocial responses" (Mednick, 1977:5). The electrodermal inadequacy is said to produce a deficit in the ability to dissipate fear, resulting in either an incapacity or a lag in curbing aggressive impulses.

Mednick has also undertaken elaborate studies of twins who were separated at birth and never met and of adopted children who were unacquainted with their biological parents. He finds higher concordance in delinquency and crime rates among twins and adoptees and their natural parents than could be accounted for by chance. The most reasonable explanation, he argues, is that there are inherited traits that in some manner produce delinquency, however such traits may be acted upon by subsequent environmental experiences. In one study, for instance (Gabrielli and Mednick, 1983), Mednick and a colleague studied 14,427 adopted children and both their biological and adoptive parents. They found a particularly strong relationship between property offenses committed by the children and by their natural parents, but no correlation for crimes of violence. "Sons of biological fathers who were chronic offenders," the authors (Gabrielli and Mednick, 1983:435) note, "showed the highest level of criminality though they had never met their fathers." If the biological mother was an offender, the likelihood of the adopted son being a lawbreaker was even slightly higher than in regard to the father. Siblings showed the highest rates of equivalent delinquency even though they had been adopted into different families.

One difficulty, of course, acknowledged by the authors, is that adoption agencies often try to place children into families that resemble their own in significant ways. It is possible that in this manner the results have been preformed by the agencies' policies. Nonetheless, recent work on biosocial correlates of delinquency seems to confirm the commonsense view that certain types of human structure and nervous system are likely to be more susceptible to social difficulty in certain kinds of environments, just as persons who are over seven feet tall stand a better chance than those under five feet of being basketball stars and those with a slow pulse rate have an edge toward becoming better distance runners. We know that height has strong genetic components, and pulse rate probably does as well. The strength of the relationships, however, does not appear so overwhelming as to suggest the utility of any widespread intervention program.

After a thorough review of a vast body of literature on the medical aspects of delinquency, Scott (1975) suggests that the evidence of association of physical and mental health factors as well as prenatal and genetic factors with juvenile delinquency is scanty, with at best an indirect linkage; for instance, physiological difficulties may produce problems in social adjustment — such as impatient and intolerant responses from others — that may in turn be associated with subsequent delinquent acts. At the moment, this seems a notably sensible summary observation, but this field of work is far from foreclosed as we attempt to gain a better understanding of delinquency. As Wilson and Herrnstein (1985:207) have observed:

> It took years of patiently following the life histories of many men and women to establish the linkage between smoking or diet and disease; it will also take years to unravel the complex and subtle ways in which intelligence, temperament, hormonal levels and other traits combine with family circumstances and later experiences in school and elsewhere to produce human character.

Similarly, Rowe and Osgood (1984:526–527), writing in the major sociological journal, the *American Sociological Review,* protest that previous sociological explanations of delinquency have "ignored or ridiculed" genetic factors, though they grant that such factors "can only be the first state of any causal sequence leading to social behavior." Their investigation, conducted with a sample of twins in all school districts in Ohio, excepting inner-city districts, where access proved too difficult, concentrated on three theoretical links to delinquent behavior: (1) genetic variation, (2) common environmental influences, and (3) specific environmental influences that affect each individual uniquely. They maintain that genetic factors contributed most to distinctions between delinquents and nondelinquents, though they take care to note that "although genetic factors are implicated, this does not mean that delinquency is either a direct result of biological differences or that it is inevitable" (1984:526). What is argued is that responses to social events and conditions are related to genetic traits and that these ought to figure more prominently than they have in current theorizing about delinquency.

Psychiatric Theories and Their Sequelae

Sigmund Freud (1856–1939)

The work of Sigmund Freud has exerted a profound influence on the manner in which human beings throughout the world evaluate behavior. Freudian concepts inevitably have been employed to attempt to explain juvenile delinquency, particularly those kinds of delinquent acts which seem to reflect personal pathology. The Freudian system in many ways is seductive and appealing, because it is a closed framework of thought; that is, once the premises are granted it becomes impossible to rebut a Freudian conclusion. In this sense, it is different from science — perhaps better, perhaps worse, but different. More than a third of a century ago, Karl Popper (1950) dismissed psychoanalysis, along with marxism and astrology, as made up of self-conforming, nonscientific theories. For Popper, the difficulty was that the theories could not be "falsified" — that is, that there is no conceivable behavior that would contradict them. In 1985, Popper continued to hold to his earlier view: "Psychological theories can be abstract, but they must have consequences that are observable," Popper noted in an interview. A mental process, such as "repression," he pointed out, cannot be observed (Goleman, 1985:18; see also Cioffi, 1985).

The self-confirming aspect of Freudian theory might be exemplified by the diagnosis of a probation officer that a delinquent under his supervision shows "neurotic tendencies." The boy is late for an appointment with the officer, who interprets such tardiness as "hostility" and indicates in his report that the hostility represents an indication of the neurosis. But had the boy been exactly on time, the officer could have defined that as "compulsivity," and had he been early that might have been viewed as "defensiveness" — and both of these could as well be regarded as neurotic manifestations.

Other writers are not as pessimistic as Popper about the scientific aspirations of psychiatry. Edelson (1984), for instance, has set out a series of steps that psychiatrists might take to try to translate their ideas into scientifically acceptable form:

- A clearly stated hypothesis and an explanation of how it accounts for the data reported.
- Separating the facts reported from the analyst's interpretation of them.
- Specifying what, if it had occurred, might have led to rejecting the hypothesis, and showing how such events might have led to a revision.
- A statement of rival explanations and how the data favor one hypothesis over others.
- A consideration of factors, such as suggestion, that might contaminate the findings.

This agenda, which essentially asks that the methods of science be applied to psychoanalysis, is germane to other theories as well, and its ingredients should be kept in mind throughout our continuing review of ideas about delinquency.

The major scientific difficulty with the Freudian system as it applies to delinquency is that it is not predictive. It is one thing to say that a young boy who kills his father after the father has beaten his mother is acting out an unresolved Oedipal fixation, but quite another to predict which young men will murder their mothers. Interpreters often fall back upon psychiatric explanations because they are omnipresent and therefore helpful in the face of puzzlement, but their apparent aptness does not necessarily make them accurate.

Freud, the progenitor of the psychiatric school, was born in Moravia and completed his medical training in Vienna. He first worked as a research scientist, dissecting fish and coming close to making what would have been the important discovery of the value of cocaine as an anesthetic for eye operations. He did employ cocaine as a counteractive agent for a friend addicted to morphine — and thereby compounded the friend's troubles severely. Freud himself also used cocaine, sometimes heavily, for ten years, until he stopped completely in 1896 (Masson, 1985). In part because he experienced anti-Semitism in his post at the university, Freud took up private medical practice. In this role, he initially worked with hypnotism, discovering, in collaboration with Josef Breuer, that hysterical patients under hypnotism would render up information bearing directly on the reasons for their psychosomatic condition. Once out in the open, the material could be dealt with, and the illness would dissipate. Soon after, Freud found that he could dispense with hypotism and seemed able to help patients by allowing them to talk openly, their "free associations" providing the key to their difficulties. This represents, in much truncated form, the treatment method of psychiatry; its theory, of course, need have no relationship to the value of the treatment. That is, treatment can succeed or fail without validating the accuracy of the theoretical postulates upon which it is built.

Psychiatry itself is constructed upon Freud's famous triad of forces operative in the human personality: the *id,* or biological urges and wants; the *superego,* the learned dictates of the social system; and the *ego,* the I, the force that mediates among the demands of the id, the obstacles of the environment, and the pressures of the superego. We are forced to inhibit or at least control our biological urges from childhood on and develop frustrations and insecurities as a result. We suffer disappointments in love, professional failures, economic insecurity, and a variety of other problems that, in a person not sufficiently healthy emotionally, can trigger illness or antisocial behavior such as delinquency. We sometimes do not ourselves understand why we feel or act as we do, because the reasons, too hurtful to be faced directly, lie buried in our unconscious. Particularly important in the conflicts we must resolve is that identified for men as the Oedipus complex and for women as the Electra complex. Its basis is that boys yearn for the exclusive love of their mothers, and girls for that of their fathers. This brings them into conflict with the other parent. An inability to resolve the conflict — to move beyond this parental attachment and hostility — can, Freudians insist, cause aberrant behavior and problems in social living.

A recent experiment by Silverman, Lachmann, and Milich (1983) represented an unusual attempt to demonstrate the validity of Freud's Oedipus theory. Silverman flashed subliminal messages on a screen before male schizophrenics and found that the message "Mommy and I are one" temporarily reduced symptoms in certain types of the schizophrenics. Though the results are hardly notably persuasive, the technique is one of many interesting approaches being used today to try to demonstrate or destroy psychiatric postulates. On other fronts, the Freudian system has come under increasingly harsh attack. Neurologists, for instance, maintain that the tripartite division of the mind into id, ego, and superego is a primitive construction, not supported by the complex processes of the brain's function. Recently, a German psychologist (Eschenroder, 1984) took Freud to task on one of his classic studies, that of Hans, a five-year-old who feared horses, saying that they would bite and assail him. When he saw a horse, he would sob hysterically. Freud maintained that Hans suffered from an Oedipal conflict, with fear of his father being translated into imagery involving horses. Eschenroder, however, suggests that Hans was brainwashed into providing fuel for Freud's theories by questions suggested to the father by the analyst, and that Hans's trauma was in truth the consequence of his having witnessed a street accident in which a carthorse struggled desperately to release itself after being trapped by its harness.

A typical Freudian interpretation might be applied to the common delinquency offense of shoplifting. That a male offender took a fountain pen or a flashlight could be deemed to stem from fears of castration, with the stolen items said to represent "phallic symbols." Things stolen, whether lingerie, lipstick, sweaters, or pup tents, are believed often to possess meaning for the pilferer — though he or she may not be aware of such meaning. In addition, the shoplifting could well represent an unconscious attempt to punish parents for some real or imagined grievance the delinquent has against them. The offense also could be committed, Freudians say, to get attention that is not forthcoming when the delinquent behaves satisfactorily. Delinquency also might reflect a desire for punishment growing out of a sense of guilt or an interest in obtaining treatment because of a feeling of anxiety that cannot be traced to a particular source.

Another Freudian interpretation is that offered by Nyswander (1956:64, 65) for hard drug use; the theory, like most such ideas, is interesting but not demonstrable:

> Is there a correlation between an adolescent's experiencing of the yearnings accompanying his own developing sexuality and his attempts to find gratifications by means other than the normal maturation of this phase of his life?
> Consider that narcotics are known to diminish sexual activity to the zero point. We know from the action of morphine on the central nervous system that the addict feels as satisifed . . . as if he had already performed coitus. In this light the adolescent's search for his next shots appears to be an activity which supplants looking for a "hot" date. On questioning, he may relate that his few attempts at sexual relationships have been attended with considerable fear and relatively little satisfaction. Furthermore, it has been established that mixed groups of addicts do not indulge in any form of sexuality.
> . . . The addict usually gives up drugs at the time of life when sexuality begins to diminish. In effect, he manages to live his life in such a way as to avoid the normal gratification of sexual longings as experienced by others.

Herbert Quay (1983:I, 332) has deftly summarized the manner in which the psychiatric school seeks to explain delinquency. Individuals with weak superegos, he notes, are presumed to be likely candidates for delinquency. Also, "Ego defects that impair contact with, and realistic interpretation of, the environment can also lead to crime. Individuals with weak egos and those seeking punishment because of unconscious guilt feelings are likely to fall into the anxious and immature group" (1983:332). Such ego and superego defects generally are ascribed to disturbed parent-child relations, usually resulting from psychological problems of the mother. This last position, of course, is one of several psychiatric postulations that has put the theory into disrepute with feminists. Quay's (1983:342) summary of the psychiatric and psychoanalytical theories in regard to crime is well put:

> In many ways these explanations are appealing, if only for their simplicity. Weak superegos can often be "found" in criminals, particularly if criminal behavior is accepted as evidence for the weakness. Also, many criminals seem to show unconscious desires for punishment by leaving fingerprints or other incriminating evidence at the scene of the crime; but this may also be explained by the empirical finding that a high level of anxiety impedes deliberate thinking. Psychoanalytical

theory, in addition to the unobservable nature of its basic explanatory constructs and its reliance on instinctual drives . . . , does not provide adequate room for . . . environmental factors and the processes of learning.

Despite these reservations, Quay points out that long-forgotten early events, as noted by psychiatrists, certainly can have lasting effects, but he notes that we now believe that intervening experiences can diminish or eliminate the importance of such events.

Psychological Theories

Psychologists have not been prominent in the study of juvenile delinquency, though, given the early significance of Hall and his contemporaries, it might have been assumed that they would have played a leading role. But early psychology was closely tied with philosophy, and soon after it took its empirical turn, the study of delinquency was preempted in the United States by sociologists. Only after the Second World War did multidisciplinary academic departments devoted to investigating crime and delinquency begin to develop in response to the obvious position that to understand so variegated a phenomenon as delinquency it is essential to coordinate its study among a variety of specialists — sociologists, economists, psychologists, historians, jurisprudents, social workers, and others.

Very often — much too often — psychological work on delinquency has taken the route of using long-existing tests on cohorts of delinquents and nondelinquents and attempting by this means to distinguish the groups. In part, this is the result of the accessibility of the samples: like students, another favorite target of psychological experimentation, delinquents can be induced rather easily to participate in such exercises. They do so partly out of boredom, partly out of curiosity, and partly because they are amenable to the solicitations of the experimenters. Sometimes, though, "subjects" resent the intrusions, a matter that obviously can affect the results. Görling (1966:145), writing from the perspective of the delinquents, notes of psychologists:

> They wanted to know everything, likes and dislikes, interests, what it had been like when we were kids. About our parents, brothers, and sisters. Did we lay girls, and since when. And then we had to interpret various words. It was like eating yourself up in daily portions. Afterwards, you felt gnawed to pieces and hollowed out, squeezed dry and quite empty. It almost hurt you all over.

There has been a tradition in psychological research of this nature with delinquents to use such tests as the Minnesota Multiphasic Personality Inventory (MMPI) and intelligence tests, plus a very large inventory of other schedules aimed at assessing personality traits. In a typical inquiry, for instance, the authors (White, Labouvie, and Bates, 1985) found on the basis of administration of a test of "sensation seeking" that self-reported delinquents scored significantly higher on the distribution scale of the test. The results, of course, could be the product of the delinquent behavior rather than the other way around, yet it is recommended that it might be useful to fight delinquency by providing high sensation seekers with socially approved opportunities to meet their expressed needs. Such outcomes, usually the product of careful and sophisticated work, though they may distinguish delinquents from nondelinquents, provide only slanting insights on why the persons with particular test scores got into trouble. Most often, many others with similar personality profiles have avoided difficulties, and some with "better" profiles have gotten into trouble. In addition, virtually all of the testing has been done after the youths have had run-ins with the law, and their experiences in such regard seem very likely to influence the way they respond to personal interviews or paper-and-pencil psychological tests. That self-images, for instance, are lower for delinquents than nondelinquents may be no more than a consequence of the fact that they like themselves less because they have been caught and convicted and now are resident in an institution.

Having noted such reservations about the run-of-the-mill psychological research on delinquency, we can turn to several formulations that have gone beyond these limits and striven to establish sophisticated theoretical statements based upon empirical findings.

Conditioning Theory

H. J. Eysenck is the leading proponent of the view that failure of a person to incorporate satisfactorily the dictates of society represents the major explanation for subsequent delinquent behavior. This, of course, is congruent with Freud's idea that an inadequate superego can cause difficulties in living, but Eysenck discards Freudian theorizing as little more than idle speculation, and he has been one of psychiatric treatment's severest critics, largely through his insistence that the "cure" rate for such treatment is no better for persons who receive it than for those who were equally disturbed and unable for various reasons to begin treatment. For members of both groups, Eysenck insists, about two thirds reexamined two years later have improved considerably.

Eysenck (1964) points out that conscience, in the main, is instrumental in making us behave in a morally and socially acceptable manner and that the acquisition of a satisfactory conscience is the culmination of a long process of conditioning. His research work, Eysenck notes, has demonstrated that extroverted persons, both normal and neurotic, are more difficult to condition — that is, to train — than introverted persons. He then points out that extroverts tend to get into more trouble than introverts. A study of 993 male freshmen at the University of Minnesota, for instance, found that members of the extrovert group had experienced significantly more automobile accidents than individuals with other personality types. Similarly, pilots in South Africa who had had flying accidents in training schools were found to be much more extroverted that those who completed this period without any accidents. Eysenck also cites a study of sexual delinquency among young women — often a cause of filings against them in juvenile court — that found the same distinctive personality differences.

To his credit, Eysenck regards his theory as very tentative, requiring much more confirmation before it can be given credence. He poses the question that in the previous chapter we noted as essential (and often absent) for theorists: "Are there any contradictory data that might lead us to doubt the validity of our theory?" He notes that most of the studies have been done on incarcerated persons and that such results as "high emotionality" might represent a response to their present residence. He argues against this thesis, however, pointing out that persons in prison for ten days score about the same as those there for ten years. But then he graciously grants that "nonetheless, it must be admitted that this is a point which requires much further study" (1964:134).

Eysenck then takes up the most vulnerable aspect of his theory, one that may well have occurred by now to students thinking about his ideas. It is obvious that not all persons receive the same conditioning or indoctrination. As Eysenck (1964:135) grants:

> We know . . . that in middle-class families there tends to be much greater stress on moral and social behavior, and firmer control over aggressive and sexual modes of conduct, whereas in some working-class families, far from frowning on aggressive conduct and applying conditioning methods to suppress it, there is rather a tendency to encourage it and to take pride in the prowess of the growing boy. We also know that there are considerable differences in childrearing practices of different nations.

But Eysenck then argues that for most persons conditioning is imposed by parents strongly arguing for law-abiding patterns (see, for instance, the remarks of the mother of the New York young man shot by Bernhard Goetz reported in the previous chapter; also West, 1963). He grants, however, that some youngsters — say, those with parents deeply involved in crime — are apt to be conditioned into similar kinds of patterns as the parents.

The conditioning position taken by Eysenck has to be regarded in precisely the way he offers it, as a tentative set of ideas whose more precise formulation and accuracy require a good deal more experimental work. It may be that he has pointed out an important path that psychologists need to cultivate; or he may be setting up signposts leading to a theoretical dead end.

Frustration-Aggression Hypothesis

The ideas about conditioning advanced by Eysenck represent a global theory of delinquency; that is, if correct, they could account for all forms of the behavior in terms of unsatisfactory response to social demands. Other theories focus only on certain aspects of delinquency. The frustration-aggression hypothesis, particularly prominent among these, deals virtually exclusively with acts of violence.

The idea that frustration produces an aggressive response was first formulated by Dollard and his associates in 1939. It grew out of psychoanalysis and out of the then-current interest in psychology in stimulus-response patterns. Such patterns were concerned with the reaction of an organism to the intrusion of new phenomena, from such direct matters as the eye-blink reflex as a reaction to a sudden beam of light to the manner in which a person responds to a magnificent painting. For Dollard and his associates, frustration was "an interference with the occurrence of an instigated goal-response at its proper time in the behavioral sequence" (Dollard et al., 1939:7). More simply put, the theorists were saying that a person became frustrated if he or she was kept from attaining the satisfactions expected when the person thought they would be achieved. Such frustration would arouse aggression either against the source inflicting the frustration or against a more convenient object. The theory also contained a notion of catharsis: it suggested that the expression of aggression would alleviate the frustration and allow the organism to return to a more satisfactory state. Laboratory studies have confirmed this notion: Hokanson and Burgess (1962), for instance, demonstrated that male subjects exhibited a sharp increase in systolic blood pressure when angered and displayed a faster return to their regular blood pressure level if they could punish their insulter than if they could only behave in a nonaggressive manner.

In a review of the scientific status of the frustration-aggression hypothesis almost forty years after its initial enunciation, Berkowitz (1978) points out that it certainly does not account for all aggression: a soldier, he notes, might kill an enemy without anger, seeking to end the war and to protect himself, while a Mafia "hit man" might kill a competitor with no emotional involvement. Some theorists also have suggested that prior learning might influence whether frustration will be responded to with aggression or whether the person thwarted will withdraw and retreat. But Berkowitz, citing animal experiments, believes that aggression may be an inherent response to frustration: he points out that socially isolated pigeons, suddenly deprived of food, will attack another pigeon in their cage (Azrin, Hutchinson, and Hake, 1966). After a thorough and careful review of experimental work on the frustration-aggression hypothesis, Berkowitz concludes that frustration is translated into pain and that, while responses to pain may take numerous forms, it generally "elicits fairly specific reactions that incline the organism to be aggressive" (1978:705).

The frustration-aggression theory can provide some significant insight into the wellsprings of delinquency. It helps explain why the deprivations suffered by working-class children may be instrumental in fueling the higher level of openly aggressive forms of delinquency that they manifest. And it can help us to understand the sudden violent outbursts of delinquents who are unable to get their own way in an encounter. Obviously, the theory suggests that it is not a particularly good idea to frustrate a person needlessly if that person does not have a legal channel by means of which to respond to such frustration. But frustration also can be enabling: it can propel persons to seek alternative and better ways to solve their dilemmas. Frustration also seems inevitable because none of us are going to be able to have everything we want when we want it, no matter how effectively we manage to keep our desires in check.

The frustration-aggression hypothesis, thus, offers an interesting range of interpretative insights into some possible wellsprings of violent forms of delinquency and suggestive pathways to try to reduce such behavior. It is this utility that accounts for the continuing vitality of the theory and for its prominent position among psychological schemes bearing upon delinquent behavior.

Operant-Utilitarianism: Wilson and Herrnstein

Crime and Human Nature, by James Q. Wilson and Richard J. Herrnstein (1985), undoubtedly has been the most widely heralded contribution to the theory of delinquency in half a century or more. Wilson, a political scientist, and Herrnstein, a psychologist, both at Harvard University, intrude an alien, antagonisic, and, often, a refreshingly different disciplinary perspective into the field. They assiduously reexamine many earlier studies that have been rejected as inept and insist that, however flawed such studies may be in terms of contemporary research standards, they set out findings that make good sense and that can be supported by more sophisticated recent inquiries overlooked because of the parochial interests and intellectual biases of most scholars in the field of delinquency. Wilson and Herrnstein have been criticized, however (and correctly so), for using these research materials in a self-serving manner; in a particularly telling counterpunch, Kamin (1986:24) makes the following point:

> Tiny snippets of data are plucked from a stew of conflicting and often nonsensical experimental results. Those snippets are then strung together in an effort to tell a convincing story, rather in the manner of a clever lawyer building a case. The data do not determine the conclusions reached by the lawyer. Instead the conclusions toward which the lawyer wants to steer the jury determine which bits of data he presents.

Wilson and Herrnstein range over a wide array of items that they think are significantly related to explanations of delinquency—most notably race and intelligence—but their work most reasonably belongs with that of the psychologist theorists. Their most explicit theoretical statement has considerable elements of the utilitarianism of Bentham and Beccaria, which we discussed earlier, and the social control ideas of Hirschi, which we will examine later. The theory states (1985:61):

> The larger the ratio of rewards (material and nonmaterial) of noncrime to the rewards (material and nonmaterial) of crime, the weaker the tendency to commit crimes. The bite of conscience, the approval of peers, and any sense of inequity will increase or decrease the total value of crime; the opinions of family, friends, and employers are important benefits of noncrime, as is the desire to avoid the penalties that can be imposed by the criminal justice system. The strength of any reward declines with time, but people differ in the rate at which they discount the future. The strength of a given reward is also affected by the total supply of reinforcers.

This is something of a grabbag of ideas. The first sentence is no more or less than pure utilitarianism. The authors, however, are well aware of the deficiencies of so bald a statement standing alone, so they buttress it with an inventory of those things which incline toward crime and those which inhibit it (for example, the bite of conscience and the penalties that might flow from being apprehended). Then they hedge the theory with a pair of reservations that vitiate any exactness: "people differ" and "the strength of any reward declines with time." Finally, the theory moves into an even more abstract, difficult-to-test realm: "The strength of any reward is . . . affected by the total supply of reinforcers"—a rather fancy way of saying, "Well, it depends . . ."

Wilson and Herrnstein grant that there are large hunks of tautology in their ideas ("a person will do that thing the consequences of which are perceived by him or her to be preferable to the consequences of doing something else") but take the rather odd position that they can salvage a tautology by "plausibly" describing its ingredients (1985:43). They do so at one point in their work by reviewing in particularly expansive detail the ideas of the constitutional theorists, including Lombroso and the Gluecks, and concluding that "the predictors

VANILLA

HOT FUDGE

chon
Day

"And now I want to thank you very much."

Psychologists argue that the response the server chooses can affect the child's future behavior.

of crime are genetic to some degree" and that it therefore follows "that crime should be too" (1985:209). There is mounting evidence, Wilson and Herrnstein insist, that offenders on the average differ from nonoffenders in physique, intelligence, and personality.

Obviously, the revisionist views of the Harvard professors have not escaped criticism. Jack Gibbs (1985:381) of Vanderbilt University, a particularly astute scholar, praises them for being able to "avoid the usual shrillness" found in "interdisciplinary warfare." Gibbs labels their theory "operant-utilitarian," finding its roots in operant psychology and economics. He believes that Wilson and Herrnstein might have done better to carry out original research to try to support their theory rather than relying on materials published with other aims. He also finds the work "amorphous," that is, failing to set forth a series of carefully enunciated premises (1985:383) or to demonstrate "the slightest concern about the empirical applicability of their terms." Gibbs also believes that the twenty pages devoted to resurrecting constitutional theories of delinquency causation are outside the bounds of the major theoretical statement, therefore a "puzzling" inclusion. Gibbs (1985:387) further echoes the general response to Wilson and Herrnstein by the scholarly community that traditionally has been concerned with the subject of delinquency:

> It is unfortunate that Wilson and Herrnstein did not devote the space and energy invested in [a number of chapters] to a clarification of their theory by stating explicit premises and deducing testable conclusions. Instead, we have another discursive, untestable theory, something that has never been in short supply. Hence, despite Wilson and Herrnstein's serious scholarship, their book will not lead criminologists out of the wilderness in which they now wander.

Summary

Theories about the cause of delinquency that focus on constitutional differences between individuals abound. There is something marvelously appealing about the possibility of locating something that will predetermine human behavior, so that there no longer will be any uncertainty about what will happen. Poverty, greed, abuse — such kinds of social deprivation provide only unhappy explanations of illegal behavior, because they tell us that we are in part responsible for allowing such conditions to emerge and to flourish, and because they at least subtly suggest that there exists within each of us a potentiality for lawbreaking should the right conditions prevail. If we could determine what kinds of genetic arrangements lead to lawbreaking, we could isolate the carriers or perhaps in time engineer changes that would remedy the deficits. The matter is highly reminiscent of the old Calvinistic doctrine of predestination, which declared that certain persons had already been singled out for divine grace and salvation. The question of whether you or I were among the chosen became too intolerable a burden to carry through life, so the doctrine gradually became transformed, now suggesting that those elected by God could read that verdict most clearly by seeing what fate had been decreed for them in this world: the well off, the successful, obviously also were the blessed, and it was they who would gain heavenly status after their transition period here on earth.

In the same manner, hereditary theory, as Goshen (1974:17) has noted, is "an elitist view . . . which places the theorist himself in the most elite position, with the delinquent in a congenitally inferior position." In this chapter, we have seen how Goring used more advanced experimental techniques to rebut Lombroso's strikingly primitive views of the cause of crime but how, nonetheless, Goring fell into essentially the same kind of trap as Lombroso, insisting that he was able to identify a distinctively different person, a physically predetermined delinquent type. Years later, a cadre of Harvard scholars — Hooton, an anthropologist, Sheldon Glueck, a lawyer, Wilson, a political scientist, and Herrnstein, a psychologist — all would hark back to these compelling themes. At the same time, other investigators would look at XYY chromosomes, EEG brain patterns, intelligence scores, left-handedness, and an array of other factors, seeking for the interpretative Grail in regard to delinquency. At the moment, the verdict on such efforts has to be that allowed to juries in Scotland, who need not choose only between guilt and nonguilt: they have the option of declaring, "Not proven."

Psychiatry and psychology, like the biological theories, have focused on the individual (rather than the group or the society) as the target for understanding the emergence of delinquent behavior. Their reasoning is this: whatever attitudes a group holds, reinforces, or transmits ultimately become effective only when they penetrate the psyche of the individual. To examine what a social system values will never tell you what each person within that system holds dear and what set of ideas each person will respond to. All ideas are filtered by the individual psyche; besides, there are so many ideas available, so many different things stressed, that it is feckless to try to deduce individual actions from such variegated conditions.

Freudian psychiatry and its contemporary offshoots have exerted a strong influence on attempts to understand delinquent behavior. At the moment under serious attack, particularly as a method of treatment (the "talking cure" it is sometimes called), psychiatry has the advantage of being able to "explain" virtually any event and the disadvantage of not being readily susceptible to testing or being predictive, two essential attributes of a body of knowledge seeking scientific repute. Psychology, relatively late into the field in terms of the attention it has accorded to delinquency, has yet to shape its materials in ways that make them particularly relevant for an understanding of behaviors that not only depart from some sets of social norms but also violate specific rules enunciated by legislative and judicial bodies. In this chapter, we focused on Eysenck's conditioning theory, the theory of frustration-aggression, and the newly enunciated operant-utilitarianism of Wilson and Hernstein as representative of the kinds of insights that psychology can bring to an understanding of delinquent acts. Other and more comprehensive views undoubtedly will emerge during the coming decades.

References

Adorno, Theodor W., Frenkel-Brunswick, Else, Levinson, Daniel J., and Sanford, R. Nevitt. 1950. *The Authoritarian Personality.* New York: Harper and Row.

Agnew, Robert. 1983. Physical Punishment and Delinquency: A Research Note. *Youth & Society* 15:225–236.

Anderson, C. L. 1936. Epilepsy in the State of Michigan. *Mental Hygiene* 20:441–462.

Andrew, June M. 1980. Are Left-Handers Less Violent? *Journal of Youth and Adolescence* 9:1–9.

Azrin, Nathan H., Hutchinson, R., and Hake, D. F. 1966. Extinction-Induced Aggression. *Journal of Experimental Analysis of Behavior* 9:191–204.

Bartholemew, Allen A., and Sutherland, G. R. 1973. Chromosome Survey of Persons Charged with Murder. *Australian and New Zealand Journal of Criminology* 6:251–256.

Berkowitz, Leonard. 1978. Whatever Happened to the Frustration-Aggression Hypothesis? *American Behavioral Scientist* 21:691–708.

Bond, Earl E., and Appel, Kenneth E. 1931. *The Treatment of Behavior Disorders Following Encephalitis.* New York: Commonwealth Fund.

Borgaonkar, Digamber S., and Shah, Saleem A. 1974. The XYY Chromosome Male — Or Syndrome? In *Progress in Medical Genetics,* vol. 10, edited by Arthur G. Steinberg and Alexander G. Bearn, 135–222. New York: Grune and Stratton.

Cavan, Ruth S. 1969. *Juvenile Delinquency: Development, Treatment, Control.* 2nd ed. Philadelphia: Lippincott.

Cioffi, Frank. 1985. Psychoanalysis, Pseudo-Science and Testability. In *Popper and the Human Sciences,* edited by Gregory Currie and Alan Mosgrove, 13–44. Hingham, Mass.: Kluwer.

Cortes, Juan B., and Gatti, Florence M. 1972. *Delinquency and Crime: A Biopsychosocial Approach.* New York: Seminar Press.

Craig, Maude M., and Glick, Selma. 1963. Ten Years' Experience with the Glueck Social Prediction Scale. *Crime and Delinquency* 9:249–261.

Dollard, John, Miller, Neal E., Doob, Leonard W., Mowrer, O. H., and Sears, Robert R. 1939. *Frustration and Aggression.* New Haven: Yale Univ. Press.

Dorus, Elizabeth, Dorus, Walter, Telfer, Mary A., Litwin, Samuel, and Richardson, Claude E. 1976. Height and Personality Characteristics of 47, XYY Males in a Sample of Tall, Non-Institutionalized Males. *British Journal of Psychiatry* 129:564–573.

Driver, Edwin D. 1960. Charles Buckman Goring. In *Pioneers in Criminology,* edited by Hermann Mannheim, 335–348. London: Stevens.

Duvoisin, Roger C. 1984. *Parkinson's Disease.* 2nd ed. New York: Raven Press.

Edelson, Marshall. 1984. *Hypothesis and Evidence in Psychoanalysis.* Chicago: Univ. of Chicago Press.

Ekman, Gosta. 1951. On Typological and Dimensional Systems of Reference in Describing Personality. *Acta Psychologica* 8:1–24.

Eschenroder, Christof T. 1984. *Hier irrte Freud: Zur Kritik der Psychoanalytischen Theorie and Praxis.* Munich: Urban & Schwarzenberg.

Eysenck, Hans J. 1964. *Crime and Personality.* Boston: Houghton Mifflin.

Fancher, Raymond, E. 1985. *The Intelligence Men: Makers of the IQ Controversy.* New York: W. W. Norton.

Fitzhugh, Kathleen B. 1973. Some Neuropsychological Features of Delinquent Subjects. *Perceptual and Motor Skills* 36:494.

Flor-Henry, P. 1978. Gender, Hemispheric Specialization and Psychopathology. *Social Science and Medicine* 12B:155–162.

Gabrielli, William, and Mednick, Sarnoff. 1983. An Adoption Cohort Study of Genetics and Criminality. *Behavior Genetics* 13:435.

Gelb, Steven A. 1986. Henry H. Goddard and the Immigrants, 1910–1917: The Studies and Their Social Context. *Journal of the History of the Behavioral Sciences* 22:324–332.

Gibbens, Trevor C. N. 1963. *Psychiatric Studies of Borstal Lads.* New York: Oxford Univ. Press.

Gibbs, Jack. 1985. Review Essay: Crime and Human Nature. *Criminology* 23:381–388.

Glueck, Sheldon, and Glueck, Eleanor T. 1950. *Unraveling Juvenile Delinquency.* New York: Commonwealth Fund.

———. 1952. *Delinquents in the Making: Paths to Prevention.* New York: Harper.

———. 1965. *Ventures in Criminology: Selected Recent Papers.* Cambridge, Mass.: Harvard Univ. Press.

———. 1968. *Delinquents and Nondelinquents in Perspective.* Cambridge, Mass.: Harvard Univ. Press.

———. 1974. Replies to Criticisms. In *Of Delinquency and Crime: A Panorama of Years of Search and Research,* by Sheldon Glueck and Eleanor T. Glueck, 226–320. Springfield, Ill.: Thomas.

Goddard, Henry H. 1915. *The Criminal Imbecile.* New York: Macmillan.

Goleman, Daniel. 1985. Pressure Mounts for Analysis to Prove Theory Is Scientific. *New York Times* (January 15):18.

Goring, Charles B. 1913. *The English Convict: A Statistical Study.* London: His Majesty's Stationery Office.

Görling, Lars. 1966. *491.* New York: Grove Press.

Goshen, Charles E. 1974. *Society and the Youthful Offender.* Springfield, Ill.: Thomas.

Hartl, Emil M., Monnelly, Edward P., and Elderkin, Roland D. 1982. *Physique and Delinquent Behavior: A Thirty-Year Follow-Up of William H. Sheldon's "Varieties of Delinquent Youth."* New York: Academic Press.

Hokanson, Jack E., and Burgess, Michael. 1962. The Effects of Three Types of Aggression on Vascular Processes. *Journal of Abnormal and Social Psychology* 64: 446–449.

Hooton, Earnest A. 1939. *The American Criminal: An Anthropological Study.* Cambridge: Harvard Univ. Press.

Hsu, L. K. G., Wisner, Katherine, Richey, E. T., and Goldstein, C. 1985. Is Juvenile Delinquency Related to an Abnormal EEG? *Journal of the American Academy of Child Psychiatry* 24:310–315.

Humphreys, Lloyd G. 1957. Characteristics of Type Concepts with Special Reference to Sheldon's Typology. *Psychological Bulletin* 54:218–228.

Jacobs, Patricia A., Brunton, Muriel, and Melville, Marie M. 1965. Aggressive Behavior, Mental Subnormality and the XYY Male. *Nature* 208:1351–1352.

Janssen, B., and Whiting, H. T. A. 1984. Sheldon's Physical-Psychical Type Revisited. *Journal of Research in Personality* 18:432–441.

Joneja, M. G., Travill, A. A., and Scott, G. D. 1972. Chromosomal Studies of Prison Inmates with Relationship to Offense Characteristics. *Canadian Psychiatric Association Journal* 17:147–148.

Kamin, Leon. 1986. Is Crime in the Genes? The Answer May Depend on Who Chooses What Evidence. *Scientific American* 254:22–27.

Klinefelter, Harry F., Reifenstein, E. C., and Albright, F. 1941. Syndromes Characterized by Gynecomastia Aspermatogenes Without A-Leydeigism and Increased Excretion of Follicle Stimulating Hormone. *Journal of Clinical Endocrinology* 2:615–627.

Kreuz, Leo E., and Rose, Robert M. 1972. Assessment of Aggressive Behavior and Plasma Testosterone in a Young Criminal Population. *Psychosomatic Medicine* 34:321–332.

Lerner, Richard M. 1969. The Development of Stereotyped Expectancies of Body Build–Behavior Relations. *Child Development* 40:137–141.

Masson, Jeffrey M., ed. and trans. 1985. *The Complete Letters of Sigmund Freud to Wilhelm Fliess, 1887–1904.* Cambridge: Harvard Univ. Press.

McCord, William, McCord, Joan, and Zola, Irving K. 1959. *Origins of Crime: Evaluation of the Cambridge-Somerville Youth Study.* New York: Columbia Univ. Press.

Mednick, Sarnoff. 1977. A Biosocial Theory of the Learning of Law-Abiding Behavior. In *Biosocial Bases of Criminal Behavior,* edited by Sarnoff Mednick and Karl O. Christiansen, 1–8. New York: Gardner Press.

Meyer-Bahlburg, Heino F. L. 1974. Aggression, Androgens, and the XYY Syndrome. In *Sex Differences in Behavior,* edited by Ralph N. Richart and Raymond L. Vande Wiele, 433–454. New York: Wiley.

Montagu, Ashley. 1968. Chromosomes and Crime. *Psychology Today* 2 (October):43–49.

Moran, Richard. 1980. The Search for the Born Criminal and the Medical Control of Criminology. In *From Badness to Sickness: A Sociology of Deviance and Social Control,* edited by Peter Conrad and Joseph W. Schneider, 215–240. St. Louis: Mosby.

Nyswander, Marie. 1956. *The Drug Addict as a Patient.* New York: Grune and Stratton.

Peterson, Donald R., and Becker, Wesley C. 1965. Family Interaction and Delinquency. In *Juvenile Delinquency: Research and Theory,* edited by Herbert C. Quay, 63–99. Princeton, N.J.: Van Nostrand.

Pfeiffer, John. 1965. *The Human Brain.* New York: Harper and Row.

Popper, Karl R. 1950. *The Open Society and Its Enemies.* Princeton, N.J.: Princeton Univ. Press.

Price, W. H., and Whatmore, P. D. 1963. Behavior Disorders and Pattern of Crime Among XYY Males Identified at a Maximum Security Hospital. *British Medical Journal* 4:533–536.

Quay, Herbert C. 1983. Crime Causation: Psychological Theories. In *Encyclopedia of Crime and Justice,* edited by Sanford H. Kadish, 330–342. New York: Free Press.

Rowe, David C., and Osgood, D. Wayne. 1984. Heredity and Sociological Theories of Delinquency: A Reconsideration. *American Sociological Review* 49:526–540.

Sandberg, Avery A., Koepf, George F., Ishirara, T., and Hauschka, T. S. 1961. An XYY Human Male. *Lancet* 2:488–489.

Scott, P. D. 1975. Medical Aspects of Delinquency. *British Journal of Psychiatry* (Special Publication No. 9):287–295.

Shah, Saleem A. 1967. The 47, XYY Chromosomal Abnormality — A Critical Appraisal with Respect to Antisocial and Violent Behavior. In *Issues in Brain/Behavior Control,* edited by W. Lynn Smith and Arthur A. Kling, 49–67. New York: Spectrum.

Shapiro, Harry L. 1981. Earnest A. Hooton, 1887–1954: *In Memoriam con Amore. American Journal of Physical Anthropology* 56:431–434.

Sheldon, William H., Hartl, Emil M., McDermott, Eugene. 1949. *Varieties of Delinquent Youth: An Introduction to Constitutional Psychiatry.* New York: Harper and Row.

Sheldon, William H., and Stevens, Stanley S. 1941. *The Varieties of Temperament: A Psychology of Constitutional Differences.* New York: Harper.

Sheldon, William H., Stevens, Stanley S., and Tucker, William B. 1940. *The Varieties of Human Physique: An Introduction to Constitutional Psychology.* New York: Harper.

Silverman, Lloyd, Lachmann, Frank, and Milich, Robert. 1983. *Search for Oneness.* New York: International Universities Press.

Sutherland, Edwin H. 1956. Varieties of Delinquent Youth. In *The Sutherland Papers,* edited by Karl Schuessler, Alfred Lindesmith, and Albert Cohen, 279–290. Bloomington: Indiana Univ. Press.

Tannenbaum, Frank. 1938. *Crime and the Community.* New York: Columbia Univ. Press.

Tappan, Paul W. 1949. *Juvenile Delinquency.* New York: McGraw-Hill.

Theilgaard, Alice. 1984. A Psychological Study of the Personalities of XYY- and XXY-Men. *Acta Psychiatrica Scandinavia* (Supplement No. 35) 69:1–133.

Toby, Jackson. 1965. An Evaluation of Early Identification and Intensive Treatment Programs for Delinquents. *Social Problems* 13:160–175.

Trevvett, Nina B. 1965. Identifying Delinquency-Prone Children. *Crime and Delinquency* 11:186–191.

Vold, George B., and Bernard, Thomas J. 1979. *Theoretical Criminology.* 2nd ed. New York: Oxford Univ. Press.

West, Donald J. 1963. *The Habitual Prisoner.* New York: St. Martin's Press.

White, Helen R., Labouvie, Erich W., and Bates, Marsha E. 1985. The Relationship Between Sensation Seeking and Delinquency: A Longitudinal Analysis. *Journal of Research in Crime and Delinquency* 22:197–211.

Wilson, James Q., and Herrnstein, Richard J. 1985. *Crime and Human Nature.* New York: Simon and Schuster.

Wolfgang, Marvin E. 1977. Foreword to *The Biosocial Bases of Criminal Behavior,* edited by Sarnoff Mednick and Karl O. Christiansen, v–viii. New York: Gardner Press.

CHAPTER 5

Ecology, Strain, Anomie, Subcultural, and Labeling Theories

© Barry Kirk, Black Star

The dominance by sociologists of teaching and research on the subject of juvenile delinquency is reflected in the wide range of theoretical contributions rooted in concepts that are important to the sociological enterprise. As their name implies, sociologists are concerned primarily with the larger society rather than with the individual when they seek explanations of behavior. Their theories tend to focus on matters such as relating conditions of life in the slums and ghettos to, say, car theft or the formation of gangs of juveniles. And, of course, explanations of that sort tend to fall short when it comes to understanding why one particular black slum child — to take a recent illustration (Wideman, 1984) — becomes a professor of English literature at the University of Wyoming and a distinguished novelist while his younger brother is sentenced to life imprisonment as an accessory for murder during an attempted holdup. Both brothers were exposed to essentially the same upbringing, but it obviously produced different results. It can always be argued that something essential differed in the environment of the brothers: after all, being a younger brother has a different meaning than being an older one; and besides, the parents were of different ages when they raised each of the children. In addition, the experiences of the youths undoubtedly varied significantly in school and in the neighborhood. These dissimilar conditions could have been instrumental in fashioning the distinctive life paths of the brothers. The particular story, though, developed in an even more puzzling fashion when, during the summer of 1986, the professor's son, a highly regarded high school student and athlete, was charged with stabbing a friend to death during a camping trip in Arizona.

Courtesy United Nations/Claudio Edinger

Sociological theories emphasize such factors as slums and ghettoes in the propagation of delinquency.

It also is true that the same experience produces varied impressions upon a number of individuals exposed to it. Four persons held up at gunpoint are apt to react with a considerable range of responses: one will cry, another smile, the third look grim, while the fourth lurches forward to attack the aggressor. Later, each of the four may report very different lessons and very different effects from the episode. One can barely remember it, for instance, while another has recurrent nightmares. Many sociologists concentrate on statistical regularities, that is, on the numerical likelihood of the occurrence of delinquency in certain kinds of social groupings, but they tend to ignore the fine details of the process by means of which social conditions are translated by a particular individual into delinquent behavior.

When they first began to study juvenile delinquency, sociologists were closely affiliated with a social work tradition. Many of the pioneer sociologists had strong religious backgrounds; their goal was to employ social science for the betterment of humankind (Geis, 1964). The juvenile court, as we will see, was a notable product of this tradition. So was the very strong emphasis on indeterminate sentences, which were based on the assumption that social scientists could satisfactorily diagnose and treat criminals and delinquents and therefore ought to be given the authority to base sentence lengths on their own judgments of what was required for rehabilitation and not on the nature of the offenses alone.

Today, the pendulum has swung much more toward skepticism about the capabilities of treatment and toward the view that the character of the delinquent act itself, not the nature of the delinquent, should determine punishment. Some sociologists too have abandoned study of groups of individuals and turned their attention exclusively to social conditions as the primary determinants of delinquency. Their agenda for reform can range anywhere from a call for the construction of additional playgrounds to recommendations for significant changes in social structures.

The Ecological School: Clifford R. Shaw (1895–1957) and Henry D. McKay (1899–1980)

Serious sociological study of juvenile delinquency got underway in the city of Chicago, the site in 1899 of the establishment of the country's first juvenile court. The sociology department at the University of Chicago, largely under the impetus of Robert E. Park, a journalist turned academic, undertook to examine the environment surrounding it, with particular emphasis on problems and persons not in the mainstream of life (Matthews, 1977). Universities traditionally have been located in remote places, away from metropolitan areas — witness Oxford and Cambridge, among many others — presumably so that students may pursue their learning unimpeded by urban distractions. But Chicago, founded with Rockefeller money, contradicted the ancient tradition, and its sociologists elected to exploit their situation. The result was a series of brilliant monographs that have endured as classics of urban study: Nels Anderson's *The Hobo* (1923), Harvey Zorbaugh's *The Gold Coast and the Slum* (1929), Paul

Cressey's *Taxi-Dance Hall* (1932), Ruth Cavan's *Suicide* (1928), and Louis Wirth's *The Ghetto* (1928) were among the more prominent investigations.

The subject of delinquency in Chicago became the particular province of Clifford Shaw and Henry McKay, both trained in the university's sociology department, though neither completed his Ph.D. because of an inability (or unwillingness) to pass the foreign language requirement. Shaw was gregarious, charismatic, a leader. Almost half a century later, Charlotte Kobrin, the wife of one of Shaw's co-workers, remembers thinking when she first met Shaw: "This must be what Abraham Lincoln was like." McKay was soft-spoken, modest, and retiring. Both men were rural products, part of the great migration from the surrounding countryside into the hub city of the Midwest. Shaw was from Luray, Indiana, a crossroads town with a few houses; McKay was from Orient, South Dakota. They came together at the Institute for Juvenile Research, established in the late 1920s with private funding (Finestone, 1976). There they collaborated on theoretical work that earned them a distinguished reputation in the annals of the study of juvenile delinquency (Snodgrass, 1972; 1976).

Areal Studies

The major thrust of Shaw and McKay's effort was to plot the ecological distribution of juvenile delinquency within the environs of Chicago. At the time that they were conducting their research, there was great concern throughout the United States regarding what was deemed to be the excessive lawlessness of members of immigrant groups. Pamphleteers deplored what they claimed was a decline in national standards of conduct, pointed out that newcomers undercut the wages of citizens by working for less money, and said that they engaged in strange and alien conduct. Immigrants were criticized for retaining allegiance to their native lands, for refusing to jump into the melting pot to be refashioned into a shape more like that of the majority population. Children of migrants often found themselves caught between the conflicting demands of two cultures —those of their new home and the "foreign" values of their parents. In a particularly vivid study, Pauline Young (1932) showed how Molokan children, from the Russian steppes, became confused. Their parents, devoutly religious, glorified manual labor, noting that Christ was a carpenter; but their non-Molo-kan friends scorned such work, looking for quick and easy sources of income. Older brothers, arrested as delinquents, would write home from reform schools extolling the freedom and the diet of institutional living—compared to the bleakness of home—and advising their younger siblings that all this was theirs if they would steal a car or rob a store.

Shaw and McKay's contribution was to demonstrate two basic points: first, that rates of delinquency varied significantly in different parts of the city; and second, that these rates remained the same over time in a given locale regardless of which ethnic group made up the bulk of the area's residents. The highest rates of delinquency were in areas contiguous to centers of commerce and industry, and particularly on the fringe of the downtown section. These were slum neighborhoods, crammed with migrants, derelicts, and the downtrodden. Absentee landlords were unwilling to rehabilitate the decaying property because they assumed that in time it would be ripped down to make way for the outward expansion of the core of the city. Dwellings often were "railroad flats," large old mansions converted into innumerable apartments where access to the rear units had to be achieved by passing through the quarters of other families. The dwellings were overcrowded and disease-ridden; sometimes persons working different shifts in places such as the Chicago slaughterhouses would share a bed, one sleeping in it while the other worked.

Successful migrants quickly moved out of these high-delinquency neighborhoods as a matter of self-protection and self-improvement, to take advantage of better schools and other amenities available elsewhere. It therefore was not race or ethnicity, Shaw and McKay insisted, that prefigured delinquency but rather —in an explanation that looked to the earliest developments of concepts of delinquency—life in a deteriorated section of the city where each day uncounted examples of wayward behavior became known to youngsters and where illegal acts represented a means of overcoming the grim reality of a marginal existence. When a group edged its way into the suburbs, as the Swedes, the Irish, and the Jews had done, its rate of delinquency dropped to the level continuously manifested in the area where members of the group now came to live (Shaw, 1929).

The theoretical implication of the mapping strategy employed by Shaw and McKay obviously was that delinquency is inculcated from a youngster's surroundings, a consequence of lawbreaking examples and a function of distress. The theory did not, of course, pinpoint why certain boys and (many fewer) girls succumbed to the delinquency ethos in their environs while others did not. But it did focus attention on criminogenic circumstances, on social conditions that breed behavior that is outlawed. Shaw and McKay's work also emphasized that a delinquent career was developed as an adjustment to life and was not an independent and individual phenomenon resulting from inborn tendencies or accidental psychological abnormalities (Burgess and Bogue, 1963:592).

Autobiographies of Delinquents

Complementing the ecological approach was an emphasis by Shaw and McKay on the collection of biographical statements by juvenile delinquents, "the boys' own stories." From a large hoard of such materials three books were published: *The Jack-Roller* (1930), *Brothers in Crime* (1938), and *The Natural History of a Delinquent Career* (1931). Shaw and McKay hoped that these documents would provide a source for generating hypotheses about delinquency. They allowed the youngsters to convey how they felt about things, rather than having researchers superimpose their judgment on the situation.

The Jack-Roller may be taken as prototypical of the genre. In it, Stanley tells of his intense hatred for a stepmother, his constant efforts to escape home by running away, and his involvement with other boys in jack-rolling, that is, robbing drunks who were presumed to be too incapacitated to offer effective resistance. Shaw makes a number of efforts to redeem Stanley, including several foster home placements. But Stanley feels ill at ease in one rather splendid setting into which he is placed, and he consistently gets into difficulty in a series of menial jobs because of his chronic inability to suffer the smallest slight, real or imagined. Ultimately, Shaw finds a traveling salesman job for Stanley that appears to provide the freedom from supervision and the ability to use his extraordinarily ingratiating personality to its best. Forty years later (1982), when located in Los Angeles, Stanley reported that he had continued to remain out of prison, though he had spent some time in a mental hospital. He was still painfully touchy about any infringement on his emotional territory: he would explode if he thought that someone had looked at him "wrong" or slighted him.

Perhaps the most obvious lesson of Stanley's story is that determination of the proper theoretical interpretations of delinquency can be extremely complicated. Was Stanley doomed by his personality to continuing social difficulty? Had Shaw salvaged him from a career in crime, or had Stanley's temerity in the face of really dangerous lawbreaking deterred him? Was his stepmother as influential in corroding his life as Stanley maintained, or had the neighborhood placed an incurable scar on his soul? And how typical was Stanley of young men who embark on careers of delinquency? In one respect, he certainly was unusual: he was very articulate, able to put together in rather dramatic form the story of his life both as a young delinquent and as an elderly man. (For an interesting contemporary autobiography by a delinquent, see Devlin, 1985.)

The Chicago Area Project

For Shaw and McKay, theory was secondary and action primary in their agenda for dealing with delinquency. They might have concluded from their work that the absentee landlords were at fault and that programs of social protest and revolt would prove the most effective path for reducing delinquency. Instead, they elected another approach, equally plausible. They sought to upgrade the neighborhoods producing high levels of delinquency by involving the indigenous population in self-improvement efforts.

This approach was based on their belief that the most serious failure of all was the failure of institutions to fill the needs of impoverished slum residents. As Kornhauser (1978:80), summarizing Shaw and McKay's work, notes:

> Family, school, and community lack the money and skills with which to attract and hold the child to a conventional course of action. They cannot provide the channels that lead to successful achievement. This incapacity is heightened by the isolation of institutions, for such institutions cannot be changed or adapted to the needs of slum children. . . . Shaw and McKay focus primarily on the family. Poor families cannot bind their children because they lack the means with which to help them realize valued goals. The slum family is also unable to communicate or enforce its special needs through organizations linked to conventional institutions. As a result, institutions outside the family are not pressured to serve the child more adequately.

This view was the basis of Shaw and McKay's famous Chicago Area Project (CAP), a remedial program undertaken during the 1930s and 1940s that has been called by Schlossman and Sedlak (1983:398) "a legendary experiment in community-based delinquency prevention." Schlossman and Sedlak studied intensively the CAP efforts in one neighborhood, that of Russell Square in South Chicago. On the basis of examination of archival materials, they concluded that the program may have been effective in reducing delinquency and that its demise — as well as the disappearance of similar endeavors — represented a significant setback in delinquency prevention work.

Russell Square was primarily a Polish neighborhood, geographically separated by steel mills and railroad tracks from places surrounding it. Juvenile delinquency was rampant in the area when the CAP moved in: fifteen well-established youth gangs were active. Gang delinquency, however, was less violent than it is today: petty theft was the most common illegal act, involving such things as raiding fruit stands, stripping cars, and snatching purses. Typical of the gangs were the Aces, described by a committee investigating conditions in the area in the following manner:

> The Aces always looked for, and managed to discover, excitement in anything that devilled someone else. They pulled trollies off the wires routinely [trolley cars, attached to overhead electrified wires, were a common form of urban transportation at this time]; snatched purses in broad daylight; were so adept at lifting fruit from peddlers' wagons that on one adventure they succeeded in running off with three bushels of apples, tossing fruit back at the storming peddler. The Aces shinnied up trees in the park, reached into the nests of sleeping sparrows, and popped them into paper bags. . . . Then they took the sparrows into St. Michael's gym where a basketball game was in progress and released the birds, one by one. They delighted in burning home-made stink bombs at social gatherings. Their vandalism made the park director's life miserable. In turn, he did his best to keep the boys out of the park. (Schlossman and Sedlak, 1983:424)

Shaw assigned several "detached workers" to Russell Square. Their task was to hang around with gang members and to develop informal, trusting relationships. The workers were to be alert to boys with serious emotional problems; these youngsters were to be referred to the Institute for Juvenile Research (IJR), where they would receive help. The workers were expected to offer a model of conventional moral and social values for emulation by Russell Square youths. The theoretical underpinning of the intervention obviously was that the absence of such standards was largely responsible for delinquent activities. The CAP also sponsored a flourishing athletic program in the neighborhood, working through St. Michael's Church, the institution that commanded near-universal allegiance in Russell Square. The athletic program became a vehicle to enlist adults in neighborhood improvement projects. The CAP, Shaw often said, did not wish to superimpose itself on the community; it sought to mobilize local residents to analyze their own problems and to sponsor appropriate remedial efforts.

At first, the CAP work met considerable resistance, primarily rooted in a distrust of outsiders, particularly academics from the University of Chicago. It was believed that university scholars had blackened the name of the Polish community in Chicago by studies portraying their children as misfits and delinquents. Shaw himself, for instance, was accused of emphasizing Stanley's Polish background in *The Jack-Roller*.

The athletic program stood at the core of CAP efforts throughout. Vacant lots were converted into playgrounds, the church basement was renovated to provide recreation rooms, and leagues were formed for baseball, basketball, football, and volleyball. There also were wood shop and arts and crafts projects, as well as a study group that attracted between 150 and 200 youths to lectures on social problems by professors and politicians, built up a 1,000-volume library, and published its own newspaper. CAP workers defied traditional social work rules by displaying a flexible, "hang-loose" attitude toward delinquency and nonconformity, in particular by trying to avoid being critical and nagging.

The project was run by the Russell Square Community Committee, whose goal was to build a new sense of potency among law-abiding residents in order to transform their neighborhood so that it would no longer give rise to or tolerate conditions that were believed to foster juvenile delinquency. Volunteers raised funds by holding bazaars, handicraft exhibits, and similar events. The CAP established a summer camp on a lake in Michigan City, Indiana, where 350 youngsters weekly went for vacation. The committee sought to rid the neighborhood of houses of prostitution and fences (receivers of stolen goods) and to restrict the access of minors to bars.

Another prong of the attack was to take every opportunity to explain to representatives of the formal agencies, such as the police, the schools, and the probation department, why troublesome children in Russell Square behaved as they did. Residents sought to soften the remote and impersonal views that strangers inevitably had of persons living in Russell Square. Particular stress was placed on reducing school truancy in the belief (one later elaborated on by other theorists) that continuing attachment to traditional institutions and values was an especially important inhibitor of delinquency. The CAP also established close connections with the Illinois Parole Board and exercised substantial control over the conditions imposed upon Russell Square residents released from prison.

Opposition to the CAP efforts focused on a number of issues. One of CAP's own workers, Saul Alinsky, believed CAP was too accommodating to vested interests, and he later (Alinsky, 1946) organized more militant movements in downtrodden Chicago neighborhoods. Law-abiding residents and government officials often felt that the program was overtolerant of misbehavior and thereby encouraged further waywardness. Professional social workers resented what they regarded as fumbling and amateur efforts, and they were not pleased with the emphasis on the superiority of local leadership to that of trained outsiders.

In the end, Shaw and McKay themselves remained uncertain whether their bold attempt to translate some loose theoretical concepts into a practical action program had been successful. They did become convinced that, given the chance, local residents in high-crime areas could organize themselves effectively to address common problems and that, because of their intimate knowledge of local conditions, they could mobilize support in ways not available to outsiders. It was maintained that there had been a two-thirds decline in police contacts with youths in Russell Square during the life of the project and that there had been a striking drop in juvenile court petitions filed against youngsters from the neighborhood. Indeed, so few petitions had been filed in the later years that the pool was not sufficiently large for meaningful statistical analysis. These data, however, are not sufficient to demonstrate a causal linkage between the theoretical basis of CAP and its performance, a matter Shaw and McKay fully appreciated.

CAP spawned several related projects, and, indeed, projects continue to operate today in Chicago to reduce gang delinquency by hiring indigenous workers. "Modest" success is reported by Spergel (1986) for the Crisis Intervention

Service project (CRISP), which employed former gang leaders, conventional citizens, and police, as well as university graduate social work students. Evidence indicated that surveillance and interventions into crisis situations were more effective deterrents in the project than counseling strategies. Today's gangs, though, can be much more formidable than those in the days when a knife or homemade zip gun served as a dangerous weapon. Gang workers now report groups in Los Angeles with access to .357 magnum pistols, hunting rifles with pinpoint scopes, and U21 semiautomatics from Israel (Barich, 1986; see also Slayton, 1986).

Additional Ecological Work

There has been some confirmation of Shaw and McKay's ecological insights in other geographical settings. Wallis and Malifant (1967), for instance, found high delinquency rates persisting in the slum boroughs of London for over forty years, despite alterations in the ethnicity of residents. These rates correlated with census factors such as education, overcrowding, and underemployment. The areas, however, were marked by a relatively low rate of suicide and divorce. This last finding underlines one of the interpretive vulnerabilities of ecological studies, first pointed out by Robinson (1950). An area may show certain traits, Robinson noted, but this need not mean that such traits are characteristic of the individuals being studied. Thus, a slum area may manifest a relatively low divorce rate, but the delinquents in that area could all conceivably be from broken homes; the areal rate itself does not necessarily predict what will be true of particular individuals living in the area.

Some of the positions of Shaw and McKay have not gone unchallenged. Jonassen (1949) pointed out, for example, that only five pages after they had claimed that the nature of the group dwelling in an area was unimportant to a continuing high rate of delinquency, Shaw and McKay (1942:440) had written:

> In communities occupied by Orientals, even those communities located in the most deteriorated sections of our large cities, the solidarity of Old World cultures and institutions has been preserved to such a marked extent that control of the child is still sufficiently effective to keep at a minimum delinquency and other forms of delinquent behavior. [see further Fujimoto, 1978]

Later, in a study in Baltimore, Lander (1954) maintained that it was not socioeconomic conditions but rather "anomie" — a sense of alienated aimlessness — that led to delinquency in certain geographic settings in a city. But Chilton (1964) and Gordon (1967), by analyzing census data for Detroit, Chicago, and Indianapolis, refuted Lander's claim: slum conditions measured by items such as unemployment and family income were found to be major correlates of illegal youthful behavior.

A particularly interesting extension of the work of Shaw and McKay was recently undertaken by Bursik (1984). He reanalyzed data collected by the IJR in Chicago for the period 1940 through 1970, using more modern statistical techniques than those available to Shaw and McKay. The major finding was that the pattern of delinquency remained much as Shaw and McKay had seen it for 1940, 1960, and 1970, with particular neighborhoods demonstrating consistent rates regardless of changes in population. For 1950, however, Bursik found a very different condition. Between 1940 and 1950, as a result of U.S. Supreme Court decisions, racially restrictive covenants in housing were banned. Because of this, blacks moved into adjoining white areas in unprecedented numbers; the number of racially mixed census tracts in Chicago (those having more than 1 and less than 97.4 per cent black composition) increased from 135 in 1940 to 204 in 1950. For a time, this black population movement generated violent opposition that was reflected in much higher than common delinquency rates (see further Heitgerd and Bursik, 1987). Suttles (1972) believes that gangs of white delinquents were one of the major forces against what was defined as a black invasion. In 1960 and 1970, however, the delinquency-ecology relationship had returned to the patterns suggested earlier by Shaw and McKay.

New residential patterns that have significantly altered the pre – World War II structure of cities also may play havoc with the Shaw and McKay conclusions. Cheap public housing sometimes is scattered throughout an urban area, rather than placed downtown exclusively, and satellite shopping centers and malls draw juveniles, who now also have access to cars. Patricia and Paul Brantingham (1981:49) believe that the new "mosaic urban form" will introduce more dispersion in delinquency.

The "Gang" Theorists

One of the more important discoveries of Shaw and McKay was that juvenile delinquency is something of a social event. Lone offenders proved to be relatively rare; much more often it was a pair of youths or a group that became involved in lawbreaking. Unlike adult crime, in which associates are sometimes necessary to maximize the likelihood of success, delinquency groupings seem more a reflection of a need for comradeship and a matter of more passive youngsters following the lead of aggressive peers. This, as we noted in Chapter 2, has served as an important tie between delinquency theory and the more general direction in thinking about childhood and youth. It has also, as we shall see, preserved much of the focus of thinking about delinquency on lower-class communities, despite questions that, as we saw in Chapter 1, can be raised about such a focus.

Groups of delinquent youths — gangs — also have served as a means of protection and identification in American slums. Typically, gang members consort with those who share a similar heritage, usually of a racial or ethnic nature. There are white gangs and Latino gangs and black gangs, for instance, and these groups compete for recognition. Their conflicts at times seem choreographed, much like the action in the well-known theatrical play and motion picture *West Side Story*. Quarreling erupts over "turf," that is, which group has "rights" over which particular segment of the ghetto neighborhood. Acrimony also is apt to arise over girls, with gang members manifesting a stereotypical protective posture in regard to "their" women.

The word *gang* was used in English as early as 1340 to denote "a number of things used together," and in time it came to designate a ship's crew or companies of mariners. The word soon came to carry a derogatory designation. When

Gang behavior as depicted in the film *The Wild One.*

Samuel Johnson compiled his dictionary in the late 1700s, he indicated that *gang* was "seldom used but in contempt or abhorrence," a view borne out in Shakespeare's *Merry Wives of Windsor,* where a character cries out against "panderly rascals" and notes that "there's a knot, a gang, a pack, a conspiracy against me." The term *gang,* interestingly, is very infrequently used by teen-agers to describe their group; rather it is the "clique," the "club," the "team," or "boys." The nomenclature employed seems to represent an attempt to differen-tiate their association from that of "gangsters" (Merwin, 1960:22).

Anthropological research indicates clearly that gangs are not necessarily a consequence of the condition of adolescence. Margaret Mead (1928) demon-strated that in Samoan culture, for instance, adolescence constituted a placid and barely discernible period of transition from dependence to independence and involved a smooth passage into adult status. That gangs come to exist in a society, therefore, obviously is a reflection of the structure of that society — how it treats young persons and how those young persons come to respond to their condition.

The Early Theorists

Theorists of delinquency, primarily sociologists, have found gangs particu-larly useful organizations for analysis. All paths involving study of gang behavior fan out from the pioneering investigation conducted in the 1920s by Frederic M. Thrasher, another of the brilliant group of scholars connected with the University of Chicago. Thrasher was born in 1892 and worked for a time as a newspaper reporter before embarking on the study of sociology. His book, *The Gang* (1927), was based on investigation of 1,313 juvenile groups in Chicago. Like the work of Shaw and McKay, it stressed ecological patterning, and it emphasized that gangs were the training grounds for adult criminal activity. Thrasher further noted that incarceration often fails to inhibit gang activity because it lends prestige to the young person, who after release can claim a toughening experience that is admired by others of the group. Thrasher also was the first writer to highlight the importance of the fence as a key figure in crimes against property committed by gang members.

Like that of Shaw and McKay, Thrasher's primary aim was to portray a social phenomenon so that curative action might be undertaken. A major theoretical postulation was to criticize psychological theories as inadequate; a review of *The Gang* notes, for instance, that "to treat the gang member as an isolated person, to compute his intelligence quotient, to call him psychopathic is to leave the full causation of his conduct untouched" (K. Young, 1927:51). Otherwise, the theory was more implicit than overt, with Thrasher's work suggesting that gang membership represented a normal and reasonable response to prevailing conditions. It would remain for later theorists to try to spell out precisely what those conditions might be which fostered gang behavior and what gang memberships offered to those who joined.

It was not until shortly before World War II that a second book appeared to advance theoretical understanding of gangs. William Foote Whyte (1943) had moved into a Boston working-class neighborhood to gather material for his doctoral dissertation at Harvard. He gained acceptance by winning the sponsorship of a gang leader, and he proceeded to take copious notes on gang activities, much like an ethnographer adrift amidst an alien tribe. Status in the gang was determined to be a key ingredient in a wide range of a member's behavior. Good bowlers, for instance, would do more poorly than usual when they played with gang leaders but would improve considerably when matched against persons with standing in the gang lower than their own.

Whyte had asked his sponsor, Doc, to let him know if he did anything wrong. What Doc tells him conveys one of the theoretical insights about gang behavior that Whyte uncovered, the ability of the leader to fashion the group's acceptance or rejection of an outsider:

> You won't have any trouble. When you come in like that, at first everybody will treat you with respect. You can take a lot of liberties, and nobody will kick. There's just one thing to watch out for. Don't spring [treat] people. Don't be too free with your money. (Whyte: 1981:292)

Whyte also noted how distinctive language styles and in-group words fostered a separateness and a pride among the gang members. He thereby pinpointed a particularly important theoretical issue regarding gangs: that they offer to their members rewards that may not be available to them otherwise — acceptance, status, achievement, excitement, money.

Strain Theory: Albert K. Cohen's Delinquent Boys (1955)

Clearly and interestingly written, carefully argued, Cohen's *Delinquent Boys* postulated a number of theoretical positions about gang behavior as a form of juvenile delinquency that established and invigorated some of the most exciting theoretical work in the field of delinquency.

Cohen's work followed the earlier sociological tradition of research about particular American communities to pinpoint the value system and cultural emphases of our society. In their study of Middletown, U.S.A., (which actually was Muncie, Indiana), the Lynds (1929) noted the extraordinary emphasis on success and the derogatory attitudes toward persons who had not been able to achieve such success. Warner and Lunt (1941), conducting their research at a site they called Yankee City (actually Newburyport, Massachusetts), demonstrated the importance of the community's class structure and showed how a person was placed in one or another of the social classes. The information gathered in these inquiries was later employed by Williams in *American Society* (1970) to inventory American values. A value can be determined in a shorthand manner by discovering which choice an individual makes when confronted with alternatives: given the discovery of a ten-dollar bill, for instance, what use would he make of it?

It is essentially the nature of our culture that leads to the formation of delinquent gangs, according to Cohen. His basic theme is highlighted in the following sentence: "The same value system, impinging upon children differently equipped to meet it, is instrumental in generating both delinquency and respectability" (1955:137). Middle-class youths yearn for their own cars because the possession of an automobile is an important symbol of self-esteem in America. The shiny grillwork and the plush upholstery of a new automobile is almost everywhere accorded respect, and ownership of such a vehicle connotes success and importance. Some youths are given cars by affluent parents, or they have available to them means by which within a reasonable time they can come to afford cars. Youths from the middle class who have to postpone ownership of a car have numerous compensating satisfactions, and what they have could be seriously jeopardized if they were to violate the law and steal cars. The risk is hardly worth the small gain for them.

Lower-class youths, including gang members, also have been efficiently and almost mercilessly tutored by advertising and word of mouth regarding the importance of automobile ownership. They may not have compensating sources of self-esteem. Nor, particularly in the case of gang boys, are they apparently as fearful of the punitive consequences or as hopeful about future prospects as middle-class youths. Stealing a car becomes a reasonable way to achieve what everybody in the society has learned is important.

Gang delinquency, Cohen maintains, constitutes a solution to problems of adjustment to which the established culture provides no satisfactory solutions. Delinquency is a gang member's response to his problems in regard to status and self-respect. Gang members, Cohen (1955:133) observes, "never quite escape the blandishments of middle-class society." The gang provides "moral reassurance" against "gnawing doubts" and gives "repeated, emphatic and articulate support" to the member. Cohen (1955:26) emphasizes the following attributes and functions of the juvenile gang:

> The delinquent subculture, with its characteristics of non-utilitarianism, malice, and negativism, provides an alternative status system and justifies, for those who participate in it, hostility and aggression against the sources of their status frustration.

In essence, then, as Cohen sees it, the theoretical path to understanding gangs is by means of focus on what he regards as a common pattern of culture in the United States, associated with an inability of many lower-class youngsters to achieve by legitimate means things that they have come to believe are important. The solution of the problem is hardly self-evident if Cohen's understanding of its nature is accurate. "How, " he (1955:177) asks at one point, "can we change the norms of the middle-class world so that a [youngster's] working-class characteristics do not relegate him to an inferior status?" And "what price are we willing to pay for this or that change?" Cohen (1955:177) compares the reformative dilemma with that confronting some schoolteachers: do they "reward the 'meritorious' and implicitly humiliate the handicapped, or . . . abandon this system of competition and invidious discrimination and abandon therewith a most powerful spur to the development of the kind of character most of us so highly prize?" What Cohen's analysis indicates clearly is that, even if correct, theoretical insight does not necessarily guarantee — or even make worthwhile — curative action.

Cohen's thesis derives support from a recent study of juvenile delinquency in The Hague, the capital city of the Netherlands. The investigators (Junger-Tas and Junger, 1984) indicate that the much higher rate of delinquency among boys compared to girls is a function of socialization, in which boys' emphasis is on autonomy and independence, while girls tend to stress emotional ties with parents and family. When boys fail in conventional efforts, they more than girls, the Dutch writers believe, will try to find compensations for loss of status. One way is to turn away from society. Junger-Tas and Junger found that failure in school was a particularly powerful precursor to delinquency. It resulted in frequent truancy and the development of a "tough-guy" attitude. If boys do not get any reward from conventional systems, they will move toward delinquent peer groups. The Dutch research team recommends that remedial efforts be concentrated on school reforms, because education is "an open and accessible system" compared to the "private sphere of the family" (1984:58).

Anomie Theory: Richard A. Cloward and Lloyd Ohlin, Delinquency and Opportunity (1960)

The idea of a delinquent subculture — a distinctive mode of life found among gang boys — which was put forward by Cohen, has formed the basis for several succeeding theoretical statements about the nature of gang existence. The major difference between Cohen's report and the work of those who have followed him lies in the stress by later writers upon different types of delinquent adjustments and styles and their quarrel with Cohen regarding whether in fact gang boys are primarily reacting to middle-class values.

The second major postwar contribution to the theoretical understanding of gang delinquency, that by Cloward and Ohlin, seeks to answer two fundamental questions. First, why do delinquent norms or rules of conduct develop? And second, what are the conditions for various systems of delinquent norms — such as those involving violence in contrast to those favoring theft or those pertaining to drug use? By subdividing gangs into distinctive types, Cloward and Ohlin more clearly were able to describe aspects of the phenomenon being examined.

For Cloward and Ohlin, it is the character of delinquent neighborhoods that breeds gang-member imitation, most particularly the absence of opportunity to succeed in a manner other than that offered by crime and delinquency. They offer the following prescription for reform of gang misbehavior (1960:211):

> The major effort of those who wish to eliminate delinquency should be directed to the reorganization of slum communities. Slum neighborhoods appear to us to be undergoing progressive disintegration. The old structures, which provided social control and avenues of social ascent, are breaking down. Legitimate but functional substitutes for these traditional structures must be developed if we are to stem the trend toward violence and retreatism [i.e., drug use] among adolescents in urban areas.

The theoretical speculations of Cloward and Ohlin provided a framework for intervention programs during the years when the national government poured funds into efforts to alleviate problems of social inequity. In New York, the Mobilization for Youth program stressed the creation of work opportunities for youths in order to direct them away from gang activities. Leaders of the Mobilization program indicated what they regarded as some of the sources of the problem.

> The educationally deprived of our slums not only lack the skill and academic knowledge required for advancement, they are often so undereducated as to be unable to fulfill the simple requirements of an application process, from reaching the employment office to filling out necessary forms. In addition, lower-class youngsters, because of their own distinctive socialization, often lack such middle-class graces as good speech, promptness, neatness, and politeness. This handicaps them in work settings which tend to be mechanized, routine, and formal. It is not surprising, therefore, that they are as often fired for poor work attitudes as for poor performance. (Brager and Purcell, 1967:121)

The supposition that working-class boys aspire to higher social levels and that their behavior is part of a frustration process is a major departure from the popular and reformist concepts we discussed in Chapter 2. And it is somewhat supported by empirical research by Rivera and Short (1967), who found that responses to the question: "thinking realistically, what sort of work do you actually think you'll be doing ten years from now?" fell into three major patterns. First, all youths expected to attain a position well above their present status. Second, racial differences were the reverse of what might be expected within both the gang and the nongang categories, with blacks anticipating greater achievement than whites. With race controlled, however, the expectations of gang boys were lower than those of nongang boys, taking into account the current status they occupied.

The conclusions about opportunity structure of Cloward and Ohlin (1960:193) are similar to themes found in the Chicago Area Project:

> What is necessary is to introduce a measure of variety into the occupational horizons of these youngsters. They must be taught that better worlds exist and that these worlds are populated with flesh and blood people with whom they may interact. Persons such as detached workers and school teachers fit the bill quite nicely. The problem lies in the tasks of getting close enough to the boys to be taken seriously and in encouraging a sense of emulation and a willingness to seek a more pervasive and final separation from the neighborhood milieu.

In short, Cloward and Ohlin agree with Cohen that delinquent youths can be reclaimed from lawbreaking careers by becoming integrated into a middle-class world. This, in itself, is a long-standing feature of both popular and theoretical thinking about delinquency. They differ in that they do not see delinquency as an angry reaction to middle-class values and as an attempt to establish the same values in a lower-class setting by offering esteem and reward for delinquent acts. They see delinquency as a response to the opportunities available to the lower-class youth. The more adept of the slum youngsters move into racketeering and other high-status crimes; the less capable end up as dropouts and drug users, since successful crime, like successful business, is discriminating in whom it allows to enter its world.

The emphasis of Cloward and Ohlin is that delinquents behave in a perfectly rational manner in making choices in an environment in which such choices are limited. Lee Steiner (1960:181) has pinpointed such a belief in the following analysis:

> In studying the delinquent, we must face the reality that he is responding in the best way he knows how, with the only set of emotions he has, and to the only surroundings he knows. If we accept the truism that within the limits where we have a choice, each of us selects that behavior which is most pleasing and rejects that which is most distasteful, we must conclude that the delinquent's behavior seems logical to him. The task of therapy is to make this behavior seem illogical. The delinquent must first *want* another way of behavior.

For Cloward and Ohlin, there would be little chance to persuade youths that their behavior is illogical unless this might be done by confronting them with a harsh appraisal of the likely consequences if they continue on their path. But such a warning would be contradicted by examples of the successful gangsters that they see all about them. Only if satisfactory opportunities that on balance are more attractive than those of delinquency are opened up for them are they likely to abandon their course, according to Cloward and Ohlin. Otherwise, as Malcolm X (1965:316) clearly noted:

> Ghetto teen-agers see the hell caught by their parents struggling to get somewhere. . . . The ghetto teenagers make up their own minds that they would rather be like the hustlers whom they see dressed "sharp" and flashing money and displaying no respect for anybody or anything. So the ghetto youth become attracted to the hustler worlds of dope, thievery, prostitution, and general crime and immorality.

In a thoroughgoing review of the implications of the Cloward and Ohlin approach for public programs of delinquency prevention, Daniel P. Moynihan (1969), now a United States senator from New York, argues that the lawyers in government who framed delinquency control efforts during the 1960s were neither "especially familiar with" nor "temperamentally attuned" to the social science theories on the subject that we have been reviewing here. Besides, Moynihan insists, the theories themselves were inadequate in regard to truly guiding public policy. He acidly notes the following about the federal efforts of that period (1969:170):

> This is the essential fact: *The government did not know what it was doing.* It had a theory. Or, rather, a set of theories. Nothing more. The U.S. government at this time was no more in possession of confident knowledge as to how to prevent delinquency, cure anomie, or overcome that midmorning sense of powerlessness, than it was the possessor of a dependable formula for motivating Vietnamese villagers to fight Communism. At any time from 1961 to 1964 an afternoon of library research would have established that the Cloward-Ohlin thesis of opportunity structure, though eminently respectable, was nonetheless rather a minority position, with the bulk of delinquency theory pointed in a quite different direction.

Moynihan undoubtedly overstates the declassé position of the Cloward-Ohlin position: in truth, delinquency theory was pointing (and still points) in a considerable variety of different directions, and Cloward and Ohlin's thesis was one of the more prominent of those thrusts. Indeed, the theories that we have been reviewing might well be compared in this respect to that famous horse rider portrayed by the Canadian mathematician-humorist Stephen Leacock, the man who got upon his mount and rode off wildly in all different directions.

Moynihan in particular faults Cloward and Ohlin for neglecting the role of the family in the genesis of delinquent acts. He cites with approval Bordua's (1961:134) observation that opportunity structures may indeed be blocked for delinquent youths but that "this seems, often, the end product of a long history of their progressively cutting off opportunity and destroying their own capacities which may begin in the lower class family." Moynihan, of course, is mostly suggesting that a great many different things can be important in producing delinquent behavior. He thinks the family is especially important; Cloward and Ohlin find the social conditions of the neighborhood more significant. Both probably have hold of a piece of the whole truth. The causes of a delinquent act obviously are multiple; how do you put into the equation, for instance, the keys inadvertently left in a car that tempt a youngster to steal it, though he seemingly had no intention or overt interest in doing this until an ill wind blew his loose-fitting hat through the car window and he noticed the keys when he went to retrieve the hat? Indeed, what causal role is to be attributed to the wind? Or to the fact that he was wearing a hat?

Subcultural Theory: Walter Miller on City Gangs

Miller, the third of the postwar triumvirate of contributors to theory in this area, is a social anthropologist from the University of Chicago who worked for more than half a dozen years, primarily in Roxbury, Massachusetts, with delinquent gangs. For Miller, gang behavior was no more nor less than an expression of a culture that prevailed in the slum neighborhoods. His thesis is summarized in the following paragraph:

> In the case of "gang" delinquency, the cultural system which exerts the most direct influences on behavior is that of the lower class community itself — a long-established, distinctively patterned tradition with an integrity of its own — rather than a so-called "delinquent subculture," which has arisen through conflict with middle class culture and is oriented to the deliberate violation of middle class norms. (Miller, 1958:5)

Miller believes that delinquency is engaged in repeatedly, systematically, and regularly, by rational, understandable people as a routine and expected part of their ordinary conduct of life. The distinctive lower-class culture that Miller describes is said to be marked by female-based households and a pattern of serial monogamy — that is, many marriages, one after the other. In their adaptation to lower-class cultural traits, boys come to expect to get into trouble; they assert their toughness, display "smartness," emphasize the ability to outwit or con others, and seek excitement. They accept the dictates of what they see as "fate" and are constantly concerned with the maintenance of their individual autonomy. According to Miller, gangs are built around individuals belonging to four distinct social subcultures — they are males, adolescents, and urban residents who are equipped only for low-skilled manual work. Like that of the other theorists, Miller's work accepts the aims of the delinquents as essentially those of all humans and suggests that alternative ways of satisfying such aims represent the most efficient tactic for diverting them into law-abiding channels. He notes, for instance, that theft is overwhelmingly the major behavior of delinquents. Provide law-abiding substitutes for these goals — meaning the ability to acquire money to subsidize a reasonable amount of acquisition and pleasure — and the incentive for theft will be vitiated, Miller argues.

Miller's work has been the most severely criticized of the gang theorists. Kornhauser (1978:208), for instance, says that "the subculture of the lower class, as portrayed by Walter Miller, exists only in his imagination. Moreover, whatever their status in fact or fancy as components of a subculture, the traits described by Miller are not related to delinquency."

Undoubtedly the strongest attack on Miller's position is that of Ryan (1971:123–125), who calls it "obnoxious" and lambastes what he believes is a lamentable American habit of "blaming the victim" for the victim's difficulties. He says that we tend to regard social problems as if they are the fault of the person who suffers from them rather than the responsibility of those forces or individuals who cause the suffering. A rape victim is blamed for hitchhiking or for wearing "provocative" clothing; all the blame should be affixed, Ryan argues, onto the rapist, who flagrantly broke the law. It is his fault only. Caricaturing victim-blaming techniques, Ryan tells of the U.S. senator during an investigation of the origin of the Second World War who bellowed: "What was Pearl Harbor doing there?" when inquiring about the 1941 Japanese aerial attack on that Pacific outpost. In regard to Miller's position, Ryan argues that the "focal concerns" identified with the lower class actually are values shared by all Americans. Who among us, he asks, prefers the opposite of such concerns — boredom, stupidity, subjugation, and weakness?

Gang Theories Generally

The "gang theories" have been extraordinarily important in rejuvenating and focusing intellectual attention on the explanation of processes that contribute to the genesis of juvenile delinquency. Indeed, it is one of the striking ironies of scholarship that there is more sophisticated theory dealing with juvenile law-breaking than there is with adult crime, though the latter by most standards is far more important. This situation may be attributable to the unusually great importance that Americans attach to youthfulness and our deep social concern with waywardness within that age group. Foreigners often comment on the intense identification of Americans with the young and, indeed, on Americans' own interest in "staying young" as long as possible. Our military people, for instance, are regarded as particularly kind to children, and parents in the United States are said to be especially indulgent to their offspring. These cultural values may lie at the root of the great concern with delinquency, along with a national spirit of optimism, a belief that wayward youngsters can be "saved" and that with help and a bit of luck they too can realize the American dream of success.

Labeling Theory _____

Labeling theory as an explanation of juvenile delinquency enjoyed a decade-long period of prominence before logical and empirical reservations undercut belief in its ability effectively to capture the essence of the causal pattern of delinquent behavior. Essentially, labeling theory rests on the supposition that human beings respond to the definitions placed upon their behavior by others, especially those who have power. If I am called a "bad boy" and treated as such, I come to introject that image of myself and behave in the manner that others have maintained is my mode. This happens particularly when there are available to me no countervailing definitions of what I am; that is, when nobody tells me that I am good, decent, and acceptable. As Fine (1977:167) observes, the labeling process "amplifies the very phenomena it is intended to suppress."

There is a large body of social science literature that testifies to at least the partial truth of this formulation. Particularly impressive are reports of brain-washing, as practiced in the early days following the Chinese Revolution. An American couple tells how the Chinese, after arresting them for espionage, isolated them from anybody who would offer them social support. The Ricketts had been in China on a study fellowship and had at times dined with the American naval attaché, gossiping with him about what they had seen at the university and elsewhere. The Chinese said that this represented traitorous behavior, because it provided a potential enemy with inside information. They asked the imprisoned Ricketts to put in writing an explanation of their behavior and each time laconically rejected their statement. The Ricketts tried harder, desperately searching their minds for a version of events that would satisfy their uncommunicative captors. Occasionally they would be treated more leniently, for reasons they could not fathom, and after that they would be dealt with more harshly. In typical brainwashed style, they more and more came to accept the

Drawing by Chas. Addams; © 1936, 1944 The New Yorker Magazine, Inc.

*"You are trustworthy, loyal, helpful, friendly,
courteous, kind, obedient, cheerful,
thrifty, brave, clean, reverent."*

A labeling process in action outside the justice system.

reality of those who ruled over them in prison; they introjected the label that the captors pinned upon behavior that at best could be regarded by an objective outsider as ambiguous (Rickett and Rickett, 1957; see also Lifton, 1961).

Similarly, social psychologists for years have conducted experiments that demonstrate that we tend to place credence in persons who seem important, even though the message they transmit may be no different than that of a person who is unprepossessing. Dress a person in a three-piece suit, let him grow a beard, and what he says will prove more believable to most audiences than the same message delivered by the same person dressed in jeans and looking casual and unimpressive (Wilson and Rachal, 1977).

The Development of Labeling Theory

Labeling theory is built upon early work by two prominent students of crime and delinquency, Frank Tannenbaum and Edwin Lemert. Tannebaum had served time in prison as a wartime conscientious objector. Partly because of this experience, he began a scholarly career at Columbia University specializing in criminology. He coined the phrase *dramatization of evil* to describe the tendency of authorities to paint deviants in a light that undermines their self-esteem and thrusts them outside the pale of conventional life (Tannenbaum, 1938). He suggested that we treat people in terms of the categories into which they are placed rather than in the fullness of their humanity. A boy may be a Catholic, a dog lover, an ardent baseball fan, someone who is kind to his sister, a reflective, nature-loving person, and a delinquent caught at shoplifting. It is this last label that will tend to suffocate the others, and in terms of which we are apt to deal with him. The label may well keep him from staying comfortably in school (teachers and other pupils are apt to shy away from him), from getting a good job, and from associating with conforming youngsters. The only route left open to him that will allow ready access may be that in the world of delinquency.

Lemert (1951), the second of the major early labeling theorists, differentiated between "primary" and "secondary" labeling processes. He granted that there is little or no labeling of a youngster by the authorities until that youngster does something that gets him into difficulty. The secondary labeling process occurs after the initial encounter with authorities because of lawbreaking, and it is this phenomenon that is said by Lemert to have the potential of strengthening a commitment to antisocial actions.

Labeling theory was employed to justify reducing any stigma that might come to adhere to persons who have the possibility of contact with law enforcement forces. It was argued, for instance, that it would prove more efficacious to release a youngster, or to ignore his behavior, than to place a label of "delinquent" onto him. Policies of benign neglect and "radical nonintervention" were advocated instead of official action in the face of delinquency (Schur, 1971). The analogy sometimes was made to the temper tantrums of infants, about which the accepted wisdom is that ignoring the behavior is likely to prove the most effective way of eliminating it, since the infant soon discovers that the tantrums will not get the desired results.

Criticisms of Labeling Theory

In delinquency, however, the situation is apt to prove a good deal more complicated than with temper tantrums. For example, delinquent behavior is likely to be undertaken in order to achieve a good many more things than the attention of one's parents, though sometimes, of course, that is one of its goals. Also, if delinquent acts result in the acquisition of fame and fortune of sorts, it hardly seems likely that they will be abandoned if the authorities overlook them. As another example, at least some persons who are labeled do not passively accept the designation and act in terms of it, but resist its imposition and set out to demonstrate the inaccuracy of the label (Gove, 1975). If I am called cheap by my friends, I may still never reach for a check, but there is also some likelihood that I will become more generous in order to avoid their aspersions

© Leonard Freed, Magnum

The labeling process begins at this moment, according to some theorists.

and to gain their approval. Labeling, in such terms, can be seen to be considerably more complex than indicated by its early advocates, who were apt to regard
all delinquents as fundamentally decent persons who had been thrust into
undesirable molds by the nastiness of their remorseless oppressors. In this
sense, the labeling theory — as do many theories — fit well with the tenor of the
political period in which it came to favor, a period of iconoclasm and hostility to
authority during the Vietnam War period. The roots of a theory and its political
character, though, do not in any way speak to its accuracy. For labeling, decline
of its acceptance in recent times seems to lie primarily in a growing belief that it
greatly oversimplifies the process producing juvenile delinquency. Gibbs (1972),
for instance, points out that labeling is a ubiquitous and unavoidable process: it
occurs constantly through group and general social disapproval and not only by
means of official mechanisms. Delinquents themselves usually are perfectly
aware of the definitions of their behavior by others and hardly need official
verification. In many cases, in fact, they themselves are their own severest
critics.

In a Swedish review of labeling theory, Knutsson (1977) notes that it has
proven to be particularly popular with college students. He believes that this
may be because the theory, if accepted, relieves persons of moral responsibility
for their actions: according to the theory, they are governed by "forces" that
they do not know and cannot influence. "As viewed by labeling theory in its
most popular form," Knutsson writes (1977:53), "the deviant starts by doing
what everybody else does but has the bad luck to get caught and labeled."
Knutsson (1977:56) finds the theory "unclear and dubious" but grants that it

has provided "interesting insights into the deviant's behavior as seen from his own viewpoint."

That the label is not superimposed until some wayward behavior occurs represents a notably weak link in labeling theory postulates. As Akers (1967:463) has noted: "One sometimes gets the impression from reading [label-ing] literature that people go about their own business and then 'wham' — bad society comes along and slaps them with a stigmatized label." Some labeling theorists attempt to counteract this criticism by saying that all of us engage in acts that could be viciously labeled, but only a portion of us are selected out for such treatment — and that members of this group are largely from the economi-cally depressed segment of society.

By and large, research tests have experienced difficulty demonstrating a labeling effect, though Klein (1986) recently reported that of delinquents ran-domly released, referred to court, or diverted, those released were least apt to be among the 60 per cent who committed another offense. Miller and Gold (1984), however, found that among eighty-three youths who had committed delinquent acts those who had been apprehended did not feel more frequently labeled by parents and teachers than those who remained undetected. Persons caught, however, showed a 7 per cent greater likelihood of becoming more severely delinquent. The researchers believe that arrest — in contrast to trial or incarceration — is the most "iatrogenic" (something that worsens the effect it seeks to cure) point in the system of juvenile justice, though they were unable to discover from their research why this might be so.

The most sophisticated review of labeling theory has been done by Walker (1980), who distinguishes seven forms of the process. These are called (1) *suspicion*, whereby the offender may become more likely to be suspected of subsequent offenses, especially those resembling his original offense; (2) *em-ployment disqualification*; (3) *ostracism*, whereby the offender may lose friends or, perhaps, family support; (4) *damaged self-image*, in terms of which an offender might be inclined to regard illegal behavior as consistent with his "nature" or to believe that he has little to lose by further lawbreaking; (5) *antilabel reaction*, whereby an offender may reject the label as unfair and become determined to prove that this is true; (6) *antilabeler reaction*, in terms of which the labeled person might reject the values of society as unfair or exces-sively censorious and might devote himself to exposing the shortcomings of the society; and (7) *martyrdom*, in which the labeling could be defined by others as a great moral wrong and thereby enlist support for the person and the person's cause. Walker points out that the last three reactions tend to be ignored by labeling theorists and that the evidence for the first five effects is "scrappy and equivocal" (1980:143). He notes, for example, that studies demonstrating that prosecuted juvenile delinquents are more likely to commit further delinquencies than unprosecuted delinquents could be interpreted in support of items 3 and 4 in the foregoing list; but they also could satisfactorily be explained by the idea that many of the prosecuted delinquents came to realize how mild were the results of their offending. Walker (1980:143) believes that "the assumption that stigma is an automatic and harmful consequence of conviction is to a consider-able extent a legacy of an earlier era in which penal systems were deliberately designed to ensure that this was so." Nowadays, he believes, it is not easy to point to a measure that is deliberately stigmatizing, and much more sophisticated research needs to be done before labeling can be taken seriously as an explanation of delinquent behavior.

Neutralization and Drift

Neutralization

If delinquents do not become significantly influenced by labeling, what tactics are they likely to employ to keep up their self-esteem and counteract derogatory designations? This question has been addressed by Gresham Sykes and David Matza (1975) in a classic delineation of the rationalizations that delinquents employ to blunt judgments about the absence of compassion for others shown in acts of violence and predatory crimes. Sykes and Matza suggest five major self-justifying techniques: delinquents are said to (1) "condemn the condemners," that is, to indicate that those who denounce their behavior are themselves really no better than they are; look at white-collar criminals, such as tax evaders, the delinquent says; (2) deny responsibility for the behavior, claiming that their act was due to forces beyond their control, such as drug use or unloving parents; (3) deny injury, maintaining that what they have done has really harmed no one; after all, the store they robbed has insurance and, besides, it will pass on the loss to the customers in the form of increased prices; (4) deny the victim, claiming that whoever was robbed or hurt only got what that person deserved; another form of the same process (Minor, 1981) is to prey upon absent or unknown victims and thereby avoid identifying with the depredations these persons suffer; and (5) appeal to higher loyalties, stating that support and assistance for friends and the gang are more important than anything else.

If delinquents require and employ such "techniques of neutralization," this would indicate that they have incorporated into their thinking the usual definitions of acceptable behavior and feel a compelling need to placate their consciences for what they have done. There is a considerable research literature on the issue, but it tends to focus on the question of whether a potential delinquent beforehand—often in terms of interpretation of a written scenario—would justify a given delinquent behavior by a neutralization technique. Ball and Lilly (1971), for instance, found that sixth-grade pupils living outside the city were more likely to "accept" neutralizations than tough urban high school students; that is, they were more apt to believe that certain acts were excusable if certain conditions prevailed. Typically, for instance, the question is asked: "Would you feel guilty for cheating on a test if the instructor deliberately gave an overly difficult or tricky test?" Those more willing to cheat under the specified condition presumably would have an excuse in place were these circumstances to develop. This line of inquiry, however, somewhat deflects the thrust of the Matza and Sykes position. Its core point appears to be that delinquents offer explanations for their acts that are aimed at blunting more unpleasant definitions of such behavior and that the employment of such explanations indicates something of a feeling of unease with the behavior. Few delinquents, for instance, are apt to say, "I robbed that crippled old man because I'm a no-good kid and I wanted to have some fun at the arcade and he was an easy target, so I stole his money. I enjoy robbing old men almost as much as beating blind old women and young, helpless kids."

In an interesting test of the Sykes-Matza proposition, the Schwendingers (1967:96) asked groups of delinquents and nondelinquents to respond to a vignette, which read as follows:

> I want you to act out this story: some teenagers are arguing over whether they should beat up an Outsider who insulted their club. An Outsider is someone outside their circle of friends. Those who are in favor of beating him up argue with the others about it. The others are finally convinced that the Outsider should be beaten up by the entire group.

The same general format was followed in additional enactments involving victimization of a Rich Teenager and of a Businessman, using appropriate scenarios. The Schwendingers argue that if Sykes and Matza are correct there should be moral justifications expressed. However, the delinquents who objected to the retribution were almost entirely concerned with tactical rather than moral issues: the intrusion of the Outsider's friends, police apprehension, or stakes too small for the risk. Nondelinquents were the ones who raised moral issues. But the Schwendingers grant that the delinquents may have been expressing viewpoints that would carry weight with their fellow gang members and that group decision processes can differ significantly from individual explanations of behavior.

Drift

The key arguable element of the Sykes and Matza position, then, becomes whether delinquents truly employ neutralizations because they feel guilty about their lawbreaking. Matza (1964) has put forward the view that delinquents "drift" into their waywardness, that they usually behave in a satisfactory manner but will on rare though episodic occasions release themselves from social constraints and break the law. To test his view, he asked 100 institutionalized delinquents to respond to vignettes depicting situations such as a mugging, fighting with a weapon, armed robbery, auto theft, stealing from a warehouse, vandalism, and stealing a bike. On the average, 2 per cent of the respondents approved of the acts, 40 per cent were indifferent, 30 per cent mildly disapproving, and 28 per cent indignant. Matza (1964:49) finds in these answers evidence that "adherents of the subculture of delinquency seem little committed to the misdeeds inherent in it."

Attacks on this conclusion raise an experimental point that we have seen come home to plague earlier theories of delinquency: that Matza failed to employ a control group. It also has been suggested that institutionalized delinquents are apt to be wary of expressing any but conventional views because their standing in the institution and their opportunities for release might be affected. Hindelang (1970), using a population from a middle-class section of Oakland, California, and employing self-reports to measure involvement in delinquent activities, found, contrary to Matza, that persons involved in delinquent activities approved of such behavior much more than those who had reported that they had avoided such involvement. He believed that his results support the position of Cloward and Ohlin and of Cohen that delinquents come to have attitudes distinctively different from nondelinquents. "It is not necessary to postulate the mechanism of 'drift' or of the 'techniques of neutralization' if in fact delinquents do not have moral inhibitions which normally restrain them from delinquent involvement," Hindelang (1970:508) maintained. But there are a bevy of methodological questions that can readily be raised about Hindelang's results as well. Self-report scales are always suspect (see Chapter 1); and when a researcher combines two pencil-and-paper measures, the first of delinquent activity and the second of attitudes, we have at best only second-hand measures of those things in which we are directly interested. A natural experiment in which delinquents were able to express their views in a way distinctive from a researcher's staged experiment would be able to provide more believable evidence on the issues being considered; even better, naturalistic observations on how delinquents in fact acted in regard to "neutralization" tactics and solid information on their delinquent careers would decidedly advance the debate on this crucial aspect of delinquency theory.

Summary

Dominance by scholars with training in sociology of the study of juvenile delinquency has led to the enunciation of a wide range of theoretical statements that focus on group processes and on social values as the key elements in producing wayward behavior by young persons. The work began at the University of Chicago as part of a renowned effort by its sociology faculty to determine the ecological patterns of the city in which the university was located. *Ecology*, a biological term, refers to the relationship between an organism and its environment. Chicago sociologists assumed that different parts of a city create and support special kinds of life-styles, just as a rain forest nurtures its special kind of animal and plant life and exists on the basis of delicate symbiotic relationships between plants and wildlife found in its midst.

Chicago, at the time the second largest metropolitan area in the United States (trailing only New York in population), was divided into areas that researchers designated by concentric circles drawn from the core of the city. This work on delinquency, carried out by Clifford Shaw and Henry McKay, among others, demonstrated that delinquency in general tends to be higher the nearer a neighborhood is to the center of the city. Particularly deteriorated neighborhoods exist right beyond the limits of the business area because owners and investors anticipate that property values will appreciate dramatically in time, as the business community moves outward. Therefore, they allow the housing they own to crumble because their prime interest is in holding onto the land until it becomes valuable as the site for new construction. It is in such areas that the new immigrants, both from abroad and from impoverished sections of the country, come to congregate, and where the delinquency rates are notably high. Shaw and McKay stressed that such neighborhoods, so long as they remain slums, will produce large numbers of lawbreakers regardless of which ethnic group resides there, be it Scandinavians, Germans, blacks, Hispanics, or other newcomers. Subsequent research has challenged this early assumption in regard to Orientals, whose especially close-knit family patterns and high achievement motivation may save youngsters from involvement in delinquency. But with the influx of unskilled and poorly educated Asians into the United States in the wake of the Vietnam War, Shaw and McKay's hypothesis may turn out to demonstrate more nearly universal application.

Work with inner-city dwellers by Chicago school sociologists was largely based on pragmatic rather than explicitly theoretical grounds. Shaw and McKay placed particular reliance on mature law-abiding persons living within a slum area to be able to establish programs that would keep the youth out of trouble. This reliance, of course, conflicted with the convictions of trained social workers and other professionals who believed that special kinds of skills and disciplined attitudes were essential to redirect human behavior. At the moment, it is arguable which emphasis is the more correct; it seems likely that each has some truth on its side and that the need is for a multifaceted program that takes advantage of what works, whatever its source, and discards unproductive pretensions.

Chicago sociologists, led by Thrasher, inaugurated the study of juvenile gangs, a line of inquiry that has produced most of the sophisticated and provocative theoretical reasoning in the area of juvenile delinquency. Thrasher saw gangs forming as adolescent play groups and then, in certain social settings, becoming more troublesome and isolated from mainstream life as the members caused difficulty and threatened the well-being of law-abiding citizens. Cohen, who pioneered contemporary gang studies, declared that gang members find solace in such groups because they are severely handicapped in efforts to achieve the kinds of things valued by a middle-class society and, inevitably, by them also. If you can't obtain recognition by having a good car, a nice parental home, expensive clothes, good grades, or a star position on an athletic team, you can spurn all of those things and set up your own rules. In that realm, the most lucrative shoplifting heist, the greatest display of courage in gang warfare, the snazziest gang costume and hairstyle, and similar badges of achievement make the gang functional for those who, primarily for reasons of their original social handicaps, cannot succeed in conventional realms.

Cohen's theory, with elements of the process that psychologists call "reaction formation," was challenged at some points but primarily refined by Cloward and Ohlin, who found entrance into delinquency not merely a passive surrender to an inability to achieve middle-class values but dependent upon a person's own traits and the opportunities offered in the neighborhood. Some youngsters lack the qualities to achieve either middle-class or gang status: they might fall into what Cloward and Ohlin called a retreatism pattern, marked in particular by withdrawal from social striving and typified by drug usage. Opening up avenues of access to middle-class achievement, particularly through educational enhancement and job opportunities, seemed to Cloward and Ohlin to represent the most promising prong of any attack on delinquency.

A rather different theoretical pronouncement emerged from Miller's study of gangs in Roxbury, a Boston neighborhood. Miller did not believe that middle-class concerns dictated gang activity but rather that such activity represented the product of another ethos, one found only in the slums. Miller delineated a core of "focal concerns," including such things as toughness and a desire for excitement, that he believed underlay the structure of juvenile gang activity. Probably the most severely criticized of the major gang theories, Miller's postulations have been attacked on the ground that they do not either truly or exclusively mirror working-class culture.

Labeling theory came into prominence at the time that American society was in a particularly critical mood about the trustworthiness and the reliability of persons exercising authority. The theory maintains that youngsters who are officially declared to be delinquent will be pushed even more deeply into such behavior because they will see themselves in terms of what they are said to be and because other channels of behavior will be closed to them. Teachers insisting that certain pupils are "bad," the labeling theorists argue, reinforce the very badness they supposedly want to suppress. But labeling theory has run into a large number of obstacles in its attempts to obtain empirical support for its propositions. Its most prominent deficit lies in the fact that it cannot be used to explain the original delinquency — the act that elicited the label in the first place. It may well be that it is the same forces that create later delinquency, not the labeling at all. In addition, there are a whole variety of adaptations that persons can make to being labeled in a derogatory manner, one of which, obviously, is to reform so that the label is refuted.

Other work related to self-image theory has focused on the techniques — the rationalizations or neutralizations — that are employed by delinquents to make them immune from having to deal with derogatory feelings and attributions. Sykes and Matza identified a number of responses, such as condemning the condemners, that they maintained are employed by delinquents. Research, however, has failed to provide much support for the idea that delinquents feel any special need to have their behavior redefined in more "acceptable" ways. It seems likely that the accolades they get from their peers for successful delinquency may be more immediate and more important than the more remote judgments of the larger society.

That delinquents "drift" into their lawbreaking behavior, a view advanced by Matza, is the last of the theoretical notions reviewed in this chapter. Matza maintains that delinquency is not inexorably caused by any particular constellation of circumstances but that most youngsters commit a large variety of acts, some few of which are delinquent. Many of the illegal acts are essentially chance occurrences — a response to an opportunity or a routine involvement that is common to all persons of a particular age. Sometimes these acts will be repeated, perhaps because the experience was enjoyable or perhaps the circumstances are rather readily at hand. Most of the youngster's activities, nonetheless, are well within the limits of acceptable behavior. In time, some persons "drift" deeper and deeper into patterns of delinquency, although throughout they also persist in doing most things in a perfectly lawful manner.

References

Akers, Ronald. 1967. Problems in the Sociology of Deviance: Social Definitions and Behavior. *Social Forces* 46:455–465.

Alinsky, Saul D. 1946. *Reveille for Radicals*. Chicago: Univ. of Chicago Press.

Anderson, Nels. 1923. *The Hobo.* Chicago: Univ. of Chicago Press.

Ball, Richard A., and Lilly, J. Robert. 1971. Juvenile Delinquency in an Urban County. *Criminology* 9:65–85.

Barich, Bill. 1986. The Crazy Life. *The New Yorker* 62 (November 3):97–130.

Bordua, David J. 1961. Delinquent Subcultures: Sociological Interpretations of Gang Delinquency. *Annals of the American Academy of Political and Social Science* 338:119–136.

Brager, George A., and Purcell, Francis P. 1967. Community Action Against Poverty. New Haven: College and Univ. Press.

Brantingham, Paul J., and Brantingham, Patricia L. 1981. *Environmental Criminology.* Beverly Hills, Calif.: Sage.

Burgess, Ernest W., and Bogue, Donald J., eds. 1963. *Contributions to Urban Sociology.* Chicago: Univ. of Chicago Press.

Bursik, Robert J., Jr. 1984. Urban Dynamics and Ecological Studies of Delinquency. *Social Forces* 63:393–413.

Cavan, Ruth S. 1928. *Suicide.* Chicago: Univ. of Chicago Press.

Chilton, Roland J. 1964. Continuity in Delinquency Area Research: A Comparison of Studies of Baltimore, Detroit, and Indianapolis. *American Sociological Review* 29:71–83.

Cloward, Richard A., and Ohlin, Lloyd E. 1960. *Delinquency and Opportunity.* New York: Free Press.

Cohen, Albert K. 1955. *Delinquent Boys.* New York: Free Press.

Cressey, Paul. 1932. *Taxi-Dance Hall.* Chicago: Univ. of Chicago Press.

Devlin, Mark. 1985. *Stubborn Child.* New York: Atheneum.

Fine, Bob. 1977. Labelling Theory: An Investigation into the Sociological Critique of Deviance. *Economy & Society* 6:166–193.

Finestone, Harold. 1976. *Victims of Change: Juvenile Delinquents in American Society.* Westport, Conn.: Greenwood Press.

Fujimoto, Tetsuya. 1978. *Crime and Delinquency Among Japanese-Americans.* Tokyo: Chuo Univ. Press.

Geis, Gilbert. 1964. Sociology and Sociological Jurisprudence: Admixture of Lore and Law. *Kentucky Law Journal* 52:267–293.

Gibbs, Jack P. 1972. Causation and Theory Construction. *Social Science* 52:815–826.

Gordon, Robert A. 1967. Issues in the Ecological Study of Delinquency. *American Sociological Review* 32:927–944.

Gove, Walter R. 1975. The Labelling Perspective: An Overview. In *The Labelling of Deviance: Evaluating a Perspective*; edited by Walter R. Gove, 3–20. New York: Wiley.

Heitgerd, Janet L., and Bursik, Robert J., Jr. 1987. Extracommunity Dynamics and the Ecology of Delinquency. *American Journal of Sociology* 92:775–787.

Hindelang, Michael J. 1970. The Commitment of Delinquents to Their Misdeeds: Do Delinquents Drift? *Social Problems* 17:502–509.

Jonassen, Christen T. 1949. A Re-Evaluation and Critique of the Logic and Some Methods of Shaw and McKay. *American Sociological Review* 14:608–617.

Junger-Tas, Josine, and Junger, Marianne. 1984. *Juvenile Delinquency: Backgrounds of Delinquent Behavior.* The Hague: Ministry of Justice.

Klein, Malcolm W. 1986. Labeling Theory and Delinquency Policy: An Experimental Test. *Criminal Justice and Behavior* 13:47–79.

Knutsson, Johannes. 1977. *Labeling Theory: A Critical Examination.* Stockholm: National Swedish Council for Crime Prevention.

Kornhauser, Ruth R. 1978. *Social Sources of Delinquency: An Appraisal of Analytic Models.* Chicago: Univ. of Chicago Press.

Lander, Bernard, 1954. *Toward an Understanding of Juvenile Delinquency.* New York: Columbia Univ. Press.

Lemert, Edwin M. 1951. *Social Pathology.* New York: McGraw-Hill.

Lifton, Robert J. 1961. *Thought Reform and the Psychology of Totalism.* New York: W. W. Norton.

Lynd, Robert S., and Lynd, Helen. 1929. *Middletown: A Study in Contemporary American Culture.* New York: Harcourt, Brace.

Malcolm X. 1965. *The Autobiography of Malcolm X.* New York: Grove Press.

Matthews, Fred H. 1977. *Quest for an American Sociology: Robert E. Park and the Chicago School.* Montreal: McGill-Queen Univ. Press.

Matza, David. 1964. *Delinquency and Drift.* New York: Wiley.

Mead, Margaret. 1928. *Coming of Age in Samoa.* New York: Morrow.

Merwin, Donald J., ed. 1960. *Reaching the Fighting Gang.* New York: New York City Youth Board.

Miller, Michael O., and Gold, Martin. 1984. Iatrogenesis in the Juvenile Justice System. *Youth & Society* 16:83–111.

Miller, Walter B. 1958. Lower Class Culture as a Generating Milieu of Gang Delinquency. *Journal of Social Issues* 14, no. 3:5–19.

Minor, W. William. 1981. Techniques of Neutralization: A Reconceptualization and Empirical Examination. *Journal of Research in Crime and Delinquency* 18:295–318.

Moynihan, Daniel P. 1969. *Maximum Feasible Misunderstanding: Community Action in the War on Poverty.* New York: Free Press.

Rickett, Allyn, and Rickett, Adele. 1957. *Prisoners of Liberation.* New York: Cameron.

Rivera, Ramon J., and Short, James F., Jr. 1967. Occupational Goals: A Comparative Analysis. In *Juvenile Gangs in Context,* edited by Malcolm W. Klein and Barbara Meyerhoff, 70–90. Englewood Cliffs, N.J.: Prentice-Hall.

Ryan, William. 1971. *Blaming the Victim.* New York: Pantheon.

Robinson, William S. 1950. Ecological Correlates of the Behavior of Individuals. *American Sociological Review* 15:351–357.

Schlossman, Steven, and Sedlak, Michael. 1983. The Chicago Area Project Revisited. *Crime and Delinquency* 29:398–462.

Schur, Edwin M. 1971. *Labeling Deviant Behavior.* New York: Harper and Row.

Schwendinger, Herman, and Schwendinger, Julia. 1967. Delinquent Stereotypes of Probable Victims. In *Juvenile Gangs in Context,* edited by Malcolm W. Klein and Barbara Meyerhoff, 91–105. Englewood Cliffs, N.J.: Prentice-Hall.

Shaw, Clifford R. 1929. *Delinquency Areas: A Study of the Geographic Distribution of School Truants, Juvenile Delinquents, and Adult Offenders in Chicago.* Chicago: Univ. of Chicago Press.

———. 1930. *The Jack-Roller: A Delinquent Boy's Own Story.* Chicago: Univ. of Chicago Press.

———, McKay, Henry D., and McDonald, James F. 1983. *Brothers in Crime.* Chicago: Univ. of Chicago Press.

———, and McKay, Henry D. 1942. *Juvenile Delinquency and Urban Areas: A Study of Rates of Delinquency in Relation to Differential Characteristics of Local Communities in American Cities.* Chicago: Univ. of Chicago Press.

———, and Moore, Maurice E. 1931. *The Natural History of a Delinquent Career.* Chicago: Univ. of Chicago Press.

Sheu, Chuen-Jim. 1986. *Delinquency and Identity: Juvenile Delinquency in an American Chinatown.* Albany, N.Y.: Harrow and Heston.

Slayton, Robert. 1986. *Back of the Yards: The Making of a Local Democracy.* Chicago: Univ. of Chicago Press.

Snodgrass, Jon. 1972. The American Criminological Tradition: Portraits of the Men and Ideology in a Discipline. Ph.D. dissertation, University of Pennsylvania.

———. 1976. Clifford R. Shaw and Henry D. McKay: Chicago Criminologists. *British Journal of Criminology* 16:1–19.

———, ed. 1982. *The Jack-Roller at Seventy: A Fifty-Year Follow-up.* Lexington, Mass. Lexington Books.

Spergel, Irving A. 1986. The Violent Gang Problem in Chicago: A Local Community Approach. *Social Service Review* 60:94–131.

Steiner, Lee. 1960. *Understanding Juvenile Delinquency*. Philadelphia: Chilton.

Suttles, Gerald D. 1972. *The Social Construction of Communities*. Chicago: Univ. of Chicago Press.

Sykes, Gresham M., and Matza, David. 1957. Techniques of Neutralization: A Theory of Delinquency. *American Sociological Review* 22:664–670.

Tannenbaum, Frank. 1938. *Crime and the Community*. Boston: Ginn.

Thrasher, Frederic M. 1927. *The Gang*. Chicago: Univ. of Chicago Press.

Walker, Nigel. 1980. *Punishment, Danger and Stigma: The Morality of Criminal Justice*. Oxford: Basil Blackwell.

Wallis, C. P., and Maliphant, R. 1967. Delinquent Areas in the County of London: Ecological Factors. *British Journal of Criminology* 7:251–284.

Warner, W. Lloyd, and Lunt, Paul S. 1941. The Social Life of a Modern Community. New Haven, Conn.: Yale Univ. Press.

Whyte, William F. 1943. 3rd ed. 1981. *Street Corner Society: The Social Structure of an Italian Slum*. Chicago: Univ. of Chicago Press.

Wideman, John E. 1984. *Brothers and Keepers*. New York: Holt, Rinehart and Winston.

Williams, Robin, M., Jr. 1970. *American Society: A Sociological Interpretation*. 3rd ed. New York: Knopf.

Wilson, James Q., and Rachal, Patricia. 1977. Can the Government Regulate Itself? *The Public Interest* 46:3–14.

Wirth, Louis 1928. *The Ghetto*. Chicago: Univ. of Chicago Press.

Young, Kimball. 1927. The Gang and the Modern World. *New Republic* 51 (June 1):51.

Young, Pauline V. 1932. *The Pilgrims of Russian-Town*. Chicago: Univ. of Chicago Press.

Zorbaugh, Harvey. 1929. *The Gold Coast and the Slum*. Chicago: Univ. of Chicago Press.

CHAPTER 6

Critical, Differential Association, and Control Theories

The final three theories to be reviewed are based on very different foundations than those discussed in previous chapters. The critical or Marxist theory finds its vitality in economic and political factors, particularly modes of production, and believes that such factors lie at the root of juvenile misbehavior. The differential association theory, the second position to be discussed in this chapter, is based on learning principles. Differential association theory maintains that persons learn criminal behavior from others. Control theory, the third to be discussed here, at the moment enjoys the greatest acceptance among persons studying juvenile delinquency. For control theorists, delinquency represents a falling away from the grip of mechanisms that produce conformity; control theory seeks to pinpoint which particular mechanisms are most important and to formulate a series of statements in terms of which we might be able to predict who will prove to be a delinquent.

Each of these theories, whatever its inadequacies, contains a good deal of intellectual force; it can make thought more organized and more direct and can pose questions about the genesis of delinquency that need careful consideration if we are truly to understand the behavior.

Critical Theory ————————————————————

Origins

Much of the contemporary world is ruled by the ideology of Marxism — indeed, during the 1950s for the first time in centuries the Bible was replaced by Karl Marx's *Das Kapital* as the best-selling book in the world (Rostow, 1959:39). Marxist theories seek to explain virtually all human behavior of any consequence; inevitably, they have been brought to bear on attempts to comprehend crime and delinquency, though some scholars argue that, since Marx wrote little on the subject, "it would be fruitless to attempt a comprehensive theory of deviance and social control based on a re-examination of classic Marxist texts" (Ferrajoli and Zolo, 1986:84). Nonetheless, there is a considerable body of current Marxist writing known as *critical criminology*.

The essential theme of critical theory is that delinquency is rooted in the inequities of the distribution of wealth in capitalist countries. Such inequities are said to produce a struggle among members of different classes. The leaders under capitalism (members of the so-called *grand bourgeoisie* class) are said to exploit the masses (the *proletariat*). Ultimately, Marxists postulate, the system will rot on its own, though the process can be speeded up by revolt on the part of the oppressed; all they have to lose, Lenin maintained in his rallying cry, is their chains.

The traditional hostility of critical writers to religion is based on the Marxist doctrine that religion is the "opiate of the masses"; that is, by turning people's attention away from their exploitation in this world toward anticipation of reward in another world, religion is said to serve the cause of capitalists, who prefer a quiescent laboring force. Critical theorists believe that all social conditions pass through a dialectical process. The process begins with conditions as they exist — the *thesis*, this situation is called. A thesis generates an opposing

Critical theory postulates that delinquency in capitalist societies results from inequities in the distribution of wealth. The controlling power of the wealthy is mediated through law enforcement.

position, an *antithesis*, and thereafter, the two positions—the thesis and its antithesis—become fused into a *synthesis*, which itself becomes a new thesis as the process continues. The ultimate end of this ongoing sequence is said to be the disappearance of capitalism and the emergence of communism, under which there is no private ownership and each person receives his or her just due.

Critical criminology finds its heritage in the writings of Karl Marx (1818–1883), a German-born political economist who lived most of his adult life in London in genteel poverty (Sowell, 1985). Marx eked out a livelihood for his family writing newspaper pieces, many of them for a New York paper, and he was subsidized at times by his collaborator, Friedrich Engels (1820–1895). Engels's father owned a mill in Manchester, England.

The essence of the Marxist position lies in the idea of *surplus value*. In any economic system, people produce wealth. In a fair system, Marx maintained, they ought to share fully in the wealth they produce. Under capitalism, much of what they produce goes to those who control the resources and who thereby are able to exert power over the government and the way it does things. If, for instance, I own 1,000 shares of stock in General Motors, I will receive cash dividends on a quarterly basis, though I will have done nothing whatsoever to earn this money; the stock may be something I inherited. If I own enough stock, I can endlessly sun myself on the beaches as funds flow to me, funds made available through the labor of others. Those others, the workers, are receiving less than they deserve, critical theorists insist, while I am getting more than I deserve. This situation puts them and me into conflict, because I would prefer to get even higher dividends—by reducing salaries, for instance, or firing people or, at the very least, working them as hard as possible to increase their productivity. They, on the other hand, have an understandable interest in keeping more of the wealth that they have produced and reducing my share.

Causes of Juvenile Delinquency

From such conflicts of interest between capitalists and workers, crime and delinquency are believed to be generated. In regard to delinquency, for instance, there will be pressure on a manufacturing company to hire more girls and women because they can be paid less money—at least, this was so before affirmative action and comparable worth became national issues. Moving women out of their homes and into factories could be a cause of misconduct on the part of their unsupervised children. Similarly, prostitution is regarded by Marxists as a consequence of low wages that keep a laborer from getting married and force him to resort to the sexual services of a prostitute. The prostitute herself is said by critical theorists to be made to enter that trade because of the absence of satisfactory employment opportunity (Barnett, 1976). Similarly, in Sinclair's (1983:21) view, "during the Industrial Revolution, the availability of children for exploitable labor was used by industrialists as a lever to pressure the larger work force to labor for lower wages." Sinclair suggests that the juvenile justice system originated because of fear among persons in the upper classes of youngsters who were neither in school nor employed. Juvenile delinquency, she maintains, was "invented" in order "to ensure the perpetuation of the rule of the bourgeosie and its concept of childhood." The following is Sinclair's reform agenda (1983:25):

> there can be but one real solution to our juvenile justice problem, the radical/Marxist theorists agree—a humane socialist society which would eliminate the feelings of powerlessness and inadequacy of the young. . . . No one group would be predestined to occupy the lowest paying, most menial jobs. Every job in society would be given dignity and all members of society would share in these jobs which must be performed. The elimination of competition, the guarantee of a decent living, the elimination of the excessive accumulations of private property and wealth would create a true democracy.

Delinquency, then, is seen as no more nor less than the consequence of the capitalistic economic system. Colvin and Pauly (1983), for instance, offer what they call a "structural-Marxist" theory of "serious patterned delinquent behavior." They suggest that under capitalism the lives of lower-class youths are marked by "coercive . . . relationships encountered in various socialization contexts," such as the home, the family, and the workplace. The experiences of lower-class youths, it is argued, produce negative or alienated bonds that lead to serious delinquency. This alienation is done to the potential delinquents both "by deliberate design and subtle mechanisms" (1983:537). In school, for instance, intelligence tests for tracking are said to be ruling-class tactics to keep working-class youths down. The intelligence tests, Colvin and Pauly argue, measure "initial bonds," which are poorer in lower-class families, and not innate intelligence. Youths programmed to fail are kept from the mainstream of society, and they bond with peers who are the same as themselves and inevitably come into conflict with the legal authorities. Under a communist regime, critical theorists insist, delinquency would completely disappear because there would be no reason whatsoever for persons to commit acts against others or against the state, since they are not themselves being victimized and the state essentially is themselves: to act against it would be to act against their own best interests.

Criticisms of Critical Theory

A notable difficulty with this view of delinquency has been the absence of evidence that would substantiate it in those societies claiming to follow Marxist principles. Those sympathetic with communism, for instance, find the continuing high level of delinquency in the Soviet Union embarrassing. Critical criminologists in the United States and the United Kingdom often dismiss the issue by saying that the Soviet Union is not truly a communist society and therefore does not offer an accurate test of Marxist principles. Writers in the Soviet Union themselves are apt to engage in a form of double-talk when trying to interpret delinquency in their midst. "It is," Sakharov (1977:37) writes more than half a century after the Russian Revolution, "an abominable heritage of the past that ultimately will disappear totally." Sakharov notes that several Soviet writers have concluded that biological factors must be regarded as the primary cause of delinquency, because there is absolutely nothing in the social structure of their country that might account for the phenomenon, but he dismisses this explanation in favor of one suggesting "a lag of social consciousness behind reality" (1977:47); that is, persons in the Soviet Union continue to commit delinquent acts because they do not adequately understand that they have no reason to do so. Sakharov does grant that there may be "unsatisfied needs" in the country that could cause lawbreaking. These are said to be the function of things such as crop failures, war, and natural catastrophes, matters that are but "temporary and transitional." The entire analysis by Sakharov, self-conscious and fundamentally unpersuasive, is in accord with Engels's dictum that under a communist regime "the motivations for stealing will be eliminated" and "only the mentally ill will steal."

Explanations for the ongoing delinquency problem in Cuba take much the same form as those manifested in the Soviet Union. The remnants of capitalist thought often are blamed, and it is maintained that Cuban youths are the targets of a concerted effort by the United States aimed at their corruption. There also are fears that the selection of the most promising students for study in special schools may create an elite group, whose existence will contribute to jealousy and subsequent delinquency. Fidel Castro, leader of the government, addressed this point in a recent speech:

> Sometimes too much is allowed and all faults are tolerated. Thus there are some parents that, if their child comes home with a towel or some other object which is not theirs, force him to return it, make him apologize and criticize his actions. There are also other parents who do not yet have the consciousness . . . so that we sometimes have cases of theft in schools.
>
> Another way that families influence their children negatively is that . . . because they made a foreign trip, or because a friend brought them some gift, immediately adorn the child with the foreign gift. . . . Leave it home and don't

allow the child to come to school with this superspecial gift which the others do not have and cannot have. (Salas, 1979:26–27)

The data available to us from Cuba on juvenile delinquency are far from complete, but it seems from what we know that it differs there very little from what is found in other socialist and in capitalist societies. It appears to be concentrated among lower-class urban male youths with low educational achievement. Property offenses constitute the largest category of juvenile crime, with consumer goods such as clothes, radios, and tape recorders most sought after by offenders. The overrepresentation of adherents of Afro-Cuban religions seems to indicate, Salas (1979:33–34) notes, that race still may be a factor to consider. Cuba also has juvenile gangs that seem to be very similar to those found in capitalist societies.

Recent Thought

The critical theorists have in recent years often fallen to quarreling among themselves, debating over abstruse points of doctrine. Debate (see, for example, Norrie, 1982) sometimes concentrates on precisely what it was that Marx meant in some relatively ambiguous writing rather than on the accuracy of one or another critical viewpoint.

Some critical theorists believe that all delinquents should be regarded as victims of a mean-spirited political and economic system in Western societies. Others believe that Marx preached that criminals were to be ruthlessly cast aside rather than glorified as martyrs, that these offenders constituted a *lumpenproletariat*, that is, a bunch of thugs who prey upon members of the working class and hold back the aspirations of that class for revolution. Marx and Engels scathingly described the lumpenproletariat as a

parasitic class living off productive labor by theft, extortion and beggary, or by providing "services" such as prostitution and gambling. Their class interests are diametrically opposed to those of the workers. They make their living by picking up the crumbs of capitalist relations of exchange, and under socialism they would be outlawed or forced to work. . . . They are open to the bribes and blandishments of the reactionary elements of the ruling classes and the state; they can be recruited as police informers and the armed elements of reactionary bands and "special" state forces. (Hirst, 1972:41)

Besides providing a taste of the special kind of rhetoric used by critical theorists, the quotation highlights the derogatory attitude held by some Marxist writers toward criminal offenders, a position in sharp contrast to that of others who regard them as political victims of an unfair system (see e.g., Quinney, 1973).

In addition, the postulates of critical theory, like those of psychiatry, have not proven readily adaptable to the demands of science. Most of the statements are not susceptible to proof or disproof; they have to be accepted or rejected as a matter of faith. When crude empirical tests are at times attempted, the theories often prove inadequate. Sharpe (1984:14), for instance, has pointed out that the Marxist insistence that capitalism and crime go hand in hand does not hold up when the rates of lawbreaking in preindustrial and capitalistic England are analyzed: the rates "do not seem to have changed much between the fourteenth century and 1800," he notes.

In a thorough review of the contributions and standing of critical theory, Shichor (1980:14–15) reaches the following conclusions:

1. There is a tendency to oversimplification because of the limitation of explanation of lawbreaking to basically one factor, namely political-economic power relationships.
2. There is an overpoliticization of crime, so that crime becomes political activity and many political activities become defined as crimes.
3. Critical theory has been marked by an opposition to reform measures since they tend to reinforce the current system. Critical theorists often support intolerable circumstances rather than desirable change because they believe that the worst possible conditions will produce unrest and revolt. Such an attitude can be regarded as cold-bloodedly expedient and indicative of a lack of sensitivity about immediate human needs.
4. There is failure to acknowledge that, so far, societies that have followed the Marxist line are totalitarian, tend to use repressive measures more readily than most capitalist societies, and have a ruling class that is neither open nor easily approachable.
5. The theories have been marked by an overemphasis on political activism with a corresponding neglect of research. Much of the work seems to represent ideological posturing, rhetoric, or criticism of others.
6. Critical theorists possess an oversimplified view of capitalist society and its legal system.

Obviously, the final verdict on the relationship between economic and political systems and their effect on the type and kind of juvenile delinquency has not yet been rendered. It may well be that what appear to be high rates of crime and delinquency in some capitalist countries are a function of a relatively high degree of freedom that they offer in comparison with the totalitarian regimes. It is far easier to discourage and to control crime when the government is willing and able to adopt tyrannical countermeasures in the name of order. Chile under a right-wing dictatorship seems less crime-ridden than Brazil, under a more democratic regime. The same seems true of East and West Berlin. In this regard, delinquency may be a consequence of better living conditions, and perhaps of more glaring distinctions between the have-nots and the haves. Such a possibility, of course, requires much better demonstration before it can be accepted, but it is in line with the views of at least one set of highly regarded scholars:

> The evidence is substantial that social, industrial, and commercial progress is accompanied by an increase in criminal activity. For as you expand the bounds of human freedom and economic and social potential, you equally expand the bounds of potentiality for nonconformity and delinquency and crime. As legitimate opportunities increase so also do illegitimate opportunities. (Morris and Hawkins, 1970:49)

Differential Association _____

Edwin H. Sutherland (1883–1950)

The theory of differential association is undoubtedly the best-known and the hardiest survivor among all the explanations put forward in the United States to account for lawbreaking behavior. The theory has been widely criticized, largely on the ground that it is just about impossible to test. It also has been said to represent too great an emphasis on selected principles of learning theory, that is, of ways in which people acquire information and ideas on the basis of which they act. But despite a long record of hard handling, differential association remains widely known and basically important. Its importance perhaps rests most fundamentally on three conditions: (1) the enunciator of the theory, Edwin H. Sutherland, is generally regarded as the keenest intellect to have addressed sociological issues of crime and delinquency; (2) Sutherland taught several scholars who themselves have made outstanding contributions to the field and have kept alive his ideas, persons such as Donald R. Cressey and Albert K. Cohen; (3) Sutherland incorporated his ideas into what continuously was the best-selling textbook in criminology, a volume that (revised after Sutherland's death by Cressey) went through ten editions between 1924 and the 1980s; (4) Sutherland's theory of differential association makes a good teaching vehicle; its postulates are set out in an orderly manner, and its logic can be impressive; and (5) the theory represents a repudiation of psychiatric ideas and thus fits well with the general social emphasis in thinking about juvenile delinquency in the United States.

The theory of differential association first appeared as a systematic formulation in 1939 in the third edition of Sutherland's *Principles of Criminology*, although the basic ideas involved in it had been expressed in partial form in earlier editions of the text. Sutherland regarded it as a comprehensive scheme that might be applied to account for most, if not all, lawbreaking behavior. Sutherland himself seemed to vary in his assessment of the sophistication of the theory. At times, he indicated that it was a rough, tentative formulation that required considerable fine tuning. But in the latter part of his career he often came to its defense with acumen and vigor.

Sutherland had come to the study of crime and delinquency by a route familiar to many early workers in the field. His father was a prominent Baptist minister who spent most of his adult life as president of a sectarian college in Grand Island, Nebraska. Sutherland was regarded as a person "imbued with sincerity and objectivity," "soft-spoken," a man of "paternal wisdom" (Odum, 1951:348). Of Scottish heritage, he received his A.B. from Grand Island College and his Ph.D. from the University of Chicago, first enrolling in the Divinity School but later switching to sociology. His explanation for the change in major subjects foreshadows his theoretical notions of the importance of association on behavior. He wrote:

> When I entered Dr. Henderson's [sociology] course, I received personal attention. He spoke to me, knew me, was interested in me. Consequently, I was interested in pursuing sociology, and interested in the type of sociology that Professor Henderson presented. (Geis and Goff, 1983:xiv)

Sutherland taught for six years at William Jewell College in Liberty, Missouri, then at the University of Illinois, the University of Minnesota, the University of Chicago, and finally, and for most of his career, at Indiana University. Albert K. Cohen, whose work we discussed earlier, recalls a seminar that he took with Sutherland at Indiana:

> It was not only that we felt that Sutherland was at the frontier, we felt that we were at the frontier. Although most of us were beginning graduate students, we felt that we were participating in this work of pushing back frontiers. I believe that any of Sutherland's students of those days will tell you that Sutherland, for all the tenacity of his views, was never overbearing, never didactic, never arrogant. He invariably treated his students with respect, never humiliated them, always made them feel that we were partners in a quest. (Geis and Goff, 1983:xxviii)

The Theory and Criticisms of It

Sutherland's best-known contribution to criminology was the coining of the phrase *white-collar crime* and the production of a book and several pioneering articles on the subject. White-collar crime, like street crime and juvenile delinquency, was said to be explicable by his theory of differential association. The theory contains nine integral points (Sutherland and Cressey, 1978):

It begins by asserting that *criminal behavior is learned*. Many persons have objected to the broad brush with which this point is painted, noting that it is possible to stretch the term *learning* to include virtually any aspect of behavior —even those that appear spontaneous. The chief objection has been the use of learning to account for a variety of casual, occasional, or episodic delinquent behaviors. Does a youthful arsonist need to learn how to set fires, or is it more reasonable to presume that he knows how to light a match and presumably on his own makes the connection between a legal lighting of, say, a cigarette and the illegal torching of a dwelling?

Explicating the first point, Sutherland specifies as a second point that *criminal behavior is learned in interaction with other persons in a process of communication.* This broad formulation merely fleshes out in general terms how we come to learn things from others. There is little precise indication of the actual procedures by which a delinquent orientation is transmitted. In fact, it seems very likely that the point made may be accurate only in the most general sense: delinquent acts certainly seem possible to learn from the mass media or other stimuli: there is, indeed, a considerable literature that maintains that television and pornography both inculcate ideas of delinquent behavior that require no mediation by other persons.

While there can be little doubt that in certain environments, delinquents learn from others a variety of delinquent norms, there is no gainsaying that such learning seems to have different outcomes for those exposed to essentially the same kinds of persons. Kobrin (1951) showed that in depressed areas, youngsters experience a variety of conflicting types of interactions—some with delinquent emphases, others nondelinquent, and still others antidelinquent. It frequently seems to be an accident or adventitious circumstance that creates delinquent behavior. Certain criminal careers emerge without any delinquency in a person's background, whereas other active delinquents cease lawbreaking

The essence of differential association theory is that behavior, legitimate and illegitimate, is learned in intimate interactions with other people.

as they grow older. The process by which such things occur seems more complicated than merely determining whom they interact with and how: indeed, a standard (and not particularly fair) criticism of differential association is that it ought to predict enormous criminal behavior among prison guards, because they associate to a great extent with inmates. But Sutherland, as we shall see, implies more than a mere count of interactions with other persons as the predictive basis of delinquent activity.

One of the more intriguing sidebars to Sutherland's position has been suggested by Short and Strodtbeck (1965) on the basis of their work with gangs in the city of Chicago. They discovered that boys dropped their association with their gang if the girl with whom they had been having sexual intercourse became pregnant. They married and the new husband used as an excuse for disaffiliation with the gang that "the old lady" (his wife) didn't want him "hanging out with the guys." This excuse was hardly an accurate statement; in most realms of his behavior, the husband did pretty much as he liked. But he appreciated that gang activity was dangerous, and he was willing to take refuge in an excuse that he knew would be accepted. If he withdrew from the gang, the chances that he would cease his lawbreaking career improved dramatically. Conversely, if his girl did not become pregnant, he would continue with the gang and probably end up in increasingly more serious difficulty with the law. The enigma raised by this set of circumstances, of course, is that the key variable separating the first group from the second group of gang members is the chance that a girlfriend would conceive. This is hardly the kind of circumstance upon which a convincing causal explanation of continuing delinquent behavior can be built, and it illustrates that the theories that we have, given the nature of the behavior being examined, might have to be kept at a general level, rather than reduced to a level of explanation that can account for the delinquent act of any particular individual.

If individuals acquiring delinquent habits or propensities were exposed only to situations, circumstances, and interactions of a delinquent nature, it would be relatively easy to comprehend how the process of communication brings about delinquent behavior. In view of the enormous variation in standards and personalities to which any individual in our society is exposed, it becomes exceedingly difficult to discern those critical elements that induce delinquency without the intervention of some additional principle.

Sutherland's third point is that *criminal behavior is acquired through participation within intimate personal groups.* This particular stress suggests that the roots of delinquency must be sought in the socializing experiences of the individual. Unfortunately, the process of socialization is far from being effectively understood by scholars. In most instances, the terms setting out such interpersonal processes have been descriptive and often tautological. Through the intervention of concepts such as role-playing, we assume that the individual will develop certain of the characteristics of family and age-level groups, though we cannot indicate how this process takes place. This problem becomes especially cogent when we recognize that the behavior to which the developing individual is exposed is often highly inconsistent.

Sutherland's fourth emphasis indicates that *the criminal learning process includes* not only techniques of committing crime but also the shaping of *motives, drives, rationalizations, and attitudes.* Techniques for delinquency can involve high degrees of skill: picking pockets (and not getting caught at it) demands a considerable adroitness (Maurer, 1955). Being a successful juvenile prostitute demands knowing how to hustle customers, collect money, buy protection, deal with a drunken or violent john, and a considerable number of other "qualifications."

Fifth, Sutherland attempts to narrow his focus by indicating the kinds of pressures that move the learning process in the direction of acceptance of illegal pursuits. Careful to keep his theory within legal definitions of behavior, Sutherland stipulates that *the specific direction of motives and drives is learned from definitions of the legal codes as favorable or unfavorable.* There is considerable ambiguity in this tenet: it suggests that at certain phases of our development we learn that our motives are either contrary or favorable to law codes on the basis of how the group about us reinforces our attitudes through its own views. The broad reference to "direction of motives and drives" almost leaves more questions unanswered than it clarifies. Besides, the development of delinquent attitudes seems to be not quite the studied or formal process that Sutherland describes. Before a person accepts the attitude, for example, that "only suckers work," a variety of subtle and reinforcing attitudes have to be absorbed, into which a knowledge of legality and illegality probably does not figure very much.

Sixth, Sutherland attempts to answer the dilemma posed by the issue previously noted by establishing the principle of "differential association," which represents the core of his theoretical position. According to this postulate, *a person becomes delinquent because of an excess of definitions favorable to violation of the law over definitions unfavorable to violation of the law.* This aspect of the theory indicates that understanding of delinquency can best be sought in the character of the associations an individual establishes. It was adherence to this position that made Sutherland a staunch opponent of the individualistic explanations of psychiatry. This doctrine, however, is extremely difficult to test. The difficulty is acknowledged by Cressey (1960), who suggests that quantification may be held as an ideal, but one unlikely to be realized, though the theory implies that it seeks to offer testable propositions. It is virtually impossible to determine with any accuracy how associations "favorable to the violation of the law" are established and to measure them in comparative terms. In the first place, identification with others and with behavior patterns involves a great many supporting, contrasting, and conflicting elements. Identification may be intimate with and even sympathetic to delinquent elements without necessarily producing delinquent behavior. It seems doubtful whether any standard of behavior to which an individual is exposed may be assessed wholly in terms of attitudes favorable or unfavorable to the law.

As a means of demonstrating with greater clarity the character of the associations that have a subsequent effect on behavior, Sutherland states his seventh point, that *differential association may vary in frequency, duration, priority, and intensity.* But there is no suggestion regarding which of these elements is apt to be more important than the others or, indeed, anything beyond this specification of elements of the learning process. Frequent contacts may promote feelings of boredom and indifference; one intense experience may overwhelm all prior learning — or it may not.

Sutherland's eighth point concerns the nature of learning and, again, is primarily a didactic statement of common behavioral science understanding rather than a contribution that moves the theory very far forward: *learning criminal and delinquent behavior,* Sutherland asserts, *involves all the mechanisms that are involved in any other learning.* The key problem is not that Sutherland is wrong; it is that he casts into the spotlight a theoretical problem that has plagued students of human behavior since time immemorial. If delinquency is to be understood as learned like anything else — say, basketball skills, cooking, patriotism, and flirting — then any theory that can unravel its ingredients will at the same time have to set before us an understanding of all human action. Sutherland's propositions can hardly pretend to approach so stunning an intellectual achievement and in that regard can be regarded as extraordinarily overambitious, or, perhaps, simplistic. Critics have at times faulted them on both of these grounds.

As his next-to-last proposition Sutherland stressed that *learning differs from pure imitation,* and his last point is a reminder that *while criminal behavior is an expression of general needs and values, it is not explained by these general needs and values because noncriminal behavior is an expression of the same needs and values.* This injunction, well taken, indicates that the oversimplified generalizations sometimes employed to account for delinquency — such as the view that a youth steals because he craves "esteem" or kills because he is "unhappy" or robs because he wants "money" — have no real scientific merit. Persons, criminal and noncriminal, are motivated by much the same needs and values. They become or do not become delinquents on the basis of their unique responses to common drives for prestige, happiness, success, power, wealth, and numberless other human aspirations. I may feel a pressing need for money and take an extra weekend job pumping gas, or try to borrow some from a friend, or shrug my shoulders and figure that this time I'll do without. Another person, feeling the same need, may hold up a fast-food outlet.

Cressey (1960), in later reviews of Sutherland's position, has acknowledged some of the reservations expressed here. According to Cressey, however, Sutherland's theory represents fundamentally an attempt to explain the epidemiology of crime, that is, the rates and distribution of the activity in the social structure, though it also is effective in indicating the ways in which individuals enter upon lawbreaking acts. Cressey suggests that differential association might appropriately be referred to as a principle rather than a theory.

The inability of differential association to lend itself to research represents its most severe handicap. After a thoroughgoing review of the Sutherland postulates, for instance, DeFleur and Quinney (1966:22) reached the following conclusion:

> The present analysis has shown the theory to be at such a high level of abstraction that it is not possible to test it directly with empirical data. In fact, until fundamental problems of taxonomy concerning criminal behavior and various factors associated with its etiology are clarified, empirical testing of the theory will remain a very difficult problem at best.

In the most sophisticated empirical test of differential association to date, Tittle, Burke, and Jackson (1986) concluded that favorable definitions increase criminal motivation and respondents' self-prediction of future criminal behavior for five offenses, but not for the smoking of marijuana. But the theory was found to leave out "some important variables" and to "fall considerably short" of completely explaining crime (1986:425).

In addition, the theory is unable to account for the processes by which individuals respond differentially to similar situations. Sutherland attempted to explain such differential responses by means of different perceptions individuals develop with respect to past associations (or differential association), but such an explanation is tautological, since it offers an explanation based upon the very principle it purports to examine. There is no way out of this dilemma unless we take into account the differences in human perceptions of the variety of common experiences to which individuals are exposed. This would involve some social-psychological concept of the reasons for variations in the human mechanisms of social response. As Hirschi and Rudisill (1976:19) have noted, differential association "by declaring individual properties irrelevant, or at least inessential, has had the effect of dampening interest in their exploration." Similarly, Mays (1963:87) faults Sutherland's theory for failure to take account of hidden or unconscious factors influencing behavior and for being "legalistic." The theory, he maintains, "takes us a little way and then abandons us to doubt." Nigel Walker (1965:95) has perhaps the harshest criticism of differential association. He believes it and many theories of crime and delinquency "begin with the observation of the obvious, generalize it into a principle, and are eventually reduced again to a statement of the limited truths from which they originated." It is notable that the last two critics of differential association are non-Americans. Scholars in the United States tend to be much more respectful of Sutherland's work, perhaps because he exerted so strong an influence on American criminology and their own studies.

Control Theory

Sources and Advantages of Control Theory

A particularly important reason for the current dominance of control theory as the interpretive schema for understanding juvenile delinquency is that, unlike differential association, it offers a considerable number of testable propositions. Such propositions take the form of "if-then" statements: if something exists, then it foretells that something will happen. Such formulations allow for experimental testing and confirmation and rebuttal, and many academics, by and for whom theories are to a considerable extent formulated, earn their living and reputations by experimentation.

Testable propositions are indeed what genuine science is all about, and in this regard control theory clearly has moved the study of juvenile delinquency several giant steps forward. Cohen and the team of Cloward and Ohlin examined writings about delinquents and browsed intellectually in the field before setting out their theories. Miller, trained as a social anthropologist, lived among gang members in Massachusetts and conveyed in a descriptive way his sense of those things which he thought important.

Control theory, on the contrary, is based on an elaborate series of questions administered to juvenile delinquents and nondelinquents in northern California. The differences in responses between the two groups are then tied, with consummate skill, into a series of "little" theories, and then these are wrapped into a package to contain the grander control theory itself.

The keynote work on control theory is that of Travis Hirschi (1969), appearing in his monograph *The Causes of Delinquency*. Hirschi, born in 1935 in Rockville, Utah, first propounded his theory on the basis of work done for his Ph.D. at the University of California, Berkeley. Hirschi takes his cue from a classic of sociology, Emile Durkheim's *Suicide*, in which the French theoretician wrote:

> The more weakened the groups to which [the individual] belongs, the less he depends on them, the more he consequently depends on himself and recognizes no other rules of conduct than what are founded on his private interests. (Durkheim, 1951:209)

The Theory

Essentially, control theory insists that adult-run institutions in the social system train and press those with whom they are in contact into patterns of conformity. Schools train for adjustment in society, peers press the ethos of success and conventional behavior, and parents strive to inculcate law-abiding habits in their youngsters, even, Hirschi stresses, parents who themselves play fast and loose with the rules. The theory rests on the thesis that to the extent that a youngster fails to become attached to the variety of control agencies of the society, his chances of engaging in delinquency are increased. This doctrine edges very close to self-evidence in its insistence that close affiliation with law-abiding people, groups, and organizations is predictive of law-abiding behavior, but it is notably rich in subordinate statements and findings, some of them far from obvious.

Four aspects of affiliation are addressed by the theory: (1) *attachment*, (2) *commitment*, (3) *involvement*, and (4) *belief*. (For students interested in mnemomic devices, these probably can best be recalled from memory as words beginning with *a, b, c,* and then *i*).

Attachment refers primarily to affectional ties with persons such as parents, teachers, and peers. *Commitment* refers to the cost factors involved in delinquent activity. People are committed to conventional activities and have invested something in their ultimate success, an investment that they are wary of risking in delinquent acts. Commitment might involve things such as the aspiration of going to college and obtaining a high-status job. *Involvement* concerns matters such as time spent on homework, that is, participation in activities related to future goals and objectives. *Belief* refers to a conviction about the legitimacy of conventional values, such as the law in general and criminal justice mandates in particular.

Hirschi insists that there is no important relationship between social class, as traditionally measured, and delinquency; thus, a person in any class — lower, middle, or upper — who defaults on liaisons with the important formative agencies in our society will be much more apt to find himself or herself on a path that ends in delinquent activities (see, however, Seagrave and Hastad [1985] for a different view). Among important considerations, control theory stresses strongly "the bond of affection for conventional persons." "The stronger this bond, the more likely the person is to take it into account when and if he contemplates a criminal act" (Hirschi, 1969:83). What happens essentially, the theory suggests, is that persons confronted with the possibility of behaving in a law-violative manner are likely to ask of themselves: "What will my mother — or my father — think if they find out?" To the extent that persons believe their parents will be disappointed or ashamed, and to the extent that they care that the parent will feel so, they will be constrained from engaging in the sanctioned behavior. Positive answers to the following two family-related questions also correlated with nondelinquent behavior: "When you come across things you don't understand, does your mother (father) help you with them?" and "Does your mother (father) ever explain why she (he) feels the way she (he) does?" (1969:90). In regard to items such as these, Hirschi (1969:91) reaches the following conclusion:

> The intimacy of communication between child and parent is strongly related to the commission of delinquent acts. Only five percent of the boys who often discuss their future plans and often share their thoughts and feelings with their fathers have committed two or more delinquent acts in the year prior to administration of the questionnaire, while 43 percent of those never communicating with their fathers about these matters have committed as many delinquent acts. . . . [But] those who spend much time talking with their parents are only slightly less likely than those who spend little time talking with their parents to have committed delinquent acts. All of which suggests that it is not simply the fact of communication with the parents that is crucial in affecting the likelihood that the child will recall his parents when and if a situation of potential delinquency arises.

School similarly is significantly related to delinquent and nondelinquent behavior. The better a student does in school, the less likely he or she is to have committed a delinquent act. In part, of course, doing well in school relates to ability, so that control theory came to insist that intelligence and delinquency have some association (Hirschi and Hindelang, 1977). Hirschi uses school issues as a stalking point to demonstrate how control theory differs from the strain theory of Cohen. He suggests that Cohen believes that delinquency is caused by lower-class boys' adopting middle-class values and, when unable to meet them, rebelling and transmuting and caricaturing such values. But Hirschi's nondelinquents, much more than the delinquents, respond positively to the question: "Do you care what teachers think of you?" and he believes this demonstrates the empirical strength of his position in contrast to strain theory ideas. Hirschi (1969:127) summarizes his views about school succinctly and generalizes them to the essence of his theoretical beliefs in these words:

> The boy who does not like school and does not care what teachers think of him is to this extent free to commit delinquent acts. Positive feelings toward controlling institutions and persons in authority are the first line of social control. Withdrawal of favorable sentiments toward such institutions and persons at the same time neutralizes their moral force.

There is, it seems, something in these words that might give pause. They indicate that obedience breeds conformity, and conformity eschews delinquency. But such an antidelinquency script has to depend heavily on the virtue of the authorities. The second and third sentences of the paragraph above are precisely the prescription that developed into unthinking adherence by the German youth to the terrible principles of the Nazi party before and during the Second World War (Becker, 1946). Ideally, an element of judgment intrudes into the situation, one in terms of which persons determine for themselves whether authorities *merit their approbation and emulation.* No such intermediate consideration is relevant for the theory itself: it presumes that the authorities are good and decent, and it advocates enhancing allegiance to them if delinquency is to be avoided.

Control theory takes a number of sideswipes at the gang theorists in passing, suggesting that they romanticize the bonhomie of gang existence. Persons most closely attached to their friends, Hirschi found, tend to be less delinquent than others. He believes that, folk wisdom aside, delinquents are not likely to make sacrifices to the requirements of the group, that delinquent gangs, unlike conforming groups, are marked by "distrust and suspicion" (1969:134; but see Giordano, Cernkovich, and Pugh [1986:1170], who argue that the "cold and brittle" image of delinquents' friendships and the "intimate fraternity" characteristics of those of nondelinquents are "oversimplified").

In addition, nondelinquents, control theory maintains, have high stakes in conformity: they want to achieve conventional goals. This, of course, is distinctively different from strain theory, which suggests that conventional aspirations are typically a source of motivation to delinquency. In this regard, smoking, "riding around in a car," and dating are discovered to be precursors and concomitants of delinquent behavior. Hirschi interprets this finding as indicative of premature striving for adult status, an inappropriate shedding of adolescent behavior that is associated with delinquency. Smoking for Hirschi is the equivalent in causal significance to the tattoo, "a starting point for the development of a delinquent self-image," and the earlier smoking is begun the more likely the child is to commit delinquent acts. Among those youngsters who spend five or more hours a week riding around in a car, the proportion having committed a delinquent act was found to be twice the proportion for those who spend no time in such activity. Similarly, those who found adolescence "boring" were more likely to be in the ranks of the delinquents.

In addition, belief in the moral validity of the law was consistently related to nondelinquent outcomes. Finally, ambition was shown to reduce the chances of delinquency: as Hirschi puts the matter (1969:227), "the greater one's acceptance of conventional (or even quasi-conventional) success goals, the less likely one is to be delinquent, regardless of the likelihood that these goals will some day be attained." Summarizing his position, Hirschi (1969:iii) notes the following:

> The theory I advocate sees in the delinquent a person relatively free of the intimate attachments, the aspirations, and the moral beliefs that bind most people to a life within the law. In prominent alternative theories, the delinquent appears either as a frustrated striver forced into delinquency by his acceptance of the goals common to all of us, or as an innocent foreigner attempting to obey the rules of a society that is not in position to make the law or to define conduct as good or evil.

Critiques of Control Theory

There are at least two fundamental vulnerabilities of control theory. First, it relies exclusively on responses to inquiries and not on behavioral measures. The responses, of course, are supposed to represent truly what the person actually believes and to correspond to how that person behaves. When I say that I am respectful of a teacher's opinion, Hirschi has to assume that I really am so, that I will in fact think twice about what a person in authority might believe of me before I commit a delinquent act. It is arguable that Hirschi's assumption is factually accurate. Second, the measure of delinquency on which control theory is based is a self-report measure, and again there has to be uncertainty about the accurate congruence between what persons say they do or have done and what in fact represents their behavior. So in essence control theory is a measure of the relationship between two sets of questionnaire responses, both of which may be only partially, if at all, accurate indicators of the behavior that they are presumed to determine. (See the discussion of the validity of self-report studies in Chapter 1.)

Later studies have also quarreled with and extended some of Hirschi's conclusions. Using questionnaires administered to 3,065 adolescents, Krohn and Massey (1980) concluded that commitment was more closely related to delinquent behavior than either belief or attachment and that control theory was more predictive for less serious than more serious offenses and for female more than male delinquency.

In addition, it has been said that Hirschi does not consider how the four elements of his theory—attachment, belief, commitment, and involvement—might act simultaneously in regard to delinquent behavior. Wiatrowski, Griswold, and Roberts (1981), in trying to distinguish statistically among all the elements of the theory, found that the important explanatory variables were attachment to parents, dating, attachment to school, belief, and involvement; in short, that "a different picture emerges than when applying simpler forms of analysis" (1981:537). These authors also believe that social class and ability are essential components of a schema of delinquency explanation. In addition, Hirschi has been criticized for assuming causal relationships among his variables, when only longitudinal data, which he does not possess, would support such a conclusion (Gomme, 1985:577).

Elliott and Voss (1974) further insist that, on the basis of data they collected, school failure itself contributes to delinquency, but after the person drops out his or her rate of delinquency declines significantly. So, as they see it, it is not the absence of attachment to the school that causes the delinquency, but rather the painful experiences of discomfort and failure while in the school system that trigger misbehavior. Elliott and Voss (1974:205) believe that "school is the critical context for the generation of delinquent behavior." The same authors disagree with Hirschi's observation that peer involvement inhibits delinquent activity. Instead, they report (1974:205) that "a strong commitment to one's peers was conducive to delinquency, regardless of the extent of delinquency in that group." For them, this suggests that "the peer culture itself is conducive to delinquency." This last finding has been further explicated by Thompson, Mitchell, and Dodder (1984:12), who point out that the validity of Hirschi's theory "rests almost entirely on his own research." They found, also employing questionnaires, that the relationship between delinquency and attachment to conventional attitudes diminishes to the point of being virtually nonexistent when the effect of delinquent companions is controlled; or, put another way, that delinquent companions as a causal explanation overwhelms the remainder of Hirschi's ideas about the roots of delinquency. They note that this conclusion might be taken as possible support for differential association theory as well as for refutation of control theory.

The dispute about the effect of dropping out of school on delinquency (see generally Natriello, 1986) is far from settled, however. Thornberry, Moore, and Christenson (1985), for example, recently reported what they believed were methodological shortcomings in previous studies. Their reexamination of the issue concluded that Hirschi is correct and Elliot and Voss incorrect and that there was an "ineluctable conclusion": that "dropping out of school is positively associated with later crime" (1985:3).

More recently, Hirschi (1983) has proposed, as an extension of control theory, that if a youngster works he is more apt to engage in delinquency because parents lose a certain degree of control and there is less dependence. But Gottfredson (1985), in a comprehensive test of the relationship between holding a job while in school and self-reported delinquency, discovered that working does not have an effect on delinquency. Nor does working have a detrimental effect on commitment to education, involvement in extracurricular activities, time spent on homework, attachment to school, or attachment to parents. Though working did decrease school attendance for some groups of students, these effects did not translate into increases in delinquent behavior.

Summary

This chapter has considered three major theories that play a significant role in present-day discussions of the causes and correlates of juvenile delinquency —critical theory, the theory (or principle) of differential association, and control theory. Each has strong adherents, persons who are persuaded that it offers the best insights into the genesis of youthful waywardness.

Critical theorists insist that it is a feckless enterprise to look at the individual delinquent in an effort to comprehend his or her behavior: delinquency's fundamental cause, they maintain, lies in the economic and political arrangements within the social system. They see capitalism and the profit motive as the real culprits in the creation of social ills. Class warfare, the critical theorists believe, underlies contemporary life in capitalist societies and results in the exploitation of those who are shut off from realization of the benefits that the society offers. These outcast persons resort to delinquent behavior in order to survive: their fate is the inevitable consequence of pressures exerted on them to be satisfied with less than a fair share of the benefits of the system. In this sense, delinquents are seen as political protesters, demanding that equity be established, so that they too can enjoy an adequate income, free access to education and medical care, regular employment at decent wages, and similar satisfactions. For them to gain such benefits, those who have more than they reasonably need would have to have things taken from them, because they will not readily yield up what they have. Thus, critical theorists often call for major social change that would produce rule by the "people" and the confiscation of what are seen as "ill-gotten" gains of the upper class.

On the specific issue of juvenile delinquency, critical theorists would argue, among other things, that the educational system is deliberately geared to create failures, because it is fashioned in the interests of the upper class. Slum schools get the poorest teachers, counsel minority students (who attend such schools because they cannot afford to live in better neighborhoods) into dead-end work, and aim to create a placid, tractable work force. Deliberate creation of a "satisfactory" rate of unemployment means that those who obtain work are careful to labor hard and uncomplainingly at wages less than the value they create because of fear of being laid off. Delinquents cannot adjust to the unappetizing lower-class existence and break the law to improve their conditions and add a bit of zest to their lives. They are punished in order to teach a lesson to those who might also be inclined to rebel, so that they can appreciate that delinquency is dangerous.

Critical theory enjoys a powerful position in some scholarly circles in capitalistic societies, particularly in social science thought in the United Kingdom and Canada. Critical theorists are particularly adept, as the title of the school indicates, at being critical: they can point out with considerable insight the apparent shortcomings of political-economic systems in which human beings are destined to enjoy very different fates, very often primarily because of the chance circumstance of who their parents are. Where critical theory falls very flat, its opponents claim, is in its blueprint for reform. It has difficulty finding any existing communist society that it can proclaim as having achieved the nirvana the critical theorists paint as the product of the elimination of capitalism; indeed, while considerable improvements have been made in some aspects of life in places such as China and Cuba, few persons would argue that they represent the Garden of Eden sites that the critical theorists seem to foretell. In particular, communist countries place restrictions upon human freedoms, most particularly the freedom to dissent openly and the freedom to travel freely. Nor are they willing to open up the political process to competing viewpoints. In Shanghai, for instance, more than 30,000 students rioted late in 1986, demanding freedom, democracy, and human rights (see generally Edward, Henkin, and Nathan, 1986). A powerful test of the claimed superiority of the critical doctrines might well be to allow freedom of movement to all peoples and to count the direction in which populations would go: there is no gainsaying that they would flow in great numbers from the socialist societies toward the capitalist world.

Recently, many critical scholars working in the field of delinquency have moved toward a more centrist position, abandoning what they label as the "left idealist" position for one called "left realist" (Lea and Young, 1984). They now argue for reforms typically advocated by liberals rather than revolutionaries, reforms such as tighter control of the police by citizen groups and making life inside prisons "as free and normal as possible" (Lea and Young, 1984:267).

Differential association, the second of the triumvirate of theoretical positions discussed in the chapter, is essentially a social learning theory, and it has enjoyed a very strong position in attempts to comprehend juvenile delinquency. Formulated by Edwin H. Sutherland, a leading scholar in the field, differential association is made up of a string of postulates that stress the introjection of attitudes favorable to lawbreaking as the precursor to violative actions. Major criticism of the Sutherland position has focused on an inability to operationalize its tenets in order to demonstrate their accuracy or falsity experimentally. It is also argued that the idea that criminal behavior is learned is tautological, if not positively incorrect. The formula would be true only if all behavior were learned, that is, if there were not genetic correlates of human action. The tautological nature of the position is seen in its retrospective character: it is easy enough to insist, after the act, that this or that factor played into the wrongdoing, but it seems improbable that examination of associations will allow satisfactory prediction of the delinquency before it occurs.

The third position, control theory, is the most popular explanatory system at the moment. Originated by Travis Hirschi, it is built upon a commonsensical idea, that the more attachments a youngster has to law-abiding persons and ideas, the more likely that youngster is to conform. In this sense, the theory represents an extension of differential association. But its particular strength is that it pinpoints with considerably more precision than other theories those elements of personal and social existence which appear to play a particularly powerful part in immunizing a person from delinquent acts. Such things as concern for the opinions of others, desire to succeed, and success in school are set out as matters that inoculate a young person against delinquency. In this regard, the postulates of control theory are readily susceptible to testing. Such tests have added considerable refinement and occasional rebuttal to the tenets first set out by Hirschi on the basis of his work with school pupils in northern California. For scientific purists control theory is susceptible to the criticism that it is built upon secondary sources, that is, upon responses to questionnaires (in contrast to behavioral samples) about attitudes and actions, in addition to questionnaires about delinquent behavior.

References

Adamson, Walter L. 1985. *Marx and the Disillusionment of Marxism*. Berkeley, Calif.: Univ. of California Press.

Barnett, Harold C. 1976. The Political Economy of Rape and Prostitution. *Review of Radical Political Economy* 8:59–68.

Becker, Howard P. 1946. *German Youth: Bond or Free*. London: Kegan Paul, Trench, Trubner.

Colvin, Mark, and Pauly, John. 1983. A Critique of Criminology: Toward an Integrated Structural-Marxist Theory of Delinquency Production. *American Journal of Sociology* 89:513–551.

Cressey, Donald R. 1960. Epidemiology and Individual Conduct: A Case from Criminology. *Pacific Sociological Review* 3:47–58.

DeFleur, Melvin L., and Quinney, Richard. 1966. A Reformulation of Sutherland's Differential Association Theory and a Strategy for Empirical Verification. *Journal of Research in Crime and Delinquency* 3:1–22.

Durkheim, Emile. 1951. Suicide [1897]. Translated by John A. Spaulding and George Simpson. New York: Free Press.

Edward, R. Randle, Henkin, Louis, and Nathan, Andrew J. 1986. *Human Rights in Contemporary China*. New York: Columbia Univ. Press.

Elliott, Delbert S., and Voss, Harwin L. 1974. *Delinquency and Dropout*. Lexington, Mass.: Lexington Books.

Ferrajoli, Luigi, and Zolo, Danilo. 1986. Marxism and the Criminal Question. *Law and Philosophy* 4:71–99.

Geis, Gilbert, and Goff, Colin. 1983. Introduction to *White Collar Crime: The Uncut Version*, by Edwin H. Sutherland, ix–xxxiii, New Haven, Conn.: Yale Univ. Press.

Giordano, Peggy G., Cernkovich, Stephen A., and Pugh, M. D. 1986. Friendships and Delinquency. *American Journal of Sociology* 91:1170–1202.

Gomme, Ian M. 1985. On the Statistical Testing of Causal Ordering in Delinquency Research. *Canadian Review of Sociology and Anthropology* 22:574–578.

Gottfredson, Denise C. 1985. Youth Employment, Crime, and Schooling: A Longitudinal Study of a National Sample. *Developmental Psychology* 21:419–432.

Hirschi, Travis. 1969. *Causes of Delinquency*. Berkeley, Calif.: Univ. of California Press.

———. 1983. Crime and the Family. In *Crime and Public Policy*, edited by James Q. Wilson, 53–63. San Francisco: Institute of Policy Studies.

———, and Hindelang, Michael J. 1977. Intelligence and Delinquency: A Revisionist Review. *American Sociological Review* 42:571–587.

———, and Rudisill, David. 1976. The Great American Search: Cause of Crime 1876–1976. *Annals of the American Academy of Political and Social Science* 423:14–22.

Hirst, Paul Q. 1972. Marx and Engels on Law, Crime and Morality. *Economy and Society* 1:28–56.

Kobrin, Solomon. 1951. The Conflict of Values in Delinquency Areas. *American Sociological Review* 16:653–661.

Kolakowski, Leszekk. 1978. *Main Currents of Marxism*. Translated by P. S. Fall. Oxford: Clarendon Press.

Krohn, Marvin D., and Massey, James L 1980. Social Control and Delinquent Behavior: An Examination of the Elements of the Social Bond. *Sociological Quarterly* 21:529–543.

Lea, John, and Young, Jock. 1984. *What Is to Be Done About Law and Order?* Harmondsworth: Penguin.

Maurer, David. 1955. *Whiz Mob.* New Haven, Conn.: College and Univ. Press.

Mays, John B. 1963. *Crime and the Social Structure.* London: Faber and Faber.

Morris, Norval, and Hawkins, Gordon. 1970. *The Honest Politician's Guide to Crime Control.* Chicago: Univ. of Chicago Press.

Natriello, Gary, ed. 1986. *School Dropouts: Patterns and Policies.* New York: Teachers College, Columbia Univ.

Norrie, A. W. 1982. Marxism and the Critique of Criminal Justice. *Contemporary Crisis* 6:59–73.

Odum, Howard. 1951. Edwin H. Sutherland, 1883–1950. *Social Forces* 29:348–349.

Quinney, Richard. 1973. *Critique of Legal Order: Crime Control in Capitalist Society.* Boston: Little, Brown.

Rostow, Eugene V. 1959. *Planning for Freedom: The Public Law of American Capitalism.* New Haven, Conn.: Yale Univ. Press.

Sakharov, A. B. 1977. On the Conception of the Causes of Crime in Socialist Society. *Soviet Law and Government* 15:37–54.

Salas, Luis. 1979. *Social Control and Deviance in Cuba.* New York: Praeger.

Seagrave, Jeffrey O., and Hastad, Douglas N. 1985. Evaluating Three Models of Delinquency Causation for Males and Females: Strain Theory, Subculture Theory, and Control Theory. *Social Forces* 18:1–17.

Sharpe, J. A. 1984. *Crime in Early Modern England, 1550–1750.* London: Longman.

Shichor, David. 1980. The New Criminology: Some Critical Issues. *British Journal of Criminology* 20:1–19.

Short, James F., Jr., and Strodtbeck, Fred L. 1965. *Group Process and Gang Delinquency.* Chicago: Univ. of Chicago Press.

Sinclair, Catherine M. 1983. A Radical/Marxist Interpretation of Juvenile Justice in the United States. *Federal Probation* 46 (June):20–28.

Sowell, Thomas. 1985. *Marxism: Philosophy and Economics.* New York: Morrow.

Sutherland, Edwin H, and Cressey, Donald R. 1978. *Criminology* 10th ed. Philadelphia: Lippincott.

Thompson, William E., Mitchell, Jim, and Dodder, Richard A. 1984. An Empirical Test of Hirschi's Control Theory of Delinquency. *Deviant Behavior* 5:11–22.

Thornberry, Terence P., Moore, Melanie, and Christenson, R. L. 1985. The Effect of Dropping Out of School on Subsequent Criminal Behavior. *Criminology* 23:3–18.

Tittle, Charles R., Burke, Mary Jane, and Jackson, Elton F. 1986. Modeling Sutherland's Theory of Differential Association: Toward an Experimental Clarification. *Social Forces* 65:405–432.

Vermes, Miklos. 1978. *The Fundamental Questions of Criminology.* Translated by I. Decsenyo. Leyden: A. W. Sijthoff.

Walker, Nigel. 1965. *Crime and Punishment in Britain.* Edinburgh: Univ. Press.

Wiatrowski, Michael D., Griswold, David B., and Roberts, Mary K. 1981. Social Control Theory and Delinquency. *American Sociological Review* 46:525–541.

PART III

Methods of Control

CHAPTER 7

Precedents for the American Juvenile Justice System

HIGHWAYMAN AT 17

BURGLAR AT 17

BURGLAR AT 18

MURDERER AT 19
HANGED AT THE TOMBS

PICKPOCKET AT 15

HIGHWAYMAN AT 18

PICKPOCKET AT 13

HIGHWAYMAN AT

With this chapter, we turn from ideas and theories about juvenile delinquency to a consideration of the ways in which society has responded to it. Much of our focus in this chapter will be on the development and characteristics of the American juvenile justice system. In the process we shall examine the early precedents for that system, looking mainly at the nineteenth century and at the institutions that served as a background for much that characterizes the juvenile justice system in our own time. In subsequent chapters, we shall explore the creation, evolution, and operations of the central institution of the modern juvenile justice system in America, the juvenile court. We shall see, as well, the ways in which young people find themselves under the court's jurisdiction, and those institutions whereby the juvenile court seeks to treat young offenders. We shall conclude this section, in Chapter 12, with a comparative look at juvenile justice systems in other societies.

In Chapter 2 we noted, as a main line of development in ideas about juvenile delinquency during the nineteenth century, the increasing sense of the distinctive characteristics of the child. In the American juvenile justice system prior to about 1900, the main line of development was consistent with this viewpoint. Above all, it involved a growing recognition that juvenile crime demands distinctive institutional responses and that laws and institutions designed for adult offenders are inappropriate for youngsters. In this chapter, we shall see how this recognition was put into practice in ways that led to the creation of a distinctive juvenile justice system and to the juvenile court.

Ancient and Medieval Responses to Juvenile Crime _____

To gain some perspective on the evolution of a distinctive juvenile justice system, it is useful to look back into history at the treatment of juvenile crime in earlier times. As we saw in Chapter 2, ancient and medieval societies lacked institutions specially oriented toward children, and children were dealt with primarily in terms of the institutions and needs of an adult world. What was true in the social realm was true in the legal realm as well. Those who dealt with children who broke the law often recognized that children could not be held to the same standards as adults. In particular, ancient and medieval jurisprudence acknowledged that young people could not always be expected to understand the difference between right and wrong as well as adults should. Nevertheless, Western systems of criminal justice provided no separate laws or institutions for juveniles even through the early modern period.

Roman Law

The best accounts of ancient responses to juvenile crime come from Rome. The early codification of Roman law, known as the Twelve Tables (c. 488–451 B.C.), made clear that children were criminally responsible for breaking the law and that such children were to be dealt with in the context of the larger criminal justice system (Nyquist, 1960). The only allowance made for young people was in the severity of punishment imposed for specific crimes. Thus, for example, under the Twelve Tables, theft of crops at night was considered a capital offense, but an offender under the age of puberty was to be given only a flogging. Similarly, an adult caught in manifest theft was subject to flogging and enslavement to his victim; a young offender would receive corporal punishment only at the magistrate's discretion and was required to make restitution rather than to enter slavery (Ludwig, 1955).

This basic approach to juvenile crime, in which children were held criminally responsible for breaking the law, though they might be treated with some leniency, remained in force throughout Roman history, although during the republic (c. 500–31 B.C.) and the empire (31 B.C.–A.D. 476), Roman law showed an increasing recognition of stages in life. In the Roman Empire, children were classified as *infans, proximus infantiae,* and *proximus pubertati.* In general, the child, if *infans,* was not held criminally responsible, while those approaching puberty were held liable if capable of understanding the difference between right and wrong. For much of Roman history, *infantia* meant simply the incapacity to speak, but in the fifth century A.D., this age was fixed at seven years, and youngsters under that age were considered wholly exempt from criminal liability. Puberty as a legal category was fixed at fourteen for boys and twelve for girls, and those above that age were held criminally liable. For children between seven and puberty, the key criterion seems to have been the apparent capacity of the child to distinguish between right and wrong (Nyquist, 1960; Jolowicz, 1957; Buckland, 1963).

Medieval Law

Laws from medieval Europe were not far different from those of ancient Rome. Medieval Teutonic law stood out in exempting young children from the full force of criminal prosecution, with different sources pointing to ages of criminal minority varying from seven to fifteen (Nyquist, 1960). The fragmentary evidence from Anglo-Saxon Britain indicates a system of laws that actually began criminal responsibility prior to age seven, with youngsters being liable even for capital punishment, although, during the reign of King Aethelstan (c. A.D. 924–939), the monarch ordered that "no younger person should be slain than XV years" (Ludwig, 1955:15–16; Sanders, 1970:4).

The English Common Law Tradition ⸺⸺⸺⸺⸺⸺

English medieval judgments and practices ultimately crystallized in the English common law tradition, a tradition of legal thought and practice that guided jurisprudence not only in Britain but in America as well. The term *common law* refers to that body of law, going back to the Middle Ages, that grew out of judicial decisions rather than resulting from specific legislation. In regard to juvenile offenders, it evolved into a fairly fixed form by the seventeenth and eighteenth centuries.

Following the Norman Conquest in 1066, and during much of the medieval period, English law held children criminally responsible from birth. However, it seems certain that few children under the age of seven actually faced legal penalties for criminal acts: pardons after conviction appear to have been virtually inevitable in such cases. Thus, by the 1300s, many English courts had come to treat even the formality of a trial as unnecessary in the disposition of a case involving a child under the age of seven. Although the practice of judgment and pardon remained a part of English criminal justice until about the middle of the fifteenth century, it ultimately withered away. Some time prior to 1600, such younger children ceased to be required to appear for trial on criminal charges (Ludwig, 1955).

Insofar as older children were concerned, specifically those between seven and fourteen, English common law evolved in much the manner of Roman law. Medieval jurisprudence did not provide blanket pardons for children in this age group but looked mainly to considerations other than chronological age in the disposition of cases: apparent maturity, severity of punishment for the crime, capacity to understand the difference between right and wrong, and evidence of malice were all taken into account by judges trying older children. Thus, again like Roman law, medieval English legal practices recognized a period of "conditional responsibility," preceding puberty, such that cases of such offenders had to be taken individually, with great attention being paid to the circumstances in which an offense had been committed (Ludwig, 1955).

By the seventeenth century, these practices, with roots in the Middle Ages and reinforced by Roman law, had become dominant in English law. Michael Dalton, to whom we referred in Chapter 3, bore this out, indicating that there was both some flexibility and some common practice in the administration of justice in his day. Describing, for example, the disposition of homicide cases, he wrote (Sanders, 1970:11):

> An infant of eight yeares of age, or above, may commit homicide, and shall be hanged for it, *viz.* If it may appeare (by hyding of the person slaine, by excusing it, or by any other act) that he had knowledge of good and evill, and of the perill and danger of that offence. . . . But an infant of such tender yeares, as that he hath no discretion or intelligence, if he kill a man, this is no felonie in him.

According to the great eighteenth-century English legal scholar William Blackstone, writing of seven- to fourteen-year-olds guilty of crime, "the capacity for doing ill, or contracting guilt, is not so much measured by years and days, as by the strength of the delinquent's understanding, and judgment," an approach to determining criminal responsibility that had been the practice from the fourteenth century (in Abbott, 1938:II, 342).

This English common law tradition also operated in the American colonies and was retained throughout the early period of American nationhood. Chancellor James Kent, whose *Commentaries on American Law* (1826–1830) were intended to systematize legal practices in the United States, echoed Blackstone's principle that "the responsibility of infants for crimes by them committed, depends less on their age, than on the extent of their discretion and capacity to discern right and wrong" (Kent, 1827:II, 191).

Such an understanding of juvenile crime, although it recognized at least the potential legal incapacity of the young offender, was something very different from the popular and theoretical ideas about juvenile crime that have developed in more recent times. The focus on the individual young offender and his or her capacity—central to both Blackstone and Kent—implied an utter lack of recognition of juvenile crime as a special *category* of offending. And it implied, as well, no duty on the part of society to respond in a distinctive institutional way to the youngster who was held liable for the commission of an offense.

The Punishment of Young Offenders in the Early Modern Era

General Attitudes. One measure of how unaware the early modern criminal justice system was of any special problems posed by juvenile crime may be seen in the fact that juvenile offenders were subject to the same punishments as those faced by adults. Since, prior to 1800, incarceration was almost unknown as a sentence, convicted juveniles, like their adult counterparts, were often subjected to rather harsh corporal punishment. Wiley B. Sanders, having collected a great number of cases heard in the Old Bailey between 1681 and 1836, finds many instances of severe corporal punishment inflicted upon youngsters convicted of crime. In 1686, for example, a ten-year-old boy found guilty of stealing thirty yards of "Lemon-colour'd Satin Ribbon" was ordered whipped (Sanders, 1970:23). In 1690, another ten-year-old boy, convicted of stealing two gold rings and some money, was ordered "burnt in the hand" (1970:26). Whipping and burning the hand were the most common forms of corporal punishment applied, regardless of the offender's age, and were exercised frequently as a part of English justice. Similar practices seem to have obtained in the colonies of North America.

No less common as a response to crime was the removal of the offender— adult or juvenile—from his or her old environment, chiefly through what was known as "transportation." In the seventeenth and eighteenth centuries, this could mean the sending of the offender to America or Australia. Paupers as well as criminals faced "transportation" during this period as the British Empire populated at least some of its dominions by sending its "undesirables" to new homes in new worlds.

About the only sanction specifically aimed at juvenile offenders was the occasional decision to bind a young offender out to a local tradesman as an apprentice, a practice pursued in the colonies as well. Given the presence of such an institution as apprenticeship aimed at young people between fourteen and twenty-one, it is not surprising that it should have been used as a way of dealing with delinquents. As we shall see, English law had long provided for a similar binding out of pauper children, and it was easy to extend the practice to delinquents. However, binding out seems to have been less frequently used by the courts than the more common forms of corporal punishment.

Capital Punishment. Finally, however, the courts could also impose capital punishment on any young offender over the age of seven, including children between seven and fourteen, should the court find them able to discriminate between right and wrong. During the period up to 1800, moreover, English— and American colonial—law recognized many crimes as capital offenses. According to Blackstone, in 1765–1769, the capital statutes in force numbered 160, and the number was growing: an 1823 estimate assessed the number as 200, and some authorities of about the same period believed it to be even higher (Radzinowicz, 1948). Children were subject to these laws; they could be sentenced to death.

And, in fact, children were sometimes sentenced to be executed. In 1690, for example, a fourteen-year-old boy, found guilty of picking pockets and of robbery, was sentenced to die and was hanged. In 1735, a ten-year-old girl, an apprentice who stole some money in her master's house, was sentenced to be executed. Others — described as children but of indeterminate age — received the same sentence during this period. And, of course, this practice was not confined to England, for the colonies, too, recognized many capital crimes and also subjected young people above the age of exemption to sentences of death. Indeed, some colonies, notably those settled by Puritans, had even stricter laws than the Mother Country. As we noted in Chapter 2, even incorrigibility was a capital offense in colonial Massachusetts.

It is difficult to know how often any sentences of death were carried out. For all the harshness of the Massachusetts law, for example, there were no cases in which such incorrigible youths were actually executed; usually they were taken from their parents and apprenticed to another family (Morgan, 1966). English history is also unclear. Often, it seems, very young children sentenced to die — those of, say, nine or ten — would ultimately have their sentences commuted to transportation (see, e.g., Radzinowicz, 1948). Then, too, as Anthony M. Platt has noted, the severity of the law might be mitigated simply by a refusal to prosecute or by securing a pardon. The scholar B. E. F. Knell, cited by Platt, surveyed some 103 cases of children, aged eight through thirteen, sentenced to death between the years 1810 and 1836 for stealing. Not one was actually executed (Platt, 1977:196–197). Nevertheless, capital punishment had been applied, if somewhat infrequently, well into the 1700s, and for older youth it was anything but unusual. Radzinowicz reports, for example, that, in 1785, eighteen of twenty offenders executed in London were under eighteen years of age (1948:14). Executions were rare, but not unknown, even into the nineteenth century.

Thus we see that in the English common law tradition, young offenders could receive lenient treatment, but, for those over the age of seven, leniency was by no means guaranteed. Moreover, and more significantly, except for the occasional imposition of an apprenticeship on a young offender, the English tradition offered no separate institutions for the handling of juvenile delinquents. Those who were accused of crimes and prosecuted for them went through the same court procedures and, if found guilty, faced the same punishments as did adults.

Toward a Legal Recognition of Juvenile Delinquency _____

During the nineteenth century in both England and America, much that we have seen in regard to the treatment of children by the legal system underwent great change. For many people, that children — even children who had committed crimes — should be treated as if they were only small adults was unthinkable, and the nineteenth century saw the triumph of their views in the criminal justice system, both here and abroad.

It is useful, at this point, to review some of the material we discussed in Chapter 2. As we saw there, the opening of the nineteenth century was the setting for major changes in Western conceptions of childhood and youth, summarized most simply by the emergence of the view of the child as a peculiarly malleable creature, easily molded to good or ill by the world around it. Such an emerging conception of childhood influenced not only notions of proper child-rearing techniques but thinking about those children who got into trouble. Rejecting such notions as infant depravity or inclinations to wrongdoing, many people began to question the kinds of influences to which young offenders were subjected, and, setting their sights on the reform rather than punishment of such youngsters, these people sought new approaches to solving the problem of juvenile delinquency.

As we also noted, America during the early years of the nineteenth century was a changing society, one in which the consciousness of juvenile crime was rapidly rising. In particular, urbanization and delinquency were closely connected in the minds of many, who believed that the children of the urban poor — and particularly the children of urban immigrants — were especially susceptible to the dangers of urban life and, thus, to delinquency. For these reformers, as we discussed in Chapter 2, the causes of delinquency were mainly environmental, and juvenile crime itself was seen as more of a moral problem than a problem for the criminal justice system. Again, it is here that we see the beginnings of our contemporary understanding of juvenile delinquency as a special category of deviant behavior. Not surprisingly, here, too, we see the bases of institutional responses to juvenile delinquency as such in the United States.

The Rise of Public Schooling: An Early Approach to Prevention

Education had long been understood by Americans to be a significant social force, a force for inculcating proper values and beliefs. It was a hallmark of Puritan child rearing, but elsewhere in colonial America, education had also been assigned great importance. With the emergence of the new nation, many people continued to see education as essential to the development of a healthy and prosperous American republic.

It is not surprising, then, that faced with the challenges of a changing America, and particularly with the challenges posed by immigration and urbanization, many men and women turned to education as a solution. There was a widespread belief, especially among those middle-class Americans who dominated early reform movements, that education could help bring the children of the urban and immigrant poor into the mainstream of American society and, thus, could help to prevent the problems that appeared to be increasingly pressing in urban life. Along with this, they believed that giving an education to poor and immigrant youngsters could do much to prevent juvenile crime. The school was, in fact, one of the first American attempts to create a distinctive institutional response to juvenile crime.

Some of the earliest educational efforts in this direction were privately supported. Throughout the opening years of the nineteenth century, reformers, philanthropists, and civic leaders encouraged the creation of "charity schools," "infant schools," and similar institutions whose purpose it was to educate but, above all, to inculcate discipline and "moral character" in the children of the urban poor (see Nasaw, 1979). Children from more affluent families could attend private schools in which more clearly intellectual concerns were thought appropriate.

This view of education as a barrier to delinquency was especially important, however, in the founding of the earliest American public school systems during the early part of the nineteenth century. The most notable of these systems was established in Boston even before the opening of the nineteenth century, and it served as a model for similar systems in other cities. Stanley K. Schultz, the foremost historian of the early days of the Boston public schools, has demonstrated the importance of preventing delinquency in the thinking of those who brought that system into being.

The Boston public school system was established by the Education Act of 1789, which provided for schools open to all residents of the city and was administered by a democratically elected board. From the beginning, the schools were expected to have moral as well as intellectual purposes, preparing Boston's young people to grow into virtuous and useful citizens. As Boston grew, the moral purposes came to seem increasingly important (Schultz, 1973). As Schultz (1973:254) points out, by the 1820s and 1830s, the champions of public education in Boston had assigned a crucial role to the schools in training the children of the "lower classes," making them more civilized and less of a potential threat to the social order.

Such views were not, of course, confined to Boston. Wherever proponents of public education sought to make their case they urged the power of education to uplift the masses and, thus, to help prevent crime and delinquency. As Kaestle (1976) has shown, there was an important measure of democratic ideology in the argument for public schooling, for its proponents urged education as a basis for equality of opportunity. But, as he has rightly stressed, the key was always an "overriding concern for the poor and the immigrant," with emphasis on the power of education to lessen the apparent danger such people — and their children — posed to society (Kaestle, 1976:183). Kaestle describes the argument for free schooling in England in words that apply to the United States as well. The proponents of public schooling in Boston, New York, Philadelphia, and elsewhere argued that, in Kaestle's words, "Prevention was better than punishment. Wherever schools were opened, prisons would be closed" (1976:181).

The establishment of public schools in the United States was strongly influenced by the growing concern about delinquency in the early nineteenth century. The belief that schooling could help to prevent delinquency was the product of that environmentalism and that reevaluation of childhood which we saw in Chapter 2.

The Houses of Refuge

Still, whatever the hopes of those who put their trust in public education, juvenile crime was a fact of life in early-nineteenth-century America, and many men and women turned their attention not only to the possibilities of preventing delinquency but also to the difficult question of how society could best respond to those juveniles who committed crimes. But the reformers' approach to that question was not that which had been addressed by Blackstone or even Kent, who focused on legal issues of capacity and prosecution. For many men and women, it was more one of how society should respond to juvenile offenders in a way that fully respected the unique character of the child. One of the earliest answers, and one of the most influential, lay in the early-nineteenth-century movement in various parts of the United States to create what were called "houses of refuge."

To understand this movement, it is necessary to remember that, as we have already noted, in English tradition and in colonial America, juveniles guilty of crime were subject to roughly the same punishments that faced adult offenders. This continued to be the case in the early nineteenth century, when the use of imprisonment as a punishment for crime came to be fairly common in both England and America. It is easy to forget that the use of prison in this way is a relatively recent practice, datable to about the end of the eighteenth century. Prior to that, most punishment — apart from "transportation" — was corporal and was inflicted fairly swiftly. Public whippings, confinement in stocks or pillories, forms of mutilation such as cropping the ears, or, of course, punishment by death awaited most of those convicted of crimes. Jails served mainly to hold people awaiting trial or awaiting punishment; they were places of detention, not of punishment. Beginning in the late eighteenth century, however, one may see in Western thinking a general revulsion against brutal treatment of criminals. Prison came to be seen as a humane alternative to older forms of punishment, and confinement came to appear a more appropriate response on society's part to criminal acts.

In the early days, this new approach was readily applied to juveniles as well. Thus, in New York in 1820, a boy eight years old was convicted of burglary in the theft of a jewelry box, and the judge sentenced him to three years in the state prison (Bremner, 1970). Though younger than most, he probably did not lack youthful companions when he got there, nor would others. About seventy-five boys aged twelve to sixteen were sentenced to prison in New York each year. Although there were some differences in the treatment of children in prison — boys were not, for example, put to labor — they were, in general, allowed to mix with the adult convicts as members of the general prison population.

This last fact was, to many, an unconscionable state of affairs. As we saw in Chapter 2, children were coming to be seen as quite malleable creatures, easily made to respond to powerful influences. In a strong family, for example, children would come to feel awe and respect for their parents and could be molded into upright citizens. However, when children were exposed to bad influences, then the opposite result would be likely to prevail. And mixing with adult criminals in jail meant that young offenders were exposed to the worst influences of all. As a group of New York reformers reported to that city's common council, given the mixing of children with adult criminals in prisons, "it is in vain to expect that a sentence condemning a child to the Penitentiary will have any beneficial effect on his morals; on the contrary it is probable that his vicious inclinations will be strengthened by association with experienced Villains" (in Abbott, 1938:II, 344). For these reformers, what was needed was a way to separate juvenile criminals from adults. Only in this way could young people who had gone wrong be properly removed from an evil environment and, thus, be remade into good and useful adult citizens.

The perception of a need for separate facilities was not entirely original in the early nineteenth century. As far back as the 1730s, the English philosopher George Berkeley had proposed the setting up of "bettering houses for bringing young gentlemen to order," and, indeed, he saw excellent precedent for such "houses" in similar ones that had been tried earlier in Amsterdam (Radzinowicz, 1948:263). In 1758, Sir John Fielding had established a house of refuge for orphan girls in London, meant especially to save such girls from prostitution (Sanders, 1970). In the 1770s, the English reformer John Howard, having been impressed by the house of refuge in Amsterdam, recommended a thorough-going reform of English prisons, noting especially the corruptibility of juvenile inmates and urging, too, the separation of inmates by both age and sex (Hawes, 1971). In 1788, the Philanthropic Society of London opened an institution to serve the children of convicts along with other poor and delinquent children. However, such efforts were, at best, isolated and had not spread far, certainly not to North America.

The New York House of Refuge. Nevertheless, concerned about both the growing problem of juvenile delinquency and the imprisonment of young children, many Americans began to take more seriously the need for a special institution for juvenile offenders. The pioneering effort to alleviate this problem took place in New York, where, under the leadership of John Griscom and Thomas Eddy—the latter of whom was also active in educational efforts directed toward the city's poor—a group began serious discussions of what they called "the perishing and dangerous classes" of the city. This resulted in the founding, in 1817, of the Society for the Prevention of Pauperism in New York City. With Griscom as chair, the society quickly recognized that juvenile delinquency was the most pressing problem related to pauperism and, in keeping with the general attitudes of reformers from this period, that "the children of neglectful, intemperate, vicious parents, and those which are trained to sin, should be *saved from prison,* even though they may have been guilty of actual crime." As Griscom himself argued, "an institution was wanting in which juvenile delinquents might be taken care of, and rescued from the inevitable ruin which awaits them when thrown into bridewells and prison, in company with adult criminals" (John Griscom, 1860:337).

Others joined Griscom in his concern for juvenile delinquents, and by the end of 1823, enough sentiment had developed for the creation of such an institution for juvenile offenders for Griscom to call a public meeting on the subject. This meeting led to the founding of the Society for the Reformation of Juvenile Delinquents, a new organization intended to agitate at both the city and the state level for the establishment of institutions devoted solely to the correction of juvenile offenders (Hawes, 1971). The need for such institutions was clear, given the organization's leading ideas. In a petition to the state legislature, organization leaders appended a long list of juveniles, most between ages eleven and fourteen and many arrested only for being homeless, who had been committed by the courts to a penitentiary. A house of refuge, its proponents urged, would provide "a course of treatment, that will afford a prompt and energetic corrective of their vicious propensities, and hold out every possible inducement to reformation and good conduct" (in Abbott, 1938:II, 348). On January 1, 1825, with six boys and three girls, the house of refuge began its operations in New York (Hawes, 1971).

Within a few years, other, similar houses of refuge were established in other American cities. Boston established its House of Reformation in 1826, and Philadelphia, its own House of Refuge in 1828. All of these institutions were fairly similar in organization and purpose. Each, like the New York one, was founded by private individuals and, while receiving some state financial support, was primarily dependent on private money and management. In addition, all the early houses took in as inmates not only youngsters who had been convicted of crimes but also some who appeared likely to fall into crime — orphans or abandoned children, vagrants, and, in a few cases, those found unmanageable by their parents. Children assigned to the houses were given indeterminate sentences — they were to stay until the managers believed a reformation had been accomplished (or until the youngster reached adulthood) and not for any predetermined length of time (Beaumont and Tocqueville, 1833).

Order and Discipline in the Houses of Refuge. The houses were also quite similar in having strict, regular orders of discipline, justified on the basis of the delinquent's apparent need for such elements in his life. These systems not only were based on concepts of juvenile delinquency but cohered, as well, with general trends in thinking about crime and punishment. For adult prisons as well as juvenile houses of refuge, the belief was widely accepted that inmates needed exposure to a life of order and discipline — both as a measure designed to assist in rehabilitation and as one necessary to keep the institution functioning (Rothman, 1971). In the house of refuge, the quest for order took shape in several ways.

The most obvious measure for reinforcing order in the houses of refuge lay in adherence to very tight daily schedules, with regular hours for rising and retiring, meals at set times, and regular periods set aside for workshop training and for schooling. Although there might be some seasonal variations, the schedule was to be observed daily, without deviation. In addition, supplementing both the orderliness of the schedule and the aims of the houses of refuge, regular hours were set aside daily for religious observances and prayers (Beaumont and Tocqueville, 1833; Bremner, 1970).

Both orderliness and the aims of reformation were served, too, by an effort to classify all of the inmates according to their moral conduct, from best to worst, with members of each group receiving differing privileges and privations. In Boston, inmates were divided into three "Bon Grades" and three "Mal Grades," those in the highest "Bon Grade" being "those who make *positive*, REGULAR, and CONTINUED effort to do right," while those boys "who are *positively*, REGULARLY AND CONTINUALLY inclined to do wrong" were committed to the lowest "Mal Grade." Boys in the first "Bon Grade" were actually allowed to leave the house on their own, to be trusted, to wear "the undress uniform," and to receive other privileges. Those in the lowest "Mal Grade" faced severe privations — including a diet confined to bread and water, wearing shackles, or solitary confinement (Beaumont and Tocqueville, 1833:221).

Such a strict approach to discipline was the hallmark of the house of refuge system. Although all of the houses depended on a monitoring system, in which elected inmates were chosen to watch over the others, it was very clear that, as one observer of the Boston house wrote, "The boys are and ever have been . . . under the sole absolute control of the superintendent," and, he added with approval, "The extent of their subjection, we might say devotedness, can be conceived by those only who have witnessed it. . . . Each boy knows that whatever he is commanded to do, he *must* do, and, the necessity being apparent, he does it" (House of Reformation, 1832:385). However, for those who did depart from the rules of discipline, punishment was to be swift and sure. Its main forms involved the loss of privileges. Corporal punishment was to be used only as a last resort. Nevertheless, as one may have noted in looking at Boston's lowest "Mal Grade," punishments could be as severe as a bread-and-water diet or solitary confinement. Or, as one writer noted, punishment might even take a more innovative twist, as in this Boston classroom (House of Reformation, 1832:383):

> In one room a large boy was reading aloud to several smaller ones. He had a badge, and was a monitor. One of his auditors had a bandage over his eyes, which he did not offer to remove. He had abused the use of his vision in not attending to his book, and was therefore deprived of it. We learned that the system of privations, practised in the house, is an improvement on the Jewish law of "an eye for an eye, and a tooth for a tooth." If a boy make an improper use of his hands, they are confined; if his eyes depart from their proper object, they are bandaged.

Through such privations, and their threat, discipline was to be maintained.

We have already noted that children guilty of crimes and those thought to be potential criminals could alike be committed to a house of refuge, but it must be stressed again that the guiding principle behind any committal was a belief on the part of city officials that the child could not receive a proper upbringing from his or her own parents. This may have been the most significant feature of the house of refuge, and it was also, in some ways, the most controversial.

Parens Patriae

A key assumption made by the house of refuge system was that, in certain situations, the state had a right, for its own good and for the good of the child, to intervene in the life of a family and to take over the upbringing of a child, and that the matter was more one of social concern than of criminal justice as narrowly conceived. In the house of refuge system this meant that children could be committed to the institution without regard to the rights of either the child or its parents. This was true even to the point where children were committed with no regard for due process of the law; certainly without regard to the usual right of trial by jury (Fox, 1970). Moreover, because sentences to the house of refuge were indeterminate, parents lost all control over their children, too. Schlossman (1977:27) quotes the manager of the New York house as claiming, in 1829, "Parents or guardians, from the time [the child] is legally sentenced to the Refuge, lose all control over its person." The state thus assumed enormous powers under the house of refuge system. How was this assumption of powers justified?

The justification was, in fact, both formal and traditional. The formal justification was elaborated in the 1830s, in the United States, in the invocation of a legal doctrine known as *parens patriae*. A doctrine of somewhat uncertain origin, but with roots in the Middle Ages, *parens patriae* was an assertion of the right of the state to assume the wardship of a child when the natural parents or testamentary guardians were adjudged unfit to perform their duties. The doctrine developed slowly and mainly in response to litigation having to do with the rights of infants to inherit property. In most such suits, dating back to the fourteenth century, the power of the crown was invoked to protect the rights of infants. But going back to the time of Edward I in the thirteenth, *parens patriae* was invoked, as well, for the protection of such others as the mentally retarded and the mentally ill, the former, at least, "being adjudged ever to be, as it were, below full age," in the words of one medieval legal theorist (Cogan, 1970:160; see also Rendleman, 1971). A similar equation had also been known in Roman law (Ludwig, 1955). Indeed, one myth even has it that *parens patriae* was initially a doctrine having to do only with the incapacitated but became extended to children as a result of a printer's error, when the word *enfant* was accidentally substituted for *ideot* in a text; the tale, however, seems without validity (Rendleman, 1971).

In any event, if the doctrine was developed mainly out of disputes having to do with rights of property and inheritance, it was greatly extended during the sixteenth and seventeenth centuries. England had passed numerous laws for the protection and regulation of the poor during this tumultuous period of her history, and the king as *pater patriae* was given the duty of protector of charities in the country. In addition, the regulation of card playing, gaming, and sporting was also said, in about 1600, to be the right of the state, under the doctrine of *parens patriae* (Cogan, 1970). By the eighteenth century, then, *parens patriae*, understood as the right of the state to intervene in private affairs, was well established. The doctrine would continue to be applied with increasing scope to family matters. In two celebrated cases, the right of the court to decide on the guardian of a child was asserted and, again, *parens patriae* was involved: "The Crown, as *Parens patriae*," it was declared, "was the Supreme Guardian and the Superintendent over all Infants" and, hence, could intervene in the family on a child's behalf (1970:174).

Ex Parte Crouse

It was in America, however, that this doctrine of *parens patriae* was first invoked in ways relating to juvenile delinquency, and, indeed, its invocation grew directly out of a case involving one of the early houses of refuge. The decision in the case, rendered in 1838, was known as *Ex parte Crouse*. Briefly described, the decision arose when the mother of a young girl named Mary Ann Crouse filed a complaint declaring the girl incorrigible, a complaint resulting in Mary Ann's committal to the Philadelphia House of Refuge. Her father, upon learning of this, immediately filed a petition of *habeas corpus*, which was denied, whereupon he sued on constitutional grounds, charging that his daughter had been imprisoned without jury trial and should be released. The court denied the suit, approving Mary Ann's committal and, more significantly, denying that the due process rights applied to children. The court justified its denial on the grounds of *parens patriae* (Schlossman, 1977).

According to the court, the state had a major duty to children under the doctrine of *parens patriae.* Above all, it had the duty to protect the child from an improper upbringing. Mary Ann, the judges declared (*Ex parte Crouse,* 4 Wharton (Pa.) 9, 1838), "had been snatched from a course which must have ended in confirmed depravity: and not only is the restraint of her person lawful, but it would have been an act of extreme cruelty to release her from it." And the court asked, rhetorically, "May not the natural parents, when unequal to the task of education, or unworthy of it, be superseded by the *parens patriae,* or common guardian of the community?" Its decision answered that the community could, indeed, supersede the natural parents in such a case. Such a decision clearly accorded with the more general views of reformers about juvenile delinquency, its causes, and the most productive responses to it. In the words of Mennel (1973:24), "it gave refuge and reform school authorities the best of two worlds: it separated delinquent children from their natural parents, and it circumvented the rigor of the criminal law by allowing courts to commit children, under loosely worded statutes, to specially created 'schools' instead of jails."

As we shall see in Chapter 7, *parens patriae* did not go unchallenged. In the post–Civil War years, in particular, the doctrine received strong criticism, and there were even a few judicial decisions undermining its authority. In our own time, as we shall also see, the doctrine has been severely tested. But in the era prior to the Civil War, when the foundations were laid for an American juvenile justice system, *parens patriae* provided a strong legal justification for developing practices.

A Second Stream: The English Poor Laws

But if the doctrine of *parens patriae* was important, it was not the only precedent for state guardianship that would underlie the establishment of early houses of refuge. Another, perhaps even more important, may be traced to what Rendleman (1971:205) has described as the "mechanisms, definitions, and dispositions developed in feudal England to deal with poverty." These mechanisms were embodied most clearly in the Poor Laws of England and colonial America, and though they did not explicitly invoke *parens patriae,* they still provided for the intervention of the state into intrafamily affairs and for the supervision of juveniles deemed to need it. Here was a major element in the statutory background to the modern American juvenile justice system.

English legislation of this sort may be easily seen in the sixteenth century in the form of laws ordering the apprenticing of poor children. For example, under Henry VIII, in 1535, it was enacted (in Bremner, 1970:I, 64):

> Children under fourteen years of age, and above five, that live in idleness, and be taken begging, may be put to service by the governors of cities, towns, etc. to husbandry, or other crafts or labours.

The important "Statutes of Artificers" of 1562 went even further, providing for the separation of pauper children from their parents and apprenticing them

(Rendleman, 1971), a provision that was maintained in the Elizabethan Poor Law of 1601: the church wardens of every parish were given the right to take children from any parents who "shall not . . . be thought able to keep and maintain their children" (in Bremner, 1970:I, 65).

Such practices were maintained under colonial American laws as well. In Virginia, legislation supported the building of several "workhouses," in which children could learn a variety of trades, and county commissioners along with parish vestry were empowered, in the words of 1668 legislation, "to take poor children from indigent parents and to place them to work in those houses" (in Bremner, 1970:66). A Connecticut statute of about 1673 gave the town selectmen and overseers of the poor a similar right to take the children of poor parents who "shall suffer their children to live idly or misspend their time in loitering" from those parents and to bind them out as apprentices (Bremner, 1970:68). And the records indicate that such action was not uncommon in other colonies as well.

These poor laws provided an important background to the American juvenile justice system for two reasons. First, like *parens patriae,* they justified state intervention into family life when, significantly, a child's parents or guardians appeared to those in authority to be unfit for child rearing. Indeed, Rendleman has suggested that the real significance of *Ex parte Crouse* lay not simply in its invocation of *parens patriae* but, more, in its application of *parens patriae* to precedents already present in the poor laws. Second, as stated, the poor laws were easily suited to use in regard to delinquent children. Indeed, they probably were used that way since, at the time of their formulation, such terms as *vagrant, wayward,* and *delinquent* were virtually synonymous and were intended to be so. As late as 1875, Mary Carpenter argued that "there is no distinction

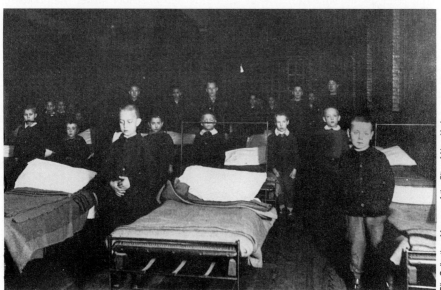

Workhouse for boys in the nineteenth century.

between pauper, vagrant, and criminal children, which would require a different system of treatment." All were, or were likely to become, a problem for the community (Fox, 1970:1193). By the opening of the nineteenth century, then, there was ample precedent for state intervention into family life. The houses of refuge represented a pioneering effort to apply that precedent to the problems of juvenile delinquency.

Parens Patriae Put into Practice: Other Approaches to Juvenile Delinquency in Nineteenth-Century America

The house of refuge model was the dominant one for most of the first half of the nineteenth century. If the three privately financed and run private houses were not always emulated, as such, when the various states sought to implement their own plans for dealing with juvenile delinquency, they drew heavily on the example provided by the houses of refuge in order to create state-supported "reform schools." Most states outside the South established such schools prior to the Civil War; the southern states followed suit by about the opening of the twentieth century.

Little distinguished the state institutions from the earlier houses of refuge. Most adopted the system of housing inmates in dormitorylike — one might say "prisonlike" — quarters; like the houses of refuge, the state institutions depended upon a structured environment and offered both vocational and academic educational programs. The state schools may have allocated a bit more time to academic education (hence the name *reform school* rather than *house of refuge*), but beyond this difference, there was little else. All, too, relied on indeterminate sentencing and had the moral uplift of the inmate as a central goal (Mennel, 1973). However, despite the apparent success of the house of refuge model, even by mid-century some major problems had begun to appear, and some severe criticisms were leveled against it.

Criticisms of the Houses of Refuge

Criticisms of the houses of refuge focused on a number of elements. For one, although the house of refuge was supposed to be rehabilitative, it often appeared to be as much a prison as a place of refuge. Thus, within just a few years of its opening, the New York House of Refuge had been surrounded by high stone walls and contained several large stone buildings housing individual jail cells. The house's manager not only recognized but even approved of the jaillike characteristics of the institution (Schlossman, 1977).

Still more troubling, however, was the apparent failure of the houses of refuge to bring about anything like the levels of reformation for which their founders had hoped. Almost from the beginning, the managers of the houses of refuge faced severe disciplinary problems, and, as Hawes (1971) found, serious incidents occurred almost daily. Children frequently escaped from the confinement of a house of refuge, and many grew abusive and even violent toward the teachers and other employees. The house staff often reacted violently, even though corporal punishment was supposed to be used only as a last resort. When one 1826 escapee was returned to the New York House of Refuge, he was whipped "with a cowskin up on his bare back" and then placed in solitary confinement, on a bread-and-water diet, for three days (Hawes, 1971:47–48).

Such punishments were not uncommon, nor, despite the official policy, were they used only as a last resort. According to one former employee of the New York House of Refuge, "Corporal punishments are usually inflicted with the cat or a rattan. The latter punishment is applied in a great variety of places, such as the palm and back of the hands, top and bottom of the feet, and lastly, but not rarely or sparingly, to the posteriors over the clothes, and also on the naked skin" (Schlossman, 1977:35). Although extremely brutal floggings were commonplace in adult prisons as well (Lewis, 1965), corporal punishment seemed to be especially troubling in a house of refuge. According to Mennel (1973), the Boston House of Reformation's reputation for excessiveness in disciplinary practices was such that, at one point, city magistrates simply refused to commit children to it.

But perhaps most serious of all, in the view of many critics, was that, despite the presence of formally rigid classification schemes, the houses of refuge were doing an inadequate job of separating hardened young inmates from those who had been admitted for relatively minor offenses. Thus, the prisonlike refuges and reformatories, contrary to intent, were perpetuating some of the same problems they had been created to prevent by mixing the corruptible with the already corrupt. "The most vigilant supervision," complained one critic, "cannot prevent opportunities for the relation, by the older and more vicious, of all the details of a corrupt life, the explanation of technical terms, and practical application of skill, which would in many instances entirely neutralize the moral and religious training however thorough" (Rockwell, 1867:338). The reformatories were thus becoming schools for crime rather than for reformation.

In large part, the failure of the houses of refuge grew out of the difficulties inherent in the emerging conceptions of childhood and youth we discussed in Chapter 2. Muncie (1984) has described these difficulties in regard to England, and his remarks are relevant to the United States as well. The houses of refuge were built on a growing admiration for childhood's natural virtues, but the youngsters who constituted the clientele for a house of refuge rarely conformed to the ideals presented by child-rearing literature. They had already learned too much to look upon adults with that mixture of affection and dutifulness so prized in the literature. And when they failed to respond as ideals had predicted, the houses' managers reacted with harshness (see also Brenzel, 1983). In any case, the various failures of the houses of refuge led many Americans to seek solid alternatives to the house of refuge model.

The Cottage System

One of the most significant of such alternatives was developed in the 1850s, taking shape in what was known as the "family system" or "cottage system." Introduced in this country in the Massachusetts Industrial School for Girls, which began operation in 1854, and the Ohio Reform School (1857), the cottage system sought to depart from the prisonlike "congregate system" prevalent at the older institutions for juvenile offenders. Rather than house delinquents in large dormitory facilities, bringing them together under strict routines in workshops, the family system placed anywhere from one to three dozen inmates with similar characteristics in separate small houses under the supervision of a surrogate father or mother. The "family" thus created was to work, live, and attend school together, mixing only rarely with the inmates placed in other "families" (Schlossman, 1977:38).

The advantages to the cottage system were believed to lie in the opportunities it provided for a closer supervision of the inmates and for supervision, too, of a better quality. Clearly, for example, it was easier, with inmates housed in separate buildings, to enforce the kind of classification system that many believed necessary to bring about reform. The institution would not become a breeder of further crime.

Beyond that, however, the congregate system could be seen as faulty simply by virtue of its size. Congregate institutions were too impersonal—the officers "find it sometimes too difficult to learn even the *names* of their charges," wrote one critic (Rockwell, 1867:378)—and this problem, understood in terms of nineteenth-century conceptions of delinquency, was a severe one. As most people believed, not only did delinquents tend to come from poor and badly ordered family backgrounds, but the family was itself taken to be the seat of discipline and good behavior. Thus, as Rockwell (1867:378) argued, "Reformation must be, from its very nature, a work of close individual culture, and just so far as we assimilate institutions to the warmth, nearness, and limit of families, we increase the probabilities of success in it."

Thus, the cottage system was expected to address directly a major factor in juvenile delinquency as it was understood in the nineteenth century. In the words of its Ohio proponents (in Bremner, 1970:I, 706), the inmates were there "because they either never enjoyed the sweet of a good family home, or the family influences surrounding them were bad," and, in the true language of *parens patriae,* they argued that it was the responsibility of "the State" to come as near the idea of a well regulated, honest family, as is possible under the circumstances.

The cottage system had great impact on American approaches to delinquency. As Schlossman has observed, by the end of the nineteenth century, the cottage system had become "the conventional wisdom in American correctional ideology" (1977:49).

The Massachusetts Industrial School for Girls

The cottage system was not, however, an unalloyed success, as Brenzel (1983) has shown in her study of the Massachusetts Industrial School for Girls. This school at Lancaster began under the influence of the kinds of ideas we have been tracing thus far, but also in the belief that girls from poor families faced special dangers because of the weakness of their sex and, too, that girls needed special training that would instill in them the proper feminine virtues. The school at Lancaster was supposed to do this, through all the special strengths of the cottage system.

Almost from the beginning, however, there were problems. Chief among them was the apparently simple question of how to group the girls in the various cottages. Girls were sent to Lancaster for many reasons; the staff had many uses for the school. Some were abused children, sent to Lancaster for their own safety. Others were "incorrigibles," placed into custody at the request of their parents. Indeed, Brenzel (1983) has uncovered evidence that parents sometimes fabricated charges of incorrigibility in order to enable their daughters to take advantage of the educational opportunities Lancaster offered. Still others had been found guilty of crimes — usually stealing or prostitution. In theory, all were "children" and, thus, reformable. Thus, they were grouped together, without regard to background.

The practice was, however, a dangerous one, as many recognized. Some of the girls appeared to be "hardened" when they arrived and, thus, able to corrupt the more innocent among them. And, indeed, the presence of apparently hardened youngsters made the philosophy behind Lancaster difficult to maintain. As Brenzel shows, relatively shortly after the school's founding, those responsible for it had come to see its inmates more as delinquents than as children and to stress the punitive, custodial character of the institution over its redemptive purposes (1983). This tendency continued to gain strength as the institution grew and developed. The cottage system, as an institutional alternative to older house of refuge models, ultimately did not go very far in the directions that reformers desired, at least as it was put into practice at Lancaster.

Charles Loring Brace and the "Placing-Out" System

However, other reformers of the period went somewhat further in their efforts to move away from a prisonlike approach to dealing with juvenile offenders. Among the most influential of these was Charles Loring Brace. Brace, who had studied for the ministry and who, in 1850, made a tour of European philanthropic and correctional institutions, became deeply involved in problems of crime and delinquency while engaged in philanthropic work in New York. His duties at the time included working for the reform of adult prisoners on Blackwell's Island and "the squalid poor" in the Five Points district, one of New York's most depressed areas. Describing the effort as "Sisyphus-like work," Brace (1880:77, 78) was soon struck with "the immense number of boys and girls floating and drifting about our streets, with hardly any assignable home or occupation, who continually swelled the multitude of criminals, prostitutes, and vagrants." Here, he recognized, was an especially serious problem: little could be done about the problems of urban life if such youngsters could not be reached and reformed.

Thus, Brace, with some associates, began an attack on many areas of juvenile problems, under the umbrella of the Children's Aid Society of New York, organized in 1853 and incorporated in 1856 with Brace as its executive officer. Among its many projects, the society organized workshops for teaching trades to youngsters and established lodging houses for homeless "street boys." But its more ambitious project, aimed directly at urban delinquents, was an elaborate "placing-out" system set up to remove unfortunate youngsters from the urban slums, placing them in new homes in which they might be subject to more wholesome influences. Indeed, such youngsters were to be removed from the

Boys "placed out" by the Children's Aid Society.

urban environment altogether and placed in the homes of rural families in the "west."

The effects of such a placing-out system were, in Brace's mind, to be significant. For one thing, placing out would put the youngster into a good home and into a proper family. Like other reformers, Brace believed that the nature of a child's family had much to do with its fate and that poor, urban parents were by and large unfit to raise their children. For another, Brace felt that there was and would always be a need for agricultural labor: placing youngsters with farm families not only gave them a trade but gave them a trade with a future. Finally, like many Americans, Brace believed that there was virtue in rural life. He had, as one scholar observed, a powerful faith in what he described as exposing children to "pure country air instead of the gases of sewers, trees and fields in place of narrow alleys" (Langsam, 1964:19; see also Bremner, 1970). And, too, he was quite happy to get a class of potential troublemakers out of the city.

The importance of this last motive should not be underestimated. Brace had, after all, entitled his own account of his life's work "The Dangerous Classes of New York," and he meant the appellation to be taken seriously. Juvenile delinquents were not simply unfortunate themselves but positively dangerous to the very fabric of society: "Let but law lift its hand from them for a season, or let the civilizing influences of American life fail to reach them," he declared, "and, if the opportunity offered, we should see an explosion from this class which might leave this city in ashes and blood" (1880:29). He likened such people in New York to those who had led a mid-century "communist outbreak" in France. And, even if his worst prediction might not be realized, Brace had only to note that, at the very least, such young delinquents, grown up, would be given the right to vote (Children's Aid Society, 1854:13). Hence, their reform was essential; their presence in the city, a cause for concern.

So, although some children were placed in foster homes in New York City, the Children's Aid Society sent many urban delinquents out of the city and into rural areas of New York State — and beyond. Youngsters taken from the city streets might be dispatched to such midwestern states as Iowa, Missouri, and Michigan, with the largest number in the early years going to Indiana. But some children were sent as far south as Florida and as far west as Texas while the system was in operation. In all, in the years between the program's inception in 1853 and Brace's death in 1890, around 92,000 youngsters were "placed out" by the society. The program continued until 1929, but after about the mid-1890s it involved only token placements (Langsam, 1964).

For many of those sent out of the city, the experience seemed a good one. Some of the children wrote back to the society in ways that could only have made Brace and his co-workers feel good, reporting a love of the country and the development of all the right habits. Many of those who received the children could report, as did one, that in his new home a youngster "is quite well and contented, and we are very well pleased with him" (Children's Aid Society, 1855:43). Moreover, Brace could also point to some objective successes in his program. A number of the boys grew up to be independent and prosperous farmers, and some went beyond even that: by 1901, the society's records showed that alumni of the system included nineteen clergymen, seventeen physicians, twenty-six bankers, thirty-four lawyers, and even three governors of states or territories (Langsam, 1964:30).

Still, Brace's program was not without problems. As was the case at Lancaster, there is evidence that some poor parents used Brace's program as a quasiemployment agency for their children (Zelizer, 1985), an interesting commentary on Brace's own ideas about the urban poor. From the other side, it also seems that many of the farm families who received children from what came to be known as "orphan trains" (Brace sent homeless children as well as delinquents out of the dangerous New York environment) saw in the placing-out program a chance to get cheap help. According to one veteran of the program, the arrival of the children into their new community was like a "slave auction": the youngsters "stood on the courthouse steps . . . and people felt their muscles." He concluded, "A lot of folks were looking for free farm labor" (Jackson, 1986:101). And the program also aroused opposition. Some western communities felt they were being asked to absorb New York's criminal element, and, not surprisingly, some of the children sent west did commit crimes. Brace was convinced that reports of such cases tended to be greatly exaggerated — "a theft of one lad is imputed to scores of others about him," Brace complained (1880:243) — but the problem was nevertheless a real one, and one the society had to face for the life of the enterprise. Other opposition came from the Catholic church, which feared efforts on the part of the society to draw Catholic youngsters into the Protestant fold — an effort Brace denied was taking place. Nevertheless, Brace's efforts were a significant response to what many had seen as the failure of such institutional efforts at the houses of refuge and reform schools.

Other Nineteenth-Century Experiments

Charles Loring Brace was not the only nineteenth-century American to seek what might be called anti-institutional approaches to juvenile delinquency. Among the more influential of those who joined him in such an effort were Samuel Gridley Howe and, near the close of the century, William R. George.

Howe was troubled by the character of houses of refuge and of state-funded reform schools, which he saw as little better than prisons. He felt that most juvenile offenders committed to such institutions were more likely to be harmed than rehabilitated. Beginning in the 1860s, Howe proposed several alternatives to existing approaches to delinquents. Working in Massachusetts, he initially sought to create a plan for leasing small farms to be colonized by young offenders. Failing this, he proposed that the state place young offenders with upright families who would agree, for a stipend, to give the youngsters a proper upbringing. Howe was also an ardent opponent of institutions for delinquents, whatever form those institutions might take (Schlossman, 1977).

Military Schools. One institution that did begin to take on significance during the latter part of the nineteenth century was the military school. As Mennel (1973) has described them, these institutions served as, essentially, private reform schools for the children of middle- and upper-class families, children whose behavioral problems caused difficulties at home. Few were actually delinquents; the presence of such tough cases was something the schools themselves did not want (although, as Mennel points out, had some of them been poor they would probably have been characterized as delinquent in the setting of late-nineteenth-century America). But the schools were often represented as institutions that could prevent problem children from becoming delinquents, and this had much to do with their success.

The George Junior Republic. But perhaps the most innovative response to juvenile delinquency in the late nineteenth century was the creation of "junior republics," modeled after the George Junior Republic in New York State. William R. "Daddy" George (1866–1936) was a New York businessman whose work in Five Points and other rough areas of the city gave him an interest in the city's youth gangs. At one point, he recruited his own "Law and Order Gang" to try to combat the problems he saw among youngsters. In 1890, he founded a "fresh air camp" in rural New York for the benefit of Manhattan street children. But, as Mennel (1973) has said, George came to see that the camp promoted dependency rather than the self-discipline and self-reliance that would serve as antidotes to delinquency, and, by 1895, he changed the camp into a year-round "junior republic" where everything was to be paid for by the labor of the youngsters and where the campers were given the responsibility of electing their own representatives to devise and administer the laws of the camp. George himself retained veto power over the children's decisions.

The George Junior Republic was administered like a self-contained little village. There were stores, a post office, a farm, a courthouse, and "capitol." All were run by the youngsters, who achieved varying levels of wealth based on their individual "industry." Those who broke the law were forced to answer to a court of their peers, and the punishments could be severe. According to Holl (1971), most convicted offenders were sentenced to hard labor without wages. During the early days of the republic, the stigma of offense was made even more visible by the requirement that the convicts wear stripes. Housed in the republic's jail and guarded by youthful "citizens" of the republic, the young offender was made to feel the seriousness of his misbehavior.

The George Junior Republic was not without its detractors. Anti-institutional and contrary to the dominant, paternalistic ideologies of the houses of refuge and the reform schools, the junior republic received strong criticism and opposition from state charitable agencies and other sources. Internal troubles also plagued the republic from its earliest days. For a variety of reasons, the George Junior Republic did not really survive in anything but its name beyond the end of World War I. But during its heyday around the turn of the century, it attracted a great deal of interest. President Theodore Roosevelt was a vocal admirer of George and of the junior republic, and George's republic inspired others elsewhere in the United States. Mennel (1973) has noted that self-government was even introduced into a few existing reformatories. Whatever the ultimate failure of George's republic, it was an important expression of the continuing sense, among many Americans, of a need for genuinely distinctive measures in the handling of juvenile crime.

Probation

One other approach to juvenile delinquency was developed during the first half of the nineteenth century, and that was probation. Although, as we shall see in subsequent chapters, probation became a major component of the juvenile justice system in the twentieth century, its beginnings were quite inauspicious. In the early 1840s, shoemaker John Augustus was visiting one of Boston's municipal courts and met a man who had been brought before the court as a "common drunkard." Augustus approached the man and, convinced of his desire to reform, urged the judge to release him in Augustus's care, which was done. At Augustus's urging, the man "signed the pledge" and, appearing in court three weeks later, had adopted an "industrious and sober" life. Augustus then began, as a regular practice, bailing out and supervising others brought before the court on charges of drunkenness (Augustus, 1852:5).

During 1843, Augustus began to broaden his efforts to those charged with other crimes including, late in that year, two little girls aged eight and ten and an eleven-year-old boy, all of whom had been charged with stealing. In these cases, too, Augustus's supervision was successful, and, despite some opposition from the police, he began to deal relatively frequently with juvenile offenders. By 1846, he had arranged with the Police Court in Boston to continue the cases of about thirty children from nine to sixteen years of age, placing the children under his supervision and, with the cooperation of the court, administering a regular system of probation. The children reported to him, and he took on himself the responsibility to "note their general conduct, see that they were sent to school or supplied with some honest employment, and . . . make an impartial report to the court, whenever they should desire it" (in Sanders, 1970:375). Boston authorities seemed well pleased with the scheme, on the grounds that the children released to Augustus showed marked improvement and, as Schlossman (1977) has noted, that it was cheaper than creating new institutions. In any case, by 1852 he had supervised the probation of 116 boys under the age of sixteen, and about 80 per cent had avoided further trouble with the law (Hawes, 1971).

Augustus died in 1859, but other volunteer probation officers carried on his work until 1869, when the state of Massachusetts began to supervise the practice. Creating the office of state visiting agent, the legislature gave that officer ultimate responsibility for supervision of all children who had come under the care of the state, including the responsibility to appear "in behalf of the child" at hearings held for the purpose of committing children to state reform schools. In addition, the state, in a related action of 1870, provided for separate trials for juvenile offenders (Hawes, 1971).

The system established by Augustus thus received the imprimatur of legislation, and it was, by all accounts, a successful one. Usually, in a juvenile hearing, the judge met privately with the young offender and the state visiting agent, most commonly simply accepting the agent's recommendation for the disposition of a case. If the juvenile were put on probation, the visiting agent served as probation officer, checking on the probationer's behavior. Subsequently in the nineteenth century, probation laws were passed by five other states (Ludwig, 1955). Probation became, by the early twentieth century, a key feature in society's response to juvenile delinquency.

Summary

The early history of juvenile justice paralleled, in significant ways, the histories of childhood and of emerging concepts of delinquency. At a time when Western civilization was becoming increasingly "child-centered," one can see the steady growth of approaches to delinquency that aimed to set young offenders apart from adult criminals and focused on discovering ways of addressing the unique characteristics of the child in an effort to produce moral reform.

Up through the early modern period in Western history, there were no such efforts. Although allowances were made for age in dealing with young offenders, children accused and convicted of crime were generally treated like adult offenders. With the opening of the nineteenth century, however, this began to change, as Western society in general — and American society in particular — saw the creation of a range of institutions designed to deal specifically with juvenile delinquents. Among the first, and most significant, were the houses of refuge established in the largest cities. These houses succeeded in separating juvenile offenders from adult criminals. They did not, however, entirely succeed at providing an alternative to punitive, prisonlike institutional responses to juvenile crime.

Throughout the nineteenth century, the issue of creating appropriate institutional responses to juvenile crime remained significant. At one level, this meant establishing alternative institutional forms. These included the "cottage system" as well as such private approaches as those embodied in military schools and "junior republics." At another level, this led to such "anti-institutional" responses as those involved in Brace's "placing-out" system or probation. The precedent set by such responses as these, and particularly by probation, continues to have great influence on American juvenile justice, as we shall see in subsequent chapters.

No less significant were the legal precedents set in the nineteenth century, and particularly the establishment of *parens patriae* as a fundamental basis for institutional approaches to juvenile crime. *Parens patriae* (and the interpretive background lent by the English poor laws) justified the kind of state intervention into families and child rearing that seemed essential to such approaches to delinquency as the houses of refuge. At the close of the nineteenth century, and for the first two thirds of the twentieth century, *parens patriae* served as the cornerstone of the juvenile court, the culmination of attempts to define juvenile delinquency as a special category of legal concern.

The foundation and the evolution of the juvenile court grew out of the practices developed in the early nineteenth century. The story of the juvenile court's development is the focus of the chapter that follows (Chapter 7).

References

Abbott, Grace, ed. 1938. *The Child and the State.* 2 vols. Chicago: Univ. of Chicago Press.

Augustus, John. 1852. *John Augustus: First Probation Officer.* Rept. New York: National Probation Association, 1939.

Beaumont, Gustave de, and Tocqueville, Alexis de. 1833. *On the Penitentiary System in the United States, and Its Application in France.* Translated by Francis Lieber. Rept. New York: Augustus M. Kelley, 1970.

Brace, Charles Loring. 1880. *The Dangerous Classes of New York, and Twenty Years' Work Among Them.* 3rd ed. Rept. Montclair, N.J.: Patterson Smith, 1967.

Bremner, Robert. 1956. *From the Depths: The Discovery of Poverty in the United States.* New York: New York Univ. Press.

———, et al., eds. 1970. *Children and Youth in America: A Documentary History.* 3 vols. Cambridge, Mass.: Harvard Univ. Press.

Brenzel, Barbara M. 1983. *Daughters of the State: A Social Portrait of the First Reform School for Girls in North America, 1856–1905.* Cambridge, Mass.: MIT Press.

Buckland, W. W. 1963. *A Textbook of Roman Law from Augustus to Justinian.* 3rd ed., rev. by Peter Stein. Cambridge: Cambridge Univ. Press.

Carpenter, Mary. 1853. *Juvenile Delinquents: Their Condition and Treatment.* Rept. Montclair, N.J.: Patterson Smith, 1970.

Children's Aid Society. 1854. *First Annual Report of the Children's Aid Society.* Rept. New York: Arno Press, 1971.

Children's Aid Society. 1855. *Second Annual Report of the Children's Aid Society.* Rept. New York: Arno Press, 1971.

Cogan, Neil. 1970. Juvenile Law, Before and After the Entrance of *"Parens Patriae." South Carolina Law Review* 22:147–181.

Foucault, Michel. 1977. *Discipline and Punish: The Birth of the Prison.* Translated by Alan Sheridan. New York: Pantheon.

Fox, Sanford. 1970. Juvenile Justice Reform: An Historical Perspective. *Stanford Law Review* 22:1187–1239.

Gillis, John R. 1974. *Youth and History: Tradition and Change in European Age Relations, 1770–Present.* New York: Academic Press.

Hawes, Joseph M. 1971. *Children in Urban Society: Juvenile Delinquency in Nineteenth-Century America.* New York: Oxford Univ. Press.

Holl, Jack M. 1971. *Juvenile Reform in the Progressive Era: William R. George and the Junior Republic Movement.* Ithaca, N.Y.: Cornell Univ. Press.

House of Reformation, The. 1832. *New England Magazine* 3:382–390.

Jackson, Donald Dale. 1986. It Took Trains to Put Street Kids on the Right Track Out of the Slums. *Smithsonian* 17, no. 5:94–103.

John Griscom. 1860. *American Journal of Education* 8:325–347.

Jolowicz, H. F. 1957. *Roman Foundations of Modern Law.* London: Oxford Univ. Press.

Kaestle, Carl F. 1976. Between the Scylla of Brutal Ignorance and the Charybdis of a Literary Education: Elite Attitudes Toward Mass Schooling in Early Industrial England and America. In *Schooling and Society: Studies in the History of Education,* edited by Lawrence Stone, 177–191. Baltimore, Md.: Johns Hopkins Univ. Press.

Kent, James. 1827. *Commentaries on American Law.* 4 vols. Rept. New York: Da Capo Press, 1971.

Langsam, Miriam Z. 1964. *Children West: A History of the Placing-Out System of the New York Children's Aid Society, 1853–1890.* Madison, Wisc.: State Historical Society of Wisconsin.

Lewis, W. David. 1965. *From Newgate to Dannemora: The Rise of the Penitentiary in New York, 1796–1840.* Ithaca, N.Y.: Cornell Univ. Press.

Ludwig, Frederick, J. 1955. *Youth and the Law: Handbook on Laws Affecting Youth.* Brooklyn, N.Y.: Foundation Press.

Mennel, Robert M. 1973. *Thorns and Thistles: Juvenile Delinquents in the United States, 1825–1940.* Hanover, N.H.: Univ. Press of New England.

Morgan, Edmund S. 1966. *The Puritan Family: Religion and Domestic Relations in Seventeenth-Century New England.* Rev. ed. New York: Harper.

Muncie, John. 1984. *"The Trouble with Kids Today": Youth and Crime in Post-War Britain.* London: Hutchinson.

Nasaw, David. 1979. *Schooled to Order: A Social History of Public Schooling in the United States.* New York: Oxford Univ. Press.

Nyquist, Ola. 1960. *Juvenile Justice: A Comparative Study with Special Reference to the Swedish Child Welfare Board and the California Juvenile Court System.* London: Macmillan.

Platt, Anthony M. 1977. *The Child Savers: The Invention of Delinquency.* 2nd ed. Chicago: Univ. of Chicago Press.

Radzinowicz, Leon. 1948. *A History of English Criminal Law and Its Administration from 1750: The Movement for Reform, 1750–1833.* London: Stevens and Sons.

Rendleman, Douglas. 1971. *Parens Patriae:* From Chancery to the Juvenile Court. *South Carolina Law Review* 23:205–259.

Rockwell, Mrs. S. N. 1867. Facts and Thoughts About Reform Schools. *American Educational Monthly* 4:257–261, 295–298, 335–339, 375–378, 415–418.

Rothman, David J. 1971. *The Discovery of the Asylum: Social Order and Disorder in the New Republic.* Boston: Little, Brown.

Sanders, Wiley B., ed. 1970. *Juvenile Offenders for a Thousand Years: Selected Readings from Anglo-Saxon Times to 1900.* Chapel Hill, N.C.: Univ. of North Carolina Press.

Schlossman, Steven L. 1977. *Love and the American Delinquent: The Theory and Practice of "Progressive" Juvenile Justice, 1825–1920.* Chicago: Univ. of Chicago Press.

Schultz, Stanley K. 1973. *The Culture Factory: Boston Public Schools, 1789–1860.* New York: Oxford Univ. Press.

Zelizer, Viviana, A. 1985. *Pricing the Priceless Child: The Changing Social Value of Children.* New York: Basic Books.

CHAPTER **8**

Development of the American Juvenile Justice System

Courtesy A. Binder

Although the development of a distinctive juvenile justice system started with the efforts of early-nineteenth-century reformers that led to the first house of refuge, some of the most significant practices and approaches to juvenile crime did not take shape until the latter part of the nineteenth century, during the period historians call the Progressive era. Extending roughly from the 1880s to the coming of World War I, the Progressive era represented a time of great turmoil in American social and intellectual life and in the establishment of the American juvenile justice system. As we saw in Chapter 2, an unprecedented wave of immigration and a quickening pace of urbanization made many Americans aware of juvenile deliquency to a degree that had not been known before. Intellectual developments — including the "discovery" of adolescence — contributed to this growing awareness of delinquency. And most of those who examined the problem were convinced that existing approaches to it, including the long-established houses of refuge and state-sponsored reform schools, were not doing enough to combat juvenile crime. The Progressive era saw the development of new approaches to deliquency, approaches that have come down to our own time.

The chief focus of Progressive era reformers was on the effort to "decriminalize" juvenile deliquency. These reformers sought to remove youngsters accused of crime from the ordeal of criminal proceedings. Their effort ultimately succeeded, taking shape in the founding of special "juvenile courts" designed to deal with young offenders in ways that focused on treatment rather than

Inmates at work in an early reform school.

prosecution. The first of these courts was founded in Chicago in 1899. It was the predecessor of juvenile courts now operating in every state in the union.

The Founding of the Juvenile Court _____

The Problems of Juvenile Justice in Illinois and Chicago

Chicago in the 1890s was in a peculiar situation. A city of over a million people, its population had more than doubled in the preceding decade, swelled largely by immigrants from all over Europe. As had happened in the older cities of the Northeast, such rapid growth had brought about difficult conditions and a shocking increase in juvenile delinquency (Hawes, 1971). And, also as in the older cities, the municipal services were quite unequal to the task of responding to urban problems, including the problems of juvenile delinquency.

But Chicago faced special difficulties in regard to juvenile delinquency. An 1855 ordinance had established a Chicago Reform School to deal with both delinquent children and those with other problems, such as neglect or abandonment. Like earlier institutions in other cities, the Chicago school was guided, at least implicitly, by principles of *parens patriae,* and it was to be an institution for the protection as well as the reformation of youngsters. Only a small proportion of those committed to the school prior to its destruction in the great Chicago fire of 1871 were sent there for criminal offenses.

By the end of the 1860s, however, the Chicago school, also like many other institutions, was acquiring a bad reputation. The best evidence indicates, as the legal historian Sanford Fox (1970:1215) argues, that the courts were "turning against the institution," committing youngsters to it only when there was no alternative. But the most serious problem for juvenile justice in Chicago and the rest of the state came in 1870, in a decision of the Illinois Supreme Court in the case *People ex. rel. O'Connell v. Turner* (55 Ill. 280). Daniel O'Connell was a youngster who had been committed to the Chicago Reform School on the vaguest of grounds. He had not been convicted of any crime; indeed, he had not been accused of any crime. His father filed a writ of *habeas corpus* to get Daniel released, and the Supreme Court found for the father. The words of the court were a direct challenge to *parens patriae* as a basis for the state's approach to juvenile offenders (in Fox, 1970:1217):

> It is claimed that the law is administered for the moral welfare and intellectual improvement of the minor, and the good of society. From the record before us, we know nothing of the management. We are only informed that a father desires custody of his child; and that he is restrained of his liberty. Therefore, we can only look at the language of the law, and the power granted.

According to the court, the state could claim no legitimate right to interfere with the relationship between parent and child. The result was that Illinois courts lost all jurisdiction over young people deemed to be in trouble, at least over those who, like O'Connell, had not been found guilty of crime.

The *O'Connell* decision also meant that the focus of the state's treatment of delinquents had to be essentially within the confines of the criminal justice system. Minor offenders were usually sentenced to county jails. More serious young offenders were sentenced to an inadequate state reform school in Pontiac, an institution that was little more than a "minor penitentiary" (Platt, 1977:102–103). For the most part, children were subject to the same criminal proceedings as adults. If arrested, the child was held in jail with adult prisoners; the young offender was then taken before the grand jury for indictment and before a petit jury for trial. If found guilty, the delinquent was sentenced to either the city prison or the Cook County jail. In 1898, the year before the establishment of the juvenile court, 575 boys were confined in the county jail; 1,983 boys were committed to the city prison (Hurley, 1925).

Reformers saw several reasons to be concerned about the situation. For one thing, by all accounts conditions for children held in jail were appalling. Not only was there the traditional problem of mixing children with older criminals, but reformers found problems of filth, vermin, and psychological terror as well. This led many judges to let young offenders off with no sentence at all, since they could not bring themselves to commit a youngster to such conditions. Children became brutalized by a stint in jail; they might also be encouraged in crime by knowing that, even if they were convicted, there was a good chance of facing no punishment at all (Adams, 1935).

It should not be thought that such conditions were confined to Chicago. Edward L. Ayers (1984), in a study of crime and punishment in the nineteenth-century southern United States, has described similar if not worse conditions in

A boy's cell in a nineteenth-century prison.

that region in the 1890s. In Georgia, for example, over a third of the convicts in the state penitentiary were under twenty years old, and eighteen of them were below the age of twelve. Southern juvenile delinquents were as likely as older criminals to be sentenced to chain gangs under the South's notorious convict lease system. And they were also exposed to the bad influence of adult criminals and to homosexual assaults. Not surprisingly, southern voices spoke strongly against such conditions.

Creation of the Illinois Juvenile Court

But it was in Chicago that such voices had their greatest influence, as reformers not only sought to change the conditions of custody for juvenile delinquents but argued that the root of the problem lay in the fact that a young offender should have to face the criminal justice system at all. Timothy D. Hurley, a Chicago judge who had served as chief probation officer for the court, wrote of the subjection of young offenders to a court trial, "Imagine such a solemn farce of proceedings, the nature of which the child rarely understood." And, if convicted, Hurley (1925:320–321) wrote, the child's future was forever tarnished: "Henceforth, among men, he was a *criminal.* No matter where he went, no matter low long he lived, the foul taint of the convict remained with him." The problem was, then, to find ways of treating young offenders without putting the taint of criminality on them.

Agitation for major change came as early as the 1880s, led chiefly by the Chicago Woman's Club. Through its committees, the club sought to alleviate conditions in existing institutions, adding matrons to the jail staff, for example, and sponsoring a school for boys awaiting trial or serving sentences in the jail. As early as 1892, the Woman's Club's Jail Committee suggested a special juvenile court, and by 1895 the club sponsored a bill to go before the Illinois legislature providing for a separate court for children and a probation staff. The bill made little progress, but it did provoke a great deal of interest among other citizens and groups (Lathrop, 1925).

By 1898, the juvenile court movement had become quite strong. Under the leadership of Julia Lathrop, a member of the State Board of Charities, such organizations as the Chicago Bar Association and the Catholic Visitation and Aid Society threw their weight behind the juvenile court idea, and in early 1899, a bill creating such a court was passed. The juvenile court went into operation in that year (Hurley, 1925).

The juvenile court in Chicago brought together and put into practice many of the concepts of delinquency that had become current during this period. Aimed at "dependent, neglected, and delinquent children" alike, the court was intended to address the problems of those under the age of sixteen, who did not have "proper parental care or guardianship" as well as those found guilty of breaking the law (in Abbott, 1938:II, 393). In this, of course, the court was consistent with the doctrine of *parens patriae,* and this was, in fact, its intention. According to a state's attorney at the time, "The fundamental idea of the law is that the State must exercise guardianship over a child found under such adverse social or individual conditions as develop crime" (in Hurley, 1925:325–326). The obvious constitutional problem posed by the earlier *O'Connell* decision was simply ignored, raised by neither the legislature nor, subsequently, the legal community (Fox, 1970:229).

The broad definition of delinquency institutionalized by the act has, we should note, led such critics as Platt (1977) and Fox (1970) to question the humaneness of the motives of those who worked for the juvenile court's creation. Platt has emphasized the extent to which the "child-saving movement" that helped to bring about the juvenile court in Illinois drew its support from wealthy and powerful members of the community. Thus, he argues (1977:xxii), the movement might best be understood as an effort to "achieve order, stability, and control, while preserving the existing class system and distribution of wealth."

Platt's image of the Illinois reformers, which has been very influential, is not without foundation. We noted in Chapters 2 and 7 the class biases present in the earliest development of a concept of juvenile delinquency in nineteenth-century America. We also noted in Chapter 7 the interest of such reformers as Brace in maintaining social order. Still, Platt may be said to overstate his case. As Ryerson (1978) has noted, one can deny the humanitarian character of the reformers' motives only if one is prepared to equate humaneness with nonintervention. In fact, the diverse men and women who led reform in Illinois had equally diverse motives — some tied to a concern for the child, some to social conservatism, and some to social reform — a point Platt himself concedes (1977:XXV). But motives are never easy to lay bare. Much clearer, historically, is the important background the Illinois reformers provided for the American juvenile justice system. To see this background, we must turn to a more detailed description of the 1899 Juvenile Court Act.

The Illinois Juvenile Court Act, 1899

The Illinois Juvenile Court Act of 1899 gave the court the kind of broad powers and purposes in keeping with *parens patriae*. The act specified, "Any reputable person, being resident in the county, having knowledge of a child under the age of 16 in his county who appears to be either neglected, dependent or delinquent, may file with a clerk of a court having jurisdiction in the matter a petition in writing, setting forth the facts, verified by affadavit." The act gave courts authority to appoint "discreet persons of good character" as probation officers (interestingly, they were "to receive no compensation from the public treasury"). The probation officers were expected

> to make such investigation as may be required by the court; to be present in court to represent the interests of the child when the case is heard; to furnish the court such information and assistance as the judge may require; and to take such charge of any child before and after trial as may be directed by the court.

The court, in the act, was directed "to hear and dispose of the case in a summary manner." A delinquent child could be allowed to remain at home subject to the supervision of a probation officer, "placed in a suitable family home, subject to the friendly supervision of the probation officer," or committed to "a training school for boys," "an industrial school for girls," or any county institution for the care of delinquents. If the offense was a violation of a criminal code, a boy over the age of ten could be sent to the state reformatory and a girl over ten to the state Home for Juvenile Offenders.

Any child found dependent or neglected by the court could be committed "to the care of some suitable State institution, or to the care of some reputable citizen of good moral character, or to the care of some training school or an industrial school, or to the care of some association willing to receive it."

The act further specified, "No court or magistrate shall commit a child under twelve (12) years of age to a jail or police station. But if such child is unable to give bail it may be committed to the care of the sheriff, police officer or probation officer, who shall keep such child in some suitable place provided by the city or county outside of the enclosure of any jail or police station." (As we shall see in Chapter 10, it is interesting that bail was allowed for juveniles in 1899. Later, in most states, this would not be the case.) The act forbade confinement of children in any building or settings that contained "adult convicts."

In the juvenile court itself, the procedure was to be very different from that accorded to adult defendants in a criminal proceeding. Procedural informality was to mark the court. The "solemn farce" (Hurley, 1925:329) of the jury trial was to be avoided, and hearings were to involve chiefly the judge, the child, his or her parents, and the probation officer — serving as an expert. In the proceedings, the judge's concern was to be less with the juvenile's guilt or innocence of a specific act than with the need of the state to assume the child's guardianship. In the words of one of the pioneer judges of the Chicago court, Julian W. Mack (1925:314), no longer did the court ask of the juvenile, "Are you guilty or innocent . . . ? We ask at this time, 'What are you? How have you become what you are? Whither are you tending and how can we direct you?'" Accordingly, the juvenile court relied heavily on reports not only from probation officers but also from social workers, psychologists, and other members of the developing "helping professions."

As the act itself makes clear, the new juvenile court sought to make heavy use of probation rather than incarceration in the disposition of cases. Ideally the child would be returned to his family, but, rather than being left to the care of the family alone, the youngster's life would now be supervised by a probation officer with broad powers of surveillance and intervention. The court's proponents had not only recognized the failure of contemporary institutions but also sought to draw on potential strengths of the family in bringing about reform. With a probation officer who could, in a sense, treat and educate the natural family, a more thoroughgoing reform was believed possible (Schlossman, 1977). Quite obviously, probation and the probation officer represented not only what was newest about the juvenile court system but a key to its success or failure.

The philosophy of the act was summarized in its last paragraph:

> This Act shall be liberally construed, to the end that its purpose may be carried out to-wit: That the care, custody and discipline of a child shall approximate as nearly as may be that which should be given by its parents, and in all cases when it can be properly done the child be placed in an approved family home and become a member of the family by legal adoption or otherwise.

The Illinois Juvenile Court Act was a critical step in the institutionalization of a distinctive juvenile justice system.

One should not overemphasize the uniqueness of the Illinois juvenile court. As such critics as Fox (1970) and Caldwell (1961) have stressed, its main significance lay in the extent to which it codified and elaborated on existing ideas, giving an unprecedented legal sanction for *parens patriae* and providing new opportunities for welfare-oriented approaches to delinquency, while not really removing delinquents from the legal system. And, despite the use of probation, the juvenile court made few changes in the institutional treatment of delinquents. There were, for example, no changes in the administration and character of the state reform school as a result of the creation of the juvenile court. Nevertheless, the creation of the court itself was a major episode in the history of American delinquency, one with profound and continuing implications.

The Spread of the Early Juvenile Courts _____

Ben Lindsey and the Denver Juvenile Court

If, as we have noted, the Illinois juvenile court served as a prototype for other states, surely another significant, influential voice on behalf of juvenile courts came not from Chicago but from Denver, Colorado. Ben B. Lindsey — who came to be known as "the kids' judge" (Schlossman, 1977:125) — was, in the early twentieth century, a major force for the establishment and development of a juvenile court ideal.

In 1900, Lindsey, a politically active lawyer of Denver, was appointed to the office of judge of the county court. Shortly after assuming his post, he was asked to hear a case of larceny, which, he was told, "would not take two minutes." Agreeing to do so, he was presented with a frightened young boy, accused of having stolen coal from the railroad tracks. Given no alternative but to send the boy to the state reform school, Lindsey did, but, when the boy's mother began to scream and sob, Lindsey suspended the sentence and decided to look into the case himself. The family was poor and suffering; Lindsey placed the boy on probation and began, as he said, "to think over this business of punishing infants as if they were adults and of maiming young lives by trying to make the gristle of their informed characters carry the weight of our iron laws and heavy penalties" (Lindsey and O'Higgins, 1911:82–83). Locating a section of a Colorado school law of 1899 defining the habitual truant and the incorrigible child as "a juvenile disorderly person," Lindsey believed he had found the answer to his problem (1911:86–87): "A juvenile disorderly person! Not a criminal to be punished under the criminal law, but a ward of the state as *parens patriae.*" Invoking that important doctrine, Lindsey requested the district attorney thenceforth to file complaints against children under this Colorado school law. Thus began the Denver juvenile court.

The hallmark of Lindsey's Denver court was its informality, as Lindsey sought to establish rapport with the youngsters brought before him. In keeping with G. Stanley Hall's notions of adolescence, Lindsey argued that children were naturally neither moral nor immoral, but *un*moral because not fully formed. "They are," he wrote, "little savages, living in a civilized society that has not yet civilized them, often at war with it, frequently punished by it, and always secretly in rebellion against it, until the influences of the home, the school and the church gradually overcome their natural savagery and make them moral responsible members of society." The juvenile court's task was to aid these other civilizing forces, and this could not be done unless the young offender saw the court as a helpful friend rather than an arm of a punitive, impersonal legal system (1911:134–135).

The goal in Denver, as in Chicago, was to keep children out of the institutions of the criminal justice system, including the state reform school, and to rely heavily on probation. Lindsey, in his effort to make probation effective, used the informal approach and sought to create a friendship with the young offender in such a way as to make those on probation feel that continuing good behavior was an obligation not to society but to Judge Lindsey himself. "I can *help* you, Harry," he told one boy. "But you've got to carry yourself. If I let boys go when they do bad things, I'll lose my job. The people will get another guide, in my place, to punish boys, if *I* don't do it. I can't let you go" (1911:141).

In addition, Lindsey established remarkable Saturday-morning "report sessions" at which he met with his probationers, receiving reports from them (supplemented by reports from their teachers) on their behavior. Beginning with a little talk, Lindsey would then ask individual youngsters to stand before the group and discuss openly both good and bad reports. An account of one of these sessions shows much about how Lindsey worked. To one youngster who had been doing particularly well, Lindsey would say, expansively, "Skinny, you've been doing fine lately; had a crackerjack report every time. . . . That's great. Shake, Skin. You're all right you are." By contrast, when he had to deal with Eddie, crying because he had not been so good, Lindsey was finally forced to sentence the boy to reform school. Sobbing, Eddie asked for another chance, but was turned down. "I'm sure that after a year or two you'll be glad I sent you to the school," Lindsey told him. "And I'll be up there in a few days to see you, Eddie, myself. What's more, I know some boys up there — friends of mine, that'll help you, Eddie; be friends to you" (in Levine and Levine, 1970:205–206).

In its assumptions and procedures, Lindsey's Denver court embodied the juvenile court ideal. Making extensive use of probation, basing its operations on the doctrine of *parens patriae* rather than that of adult due process, and seeking to focus on counseling over prosecution, the Denver court and others like it tried to decriminalize juvenile delinquency and to take a "parental" approach to those who were viewed as society's victims rather than as criminals or even as a potentially criminal element.

The Establishment of Juvenile Courts in Other States

The spread of the juvenile court idea was rapid, based on the Chicago model and encouraged by such proponents of the court as Ben Lindsey. Wisconsin and New York established juvenile courts in 1901, Ohio and Maryland in 1902, even anticipating Lindsey's Colorado efforts. By 1912, twenty-two states had juvenile court laws, and by 1928, only two states lacked some kind of juvenile court system. The last of these, Wyoming, finally fell into line in 1945 (Platt, 1977; Mennel, 1973).

It was not the case that juvenile court systems were uniform throughout the states, nor even that every state directly followed the Illinois model. John R. Sutton (1985:116), in a comparative analysis of early juvenile courts, has shown the differences among them. According to Sutton, there were "five legal innovations" that reformers supported in trying to establish juvenile courts. These were "(1) the explicit labeling and definition of delinquency as an offense category, (2) the labeling and definition of neglect and dependency, (3) the requirement of separate pre-adjudicatory detention for juveniles and adults, (4) the requirement of a separate trial and/or 'docket and record' for juveniles, and (5) the establishment of a specialized juvenile probation service." All of these were part of the Illinois act, as we have seen.

Sutton shows that states responded differently to these innovations. Most sought to "label" delinquency, neglect, and dependency in their juvenile court acts, but the labels were often vague and contradictory in the legislation, ultimately becoming, as we shall see, a major issue in juvenile justice policy. Separate detention was provided for with — or even before — the establishment of the juvenile court in many states, but other states were slow to make such a provision. North Dakota did not require separate detention until 1969; Maine, until 1977 (Sutton, 1985). Provisions for separate hearings and for probation generally were a part of the establishment of juvenile courts.

There were, then, some differences to be seen in the early juvenile courts. Nevertheless, the establishment of these courts and their main features provided the framework for juvenile justice in twentieth-century America.

Early Developments in the Juvenile Courts _____

Strengthening Parens Patriae

The early years of the juvenile courts were marked by great optimism about their character and potential. From the earliest days of their development, these courts seemed to offer a real alternative to the treatment of delinquency as a species of criminality and a field for the reform of young people and even of society. And, indeed, in the earliest years of the twentieth century, society continued to build on the assumptions and ideals that lay behind the juvenile courts. In particular, the doctrine of *parens patriae* was actually strengthened in its influence on American responses to delinquency.

One may see this in several ways. For one, the juvenile court laws were often supported by other legislation fully based on *parens patriae*. The first decade of the twentieth century saw the passage of "parental delinquency" laws that specified "contributing to the delinquency of a minor"; these laws held parents liable for neglect of their children. Colorado, with the encouragement of Lindsey, provided jail sentences and fines for parents who neglected their children. Kansas parents could be fined up to $1,000 or imprisoned for contributing to delinquency in their children (Mennel, 1973). (See the discussion in Chapter 14.)

This period also saw the rise of family courts in several American cities and states. These courts were intended to deal not only with juvenile delinquency but also with the kinds of family problems that seemed to contribute to delinquency. The first of these was founded in 1914, in Cincinnati, when the juvenile court and the domestic relations court were joined to address problems of family life and delinquency (Mennel, 1973). The extent to which this effort was tied to the concerns that had produced juvenile courts — and even houses of refuge — should be clear. The cause of delinquency was assigned, most pertinently, to improper family life and parental care. The state, supported by *parens patriae,* had the duty to prevent delinquency by taking a role in the rearing of "endangered" children.

And, indeed, throughout the early years of the court, the doctrine of *parens patriae* was itself more fully established in the legal community. A 1905 Pennsylvania decision, *Commonwealth v. Fisher* (213 Pa. 48, 1905), upheld the legal foundations of juvenile court law in that state (Mennel, 1973). This was the tendency of other states as well. In 1908, for example, the Supreme Court in Idaho in *Ex parte Sharpe* (15 Idaho at 127, 1908) upheld the state's juvenile court act, justifying the state's depriving a young person of freedom without due process in language clearly based on *parens patriae:*

> [The juvenile court's] object is to confer a benefit both upon the child and the community in the way of surrounding the child with better and more elevating influences and of educating and training him in the direction of good citizenship and thereby saving him to society and adding a good and useful citizen to the community. This, too, is done for the minor at a time when he is not entitled, either by natural law or the laws of the land, to his absolute freedom, but rather at a time when he is subject to the restraint and custody of either a natural guardian or a legally constituted and appointed guardian to whom he owes obedience and subjection. Under this law the state, for the time being, assumes to discharge the parental duty and to direct his custody and assume his restraint. . . .
>
> It would be carrying the protection of "inalienable rights," guaranteed by the Constitution, a long way to say that guarantee extends to a free and unlimited exercise of the whims, caprices, or proclivities of either a child or its parents or guardians for idleness, ignorance, crime, indigence or any kindred dispositions or inclinations.

Thus, although one can find a few early decisions limiting the juvenile courts' powers — in *Mill v. Brown* of 1907 (31 Utah 473, 1907), for example, the Utah Supreme Court released a child from the reformatory because the state had not adequately demonstrated the incompetence of the parents — and although there were a few legal critics of the courts and of *parens patriae* as a doctrine, for the most part the early years of the courts also represented a strengthening of the acceptance of *parens patriae* as the basis for society's response to juvenile offenders in America (Ryerson, 1978).

This was true not only at the level of the state courts but even at that of the United States Supreme Court. For example, in *People v. Lewis* (260 N.Y. 171, 1932, cert. den. 289 U.S. 709, 1933), an appeals court in New York reversed a decision of a juvenile court on the ground of inadequate procedure. Lewis, a boy of fifteen, after a most informal court hearing, had been committed to an industrial school for up to six years for theft. The highest court of New York reversed the decision of the appeals court, arguing that the goal of helping rather than punishing in the juvenile court made constitutional safeguards for due process unnecessary. (A strongly worded dissent, it should be noted, did attack the concept of *parens patriae* as justification for not requiring due process.) The *Lewis* case went on appeal to the U.S. Supreme Court in the early 1930s, but the Supreme Court refused to hear the case.

This consensus in court decisions does not mean, however, that the early juvenile courts lacked their critics. As Ryerson (1978:8) has suggested, "the honeymoon of the juvenile court with the public was remarkably brief." Indeed, criticism of the courts began fairly soon after their establishment as a range of problems began to appear in their administration and in their apparent impact — or lack of impact — on the problems they were intended to solve.

A Juvenile Court Ideal — And a Criminal Justice Approach

Several major concerns appeared frequently in discussions of the courts. One of these was that the courts, whatever their ideals, really did little to change the treatment of juvenile offenders. We have already noted that the Illinois act had no effect on the character of the state's inadequate, prisonlike reform school, and this seems to have been the case in other states as well. Beyond that, whatever the intent of early reformers and despite the presence of such men as Ben Lindsey, most juvenile courts functioned as institutions very close to criminal courts. Despite the ideal of focusing on the child rather than the crime, the tendency in practice was toward criminal proceedings and toward a concern with questions of guilt or innocence (Ryerson, 1978; Fox, 1970). Moreover, the atmosphere in many if not most juvenile courts was far from familial, with juvenile court judges relying heavily on threats and coercion rather than on friendship and advice (Platt, 1977:151).

Steven Schlossman (1977) has illustrated this aspect of juvenile court evolution thoroughly in his detailed account of the Milwaukee court. That court was established in 1901 as a result of the efforts of reformers much like those in Chicago. Founded on the doctrine of *parens patriae,* it was specifically intended to decriminalize juvenile delinquency and to provide an opportunity for rehabilitation rather than punishment as a response to juvenile crime. But, as Schlossman points out, the reality was often far from the ideal.

For one thing, Schlossman's evidence reveals, court transcripts in Milwaukee show judges and probation officers who relied mainly on fear and short-term imprisonment — detention — to render children cooperative. Although the majority of children were placed on probation rather than institutionalized, probation officers themselves — keys to the system in Milwaukee as in Chicago — were often petty moralists, eager to find the smallest faults in their clients and to see those faults as evidence of delinquent tendencies. Indeed, contrary to the prevailing ideology of the innate goodness of the child, those who administered juvenile justice in Milwaukee seemed far more ready to look for signs of criminality. Milwaukee judges and probation officers sought to incriminate children and their parents, not to find sources of family strength.

Many of the courts' early champions were aware of such problems and, indeed, directed their own criticism at the courts' operations. Such writers as Grace Abbott (1936) and Miriam Van Waters (1925) objected to the way in which the courts approximated criminal proceedings and argued that, if anything, the courts had to be more parental in their treatment of young people. They had to embody more fully the doctrine of *parens patriae.*

The Problem of Recidivism. This response on the part of such people as Van Waters and Abbott is important because it not only captured the gist of what might be called a "reform" criticism of the courts — that they did not put juvenile court ideals adequately into practice — but also responded to a criticism of the courts from a different direction. This was the criticism that the courts did not adequately respond to delinquency itself. A substantial number of critics of the early juvenile courts believed that the juvenile courts were ineffective at both reforming young offenders and protecting society from juvenile crime. These critics pointed to a high rate of recidivism among youngsters brought before the juvenile courts.

The problem of recidivism was hotly debated in the early days of the courts. Such defenders as Van Waters cited figures which appeared to indicate that the courts were reducing juvenile crime and, above all, that their efforts helped to reduce repeat offenses among juveniles (Van Waters, 1925). Other people saw very different results from the juvenile court. Surveys from the 1920s showed recidivism rates as high as 61 per cent among youngsters who had been through the program offered by the juvenile courts. Later surveys pointed to recidivism rates as high as 88 per cent (Finestone, 1976; Caldwell, 1961). To many Americans, such rates were strong evidence that the courts were not doing their job and that parental approaches were doomed to fail. Instead, these critics argued for more punitive responses to juvenile offenders, based on a recognition of juvenile delinquency as, above all, a species of crime to be answered by the full force of the criminal law. This debate, in particular, has remained constant in discussions of juvenile delinquency, not only in the United States but, as we shall see in Chapter 12, in other countries as well (see also the discussion in Platt, 1977).

The Failings of the Courts' Personnel. There were other criticisms of the juvenile courts from this period. Most notably, critics worried about the character and qualifications of those who administered the courts, especially the judges and probation officers, who often seemed poorly prepared for their jobs and unsympathetic to the young people brought before them. In addition, in many jurisdictions the courts suffered severe caseload problems, and the overcrowding of the courts made it increasingly difficult for judges, probation officers, and other professionals to give individual children the kind of time the court's ideal seemed to demand. There were too many children to allow judges and probation officers to establish close, "parental" relationships.

The U.S. Children's Bureau. None of these criticisms fell on deaf ears. In 1912, the federal government established the U.S. Children's Bureau to look into a broad range of matters affecting the welfare of American children (Mennel, 1973), and in 1918 the Bureau turned its attention to American juvenile courts. The bureau's investigators found that, to a shocking degree, those courts failed to live up to the juvenile court ideal. Although most did provide for separate hearings for juveniles accused of crimes, the bureau pointed to severe problems in the conduct of those hearings and singled out, as well, a widespread tendency to place accused youngsters into detention. This all too often meant detention in a county jail, where young offenders and adult criminals were indiscriminately boarded together. Such detention was often, one should note, in violation of state law (see Chapter 11). Under such conditions, the bureau concluded, the juvenile court ideal was unlikely to be realized (Ryerson, 1978).

Continuing Debate. Criticism of the juvenile courts mounted during the 1930s and 1940s, particularly as academic social scientists and others turned more and more attention to the problem of juvenile delinquency. We have already noted at least some dissatisfaction in the legal community over due process, even if the appellate courts continued to uphold the juvenile courts and their foundations in *parens patriae*. By removing juveniles from the criminal justice system, these scholars argued, the courts were also denying to youngsters many of the basic protections of due process—the right to trial by jury, for example, or the right to representation in what were really legal proceedings. These issues had been raised, of course, as long ago as the *Crouse* decision, discussed in Chapter 7, and they were raised, as well, in such cases as *O'Connell* and *Fisher*. Although they did not figure significantly in the early days of the juvenile court—when, as we have seen, the higher courts tended to support *parens patriae*—as we shall see in the pages to come, they became increasingly important after World War II.

Other criticisms focused on the juvenile courts' inability to engage in the proper treatment of delinquents, especially as sociologists developed more sophisticated ideas about deviance and delinquency, and even on the stigma—the perhaps debilitating stigma—attached to youngsters who, for whatever reason, were taken before the courts. This issue was especially important in the work of the sociologist-lawyer Paul Tappan, whose research in the New York City court, consistent with the labeling theories of Tannenbaum and Lemert, demonstrated how a loose administrative application of legal classifications to girls coming before the court "led to their effective stigmatization in the network of metropolitan welfare agencies" (in Lemert, 1970:28). In this and in other ways, many of the theoretical perspectives on delinquency discussed in Chapters 3–6 also informed criticism of the juvenile court.

Still, for all the criticism, and for all the validity of that criticism, the juvenile court system remained the primary approach to juvenile delinquency through World War II and into our own time. Beginning with the war era, however, and particularly with the 1960s, the juvenile court system underwent still closer and more skeptical investigation from many Americans and underwent modifications that had noticeable effects on the courts' bases and operations.

The Great Juvenile Delinquency Scare _____

One reason for this increasing scrutiny directed toward the juvenile courts in the post–World War II era lay in a heightened sense on the part of many people of the significance of juvenile delinquency as a problem in American life. That was especially true for the late 1940s and the decade of the 1950s.

Robert Mennel (1973:196) has described 1940 as a year that "represents several landmarks in the history of juvenile delinquency in the United States." It showed, above all, a strong commitment on the part of the federal government and others to the welfare of American youngsters and to the fight against delinquency through such activities as a White House Conference on Children and the approval by the American Law Institute of a model Youth Corrections Authority Act to provide guidelines to state governments on handling young offenders. But it was important in other ways as well. With the coming of the 1940s, and particularly of World War II, Americans began to develop a heightened consciousness of juvenile delinquency as a problem in their midst and as a problem that threatened the very fabric of American life. By the 1950s, many people believed that the matter had assumed crisis proportions, and they began to devote great attention and concern to what could be done about delinquency. It is no exaggeration to say that the late 1940s and early 1950s were the setting for a great American juvenile delinquency scare.

World War II and the Postwar Era: A Sense of Crisis

Gilbert (1986) has traced the main outlines of the juvenile delinquency scare. Beginning in late 1942 and early 1943, many Americans began to believe that crimes committed by youngsters were on the rise. The explanation for this increase seemed clear to them. The impact of the war had produced severe dislocations in American families, leading to a neglect of the children and, accordingly, to an outbreak of delinquency. There appeared to be evidence to support such an impression. "Zoot-suiters" in Los Angeles, "Victory Girls" who surrounded troop-training facilities, and other apparently rootless youngsters shocked many Americans. FBI statistics appeared to indicate a growing rate of crime by juveniles. Popular magazines picked up such evidence and made it appear to indicate a crime wave among American youth. Although the figures were debatable, to say the least, public concern was high, fueled by such visible figures as J. Edgar Hoover, director of the FBI, and the U.S. attorney general, Tom Clark. This concern lapped over into the postwar era, in terms of both popular ideas and governmental focus. The governmental focus translated into a range of activities, including a 1946 National Conference on the Prevention and Control of Juvenile Delinquency, a Senate Continuing Committee on the problem, and a 1950 White House Conference on Children.

Throughout the late 1940s and early 1950s, as Gilbert shows, these various bodies—particularly the FBI and the Continuing Committee—did much to keep the problem of delinquency in the public eye. Working with local groups and with the media, the committee's staff sought to address the sources of delinquency and to explore different approaches to combating it. The FBI sponsored a series of conferences on the subject and disseminated new ideas and theories to workers in the field. Although it was not the purpose of the Continuing Committee or the FBI to engage in scare tactics—and the FBI took what Gilbert shows to be a particularly responsible approach to the various findings and theories on juvenile delinquency—the upshot was, nevertheless, a strong public interest in and reaction to what appeared to be a growing problem in American society.

The Media and Delinquency: A Fifties Fear

We have already presented some evidence of this public interest when, in Chapter 2, we discussed recent popular concepts of delinquency, particularly as those concepts were embodied in such forms as the "JD films" of the mid-1950s and thereafter. Such films played on the popular concern of the period and, indeed, did much to increase it. But this popular consciousness of delinquency had more formal manifestations, as well, and these were a major part of the American response to juvenile delinquency after World War II. They took shape, as Gilbert shows, in a campaign to link delinquency to the American mass media.

Although this campaign took place on many fronts, it almost certainly came to a head in the mid-1950s through the activities of the United States Subcommittee to Investigate Juvenile Delinquency. The subcommittee was founded in 1953 but became especially visible after 1955 when Senator Estes Kefauver of Tennesse assumed its chair. The subcommittee investigated a range of causes of delinquency, receiving testimony from some of the era's most distinguished people with expertise in delinquency. But much of the focus was on the media. The television, radio, and film industries were all examined, and special attention was given to comic books, particularly those which made extensive use of violence. The subcommittee's hearings focused American attention on the possibility that the violence to which youngsters were exposed through American popular media was an important contributing factor in what appeared to be a juvenile crime wave (Gilbert, 1986).

The most significant figure in the Kefauver hearings and in seeking to forge links between popular culture and juvenile delinquency was Dr. Fredric Wertham, a leading American psychiatrist. Wertham had a long career of applying psychiatric theory and techniques to problems of crime and treatment, as well as in civil liberties activities and in championing civil rights. Going back to the late 1940s, Wertham began to argue that the violence in American popular culture was a powerful corrupting force among American youth and a leading cause of juvenile delinquency. His 1953 book, *The Seduction of the Innocent,* provided an influential statement of this argument, and the Kefauver hearings gave him a national forum from which to present it to a wider audience. A measure of Wertham's ideas may be gained from a passage in his final book, *A Sign for Cain,* published in 1966. Mass-media violence, he wrote, desensitized youngsters to the real suffering violence entailed. Beyond that, it even encouraged violent acts by children (1966:285):

> Murders by children connected with a mass-media factor keep on occurring. A boy of eight sexually abused a four-year-old girl and strangled her to death with a clothesline. Neighbors described him as "a normal, very nice boy from a wonderful family." Young as he was, he already had a real Superman complex. Other children called him The Boss. He used to talk about Bat Masterson and tell "stories about Batman and the people from other planets." The charge against him: "juvenile delinquency — homicide."

Wertham identified other factors leading to delinquency — racism, for example, as well as drugs and an ineffective juvenile justice system. But the attack on the American mass media figured strongly in his works and made Wertham himself a prominent figure.

Reports from the Kefauver subcommittee recognized that juvenile delinquency was the product of more than violent comic books or television shows, although, we should note, the debate over the effect of violence in the mass media on juvenile behavior remains lively. But the significance of the hearings did not lie in any theoretical advance they may have made in the understanding of juvenile delinquency. Rather, the significance of the hearings and of the campaign to link juvenile delinquency to the mass media, like that of the larger juvenile delinquency scare, lies in its indication of the extent to which many of the answers that preceding generations of juvenile delinquency workers had supplied to the problem of juvenile crime were widely viewed as inadequate. Wertham himself, for example, questioned the assumptions underlying *parens patriae* — as well as those underlying much delinquency theory — by citing cases of young offenders from good homes.

A Sense of Crisis: Mounting Criticism of the Juvenile Courts

This questioning went beyond the Kefauver hearings and the 1950s scare and led, ultimately, to an increasing skepticism about American society's major institutional response to juvenile delinquency, the juvenile court system. To some critics, the court was failing to do its duty because of its conservatism, because it was unable or unwilling to address the fundamental social and economic causes of delinquency. To others, the court was a failure precisely because of its welfare orientation, because it failed to punish youngsters who were, after all, guilty of criminal behavior. One judge, writing in 1954, made this case clearly (in Platt, 1977:156, n. 67):

> I cannot comprehend the reasoning that suggests that marauding gangs of little hoodlums armed with guns, knives, switch knives and other illegal weapons are to be considered as a matter of law incapable of committing the crime of murder. Infants under the age of 21 years, according to statistics, perpetrate a high percent- age of the heinous crimes committed throughout the country, and the situation has reached such serious proportions that it is a threat to the public welfare and safety of law-abiding citizens. . . . Murder by an individual criminal is bad enough but when it appears that a confirmed criminal has organized a group of teenagers for the sole purpose to murder and rob, then the time has come to examine the underlying philosophy of the treatment of juvenile offenders.

Such words as these recall earlier debates about the juvenile court and show the depth of pessimism at least some observers felt about the institution, and about the problem of delinquency, at the height of the 1950s scare.

And, indeed, this pessimism remained an important legacy of the 1950s, becoming a prominent feature of American thinking about delinquency during the 1960s and, as we shall see, beyond. One may note, for example, a 1967 report, *The Challenge of Crime in a Free Society*, by the President's Commission on Law Enforcement and Administration of Justice. The commission made a sweeping investigation of juvenile court practices and procedures and concluded in its report (Ryerson, 1978:146, 147), "The juvenile court has not succeeded significantly in rehabilitating delinquent youth, in reducing or stemming the tide of delinquency, or in bringing justice and compassion to the child offender." And the failure was seen to be more than one of the court's not living up to its own ideals, something earlier reformers had charged. According to the report, the real problem lay in the fact that delinquency represents "a pattern of behavior which is induced by a multitude of pervasive societal influences well beyond the reach of actions by any judge, probation officer, correction counsellor or psychiatrist" (Ryerson, 1978:147). Juvenile crime, that is to say, could resist the best-intentioned efforts of the juvenile courts to prevent it.

Due Process

One may trace several important developments in the American juvenile justice system to the turmoil and pessimism that had become so visible by the 1960s. Later in this chapter and in Chapter 10 we shall discuss legislative attempts to "recriminalize" at least some juvenile offending. In Chapter 11 we shall examine concerns about the character and effectiveness of detention and institutionalization for young offenders. In this chapter, however, we will focus on the one issue that had the most visible legal impact on the juvenile courts themselves, the issue of due process.

During the period we have been discussing, some of the most significant criticism of the courts — frequently expressed from the mid-1950s and through the following quarter century — came from those who, recognizing the failure of welfare-oriented approaches, believed that the juvenile courts could no longer justify what these critics saw as an invasion of personal rights on "humanitarian" grounds. The informality of the courts and the effort to "decriminalize" delinquency meant that children brought before the juvenile courts did not enjoy such benefits of due process as the right to counsel, to trial by jury, or, in many states, to appeal. This, to many critics, gave young offenders the worst of both worlds. Such youngsters were subject to removal from home and institutionalization, with none of the protections the law gave to adults accused of crime.

We have already noted that, even from the earliest days, the juvenile courts faced legal challenges and criticisms. The purpose of the juvenile court was to ensure that juvenile offenders should not be subjected to the rigors of criminal proceedings. In Chicago and elsewhere, the aim was to establish informal hearing procedures involving the youngster, the judge, and the appropriate experts, and to focus less on questions of guilt and innocence than on questions of the young person's welfare. But, again, that also meant that such hearings did not involve the traditional features of Anglo-American jurisprudence. That is to say, unless there were exceptional circumstances, youngsters brought before the juvenile court did not receive trials by jury, nor did they have the right to counsel in an adversarial proceeding. Put more simply, juvenile offenders could be subject to the sanctions of the law — even to commitment to a state institution for an indeterminate period — without receiving the due process of law. And this point was argued from the earliest days of the juvenile courts, as we have seen, in such notable cases as *Commonwealth v. Fisher.*

For the most part, during the early years, as we have also noted, the higher courts tended to uphold the juvenile courts, on the basis of *parens patriae.* Certainly through the 1920s there was some criticism of the courts on grounds of due process, but such criticism had little impact on either the courts or their practices. Although several cases challenging the juvenile court on due process grounds were mounted during that period, going as far as the United States Supreme Court, they had little effect.

In part this was because, as Binder (1984) has shown, more general American attitudes toward due process were not as strongly developed in the early twentieth century as they are in our own time. As he demonstrates, the due process protections of the United States Constitution were not applicable in state criminal trials at the beginning of the twentieth century and were made applicable very gradually in subsequent years. Rights for children came only after they were established for adults, and as the current era of concern for the welfare of children proceeded.

Binder points out that the phrase *due process of law* was first used in a reaffirmation of the Magna Carta in 1354. Essential due process protections were incorporated into the United States Constitution by the first ten amendments, the Bill of Rights. But in 1833, in *Barron v. Baltimore* (7 Peters 243), the Supreme Court ruled that the Bill of Rights applied only in federal courts, not in state courts. Even the Fourteenth Amendment, ratified in 1868, did not change matters, although it firmly restated (from the Fifth Amendment), "nor shall any state deprive any person of life, liberty, or property, without due process of law." A series of decisions of the Supreme Court between 1873 and 1905 made it clear that states were not required to conform to the provisions of the Bill of Rights, even given the words of the Fourteenth Amendment. And, it should be remembered, the first juvenile court came into being in 1899.

But, in 1925, the Court started reversing itself, and by 1969 virtually all guarantees of the Bill of Rights for procedural protection were made applicable to the states. The 1960s represented an especially important decade in this, for, according to Binder (1984:361), "Nine of the ten guarantees in the first eight amendments that are now applicable to the states were made so between 1962 and 1969." He cites several reasons for this change, traceable back to the 1930s, as the government, and later the courts, recognized that the well-being of the public was an affirmative governmental responsibility. But, whatever the cause, it is clear that the 1960s saw an expanded interest in the role of due process in juvenile courts and in society's response to juvenile delinquency as well.

Forces for Change: California and New York _____

Some of the pressure for change in juvenile court practices in light of due process questions came from within the states themselves and as a result of over a half century of experience with the courts. These were especially visible in the California Juvenile Court Act of 1961 and in the New York Family Court Act of 1962.

California

The California act was based on the recommendations of a commission appointed by the state's governor to study matters related to dependent and delinquent children. The *Report of the Governor's Special Study Commission on*

Juvenile Justice (Parts I and II), submitted in 1960, proposed a new juvenile statute and contained thirty-one specific recommendations.

The law to which the commission directed its attention was enacted in 1937, but many of its essential features dated from 1915. Governing the juvenile court, the law embodied the main features of *parens patriae,* providing that the juvenile offender should receive "care, custody, and discipline" that would "approximate as nearly as possible that which should be given by his parents." The commission found that the court, in operation, hardly approximated the ideal and pointed out a number of fairly specific problems (*Report of the Commission,* 1960a:12):

1. There is an absence of well-defined, empirically derived standards and norms to guide juvenile court judges, probation, and law enforcement officials in their decision making. Consequently, instead of a uniform system of justice, varied systems based upon divergent policies and values scales are in evidence. Actually, whether or not a juvenile is arrested, placed in detention, or referred to the probation department, and whether or not the petition is dismissed, probation is granted, or a CYA commitment is ordered by the juvenile court, seems to depend more upon the community in which the offense is committed than upon the intrinsic merits of the individual case.
2. Basic legal rights are neither being uniformly nor adequately protected under present juvenile court provisions and procedures.
3. The relatively independent status of the official agencies in the juvenile justice processes has produced inconsistencies in philosophy, imperfect coordination of efforts, and disparity in administration.
4. The quality of rehabilitative services is of questionable effectiveness and, in many instances, case decisions seem to be based upon considerations of expediency and administrative convenience rather than upon the objectives of rehabilitation and social justice. This is partly because juvenile courts and official delinquency control agencies have been seriously overtaxed by the sizable growth in the number of children brought to their attention without commensurate increases in available services, staff, or treatment facilities.
5. There is excessive and unwarranted detention of children in the state.
6. The present juvenile court statute contains numerous ambiguities and contradictions and is in urgent need of revision and reorganization.

These were criticisms that went to the heart of the juvenile court system.

To be sure, the commission did not question the basic foundation of the court in *parens patriae,* in the right of the state to "provide some or all parental guidance and assistance to children in need or in trouble," nor did it favor any change in the "relatively informal atmosphere" that had long been intended to distinguish the juvenile court (1960a:12–13). But it did recommend some significant changes, which were adopted in the 1961 law: three classes of minors subject to the law were established, a two-stage hearing process was adopted, and certain rights regarding counsel were made clear.

Differentiating Among Types of Children Subject to Court Jurisdiction. The prior law made young people subject to juvenile court proceedings for a great variety of reasons. It could place under the court's jurisdiction the child

(a) who is found begging, receiving or gathering alms, or who is found in any street, road, or public place for the purpose of so doing, whether actually begging or doing so under the pretext of selling or offering for sale any article, or of singing or playing on any musical instrument, or of giving any public entertainment or accompanying or being used in aid of any person so doing . . .

(d) whose home is an unfit place for him, by reason of neglect, cruelty, or depravity of either of his parents, or of his guardian or other person whose custody or care he is . . .

(j) who is a habitual truant from school within the meaning of any law of this state . . .

(m) who violates any law of this State or any ordinance of any town, city, or county, of this State defining crime.

The act was structured such that a ward of the court could just as easily be an eight-year-old who was neglected, a twelve-year-old who stayed away from school regularly, or a nineteen-year-old who committed many armed robberies.

The revised code, identifying three separate classes of minors subject to the court's jurisdiction, made distinctions based on the nature of the problem that brought the child to the court's attention and on the appropriate alternative possible treatment. Each class was described in a separate section of the code. Section 600 specified dependent and neglected children, Section 601 status offenders, and Section 602 included violators of any criminal law or ordinance. For each section there was a separate listing of allowed dispositions. For example, a 602 minor, but not a 600 or 601 minor, could be committed to a state institution under the authority of the California Youth Authority; a 602 minor and a 601 minor, but not a 600 minor, could be committed to a county juvenile home, ranch, or camp; but all three types could be placed in a suitable private facility or foster home.

This aspect of California law was to undergo some refinement. Court decisions about "statutory vagueness" or the failure of statutory language to provide adequate notice of what behavior brings a child within juvenile court jurisdiction led California to amend Section 601 by deleting broad language that could bring before the court any child "who from any cause is in danger of leading an idle, dissolute, lewd or immoral life." Nevertheless, the distinction itself represented an important change in California juvenile court law.

Legislative Reform and Due Process. Other changes inaugurated by the 1961 California law more clearly addressed due process concerns. Prior to 1961, California law stipulated that "the court shall proceed to hear and dispose of the case in a summary manner." That led in practice, according to the *Report of the Commission* (1960a:28), to a failure of the juvenile courts to "distinguish between the jurisdictional facts and the social data at the hearing." This meant that court decisions were often rendered before any charges had been substantiated.

In response, the 1961 law provided for a two-stage hearing procedure, consisting of an adjudicatory (or jurisdictional) hearing followed by a dispositional hearing. In the first stage, the court considers only whether the allegations against the young persons are true; that is, whether the minor comes under Section 600, 601, or 602. The purpose of the adjudicatory hearing is comparable to the purpose of the trial in criminal court in the determination of guilt or innocence, although the standard of proof in the 1961 law for the juvenile court was "preponderance of evidence" rather than "beyond a reasonable doubt," as in a criminal court. This first-stage hearing was intended to force the juvenile court to deal adequately with the allegations that brought youngsters under its jurisdiction.

Due process also became an issue in the 1961 law's attention to the right of juvenile offenders to counsel. Before 1961, California juvenile court law did not specifically state that a minor had the right to counsel, and there was no duty to provide counsel if a youngster or the family could not afford to do so. The new law mandated provision for counsel for 602 offenders charged with felonies; the court was required to appoint counsel (usually from the public defender's office) if the minor could not afford one. In addition, all minors brought to the court's attention had to be informed of their right to have counsel present at juvenile court hearings.

The 1961 California statute, influential in other states, brought some major changes to the juvenile court. It showed, moreover, the growing awareness of the significance of due process concerns in the deposition of juvenile court cases.

New York

Changes wrought by the New York Family Court Act of 1962 were similar to those created by the 1961 California act but arguably went beyond the provisions of the California law in regard to due process (Brantingham, 1979). Sources for change in New York were varied. Much impetus came from the Judicial Conference, assigned the task of recommending a reorganization of the state's courts. The Judicial Conference reported to the governor of New York in November 1958, recommending the establishment of a statewide Family Court. The Family Court was to be given power over a wide range of cases, including those involving child neglect, custody, adoption, support of dependents, establishment of paternity, proceedings for conciliation of spouses, guardianship, and "crimes and offenses, except felonies, by or against children" (Paulsen, 1963:423).

"PINS." As did California, New York adopted a system distinguishing among three kinds of youngsters subject to the Family Court's jurisdiction: criminal children; children brought before the court by reason of dependence, neglect, or abuse; and those who engaged in troublesome but noncriminal behavior. A youngster included in the last category was considered a "person in need of supervision" and was identified as a boy under sixteen or a girl under eighteen who was a habitual truant or who was incorrigible, ungovernable, or habitually disobedient and beyond the control of parent or other guardian. Young people under this classification quickly came under the acronym PINS. This consolidation and labeling, according to Brantingham (1979:268), "made the entire category of troublesome behavior jurisdiction . . . visible in a way it had not been before." And this aspect of the New York act, along with the similar distinction drawn in the California law, was highly influential. As

Brantingham notes (1979), during the 1960s and 1970s, similar provisions were adopted by twenty five other states — along with such appropriate acronyms as "CINS" or "CHINS" (Child in Need of Supervision), or "JINS" (Juvenile in Need of Supervision).

Due Process Reforms. The New York Family Court Act also resembled the California law in providing for a two-stage hearing process, carefully distinguishing between "adjudicatory hearings" and "dispositional hearings." Where the New York act goes beyond California law, however, is in regard to right to counsel. The act itself articulates a legislative finding "that counsel is often indispensable to a practical realization of due process of law and may be helpful in making reasoned determination of fact and proper orders of disposition." To implement this, the act establishes a system of "law guardians" whose function it is to represent individuals brought before the Family Court, including delinquent youngsters and PINS, and at public expense (Paulsen, 1963:433–434). Lawyers had not previously been barred from the New York juvenile courts, although their presence had been rare. Following the 1962 restructuring of the courts, their presence became common and shifted much of the focus of hearings to encompass issues of due process (see Prescott [1981] for a good, journalistic account of the family court's operation in New York City).

The changes in California and New York, influential on other states, came largely from internal sources — from commissions formed to examine the states' legal systems and, one might note, also from agitation within the legal community. In both California and New York, some impetus for change came from private attorneys and legal aid societies dissatisfied with the juvenile courts' operations (see Lemert, 1970; Prescott, 1981). These internal forces for change were buttressed, beginning in the middle of the 1960s, by the powerful stimulus of a series of United States Supreme Court decisions that called for the provision of due process in juvenile court cases.

Supreme Court Decisions

Kent v. United States

The first of the Supreme Court decisions to call for due process was *Kent v. United States* (1966). Morris A. Kent, Jr., was fourteen years old when he initially came under the authority of the juvenile court of the District of Columbia. He had been arrested for breaking into several houses as well as for trying to snatch a woman's purse. The court placed Kent on probation in the custody of his mother but under the sporadic monitoring of probation officers.

About two years later, when Kent was sixteen, his fingerprints were found in the apartment of a woman whose wallet had been stolen and who had been raped. He was still on probation at the time. Under interrogation by police after the second arrest, Kent admitted the rape and the theft of the wallet and also volunteered information regarding many other offenses of housebreaking, robbery, and rape.

A code of the District of Columbia allowed a juvenile court judge to waive jurisdiction to the adult criminal court for a child sixteen years of age or older charged with a serious crime, "after full investigation." As we shall see in Chapter 10, such provisions are common in state codes. The juvenile court judge in the Kent case waived Kent to the criminal court without a hearing, apparently interpreting the requirement of "full investigation" to mean private consultation and reflection. The judge did not confer with Kent or Kent's attorney, ignored the attorney's motions stemming from a belief that Kent suffered from "severe psychopathology," made no findings, and gave no reasons for the waiver.

After the waiver order, Kent was indicted by a grand jury and tried by the United States District Court for the District of Columbia. The jury found him guilty on six counts of housebreaking and robbery but "not guilty by reason of insanity" for rape. He was sentenced to a total of thirty to ninety years in prison for the housebreaking and robbery convictions. If Kent's case had remained in juvenile court, he could have been institutionalized for no more than five years.

Kent's appeal reached the U.S. Supreme Court, with the argument that the juvenile court's waiver of jurisdiction had not been properly conducted, that there had been no "full investigation" as the law required, and, thus, that the case should not have been waived to the criminal court. The Supreme Court agreed. The juvenile court's action had been arbitrary, the court decided, and, thus, invalid. According to the court's decision, a youngster accused of crime is entitled to certain minimum rights and procedures before a waiver is granted. Because Kent had not been accorded those rights, the case was remanded to the District Court for a new hearing on waiver (*Kent v. United States*, 383 U.S. 541, 1966).

In Re Gault

The action in *Kent* to require minimum procedural standards in the determination of waiver was followed the next year, 1967, by *In re Gault* (387 U.S. 1), which stipulated minimum standards in adjudicatory hearings. Along with *Ex parte Crouse*, the 1838 case that established *parens patriae* in the American judicial system, *In re Gault* — which had entirely the opposite effect — is one of the two most notable decisions in the history of the American juvenile justice system.

Fifteen-year-old Gerald Gault and a friend were arrested by a deputy sheriff in Gila County, Arizona, on the basis of a complaint by a neighbor of the boys. She complained about a telephone call that involved lewd and indecent remarks. (The actual remarks, as quoted in Prescott [1981:71], consisted of three questions: "Do you give any?" "Are your cherries ripe today?" and "Do you have big bombers?"). When arrested for the call, Gault was under probation as a result of previously having been in the company of another boy who had stolen a wallet.

After his arrest, Gault was taken to a detention home where he was kept for several days. His parents were not notified of the arrest, of his custody in the home, or of a petition filed with the juvenile court for an initial hearing. In a subsequent adjudicatory hearing, Gault and his parents were not formally notified of the charges against him, there was no right to counsel, there was no right to confrontation and cross-examination (the offended woman never even appeared at the hearing), there was no privilege against self-incrimination — Gault's admissions of guilt were accepted with an absence of procedural safeguards — and there was no right either to a transcript of the proceedings or to appeal to a higher court in Arizona. As a result of the findings of the hearing, Gault was committed to an institution for six years. It should perhaps be pointed out that the penalty in the Arizona Penal Code for a person who "in the presence or hearing of any woman or child . . . uses vulgar, abusive, or obscene language" was a fine of $5 to $50 or imprisonment for not more than two months. And for an adult, in contrast to Gault, even that comparatively slight punishment could occur only after a trial with due process protections.

S. Harris

*"Six months for possession of a cigarette? I got thirty
days for possession of a deadly weapon."*

Gault was committed to an institution for six years. If he had
been an adult, the maximum penalty for the offense would
have been a small fine or imprisonment for two months.

The wording of the *Gault* decision, written by Justice Fortas, showed clearly that the U.S. Supreme Court was appalled by the treatment of Gault in Arizona's court system. It is likely that a court of an earlier era would have responded much differently. But, in the late 1960s, there was shock bordering on outrage (at 27):

> Ultimately, however, we confront the reality of that portion of the Juvenile Court process with which we deal in this case. A boy is charged with misconduct. The boy is committed to an institution where he may be restrained of liberty for years. It is of no constitutional consequence — and of limited practical meaning — that the institution to which he is committed is called an Industrial School. The fact of the matter is that, however euphemistic the title, a "receiving home" or an 'industrial school" for juveniles is an institution of confinement in which the child is incarcerated for a greater or lesser time. His world becomes "a building with white-washed walls, regimented routine and institutional hours. . . . " Instead of mother and father and sisters and brothers and friends and classmates, his world is peopled by guards, custodians, state employees, and "delinquents" confined with him for anything from waywardness to rape and homicide.

Given the character of institutionalization, the proceedings of the juvenile court were, according to the decision, improper. "Under our Constitution," Justice Fortas stated, "the condition of being a boy does not justify a kangaroo court." Noting that Gerald appeared to have come from a good home, the justices questioned why, given traditional notions underlying the juvenile court, the judge did not explore the possibility that the boy could have been "disciplined and dealt with at home." And, echoing earlier critics of the juvenile court, Justice Fortas noted the remarkable gap between the juvenile court's ideal and its reality.

> Indeed, so far as appears in the record before us, except for some conversation with Gerald about his school work and his "wanting to go to . . . Grand Canyon with his father," the points to which the judge directed his attention were little different from those that would be involved in determining any charge of violation for a penal statute. (At 28)

This led to the Supreme Court's most significant point:

> The essential difference between Gerald's case and a normal criminal case is that safeguards available to adults were discarded in Gerald's case. The summary procedure as well as the long commitment was possible because Gerald was 15 years of age instead of over 18. (At 29).

It was as a result of such considerations that the Court found that Gault had been unconstitutionally confined in a state institution because he was denied his right to due process. And, on specific requirements of due process, the Court ruled:

> Due process of law requires notice of the sort we have described — that is, notice which would be deemed constitutionally adequate in civil or criminal proceedings. It does not allow a hearing to be held in which a youth's freedom and his parents'

right to his custody are at stake without giving them a timely notice, in advance of the hearing, on the specific issues that they must meet. (At 33, 34)

We conclude that the Due Process Clause of the Fourteenth Amendment requires that in respect of proceedings to determine delinquency which may result in commitment to an institution in which the juvenile's freedom is curtailed, the child and his parents must be notified of the child's right to be represented by counsel to be retained by them, or if they are unable to afford counsel, that counsel will be appointed to represent the child. (At 41)

It would indeed be surprising if the privilege against self-incrimination were available to hardened criminals but not to children. The language of the Fifth Amendment, applicable to the States by operation of the Fourteenth Amendment, is unequivocal and without exception. (At 47)

Absent a valid confession adequate to support the determination of the Juvenile Court, confrontation and sworn testimony by witnesses available for cross-examination were essential for a finding of "delinquency" and an order committing Gerald to a state institution for a maximum of six years. (At 56)

In summary, the Court made the following rights and privileges mandatory in juvenile adjudicatory hearings where there could be a commitment to a state institution for "delinquency": timely notice of specific issues in advance of the hearing, notification of right to counsel and appointment of counsel if the family cannot afford one, protection against direct and implied coercion in confessions, and sworn testimony subject to an opportunity for cross-examination.

The Court did not rule on the questions of lack of provision for appellate review, the failure to provide a transcript of the hearing, and the failure of the juvenile court judge to state reasons for his decisions.

The Court's decision was not unanimous, and in a strong dissent, Justice Stewart made clear both his feeling that *Gault* undermined *parens patriae* and that *parens patriae* itself should remain a fundamental part of juvenile court proceedings. He wrote:

And to impose the Court's long catalog of requirements upon juvenile proceedings in every area of the country is to invite a long step backwards into the nineteenth century. In that era there were no juvenile proceedings, and a child was tried in a conventional criminal court with all the trappings of a conventional criminal trial. So it was that a 12-year-old body named James Guild was tried in New Jersey for killing Catharine Beakes. A jury found him guilty of murder, and he was sentenced to death by hanging. The sentence was executed. It was all very constitutional. (At 79–80)

Stewart's dissent shows the extent to which what had by then become traditional views of juvenile justice remained important.

And, in fact, despite Stewart's fears, statements in both the *Kent* and the *Gault* decision made it clear that the Court was not entirely rejecting the older juvenile court ideal. Instead, it was attempting to remove blatant abuses from juvenile court procedure without destroying its central orientation — at least in theory — of compassionate concern for the child. As Schultz and Cohen have argued (1976), *Gault* saw the failure of the juvenile court system as a failure of operations, not philosophy. In *Gault,* for example, the Court asserted that "the observance of due process standards, intelligently and not ruthlessly administered, will not compel the States to abandon or displace any of the substantial benefits of the juvenile process' (at 21).

Subsequent Decisions

That attempt to balance procedural fairness with the spirit of *parens patriae* has, in fact, led to a series of decisions over subsequent years that have seemed, in many ways, contradictory. In 1970, the Court decided in *In re Winship* (397 U.S. at 368) that the standard of proof in juvenile court for delinquency hearings must be "beyond a reasonable doubt" rather than the more usual basis of "preponderance of the evidence," upholding the tendency toward due process. In a dissenting opinion, however, one justice, Warren Burger, questioned whether such an emphasis on due process would not severely endanger what he saw as a necessary degree of flexibility in the institution.

And, indeed, in *McKeiver v. Pennsylvania* (403 U.S. 528), rendered in 1971, the Court tilted in the direction of *parens patriae* by ruling against the requirement of a jury trial in juvenile court proceedings. Subsequently, however, in 1975, in *Breed v. Jones* (421 U.S. 519), the Court again upheld due process by holding that a youngster had been unconstitutionally placed in double jeopardy by being waived for trial in a criminal court after an adjudicatory hearing in which the allegations against the youngster were sustained.

The record is, thus, not wholly clear. But it is certain that after *Kent* and, particularly, *Gault,* the issue of due process has become a central one in the continuing development of the juvenile courts.

The Impact of Due Process

Just as the record of court decisions on due process is not wholly clear, neither is the impact of *Kent, Gault,* and other decisions on the juvenile court system itself. Although we shall discuss this question in more detail in Chapter 10, we may note certain broad issues to which it has given rise at this point. In general, we may note that, despite the major decisions we have discussed here, juvenile courts continue to retain broad powers over those youngsters who come under their jurisdiction. At the same time, one can see areas in which due process decisions have had a real influence on the operations of the courts. Binder and Binder (1982), for example, have traced a number of decisions in which the courts have had to face due-process-based challenges at almost every level of their operation and have shown how such challenges have made juvenile delinquency professionals cognizant of the *issue* of due process when formulating programs for the treatment of delinquency.

Platt (1977), examining one particular due process issue, has focused on the impact of the right to counsel on juvenile court processes and has found somewhat mixed results. According to Platt, the introduction of lawyers into the juvenile court has not really led to the development of the adversarial criminal proceedings of traditional Anglo-American jurisprudence. To the contrary, he argues, most attorneys who take juvenile cases tend to operate within the older, informal patterns of the juvenile court, assuming the role of negotiator between judge and family and, for the most part, accepting the older welfare-oriented approaches on which the court was based. To the extent that Platt is right, such decisions as *Gault* have changed the form but not the substance of juvenile court proceedings.

Wisconsin: A Case Study

Perhaps the easiest way to see the development of American attitudes and the impact of *Gault* and other decisions is to follow the evolution of juvenile court law in a single American jurisdiction. We have chosen Wisconsin as a fairly typical example of a system that has had to confront some of the legal changes and challenges we have discussed.

The Wisconsin juvenile court dates back to the early years of the twentieth century. Following the precedent of the Illinois law of 1899, Wisconsin enacted Chapter 90 of the Laws of 1901, creating in Milwaukee County the first juvenile court in the state. Like the Illinois law, the one in Wisconsin was aimed at the control and rehabilitation of dependent, neglected, and delinquent children below the age of sixteen. It allowed the juvenile court to " . . . commit the child to the care and guardianship of a probation officer . . . and allow said child to remain in its home . . . "; place the child with "a suitable family, subject to the friendly supervision of the probation officer"; "commit the child . . . to an industrial school"; or "commit the child to the care and custody of some association or institution that will receive it, embracing in its objects the care of neglected, dependent or delinquent children" (Section 6).

In 1905 (Chapter 496, Laws of 1905), certain acts of misconduct were specified as justifying the label "delinquent" for a child:

> The words "delinquent child" shall include any child, under the age of sixteen years . . . who is incorrigible; or who knowingly associates with thieves, vicious or immoral persons; or who is growing up in idleness or crime; or who knowingly patronizes any place where any gaming device is or shall be operated; or who knowingly visits or enters a house of ill-repute; or who patronizes, visits, or enters any stall, saloon, or wine room, or any saloon frequented by men or women of bad repute; or who attends, visits or enters any dance held in any room or hall in connection with a saloon, unless accompanied by parents or legal guardian; or who loafs or congregates with groups or gangs of other boys at or about railroad yards or tracks; or who habitually uses obscene, vulgar or profane language, or is guilty of immoral conduct in any public place, or about any schoolhouse.

Thus, in Wisconsin, in 1905 a youth below the age of sixteen did not have to commit a criminal offense to be considered "delinquent." Indeed, a boy could be designated "delinquent" if he visited a saloon or if he congregated with other boys at a railroad crossing.

In the early years, it should be noted, Wisconsin juvenile court law required a preliminary hearing for youths charged with more serious crimes and permitted release of a youth on bail. Both of these provisions were dropped as the law matured.

In 1911, the upper age for delinquency was set at seventeen for girls and sixteen for boys, and in 1929 the upper age became seventeen for both sexes.

The 1911 act, too, expanded the applicability of juvenile court legislation to all counties.

The constitutionality of Wisconsin's juvenile court law was considered by that state's supreme court in 1918. The case was an appeal from a court in Milwaukee County that had placed two boys on probation after declaring them delinquent. Lawyers for the youths argued that the law was unconstitutional because it did not allow a jury trial and authorized criminal conviction without due process. The Wisconsin Supreme Court, like other state courts previously and subsequently, declared that the *parens patriae* philosophy was appropriate in the judicial handling of juveniles (*State v. School, State v. Pollard,* 167 Wis. 504, 167 N.W. 830, 1918). The following sentiment has been repeated many times (167 Wis. at 509, 167 N.W. at 831):

> It is sufficient to say on this point that the proceedings under this law are in no sense criminal proceedings, nor is the result in any case a conviction or punishment for crime. They are simply statutory proceedings by which the state in the legitimate exercise of its police power, or, in other words, its right to preserve its own integrity and future existence, reaches out its arm in a kindly way and provides for the protection of its children from parental neglect or from vicious influences and surroundings, either by keeping watch over the child while in its natural home, or where that seems impracticable, by placing it in an institution designed for that purpose.

Several other constitutional challenges followed in Wisconsin, but the law was upheld by its Supreme Court in each case. A quotation from the decision *In re Alley* (174 Wis. at 91–92, 182 N.W. at 362, 1921) dramatically contrasts with later sentiments of the U.S. Supreme Court and the Wisconsin Supreme Court itself. Time and circumstances were not yet on the side of concern for due process rights:

> This law was not designed as a method of punishment for crimes committed by juveniles. Every section and paragraph of the statute is permeated with the benevolent purpose of improving the child's condition and not with punishing his past conduct. The whole object and purpose of this law will be defeated if it is construed and applied as a punitive statute.

Subsequent years saw many changes in procedural details. However, even a major revision of Wisconsin's juvenile court law in 1955 did not alter its paternal, nonadversary emphasis. While a jury trial could be held on demand of the petitioned minor, the hearing could be as informal as the judge desired. The judge, at will, could waive the presence in court of the youth, the right to appointed counsel was at court discretion, there was no provision for confrontation and cross-examination of witnesses, and there was no stated privilege against self-incrimination.

Perhaps because of the major revision in 1955, there is no evidence of effort in Wisconsin to introduce the profound changes in juvenile law that came about in California and New York in the early 1960s. But it would seem worthy of note in passing that in 1967 an article by Lemert was published in Wisconsin that extolled the changes in juvenile law that had occurred in California several years earlier. Even that article produced no noticeable impact on relevant legislation in Wisconsin.

Interestingly, a note in the *Wisconsin Law Review* (Dix, 1966) pointed out that many youngsters in Wisconsin (up to 1965) were transferred to adult correctional facilities for custody after being declared delinquent by a juvenile court with the usual lack of full constitutional protections. In 1964, for example, 170 youths who had been committed to juvenile institutions by juvenile courts were administratively transferred to adult correctional institutions. The note, written before the *Gault* decision appeared, states (1966:905):

> The asserted dichotomy between juvenile and adult correctional institutions does not, in an advanced correctional system, seem substantial enough to warrant finding in constitutional due process an absolute prohibition of transfer. But, on the other hand, this admission casts doubt on the validity of the reduced standard of procedural regularity in the juvenile "trial" system; if the consequences of a juvenile commitment are no different from those of an adult commitment, how can the failure to extend full procedural due process at "trial" be justified?

Still, despite such sentiments as those of Dix, the mid-1960s saw no general rethinking of juvenile court policies and procedures in Wisconsin. Interestingly, this would be the case even in the face of such Supreme Court decisions as *Kent* and *Gault,* although, of course, the state had to adjust to the legal demands of those decisions.

About six months after the *Kent* decision, the Wisconsin Supreme Court decided a case (*Winburn v. State*, 32 Wis. 2d 152, 145 N.W. 2d 178, 1966) that involved the issue of insanity as a defense in juvenile court. The influence of *Kent*, in which the U.S. Supreme Court had ruled that a youth is entitled to the "essentials of due process and fair treatment" (including effective legal counsel), was shown in lengthy and frequent references to the decision. It was also shown in such statements as "The philosophy behind the juvenile act is rehabilitation and treatment, but what may appear to a juvenile worker or judge as treatment may look like punishment to the juvenile" (32 Wis. at 161, 145 N.W. at 182). One may compare that statement with the above quotation from *In re Alley* to see the impact of *Kent* on the Wisconsin Supreme Court.

Such a revised view did not, however, have immediate impact on legislation, not even after the reinforcement provided by the 1967 *Gault* decision, which had so clearly specified fundamental rights to be observed in a juvenile proceeding. Indeed, the Wisconsin legislature failed to modify those portions of its juvenile law which were made unconstitutional by the *Gault* decision. For example, Wisconsin law made the appointment of counsel discretionary whereas *Gault* made it mandatory, and Wisconsin law allowed waiver of the presence of the child by the court at any stage of the hearing whereas *Gault* insisted on the right of the child to confront and cross-examine witnesses. The Wisconsin courts were bound by the decision of the U.S. Supreme Court, of course, and so there was the anomalous result of actual juvenile court procedure that satisfied constitutional requirements but was at variance with the provisions of state law. This remained the state of affairs in Wisconsin for some time. Writing in 1976, Larson commented (1976:263, 264):

> Eight years have passed since *Gault* first outlined the procedural requirements of due process of law with respect to juvenile justice. While Wisconsin courts are guided by the law as prescribed in appellate decisions, the Wisconsin statutes offer

no assistance in several areas because the state legislature has failed to correct unconstitutional statutory provisions. At each of the five legislative sessions since *Gault* was decided, one and sometimes several bills have been prepared to update the children's code, all of which have died in committee.

Such a haphazard approach to juvenile justice reform characterized the state's response to subsequent decisions. The *McKeiver* decision of the U.S. Supreme Court, denying the right to trial by jury in juvenile court, had no effect in Wisconsin because a jury trial was permitted when an appropriate demand was made. But Wisconsin law did allow the finding of fact in juvenile court on the basis of a preponderance of the evidence before *Winship,* so a shift to a standard based on "beyond a reasonable doubt" was required after that Supreme Court decision in 1970.

Finally, in 1978 Wisconsin changed its waiver statute to provide specific procedures and substantive criteria for that decision regarded by the U.S. Supreme Court as "critical" in *Kent.*

In Wisconsin, then, the impact of *Gault* and other influences supporting the recognition of due process in juvenile courts has not produced anything like a revolution in juvenile court proceedings. Rather, the reaction has involved more of a piecemeal response to individual high court decisions as those decisions have been handed down. And this has been the case in other states and other juvenile court systems. Prescott (1981), for example, has documented the extent to which more traditional, paternalist approaches—and even judicial arbitrariness—have remained the norm in New York City's juvenile justice system, despite the Family Court Act of 1962 and the impact of Supreme Court decisions.

Nevertheless, by introducing due process concerns into juvenile court proceedings, such varied forces as the New York and California acts from the early 1960s and the significant Supreme Court decisions handed down beginning in the latter part of the 1960s have affected much of the formal operation of the juvenile courts, much of what goes on in those courts day by day. We shall see this when, in Chapter 10, we examine the operations of the courts in more detail.

Due Process and the Juvenile Court Ideal

Gault and other Supreme Court decisions have been critically important in forcing a general rethinking of juvenile courts and their role in society, particularly in light of the apparent failure of the courts to stem what some see as a tide of juvenile crime. These decisions, that is, have occurred within the framework of the continuing debate between welfare- and criminal-justice-based, punitive approaches to juvenile crime, and they have played a role in the character and impact of that debate.

Anticipating a more detailed discussion in Chapter 10, we may note here that the mid-1970s saw a conservative trend in thinking about juvenile delinquency as such influential figures as James Q. Wilson and Ernest van den Haag argued for a more punitive approach to crime in general. Their views were supported by the despairing emphases of such criminologists as Robert Martinson, who, in 1974, made the then-famous assertion "nothing works" (quoted in Miller, 1979:84). That point of view was not confined to scholars and other academics.

In 1977, a joint committee of New York University's Institute of Judicial Administration and the American Bar Association formulated a set of *Standards for Juvenile Justice* that, in line with the punitive notions of such figures as Wilson and van den Haag, proposed what was essentially a "recriminalization" of juvenile delinquency. Tellingly, the committee coupled its criminal justice approach with a concern for due process for juveniles brought before the court.

One sees the committee's model for juvenile justice in several of the underlying principles that it cited to govern its proposals. Thus, for example, the committee argued that sanctions for juvenile offenders should be "based on the seriousness of the offense committed, and not merely the court's view of the juvenile's needs," a clear rejection of the philosophy underlying the founding of the juvenile courts. The committee also argued that noncriminal offenses should be removed from the juvenile court's jurisdiction and that the court should become, in effect, a separate criminal court for juveniles. At the same time, the committee's view of procedural protections went beyond even *Gault*, urging the requirement of written decisions, the right to appeal, and other safeguards that the Supreme Court had not addressed in that case. The committee's emphasis was not entirely on punishment. It also made the argument that in the disposition of cases, juvenile court judges should seek to impose the "least restrictive alternative" when any sentencing was required. But the thrust of the committee's report was to reject older, welfare-based approaches to juvenile delinquency and to treat juvenile delinquency as, in fact, juvenile crime (Paulsen, 1979).

The report of the committee did not lack impact. As early as 1977, the state of Washington used it as a basis for redrafting its juvenile code. Echoing older notions that the juvenile court should be capable of responding to the needs of youngsters, the code caught the newer spirit by saying, "it is further the intent of the legislature that the young, in turn, be held accountable for their offenses." The protection of society, rather than the rehabilitation of the young, was the explicit center of the new Washington code. In 1977–1978, New York took a similar, if more modest, step through a series of bills that required confinement, including a mandatory period of secure confinement, for youngsters over the age of thirteen found guilty of committing certain "designated felony acts" (1979:221–223). We shall see other efforts along these lines in Chapter 10, where we discuss in detail the juvenile court's operations.

It would, of course, be incorrect to say that such decisions as *Gault* and *Kent* made possible the New York laws and the Washington code. Indeed, their intent was precisely the opposite: it was to protect the rights of young people while maintaining a focus on the rehabilitation of those found to be delinquent. Nor would it be correct to say that "recriminalization" represents the only trend in juvenile justice today. As we shall see in looking at the operations of the courts, much of the traditional welfare-oriented approach to delinquency remains at the center. And, as we shall see in Chapter 11, the conservative tendencies of the 1960s and 1970s we have documented here were to some extent counterbalanced by liberal efforts to "deinstitutionalize" the treatment of juvenile offenders. Nevertheless, questions of due process and of recriminalization have made the most notable impact on the operations of the juvenile justice system during the past two decades.

Summary _____

The American juvenile justice system has a complex historical background. Its roots go well back into the nineteenth century, to the doctrine of *parens patriae* and to the effort to set young offenders apart from adults. The main approaches to juvenile justice in America were fixed at the close of that century with the founding of the Illinois juvenile court. The Illinois court served as a model for the juvenile courts that are now found in every state in the United States.

But the history of the juvenile courts themselves has not been a story of unbroken development. Almost from the beginning, the juvenile courts have faced strong criticisms and challenges and have had to respond, at least to some degree, to those challenges. These challenges have come from several fronts. One has been that the courts themselves, in their daily operations, have been held up to the ideals that led to their establishment and have often been found lacking. Expected to play a parental role for delinquents and other troubled children, the juvenile courts have often been overcrowded and incompetently staffed, leading to an abrupt, unsympathetic treatment of youngsters coming under the courts' jurisdiction.

Other criticisms have focused on the courts' apparent inability to reduce juvenile crime. Referring to what they see as high rates of recidivism, critics who make this charge often claim that the treatment focus of the juvenile court is inadequate in the face of a youthful criminal element and that more punitive, criminal-justice-oriented approaches are necessary instead. Other critics, who have seen the same problem of high recidivism, have responded that, if anything, the courts have not been parental enough and that more effective, treatment-based approaches are necessary if juvenile crime is to be reduced. The debate between these two groups goes back to the very earliest days of the juvenile courts. It has continued into our own time, underlying many of the other issues raised about the courts.

But, certainly, the major issue in the recent history of the American juvenile courts has been that of due process. Although there were early challenges to the juvenile courts on due process grounds — as there had been challenges to previous American approaches to delinquency — these challenges had been unsuccessful. With the establishment of the juvenile courts, the doctrine of *parens patriae* on which they were based itself became established in American jurisprudence. The constitutionality of the juvenile courts and their operations were generally upheld in America's higher courts.

The 1960s, however, saw legislative and judicial concern for the role of due process in juvenile court proceedings. In part, this may have been the product of a more general recognition of the rights of defendants — adult as well as juvenile — in criminal proceedings. These due process concerns were brought into the juvenile court systems in two major ways. First, in such states as California and New York during the early years of the decade, pressure from various sources led to major revisions in juvenile court statutes, and these revisions clearly encompassed due process concerns. The revisions distinguished between different classes of young people who might appear before the court. The revisions provided for two types of hearings for a young person brought under the courts' jurisdictions, one to establish fact and the other to address the disposition of a case. And the revisions provided for the right to counsel as well as other rights that had previously been deemed unnecessary in the informal, treatment-oriented setting of the juvenile court.

Second, from the middle of the 1960s through the 1970s, the United States Supreme Court handed down a series of decisions that required the observance of due process in juvenile court cases. Most notable were the *Kent* decision of 1966 and the *Gault* decision of 1967, each of which addressed substantive aspects of juvenile court operations and suggested major changes in them.

As we have seen, the larger ramifications of these decisions have not been clear. The Supreme Court itself has not fully rejected the older juvenile court model and has continued to hand down decisions seeking to balance that model with constitutional concerns. In the states, the impact of these decisions and of other forces for change has been piecemeal, leading to adjustments in juvenile court operations but not to any real revolution in the nature of juvenile justice proceedings. We shall consider several of these points in more detail in Chapter 10.

References

Abbott, Grace, ed. 1938. *The Child and the State.* 2 vols. Chicago: Univ. of Chicago Press.
——— 1936. The Juvenile Courts. *Survey* 72:131–133.
Addams, Jane. 1935. *My Friend, Julia Lathrop.* Rept. New York: Arno Press, 1974.
Ayers, Edward L. 1984. *Vengeance and Justice: Crime and Punishment in the 19th Century American South.* New York: Oxford Univ. Press.
Binder, Arnold. 1984. The Juvenile Court, the U.S. Constitution and When the Twain Meet. *Journal of Criminal Justice* 12:355–366.
———, and Binder, Virginia L. 1982. Juvenile Diversion and the Constitution. *Journal of Criminal Justice* 10:1–24.
Brantingham, Paul J. 1979. Juvenile Justice Reform in California and New York in the Early 1960's. In *Juvenile Justice Philosophy: Readings, Cases and Comments,* 2nd ed., edited by Frederic L. Faust and Paul J. Brantingham, 259–268. St. Paul, Minn.: West.
Caldwell, Robert G. 1961. The Juvenile Court: Its Development and Some Major Problems. *Journal of Criminal Law, Criminology and Police Science* 51:493–511.
Dix, George E. 1966. Transfer of Juveniles to Adult Correctional Institutions. *Wisconsin Law Review,* 1966:866–912.
Finestone, Harold. 1976. *Victims of Change: Juvenile Delinquents in American Society.* Westport, Conn.: Greenwood Press.
Fox, Sanford J. 1970. Juvenile Justice Reform: An Historical Perspective. *Stanford Law Review* 22:1187–1239.
Gilbert, James. 1986. *A Cycle of Outrage: Reaction to the Juvenile Delinquent in the 1950s.* New York: Oxford Univ. Press.
Hawes, Joseph M. 1971. *Children in Urban Society: Juvenile Delinquency in Nineteenth Century America.* New York: Oxford Univ. Press.
Hurley, Timothy D. 1925. Origin of the Illinois Juvenile Court Law. In *The Child, the Clinic and the Court,* 320–330. Rept. New York: Johnson Reprint, 1970.
Larson, Charles L. 1976. Development of the Law in Wisconsin in the Area of Juvenile Delinquency. *Marquette Law Review* 59:252–277.

Lathrop, Julia C. 1925. The Background of the Juvenile Court in Illinois. In *The Child, the Clinic and the Court,* 290–297. Rept. New York: Johnson Reprint, 1970.

Lemert, Edwin M. 1967. Legislating Change in the Juvenile Court. *Wisconsin Law Review* 1967:421–443.

Lemert, Edwin M. 1970. *Social Action and Legal Change: Revolution Within the Juvenile Court.* Chicago: Aldine.

Levine, Murray, and Levine, Adeline. 1970. *A Social History of Helping Services: Clinic, Court, School, and Community.* New York: Appleton-Century-Crofts.

Lindsey, Ben B., and O'Higgins, Harvey J. 1911. *The Beast.* Garden City, N.Y.: Doubleday.

Mack, Julian W. 1925. The Chancery Procedure in the Juvenile Court. In *The Child, the Clinic and the Court,* 310–319. Rept. New York: Johnson Reprint, 1970.

Mennel, Robert M. 1973. *Thorns and Thistles: Juvenile Delinquents in the United States, 1825–1940.* Hanover, N.H.: Univ. Press of New England.

Miller, Arthur S. 1979. *Social Change and Fundamental Law: America's Evolving Constitution.* Westport, Conn.: Greenwood Press.

Paulsen, Monrad G. 1963. The New York Family Court Act. *Buffalo Law Review* 12:420–441.

———1979. Current Reforms and the Legal Status of Children. In *The Future of Childhood and Juvenile Justice,* edited by LaMar T. Empey, 211–233. Charlottesville, Virg.: Univ. Press of Virginia.

Platt, Anthony M. 1977. *The Child Savers: The Invention of Delinquency.* 2nd ed. Chicago: Univ. of Chicago Press.

Prescott, Peter S. 1981. *The Child Savers: Juvenile Justice Observed.* New York: Knopf.

Report of the Governor's Special Study Commission on Juvenile Justice. 1960a. Part I: Recommendations for Changes in California's Juvenile Court Law. Sacramento: California State Printing Office.

———1960b. Part II: A Study of the Administration of Justice in California. Sacramento: California State Printing Office.

Ryerson, Ellen. 1978. *The Best-Laid Plans: America's Juvenile Court Experiment.* New York: Hill and Wang.

Schlossman, Steven L. 1977. *Love and the American Delinquent: The Theory and Practice of "Progressive" Juvenile Justice, 1825–1920.* Chicago: Univ. of Chicago Press.

Schultz, J. Lawrence, and Cohen, Fred. 1976. Isolationism in Juvenile Court Jurisprudence. In *Purusing Justice for the Child,* edited by Margaret K. Rosenheim, 20–42. Chicago: Univ. of Chicago Press.

Sutton, John R. 1985. The Juvenile Court and Social Welfare: Dynamics of Progressive Reform. *Law and Society Review* 19:107–145.

Van Waters, Miriam. 1925. The Juvenile Court from the Child's Viewpoint: A Glimpse into the Future. In *The Child, the Clinic and the Court,* 217–237. Rept. New York: Johnson Reprint, 1970.

Wertham, Fredric. 1966. *A Sign for Cain: An Exploration of Human Violence.* New York: Macmillan.

CHAPTER 9

The Front Gate to the Juvenile Justice System

In the last chapter, we examined the background of the American juvenile justice system, including key events and issues in the development of its central institution, the juvenile court. We are now ready to consider it in operation, that is, to look at what happens to youths who are processed by the American juvenile justice system. The starting point for that discussion, because of its critical screening role, is the police as a social institution. While police encounters with juveniles are typically precipitated by the complaints of other people rather than by direct observation, the police are the central "gatekeepers" of the juvenile justice system in determining who does and who does not enter. (Only a very small number of youths enter the system via referral by a parent, school, or similar source to court intake.) If, after a given encounter, an officer decides to open the gate to the justice system, referral goes to a probation or court intake officer, who independently evaluates the case. Traditionally, the probation or court intake officer decides whether or not to petition the juvenile (or family) court for a hearing. But in some states that role has been given to the office of prosecuting attorney, who, at the hearing, "represents the people." The intrusion of the prosecuting attorney into the processing chain in recent years stems from public (and, therefore, political) distress about the extent and seriousness of juvenile crime. Along with many other measures, it represents one aspect of the attempt to "get tough" with young criminals, a tendency that, as we saw in the preceding chapter, has become quite strong in recent years.

The juvenile court may send a youngster to a custodial institution if the allegations in the petition are sustained. (We shall use the term *juvenile court* in a generic way to encompass all courts devoted to juvenile matters; in some states juvenile offenses are handled in a "family court.") Or, as another alternative, the court may place the youngster under formal supervision in the community by an officer of the probation department.

For a youngster sent to an institution, the final step in justice system processing may be interaction with a parole officer. The aim of parole is to facilitate transition between institutional life and full return to the community.

The Community

Factors That Enter the Decision to Call or Not to Call the Police

A man steps out of his front door one evening and observes a group of neighborhood boys finishing the task of wrapping a substantial amount of toilet tissue around one of his trees. The boys run off, but he has recognized them. What does he do? Although he may call the parents of one or more of the boys, if he knows them, the chances are reasonably good that he will not notify the police.

On the other hand, if the man under similar circumstances had observed a group of boys assaulting an old lady and then running off with her purse, he would almost certainly notify the police. There are two principal reasons for the differing reactions in the two settings. First, the man would feel revulsion by the abuse of the lady and impelled to take some action, whereas the toilet tissue would produce no more than a "what a nuisance" reaction. And second, the man would realize that the police are too busy with more serious matters to respond to the relatively trivial boyish prank of wrapping tissue around a tree.

A person may call the police on being disturbed by a youth who is playing a radio too loudly while washing a car, if all other efforts to get change have produced only defiance; or a call may result from concern about a youth who seems to be showing psychotic behavior. These reactions illustrate that the police are the twenty-four-hour security blankets for much of the public; there is hardly a disturbing state of affairs in the community from which they are excluded from consideration as initial corrective agents. For present purposes, we will assume that a citizen observes a criminal act by a youth or what seems to be the result of a criminal act by a youth so that we can examine various factors that enter into a decision to call or not to call the police.

Certain of these factors are functions of the criminal act, the context in which it occurs, and the characteristics of the offending youth or youths. Clearly, the degree of seriousness of the act or of its outcome will influence the probability of its being reported. Assuming no risk to the informant (the presence of risk greatly complicates the issue), one is far more likely to report an offense like rape than one like minor shoplifting. Further, the degree of repetitiveness of the behavior and the individual or institution against which it is directed affect the likelihood of reporting. One may not notify the police (or some other individual who will in turn notify the police) on noticing that a youth has stolen a candy bar; however, the chances of such notification go up as the youth steals more and more over a period of time. Thus chances are greater, too, of reporting when the victim is an individual rather than an organization, particularly a large organization. And the likelihood of calling the police when criminal behavior is observed may be different if the offender is the child of a neighbor rather than an unrecognized youngster, if the offender is black rather than white, if the offender is shabbily rather than tidily dressed, if the offender is a boy rather than girl, if the offender is a boy with very long floppy hair rather than a boy with neatly trimmed hair, and so on.

Other factors that enter into a decision regarding police notification are functions of the observer. The observer of a criminal act, for example, may be in a particularly bad mood as a result of a dispute with an employer and therefore more easily irritated by all external events, so that a youthful act that would have been shrugged off at another time may precipitate anger and police notification. Now, it may seem strange that the question of whether or not a youngster is referred to the police and then enters the justice system is a function of something so irrelevant as the mood of the person who makes the original observation. But that is indeed the case. And broader institutional and community factors have similar influences. For example, the Task Force on Juvenile Delinquency of the President's Commission (1967:12) describes the role of the school as follows:

> A school, for instance, may in fact adjust many situations involving delinquency. It has an interest in offenses occurring in or harmful to the school, and it has an interest in its pupils. For children who inspire the compassionate attention of their teachers, the school may bend its efforts to secure adjustment even of wholly extra school offenses. But the school may feel it cannot afford publicly to acknowledge

these actions of its staff for fear of creating anxiety among parents and risking criticism for allocating time to nonacademic concerns.

More generally, various characteristics of an entire community and its members determine what violations of group norms are considered *deviant* and who is to be designated a *deviate* for such behavior. It is important to note in the case of youthful misbehavior and the judgment of that behavior that the outcome is an interactional process involving features of people and social groups external to the actual behavior.

For a particular observer of a youthful criminal act or its outcome, the picture becomes even more complex when one considers that people differ markedly in personal characteristics and change markedly over short time periods (as in mood fluctuations). A given person may be particularly sensitive to all evidence of youthful misbehavior and eager to report it; another may show concern only when a youth commits a very serious assaultive crime. Perhaps the first is an older retired man who has escaped to a sheltered life, while the second is a man who has had an outrageous boyhood.

Beyond such varying sensitivities, people differ in tolerance for different types of deviant behavior, in ethical and moral standards, in racial prejudice, in expectations based on the sex of a youngster, in attitudes toward the standards of the communities in which they live, and in attitudes toward law enforcement in general and the local police department in particular. And their reactions to crime will be influenced accordingly.

Evidence of the Importance of Community Members in the Specification of Deviance

The importance of citizens in the process was shown by Black and Reiss (1970). They systematically observed 281 police encounters with juveniles in three cities and noted that, excluding traffic violations, 78 per cent were initiated by calls from citizens and only 22 per cent by the police. Moreover, they found that the decision of an officer in regard to custody or release was strongly influenced by the preference of the complainant (1970:67): "Hence, it would seem that the moral standards of the citizenry have more to do with the definition of juvenile deviance that do the standards of policemen on patrol." The same conclusion was reached by Lundman, Sykes, and Clark (1980) on the basis of their replication of the Black and Reiss study "in a midwestern city of more than 500,000 in a metropolitan area of over two million people." They comment (1980:139), "In addition to citizens' exercise of discretion in the context of calling the police about a delinquent act they have witnessed, in their rolls as complainants, citizens influence arrest rates by their willingness to remain at the scene of an offense until the police arrive and by making their dispositional preferences manifest. . . . *Citizens, therefore, largely determine official delinquency rates.*"

The general reluctance of people to report a crime like shoplifting was demonstrated by Steffensmeier and Terry (1973). In their study, incidents of shoplifting were staged (rigged) in an obvious fashion so that the event would be observed by nearby shoppers. The person who observed the staged event was then given an opportunity to report the "offense" to a nearby "employer" (who was actually another accomplice in the study); only 29.2 per cent of the observers did so. Even when another accomplice acting as a second store worker asked the nonreporters if they had seen an offense take place and pointed out that the "offender" was a suspicious person, a large number of people refused to report the occurrence.

Although the results are interesting, it is, of course, difficult to generalize conclusions to the diverse array of juvenile offenses and the many different environmental conditions in which they occur. There is a bit more information when the observer is a victim of a crime. In the National Crime Survey Report entitled *Criminal Victimization in the United States, 1984* (May 1986), we find that victims reported to the police 47 per cent of violent crimes, 25 per cent of all personal theft crimes, and 38 per cent of all household offenses. The rate of reporting violent crimes was higher for women than for men and for blacks than for whites. Further (1986:8), "Stranger-to-stranger violent crimes were reported to the police at a higher rate than crimes involving nonstrangers. . . . Teenage victims of personal crimes were least likely to report crimes to the police compared to other age groups."

On the issue of the reasons for reporting or not reporting a victimization, we find (1986:8):

> In 1984, the most frequently cited reasons for reporting a violent crime to the police were to keep the incident from happening again or to others, to punish the offender, and to intervene in the current incident. . . .
> For both personal theft and household crimes, the most frequent reason for reporting the offense to the police was the desire to recover property. . . .
> The most frequent specific reason given by victims for not reporting violent crimes to the police was that the event was a private or personal matter. The most common reason cited for not reporting personal theft or household crimes to the police was that the offense was not important enough to warrant police attention. . . .
> Reasons for not reporting crimes to the police did not vary markedly for victims of different race or income groups.

Further evidence of the importance of the victim in the generation of official delinquency may be found in Hohenstein's (1969) report of a study in police discretion. He stated (1969:146), "Regardless of the seriousness of the events or the previous record of the offenders, when victims made statements to the police that they were against prosecution, offenders were 'remedialed' [that is, counseled and released] in 96 percent of the cases." Note that these results are in accord with the earlier reported ones of Black and Reiss (1970) and of Lundman, Sykes, and Clark (1980).

The community, therefore, is the first step in the process whereby the behavior of a youth is escalated to the status of deviant, delinquent, or even criminal. Behavior that is ignored, no matter how repellent it may seem in the abstract, takes on no meaning beyond the interpretations of the immediate participants, observers, and victims, if there are any. Realization of the importance of social response in the production of deviance led the historian Tannenbaum, in 1938, to lay the foundation for what later became labeling theory. He pointed out that boys in a slum area engage in a wide variety of mischievous, destructive, and possibly injurious behaviors. The behaviors are accepted as normal boys' activities by the boys themselves—it is only when the community takes responsive action (followed by the police, probation, the court, et al.) that the process of escalation and possibly labeling starts. (See Chapter 5.)

The Police

First Major Decision: To Release or Take into Custody

Offenses to Which the Police Must React. Cicourel (1968) found in one California city that 86 per cent of the offenses of juveniles that required police attention were misdemeanors or of an even less serious type—the other 14 per cent were felonies. Similarly, Black and Reiss (1970) found a 9 per cent felony rate for juveniles in three major cities, and Lundman, Sykes, and Clark (1980), in a replication of the Black and Reiss study, found a 5 per cent felony rate. In the study of Piliavin and Briar (1964), over 90 per cent of the incidents involving police and youths in a large industrialized city were "minor behaviors," and, finally, in the cohort study of Wolfgang, Figlio, and Sellin (1972), 87 per cent of the arrests were non-Index (not serious) crimes.

The Limits of Police Discretion. When a police officer confronts a youth who has been observed or is suspected of committing an offense, the officer must gather enough information at the scene to decide what to do with the youth. If interrogation of the youth and other available people together with observation of any possible evidence convinces the officer that the youth committed no offense, he or she will be released with only the filing of a report that the incident occurred (usually called a field interrogation or FI report). If that conclusion is not reached, the juvenile law of the state contains statements of the options available to the officer in more or less specific terms. In other words, the law specifies the amount of *police discretion* when there is good reason to believe that the youth committed an offense. In legal codes, good reason to believe that an offense was committed by a person or persons is referred to as *probable cause* or *reasonable cause* for so believing.

One option available to all officers is to deprive the youth of his or her liberty for a short period of time. The word *arrest* is used when an adult is deprived of liberty in that manner, but in formal and legal writing dealing with juvenile justice, the phrase *take into temporary custody* is used. (It should be pointed out, however, that operating personnel use the term *arrest* in referring to the process for all ages, and we shall do so on occasion for ease of expression.) The different phrasing is used as part of the overall effort, starting with the first juvenile court in 1899, of differentiating the juvenile from the criminal process. But there have been problems as well as gains from the phrasing. One obvious gain has been that a person who was taken into temporary custody as a youth, no matter how many times, could accurately state that he or she had not been arrested. The problems stem from the applicabilty of the huge body of laws dealing with the arrest process. As Davis (1980:3-3) has pointed out, "some courts have taken the position that the law of arrest does not apply to juveniles.

That position finds potential support in legislative statements that taking a juvenile into custody does not amount to an arrest."

But the body of laws dealing with the arrest process — commonly called the law of arrest — contains important protections for citizens from abuse by the police. To make sure that these protections apply equally to the process of taking a youth into temporary custody, some states have phrasing in their codes like the following recommendation of the Uniform Juvenile Court Act, Section 13b (drafted by the National Conference of Commissioners on Uniform State Laws, 1968): "The taking of a child into custody is not an arrest, except for determining its validity under the constitution of this state or of the United States."

Davis (1980) has presented one decision where a court in New Jersey stated specifically that criteria for lawful arrest in the case of adults apply equally to the taking into custody of juveniles. But generally, courts have not specifically addressed the issue, leading Davis (1980:3–4) to conclude, "The paucity of judicial decisions on the question is probably due to an assumption by most courts that the law of arrest is so clearly applicable to the juvenile process that the issue does not require attention."

To illustrate a juvenile law that allows wide police discretion in deciding whether or not to take a youth into custody, we have Section 625 of the Welfare and Institutions Code of California:

625. Temporary custody and detention. A peace officer may, without a warrant, take into temporary custody a minor:

(a) Who is under the age of 18 years when such officer has reasonable cause for believing that such minor is a person described in Section 601 [that is, has committed a status offense] or 602 [that is, has committed a criminal offense], or

(b) Who is a ward of the juvenile court or concerning whom an order has been made [in regard to detention or disposition] when such officer has reasonable cause for believing that person has violated an order of the juvenile court or has escaped from any commitment ordered by the juvenile court, or

(c) Who is under the age of 18 years and who is found in any street or public place suffering from any sickness or injury which requires care, medical treatment, hospitalization, or other remedial care.

In any case where a minor is taken into temporary custody on the ground that there is reasonable cause for believing that such minor is a person described in Section 601 or 602, or that he has violated an order of the juvenile court or escaped from any commitment ordered by the juvenile court, the officer shall advise such minor that anything he says can be used against him and shall advise him of this constitutional rights, including his right to remain silent, his right to have counsel present during any interrogation, and his right to have counsel appointed if he is unable to afford counsel.

That statute clearly gives an officer a good deal of discretion in the decision regarding custody. The officer may take into custody any youth where it is reasonable to believe that the youth has committed an offense, status or criminal. On the other hand, the New York Family Court Act (Section 305.2[2]) is more restrictive in specifying that "an officer may take a child under the age of sixteen into custody without a warrant in cases in which he may arrest a person for a crime." In contrast to the California statute where a youth may be taken into custody when there is probable cause that the minor has committed an offense, the New York statute limits the process to criminal offenses. In other terms, a police officer in New York is not authorized to take a youth into custody (without a warrant) where there is reasonable cause to believe the youth is in need of supervision (has committed a *status* offense). If the New York officer does feel that custody is important for a youth who has not committed a crime, the officer must convince a magistrate that a youth needs supervision so that a warrant (summons) may be issued.

Davis (1980:3-7) illustrated the "potential abuse inherent in the broad jurisdictional power to take a child into custody, specifically in situations involving noncriminal conduct" by presenting a case from California where an "appellate court expressed no concern over the fact that [a] juvenile has been taken into custody with neither warrant nor probable cause." Accordingly, he (1980:3-9) argues for the more restrictive New York approach, where a magistrate's decision is necessary for noncriminal behavior, in the following way:

> Most states grant very broad authority to police officers to take juveniles into custody in situations involving noncriminal conduct, under circumstances in which they are, in the broadest sense, endangered by their surroundings. These statutes indicate . . . that the decision to take a youth into custody is regarded primarily as a police decision. However, should it be solely a police decision when the broad jurisdictional power is invoked to take into custody a youth who is *not* charged with a criminal violation but rather, for example, is "in danger of leading a dissolute life"? Police officers generally are poorly equipped to make this sort of decision and the possibility of abuse is too hazardous to allow them to exercise it unchecked. To be sure, juveniles "in trouble" should receive help, but someone other than the officer in the street ought to assume the *primary* responsibility in the decision-making process.

Finally, in concluding this section, it is important to note that no matter how broad the jurisdictional power granted in a state code to the police for taking a youth into custody, the phrasing is of the form "may" rather than "must" take a child into custody under the stipulated conditions. That, of course, provides the basis for police discretion at the stage of first major decision.

Does that imply an officer is permitted to release a youngster (meaning no further action) suspected of committing a very serious offense, say murder or assault with a deadly weapon? The answer is: legally, yes, but practically, no. The actions of an officer are influenced by a large array of forces in addition to the cold statements in legal codes. These include the written policies of the police department, the general ethos of the department as determined by the attitude of the chief and by various peer pressures, specific directions and implied guides for actions by police supervisors, the general working conditions, and the broad expectations of the community regarding appropriate police behavior. We will consider the operation of these forces later in this chapter.

Requirements During Interrogation. Interrogation of a youth taken into custody must, according to some states' codes and according to almost all recent court rulings, satisfy *Miranda* requirements. These requirements stem

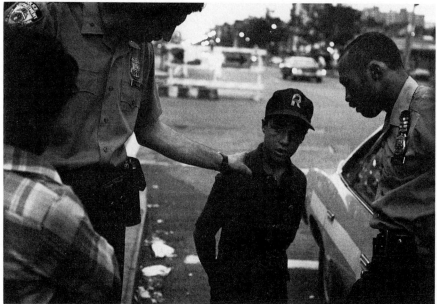

Police interrogation of a youth.

from the decision of the U.S. Supreme Court in *Miranda v. Arizona* (384 U.S. 436, 1966) and must be met before any statement made by a person in police custody may be used at a criminal trial. The Court states (at 478, 479):

> To summarize, we hold that when an individual is taken into custody or otherwise deprived of his freedom by the authorities in any significant way and is subjected to questioning, the privilege against self-incrimination is jeopardized. Procedural safeguards must be employed to protect the privilege, and unless other fully effective means are adopted to notify the person of his right of silence and to assure that the exercise of the right will be scrupulously honored, the following measures are required. He must be warned prior to any questioning that he has the right to remain silent, that anything he says can be used against him in a court of law, that he has the right to the presence of an attorney, and that if he cannot afford an attorney one will be appointed for him prior to any questioning if he so desires.

It must be emphasized that a necessary condition for the requirements of *Miranda* (the right to remain silent, the right to an attorney, and the condition that any statement made by the suspect may be used against him or her) is that the person being interrogated be in custody. The *Miranda* requirements do not apply in situations where a person is free to leave, as when a youth is interrogated by a school principal.

Some state codes have more restrictive requirements than those given in *Miranda* and in subsequent decisions of the U.S. Supreme Court that deal with the police interrogation of children (for example, *Fare v. Michael C.*, 442, U.S. 707, 1979). To illustrate, Oklahoma and Colorado require a parent or guardian to be present during the interrogation and to be advised of the *Miranda* rights — otherwise statements, admissions, or confessions of the child may not be used in court. In other states, more restrictive conditions have been set by judicial decisions based on state law (for example, the Louisiana Supreme Court, in *State in the interest of Deno,* 359 So. 2d 586, 1978, required consultation with an attorney or other fully advised adult before *Miranda* rights could be waived by a youth). Hassin (1981) has strongly argued in favor of a requirement for parental presence during the police interrogation of children. Although his arguments were directed specifically at the procedure in Israel, they have general validity. There will, of course, be problems when the parent and child are adversaries — that is, when parent and child have opposing interests. In such cases, appointment of a temporary legal counsel may be in order.

Second Major Decision: What to Do with a Youngster Taken into Custody

The Limits of Police Discretion. As in the case of the first major decision, a state code defines the limits of police discretion in deciding what to do with a youngster who has been taken into custody. As Davis (1980:3–34) has emphasized, "In terms of protecting a juvenile's rights, the decision-making process that begins immediately after he is taken into custody is perhaps an area of even greater concern than the decision to take into custody."

The alternatives commonly available to the police at this phase include outright release or release unconditionally to the custody of parents (alternatives usually called "counsel and release"), release to parents with a recommendation that help be sought from a community agency (an alternative that may fall under the rubric of "police diversion" — see Chapter 13), detention and referral to court intake (probation) in continued custody, or release to parents with the stipulation that future appearance at court intake is necessary. It is common in state statutes to require immediate notification to parents or guardian whenever a child is taken into custody whether or not there is immediate release. For example, the New York Family Court Act (Section 724) states, "If a peace officer or a police officer takes into custody under section seven hundred twenty-one . . . the officer shall immediately notify the parent or other person legally responsible for his care, or the person with whom he is domiciled, that he has been taken into custody." It is also common in statutes to have an expressed preference for release of children unless there is compelling reason for continued detention. The New York act used in the preceding illustration, for example, states, "In the absence of special circumstances, the peace officer shall release the child [to parental custody upon written promise to bring the child to a family court at a specified time]."

Despite that type of expressed preference in state codes, it has often been argued that the police overuse detention of youths and referral to the court. The Task Force on Delinquency of the President's Commission (1967:13) points out that the detention-referral process "has sometimes been employed not so much for protection of the juvenile or the community as for its shock effect on an alleged offender."

The *Uniform Crime Reports* (1985:240) gives police dispositions of juvenile offenders taken into custody as follows: handled within department and released, 30.7 per cent; referred to juvenile court jurisdiction, 61.8 per cent; referred to welfare agency, 1.6 per cent; referred to other police agency, 1.2 per cent; referred to criminal or adult court, 4.4 per cent.

Juvenile Officers. While it is typically an officer on patrol who takes a youth into custody, most medium and large police departments have a specialized organizational unit that is dedicated to juvenile matters. The unit is variously called the juvenile division, the juvenile bureau, or the youth services division, and the officers in the unit are known as juvenile officers. In smaller departments, the juvenile unit is frequently a component of investigative (detective) services. Typically, the juvenile specialist takes over in the processing of young suspects, including interrogation and investigation, after a patrol officer takes the youth into custody. In some departments, only a juvenile officer may send a youth to court intake, but more often the arresting officer may refer directly to the court if circumstances warrant.

A number of advisory groups, including the National Advisory Commission on Criminal Justice Standards (1973) and the Wisconsin Special Study Committee on Criminal Justice Standards and Goals (1975), have recommended the establishment of specialized juvenile units in all but the smallest departments. For example, the Wisconsin committee recommended (1975:36):

> In recognition of the frequency, complexity, and duration of juvenile problems coming to the attention of law enforcement, every such agency shall establish specialized support positions, in proportion to need, to enhance law enforcement services to juveniles. . . . for every complement of 13 sworn officers there shall be the equivalent of one full-time officer whose work is primarily to:
>
> a. Keep abreast of the needs of juveniles in the community;
> b. Handle all juvenile dispositions more restrictive than release;
> c. Advise supervisors of appropriate juvenile policies;
> d. Provide advice to patrol officers to assist them in improving the quality of their juvenile contacts.

Beyond that, the committee recommended a certification process for juvenile officers that included a mandatory curriculum containing courses ranging in content from the laws of arrest and the rights and liabilities of juveniles to the psychology of adolescent behavior and theories of delinquency. Clearly, the committee believed strongly that the decisions of the second stage, that is, disposition beyond outright release, should be in knowledgeable hands.

To end this discussion of juvenile divisions on an incidental note, in years prior to the current era of general acceptance of all types of police work for women, almost all women in police work were given primary assignments as juvenile officers. Walker (1980) has pointed out that the first female police officer, Lola Baldwin, was hired by the Portland, Oregon police department in 1905 for duties in "child protection." By 1925, 145 police departments had female officers, all assigned to work with juveniles. Walker (1980:139) expresses the spirit of the era as follows:

> The leaders of the policewomen's movement, moreover, stressed the idea that policewomen should project a helping image. They would not wear uniforms, would

not patrol regular beats, and would not arrest adults. Spokeswomen emphasized the traditional child-rearing role of the women. According to Mary Hamilton, the first policewoman in New York City, "the position of a woman in a police department is not unlike that of a mother in a home. Just as the mother smoothes out the rough spots, looks after the children and gives a timely word of warning, advice or encouragement, so the policewoman fulfills her duty."

Factors That Influence Police Discretion

As we pointed out above, Black and Reiss (1970), Lundman, Sykes, and Clark (1980), and Hohenstein (1969) found that the complainant or victim is very influential in the police decision of whether or not to take a youth into custody. Kinnane (1979:30), a former police officer, described other ways that the community influences the police:

> In a middle-class neighborhood the officer is not expected to intervene as often as he does in a poorer neighborhood. People see him more as a public servant than as "the Man." He is expected to overlook minor parking violations and crowds in front of bars (unless the crowd is teenage). People do not drink in alleys because they have enough money to buy a drink at the bar, and they do not spill over into the streets as easily as poorer people, for whom the "public" street is often an extension of their own limited private property. There are fewer opportunities for police intervention in a middle-class neighborhood, and thus less of a history that the officer must live up to. The major cause of his interventions in these neighborhoods is teenagers, both delinquent and nondelinquent. And the mobility of these adolescents means that the "car stop" is going to be one of an officer's major discretionary decisions. Any "souped-up" car is fair game here. A raised rear end, a loud muffler, a squealing acceleration, a large number of passengers, or any of the countless safety equipment violations (taillights, taglights, insufficient tread on tires, dashboard lights, etc., etc., etc.) justify a car stop that often leads to an alcohol or narcotics arrest, a stolen car, or a person wanted on a warrant.

Clearly, then, the community plays a critical role in the determination of whether or not a youngster passes through the front door into the juvenile justice system. We will now consider several other factors that affect police discretion, at the second stage of disposition as well as at the first stage of release or custody.

Administrative and Organizational Factors. We turn again to Kinnane (1979) for an interesting summary, in anecdotal form, of important administrative and organizational factors that influence police discretion, the first of which involves interaction between the community and the police hierarchy:

> Another administrative factor is as follows: Would anyone around complain to my superiors if I were to handle it? The role of crime fighter can be held over an officer's head, and every time he makes a decision not to arrest where an arrest could, legalistically, be made, he takes a chance that someone will complain about his alleged inaction . . .
> It was 11:40 at night—less than twenty minutes to go before shift change. The officer received a call for a group of teenagers drinking on a corner in a residential neighborhood. Seconds later he pulled up to the corner, got out of his car, and

approached the boys. By this time, of course, all the beer was sitting in the gutter so that each boy could repeat the litany of innocence: "It's not mine, I don't know whose it is." The officer picked up the beer, poured it out, and ordered the boys off the corner. "But I live right here," protested one. "I don't care where you live," was the reply. "I got a complaint" worked wonders and the boys moved on, speculating on which old lady in the neighborhood turned them in. As the officer radioed in "Complaint abated" to the dispatcher and noted the complaint number of the call on his log sheet, he looked up at the windows around the corner, just a bit worried that someone would be disappointed that six specimens of degenerate youth had not been arrested. (1979:38, 39)

> If the officer had been receiving a lot of pressure from his sergeant to "get his arrest stats up," he might have decided differently. (1979:38)

> A final factor to be considered in the exercise of discretion is . . . the pressure of one's peers. In police work the regard and respect of one's colleagues is vitally important. In order to earn and maintain this respect, he must occasionally choose a course of action that, among other things, meets with the approval of his fellow officers. He must not be "too soft," and while it is difficult to be considered "too hard" without bordering on outright brutality, he must confine his hardness to "hardened criminals." An officer who is excessively physical in his handling of juveniles, for example, will be suspected of cowardice or "bullyism." If he is excessively tolerant, the word will spread that "they're carrying away his post," i.e., getting away with much more than "they" should. Not only is his own reputation at stake, but the work patterns of his colleagues are at stake too. If a too-lenient officer has a beat for a week, the officer who inherits that beat from him has to work extra hard to repair the damage done to the system of mutual expectations between citizens and police in that neighborhood. (1979:45)

Some police departments have written guidelines for the handling of juvenile offenders, but many more do not. Thus, Klein, Rosenzweig, and Bates (1975) studied forty-nine departments in California and found little formal guidance for their juvenile bureaus. That heightened the influence of informal intradepartmental and personal forces on decision making. Not one of the thirteen cities in the research of Wilbanks (1975:175) had a written policy with specific guidelines, and the lack "seems to have resulted in considerable disagreement among the juvenile units as to exactly what constituted departmental policy."

Many advisory commissions and committees have stressed the importance of written guidelines to place desirable bounds on police discretion. For example, the Special Study Committee on Criminal Justice Standards and Goals of the Wisconsin Council on Criminal Justice (1975:31–32) recommended, "The Chief or Sheriff of every law enforcement agency in Wisconsin shall immediately begin to develop written policies governing the agency's involvement in the apprehension, detection, and prevention of delinquent behavior and juvenile crime . . . [and] interaction with juveniles in custody." The need for these written policies is summarized as follows by the Special Study Committee (1975:32). "Presently decisions are not restrained by mechanisms comparable to the principles of due process and the rules of procedure governing police decisions regarding adult offenders. Consequently, prejudicial practices by police officers can escape notice more easily in their dealing with juveniles than adults."

Wilson (1968a), from a study of eight communities, conceived of three broad types of police department on the basis of what he considered the "operating code of the department" (1968a:140). The operating code is reflected in a style of policing that shapes the way officers interacted with the public. In departments with a "legalistic style," the emphasis is on high arrest rates, minimum discretion, and vigorous action against illicit enterprises. A single standard for community behavior is assumed so that juveniles are treated the same as adults; that leads to a large number of arrests and detentions for juveniles. In departments with a "watchman style," there is emphasis on maintaining order rather than on regulating individual behavior. The seriousness of infractions is judged more by immediate consequences than on strict law interpretation. In this type of department (1968a:140), "Juveniles are 'expected' to misbehave, and thus infractions among this group — unless they are serious or committed by a 'wise guy' — are best ignored or treated informally." Finally, in departments with a "service style," which are often found in middle-class communities where there is a consensus regarding the (1968a:200) "need for and definition of public order," the emphasis is on courteousness and responsiveness to citizens with minimum heavy-handedness. In the words of Wilson (1968a:201), "with regard to minor infractions of the law, arrests are avoided when possible (the rates at which traffic tickets are issued and juveniles referred to Family Court will be much lower than in legalistic departments) but there will be frequent use of informal, nonarrest sanctions (warnings issued to motorists, juveniles taken to headquarters or visited in their homes for lectures)."

Although Wilson's typology is much too general and descriptive for predictive purposes, it does convey an important relationship between tone or ethos of a police department and the decision-making tendencies of its officers in police-citizen encounters.

In another publication, Wilson (1968b) compared two police departments that differed markedly in degree of "professionalism" in their handling of juvenile offenders. High professionalism implies recruiting officers on the basis of achievement and ability, low graft and corruption, equality in the enforcement of laws, and continuing formal training of officers. Contrary to expectations, he found (1968b:15), "In Western City [high in professionalism], the discretionary powers of the police are much more likely than in Eastern City [low in professionalism] to be used to restrict the freedom of the juvenile: Western City's officers process a larger proportion of the city's juvenile population as suspected offenders and, of those they process, arrest a large proportion." He points out the price a community may pay in achieving a highly professional police department (1968b:28). "A principal effect of the inculcation of professional norms is to make the police less discriminatory but more severe."

Sundeen (1974:62) related effectiveness of policy to departmental organization in his conclusion, from a study of forty-three police departments, that with "high bureaucratic control there exists a moderate positive association between policy and [counsel and release] rate" but with "low bureaucratic control, . . . there is no relationship between policy and rate." That is, in short, the obvious state of affairs whereby policy can affect the behavior of officers only if the policy is enforced.

Finally, Goldstein (1977) and Crank et al. (1986) have stressed the manner in which subtle forces, some emanating from the community and some from police officer associations (unions), affect the decisions of police chiefs, which in turn affect departmental policy and regulations. As an example, the chief may be pressured to change a tolerant departmental policy regarding youthful mischievousness in an area in which they congregate on the basis of the vigorous complaints of an outraged citizenry. Goldstein (1977:253) points out, "the administrator who resists demands for the traditional response runs the risk of appearing insensitive to community needs." The ultimate result may be the taking into custody of one or more youths who would never have made it through the front gate of the justice system without that community pressure.

Characteristics of Officers and Their Perceptions. In addition to the statements of law and the array of external pressures on the officer, an important contribution toward discretionary decision making comes from the set of personal characteristics of that officer. Police officers, like citizens in general, have different temperaments, moods, attitudes, biases, levels of tolerance for various types of behavior, and ethical and moral standards that influence their daily decisions, including that of what to do with a young offender. Indeed, various aspects of the data of Wilbanks (1975) indicate that the personal beliefs of the officer override all other factors in importance. In response to a question of what is most important in their decision making regarding juvenile dispositions, for example, almost half of the officers surveyed ranked their own preference first and about one third ranked departmental policy first. Garrett and Short (1975) studied the influences of socioeconomic class upon the perceptions by police officers of young male offenders. They used unstructured interviews and questionnaires with the officers in three cities. Officers tended to perceive lower-class boys as more delinquency-prone than boys from higher socioeconomic classes, using implicit personal theories linking social class, parental neglect, and delinquent behavior. Interestingly, the predictions of officers as to the future delinquency of boys was tested over a six-year period by follow-up of actual records — the predictions were generally inaccurate.

McEachern and Bauzer (1967:152) studied police dispositions in California and concluded, "no matter what the offense, some officers are more likely to request petitions [that is, refer to the juvenile court] than others, and this trend is consistent for each offense category." The proportion of referrals to the juvenile court, rather than informal adjustments, varied over investigators from a low of 0 per cent to a high of 90 per cent.

The results of Wilson (1968b) indicate that a police officer's socioeconomic background and personal difficulties with the law as a youth affect his or her referral rate (as well as degree of racial discrimination). And the findings of Goldman (1963) and of Ferdinand and Luchterhand (1970) indicate that an officer's attitude toward the juvenile court and its ancillary agencies may determine dispositional tendencies. For example, an offender may not be referred because the officer feels the court is too lenient or possible institutionalization too harmful. Finally, an experimental paradigm led Sullivan and Siegel (1972) to believe that arrest rate and disposition of juvenile offenders is a function of amount of experience — officers with more experience tend to arrest more and to adjust informally less.

Beyond individual differences, officers, of course, change over time in characteristics like mood and level of tolerance, with concomitant effects on decisions. Thus, an officer may be in a pleasant, forgiving mood at one time and release a youngster to his or her parents without further action, and in an irritable, vengeful mood at another time and send on to probation or the juvenile court the same youngster behaving much the same way.

Moreover, external forces and personal characteristics of officers interact in two primary ways. First, a given external pressure may very well produce different effects on different officers. For example, while most officers comply with a directive from superiors, a feeling of hostility toward those superiors, perhaps as a result of a salary or advancement issue, might lead a certain officer to a decision regarding a young offender that is precisely the opposite of what would be expected on the basis of the directive.

The second way external forces and personal characteristics interact is by the actual molding of the working personalities of the police by the forces. An illustration of that process is embedded in the issue of the "police personality," meaning a set of characteristics frequently associated with police officers. According to the results of several studies, police officers tend to be biased, cynical, suspicious, conservative, and authoritarian (see, for example, the review by Lefkowitz, 1975). It has been argued that one finds those features widely over police officers because people of that type are more likely to choose police work as an occupation, or that police officers come from a class in society where the features are widespread, or that the screening process into police work tends to select people who are cynical and authoritarian, or that the police setting molds the personalities of its employees. But, whatever the separate contributions of such determiners, it does seem that the socialization process of the police is the

© Leonard Freed, Magnum

Several studies have shown a tendency for police officers to be biased, suspicious, and authoritarian. Some people argue that officers show even stronger tendencies on occasion.

most powerful influence in producing a constellation of personality characteristics like those above.

Thus, Niederhoffer (1969:160) argues:

> It seems to me that the above data and conclusions support the notion that police authoritarianism does not come into the force along with the recruits, but rather is inculcated in the men through strenuous socialization. The police occupational system is geared to manufacture the "take charge guy," and it succeeds in doing so with outstanding efficiency. It is the police system . . . that is the more powerful determinant of behavior and ideology.

Skolnick (1966) refers to the set of cognitive and behavioral responses produced in officers by their conditions of employment as the police "working personality." He states, for example (1966:46), "Policemen are indeed specifically *trained* to be suspicious, to perceive events or changes in the physical surroundings that indicate the occurrence or probability of disorder."

Characteristics of Suspected Offenders and of the Offense. In 1964, Piliavin and Briar reported the results of nine months of observation of the interactions between police officers and youths in a large industrialized city. They found that police decision making was affected by an array of the personal characteristics of youths and by their manner of self-presentation, but that one factor stood out in importance—the demeanor of the youth. They report (1964:159, 160, 210):

> both the decision in the field—whether or not to bring the boy in—and the decision made at the station—which disposition to invoke—were based largely on clues which emerged from the interaction between the officer and the youth. . . . These clues included the youth's group affiliations, age, race, grooming, dress, and demeanor. Older juveniles, members of known delinquent gangs, Negroes, youths with well-oiled hair, black jackets, and soiled denims or jeans (the presumed uniform of "tough" boys), and boys who in their interactions with officers did not manifest what were considered to be appropriate signs of respect tended to receive the more severe dispositions.
>
> Other than prior record, the most important of the above clues was a youth's *demeanor*. . . . The clues used by police to assess demeanor were fairly simple. Juveniles who were contrite about their infractions, respectful to officers and fearful of the sanctions that might be employed against them tended to be viewed by patrolmen as basically law abiding or at least "salvageable." For these youths it was usually assumed that informal or formal reprimand would suffice to guarantee their future conformity. In contrast, youthful offenders who were fractious, obdurate, or who appeared nonchalant in their encounters with patrolmen were likely to be viewed as "would-be toughs" or "punks" who fully deserved the most severe sanction: arrest.

McEachern and Bauzer (1967) analyzed 1,010 records of young offenders in Los Angeles County. They found an interesting reversal consisting of bias in favor of girls for the more serious offenses and bias against them for the less serious ones. That is, girls were more likely than boys to be released for serious offenses and less likely to be released for offenses of minimum seriousness (status offenses). Overall, a youth was most likely to be referred to the juvenile court if the offense was more serious, if the youth was on probation at the time of apprehension, and if there were prior offenses. Moreover, when offense was controlled, the influence of such other factors as age and family status in determining disposition was eliminated or reduced substantially. Finally, there was no evidence of racial discrimination in the proportions of referrals to the juvenile court for different racial groups: black, .28; Hispanic .27; white .26.

Like McEachern and Bauzer, Terry (1967), in an analysis of 9,023 police dispositions in a midwestern city, found seriousness of offense and prior record as the two most important determiners of referral to the juvenile court. He points to the filtering by police in the following way (1967:178): "While the three least serious offenses comprise 65% and the three most serious offenses comprise 6% of all offenses appearing in police records, the three least serious offenses comprise only 9% of the offenses that appear in the juvenile court and the three most serious offenses comprise over 66% of the offenses appearing in the juvenile court records." In Terry's results, age ranked third in importance — older youths were more likely to be referred to the court even when controlling for offense differences. He found, too, that juveniles were more likely to be arrested if the offense in question involved an adult as co-defendant.

Cicourel (1968) observed police-juvenile interactions in two California cities and described the role of demeanor (in gesture, voice intonation, and bodily movement) in the formation of a trusting relationship between officer and juvenile. The absence or the breaking of that type of relationship leads to a tendency to invoke court referral. He also noted that prior history of the juvenile may lead to labeling as "bad" or "a punk" by the officer and to harsher disposition as a result.

Hohenstein (1969), as mentioned earlier in this chapter, found the attitude of the victim to be extremely important in influencing police decision for referral to court. To show (1969:149) "that the attitude of the victim was the primary factor influencing this decision and not the seriousness of the offense or the previous record of the offender," he pointed out that his data indicated "that an offender with a good previous record and guilty of a minor offense was more likely to be arrested (18 percent) than an offender in an event when the victim refused to prosecute (4 percent), regardless of how serious the present offense was or the length of the offender's previous record of delinquency." He did find that the arrest rate for blacks was 78 per cent as compared with 22 per cent for whites but could not rule out the contributions to that difference of factors not available for analysis in the study. In general he concluded (1969:149) "that no evidence was uncovered to support claims of bias by police in their disposition of juvenile offenders" and that age and sex of offender were not useful factors in predicting police disposition.

As mentioned above, Black and Reiss (1970) observed 281 police-juvenile encounters in three large cities. Their more important findings are that (1) 60 per cent of the encounters stemmed from rowdiness or mischievous behavior — only 15 of the 281 encounters involved allegations of felonies, (2) 15 per cent of the encounters resulted in arrest, (3) the decision to arrest or release a youngster depends strongly on the preference of the complaining citizen (1970:71) — "the police show a quite dramatic pattern of compliance with the expressed preferences of complainants," (4) the relative frequency of arrest is higher as the legal seriousness of the offense is greater, where there is evidence that links the juvenile to the deviant act, and for juveniles who are unusually disrespectful or unusually respectful toward the police, and (5) the arrest rate for black youths was higher than for whites, but the difference seemed to stem from a difference in complainants' preferences — interestingly, they report (1970:70), "citizen complainants who oversee the relatively severe dispositions of Negro juveniles are themselves Negro. The great majority of the police officers are white . . . yet they are somewhat more lenient when they confront Negro juveniles alone than when a Negro complainant is involved." They speculated that the finding of higher arrest rates for youths who were unusually respectful did not contradict the general results of Piliavin and Briar (1964) because comparable results would have been obtained if they (Black and Reiss) had used only the two categories of Piliavin and Briar — "cooperative" and "uncooperative."

As mentioned above, too, Lundman, Sykes, and Clark (1980) found similar results in their replication of the Black and Reiss study. And they similarly conclude (1980:147) "that the higher arrest rate of black juveniles is attributable to the more frequent presence of black complianants who lobby for formal police action."

Ferdinand and Luchterhand (1970) studied a sample of police dispositions of juveniles in six inner-city neighborhoods of a mid-sized eastern city and found that male black first offenders were referred to the juvenile court at a higher rate than white first offenders. No such difference was noted for female offenders or for males with prior records. They concluded (1970:521), "it would seem that when a youth's delinquency is rather pronounced, his disposition is made primarily in terms of factors immediately relevant to the case; but when delinquency is relatively mild, racial membership is a factor in his disposition." In addition to examining records, Ferdinand and Luchterhand administered a questionnaire to juveniles in their sample; it included items on attitude and family relationships. They found that the attitude of rejecting authority was taken into account in determining disposition for black youths but not for whites and that (1970:519) "the police are taking into account the offender's family structure when making a disposition of his case and that some of the differences in dispositions handed out to whites and blacks can be explained in terms of this practice by the police."

Wolfgang, Figlio, and Sellin (1972) studied a group of 9,945 boys, born in Philadelphia in the year 1945 (the studied group is called a "birth cohort" because of the common year of birth). The records of the boys were followed to adulthood in the process of studying delinquency patterns. Among the records studied were 9,956 police dispositions spanning an eight-year period. The investigators report differential treatment between black and white youths when the following factors were controlled: nature and seriousness of offense, socioeconomic status, and prior record. In particular, they found that nonwhites were arrested more frequently than whites and received more severe dispositions. To illustrate, they report that 44.6 per cent of nonwhite recidivists, as opposed to 26.9 per cent of white recidivists, were arrested rather than released in the field. Thornberry (1973) used the data of the Wolfgang, Figlio, and Sellin (1972) study for further analyses. He reports that the more serious offenders and recidivists were treated more seriously than the less serious and first-time offenders but points out (1973:93), "the most lenient dispositions were associated with white, minor offenders, and the most severe dispositions were associated with black, serious offenders." He also notes that youths of high socioeconomic status are more likely to receive an informal disposition than youths of low socioeconomic status, even when seriousness of offense and prior number of offenses are controlled.

An excellent overview of the research before 1980 in the area of police decision making with juveniles may be found in Smith, Black, and Weir (1980). Their concluding statement following the overview is as follows (1980:98, 99):

> In summary, it appears that even though the police have less information on which to base their decisions than do persons at other points in the juvenile justice system, police decision-making about juveniles is still a complex process. Which factors dominate appears to vary from jurisdiction to jurisdiction and officer to officer. While some writers have suggested that the decisions made about juveniles are more a function of who the officer is than who the juvenile is, the data seem to indicate that the process is more involved than that. Overall decisions depend on who the juvenile is, who apprehended him, what the offense is, who the victim or complainant is, and where (the community) the decision is made.

Dannefer and Schutt (1982) provide considerable support for the position that the important factors in police decision making vary from jurisdiction to jurisdiction. They found substantial bias in police dispositions in two communities of a populous eastern state, but the bias was especially notable in the more urban of the two communities (with a considerably higher percentage of minority residents).

Landau and Gad (1983) reported the results of a study of decision making by the juvenile bureaus of the London Metropolitan Police. They found the major determiners of a decision to "caution" (that is, to counsel and release rather than to prosecute) were type of offense and prior record, but that lesser, though significant, determiners were such nonlegal factors as age, ethnic group, and amount of parental control. The chances of black youths being counseled and released were considerably less than those of white youths; the difference, however, did not seem based on racial discrimination but on nonlegal variables (like parental control) on which the races differed.

Mott (1983) similarly reported on the use of cautioning by six police forces in England. Counsel and release rates over the six forces varied from 49 per cent to 60 per cent. The great majority of first offenders of all ages and of both sexes were simply cautioned, unless the offense was quite serious, the victim demanded prosecution, or the offense was denied by the youth. A comparison between first offenders who were cautioned and those who received lenient court dispositions (like discharge or a small fine) indicated no difference in recidivism rates over a two-year period. That finding and the observation that about 50 per cent of prosecuted male first offenders wound up with such lenient dispositions were used as arguments for greater use of cautioning by the police in England.

Challinger (1981) found similar results in Australia. He compared youngsters who received official police warnings with matched youngsters who were processed through the court system. Examination of recidivism over a six-year period showed that warnings were as effective as court processing in preventing recidivism.

Finally, Morash (1984) tested the hypothesis that when police have an image of a youth as a delinquent because of his or her associations, the probability of arrest increases. The study involved 519 youths whose names were drawn from the records of schools, the police, and the courts in two urban Boston communities. The investigation assessed both criminal behavior (by a self-report instrument) and the characteristics of peer groups (by interviews). In support of the operating hypothesis, it was found that (1984:107) "males with delinquent peers and those who break the law with their peers are most likely to have an arrest record . . . [and] youths who do not regularly associate with a peer group had very limited police contact." The effects of peer-group association remained when seriousness and frequency of delinquency were controlled. Morash argues, in short, that the police are more likely to arrest a youth who is perceived as delinquent and possibly dangerous because of previously being associated with delinquent peers.

A few conclusions seem warranted on the basis of certain consistencies and contradictions shown over the diverse array of studies on the factors that influence police discretion. First, arrest and subsequent referral rates to the juvenile court are higher for the more serious offenses (felonies) than for the less serious offenses (misdemeanors and status offenses). Second, a youngster is more likely to be arrested and referred by a police officer if he or she is known to have committed several prior offenses. Third, older youths are more likely to be arrested and referred than younger youths, particularly preteen youths. Fourth, the preference of the victim for arrest or release is frequently critical in determining police action. Fifth, while there does seem to be differential disposition of youths on the basis of race in some departments, there is no evidence that it is a common or widespread phenomenon. And sixth, both officer and departmental characteristics influence police decision making, but there is as yet no way of specifying a simple one-to-one relationship.

Summary

In the large majority of instances, police action in the case of a suspected young offender starts with a complaint by a citizen who may have observed or been a victim of an offense. The decision to initiate the complaint will be influenced by such factors as the seriousness of the offense, characteristics of the victim, general attitude of the community toward the particular type of offense, the number of times the offense was repeated by the youth, the mood of the observer or victim and his or her tolerance of deviance, and characteristics of the offender. The importance of the complainant in defining deviance and who is to be considered deviant is further highlighted by the substantial influence he or she has in the police officer's decision of whether or not to take a youth into custody.

State codes generally allow a good deal of discretion to police officers in the handling of juveniles, although there are differences in specific allowances. For example, New York permits an officer to take a juvenile into custody without a warrant only when the officer could have arrested an adult for the same crime.

But California permits custody of a juvenile when there is probable cause that he or she committed *any* offense.

Before a youth may be interrogated after being taken into custody, he or she must be informed of the right to remain silent and have an attorney present (to be appointed if the youth cannot afford one), and that statements made during the interrogation may be used against him or her (the Miranda warnings). In some states and court jurisdictions, there are restrictions beyond those in *Miranda* on interrogating youths, such as the required presence of a parent or guardian during interrogation.

Whether the interrogation and related investigation is very brief or very extensive, a decision must be made in regard to the disposition of the offender in custody. State codes permit outright release, release to parents or guardian without further action, release to parents or guardian with a stipulated requirement for appearance at court intake, and referral to court intake in continued custody. Police discretion enters here at its second major stage. The processing of youths in police custody prior to the dispositional decision and the decision itself are often in the hands of specialists called juvenile officers.

The decision to take into custody or not and the decision regarding disposition are influenced by an array of factors beyond community standards, complainant preferences, and the wording in state codes. These include the administrative style of the department; the mutual pressures of police officers upon each other; the personal characteristics of police officers and how these are affected by administrative and organizational pressures; the characteristics of suspected offenders — demeanor, sex, race, prior offense history, attitude; and the nature of the offense.

References

Arnold, William R. 1971. Race and Ethnicity Relative to Other Factors in Juvenile Court Dispositions. *American Journal of Sociology* 77:211–227.

Binder, Arnold, and Binder, Virginia L. 1982. Juvenile Diversion and the Constitution. *Journal of Criminal Justice* 10:1–24.

Black, Donald J., and Reiss, Albert J., Jr. 1970. Police Control of Juveniles. *American Sociological Review* 35:63–77.

Challinger, Dennis. 1981. Comparison of Official Warnings and Court Appearances for Young Offenders. *Australian and New Zealand Journal of Criminology* 14:165–169.

Chused, Richard H. 1973. The Juvenile Court Process: A Study of Three New Jersey Counties. *Rutgers Law Review* 26:488–589.

Cicourel, Aaron V. 1968. *The Social Organization of Juvenile Justice.* New York: Wiley.

Crank, John P., Regoli, Robert M., Poole, Eric D., and Culbertson, Robert G. 1986. Cynicism Among Police Chiefs. *Justice Quarterly* 3:343–352.

Creekmore, Mark 1976. Case Processing: Intake, Adjudication and Disposition. In *Brought to Justice? Juveniles, the Courts, and the Law,* edited by Rosemary Sarri and Yeheskel Hasenfeld, 119–150. Ann Arbor, Mich.: National Assessment of Juvenile Corrections, Univ. of Michigan.

Dannefer, Dale, and Schutt, Russell K. 1982. Race and Juvenile Justice Processing in Court and Police Agencies. *American Journal of Sociology* 87:1113–1132.

Davis, Samuel M. 1980. *Rights of Juveniles: The Juvenile Justice System.* New York: Clark Boardman Company.

Ferdinand, Theordore N., and Luchterhand, Elmer G. 1970. Inner-City Youth, the Police, the Juvenile Court, and Justice. *Social Problems* 17:510–527.

Ferster, Elyce Z., and Courtless, Thomas F. 1971. The Intake Process in the Affluent County Juvenile Court. *Hastings Law Journal* 22:1127–1153.

Garrett, Marcia, and Short, James F., Jr. 1975. Social Class and Delinquency: Predictions and Outcomes of Police-Juvenile Encounters. *Social Problems* 22:368–383.

Goldman, Nathan. 1963. *The Differential Selection of Juvenile Offenders for Court Appearance.* Hackensack, N.J.: National Council on Crime and Delinquency.

Goldstein, Herman. 1977. *Policing a Free Society.* Cambridge, Mass.: Harvard Univ. Press.

Hassin, Yael. 1981. Presence of Parents During Interrogation of Their Children. *Juvenile and Family Court Journal* 32, no. 3:33–42.

Hohenstein, William F. 1969. Factors Influencing the Police Disposition of Juvenile Offenders. In *Delinquency: Selected Studies,* edited by Thorsten Sellin and Marvin E. Wolfgang, 138–149. New York: Wiley.

Kinnane, Adrian. 1979. *Policing.* Chicago: Nelson-Hall.

Klein, Malcolm W., Rosenzweig, Susan L., and Bates, Ronald. 1975. The Ambiguous Juvenile Arrest. *Criminology* 1:78–89.

Landau, Simha F., and Nathan, Gad. 1983. Selecting Delinquents for Cautioning. *British Journal of Criminology* 23:128–149.

Lefkowitz, Joel. 1975. Psychological Attributes of Policemen: A Review of Research and Opinion. *Journal of Social Issues* 31:3–26.

Lundman, Richard J., Sykes, Richard E., and Clark, John P. 1980. Police Control of Juveniles: A Replication. In *Police Behavior: A Sociological Perspective,* edited by Richard J. Lundman, 130–151. New York: Oxford Univ. Press.

McEachern, A. W., and Bauzer, Riva. 1967. Factors Related to Disposition in Juvenile Police Contacts. In *Juvenile Gangs in Context: Theory, Research and Action,* edited by Malcolm W. Klein and Barbara G. Myerhoff. Englewood Cliffs, N.J.: Prentice-Hall.

Meade, Anthony 1973. Seriousness of Delinquency, the Adjudicative Decision and Recidivism—A Longitudinal Configuration Analysis. *Journal of Criminal Law and Criminology* 64:478–485.

Morash, Merry. 1984. Establishment of a Juvenile Police Record: The Influence of Individual and Peer Group Characteristics. *Criminology* 22:97–111.

Mott, Joy. 1983. Police Decisions for Dealing with Juvenile Offenders. *British Journal of Criminology* 23:249–262.

National Advisory Commission on Criminal Justice Standards and Goals. 1973. *Police.* Washington, D.C.: U.S. Government Printing Office.

National Crime Survey Report. 1986. *Criminal Victimization in the United States, 1986.* Washington, D.C.: U.S. Department of Justice, Bureau of Justice Statistics.

Niederhoffer, Arthur. 1969. *Behind the Shield: The Police in Urban Society.* Garden City, N.Y.: Anchor Books.

Paulsen, Monrad G., and Whitebread, Charles H. 1974. *Juvenile Law and Procedure.* Reno, Nev.: National Council of Juvenile Court Judges.

Piliavin, Irving, and Briar, Scott. 1964. Police Encounters with Juveniles. *American Journal of Sociology* 70:206–214.

Rubin, H. Ted. 1972. *Three Juvenile Courts: A Comparative Study.* Denver, Colo.: Institute for Court Management.

———1976. *The Courts: Fulcrum of the Justice System.* Pacific Palisades, Calif.: Goodyear.

Skolnick, Jerome H. 1966. *Justice Without Trial: Law Enforcement in Democratic Society.* New York: Wiley.

Smith, Charles P., Black, T. Edwin, and Weir, Adrianne W. 1980. *Reports of the National Juvenile Justice Assessment Centers. A National Assessment of Case Disposition and Classification in the Juvenile Justice System: Inconsistent Labeling. Volume II: Results of a Literature Search.* Washington, D.C.: U.S. Government Printing Office.

Special Study Committee on Criminal Justice Standards and Goals. 1975. *Juvenile Justice Standards and Goals.* Madison: Wisconsin Council on Criminal Justice.

Steffensmeier, Darrell J., and Terry, Robert M. 1973. Deviance and Respectability: An Observational Study of Reactions to Shoplifting. *Social Forces* 51:417–426.

Sullivan, Dennis C., and Siegel, Larry J. 1972. How Police Use Information to Make Decisions: An Application of Decision Games. *Crime & Delinquency* 18:253–262.

Sundeen, Richard A., Jr. 1974. Police Professionalization and Community Attachments and Diversion of Juveniles. *Criminology* 11:570–580.

Tannenbaum, Frank. 1938. *Crime and Community.* Boston: Ginn.

Task Force on Juvenile Delinquency. The President's Commission on Law Enforcement and Administration of Justice. 1967. *Task Force Report: Juvenile Delinquency and Youth Crime.* Washington, D.C.: U.S. Government Printing Office.

Terry, Robert M. 1967. Discrimination in the Handling of Juvenile Offenders by Social-Control Agencies. *Journal of Research in Crime and Delinquency* 4:218–230.

Thomas, Charles W., and Sieverdes, Christopher, M. 1975. Juvenile Court Intake: An Analysis of Discretionary Decision-Making. *Criminology* 12:413–432.

Thornberry, Terence P. 1973. Race, Socioeconomic Status and Sentencing in the Juvenile Justice System. *Journal of Criminal Law and Criminology* 64:90–98.

Walker, Samuel. 1980. *Popular Justice: A History of American Criminal Justice.* New York: Oxford Univ. Press.

Wilbanks, William L. 1975. *The Insertion/Diversion Decision at the Police Level.* Ph.D. dissertation, State Univ. of New York, Albany.

Wilson, James Q. 1968a. *Varieties of Police Behavior: The Management of Law and Order in Eight Communities.* Cambridge, Mass.: Harvard Univ. Press.

———— 1968b. The Police and the Delinquent in Two Cities. In *Controlling Delinquents,* edited by Stanton Wheeler, 9–30. New York: Wiley.

Wolfgang, Marvin E., Figlio, Robert M., and Sellin, Thorsten. 1972. *Delinquency in a Birth Cohort.* Chicago: Univ. of Chicago Press.

CHAPTER 10

The Juvenile Court

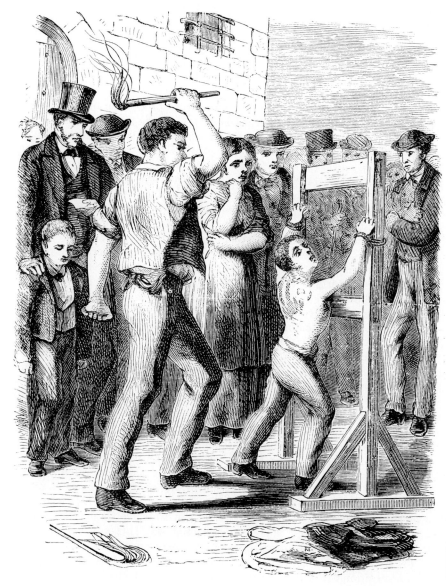

Culver Pictures, Inc.

In Chapter 9, we examined the police process starting with initial contact between officer and youth, which usually results from the complaint of a citizen. The youth may, of course, be released without being referred to the juvenile court. But in this chapter we will continue the story of juvenile justice processing by assuming that court referral is made. That referral may be by written document where the youth is immediately released to the custody of his or her parents, or by bringing the youth to a court facility while keeping him or her in police custody. The process, whether the youth is referred in custody or not, brings into operation an evaluative process by court officers that encompasses interviews with the referred youth, parents, such people as police officers and witnesses who can provide relevant information about the case, and an attorney, if one is handling the case at this point. The evaluation is often referred to as "intake screening," because it occurs at the entry point to the juvenile court and its primary function is to determine who is referred to the court for a hearing by the filing of a petition and who is screened out.

A petition for a hearing in juvenile court starts a procedure that has many of the features of a trial for an adult accused of a criminal offense. The petition requests the court to "inquire into conditions and enter such an order as may be necessary for the child's welfare" for a youth who is "in need of care and planning by the court" (or appropriate variants of the language in quotes). The petition identifies the youth by name, date of birth, sex, and address; identifies parents or guardians by names, marital status, and address; provides a statement of the facts and allegations of the case; and summarizes previous court orders concerning the minor in question.

A time for the hearing, called the adjudicatory or, in some states, jurisdictional, hearing is then set. The purpose of the adjudicatory hearing is to determine whether the youngster committed the offenses as stated, or, in more formal terms, to determine the truth of the allegations regarding misbehaving in the petition. The child is the equivalent of "guilty" in the adult court if the "allegations are sustained."

In addition to adjudicatory hearings, juvenile courts conduct each of the following types of hearing: detention, waiver or fitness, and dispositional.

When a youth is arrested by a police officer, delivered in custody to probation, and then kept in custody in a locked facility, there must be a judicial determination of the appropriateness of detention within a period of time specified in the relevant state code. The judicial determination is called a detention hearing.

A juvenile court may waive its jurisdiction to the adult criminal court when the youth does not seem amenable to its methods of rehabilitation. The lack of amenability may stem from the seriousness of the crime, the repetitiveness of the youth's criminal behavior, previous failures of the court in preventing recidivism, the age of the youth, the attitude of the youth, or some combination of these factors. A decision on this matter is made in a waiver or fitness hearing. Since the juvenile court decides whether or not to waive its jurisdiction, the expression "waiver" hearing is clear enough. But why "fitness" hearing? That use stems from the alleged goal of the hearing to determine whether the youth is "fit" for the treatment methods of the juvenile court.

The dispositional hearing follows the adjudicatory hearing, often immedi-

© Wayne Miller, Magnum

A hearing in juvenile court.

ately, and involves, as the name implies, determination of a program for re-habilitation. That program could be probation, placement in a foster home, institutionalization, or some other alternative. Clearly, there is no need for a dispositional hearing if the allegations in the petition are not sustained.

Detention

The Role of the Court Intake Officer

As discussed in Chapter 9, referral of a youth to the juvenile court by the police may be accomplished as the youth is transferred to court intake in full custody. Hufnagel and Davidson (1974:355, 356), who observed operations of the Denver juvenile court, describe the process of transfer and reception while in custody as follows:

> Almost hourly, a patrol car will turn into the alley behind juvenile hall with a child or two for the admissions office. The door is locked, and a buzzer must be pushed to notify the counselor that another child is awaiting admission. The child will pass through the door into a poorly lit office area. Behind a large counter, a juvenile hall employee waits to get basic information from the child and to relieve him or her of all valuables. If an intake screening counselor is not readily available, the child will be placed in a small locked room across from the admissions office until an interview can be arranged which will aid in determining whether or not the child will be detained pending a detention hearing before the court.

It is clear from the quotation that when a youngster is brought in custody to the court facility, an intake officer has the decision-making responsibility of release or continued detention until a detention hearing is held. The task is typically performed by a probation officer, who, in larger probation departments, is commonly designated an "intake probation officer." While recognizing that the decision regarding continued detention (as well as the screening decision to be discussed next) is the task of people who are not probation officers in some jurisdictions, we will use the terms *court intake officer, intake officer,* and *intake probation officer* interchangeably in referring to these evaluators. Creekmore (1976:125) has emphasized, "a decision to detain should presume that a petition will be recommended," but Hufnagel and Davidson (1974) found, in a Colorado court, that the system allowed a child to be detained even if a formal petition was not going to be filed.

Justifications for Detention

Typical state laws allow detention for one or more of the following reasons:

1. Release of the youth endangers the person or property of others.
2. The youth himself or herself would be subject to harm if released.
3. There is substantial danger that the youth will flee and not be available for the adjudicatory and dispositional hearings. This may be a particular concern because there is no constitutional requirement for release on bail in juvenile justice, and such release is not allowed in most states.
4. There is not adequate supervision available for the youth in the community.
5. The youth has fled from another jurisdiction and is being processed for return to that jurisdiction. The youth might be a runaway parole violator, or a runaway from an institution to which he or she had been committed.

Generally, according to Mulvey and Saunders (1982), state statutes are expressed in rather general terms rather than in the restrictive manner recommended by agencies like the National Council on Crime and Delinquency (NCCD). For example, while the NCCD recommendations include forceful language stating that children may be detained only if they are "almost certain" to run away or to commit a dangerous offense, state laws are commonly phrased to include detention for children who are "likely" to flee or endanger the community.

But whatever the legal justifications for the detention of youths, it has become obvious through studies of the detention process (see Mulvey and Saunders, 1982) that there are many extralegal factors that affect decisions to detain. The legal criteria determine who should be detained, while studies of the process in operation show who actually was detained and the special factors that apparently led to the detention decisions. Several of these extralegal factors are the following:

1. The feeling by some police and some (fewer) probation officers that a short period in jail or in a juvenile hall is the equivalent to a kick in the pants that might straighten out a young offender (see Chapter 9).
2. The concern of probation officers that release of a youngster who is brought in custody by police officers will result in severe police displeasure and endanger future rapport (Cohen, 1975b, provides some evidence of this phenomenon). That this reason may not be an overwhelming one, especially from the perspective of the police, is the frequent complaint a person in the field hears from police officers, "Why, that little bastard was back on the streets before I even got back from delivering him to juvenile hall."
3. Concern in the general community for the safety of citizens during a period of high crime, particularly violent crime by young offenders, may put pressure on justice personnel to lower considerably the release probabilities of youths taken into custody.
4. The availability of intake personnel for a thorough evaluation on a twenty-four-hour basis seems to lower the probability of detention (see, in particular, Sarri, 1974).
5. There are variations over intake officers in personal bias and variations over courts in philosophy, leading to emphasis on such factors as demeanor of the youth or number of prior offenses in certain contexts (see Sumner, 1971).

The Detention Hearing

Hufnagel and Davidson (1974:360) indicate, for the Denver court, that they observed, "if the decision is made to detain the youngster, that decision will be reviewed by the court within 48 hours." The review by the court of a probation officer's decision to detain a youth, which is required by code in most states, is the detention hearing. The specific maximum time allowance for the detention hearing varies from state to state, as does the moment that the clock starts. For example, in California, the Welfare and Institutions Code states that a minor taken into custody must be released within forty-eight hours (excluding the

nonjudicial days of Saturdays, Sundays, and holidays) from the moment of
initial custody (arrest) if a petition has not yet been filed for an adjudicatory
hearing. Further, if a petition has been filed, the minor must be brought to court
to determine whether further detention is warranted by the end of the judicial
day following the filing. Thus, in California, if a youngster is taken into custody
by the police on Monday afternoon and kept in custody, he or she must have a
detention hearing by the end of Thursday, assuming the petition is filed on
Wednesday. The allowed delay would, of course, be longer if the arrest came on
a day like Thursday or Friday that had the intervention of nonjudicial days
before the required time limitation took effect.

The Roles of Attorneys. Hufnagel and Davidson (1974:361) observed at
detention hearings in the Denver juvenile court, "Most children are now represented by counsel, and a representative of the district attorney's office attends
all hearings, arguing vigorously for detention in many of the more serious
delinquency allegation cases and taking no role whatsoever in most CHINS
cases."

As Davis (1980) has indicated, several states have declared the right to
counsel, including court-appointed counsel where the offender cannot afford
retained counsel, at every stage of the juvenile proceedings. He points out
(1980:5-7), "This represents an extension of both *Kent* and *Gault,* since they
required counsel only at the waiver and adjudicatory hearings, respectively."
(See the relevant discussion in Chapter 8.) Some states simply declare the right
to counsel without specifying that the right applies at all stages, other states
require a court-appointed counsel where the juvenile requests one but cannot
afford the expense, and still other states declare that a judge may appoint
counsel at his or her discretion. The following, from Section 633 of the California Welfare and Institutions Code, illustrates the most definitive type of granting of the right to counsel at a detention hearing: "Upon his appearance before
the court at the detention hearing, such minor and his parent or guardian, if
present, shall be informed of the reasons why the minor was taken into custody,
the nature of the juvenile court proceedings, and the right of such minor and his
parent or guardian to be represented at every stage of the proceedings by
counsel."

Several standards-setting bodies (e.g., the National Advisory Commission on
Criminal Justice Standards and Goals) and several courts (e.g., the Supreme
Court of Alaska in *Doe v. State.* 487 P. 2d 47, 1971) have mandated the right to
counsel at detection hearings — one body, indeed, stated that the right was so
critical that it should be nonwaivable.

Bail. The U.S. Supreme Court has not granted to juveniles the constitutional right to bail, although one federal district court ruling has granted juveniles in its domain the same right to bail that adults have in criminal proceedings (*Trimble v. Stone,* 187 F. Supp. 483, 1960). Wadlington, Whitebread, and
Davis (1983:300) have summarized the picture regarding bail over the states as
follows: "Four states (Hawaii, Kentucky, Oregon, and Utah) deny juveniles the
right to bail. Nine states (Arkansas, Colorado, Connecticut, Georgia, Massachusetts, Nebraska, Oklahoma, South Dakota, and West Virginia) have enacted

laws expressly granting juveniles the right to bail." In the other states, it is either not mentioned at all or left to the discretion of the court.

As Davis (1980) has pointed out, most courts have taken the position that the emphasis on release to parents at the various decision points in juvenile processing provides an adequate alternative to the bail system or that bail would be a cumbersome imposition on the juvenile court (see, e.g., *In re William M.,* 3 Cal. 3d 16, 1970; *Doe v. State,* 487 P. 2d 47, 1971; *Baldwin v. Lewis,* 300 F. Supp. 1220, 1969). He concludes (1980:3 – 43), "The protective function of the juvenile court requires that it exercise a special responsibility toward children that is not necessary or appropriate in the case of adults. . . . It sometimes happens that those circumstances warrant his detention."

Selection Criteria for Detention

Research has not shown a pattern of preference for detention on the basis of race. While Sumner (1971) found that blacks were detained at a significantly higher rate than whites, Cohen (1975b), Coates, Miller, and Ohlin (1975), Pawlak (1977), Fenwick (1982), and B. McCarthy (1985) found no such difference. According to Mulvey and Saunders (1982:277), "The lack of a clear relationship between race and the detention decision is not surprising . . . since more nonwhites are arrested initially, creating a racial imbalance from the outset."

On the other hand, several studies have shown that children of low SES are more likely to be detained than children of middle and high SES, with no difference between the latter two. Using family income and educational levels in the census tracts of the residences of youths who were candidates for detention, Cohen (1975b:25, 26) concluded, "It appears then that . . . the socioeconomic status of individuals referred to each of our courts is not substantially related to the criterion, but that in each court a greater proportion of youths from low status tracts was detained than middle and high status youths." Other indications of the relationship between low SES and a greater likelihood of detention may be found in Sumner (1971) and in Coates, Miller, and Ohlin (1975). But B. McCarthy (1985) found no evidence of a preference for detention on the basis of class.

Contrary to what one might expect from the data in Chapter 1 indicating the far greater seriousness and frequency of crime by boys as compared with girls, the available evidence shows that girls have been more likely to be detained than boys and to be held for longer periods (see Sarri, 1974; Andrews and Cohn, 1974; Pawlak, 1977; Chesney-Lind, 1977, and Pappenfort and Young, 1977). Indeed, Pawlak (1977:164) observed, "Overall, white females are detained more frequently than any other group." Contributing to that state of affairs is the high proportion of girls who have been referred to court intake for status offenses, together with the surprisingly high tendency to detain status offenders. As in the case of arrests, status offenders are more likely to be detained if they are girls than if they are boys, by a three-to-one margin according to some observers (Sarri, 1974; Chesney-Lind, 1977).

In 1969, Ferster, Snethen, and Courtless reported detention rates for various offenses over eleven jurisdictions. In all but one jurisdiction, status offenders were detained at a higher rate, mostly a much higher rate, than youths who committed crimes against persons. A similar, but less pronounced, pattern occurred in the comparison of status offenders and those who comitted crimes against property. Averaging over jurisdictions produced percentages of juveniles detained as follows: crimes against persons 7.9, crimes against property 27.8, and status offenses 42.0. Further, research reported by the Special Study Committee on Criminal Justice Standards and Goals (1975:122) indicated "that over 60% of all secure detentions were for 'status offense' reasons," and research by the Children's Research Fund (1976:3, 4) found that only 11.7 per cent of children in adult jails "were charged with serious offenses against persons. The rest — 88.3 per cent — were charged with property or minor offenses. What is most alarming is that 17.9 per cent of jailed children . . . had committed 'status offenses' . . . such as running away or truancy."

Similar patterns have been reported by Sumner (1971), by Sarri (1974), and by Pawlak (1977). To show that the array of results showing higher proportions of youths in detention for lesser offenses than for serious offenses is not purely a function of the frequencies of the various offenses, we turn to findings of Cohen (1975a, 1975b). He studied detention decisions in three juvenile courts serving large communities: Denver County, Colorado; Shelby County, Tennessee; and Montgomery County, Pennsylvania. In Denver County, 22.1 per cent of CHINS and 29.3 per cent of those with alcohol offenses were detained as compared with 22.2 per cent of those who committed property crimes and 27.4 per cent who committed violent crimes. In Shelby County, the detention percentages were as follows: unruly behavior 42.7, alcohol offense 34.0, property crime 42.0, and violent crime 55.2. Finally, in Montgomery County the percentages were unruly behavior 51.5, alcohol offense 5.0, property crime 10.2, violent crime 21.6. As a summary over the three jurisdictions that highlights the fact that detention is not predominantly for the serious offender, 40 per cent of the status offenders were detained as opposed to 38 per cent of those who committed violent crimes; 31 per cent of both alcohol and property offenders were detained.

Chused (1973) studied a random sample of over 600 files from the records of juvenile courts in three New Jersey counties. He supplemented those data with interviews encompassing court personnel, lawyers, and police officers. Perhaps most interesting in the vast array of results he reported are the great differences over the three courts in detention decision making (as well as court decision making at other processing points), despite the fact that they operated under the same state laws. For example, in one county, detention rates were uniformly high (about 85 per cent) for status offenders and for criminal-type offenders who committed serious, medium, or minor offenses. In another county, with a low detention rate (about 25 per cent), status offenders were detained at a higher rate (54 per cent) than serious criminal-type offenders (25 per cent), medium offenders (19 per cent), and minor offenders (25 per cent). The former was reported as the wealthiest county in New Jersey and generally residential, while the latter was described as a densely populated county containing the city of Trenton. The third county (containing the city of Newark) was between the others in detention characteristics (with an overall rate of 53 per cent and a rate for status offenders of 63 per cent).

Bailey (1981), in a study of more than 60,000 cases in a juvenile court of Ohio, saw no pattern of relationship between detention decision and seriousness of offense. However, when the most serious of the felonies (robbery, burglary, larceny, sex offenses) were considered separately, they were found to lead to the highest detention rates. Fenwick (1982) found no statistically significant effect for the detention decision due to seriousness of current offense, prior record, and demeanor in the hearing room. For the court he observed (in a major eastern city), the predominant factor in that decision was the variable family affiliation/disaffiliation (the degree to which the family was held together). Finally, in a study of three Massachusetts courts, Bookin-Weiner (1984) showed that family circumstances and the need for controlling an individual were the major factors determining detention decisions (see also B. McCarthy, 1985). Prior court appearances, adjudications, and offense seriousness made lesser contributions. But all these factors operated in a state where the law stipulated detention only to assure appearance in court.

Intake Screening

Intake screening involves the same sort of discretionary decision making that we discussed in the last chapter in the case of the police. Rubin (1976) has reviewed several approaches to intake decision making that differ markedly from that of intake probation officer as discretionary agent. For example, he found the process in some courts whereby (1976:91, 92), "the complaint is referred to the clerk of the court who scrutinizes the police report as to legal sufficiency. If the complaint is found sufficient a hearing is held with a judge or referee, who decides whether or not the case should go further."

Decision Making at Intake Screening

The functions of intake screening are as follows: (1) to determine whether the circumstances of the case bring it within the jurisdiction of the juvenile court, (2) to determine whether the evidence is sufficient to warrant a court hearing, (3) to decide whether the case is serious enough to require a court hearing, (4) and to arrange for a process of informal supervision if that alternative seems desirable. In the words of the Task Force on Juvenile Delinquency of the President's Commission (1967:14), "Intake is set apart from the screening process used in adult criminal courts by the pervasive attempt to individualize each case and the nature of the personnel administering the discretionary process." Moreover, as Creekmore (1976:125) states, "to ensure that the youth and parents understand the importance of this contact, the interview should begin with a careful explanation of their rights (to an attorney, to remain silent), the worker's role, the decisions available, and what effect the decisions might have on the youth."

The probation officer is, of course, expected to dismiss a case if the circumstances make it inappropriate for the juvenile court or if the evidence is not sufficient for adjudication. But as the Task Force on Juvenile Delinquency reports (1967:15):

> The jurisdictional grounds, however, are broad, and at intake most cases are
> potential subjects of the juvenile justice process — if not for specific delinquent

acts, then as incorrigibility or neglect. Most commonly, therefore, the major task at this point is to determine which cases to handle formally rather than whether a case for intervention exists. The choice is generally among dismissal (with or without referral to community service resources), unofficial handling by the court, and filing of petitions. Making that choice may call for exploration of the facts of the offense, the juvenile's background, and other facets of the case. . . .

The basic choice is between adjudication and the various nonjudicial alternatives. The selection is signified by filing a petition or deciding not to do so.

Creekmore (1976:125) summarizes the factors that should be used in intake decision making as follows:

Once the process has been explained, the interview should proceed through a two-step process. First, the complaint needs to be read and examined in factual detail and the youth questioned about the allegations. If the youth admits to the substance of the complaint, informal and formal handling or dismissal are possible. If the youth denies the complaint, only formal handling or dismissal are possible. The circumstances surrounding the offense in question need to be examined to determine if the complaint accurately represents what happened and if sufficient reason exists to file a petition based on information about this offense alone. The youth's involvement in the planning and execution of the offense, delinquent intent, and likelihood of repeating this or other offenses must also be gauged. If grounds for a petition are not found, the case should be dismissed or referred to another agency.

Filing a petition in juvenile court is the rough equivalent to filing a complaint in the adult criminal system — it brings proceedings of the court into operation. The result is an adjudicatory hearing in the juvenile justice system.

Reichel and Seyfrit (1984) reported on the use of "peer juries" in the juvenile court of Columbia County, Georgia. The peer juries consist of youths under seventeen years of age assembled by court intake officers to hear selected cases and recommend dispositions. Reichel and Seyfrit state (1984:428), "The jurors may ask questions of the youth, family, and/or the Intake Officer. Peer Jurors have the latitude to ask any questions they feel will help them understand the case and make recommendations." They may make such recommendations as restitution, curfew restrictions, or counseling but may not make such more obviously constitutionally protected recommendations as detention. The evaluative data of the investigators indicate success of the program from the perspectives of offenders, peer jury members, and parents.

The assessment of juvenile court operations by Smith, Black, and Weir (1980:128) led to the conclusion "that approximately one-half of the cases referred to juvenile courts are screened out without referral for a judicial hearing." But, as Rubin (1972) found, averages conceal wide differences in rates of filing petitions over jurisdictions. He found, for example, filing rates as low as 14 per cent and 20 per cent, in Seattle and Atlanta, respectively. Moreover, he found that referrals to probation were not always properly recorded, so there is probably a lower rate of petitioning than statistics indicate.

"Probation Workers May Not Be Tough Enough." It is important to reiterate at this point that society's extreme displeasure with juvenile criminal behavior, particularly violent behavior, has led to statutory changes aimed at hardening the process of handling juvenile offenders (see Chapter 8). In addition to general effects on court philosophy, the hardening process has consisted of reducing the role of probation, which is widely viewed as the "social worker" or compassionate side of justice, increasing the severity of punishment for juveniles (whatever euphemism may be used for punishment), increasing the adversarial role of the prosecuting attorney in juvenile hearings, and decreasing the age at which minors may be tried in adult criminal courts. Although we consider that hardening process in various other contexts, our focus at the moment is on changes that affect court intake. Thus, for example, a California statutory change in 1976 took the authority for filing a petition in the case of criminal offenses (as opposed to status offenses) away from probation and gave it to the prosecuting attorney. The probation officer could still dismiss a case or institute informal supervision, but only the prosecuting attorney, who became designated as "representing the people" in court, could petition for an adjudicatory hearing. Following the change of 1976, California's Welfare and Institutions Code (Section 653) stated:

> The probation officer shall immediately make such investigation as he or she deems necessary to determine whether proceedings in the juvenile court should be commenced. If the probation officer determines that proceedings should be commenced to declare a person . . . to be a ward of the juvenile court, the probation officer shall cause the affidavit to be taken to the prosecuting attorney. The prosecuting attorney shall within his or her discretionary power institute proceedings in accordance with his or her role as public prosecutor.

And later, in 1982, legislative action aimed at still greater influence for the prosecuting attorney further reduced the alternatives available to the probation intake officer. The change (Section 653.5 of the Welfare and Institutions Code) stipulates that "the probation officer shall cause the affidavit to be taken within 48 hours to the prosecuting attorney" in case "the offense constitutes a second felony referral to the probation officer" for a juvenile under the age of sixteen, or "the offense constitutes a felony referral" for sixteen- and seventeen-year olds. In short, the change has greatly reduced the discretion of intake probation officers in that immediate dismissal and informal handling are no longer available as alternatives to them in those types of cases.

Thomson and McAnany (1984) have pointed out that the demands for more emphasis on due process and public safety have in recent years led probation departments to skepticism and despair. Perhaps in defense against being perceived as too soft, probation departments are substituting just-deserts (punitive) approaches for the former rehabilitative ideal.

Interestingly, Harris (1986) considered the intake role of probation officers in her attempt to answer the question, "Is the juvenile justice system lenient?" She suggested that probation officers may be far less lenient than it seems on casual observation for several reasons. First, many cases are dismissed at intake for valid reasons of lack of evidence, the failure of victims or witnesses to cooperate, or the lack of credibility of a witness, while the public (including the police) may perceive only the release of "young thugs." There is support for that point in the observation by Chused (1973) that many of the cases dismissed at intake in a county he studied were so handled because the cases were largely unsolved. And second, Harris (1986) pointed out that informal probation may be just as restrictive and punitive as the formal probation that follows court processing (although, as noted below, Ferster and Courtless [1971], observed that informal probation is often little more than an empty ritual).

Informal Probation. Informal probation or informal supervision is based on an agreement among the probation officer, the minor, the minor's parents, and sometimes an attorney for a program of supervision whereby certain behavior is expected to avoid formal court proceedings. The maximum time allowed for the supervision is stated in law (e.g., three months in Illinois, six months in California); within the allowed time, the probation officer may petition the court for a hearing (or refer the case to the prosecuting attorney for petitioning) if the conditions of informal probation are not satisfied.

A probation officer, thus, has the opportunity for control over a child's life during the period of time that informal probation is allowed under state law. The child could be required to be home by a certain time every evening, attend school regularly, call the probation department every day and visit it once each week, avoid various people who may have negative influences on the child's behavior, or attend counseling sessions at a local service agency. Since that sort of supervision could significantly interfere with a child's liberty, yet occurs by an administrative procedure without judicial review, there have been many criticisms of the process of informal probation over the years. In the words of Paulsen and Whitebread (1974:127):

> Informal handling, though having the advantage of minimizing the consequences of an encounter with the police and the courts and providing a way of settling matters by an agreement, has some serious drawbacks. A child, who has never been found within the jurisdiction of the juvenile court, may be subjected to a serious interference with his freedom. In short, public authority over the life of a child can be exercised without any judicial determination that a basis for it exists.

The Juvenile Justice Standards Project of the Institute of Judicial Administration–American Bar Association (1980) recommended the complete elimination of "nonjudicial probation" as an alternative disposition at probation intake, allowing referral to a community agency as the only permissible "nonjudicial disposition" (Standard 2.4). The standards-setting group felt, in short, that informal probation was too susceptible to abuse by intake officers. On the other hand, Binder and Binder (1982) surveyed court decisions dealing with the question of the constitutionality of informal probation and concluded that the courts, contrary to opinions expressed in legal articles, were not sympathetic to making it an impermissible option. The courts seem to insist on judicial determination with the usual due process rights only when there is the possibility of profound loss of liberty, as in detention. The restriction on freedom that may come with informal probation seems to be considered minor, closer to the restrictions that accompany arrest than the loss that accompanies incarceration.

Moreover, the work of Ferster and Courtless (1971) indicates that the restrictions imposed on a child in informal probation are a good deal fewer in practice than in potentiality. During their observations of the operations of a juvenile court in a county of the "Middle-Atlantic region," they found that not much was actually done over the period of supposed supervision. In fact, substantial numbers of the children on informal supervision were never even seen by probation officers. They described informal supervision as (1971:1144) "a waiting period to see if the child encounters further difficulties; it certainly cannot be characterized as an active treatment or supervision program. This approach seems inconsistent, not only with the term 'informal probation,' but also with the prevalent assumption that certain children who have problems can be helped without court-ordered treatment." The significance of this finding is increased by the fact that some children were placed in informal probation because of presumed emotional problems.

The Choice Among Alternatives. What are the factors that lead an intake probation officer to one decision rather than to another one? Clearly, the nature of the offense and the prior record of the youngster are of consequence. Indeed, Thomas and Sieverdes (1975) found seriousness of the most recent offense to be the leading predictor of case disposition in a small southeastern city, and Thornberry (1973) found an increase in proportion of cases referred for court hearing in Philadelphia as the number of previous offenses increased. Other investigators who have shown relationships between seriousness of current offense and previous record, on the one hand, and intake decision, on the other, are Rosen and Carl (1974), Dungworth (1977), T. Carter (1979), and Fenwick (1982), although Dungworth and Carter did show that status offenders are more likely to be petitioned for such extralegal factors as social class and home environment. But marked differences have been noted over jurisdictions in the relationship between specific offense and outcome. Thus, over seven courts in Michigan, Creekmore (1976:127) found that "with the exception of offenses against persons, no apparent relationship exists between type of offense and intake decisions." As another example, Rubin (1972) found the order for likelihood of filing a petition in two cities as follows: Salt Lake City — offenses against property (59 per cent), offenses against public order (56 per cent), offenses against persons (55 per cent), status offenses (36 per cent); Seattle — offenses against persons (31 per cent), status offenses (20 per cent), offenses against property (7 per cent), offenses against public order (4 per cent).

The age of the juvenile has also been shown to be a relevant factor in decisions at intake in various jurisdictions. Terry (1967a, 1967b), in fact, found that age ranked with seriousness of offense in determining severity of disposition in a midwestern city. Ferster and Courtless (1971) similarly found that older juveniles were more likely to be referred to court than younger juveniles. But Chused's (1973) results for three counties in New Jersey did not show a distinctive pattern. In one county, there was a clear picture of higher rates of court referral for older youngsters, whether they did or did not have prior records. In another county, there was a tendency for older youngsters to be kept from court referral regardless of prior record, and in a third county there was a mixed picture. Finally, T. Carter (1979:348) found, "In the case of nonstatus offenders, intake workers are sensitive to age, apparently trying to protect younger offenders from the 'delinquent' stigma by handling their cases in an unofficial manner. However, age does not appear to be a primary consideration for the intake disposition of status offenders."

Whatever differences found in the treatment of boys and girls at probation intake seem attributable to their immediate offenses and to their prior records. Terry (1976a:225) did find, as expected, that boys were treated more severely at intake, but full analysis of the data showed, "The seriousness of the offense and the number of previous offenses appear to account for most of the relationship between the 'maleness' of the offender and the severity of the probation department disposition."

Some, but not all, investigators have reported racial factors as influential in the determination of decisions at intake. Arnold (1971), studying intakes in a southern city, found that, overall, whites were treated more leniently than Hispanics, and Hispanics more leniently than blacks. But the pattern of differential treatment varied with seriousness of offense — the difference among the three social groups was greatest with the most serious offenses. Thornberry (1973) found, as did Arnold, that blacks were more likely to be referred to the juvenile court than whites, but for Thornberry the difference was greatest for offenses of low seriousness. Chused (1973) had racial information on two of the three counties he studied and reports an inconsistent pattern where for some categories of offense seriousness, blacks were more likely to be sent to court, but for other categories whites were more likely to be sent to court. Meade (1973) reports for a southeastern county that whites were slightly more likely to be referred for formal hearings than blacks. And, finally, Thomas and Sieverdes (1975) and Terry (1967a, 1967b) report that their studies indicate that race has either no or a negligible effect on decision making at intake. In Terry's study, Hispanics were the least likely to be referred to court.

The following are some of the conclusions reached by Smith, Black, and Weir (1980:243, 249) after their thorough review of the literature on decision making at intake: (1) "the juvenile's *prior record* — the number of prior court referrals or number of previous offenses recorded — appears to be most consistently influential across all jurisdictions." (2) "The role of the *alleged offense* . . . is less clear. . . . There are definite variations between jurisdictions in which offenses are most likely to result in dismissal, informal adjustment, or referral for a court hearing." (3) *"Age* appears to be somewhat related to intake screening decisions in that younger juveniles appear not to be referred on for a formal court hearing as frequently as are older juveniles." (4) *"Family status* appears to be somewhat influential." (5) *"Socioeconomic status* and the juvenile's *school attendance or employment* do not appear to have an impact on the decisions made at the intake level." And (6) "the studies do not indicate any consistent or predominant pattern of discrimination on the basis of *race or ethnicity"* or of sex.

The Waiver Hearing

The purpose of the waiver hearing is to determine whether the juvenile court should relinquish its jurisdiction over a minor and transfer the case to the jurisdiction of an adult criminal court. As discussed in Chapter 8, the U.S. Supreme Court decided in *Kent* that waiver of jurisdiction is a "critically important" decision in the sense that it is accompanied by potentially serious consequences for the youth in question. Accordingly, the Court ordered a certain degree of procedural formality accompanied by a certain minimum of due process rights in waiver hearings.

The other decision of the Supreme Court discussed in Chapter 8 that bears on waiver hearings is *Breed v. Jones.* In it, the Court ruled that waiver to and prosecution in an adult criminal court after an adjudicatory hearing in juvenile court is constitutionally invalid because the procedure violates the double jeopardy clause of the Fifth Amendment.

Criteria for Waiving Jurisdiction

In an appendix to the *Kent* decision, the Supreme Court listed the following as suggestive criteria in the determination of waiver of a juvenile court's jurisdiction to an adult criminal court: (*Kent v. United States,* 383 U.S. at 566, 567, 1966):

1. The seriousness of the alleged offense to the community and whether the protection of the community requires waiver.
2. Whether the alleged offense was committed in an aggressive, violent, premeditated or willful manner.
3. Whether the alleged offense was against persons or against property, greater weight being given to offenses against persons especially if personal injury resulted.
4. The prosecutive merit of the complaint . . .
5. The desirability of trial and disposition of the entire offense in one court when the juvenile's associates in the alleged offense are adults who will be charged with a crime . . .
6. The sophistication and maturity of the juvenile . . .
7. The record and previous history of the juvenile . . .
8. The prospects for adequate protection of the public and the likelihood of reasonable rehabilitation of the juvenile . . . by the use of procedures, services and facilities currently available to the Juvenile Court.

Davis (1980:4-1) states, "A recent perusal of the statutes of the fifty states and the District of Columbia . . . revealed that Arkansas,Nebraska, New York, and Vermont do not provide for waiver of jurisdiction [from juvenile or family court to criminal court]." Over the jurisdictions that permit waiver, most set a minimum age (usually sixteen) and require that the alleged offense be serious. Some states permit waiver over a certain age without specification of the nature of the offense, others specify the nature of the offense but no minimum age, and still others have a unique concatenation or no limitations whatsoever on waiver. (See Davis [1980] for a listing of states that fall into each of the above categories.)

Although a few states have placed in their statutes detailed criteria for waiver determination of the sort suggested in the appendix to the *Kent* decision, most have not. As Davis (1980:4-19) points out, most jurisdictions "simply state the basis on which waiver is allowed—i.e., that the child is 'not amenable to treatment or rehabilitation' or that 'the needs of the child or best interest of the State' require that the child's case be transferred to adult court for prosecution." According to Wadlington, Whitebread, and Davis (1983), however, as new juvenile court codes are being enacted or amended, they show an increasing trend toward listing specific waiver criteria.

The implementation of a more detailed state code in the operating procedure of a juvenile court was considered by the Court of Special Appeals of Maryland in *Matter of Johnson* (304 A. 2d 859, 1973). Diane was accused of killing a two-year-old boy in a grossly negligent manner when she drove a car onto a sidewalk and struck three children (the other two children survived). She was sixteen at the time of the accident and did not hold a license to drive; her inexperience in driving was shown in the cause of the accident — putting her foot on the accelerator when she intended to apply the brakes.

The state's attorney for Baltimore requested a waiver hearing under the argument that the safety of the public required a criminal trial. As stated in *Matter of Johnson* (at 861):

> The legislature has mandated that five factors are to be considered by the juvenile judge in any waiver proceeding. Md. Ann. Code art. 22, §70-16(b). The factors are:
>
> "(1) Age of child.
> (2) Mental and physical condition of child.
> (3) The child's amenability to treatment in any institution, facility, or programs available to delinquents.
> (4) The nature of the offense.
> (5) The safety of the public."

> Not all of the five factors need be resolved against the juvenile in order for the waiver to be justifiable.

At the waiver hearing, it was established that Diane was an above-average student who seemed responsible and reliable in school with no evidence of any behavioral problems. Moreover, she was active in civic affairs and regularly attended church, where she was a member of the choir. Her minister testified at the hearing that she was "very concerned about what has happened" and that occasionally "she has been crying because of the death of the two-year-old."

The judge granted the state's request and waived the case from juvenile to criminal court with the comment (at 863) "She has not been in any difficulty and she has done well in school and has been active in school activities, has been active in community activities, but I base my decision on her age, almost seventeen when this occurred, but essentially on the very grievous nature of the offense." The judge admitted that the decision to grant waiver was a very difficult one for him.

The decision was appealed on the basis that (at 863) "the judge abused his discretion by granting waiver." The Maryland Court of Special Appeals agreed and remanded the case back to juvenile court for an adjudicatory hearing. Its decision stated (at 863), "We think it apparent that the hearing judge was unduly influenced by the 'nature of the offense' to the extent that the amenability of the appellant to rehabilitation was cast aside and not considered, or, if considered, was not afforded its proper weight." In addition, the appeals court stated that all five legislative factors must be considered actively by the hearing judge with a proper balancing among them in the arrival at a final decision. Such, the court felt, was not done in this case.

The decision of the appeals court did hint at the punitive element in the waiver decision because of the death of a two-year-old boy. Of course, the case makes one wonder about the social pressure on a judge, direct or implicit, to make a harsh decision when his or her community is deeply offended by an act or the result of an act, and communities are very deeply affected by a tragedy involving a young child. Appeals courts are more immune from that type of pressure.

In a fashion similar to the Maryland appeals decision, the Montana Supreme Court (*In re Stevenson,* 538 P. 2d 5, 1975) required that all criteria specified in the waiver statute be carefully considered and weighed in each individual case before arriving at a waiver order. But, it should be emphasized, not all courts have taken similarly restrictive positions (see Wadlington, Whitebread, and Davis, 1983).

Feld (1983) objects to the process whereby judges make waiver decisions on the basis of their clinical evaluations of youths' "amenability to treatment" or "dangerousness." His arguments are that (1983:197) "there is no valid or reliable clinical basis upon which juvenile court judges can make individualized amenability or dangerousness determinations, and that the broad discretion afforded judges to do so results in inconsistent and discriminatory application." He recommends a legislative redefinition whereby youths are excluded automatically from the jurisdiction of the juvenile court on the bases of seriousness of present offense and prior record.

Actual Due Process Rights in Waiver Hearings

In arguing for the invalidity of the waiver order in the *Kent* case because of the shabbiness of the procedure used by the juvenile court, the U.S. Supreme Court pointed out (at 554):

> We do not consider whether, on the merits, Kent should have been transferred; but there is no place in our system of law for reaching a result of such tremendous consequences without ceremony — without hearing, without effective assistance of counsel, without a statement of reasons. It is inconceivable that a court of justice dealing with adults, with respect to a similar issue, would proceed in this manner.

That would seem to specify clearly the right to counsel in waiver hearings. Yet, because Kent had an attorney at his waiver hearing and because of references to that attorney in several parts of the written decision, there have been differences in interpretation of that elementary due process right. In one legal casebook, for example, we find (Wadlington, Whitebread, and Davis, 1983:393), "*Kent* did not finally decide the issue of right to counsel at the waiver hearing, since the Court was not faced with that issue." On the other hand, in another, but equally sophisticated, legal casebook, we find (Davis, 1980:4–6), "Specifically, the Court [in *Kent*] set forth four basic safeguards required by due process during the waiver proceedings: . . . (2) The juvenile is entitled to representation by counsel at such hearings."

There is another major difference in interpretation. Appellate courts have taken differing positions on whether the *Kent* rulings are derived from the U.S. Constitution or from the juvenile code of Washington, D.C. (see a relevant discussion in Miller et al., 1985). Those differing positions determine the generalizability of the decision — if based on the Constitution, it governs waiver hearings in every court in the country, but if based on a local code, it has obviously more restricted generalizability. "Some courts," according to Miller et al. (1985:397), "regard *Kent* as a constitutionally-based decision in light of the Supreme Court's subsequent opinion in *In re Gault.*" A prime example of that is *Kemplen v. Maryland* (428 F. 2d 169, 1970). The tendency to so regard the *Kent* decision has gained increasing weight in recent years, and that means minimum due process requirements for all waiver hearings.

Unusual Jurisdictional Arrangements Among the States

In the discussion on waiver thus far, we have dealt with the process in its most typical form, where the juvenile court has original jurisdiction in a given case and holds a hearing to determine if it will waive that jurisdiction to the adult court. The array of grounds on which it will waive jurisdiction includes seriousness of offense, the maturity of the juvenile, and the likelihood of rehabilitation by the methods of juvenile justice. But there are other mechanisms and another direction for waiver.

Waiver from Criminal to Juvenile Court. In response to serious juvenile delinquency, New York State in 1978 passed harsher legislation to deal with violent young offenders. Youths of ages fourteen and fifteen were made criminally responsible for such violent or potentially violent acts as murder, kidnapping, arson, rape, robbery, and burglary, giving original jursidiction for trial to the criminal court. Youths aged thirteen were made criminally responsible for murder, again meaning original jurisdiction in the criminal court. (In this context, it is worth pointing out again that the age at which trial becomes the responsibility of the adult court in New York is sixteen.)

One motivation for that legislation in New York was the use of thirteen-, fourteen-, and fifteen-year-old youths by adults for crimes like contract murders. Even if caught, the youths would be subject only to the (rehabilitative) methods available to the family court, whereas an adult would be subject to the more severe punishments available to the criminal court. As mentioned earlier in this chapter, there is no waiver in New York from family to criminal court.

The adult criminal court that gets the case of a thirteen-, fourteen-, or fifteen-year-old who is alleged to have committed one of these serious offenses may, under Section 210.43 of New York's Criminal Procedure Law, "order removal of the action to the family court" — that is, waive its jurisdiction to the family court. The factors to be considered in making the determination, as specified in the law, are similar to the ones listed in the *Kent* as criteria for waiver in the other direction — from juvenile to criminal court. Thus, they include items like seriousness of offense, the record of the accused, and the effect of the offense on others. But the New York law lists several unique factors, such as (Section 210.43, 2): "(g) the impact of removal of the case to the family court upon the confidence of the public in the criminal justice system" and "(h) where the court deems it appropriate the attitude of the complainant or victim with respect to the motion."

Several other states have laws like that of New York, where original jurisdiction for a young offender rests with the criminal court on the basis of the seriousness of the offense (murder is most frequently specified), provided the offender's age is above a minimum (usually fourteen). Most of these states, such as Maryland, Pennsylvania, Oklahoma, Nebraska, and Arkansas, have statutory provision for waiver from the criminal court to the juvenile court.

Discretion of Prosecuting Attorney. The laws of some states, such as Wyoming and Arkansas, give the prosecuting attorney the direct authority to decide if the case initially will be heard in the juvenile court or in the criminal court. Davis (1980:2–18) describes the operation in Arkansas as follows: "If the juvenile is taken into custody without a warrant, the arresting officer must take the juvenile directly to juvenile court; however, if the child is fifteen years of age or older, the court must notify the prosecutor, who then decides whether to file a petition in juvenile court."

Prosecuting attorneys have the implicit power to choose the court where a juvenile case will be heard in states where determination is based on offense that is "charged." That may be illustrated most effectively by the District of Columbia Code. In Section 16-2301 (3) we find that a child is defined as "an individual who is under 18 years of age." But then an exception is made whereby "the term 'child' does not include an individual who is sixteen years of age or older and — (A) charged by the United States Attorney with (i) murder, forcible rape, burglary in the first degree, robbery while armed, or assault with intent to commit any such offense." Thus, if the United States Attorney (the prosecutor) chooses to charge a sixteen- or seventeen-year-old with burglary in the second degree, the juvenile's case will be heard in juvenile court, but if the choice is burglary in the first degree, the case will go to criminal court because the juvenile is no longer defined as a "child."

The Florida Juvenile Justice Act of 1981 and its amendments permit a prosecutor to file against a sixteen- or seventeen-year-old in criminal court if he or she has *previously* been adjudicated for requisite offenses, or a grand jury to charge a child with a criminal offense on probable-cause grounds. S. Carter (1984) has raised objections to these provisions, even though juvenile sanctions may be (and usually are in all but the most serious offenses) imposed after a finding of guilty.

Gillespie and Norman (1984) examined the discretionary practice in Utah whereby the prosecutor certifies juvenile offenders for waiver to a criminal court. They interviewed juvenile court personnel and analyzed official records over a four-year period. Certification was not widely used, and under 14 per cent of all certifications were for the most serious offenses of murder and rape. Further indication that the citizens of Utah were not getting the protection they may have expected from the process was in the finding that 53 per cent of those certified were neither incarcerated in prison nor given lengthy periods of institutionalization.

Davis (1980) objects vigorously to the determination of jurisdiction by prosecutors, to original jurisdiction residing in the criminal court, and to other deviations (such as concurrent jurisdiction) from the model of original jurisdiction in the juvenile court for the offenses of youths. After pointing out that the allowance of original jurisdiction in criminal court may represent social outrage at violent crime, he emphasizes (1980:2-17), "If the community's rage in response to the crime itself overcomes its sense of purpose in dealing with youthful offenders, this represents abandonment, or at least a suspension in certain cases, of the commitment to the rehabilitative ideal and a return to the purely retributive concepts prevalent in the nineteenth century."

That outrage, incidentally, has led to legislative changes making it more likely that the case of a minor will be heard in criminal court even when original jurisdiction remains with the juvenile court. In California, for example, a code change that went into effect in 1977 specifies that if a youth (of sixteen or seventeen years of age) is alleged to be an offender who committed any of about twenty listed serious crimes (Section 707, Welfare and Institutions Code), "the minor shall be presumed to be not a fit and proper subject to be dealt with under the juvenile court law." Thus, if the minor is accused of one of the listed serious crimes (like murder, arson, or forcible rape), a prima facie case of unfitness for the juvenile process is created, and the burden of proof to show fitness falls on the minor's part. In contrast, and as is generally the case in waiver hearings (or fitness hearings, as they are called in California), the burden of proof when one of the listed crimes is not alleged falls on the prosecutor to show unfitness or, in other words, the unsuitability of the youth for the methods of rehabilitation available to the juvenile court.

Similarly, in 1980, legislation in Minnesota provided that if a youth is sixteen or seventeen years of age and is accused of certain serious offenses or there is a certain combination of present offense and prior record, a prima facie case for waiver is established (see Feld, 1981). The goal of the legislation was to specify the serious offender, for purposes of the waiver decision, on the basis of age, offense, and prior record. There was, in short, a presumption that the serious offender of that type was not suited for treatment by the methods of the juvenile court. Osbun and Rode (1984) evaluated the effect of the legislation using demographic data and case history information from the juvenile court files in Hennepin County (Minneapolis). They compared number of waiver motions filed by the county attorney for periods before and after enactment of the new legislation and found no significant change. Moreover, after the legislation became effective in 1981, county attorneys chose to file waiver motions in only slightly more than half of the cases where the presumptive criteria were satisfied. And to make the legislation even more questionable, they found that the presumptive criteria (1984:199) "single out many juveniles whose records do not appear to be very serious and fail to identify many juveniles whose records are characterized by violent, frequent, and persistent delinquent activity." Clearly, then, the legislation did not have the desired effect of singling out serious offenders for criminal trials.

Because of the increasing tendency to try young offenders in criminal courts, either by making transfer easier or by shifting original jurisdiction, as well as such other factors as firmer due process rights in juvenile courts, Feld (1981; 1984) has suggested abandoning the "rehabilitative ideal" and trying all offenders (of all ages) in the same courts. Age, prior record, amenability to rehabilitation, and the suitability of available programs would then be taken into consideration at disposition. McNally (1983:36), on the other hand, argues, "Although the path of least resistance, e.g., the dissolution of juvenile court, may seem inviting to some, this overreaction may only serve to destroy 80 years of struggle for social justice." F. McCarthy (1977), however, as we shall discuss shortly, is in essential agreement with Feld.

On the other hand, Hamparian, Davis, and Jacobson (1983) reported on a state, Ohio, that had not legislated changes making it easier to waive youths to criminal court. For the year 1981, the number waved was the lowest over a four-year period. Most of the transfer actions were in response to burglary, robbery, or rape, with burglary the most serious offense in 35 per cent of the cases. Almost half of the youths had been committed to the state's Department of Youth Services for institutionalization at least once before the waiver.

The Adjudicatory Hearing

The adjudicatory hearing is functionally equivalent to the trial in criminal court in the sense that the goal is to determine the facts regarding the truth of allegations made about a person. In the criminal court, the allegations are contained in formal charges filed by a prosecutor or grand jury, while in the juvenile court, the allegations are contained in the petition for a hearing (as discussed earlier in this chapter). To help assure that decisions in adjudicatory hearings are based only on relevant facts regarding the allegations of offense, courts have prohibited the use of information in social reports until the fact finding is completed and an adjudicatory decision reached. For example, in California, it was ruled (*In re R.,* 464 P. 2d 127, 1970) that the juvenile court's review of a social study before the adjudicatory hearing constituted prejudicial error, while a Vermont ruling stated (*In re Lee,* 224 A. 2d at 919, 1966), "Such information [from a social welfare worker and other sources] was clearly not for consideration for any purpose in making findings or in deciding the case." More recently, a Maryland court (*In re Ernest J.,* 447, A. 2d 97, 1982) ruled as an error the admission of testimony by a juvenile services officer regarding the minor's earlier contacts with juvenile services. The decision in an adjudicatory hearing, in short, is expected to be based on whether the youth did or did not do what is alleged, and such social characteristics as relationship to parents and academic performance are irrelevant to the decision process.

Due Process Rights

The U.S. Supreme Court was unambiguous in its declaration in the *Gault* decision that a juvenile who has violated a criminal statute and who may be committed to an institution (1) has a right to counsel, (2) must be given timely notice of factual allegations to be considered at the adjudicatory hearing, (3) has the right to confront and cross-examine witnesses, and (4) has the right to remain silent. There remains uncertainty about due process rights in the case of an adjudicatory hearing for a status offender or where commitment to an institution is not a reasonable option for the court. (It is perhaps worth noting that Smith [1978] has argued for the extension of the rights required by *Gault* to cases where juveniles face a "loss of liberty" by possible placement in a foster or group home rather than in a state institution.) Beyond that is the question of how widely and effectively the *Gault* rulings have been put into effect in juvenile courts throughout the country even where directly applicable.

Right to Assistance of an Attorney. An immediate question that might occur to the reader of the *Gault* decision and a follower of its consequences might be: Do status offenders have the right to counsel in adjudicatory hearings? The *Gault* decision does not apply to them because they have not violated criminal statutes (so that their hearings are not normally considered "delinquency" hearings), and in most states (as we shall see in Chapter 11) they may not be committed to an institution. There is also the question of the right to counsel for other youths who are not subject to institutionalization — those in neglect, abuse, or dependency proceedings — but in the present chapter we consider only cases where the child is the offender.

As mentioned earlier in this chapter, in the section devoted to detention hearings, some states have given the right to counsel "at all stages of the proceedings" against a child. As Wadlington, Whitebread, and Davis point out (1983:458), "Since no limitation appears, the right to counsel would seem to extend to cases other than those nominally labeled 'delinquency' cases, e.g., cases of noncriminal behavior." The codes of several jurisdictions, such as Colorado, Virginia, Connecticut, and the District of Columbia, specifically indicate that the right to counsel is applicable in the case of status offenses as well as in criminal offenses ("delinquency" cases). And, finally, the remaining states specify a general right to counsel or leave the decision of appointment of counsel to the discretion of the court. As Davis (1980:5-8) comments, in such cases, "it is difficult to determine whether the right extends to cases other than those in which a violation of law is the basis for the petition."

Courts in general have not resolved the question of the right to counsel in nondelinquency cases. But the few rulings so far indicate little willingness to grant a constitutional right to counsel in the hearings of status offenders who are not subject to institutionalization, regardless of the available alternative dispositions (see, e.g., *In re Hutchins,* 345 So. 703, 1977, and *In re Walker,* 191 S.E. 2d 702, 1972).

However, it is of interest to note that Marshall, Marshall, and Thomas (1983) found, in their study of two juvenile courts in a southeastern area, that there was little difference in the formality with which status and criminal-type offenders were processed. They state that their analysis (1983:208) "indicates that statutory distinctions between legal categories (status versus criminal) have virtually no relevance for the degree of formality with which these cases are processed by the courts. Although the prosecutor appears to be somewhat more active when dealing with nonstatus offenders, there are hardly any differences with regard to the vigorousness of the defense activities."

Other Due Process Rights. In addition to the right to counsel, the U.S. Supreme Court in *Gault* declared the rights to timely notice, to confront witnesses, and to remain silent in delinquency hearings that could lead to incarceration. Subsequent to *Gault,* the Court stated that proof beyond a reasonable doubt was required during the adjudicatory phase of a delinquency proceeding (*In re Winship,* 397 U.S. 358, 1970). But the Court drew a limit to constitutional rights in *McKeiver v. Pennsylvania* (403 U.S. 528, 1971), ruling that there was no right to a jury in adjudicatory hearings. It stated in the *McKeiver* case (at 547), "The imposition of the jury trial on the juvenile court system would not strengthen greatly, if at all, the fact-finding function, and would, contrarily, provide an attrition of the juvenile court's assumed ability to function in a unique manner." Despite that strong statement, the decision did not prevent states from allowing jury trials. Indeed, we find in *McKeiver* (at 547) the following position that seems to contradict its stated concern for maintenance of the court's uniqueness: "If in its wisdom, any State feels that the jury trial is desirable in all cases, or in certain kinds, there appears to be no impediment to its installing a system embracing that feature."

A Note (1971) in a law journal shortly after the *McKeiver* decision was released pointed out that ten jurisdictions provided jury trial for juveniles in statutes and in five others there was jury trial by court mandate. An identical finding on the statutory right to jury trial was reported three years later by Levin and Sarri (1974), indicating no short-term retreat because of *McKeiver*. And Davis (1980) and Wadlington, Whitebread, and Davis (1983) report a similar picture about ten years after the *McKeiver* decision.

Interestingly, the Note (1971) questioned whether the right to a jury trial would continue in the state of Tennessee because the decision to grant the right was based on the federal constitution (and in *McKeiver* the Supreme Court ruled, of course, that there was no such right in the U.S. Constitution). But, in 1978, the Tennessee Supreme Court did rule jury trial as a matter of right under certain conditions (*State v. Johnson*, 574 S.W. 2d 739).

The California and Illinois Supreme Courts have taken opposite positions on the acceptability of a judge appointing an advisory panel to assist in fact finding and to advise the judge (who makes the actual adjudicatory decision). The California court ruled the procedure acceptable (*People v. Superior Court of Santa Clara County*, 539 P. 2d 807, 1975), whereas the Illinois court ruled that the judge must act alone (*People ex rel. Carey v. White*, 357 N.E. 2d 512, 1976).

Since the *Winship* decision requires proof beyond a reasonable doubt in delinquency proceedings (that is, where there is criminal conduct with the possibility of confinement), what is the generally accepted standard of proof in the hearings of status offenders? In many states, the standard of proof is preponderance of the evidence or clear and convincing evidence for status offenders as opposed to the stricter beyond a reasonable doubt for criminal-type offenders. A number of court rulings have upheld that difference (see, e.g., *In the Interest of Potter*, 237 N.W. 2d 461, 1976). According to Davis (1980:5-18), "Several states, however, provide that proof beyond a reasonable doubt is the standard of proof in both delinquency cases *and* need of supervision (or incorrigibility) cases." Examples of states with the strict standard of proof in both types of hearings are New York, Georgia, New Mexico, Texas, and Wyoming.

Since status offenders have not committed crimes, by definition they of course cannot be waived to adult criminal court. But a double jeopardy issue did arise in one status offense case where a petition was dismissed on the grounds of insufficient evidence. A petition was then filed for the same case and circumstances on the basis of allegations of violations of criminal law. An appeals court did not allow the hearing on the delinquency petition, arguing that it represented double jeopardy (*In the interest of R.L.K.*, 384 N.E. 2d 531, 1978).

The issues of confrontation of witnesses, self-incrimination, and timely and effective notice of allegations have not generated much attention beyond the requirements of *Gault*. And that limited attention has been directed to such more esoteric matters as the use of hearsay testimony, the need for corroborative evidence to support confessions, and whether the timely notice must satisfy the technical requirements of an indictment. In the realm of codes, Davis (1980:5-22) has indicated, "Some states by statute have expressly conferred on juveniles the rights to confrontation and cross examination, apparently intending that juveniles are entitled to those rights to the same extent they are enjoyed by adults."

Short summaries of such related topics as the right to a speedy trial, the question of vagueness in the wording of statutes dealing with status offenses, and the validity of waivers of their rights by juveniles may be found in Binder and Binder (1982).

"Due Process — Reality or Myth?"

The title of this subsection is identical to the title of an article by Sosin and Sarri (1976) that is part of a monograph devoted to research on the juvenile court. It reflects a position taken by many commentators of the adjudicatory scene (and, secondarily, of preadjudicatory and postadjudicatory court processes). F. McCarthy (1977) does not believe that the efforts by the U.S. Supreme Court in decisions like *Gault* and *Winship* have been successful in putting adequate constitutional protections into the juvenile court, and so recommended the removal of its jurisdiction over cases where there could be a loss of liberty (institutionalization). He advocated giving that jurisdiction to the adult criminal court (1977:203): "When it comes to determining whether society is justified in depriving a child of liberty . . . the proper forum for such an adjudication is in a court where the broader principles of our society find application." He argued that, despite *Gault,* the juvenile court (1977:202) "often conveyed the atmosphere of an operation based on whim and caprice" with an absence of constitutional protections valued highly in American society. For a position in agreement, see Feld (1981; 1984) and the discussion above; for one in disagreement, see McNally (1983).

Schultz and Cohen (1976) are more damning of the availability of due process for juveniles but somewhat less drastic in their recommendations. They refer to the (1976:27) "ambiguity and indecisiveness of *Gault*" and emphasize that even the limited restrictions on procedure that were stated in that decision are not uniformly followed. They propose doing away with the exchange model in juvenile court, where youths give up some rights for an orientation toward rehabilitation help, and substituting a "just deserts" or equity model, where there is punishment based on criminal misconduct but with full and real due process protections.

Sosin and Sarri (1976:194) state, "If one looks only skin-deep, it appears that the Supreme Court mandates [for due process] have been almost universally adopted by juvenile courts. However, compliance becomes less complete the more deeply one looks at the operation of the court."

Their look at the operation of the court consisted of a study based on two juvenile court samples. The first sample was obtained primarily by random selection from a listing of larger counties in the United States. Questionnaires were then sent to the selected courts for filling out by key court personnel. The second sample, selected in a more directed manner, was targeted for more intensive study. That more intensive effort involved interviews, discussions, and observations in the seven selected courts to supplement the information obtained from the more broadly sent questionnaires.

About 28 per cent of the judges in the broad sample believed (1976:193), "The Supreme Court has gone too far in protecting the rights of criminals." And about one third of the judges did not believe that a petition should be dismissed even if there is not sufficient evidence to confirm the allegations. As Sosin and Sarri (1976:194) comment, "Perhaps even here it is indicative of the state of due process in many courts that roughly one-third of the judges do not agree with this very basic premise of the Supreme Court decisions." Using a rough summary approach to measuring compliance with due process mandates of the Supreme Court, the investigators found such compliance to be about 70 per cent.

The survey results were generally confirmed in the intensive study in field sites. For example, they observed (1976:196), "Seldom in the courts visited did it appear that lawyers were vigorously defending their clients," and (1976:197), "lawyers seldom confront witnesses, and social reports are rarely used by lawyers to call witnesses." Thus, even when due process changes have been implemented, there was (1976:206) "only surface-level compliance from courts; there has been no due process revolution."

Finally, Rubin (1977:5) expressed his doubts about the implementation of due process in adjudicatory hearings as follows: "We are now in the ninth year of the post-*Gault* era and, in my view, have lagged severely in implementing both the letter and the spirit of the mandate. . . . Juvenile courts in many communities still actively discourage youth from exercising their right to counsel through a variety of approaches and with a variety of motivations."

The Dispositional Hearing

The dispositional hearing in the juvenile court is comparable to the sentencing hearing in the adult criminal court. The goal is to decide what to do with a youth after it has been determined in a fact-finding hearing (the adjudicatory hearing) that he or she has offended in a manner that justifies court jurisdiction. That determination is equivalent to the determination of "guilty" in the adult criminal court.

In a substantial number of states, there is a bifurcated hearing process where the adjudicatory and dispositional hearings are distinct and separate entities. The principal reason for the bifurcation lies in differing rules for the types and manner of presentation of evidence. Generally speaking, since the dispositional hearing is concerned with considerations of rehabilitation and correction rather than fact finding, virtually any information is admissible that bears on such matters as interpersonal relationships in general, family characteristics, health and medical history, academic achievement, types of friends, attitudes toward teachers and others in authority, and previous failures at adjustment. Thus, the social report, which, as mentioned earlier in this chapter, is not admissible in an adjudicatory hearing, is critical for the specification of individualized treatment aimed at meeting the youth's needs and protecting the public. The importance of the social report in dispositional decisions is illustrated by a court decision stating that disposition of a juvenile must be based on the characteristics of the offender rather than the gravity of the offense (*In re Patterson,* 499 P. 2d 1131, 1972) and another decision ruling that a social history used in a dispositional hearing must be up to date (*In re Smith,* 249 N.Y.S. 2d 1016, 1964). Moreover, some jurisdictions (California, for example) have specific statements in their codes that require the judge to use a social report in arriving at a dispositional decision.

The codes of some states (e.g., New York) specify that the dispositional hearing may begin immediately after the adjudicatory hearing, but delays of several weeks or longer are possible if there is a need for time to complete a social history or to receive evidence on a motion of the court or of a parent. In several states, there is a limit to the allowed delay between adjudicatory finding and the start of dispositional hearing, with special concern for youths who are being detained pending disposition. For example, in California, the delay may be up to forty-five judicial days if the youth is not detained but only ten judicial days if he or she is detained. (A judicial day, you may recall from an earlier discussion, is an ordinary working day for a court.)

Rubin (1972) studied samples of cases from juvenile courts in Atlanta, Salt Lake City, and Seattle and found that almost all dispositional hearings occurred on the same day as the corresponding adjudicatory hearing. He reports median delay between time of filing the petition and final disposition as follows: Atlanta, forty-one days; Salt Lake City, nineteen days; and Seattle, seventy days.

Where there is not statutory provision for bifurcated hearings, according to Davis (1980:6-3), "courts are usually disinclined to require a separate dispositional phase. The Missouri Supreme Court, for example, has held that if the child is found to be within the jurisdiction of the juvenile court and is adjudicated delinquent or in need of supervision, the court may proceed immediately to make a disposition in the case as warranted by statute" (see *A — S — v. Murphy,* 487 S.W. 2d 589, 1972).

The Essence of the Hearing

In a manual prepared for training programs of the National Council of Juvenile Court Judges, Arthur and Gauger (1974:54) state, "The disposition hearing in the juvenile court may be the most complicated process of the entire Anglo-American judicial system." They take that position because it is an adversarial proceeding with an admixture of recommendations by probation and social workers, reports of social and academic histories, and interactions within the court among the legal participants, the offender and his or her family, probation staff, and, perhaps, psychologists and social workers. According to Arthur and Gauger (1974:54), it is not simply a process of matching punishment to offense. "It is, rather, the matching of the needs of a complicated human being to every available facility and talent of the court and community which might best answer one particular individual child's needs, and the public's safety. It is a hearing, a judicial hearing, but with overtones of a discussion."

But that primarily represents a surface view of operations. A more philosophically oriented (and franker) picture of the dispositional hearing is provided in the following quote from a decision of the Supreme Court of Appeals of West Virginia (*State ex rel. D.D.H. v. Dostert,* 269 S.E. 2d at 409, 1980):

> The dispositional stage of a juvenile proceeding is designed to do something which is almost impossible, namely, to reconcile: (1) society's interest in being protected from dangerous and disruptive children; (2) society's interest in nurturing its children in such a way that they will be productive and successful adults; (3) society's interest in providing a deterrent to other children who, but for the specter of the juvenile law, would themselves become disruptive and unamenable to adult control; (4) the citizens' demand that children be responsible for invasion of personal rights; and, (5) the setting of an example of care, love, and forgiveness by the engines of the state in the hope that such qualities will be emulated by the subject children. While retribution is considered an unhealthy instinct and, conceivably, an immoral instinct in an enlightened society, nonetheless, State imposed retribution has historically been the *quid pro quo* of the State's monopoly of force and its proscription of individual retribution. Retribution is merely another way of saying that children are to be treated as responsible moral agents.

Due Process Rights

A dispositional hearing is obviously a critical stage in juvenile processing since it can lead to the most severe loss of liberty, institutionalization, and so it is widely accepted that it must be held in accordance with minimum due process standards. Thus, Miller et al. (1985:740) point to the right to counsel at disposition determination in the following way: "Because it is clear that in an adult criminal proceeding the defendant is entitled to counsel at sentencing . . . , it would be surprising if the Constitution did not require counsel for a group generically less able to manage their own affairs with respect to a decision of such overriding importance." Paulsen and Whitebread (1974), on the other hand, argue that there is a constitutional requirement for counsel during the dispositional hearing on the grounds that the resulting decision is of "critical importance," making the language of the *Kent* and *Gault* decisions applicable. Several court decisions (e.g., *In re Robert F.,* 293 N.Y.S. 2d 873, 1968, and *A.A. v. State,* 538 P. 2d 1004, 1975) have indeed affirmed that right using one of those arguments, or a closely related one. In any case, as Miller et al. (1985:740) point out, "as more and more juvenile codes are revised, the problem may become only theoretical, for modern codes almost invariably provide for counsel at this stage."

Prosecuting attorneys and counsels for the defense in dispositional hearings may be active advocates of the adversarial positions they represent or more passive in their approaches. In a more active role, a defense counsel, for example, may contest the harsher recommendations of the probation staff and argue for a more lenient disposition on the basis of mitigating circumstances stemming from interactions in the child's life. Similarly, the prosecutor may argue for the need to protect the public from a serious offender or one with a long history of offenses.

In accord with the differences between adjudicatory and dispositional hearings in degree of formality and related uses of evidence, it is generally accepted that not all safeguards necessary in fact finding are required for dispositional decision making. That includes the right to confront and cross-examine witnesses. And, judging from the *McKeiver* decision, there would seem no basis for a constitutionally based right to jury during a dispositional hearing. Even in the case of one state that has a codified right to jury during an adjudicatory hearing (Oklahoma), a court has ruled that the right does not extend to disposition (*Alford v. Carter,* 504 P. 2d 436, 1972).

Rubin (1985) lends a touch of reality to any discussion of due process rights in pointing out that it is common in many courts for a dispositional decision to be made before the dispositional hearing even starts. That may occur in an informal conference between judge and probation officer in the judge's chambers, in some other office, or even in a hallway. Understandably, Rubin (1985:209) emphasizes, "This approach hardly compacts with due process."

Following earlier suggestive research by Lemert (1967) and by Platt, Schechter, and Tiffany (1968) indicating that the presence of attorneys increased the likelihood of dismissal in juvenile courts, Stapleton and Teitelbaum (1972) conducted a randomized experiment to test the effects of counsel in dispositional hearings. In one of the two cities of their experiment, the presence of active and adversarial defense attorneys had little effect on dispositional outcomes, while in the other city, youths with attorneys received more dismissals. More recently, Hayeslip (1979) tested the hypothesis that the presence of attorneys in dispositional hearings will increase the likelihood of dismissal or probation, and their absence will increase the likelihood of harsher dispositions (institutionalization). He collected data on 742 hearings in a juvenile court (1979:11) "located in a moderately sized mid-western county whose population was over ninety percent white and relatively affluent." Of the 742 hearings, almost 76 per cent resulted in probation, dismissal, or simple referral to a social service agency. But, contrary to his hypothesis and much to his surprise (1979:11), "Institutional placement occurred in 22.6 percent of the hearings where no attorney was present, but occurred in 37.5 percent of the hearings where an attorney was present in defense of youths." The significant difference remained, moreover, when there was control introduced for various contaminating variables (including seriousness of offense, number of priors, and whether or not a prosecutor was present). However, he found (1979:12), "For whites, there was little difference in outcome if an attorney was present or not." On the other hand (1979:12), "When an attorney was present for nonwhites institutional placements occurred 46.2 percent of the time while when they had no attorney such placements occurred only 20.4 percent of the time."

Other individuals who have raised doubts about the proposition that the presence of counsel is associated with lighter dispositions are Lemert (1967), Susman (1973), Ferster and Courtless (1972), and Clarke and Koch (1980).

Of course, one must not, on the basis of the preceding research, jump to the conclusion that the due process requirement of representation by defense counsel is not good policy. But surely the research does indicate a need for more information about the role of counsel and what may be done to improve its effectiveness.

Alternative Dispositions Available to the Court

In broadest terms, the available dispositional alternatives are treating a youth in his or her community and institutionalizing him or her. Return to the community is usually accompanied by an order for supervision in formal probation (in contrast to the informal probation that may occur without a court order), but it may involve only return to the parents or transferring custody to another person or agency under court supervision. The process of institutionalization may be a direct one where the youth is sent by the court to a state training school or to a local facility that is subject to the court's direction (which may be operated by the probation department), or an indirect one where the youth is sent to the appropriate state department, which in turn determines actual placement.

Culver Pictures, Inc.

Placing a youth in a prison-like institution is one of the alternatives available to the juvenile court.

The specific alternatives available for disposition depend, in most jurisdictions, on whether the youngster was adjudicated as a criminal-type or as a status offender. Commonly, a status offender may not be sent to any secure institution, either a local or a state facility. (The development of that restriction since 1974 is fully discussed in the next chapter.) But some states do not distinguish between youths who commit criminal offenses and those who commit status offenses, referring to both in some such form as "delinquent children," and specify equivalent dispositions for all as designated; still other states allow institutionalization of children referred to in their codes as CHINS, PINS, or an equivalent designation for status offenders.

An interesting court objection occurred to the practice of designating all offenders as delinquent children and allowing the same range of alternatives for a young serious offender as for a truant or a runaway. The West Virginia Code 49-1-4 states that a child may be adjudicated a "delinquent child" if he or she commits an act that would be a crime if committed by an adult (short of the most serious crimes), is a habitual truant, is incorrigible or ungovernable, or is a runaway. Further, West Virginia Code 49-5-11 permits placing an adjudicated "delinquent child" in "an industrial home or correctional institution for minors." As allowed by those statutes, a juvenile court in West Virginia sent a sixteen-year-old boy to a forestry camp because he had been absent from school for fifty days. The Supreme Court of West Virginia, in *State ex rel. Harris v. Calendine* (233 S.E. 2d 318, 1977), objected in resounding terms. The essence of the decision is shown in the following quote (at 329):

> We find with regard to status offenders . . . [that] incarceration in secure, prison-like facilities, except in a limited number of cases, bears no reasonable relationship to legitimate state purposes, namely, rehabilitation, protection of the children, and protection of society.
>
> In view of the foregoing, and in view of the fact that there are numerous alternatives to incarceration for status offenders we hold that the State must exhaust every reasonable alternative to incarceration before committing a status offender to a secure, prison-like facility. Furthermore, for those extreme cases in which commitment of status offenders to a secure, prison-like facility cannot be avoided, the receiving facility must be devoted solely to the custody and rehabilitation of status offenders. In this manner status offenders can be spared contact under degrading and harmful conditions with delinquents who are guilty of criminal conduct and experienced in the ways of crime.

In accord with that perspective, the court ordered the youngster to be (at 331) "discharged forthwith from custody and restored to his liberty." Moreover, it invited actions from other children held in state institutions in violation of the guidelines enunciated in the decision — and that included directing the superintendents of all juvenile institutions in the state to post the opinion of the court in conspicuous places. (See Mones [1984] for an interesting analysis that emphasizes the importance of the *State ex rel. Harris v. Calendine* decision and related decisions of the West Virginia Supreme Court of Appeals.)

A related earlier decision in New York (*Ellery C. v. Realich,* 347 N.Y.S. 2d 51, 1973) anticipated, in a limited way, later developments on a national scale in its ruling that no person in need of supervision (PINS) may be sent to a state training school for delinquent children. That ruling was based on interpretation of the New York Family Court Act. (As an interesting aside, Ellery C., the youth in the preceding PINS case, later stabbed and killed a fourteen-year-old boy. That led to a suit against the state on the grounds that the public had not been adequately protected and that the youth's problems were exacerbated — see *Certo v. State,* 385 N.Y.S. 2d 824, 1976.)

The requirement of choice of least restrictive alternative for disposition has also been applied by courts to youths who committed criminal acts. For example, in the case *In re John H.* (369 N.Y.S. 2d 196, 1975), a court ruled as unacceptable the commitment of a criminal-type offender to a state training school on the grounds that less confining alternatives were not explored.

Finally, several states have in recent years legislated harsher alternatives for serious offenders as part of the general picture of "getting tough on crime." To illustrate, the New York Juvenile Justice Reform Acts of 1976 and 1978 called for the establishment of facilities that were physically restrictive in construction, interior characteristics, and procedures. Youths who committed certain designated felonies (such as murder, assault, rape, manslaughter, kidnapping, and robbery in the first degree) could be sent by the family court to restrictive placement for between six and twelve months followed by mandatory placement in a secure residential facility. Restrictive placement was authorized for youths down to thirteen years of age on the basis of their criminal acts, and down to seven years with two prior adjudications for felonious behavior. Further, once a restrictive order is placed by a court, it cannot be modified, set aside, or vacated. There was, thus, no pretense that the acts were not motivated by the desire for retribution and punishment for serious young offenders within the juvenile system.

Similarly, in its Juvenile Justice Act of 1977 (discussed in Chapter 8), the state of Washington created the category of "serious offender" for youths fifteen years of age and older who committed such crimes as murder, manslaughter, assault, and robbery. The act led to a set of sentencing standards that a court consults to determine commitment time. A disposition outside the allowed time range has to be justified by clear and convincing evidence.

Factors Used in Dispositional Decision Making

Studies Completed Before 1980. Terry (1967a; 1967b) studied the 246 cases processed at disposition in the Racine, Wisconsin, juvenile court over a five-year period to determine if decisions were biased on the basis of sex, ethnic and racial background, or SES. He found that females were more likely to be institutionalized than males even though they tended to have less extensive records of earlier delinquency. On the other hand, he found no evidence that the severity of disposition differed either among whites ("Anglos"), blacks, and youths of Hispanic descent or over class levels. Severity of disposition was, however, strongly influenced by the quantity and nature of previous offenses (see also Bortner, 1982).

Similarly, Ferdinand and Luchterhand (1970) found no evidence of discrimination in the dispositions of a juvenile court in a large eastern city. What little discrepancy they found between black and white youths for the less serious offenses could be accounted for by the court's desire to intervene on the basis of

a poor home environment. As they pointed out (1970:521), "Black delinquents . . . came from incomplete family situations more often than whites."

Further investigation of the effects of race and ethnicity on dispositional
decision making was reported by Arnold in 1971. His efforts were directed at the
juvenile court in a southern community with characteristics that he described as
(1971:214) "typical of many middle-sized American communities of about
250,000 population." He found that 24 per cent of "Anglos" were committed to
the state's youth authority (for institutionalization) by the court as compared
with 71 per cent of Hispanic youths and 71 per cent of blacks. But, he asked,
could those substantial differences be accounted for by differences between
groups on seriousness of offense, numbers and seriousness of prior offenses,
marital status of youths' parents, and delinquency rates in youths' neighborhoods? He found the answer to be no. Introducing statistical controls for these
variables had (1971:223) *"relatively little effect on the race/ethnicity distributions
of decisions by the judge to commit offenders to the state youth authority."*
Interestingly, analysis of the patterns and seriousness of offending led him to
the conclusion that the bias of the court was not expressed in greater harshness
toward minority-group members, but consisted (1971:211) "largely of letting
Anglos 'get off easy'!"

On the other hand, Scarpitti and Stephenson (1971) found, in a study of 1,210
adjudicated sixteen- and seventeen-year-old boys in a large eastern metropolitan county, that whites received harsher dispositions than blacks when a delinquency history index was used to control for prior records. They state
(1971:148), "It would appear that in the court studied, at least for the three
years of data collection, black boys had to exhibit a much greater degree of
delinquency commitment before the most punitive alternative was selected."
But they did find a greater tendency for boys from the lowest-SES families to be
sent to reformatories.

Thornberry (1973:90) continued the path of exploration, once more attempting to obtain a firm answer to the question: "Do blacks and members
of . . . low socioeconomic strata (SES) receive more severe dispositions than
whites and members of . . . high SES?" Using data originally collected for the
Philadelphia cohort study (see Chapters 1 and 9 for discussions of that study),
he divided dispositional outcome into two categories of seriousness: probation
and institutionalization. He placed youths into six categories where, within each
category, they were roughly equivalent in terms of seriousness of current offense
and number of prior offenses. He found (1973:95), "In all six comparisons
blacks are more likely to be institutionalized and less likely to be put on
probation than are whites," and (1973:97), "In five of the six comparisons, low
SES subjects are less likely to be put on probation and more likely to be
institutionalized than high SES subjects."

Cohen and Kluegel (1978) evaluated the pattern of conflicting results over the
studies reported by Terry, Arnold, and Thornberry in the context of the many
arguments put forth by academic sociologists that the juvenile justice system
is inherently and obviously biased against minority- and low-SES-group
members. They concluded (1978:164), "While the possible effect of court differences in the approach to juvenile justice should be considered in accounting for
the contradictory findings of previous studies, we must consider as well the
possibility that differences in the techniques of analysis have contributed to the

variation in the reported results." They proceeded to use a sophisticated method of analysis that did not rely on comparisons over race and class when other variables are controlled in some fashion but, rather, focused on (1978:166) "the more general question of how the six factors of race, class, present activity, prior record, offense type and court orientation appear to influence the severity of disposition accorded adjudicated juveniles." (See also Cohen [1975a], a federal report that contains a preliminary, but in some ways more complete, discussion of the investigation upon which the Cohen and Kluegel article was based.)

The data used in the analysis came from the case history records of male offenders referred to the Denver and Memphis juvenile courts in 1972. The two courts differed (1978:165) in that the Denver Court was "considerably more due process oriented" while the Memphis Court followed "more closely the traditional therapeutic model for juvenile courts" — that is, it was more *parens patriae* - oriented. An overview of the results of their analysis is as follows (1978:173):

> In sum, our analysis offers little support for the argument that race or class bias directly affect the dispositions given to juveniles in the Denver or Memphis juvenile courts. Rather, we found that the disposition process is most strongly influenced by prior record and type of offense in these two courts with different approaches to juvenile justice and from different regions of the country.

A clear picture of relationship between prior record and severity of dispositional decision, in support of that position, was reported by Copeland (1972) and by Chused (1973). Chused (1973) noted, as had Wolfgang, Figlio, and Sellin (1972) earlier, a tendency to impose more severe sanctions if serious dispositions were given in earlier court appearances. Interestingly, Copeland (1972) subjectively evaluated the provability of prior offenses and found that the average seriousness of provable priors was higher for juveniles who received a suspended commitment than for those sent to an institution. A less clear picture of relationship between prior record and severity of disposition was reported by Scarpitti and Stephenson (1971). They found that dispositional decision depends on the extent of prior delinquent behavior but that (1971:148) "The type of past delinquent activity does not seem closely related to the present court disposition . . . the offenses of the reformatory boys do not appear to be any more or less serious than those of the other boys." They did find (1971:148) "some slight indication" of a relationship between present offense and court disposition. Boys sent to reformatories did show proportionately more crimes against public policy than boys given other dispositions, but similar comparisons over boys given less harsh dispositions (probation or treatment in a residential or nonresidential group center) showed reversals of that pattern.

In contrast to the findings of Terry (1967a; 1967b) and also of Gibbons and Griswold (1957), Chesney-Lind (1973), Datesman and Scarpitti (1977) for status offenders), and Bortner (1982), T. Carter (1979) found that sex was not a contributing factor in predicting dispositional outcomes. Instead, he reported (1979:355), "The most outstanding finding of the present analysis is the impact of social class on disposition decisions at all levels for both nonstatus and status offenses." Lower-class youths, particularly status offenders, were more likely to be institutionalized.

Other factors that have been studied in terms of their effects on dispositions are school attendance and employment (Scarpitti and Stephenson, 1971; Chused, 1973; Cohen, 1975), family structure (Ferdinand and Luchterhand, 1970; Arnold, 1971; Chused, 1973; Cohen, 1975), age (Terry, 1967b; Chused, 1973; Cohen, 1975), and psychological characteristics as measured by the Minneapolis Multiphasic Personality Inventory (Scarpitti and Stephenson, 1971).

Before turning to a summary of the results of studies of the factors that enter into dispositional decision making, it should be pointed out that Bortner and Reed (1985) have emphasized the dangers of focusing on one aspect of court processing alone, especially final disposition. There is a complex interaction among legal variables (like prior record and current offense), extralegal variables (like sex and race), and the sequential decision processing in the court from intake to disposition. Earlier court decisions as well as legal and extralegal factors affect later decisions, an interdependence that may be lost if focus is only on one later decision point, particularly the final one. Similarly, Barton concluded that one is not likely to get a thorough understanding of the court system unless one replaces segmented approaches with a systematic research strategy like using (1976:480) "a single methodology and conceptualization in investigating decision-making at each decision point in the system."

Major Pre-1980 Findings. Smith, Black, and Weir (1980:201–203) have surveyed most of the preceding studies and summarized the state of knowledge regarding the factors that influence dispositional decision making. Abstracts from their summary follow (italics have been removed):

1. "[I]t appears that seriousness of the offense plays some role in judges' dispositional decision-making, as does, in some instances, the nature of the offense."
2. "Status offenders appear to be accorded relatively severe dispositions (institutionalization) in some jurisdictions, but this may be more a function of their family situations than of the 'offense' per se. Juveniles with similar family situations may also be accorded similar dispositions regardless of the nature of the offense which brought them before the court."
3. "It would appear that being conventionally active [in school attendance and employment] is viewed positively in some jurisdictions and that juveniles in this category receive more lenient dispositions."
4. "The studies which considered the relationship of personal factors such as race or ethnic status, age, sex, and socioeconomic status were inconsistent in their results. It would appear that these factors are important in some jurisdictions but not in others."
5. "Prior record is about the only factor which consistently appears to be related to judicial dispositional outcomes, particularly the number of prior court referrals on previous offenses."

More Recent Findings. Phillips and Dinitz (1982) studied 3,316 juvenile court dispositions in a county of Ohio over a five-year period. They evaluated the effects of offense type, prior record, prior court decisions, and offender's social characteristics on court dispositions, which were categorized as follows:

unsupervised probation, supervised probation, short detention in a local facility, and institutionalization via the Ohio Youth Commission. They found (1982:276) "no evidence that judges and referees in this court respond to a youth's race or social class in their disposition decisions." They did find, on the other hand, that seriousness of present offense and number of prior offenses (not their levels of seriousness) were important determiners of the decision to send a youth to the Ohio Youth Commission for institutionalization. But (1982:275) "Much more important than a juvenile's prior record is the severity of the court's earlier responses to his or her behavior. While a prior detention or formal supervision does not heavily affect the decision to incarcerate, a prior institutionalization is very important." They interpret the finding of the importance of prior court responses in dispositional decision making as support for certain of the arguments of labeling theorists (see Chapter 5).

Kowalski and Rickicki (1982) studied the case histories of 133 males processed in a facility of a department of youth services in a southern state. They compared the outcomes of group home or institutional placement on the basis of six variables: current offense, number of previous offenses, age, race, IQ, behavior evaluation (at a diagnostic center). They concluded that (1982:78) "postadjudicatory disposition decisions were found to be most influenced by the juveniles' [diagnostic center] behavior rating, their age, and the interaction of committing offense and number of past offenses. Similar to Cohen and Kluegel's (1978) findings pertaining to court dispositions, ours showed little systematic bias based upon the extralegal factor of race."

On the other hand, Dannefer and Schutt (1982) reported findings of racial bias in court dispositions, although the degree of bias observed in court decision making was much lower than in police decision making. Moreover, they stress a phenomenon called bias amplification, whereby police discrimination affects court discrimination. They state (1982:1129), "If there is bias at the point of police dispositions, it will ultimately translate into differences in prior record— a variable which had a stronger effect on court dispositions than any other variable studied. The effect of prior record may, in other words, include a component due to police bias."

In the most recent of this group of studies, Krisberg, et al. (1986:1) begin a monograph with the following statements: "The purpose of this paper is to explore the disproportionate incarceration of minority youth in juvenile facilities. A walk through any public detention center or training school will convince the visitor that Black, Hispanic, and Native American youths are vastly overrepresented in relation to their proportions in the general population." They start their exploration by using information from the Children in Custody (CIC) survey of the U.S. Bureau of the Census to establish that hard data were in accord with their casual observations regarding minority incarceration. And the data were indeed concordant with their casual observations. For example, in 1977, 47 per cent of those incarcerated in state training schools were minority youths (black 37 per cent, Hispanic 7 per cent, Native American 2 per cent, Asian American 1 per cent); in 1982, the percentage moved up to 54 (black 42 per cent, Hispanic 9 percent, Native American 2 per cent, Asian American 1 per cent). Using 1980 Census data, they computed incarceration rates in training schools per 100,000 comparable youths. The rates for 1982 are white 96.6, black

479.2, Hispanic 205.5, others 64.9. In other words, blacks were incarcerated in training schools at almost five times the rate of whites; the Hispanic-to-white ratio is better than two to one.

Krisberg et al. (1986) next turned to determining the reason for the differential rates. Is it discriminatory policies and practices, is it the result of inadequate resources in minority communities, or is it the result of higher rates of serious crime among minority youths? They eliminate the last of these by a reasoning process that includes analyses of FBI arrest data for Index crimes (as given in the *Uniform Crime Reports* — see Chapter 1) and self-report data on serious crime obtained in the National Youth Survey (see Chapter 1). And since the fact of inadequate resources could only account for a small part of the differences, they conclude that there is systematic discriminatory behavior in juvenile justice processing leading to the overrepresentation (and increasing overrepresentation) of minority youths in correctional facilities. They do not attribute the problem to any one process in the system, such as the dispositional decision making which is the central concern of this section, but to its operations as a whole. The results are so dramatic to them that they warn (1986:32), "In a society committed to pluralism and social justice the growing numbers of incarcerated minority youth is a harbinger of future social turmoil. This problem must be placed at the top of our national agenda to reform the juvenile justice system."

Finally, other studies following the summary of Smith, Black, and Weir (1980) have explored the effects of the following factors on dispositions: earlier detention decision (Bortner, 1982), demographic characteristics of communities (Dannefer and Schutt, 1982), and degree of effort expended by court officials in collecting extraordinary information about a juvenile's social history (Marshall and Thomas, 1983).

Summary _____

A juvenile who is arrested by the police may be brought in custody to a court intake facility or released on condition that he or she appear at the facility at a future designated time or in accordance with later notification. The central goal of intake screening is to determine the most suitable action from among the following typical alternatives: release the youth to the custody of parents or guardian, perhaps with referral to a community agency for individual or family counseling; place the youth on informal probation; petition the court for an adjudicatory hearing or refer the youth to prosecution for petitioning, whichever procedure is specified in the relevant state code. Several research studies indicate that the youth's prior record is most influential in determining severity of intake decision. The age of the youth, the nature of the immediate offense, and family status affect some decisions at certain times, but socioeconomic status (SES) and school attendance or employment seem to have no impact. And no consistent pattern of ethnic or racial discrimination has been found.

If the youth has been brought to court intake by the police while in custody, the intake officer must also decide whether he or she is to remain in custody. The legal justifications for continued detention encompass the goals of protecting the youth and the community and of keeping the youth from fleeing. But there are several extralegal factors that affect the detention decision, including the personal biases of intake officers and pressures from the police or the community. Most states have a code that requires review of a decision to detain by a judicial officer at a detention hearing. While there is no constitutional right to an attorney at a detention hearing, the right exists by statute in many states. The right to release on bail has been codified in several states, but bail is not generally available in juvenile courts.

Several studies have shown that youths of low SES are more likely to be detained than youths of higher SES, but no clear pattern of a preference for detention on the basis of race has been found. Contrary to expectation, it has been shown repeatedly in studies through the 1970s that status offenders were detained at a higher rate than criminal-type offenders, even violent offenders. And because females were more likely to be brought into the system than males for status offenses, they have widely been detained at a higher rate.

Almost all states allow the transfer of a minor from juvenile court to adult criminal court by a process referred to as a waiver hearing (so called because the juvenile court decides whether it will waive its jurisdiction). The formal grounds for waiver include seriousness of the alleged offense, prior record, degree of sophistication and maturity shown by the youth, and prospects for rehabilitation by methods available to the juvenile court. Although the U.S. Supreme Court, in its *Kent* decision, decided that waiver was an issue of critical importance that demanded minimum due process protection, various courts and legal scholars have for technical reasons interpreted the decision in different ways. But the recent tendency is to regard the right to counsel, and similar rights, as constitutionally required in waiver hearings.

The adjudicatory hearing in the juvenile court determines whether the facts of the case support the allegations in the petition filed by probation or the prosecutor. The *Gault* decision firmly established the rights to counsel, timely notice, cross-examination of witnesses, and remaining silent at adjudicatory hearings for criminal-type offenders where there is a possibility of incarceration. But those rights have not been extended to status offenders or to those not subject to institutionalization on other grounds. Moreover, the standard set in *Winship* for proof beyond a reasonable doubt in a delinquency hearing has not been extended to status offenders as a constitutionally based right. Beyond the absence of those required protections for status offenders, several observers have pointed out that the rights mandated in *Gault* and *Winship* are not being implemented on a day-to-day basis in courts throughout the country.

A dispositional hearing is equivalent to the sentencing hearing for adults. Unlike the adjudicatory hearing, which is aimed at fact finding, the dispositional hearing uses social reports directed at a youth's needs, relationships, coping skills, and deficiencies. The official goals in determining a disposition for a youth are rehabilitation and protection of the public, but punishment and retribution have been relevant concepts in the past and are coming more strongly into the picture. It is generally considered that there is a right to counsel during dispositional hearings, and that is being reflected in its inclusion in revised state codes. The principal alternative dispositions available to a juvenile court are return to the community with or without specific directives, return to the community under court-ordered probation, and placement in a local facility or a state institution (training school). In recent years, as punishment and retribution have become more prominent in response to violent juvenile crime, some states have added to their codes such harsher dispositions as placement in a facility more restrictive than a training school for minimum time periods. Several studies have explored the array of factors that enter into dispositional decision making with the general conclusions that prior record is most consistently related to dispositional outcomes; that seriousness of immediate offense has some effect on decisions; that status offenders, perhaps because of social needs, are given relatively severe dispositions; and that the factors race, ethnicity, age, sex, SES, and present school or employment activity are important in some courts at some times, but not in others or at other times.

References

Andrews, R. Hale, Jr., and Cohn, Andrew H. 1974. Ungovernability: The Unjustifiable Jurisdiction. *Yale Law Journal* 82:1383–1409.

Arnold, William R. 1971. Race and Ethnicity Relative to Other Factors in Juvenile Court Dispositions. *American Journal of Sociology* 77:211–227.

Arthur, Lindsay G., and Gauger, William A. 1974. *Disposition Hearings: The Heartbeat of the Juvenile Court.* Reno, Nev.: National Council of Juvenile Court Judges.

Bailey, William C. 1981. Preadjudicatory Detention in a Large Metropolitan Juvenile Court. *Law and Human Behavior* 5:19–43.

Barton, William H. 1976. Discretionary Decision-Making in Juvenile Justice. *Crime & Delinquency* 22:470–480.

Binder, Arnold. 1984. The Juvenile Court, the U.S. Constitution and When the Twain Meet. *Journal of Criminal Justice* 1984:355–366.

———, and Binder, Virginia L. 1982. Juvenile Diversion and the Constitution. *Journal of Criminal Justice* 10:1–24.

Bookin-Weiner, Hedy. 1984. Assuming Responsibility: Legalizing Preadjudicatory Juvenile Detention. *Crime & Delinquency* 30:39–67.

Bortner, M. A. 1982. *Inside a Juvenile Court: The Tarnished Ideal of Individualized Justice.* New York: New York Univ. Press.

———, and Reed, Wornie L. 1985. The Preeminence of Process: An Example of Refocused Justice Research. *Social Science Quarterly* 66:413–425.

Carter, Sue. 1984. Chapter 39, the Florida Juvenile Justice Act: From Juvenile to Adult with the Stroke of a Pen. *Florida State Univ. Law Review* 11:922–947.

Carter, Timothy J. 1979. Juvenile Court Dispositions. *Criminology* 17:341–359.

Chesney-Lind, Meda. 1973. Judicial Enforcement of the Female Role: The Family Court and the Female Delinquent. *Issues in Criminology* 8:51–59.

———. 1977. Judicial Paternalism and the Female Status Offender. *Crime & Delinquency* 23:121–130.

Children's Defense Fund 1976. *Children in Adult Jails.* Washington, D.C.: Washington Research Project, Inc., Children's Defense Fund.

Chused, Richard H. 1973. The Juvenile Court Process: A Study of Three New Jersey Counties. *Rutgers Law Review* 26:488–589.

Clarke, Stevens H., and Koch, Gary G. 1980. Juvenile Court: Therapy or Crime Control, and Do Lawyers Make a Difference? *Law and Society Review* 14:263–308.

Coates, Robert B., Miller, Alden D., and Ohlin, Lloyd E. 1975. *Juvenile Detention and Its Consequences.* Cambridge, Mass.: Center for Criminal Justice, Harvard Univ. School of Law.

Cohen, Lawrence E. 1975a. *Delinquency Dispositions. An Empirical Analysis of Processing in Three Juvenile Courts.* Washington, D.C.: U.S. Government Printing Office.

————. 1975b. *Pre-adjudicatory Detention in Three Juvenile Courts: An Empirical Analysis of the Factors Related to Detention Decision Outcomes.* Washington, D.C.: U.S. Government Printing Office.

————, and Kluegel, James R. 1978. Determinants of Juvenile Court Dispositions: Ascriptive and Achieved Factors in Two Metropolitan Courts. *American Sociological Review* 43:162–176.

Copeland, Greg. 1972. Juvenile Delinquency "Referrals" and Their Effect on Dispositions. *American Journal of Criminal Law* 1:296–317.

Creekmore, Mark. 1976. Case Processing: Intake, Adjudication and Disposition. In *Brought to Justice? Juveniles, the Courts, and the Law,* edited by Rosemary Sarri and Yeheskel Hasenfeld, 119–150. Ann Arbor, Mich.: National Assessment of Juvenile Corrections, Univ. of Michigan.

Dannefer, Dale, and Schutt, Russell K. 1982. Race and Juvenile Justice Processing in Court and Police Agencies. *American Journal of Sociology* 87:1113–1132.

Datesman, Susan K., and Scarpitti, Frank R. 1977. Unequal Protection for Males and Females in the Juvenile Court. In *Juvenile Delinquency: Little Brother Grows Up,* edited by Theodore N. Ferdinand, 59–77. Beverly Hills, Calif.: Sage.

Davis, Samuel M. 1980. *Rights of Juveniles: The Juvenile Justice System.* 2nd ed. New York: Clark Boardman Company.

Dungworth, Terence. 1977. Discretion in the Juvenile Justice System: The Impact of Case Characteristics on Prehearing Detention. In *Juvenile Delinquency: Little Brother Grows Up,* edited by Theodore N. Ferdinand, 19–43. Beverly Hills, Calif.: Sage.

Feld, Barry C. 1981. Juvenile Court Legislative Reform and the Serious Young Offender: Dismantling the "Rehabilitative Ideal." *Minnesota Law Review* 65:167–242.

————. 1983. Delinquent Careers and Criminal Policy: Just Deserts and the Waiver Decision. *Criminology* 21:195–212.

————. 1984. Criminalizing Juvenile Justice: Rules of Procedure for the Juvenile Court. *Minnesota Law Review* 69:141–276.

Fenwick, C. R. 1982. Juvenile Court Intake Decision Making: The Importance of Family Affiliation. *Journal of Criminal Justice* 10:443–452.

Ferdinand, Theodore N., and Luchterhand, Elmer G. 1970. Inner-City Youth, the Police, the Juvenile Court, and Justice. *Social Problems* 17:510–527.

Ferster, Elyce Z., and Courtless, Thomas F. 1971. The Intake Process in the Affluent County Juvenile Court. *Hastings Law Journal* 22:1127–1153.

————. 1972. Predispositional Data, Role of Counsel and Delinquency in the Juvenile Court. *Law and Society Review* 7:195–222.

Ferster, Elyce Z., Snethen, Edith N., and Courtless, Thomas C. 1969. Juvenile Detention: Protection, Prevention or Punishment? *Fordham Law Review* 38:161–197.

Gibbons, Don C., and Griswold, Manzer J. 1957. Sex Differences Among Juvenile Court Referrals. *Sociology and Social Research* 42:106–110.

Gillespie, L. Kay, and Norman, Michael D. 1984. Does Certification Mean Prison: Some Preliminary Findings from Utah. *Juvenile and Family Court Journal* 35(3):23–34.

Hamparian, Donna, Davis, Joseph M., and Jacobson, Judith. 1983. *Juveniles Transferred to Adult Court: Recent Ohio Experience.* Cleveland: Ohio Serious Juvenile Offender Project, Federation for Community Planning.

Harris, Patricia M. 1986. Is the Juvenile Justice System Lenient? *Criminal Justice Abstracts* 18:104–118.

Hayeslip, David W., Jr., 1979. The Impact of Defense Attorney Presence on Juvenile Court Dispositions. *Juvenile and Family Court Journal* (February), 9–15.

Hufnagel, Lynne M., and Davidson, John P. 1974. Children in Need: Observations of Practices of the Denver Juvenile Court. *Denver Law Journal* 51:355–370.

Institute of Judicial Administration–American Bar Association Juvenile Justice Standards Project. 1980. *Standards Relating to the Juvenile Probation Function.* Cambridge, Mass.: Ballinger.

Kowalski, Gregory S., and Rickicki, John P. 1982. Determinants of Postadjudication Dispositions. *Journal of Research in Crime and Delinquency* 19:66–83.

Krisberg, Barry, Schwartz, Ira, Fishman, Gideon, Eiskovits, Zvi, and Guttman, Edna. 1986. *The Incarceration of Minority Youth.* Minneapolis, Minn.: Univ. of Minnesota, Hubert H. Humphrey Institute of Public Affairs.

Lemert, Edwin M. 1967. Legislating Change in the Juvenile Court. *Wisconsin Law Review* 421:442–443.

Levin, Mark M., and Sarri, Rosemary C. 1974. *Juvenile Delinquency: A Study of Juvenile Codes in the U.S.* Ann Arbor, Mich.: National Assessment of Juvenile Corrections, Univ. of Michigan.

Marshall, Chris E., Marshall, Ineke H., and Thomas, Charles W. 1983. The Implementation of Formal Procedures in Juvenile Court Processing of Status Offenders. *Journal of Criminal Justice* 11:195–211.

Marshall, Ineke H., and Thomas, Charles W. 1983. Discretionary Decision-Making and the Juvenile Court. *Juvenile & Family Court Journal* 34:47–59.

McCarthy, Belinda. 1985. An Analysis of Detention. *Juvenile and Family Court Journal* 36:49–50.

McCarthy, Francis B. 1977. Should Juvenile Delinquency Be Abolished? *Crime & Delinquency* 23:196–203.

McNally, Roger B. 1983. Juvenile Court: An Endangered Species. *Federal Probation* 47, no. 1:32–37.

Meade, Anthony. 1973. Seriousness of Delinquency, the Adjudicative Decision and Recidivism—A Longitudinal Configuration Analysis. *Journal of Criminal Law and Criminology* 64:478–485.

Miller, Frank W., Dawson, Robert O., Dix, George E., and Parnas, Raymond I. 1985. *The Juvenile Justice Process.* 3rd ed. Mineola, N.Y.: Foundation Press.

Mones, Paul. 1984. Too Many Rights or Not Enough? A Study of the Juvenile Related Decisions of the West Virginia Supreme Court of Appeals. *Journal of Juvenile Law* 8:32–57.

Mulvey, Edward P., and Saunders, J. Terry. 1982. Juvenile Detention Criteria: State of the Art and Guidelines for Change. *Criminal Justice Abstracts* 14:261–289.

Note. 1971. Juvenile Right to Jury Trial—Post McKeiver. *Washington Univ. Law Quarterly* 605–614.

Osbun, Lee Ann, and Rode, Peter A. 1984. Prosecuting Juveniles as Adults: The Quest for "Objective" Decisions. *Criminology* 22:187–202.

Pappenfort, Donnell M., and Young, Thomas M. 1977. *Use of Secure Detention for Juveniles and Alternatives to Its Use.* Washington, D.C.: Law Enforcement Assistance Administration, Office of Juvenile Justice and Delinquency Prevention.

Paulsen, Monrad G., and Whitebread, Charles H. 1974. *Juvenile Law and Procedure.* Reno, Nev: Institute for Court Management.

Pawlak, Edward J. 1977. Differential Selection of Juveniles for Detention. *Journal of Research in Crime and Delinquency* 14:152–165.

Phillips, Charles D., and Dinitz, Simon. 1982. Labelling and Juvenile Court Dispositions: Official Responses to a Cohort of Violent Juveniles. *Sociological Quarterly* 23:267–279.

Platt, Anthony, Schechter, Howard, and Tiffany, Phyllis. 1968. In Defense of Youth: A Case of the Public Defender in Juvenile Court. *Indiana Law Journal* 43:619–640.

Reichel, Philip, and Seyfrit, Carole. 1984. A Peer Jury in the Juvenile Court. *Crime & Delinquency* 30:423–438.

Rosen, Lawrence, and Carl, Arlene. 1974. The Decision to Refer to Juvenile Court for a Judicial Hearing. In *Crime and Delinquency: Dimensions of Deviance,* edited by Marc Reidel and Terence P. Thornberry, 154–166. New York: Praeger.

Rubin, H. Ted. 1972. *Three Juvenile Courts: A Comparative Study.* Denver, Colo.: Institute for Court Management.

———. 1976. *The Courts: Fulcrum of the Justice System.* Pacific Palisades, Calif.: Goodyear.

———. 1977. The Juvenile Court's Search for Identity and Responsibility. *Crime & Delinquency* 23:1–13.

———. 1985. *Juvenile Justice: Policy, Practice, and the Law.* New York: Random House.

Sarri, Rosemary C. 1974. *Under Lock and Key: Juveniles in Jails and Detention.* Ann Arbor, Mich.: National Assessment of Juvenile Corrections, Univ. of Michigan.

Scarpitti, Frank R., and Stephenson, Richard M. 1971. Juvenile Court Dispositions: Factors in the Decision-Making Process. *Crime and Delinquency* 17:142–151.

Schultz, J. Lawrence, and Cohen, Fred. 1976. Isolationism in Juvenile Court Jurisprudence. In *Pursuing Justice for the Child,* edited by Margaret K. Rosenheim, 20–42. Chicago: Univ. of Chicago Press.

Smith, Charles P., Black, T. Edwin, and Weir, Adrianne W. 1980. *Reports of the National Juvenile Justice Assessment Centers. A National Assessment of Case Disposition and Classification in the Juvenile Justice System: Inconsistent Labeling. Volume II: Results of a Literature Search.* Washington, D.C.: U.S. Government Printing Office.

Smith, J. F., Jr. 1978. An Analysis of When Juveniles Must Be Afforded Due Process Rights. *Nebraska Law Review* 58:136–158.

Sosin, Michael, and Sarri, Rosemary. 1976. Due Process — Reality or Myth? In *Brought to Justice? Juveniles, the Courts, and the Law,* edited by Rosemary Sarri and Yeheskel Hasenfeld, 176–206. Ann Arbor, Mich.: National Assessment of Juvenile Corrections, Univ. of Michigan.

Special Study Committee on Criminal Justice Standards and Goals. 1975. *Juvenile Justice Standards and Goals.* Madison: Wisconsin Council on Criminal Justice.

Stapleton, W. Vaughan, and Teitelbaum, Lee F. 1972. *In Defense of Youth.* New York: Russell Sage Foundation.

Sumner, Helen, 1971. Locking Them Up. *Crime and Delinquency* 17:168–179.

Susman, Jackwell. 1973. Juvenile Justice: Even-handed or Many-handed? An Empirical Investigation of Decision Processes in Disposition Hearings. *Crime and Delinquency* 19:493–507.

Task Force on Juvenile Delinquency. The President's Commission on Law Enforcement and Administration of Justice. 1967. *Task Force Report: Juvenile Delinquency and Youth Crime.* Washington, D.C.: U.S. Government Printing Office.

Terry, Robert M. 1967a. Discrimination in the Handling of Juvenile Offenders by Social-Control Agencies. *Journal of Research in Crime and Delinquency* 4:218–230.

———. 1967b. The Screening of Juvenile Offenders. *Journal of Criminal Law, Criminology and Police Science* 58:173–181.

Thomas, Charles W., and Sieverdes, Christopher M. 1975. Juvenile Court Intake: An Analysis of Discretionary Decision-Making. *Criminology* 12:413–432.

Thomson, Doug, and McAnany, Patrick D. 1984. Punishment and Responsibility in Juvenile Court: Desert-Based Probation for Delinquents. In *Probation and Justice: Reconsideration of Mission,* edited by Patrick D. McAnany, Doug Thomson, and David Fogel, 137–172. Cambridge, Mass.: Oelgeschlager, Gunn & Hain.

Thornberry, Terence P. 1973. Race, Socioeconomic Status and Sentencing in the Juvenile Justice System. *Journal of Criminal Law and Criminology* 64:90–98.

Wadlington, Walter, Whitebread, Charles H., and Davis, Samuel M. 1983. *Cases and Materials on Children in the Legal System.* Mineola, N.Y.: Foundation Press.

Wolfgang, Marvin E., Figlio, Robert M., and Sellin, Thorsten. 1972. *Delinquency in a Birth Cohort.* Chicago: Univ. of Chicago Press.

CHAPTER 11

Detention, Institutionalization, Parole

Fred R. Conrad/The New York Times

We have, in preceding chapters, discussed various constitutional issues connected with the juvenile justice system's awesome power to deny a youth his or her liberty by confinement in a locked facility. In this chapter, we will look closely at the character and significance of that confinement process, which may be used as early as the very entry point to the system. As we discussed in Chapter 10, one option available to a police officer in dealing with a suspected young offender is to take the youth into custody (that is, arrest the youth) and then refer him or her to the juvenile court while the youth remains in custody. The youth may then, with concurrence of a judicial ruling coming in a short period of time (usually twenty-four or forty-eight hours), be held in continued custody up to and through adjudicatory and dispositional hearings. The process of keeping a youngster in a secure and restrictive facility up to adjudication and disposition is called *detention*. In contrast to that, *institutionalization* refers to the process of assignment of a youth to a facility for secure confinement by a court following a dispositional hearing; because of its presumed rehabilitative mission, a facility of this sort is often called a correctional institution.

Detention

Detention may be in a facility used exclusively for youths and associated with the juvenile court, or in a jail. The expression *juvenile hall* is widely used to designate the former type of holding facility. Using an arbitrary day for statistical purposes (February 1, 1985), the Bureau of Justice Statistics (1986) and the Office of Juvenile Justice and Delinquency Prevention (1986) found that 29 per cent of the youths in custody that day were being detained, while 70 per cent had been committed by a juvenile court (the remaining youths, 1 per cent, were voluntarily admitted).

Numbers of Children in Detention

According to the report of Poulin et al. (1980), about 520,000 juveniles were admitted to detention centers during a year of the mid-1970s. California alone contributed almost 140,000 to the total, or about 27 per cent of all admissions to juvenile detention centers. Fifty per cent of the total number of admissions came from five states—California, Ohio, Texas, Washington, and Florida—a grouping of states that had only about one fifth of the juvenile population.

And there are variations in detention rates within states that parallel the interstate variations. For example, a study reported by Sumner (1971) found that 36 per cent of juveniles referred to eleven county probation departments in California were detained. But the detention rate varied over counties from a low of 19 per cent to a high of 66 per cent. The highest likelihood of being detained was among those youths who offended while on probation—first offenders were detained only 25 per cent of the time.

To estimate the number of youths being held in public detention facilities each day of the mid-1980s, we may use the one-day count (February 1, 1985) of the Bureau of Justice Statistics (1986) and the Office of Juvenile Justice and

Delinquency Prevention (1986). Since there were 49,332 juveniles in custody on that day and 29 per cent of them were being detained (as noted above), we get 14,306 as the estimate of interest.

Poulin et al. (1980) also report that the number of juveniles held in an adult jail during a year of the mid-1970s was about 120,000.[1] The numbers varied from a high of over 10,000 in Wisconsin to a low of zero in each of eight jurisdictions —the District of Columbia, Arizona, Rhode Island, Delaware, Connecticut, New Jersey, Massachusetts, and Vermont. The ten states with the largest numbers of youths in jails accounted for 50 per cent of the total number of jail detainees.

Table 11.1 shows annual rates of detention for juveniles over jurisdictions per 100,000 youths aged five to seventeen. The rate for the highest state, Nevada, is more than forty times the rate for the lowest, Vermont.

A report prepared by the Office of Juvenile Justice and Delinquency Prevention of the U.S. Department of Justice (1980:25) gives 4.8 days as the average length of stay for juveniles in adult jails and 12.0 days as the average length of stay for juveniles in juvenile detention facilities. It states, further (1980:25),

TABLE 11.1   **Ranked Distribution: Annual Rates of Detaining Juveniles in Detention Centers and Jails, by State**

State	Rate[a]	State	Rate
Nevada	4,734.0	Oklahoma	1,124.3
New Mexico	3,465.8	Missouri	1,037.4
Washington	3,370.3	Kentucky	912.4
Idaho	3,366.5	West Virginia	892.9
California	2,944.7	Hawaii	887.0
Colorado	2,589.8	Iowa	803.0
Utah	2,519.4	Maryland	779.8
Wyoming	2,279.1	Illinois	743.3
Oregon	2,222.5	Louisiana	721.6
District of Columbia	2,208.8	New Jersey	664.6
Arizona	1,982.1	Maine	546.5
Tennessee	1,932.6	North Carolina	518.8
Montana	1,846.2	Kansas	490.1
Minnesota	1,715.1	Pennsylvania	483.6
Georgia	1,651.2	Mississippi	475.8
Wisconsin	1,600.8	Rhode Island	453.1
South Carolina	1,549.9	Michigan	421.1
Arkansas	1,479.8	New Hampshire	403.1
Ohio	1,414.2	Connecticut	396.7
Alaska	1,411.8	North Dakota	305.7
Alabama	1,404.3	Massachusetts	295.4
Delaware	1,325.5	New York	292.7
Virginia	1,288.0	Nebraska	205.7
South Dakota	1,240.1	Vermont	117.2
Texas	1,127.9		

[a]Rates per 100,000 juveniles aged five through seventeen.

Source: Poulin et al. (1980:20).

"The 1-day count taken by the U.S. Bureau of Census in February 1978 throughout the Nation showed that 1,611 persons classified as juveniles were being held in adult jails, 1 percent of the total persons of all ages held in an adult jail on that day."

In concluding this discussion of numbers of juveniles in jails and juvenile halls, it should be pointed out that in some states, sixteen- and seventeen-year-olds are considered adults from the perspective of the justice system (though not more generally). Smith (1980) has estimated that 32 per cent of juveniles (that is, those under eighteen) who are detained in jails are in states where they are considered adults and fall under the jurisdiction of the criminal court.

An Era of Forceful Objections to the Detention of Children

Particularly vigorous opposition to the detention of young offenders, especially those in jails, began in the late 1960s and produced significant effects on operations of the juvenile justice system during the 1970s. One of the early expressions in that lineage may be found in the report of the Task Force on Corrections, President's Commission on Law Enforcement and Administration of Justice (1967). To illustrate, the report states (1967:23):

> Far too frequently detention, although justified on a variety of grounds, is utilized as a punishment device or to impose needless controls prior to adjudication. The National Survey of Corrections referred to a county in which about two-thirds of the youngsters detained prior to hearing were subsequently placed on probation in their own homes. Clearly, the great majority of these juveniles could have awaited a hearing without detention, with little risk of failure to appear in court.

Evidence Indicating Seriousness of Offense Leading to Detention. The opposition to detention stemmed from a general concern for human rights, particularly of the downtrodden, a specific concern for the fair treatment of youngsters in the system as reflected in *Kent, Gault,* and similar Supreme Court decisions, and specific research findings and descriptions of conditions in detention facilities, particularly jails, that reinforced those concerns. We will turn to the general and specific social concerns later in this chapter and consider at this point only the research findings dealing with detention. One group of findings, as discussed in Chapter 10, contradicted the widely held belief that juvenile halls, jails, and other detention facilities contain predominantly youths who committed serious crimes. The belief is natural enough in view of the oft-stated position that a primary purpose of the system is to protect the public.

Evidence Indicating Deplorable Conditions in Jails. Reports of the surprisingly large number of children, even young children, in adult jails and the dangers to which they were exposed therein provided another source of concern about juvenile detention, as they had in earlier periods (see Chapters 6 and 7). We saw above in the report by Poulin et al. (1980) that about 120,000 children were held in adult jails during a year of the mid-1970s. But information of that sort and the resulting motivating force for change came considerably earlier. For example, a survey undertaken by the National Council on Crime and

Delinquency (see the Task Force on Corrections, President's Commission on Law Enforcement and Administration of Justice, 1967:115–212) found there were 87,951 children detained in jails during 1965 and at least another 1,300 in police lockups. Moreover, the report of survey results notes (1967:121):

> Less than 20 percent of the jails in which children are held have been rated as suitable for adult Federal offenders. Nine states forbid placing children in jail, but this prohibition is not always enforced. In 19 States the law permits juveniles to be jailed if they are segregated from adults, but this provision is not always adhered to.

Staff members of the Children's Defense Fund (1976:3) "visited 449 jails in 126 counties and 9 independent cities, almost all of which had a population of over 50,000, in the states of Florida, Georgia, Indiana, Maryland, New Jersey, Ohio, South Carolina, Texas and Virginia." They asked questions about the numbers of children jailed, the characteristics of jailed children, the services and conditions of the jails, and the legal process that preceded jailing. About half of the 449 jails held children regularly or occasionally. There were 257 children in jail on the day of the visit who were under the jurisdiction of the juvenile court (that is, they had not been waived for criminal trial), and they were overwhelmingly white males. Although minority children composed only 31.8 per cent of the jailed children, that was somewhat higher than their percentage in the general population of children. Finally, about one third of the children were fourteen or fifteen years old, and over 9 per cent were thirteen years old or younger.

Many of the articles and books that highlighted the deplorable conditions in jails presented vivid anecdotes of the effects of jailing on individual children. For example, the report of the survey of the National Council on Crime and Delinquency (Task Force on Corrections, President's Commission on Law Enforcement and Administration of Justice, 1967:121) stated:

> In Arizona in January 1965, four teenage boys, jailed on suspicion of stealing beer, died of asphyxiation from a defective gas heater when they were left alone for 11 hours in a jail.
>
> In Indiana, a 13-year-old boy, who had been in five foster homes, drove the car belonging to the last of his foster fathers to a county jail, considered one of the finest in the State, and asked the sheriff to lock him up. The boy was well segregated from adults pending a hearing for auto theft. When he had been detained for about a week, his body was found hanging from one of the bars of his cell. Next to it was a penciled note: "I don't belong anywhere."

The report of the Children's Defense Fund (1976:30) described jails visited by staff members as "very old, deteriorating, and unsafe" and failing to meet "minimal standards . . . for sewage disposal, plumbing and cleanliness." And the jails did "not provide inmates with such basic things as soap, toothpaste, toilet paper." Specific horror stories recounted are like the following (1976:30–31):

> Jon was put in a cell alone. There was no sink and nothing to drink. No pillow. The sheets were sandy and dirty. There were two bunkbeds with a toilet between

them. "Rusty, grungy. I wouldn't use it. Anyway, everyone could see in. There were bars on two sides. I could see other cells. Could see a bunch of crazy-looking people. They looked mean. I just wasn't used to seeing people like that. One was beating on the bars to get attention. There was a lot of yelling. It took a long time to get to sleep."

Fred, not yet 13, was placed in a concrete cell with two small barred windows looking out on to the street. There was a mattress and one blanket, a sink, toilet, shower. There was one old dirty cup, too soiled to drink from. Fred slept badly: "The beds were mangy, with big stains on them. I felt kind of scared. I kept walking around the cell. There was just a big thick steel door and a little round window." The light was left on all night. When Fred asked to have it turned off, "they said 'no.' They said they were afraid that I'd kill myself if it is dark. Once I threw a blanket over the light. It caught on fire."

Other accounts of harshness, abuse, and dangerous conditions in jails have been described in Sarri (1974), Wooden (1976), Goldfarb (1976), and Cottle (1977). The accounts describe unkempt, unsanitary cells where youths are subjected to brutal beatings, homosexual rape, and even murder by other inmates and, on occasion, by jail employees. Cottle (1977) interviewed children detained in jail and presented their profiles to highlight the effects of jailing. There was, for example, the case of Bobbie, a fifteen-year-old daughter of a prostitute, who was described as among the group of youngsters "who have never experienced a tender friendship and therefore do not know the meaning of tenderness" (1977:2). She was arrested along with another fifteen-year-old girl as accomplices in the murder of a pimp; both were placed in jail. Bobbie spent eleven months in a jail awaiting trial where no one came to visit her.

The progression of life in prison for Bobbie is described as follows:

> When she was first locked in her cell, she became violently ill. She felt her head getting warm as if the blood in her neck were being heated and rising hot into her brain. Then she felt as though her head was suddenly too heavy for her body to support. Her heart raced and perspiration appeared all over her body. She vomited violently, surprised that there had been no warning signs of nausea or abdominal pressure. Her fingers and toes tingled as though someone were sticking needles into them, and she was afraid that she was losing her sense of touch. Her eyesight too was affected; images became blurred and a strange scintillating arc appeared above everything she focused on, giving the impression of electrical interference. (1977:16)

> "I feel I'm getting sicker in here. Every day, just a little bit more. The place terrifies me. Sometimes I feel I'm screaming to get out, but it's all quiet. . . . I don't want to go mad. I fight against it, but it's like this large wall is moving in closer to me every day and I can't push it back anymore. There used to be a time when I thought I could, but not now. I don't know why it is either.
>
> "I've been in this jail and another one for nine months! Nine months and one week. I went in on a Monday. Monday night. Like, the first couple of months I spent time getting used to the place — getting used to it, that's a laugh — and spending my time being angry 'cause they had no right keeping me in here. Then I started to change. Sometimes when you change, you don't feel it happening. It just happens and one day you look back and say, I guess I've changed. But this time I really knew I was changing. Every day, twice a day, I would say, I'm not like me anymore. . . . They got informers in here, you know. Ladies, maybe they're police, maybe they're real prisoners. They try to break you down, get you to confess

things. One of them put a lighted cigarette on my ass one night. Honest to God, she held it closer and closer, they must have had six of them holding me down. She kept saying, 'I'll put a hole right in the middle of your goddamn ass if you don't tell us what you did.' I always wondered how come the matrons let it go." (1977:17, 18)

Three weeks before she was to be called to trial, Bobbie Dijon was found dead in her cell. She had swallowed more than a bottle of sleeping pills that she had asked a fellow prisoner to get for her. One rumor went that her brother Timmy knew about her plan to commit suicide but promised Bobbie he would never say anything. Timmy Dijon denied knowing anything of his sister's plan. Marianne Dijon did not cry upon hearing the news of her daughter's death. Her body grew stiff and she whispered, "I knew it would come." (1977:20)

Six months after Bobbie Dijon's death, Patsy Monahan [Bobbie's social worker] received a letter from a man named Stuart Post who claimed to be Bobbie's father. The letter showed no return address. It contained a twenty-dollar bill and a note saying the money was to be given to Bobbie to use any way she wanted. She was to know it had come from her father. Marianne Dijon denied ever knowing anyone by the name of Stuart Post. "Besides," she added, "it's all too late for that." (1977:21)

But Does the System Need Jails for Youths? Keve (1984) recently found that the prohibition of the jailing of children by Pennsylvania in 1979 had no perceptible effect on the juvenile justice system in that state. Similarly, Allinson (1983) reported that, while the number of juveniles in Pennsylvania jails went from 3,196 in 1975 to zero in 1981, there was no corresponding increase in the number of youngsters detained in secure juvenile facilities. Both Keve and Allinson noted an increase in the use of group home placement, foster care, and in-home detention as the use of jails decreased.

Evidence Indicating the Unreasonableness of Detention. A third group of findings that reinforced the increasing negative feelings about placing children in jails, starting in the latter 1960s, raised similar questions about placing them in juvenile halls and similar secure detention facilities. Thus, Ferster and Courtless (1972) reported that up to 25 per cent of juveniles who had been detained were released without a petition being filed for a court hearing. And Goldfarb (1976) found in one county that only 5 per cent of children who had been detained prior to court hearing were eventually sent to a state training school. While one can easily conceive of special cases where conditions change so rapidly that a detained youngster does not need a court hearing or does not need institutionalization after adjudication, one must wonder about the need for secure custody when 25 per cent of those so detained do not even have petitions filed and 95 per cent of those detained are set free prior to or by the court hearings.

Several writers have pointed out that detention for the purpose of protecting the community is a hazardous task at best on the basis of research indicating that future dangerousness is virtually unpredictable, especially on the basis of psychological states and personality features (see, for example, Monahan, 1981). Accordingly, one finds the following among the recommendations of Mulvey and Saunders (1982:285) for restricting the criteria used in detention decisions: *"elimination of any criterion that requires prediction of future behavior by detention personnel."* Allowing that the most useful guide to future dangerousness is past behavior of a similar sort, they argue (1982:285), "detention criteria should stress an individual's history of dangerous behavior (which may include the most recent crime)" but never include the "intuition or suspicions with respect to future behavior" of intake personnel.

In concluding, it is important to note that the U.S. Supreme Court in a recent decision was not sympathetic to expressions of opposition to juvenile detention on the basis of the high release rate following adjudication and the overwhelming difficulty of predicting future dangerousness. The case, *Schall v. Martin* (467 U.S. 253, 1984), dealt with the constitutionality of a New York Family Court Act authorizing detention of a child if "there is a serious risk that he may before the return date commit an act which if committed by an adult would be a crime" (at 255).

A federal circuit court had declared the act unconstitutional because the detention served as a punishment without a prior establishment of guilt in accord with due process standards. The circuit court relied heavily on statistical evidence that (at 262) "the vast majority of juveniles detained under [the act] either have their petitions dismissed before an adjudication or are released after adjudication." The Supreme Court was critical of that position in the following retort (at 272): "We are unpersuaded by the Court of Appeals' rather cavalier equation of detentions that do not lead to continued confinement after an adjudication of guilt and 'wrongful' or 'punitive' pretrial detentions. Pretrial detention need not be considered punitive merely because a juvenile is subsequently discharged."

On the issue of predictability of future behavior, the Court comments (at 278):

> We have already seen that detention of juveniles . . . serves legitimate regulatory purposes. But appellees claim, and the district court agreed, that it is virtually impossible to predict future criminal conduct with any degree of accuracy. Moreover, they say, the statutory standard fails to channel the discretion of the Family Court judge by specifying the factors on which he should rely in making that prediction. . . .
>
> Our cases indicate, however, that from a legal point of view there is nothing inherently unattainable about a prediction of future criminal conduct. Such a judgment forms an important element in many decisions, and we have specifically rejected the contention based on the same sort of sociological data relied upon by appellees and the district court, "that it is impossible to predict future behavior and that the question is so vague as to be meaningless."

Thus, the decision, written by Justice Rehnquist (before his elevation to chief justice), is clearly not responsive to arguments coming from the social sciences (indeed, the expression "the same sort of sociological data" has a pejorative ring to it). The decision of the federal circuit court on the invalidity of preventive detention in New York was reversed with the accompanying statement (at 256), "We conclude that preventive detention under the Family Court Act serves a legitimate state objective, and that the procedural protections afforded pretrial detainees by the New York statute satisfy the requirements of the Due Process Clause of the Fourteenth Amendment to the United States Constitution."

But other people at other times have been responsive to "sociological data" and to the arguments of the inequities in detaining youths, particularly in jails.

One was Senator Birch Bayh of Indiana. His office instituted a four-year examination of the role of the federal government in the prevention and treatment of delinquency that culminated in the Juvenile Justice and Delinquency Prevention Act of 1974, a very important act aimed at reducing incarceration. We shall say more about it in the next section.

Finally, there has been a major victory recently in California for those people and agencies opposed to the use of jails for the detention of youths. Under the headline "Governor OK's Limits on Juveniles in Adult Jails," the *Los Angeles Times* of September 30, 1986 (3, 21) reported:

> Legislation to sharply reduce the number of juveniles held in adult jails in California has been signed into law by Gov. George Deukmejian, it was announced Monday.
>
> The bill, authored by Sen. Robert Presley (D-Riverside), was prompted in part by the 1984 hanging death of a 15-year-old girl in a dismal cell in the rural Glenn County Jail in Northern California, but the legislation is expected to have its greatest impact in Los Angeles County, where thousands of juveniles have been incarcerated annually in adult lockups.
>
> The bill, which goes into effect Jan. 1, prohibits the use of main county jails for the detention of minors except for those being tried as adults. Rural counties without juvenile halls are given $2\frac{1}{2}$ years to develop alternatives to county jail detention.
>
> The legislation allows detention for up to six hours in police stations or sheriff's substations of juveniles over 14 years old who are accused of crimes and who are deemed to be a threat to themselves or others. Authorities will be required to keep records explaining the need for each incarceration.
>
> The bill also prohibits holding runaways or abused and neglected children in jails or police lockups.
>
> Current law allows juveniles to be held in adult jails when a local court determines that a juvenile facility is not available. Critics of the practice maintain that this provision has been used as a loophole to incarcerate thousands of youngsters a year in adult lockups, where they come into dangerous contact with mature prisoners and where some youngsters commit suicide.
>
> California Youth Authority figures show that nearly 10,000 juveniles were held for six hours or more in adult facilities in the state last year—89% of them in Los Angeles County. Advocates of changing the system maintain that the number of youngsters held in such lockups for less than six hours runs into tens of thousands a year.
>
> The governor's signature on the bill tightening restrictions on this practice marks the end of several months of sometimes bitter negotiations between advocates of change and the Los Angeles County Sheriff's Department.
>
> The department originally opposed the bill on grounds that it would cause security problems and needlessly inconvenience police officers and parents. But, after compromise amendments last month, the department did not seek a gubernatorial veto, as feared by sponsors of the legislation.
>
> However, a compromise amendment allowing limited use of police station and sheriff's substation lockups to hold juveniles caused one of the bill's sponsors, the Youth Law Center of San Francisco, to withdraw its endorsement of the legislation.
>
> Still, David Steinhart of the National Council on Crime and Delinquency, which co-sponsored the legislation, said the bill provides "probably the strongest jail rules in the country."

The newspaper article is of particular interest not only for the information it contains regarding a change in law for the jailing of youths but for its analysis of competing interests in legislative and judicial decisions on the issue of juvenile incarceration.

Institutionalization

The Predecessors to and Development of Current Institutions

Predecessors. To provide an appropriate context for this section of the chapter, it would seem useful to review briefly the material in Chapter 8 on the development in the United States of institutions for the custody of young offenders. As we saw in Chapter 8, the use of prisons to punish offenders, juvenile as well as adult, in England and America started toward the end of the eighteenth century; an illustration of that use in Chapter 6 was that of an eight-year-old given a three-year term in state prison for burglary (theft of a jewelry box). Concern about the imprisonment of children led to the first house of refuge in New York in 1825. The goal was to correct "vicious propensities" of the children in a broad effort at reformation.

Houses of refuge established shortly thereafter in Boston, Philadelphia, and elsewhere followed the New York model in being primarily dependent on private funding, in having private management, in accepting dependent and ungovernable children as well as young criminals, and in keeping their young charges for indeterminate periods of time. The houses of refuge provided operating examples when state-supported reform schools began being established during the mid-nineteenth century. The earliest reform (or industrial or training) schools were established in Massachusetts, New York and Maine (see Task Force on Corrections, President's Commission on Law Enforcement and Administration of Justice, 1967). The first of these, the Lyman School for Boys, was opened in 1846 in Massachusetts. That was followed by the New York State Agricultural and Industrial School in 1859 and the Maine Boys Training Center in 1853. By the year 1900, virtually every state had a juvenile training facility. The early institutions used the congregate or dormitory system for housing delinquents in fortresslike buildings. Beginning in the mid-1850s, many facilities were built on the cottage model with its emphasis on family living style in agricultural settings.

Aims of Institutionalization. The working philosophies of the juvenile institutions have been summarized in the Task Force on Corrections, President's Commission on Law Enforcement and Administration of Justice report (1967:141, 142) as follows:

> The term "school of industry" or "reformatory" often designated the early juvenile training facilities, thus reflecting the relatively simple philosophies upon which their development was based. Their reform programs sought chiefly to teach the difference between right and wrong. Teaching methods were primarily on a

precept level, tending to emphasize correct behavior, formal education, and, where possible, the teaching of a trade so that the trainee would have the skills to follow the "right."

Although, from the earliest period, the stated goal of these various juvenile institutions was reformation, two developments in later years produced particular reemphasis on reformation (or rehabilitation). First, following a meeting in 1870, a group of influential reformers denounced the predominant punishment philosophy in prison operations and advocated industrial training, education, rewards rather than sanctions, and the cultivation of self-respect. In short, rehabilitation rather than punishment, the reformers argued, should be the primary goal in adult prisons, the day-to-day efforts should reflect that goal (see Henderson, 1910). The second development that brought reemphasis on reformation in juvenile institutions was the set of processes that surrounded the establishment of the juvenile court in 1899. As stated in Chapter 8, the fundamental aim of all aspects of the new juvenile justice was to treat the young offender as a parent would.

But, unfortunately, as Rothman (1979:58, 59) has argued, the emphasis and reemphasis were often more at the verbal than at the operational level:

> The descent from the language of juvenile institutions to the reality of conditions is precipitous. No matter how frequently judges insisted that confinement was for treatment, training schools did not fulfill this claim. "When is a school not a school?" asked one reformatory superintendent. "When it is a school for delinquents." Reformatories were not capable of administering a grade school or high school curriculum and they did no better at vocational training. As one observer reported: "Most of the large institutions have what they call trades departments, and use them mainly for repair and construction work about the plants. . . . This gives a small amount of instruction while utilizing the labor of the inmates in reducing the expenses of the institution." Or, as the verdict of those who studied conditions at St. Charles, Illinois, put it: "Trade training of a quality which fits boys for self-maintenance is non-existent."
>
> The cottages were almost invariably overcrowded with a staff that was at once undertrained and overworked. They bore no resemblance to a normal family life. And for child guidance, the most important service that institutional psychologists or psychiatrists performed was mental testing. IQ tests were prevalent. But there was really little that the training schools could do with the results. Classification was an absurdity when cottages were overcrowded and organized essentially by age and size. Thus, one answer to the question, "What good has psychiatry been in an institution for delinquents?" was accurately enough: "To start surveys; to give us technical diagnoses and work out more and more elaborate records which no one uses."

Numbers and Types of Institutions. According to estimates by Teeters (1950) and Blackburn (1959), there were just under 170 public training schools for adjudicated young offenders in the United States at the start of the 1950s. That number includes institutions encompassed by such other names as industrial school, farm school, agricultural school, and reform school—and many schools simply given the names of benefactors or early superintendents. In addition, there were about 11 state reception and diagnostic centers, 42 forestry camps and ranches, and 135 private training schools, many run under the auspices of the Catholic Church.

The report of the Bureau of Justice Statistics (1986) on children who are held in custody gives 562 as the number of public facilities in 1985 for long-term placement and 478 as the number of such facilities for short-term placement. (See also Office of Juvenile Justice and Delinquency Prevention, 1986.) The difficulty of clearly distinguishing between facilities for dispositional placement and those for detention is shown in the following statement from that report (1986:4): "About 96% of the juveniles in long-term facilities were committed, while 86% of the juveniles in short-term facilities were detained."

Reception and diagnostic centers had been developed in several states to determine the likely causes of the personal difficulties of assigned wards, to determine reasonable approaches to treatment, to assess risks and security needs, and to select an appropriate facility for assignment. In California, for example, two reception centers were established for the evaluation of all new commitments to the state's Youth Authority. During a period of about six weeks, wards are given psychological tests, interviewed, and examined physically. Clearly, that sort of diagnostic process is intended to be directly responsive to the individualized, rehabilitative emphasis of the juvenile justice system.

As discussed in Chapter 8, the notion that the "country" had curative properties for urban delinquents was advocated at least from the mid-nineteenth century. The Children's Aid Society of New York City put the notion into practice during a later era by placing big-city youths in rural homes, and several of the early schools had agricultural emphases. With that in historical perspective, it is easy to understand why there persistently has been the expectation of positive effects of sending youths to forestry camps or ranches.

Breed (1953) has written of an early experimental camp opened in Los Angeles in 1931. Boys were supervised by probation officers while working under the direction of employees of the Los Angeles County Forestry Department. That camp and others that followed were considered so successful in the treatment of young offenders that forestry camps became an established component of California's Youth Authority in 1943. In that year (1953:705), "50 boys were transferred from county jails . . . to the Calaveras Big Trees Park where, under the supervision of skilled tradesmen, they built a camp of 100-boy capacity." Portable buildings were used, and the process of establishment was expedited because of severe overcrowding within urban institutions at the time.

The continuing interest in camps for troubled youngsters is illustrated by an article in the issue of *Newsweek* dated July 14, 1986. The opening sentence (p. 63) is, "In the Sierra Nevada mountains of northern California, teenagers who have been in trouble with the law go back-packing with their probation officers." Further in the article is the following description of a camp in Minnesota (p. 64):

> Last month seven 13- to 15-year-olds spent a rugged week at the Wilderness Canoe Base near Grand Marais, Minn. They were called the "Sheriff's Boys" because they had been referred to the camp from juvenile court as part of a treatment program for charges ranging from truancy to assault. The boys spent much of the trip fighting, staging sitdown strikes and dreaming of hot showers. One boy said he hated the required four-hour solo stint: "It was boring. You couldn't talk to

anybody." But he conceded that he had learned something: "You need friends." For kids like the Sheriff's Boys, that's an important lesson, counselors say. "By the end of the trip, they were functioning as a group," explains Wilderness camp guide Bill Reinhart. "These kids aren't used to being part of anything."

Winterdyk and Griffiths (1984) reviewed ten published evaluations of wilderness programs that were alternatives to institutionalization. They concluded that there was no evidence to support the various arguments for the efficacy of wilderness experiences in the rehabilitation of delinquents. But that lack of evidence, they state, may be due principally to the poorness of the approaches to evaluation.

Before leaving this section of the chapter, a few comments on private institutions for young offenders would seem to be in order. The two principal types of private institution are group homes and camps. In a group home, a youngster may attend a local school while living in a well-structured setting. It is typical, moreover, in a group home for the youngster to be provided with a clearly focused and directed treatment program. The emphasis in camps, as might be expected, is on the performance of outdoor manual labor. The setting and the emphasis on physical effort and personal discipline are thought, in a tradition flowing from the nineteenth century, to produce personal reevaluations of lifestyles and wholesome changes in behavior (as evidenced in the above testimonials given in the *Newsweek* quote).

Many of the private institutions are affiliated with churches. Teeters (1950:587) described Catholic institutions for young offenders as follows:

> The [Catholic] hierarchy maintains child welfare agencies and quite frequently juvenile judges refer cases to them especially if the children belong to the Catholic faith. Boys are sent to "protectories" and girls to institutions operated by the Order of the Good Shepherd. The treatment in operation in both of these institutions is perhaps more highly regimented than in the state-supported schools although it is just as probable that excessive cruelty is less frequently detected than in state reform schools. Feelings of guilt are encouraged in the hope that children will see their error and thus reform. In other words, penitence or expiation is more often the rule in these schools than in state-supported reform schools.

By the mid-1970s, according to a report by the U.S. Department of Justice (1979), there were training schools in all states and the District of Columbia, public reception and diagnostic centers in fourteen states, and forestry camps and ranches in twenty-five states. Interestingly, out of the total of 103 forestry camps and ranches in the United States at the time, 43 were in California.

The average numbers of residents per day in these facilities were as follows: reception and diagnostic centers—1,817; training schools—27,515; and forestry camps and ranches—5,567. About 80 per cent of the residents of the training schools and the reception and diagnostic centers were males, whereas 94 per cent of the residents of camps and ranches were males. About half of the residents of these facilities had been adjudicated for felonies, 26 per cent for status offenses, 19 per cent for misdemeanors, and the remainder for drug offenses.

Finally, two more recent reports of survey results (Bureau of Justice Statistics, 1986, and Office of Juvenile Justice and Delinquency Prevention, 1986) estimated the average stay for a youth committed to a custodial institution at just over five months.

Overview of Operations in Institutions

Treatment. A report of the Children's Bureau, U.S. Department of Health, Education, and Welfare (1959:697), stated:

> The word "treatment," as used in training schools today, means help given to the child — the total effort made by the school to rehabilitate the child and the after-care services in his home community. It denotes helping a child by providing a new and more satisfying experience in community living together with any special services that he may need. It includes a proper diagnosis of the child's problems and a plan of care based on that diagnosis. It implies providing an environment in which all activities are directed to getting the child ready for a successful return to community living. It covers every aspect of the child's institutional life and involves the total staff, as well as the neighboring community. Every staff member, including the cottage supervisor, teacher, clerk, maintenance man, cook, and nurse, has a definite and important contribution to make to treatment.

On the other hand, Pleune (1959) has emphasized a narrower perspective in the definition of treatment. He argues (1959:713, 714), "With grim determination to make good citizens out of delinquent children, the [training] school tries to thrust upon them the characteristics of good citizens — obedience, courtesy, respect for law, education, discipline, and work." But that (1959:714) is like "giving icepacks and aspirin to a patient with fever while ignoring the disease that causes it." To Pleune, treatment implies a psychological orientation for the staff, functioning as therapists under the supervision of a psychiatric clinic staff with a goal of "developing [each] child's capacities for healthy emotional and social growth" (1959:720).

The two perspectives on "treatment" given by the Children's Bureau, on the one hand, and by Pleune, on the other, reflect prevalent though differing attitudes. The first states, essentially, that everything that is done in an institution should be oriented toward the return of residents to their communities as law-abiding citizens, and therefore everything is a component of treatment. The second implies that treatment means the medical model with related concepts and terminological baggage. One finds in Pleune's arguments references to delinquency as a "symptom complex with multiple determinants" and as a "pathological process" and to most delinquents as "psychologically sick" (1959:714). Delinquents, according to Pleune (1959:714, 715), suffer from "a lack of constructive, dependable loving relationships" or have been exposed to "destructive aggression," and the result is "emotional injury" leading to "tension-relieving pleasure in stealing, truancy, sadistic aggression, etc."

Management. It would seem best to accept neither of these perspectives but, rather, to refer to the broad array of maintenance activities within an institution as management and to include as treatment a greater array of activities than those derived from a strictly psychiatric/medical point of view. That greater array of activities encompasses methods associated with or derived from the more formal and more theoretically based approaches to changing human behavior in socially approved directions. These methods use such names as counseling, individual psychotherapy, group psychotherapy, behavior change, and social therapy.

Education/Training. An important class of activities within most institutions falls neither under management nor under treatment in the above dichotomy. The class includes all formal education and training. It is difficult to imagine a comprehensive rehabilitative program for youngsters without education in appropriate academic subjects and training in relevant vocational spheres.

Actual Day-to-Day Operations

The segmentation of institutional efforts into treatment, management, and education/training categories is in accord with general professional usage but carries no implications for rehabilitative effectiveness. A warm relationship with a correctional officer or a shop teacher may vary well lead to greater and longer-lasting change in attitudes and in behavior than the most dynamic of psychiatric therapies. On the other hand, it has become abundantly clear that the specific maintenance activities in many institutions are motivated more by

Culver Pictures, Inc.

Educational program for institutionalized youths.

convenience for the staff than for the rehabilitation of residents. Despite the ideal of a "total effort made by the school to rehabilitate the child," one often finds in actual day-to-day operations more destructive than rehabilitative results.

Differences among correctional institutions in management directions led Cressey (1965) to place prisons on a continuum varying from authoritarian control to rehabilitation (or treatment in the broad sense). At the end of authoritarian control, there is emphasis on custody and the prevention of escapes, there are rigid relationships between staff members and inmates, but there is little interest in rehabilitation. At the other end of Cressey's continuum are the institutions that follow the model given by the Children's Bureau for training schools, where every staff member has a definite role in a broad therapeutic environment. Rather than coercion and control, there are collaborative efforts between staff members and inmates aimed at solving problems and bringing about long-range change.

As various observers have pointed out (see, for example, Duffee, 1980, and Clear and Cole, 1986), most correctional institutions, prisons and training schools alike, fall between the ends of Cressey's continuum. There must almost always be control as a dominant consideration, but that may be more or less subject to amelioration by rehabilitative goals.

Reichel (1985) studied staff decision making in assigning youths to a cottage or treatment program at a state facility for male offenders. The evidence indicated that decisions were based on the same array of variables as those used by the police and court intake officers rather than on more relevant personal characteristics. The results seemed contrary to treatment goals, but specific decisions were rationalized rather than modified when staff members became aware of information pointing to their apparent inappropriateness.

The investigation of juvenile institutions by Wooden (1976:28, 29), to which he devoted three years of diligent effort, indicated two types of training school in operation:

> The first is a miniature penitentiary with high walls surrounding the grounds. All the buildings and cell block wings therein are interlocked by long corridors. Not only are individual cell doors secured, but each wing is also locked at all times. There is almost always a self-sufficient industrial complex on the grounds — laundry, hospital, maintenance shop and any other facility needed to keep strangers out and the children in. Dubious educational and religious services are available to the children, along with the standbys of solitary confinement and of bloodhounds to locate any who run away.
>
> The second and more common type of training school is the cottage system. . . . Those in charge are "house parents" rather than "guards." The outside area is usually quiet and pleasant and bears little semblance to a penal facility. The cottages are usually small, esthetically pleasing, dorm-like structures. . . . The windows are . . . secured with heavy wire and in the event of emergencies such as fire, escape would be impossible except through the front door.

Miniature Penitentiaries. The miniature penitentiary has virtually the same array of management problems as an adult prison. The residents must be clothed, fed, guarded, protected, kept healthy, rewarded or punished when appropriate, provided leisure activities and recreation, and so on. Clear and Cole

(1986) provide a comprehensive overview of the management structures and bureaucratic operations by which those ends are accomplished with inmates who are generally resistive to regimentation — in their words, "a Herculean undertaking" (1986:288). The most critical people in the enterprise are the correctional or custodial officers, who are the line personnel in almost continual contact with inmates. According to Clear and Cole (1986:310), "The officer is both a manager and a worker — a manager to the inmates, a low-status worker to the supervisors." While maintaining close daily contact with inmates, these officers must ordinarily maintain substantial psychological distance from them because of various problems of control in penitentiarylike settings.

Cottages. The structure of the cottage makes it possible to be less oriented toward control and more toward rehabilitation. The reasons given by Clear and Cole (1986:516) are as follows:

> First, residents can be made responsible for all of a cottage's care and maintenance, and thus learn self-sufficiency. Second, the small-group atmosphere helps in the main treatment approach used in the training school — peer-group counseling. Third, cottages can be coordinated with the classification of juveniles, so that each juvenile's housing assignment is related to the degree of security required. One training school in West Virginia uses this strategy. The residents of each cottage wear T-shirts of a distinctive color. As juveniles prove themselves worthy of greater freedom, they progress through cottage assignments from those with many restrictions to those with fewer.

Camps and Ranches. In forestry camps and ranches, youngsters spend the bulk of their time in such activities as fire control, road construction and maintenance, care of livestock, construction of buildings, reforestation, care of small trees in nurseries, and the processing of wood. There is little provision for formal education, although local schools do cooperate in offering special classes, and of course the entire working experience can be considered a form of vocational training. Supplementing the work activities, according to Breed (1953), are recreational and leisure programs ranging from individual and group sports to picnics and snow parties.

The Kettle Moraine Boys School in Wisconsin, a facility that seems to fall at the benign end of Cressey's continuum (as described in Miller et al., 1985), is located on 480 acres in a state forest ("without walls, fences, or bars," 1985:898). The boys live in twelve cottages containing twenty-five boys in individual rooms. General living arrangements are described as follows (1985:896):

> Emphasis is placed upon making community living a meaningful life experience. Each boy is expected to do his share of housekeeping and groundkeeping work. A boy's day begins when he arises at 6:30 a.m. After breakfast he cleans his room, and either attends school or goes to his work assignment. Upon completion of the school day there is a period of extracurricular activities, i.e., band, chorus, varsity sports, crafts, group counseling, and so forth.

There are both a formal educational program leading to high school diplomas or, at least, to transferable high school credits and a vocational program with training in such trades as printing, welding, automobile repair, drafting, and woodworking. Although a social worker is assigned to form a "constructive relationship" with each boy, it is expected that the entire staff will interact with each boy in a therapeutic manner.

Specific Modes of Treatment

Treatment approaches used in juvenile institutions include each of the following: traditional insight psychotherapy by psychiatrists and clinical psychologists; evaluation and interpretation of interpersonal relationships in the manner of transactional analysis; emphasis on the achievement of basic needs by responsible actions in accord with the precepts of reality therapy; changing behavior according to the reinforcement procedures derived from operant learning theory; group psychotherapy oriented toward the achievement of insight and emotional control; psychodrama, in which participants are directed to act out their emotions; social therapy in cottage settings, in which the entire environment becomes a therapeutic community; and guided group interaction in nonauthoritarian cottage settings, in which group homogeneity is used in decision making and the resolution of personal problems. More details about each of these approaches may be found in Bartollas and Miller (1978).

Gendreau and Ross (1983–1984) reviewed studies that evaluated the successes and failures of various correctional treatments. They found the majority of successful programs were derived from social learning models (particularly differential association theory; see Chapter 7), while unsuccessful programs were based on "friendship" models that stressed open communication and on the medical model, in which antisocial behavior could presumably be cured much like a disease.

It is perhaps obvious that different treatments will be differentially effective with different kinds of inmates — psychodrama, for example, might produce changes in certain kinds of youngsters but not with others, who might respond well to transactional analysis. But in the 1960s, there arose a "theory of differential treatment," which led to significant institutional changes in several states, primarily on the premise that the impact of a given treatment is a function of the type of violator. The early arguments leading to this differential treatment perspective may be found in Sullivan, Grant, and Grant (1957), Grant and Grant (1959), and Jesness (1967).

Treatment and Classification. If it is accepted that the impact of treatment varies with the characteristics of violators, one needs a classification scheme to accomplish the end of fitting treatment to violator. One such scheme was derived by researchers in the 1960s on the Community Treatment Project of the California Youth Authority (see California Youth Authority, 1969, and Warren, 1971) on the basis of the developmental theory of personality that was applied to delinquency by Sullivan, Grant, and Grant (1957). The system is founded on the notion that the developing child normally acquires the skills and sensitivities necessary for dealing with his or her environment in a progressive, integrative manner. Delinquency results if the requisite skills and sensitivities are not acquired at a given developmental stage.

In the classification system, there are seven levels of interpersonal maturity

(I-levels), ranging from I_1, where the youth is infantile in interpersonal maturity, to I_7, which represents the ultimate in maturity. Delinquents are almost always at levels I_2, I_3, or I_4, where I_2 youths show unsocialized egocentrism and low frustration tolerance, I_3 youths have only beginning understanding of the needs of others and relate to others on the basis of mutual power, and I_4 youths have some sophistication in the operation of the social world, but their extreme goal-directedness produces frustration and alienation. And within each of these levels are subtypes; thus I_2 youngsters may be asocial aggressive or asocial passive; I_3 youngsters may be immature conformists, cultural conformists, or manipulators; and I_4 youngsters may be acting-out neurotics, anxious neurotics, stress or adjustment reactors, or cultural identifiers.

Once a youth was classified by level and subtype, an optimum environment, an approach to treatment, and a work assignment could be determined, or so it was argued. For example, the preferred mode of treatment for I_4 acting-out neurotic youths was insight psychotherapy, and the preferred environmental setting for an I_4 cultural identifier was one of trust and loosely defined standards (see Lerman, 1975:26, 27, for a table relating I-level typology and treatment strategies).

It is perhaps of passing interest to note that Ferdinand (1978) found substantial relationship between that I-level classification scheme and the social backgrounds of institutionalized delinquent girls. For example, the immature conformist (I_3) came from a home where punishment was erratic and intrafamily male relationships were with brothers rather than with the father, while the asocial aggressive girl (I_2) often had a violent mother who used alcohol or drugs excessively.

The most intense and damaging criticisms of differential treatment and of the I-level mode of classification is by Lerman (1968, 1975). He dismissed several evaluations of the use of I-level theory in the determination of treatment strategies and concluded that there was no evidence for effectiveness. In addition, he pointed out the following shortcomings in the overall approach: a generally specific classification method was used to prescribe very vague treatment strategies, there was evidence that the I-level method was neither reliable nor valid, and although the logic of the overall theory indicates lower delinquency rates with higher maturity levels, the empirical data do not support that expectation.

Another classification scheme for the differential treatment of institutionalized juvenile offenders is based on the work of Peterson and Quay (1961) and Quay (1964), and developed comprehensively in Quay and Werry (1972). The scheme specifies four independent dimensions of behavior that are widely found among delinquents: aggressive behavior with poor interpersonal relationships, withdrawal behavior marked by feelings of anxiety and distress, awkward and inept behavior accompanied by escapist tendencies, and socialized delinquency where adequate social adjustment leads to induction into criminal behavior by peer influence.

That overall classification, augmented by subclassification based on checklists filled out by staff members and a questionnaire completed by offenders, was used at a federal institution in West Virginia to match youths with effective treatments. Unfortunately for the system, however, a report by Gerard (1970) indicated that the general thrust was not effective. The staff in the institution did not find that there were four differentiable dimensions of behavior and felt that the attempt to match treatment to offender type created more problems than solutions.

Staff-Inmate Interactions. Bartollas and Sieverdes (1983) studied the "games" played by 561 confined juveniles in six coeducational and progressive training schools in a southeastern state. There were staff-oriented and peer-oriented games; the former were aimed at manipulating desired behaviors from staff members, whereas the latter were aimed at the enhancement of prestige and self-image. Despite the relative freedom in the institutions and the absence of brutality, gamesmanship by residents was abundant—to gain privileges, to reduce control, to gain advantages over other residents, and to expedite release. The staff-oriented game used most frequently involved attempts to impress by dramatizing positive attitudes—females were more likely than males to use flattery in the process. The investigators concluded that their analyses of gamesmanship indicate that power-oriented relationships are the mode even in progressive institutions, and that state of affairs is not conducive to rehabilitation.

Benign Rhetoric Does Not Always Imply Benign Operations

As we saw in Chapter 7 and earlier in this chapter, juvenile institutions have been severely criticized from their initial years. It would not seem possible to select a decade, starting from those initial years, during which there was no substantial castigation of the institutions in articles and books. Teeters summarized several of the criticisms in 1950, stating (1950:589), "Many reports of reform schools present a bill of particulars regarding the inadequate physical plant, the decrepit buildings, the untrained staff or its frequent turnover, the poor food, poor sleeping arrangements, overcrowding." Moreover, the institutions were reported to be "repressive and inhumane," with such "sadistic punishments" as flogging, ice-cold baths, leg chains, bread-and-water diets, and shaving the hair off the heads of girls as well as boys.

The years between 1960 and 1977 saw major social stirring in the United States, motivated to a large extent by concern for the rights and needs of the poor, minority-group members, and women. And that concern was extended to other groups and individuals who were perceived as similarly downtrodden by social processes, including juveniles incarcerated in institutions, particularly jails. Moreover, the concern in the case of incarcerated juveniles was enhanced by several parallel developments in sociology and in law. These included the rise of labeling theory and its emphasis on the social augmentation of deviant behavior by the very processes used by society in attempts to eradicate the behavior; the rulings by the U.S. Supreme Court, in the *Kent* and *Gault* decisions, on the constitutional requirements of due process in the juvenile justice system; and the reports of the President's Commission on Law Enforcement and Administration of Justice and its task forces that were highly critical of institutional processes. The reports of the President's Commission and its task forces, incidentally, were strongly influenced by the sociological thought of the day because of the predominance of sociologists on the staff of and as consultants to the commission.

The era in question, 1960 to 1977, is marked by three important developments that resulted from the general concern about social underdogs and specific concern about institutionalized youths: the publication of several semipopular books that were lurid in their condemnation of juvenile institutionalization (as well as detention), the federal Juvenile Justice and Delinquency Prevention Act of 1974, and the deinstitutionalization of young offenders in Massachusetts.

The Books. Three books will be used to illustrate the powerful denunciation of institutionalization in the semipopular press — all three, reflecting reactions to the earlier concerns rather than initiators of those concerns, came toward the end of the period: *The Concrete Cradle* by Joseph Sorrentino (1975), *Weeping in the Playtime of Others: America's Incarcerated Children* by Kenneth Wooden (1976), and *Children in Jail: Seven Lessons in American Justice* by Thomas J. Cottle (1977). The titles themselves dramatically illustrate the negative attitudes of the authors toward institutionalization.

One may wonder why a book entitled *Children in Jail* would occur in this context since the assumption might be, given the discussions during the first part of this chapter, that jails are used for the detention rather than the institutionalization of children. Jails are indeed so used in the vast majority of cases, but juvenile court judges have been known to use adult jails (or prisons) for the placement of children after dispositional hearings in juvenile courts (sometimes, according to a report by the Children's Defense Fund [1976], in violation of state law). In addition, a few states allow the transfer of a youth to a jail (or prison) if he or she is considered especially dangerous or inappropriate for the juvenile facility for other reasons, and in some cases it is possible for a youth to spend considerable time in jail awaiting transfer to a juvenile correctional institution. But by far the largest proportion of juveniles in jails (or prisons) for long-range custody consists of youths committed there by criminal courts. The trial in criminal court could have come after a waiver hearing in the juvenile court that had original jurisdiction, or the criminal court could have had original jurisdiction on the basis of seriousness of the crime. For example, in Colorado, youths as young as fourteen may be prosecuted by direct filings in a criminal court for offenses that could lead to life imprisonment for adults, and in Florida sixteen- and seventeen-year-olds may be prosecuted directly in a criminal court if there seems to be a need for "adult sanctions."

1. *The Concrete Cradle* by Joseph Sorrentino

Sorrentino, a juvenile court judge who had overcome the liabilities of a turbulent youth that included institutionalization for assault, dramatically contrasts the benign goal of rehabilitation with actual institutional operations.

On the one hand, he observes (1975:161):

> The Institute for Juvenile Court Judges states the credo that juvenile courts . . . are imbued with the goal of rehabilitation. . . . Special stress is given to providing the proper institutional environment to youthful offenders.
>
> Customarily institutions for juveniles publish statements setting forth their program objectives. They express elaborate psychological methods of reclaiming the wayward youth for constructive citizenship. At the O. H. Close School for

Reuters/Bettmann Newsphotos

A former troop barge used in the Falkland Islands, at a dock in London. New York City has agreed to lease the 396-bed barge for use as a prison to help relieve overcrowding in prisons now filled to capacity. It should be noted that, beginning at age 13, youths in New York have full criminal responsibility for certain serious crimes, and sentences up to life imprisonment are possible.

Boys, transactional analysis, as developed by Dr. Eric Berne, has been adopted as the major treatment method. The Karl Hoeton School proudly boasts a "specific treatment approach for each ward using behavior modification principles." The Ventura School for Girls says it applies "reality therapy to change delinquent behavior." The Nelles School for Boys uses "principles of operant conditioning through contingency management." Whatever the method chosen, the uniformly stated aim of juvenile institutions is to reform, not punish, delinquents.

In practice, however, he found, during an inspection tour of institutional facilities, "deplorable conditions," the use of tranquilizing drugs to keep rebellious youths in stuporous condition, overcrowded "cesspools," widespread violence and homosexual behavior, and little effort devoted to treatment or even to the most basic medical needs. Moreover, many youngsters were kept in locked facilities for minor offenses. Sorrentino encountered one girl who had been incarcerated for three months because she planned to marry her boyfriend against her mother's wishes and was defined as "incorrigible." The writer concluded (1975:166), "It seems a bizarre legal system that permits a mother to jail a daughter to prevent her from getting married."

2. *Weeping in the Playtime of Others: America's Incarcerated Children* by Kenneth Wooden

Wooden (1976) found punitive isolation in nearly every facility he visited in thirty states. He described conditions as follows (1976:129, 130):

Solitary confinement is widely used in juvenile penal institutions throughout the United States. Just about every facility I have visited in thirty states has some form of punitive isolation for those children who break rules or are otherwise troublesome. In some tragic instances, isolation is even used for punishing the mentally retarded.

Solitary confinement consists in locking a child in a small, highly secure cell by himself for a period of time — it may be one day, it may be three months or longer. The rooms are dirty, damp, vermin-infested, vile-smelling, cold in the winter and hot in the summer. They usually have a bare mattress on the floor and a toilet or hole in the floor. Total silence is the rule. No talking, no reading, no visitations.

Most of the children I saw wore only underwear. Behind heavy steel and iron doors they would sit in whatever little sunlight was available; if the door had bars, they'd rest their arms and hands on the floor beyond the cell, as if reaching out to freedom from this institutional hellhole. I would stop to talk, to make conversation, but found passive, frozen faces, concealing hurt, rage, determination or hopelessness.

Wooden found, on the one hand, that boys were frequently subjected to brutal physical punishment in institutions but that, on the other hand, girls were more commonly subjected to extreme psychological indignities. The superintendent at the Indiana Boys School in Plainfield told Wooden that in previous years when "any inmates ran, they were beaten, then thrown into solitary" (1976:50). He showed Wooden the leather straps used in the beatings. According to Wooden (1976:50):

They were 26 inches long, 3 inches wide and $\frac{1}{2}$ inch thick. The handles were stained from sweat, the ends worn thin by those who administered the beatings. The youngsters who were to be disciplined were placed on wooden racks at an appointed time (4 P.M.) "with their ass up in the air." The big debate was "should they beat the boys with their trousers on or off." When the leather strap had no effect, the guards would "take them out in the cornfield and beat the piss out of them."

As one illustration of the indignities to which girls are subjected, he writes (1976:121):

In matters of personal hygiene and cleanliness, once again, incarcerated girls suffer greater indignities than their male counterparts. Most female facilities have no individual toilets. An assortment of old pee pots, coffee cans and other crude containers are issued for disposal of body wastes. At Artesia Hall, a private institution in Texas, the girls were forced to urinate in Coke bottles for punishment. The Texas Youth Council publicly hangs a "Monthly Menstruation Report" on the door of all female cottages which lists every inmate (regardless of whether she menstruates or not) and records the onset and finish of each menses. Physical examinations of girls being admitted to the Sheldon Farm for Girls in Pennsylvania determine whether they are virgins or not. Virgins are assigned one color dress; all others wear a different color.

Examinations for venereal disease are carried out with outrageous frequency. Young ladies in custody have been known to undergo as many as three and four pelvic exams for the disease. At some facilities, ten- and eleven-year-olds are forced to submit to "vaginals" each time they are transferred to a new facility, even though they have not been released between placements. In one town in Louisiana two detectives complained to me about the county coroner, who forcefully examined all runaways: "You know when he is working because you can hear the young girls screaming at the other end of the hall."

3. *Children in Jail: Seven Lessons in American Justice* by Thomas J. Cottle

The final book in this trio of examples, that of Cottle (1977), provides descriptions of children in jail based on several years of conversations with them. A case from the book, that of Bobbie Dijon who was being detained in jail, was presented earlier in this chapter. Another youth discussed by Cottle, Fernall Hoover (again a fictitious name), was sentenced to three to five years in prison for breaking and entering and carrying a gun. He spent two and a half years in prison and was placed in solitary confinement three times, the first time at the age of sixteen. The youth described the solitary experience to Cottle as follows (1977:35):

> "First thing I realized, man, I didn't know the time. Room had no windows so I never could tell. Sometimes, you know, when you ain't sleeping you can sort of tell how many minutes passed you by. But when you're sleeping, you don't know. Ain't got no clock, ain't got no sounds to help you. You're in a cell. First I thought, I can dig it, they bring me my food, I'll make out, you know what I'm saying? But after a while they got you talking to yourself. I'd be standing in there yelling loud as I could, 'Tell me the time. *Tell me the time.*' Ain't no one going to answer you. You know that, but it don't stop you. You just keep on yelling, *'Tell me the time. Is it the day or the night?'*
>
> "Pretty soon, man, I figure I'm going crazy. I ain't even seen where I am. Suddenly the whole cell gets real light, you know, and I'm blinking my eyes so's I can get used to it. Then when I open 'em I can't see nothing. It's still black in there, 'cause I only *imagined* they turned the lights on. Then I start talking to myself, 'You ain't going crazy, man. You're doing all right. You're going to be all right. Believe me, you're going to be all right. Just hang in there.' So I tell myself, 'Think about the future, man, think about how it's going to be for you when you get out. Make it like a picture in your mind,' you know what I mean."

Another youngster, Angela, fifteen years of age, was sentenced to a juvenile institution for a period of "no less than one year" (1977:88) for breaking into a food store and stealing money and food. But she spent seven months in a county jail for women before being transferred to the correctional institution. Angela's experiences in the jail well illustrate the sexual dangers to which youngsters are exposed in adult facilities. She stated (1977:91):

> "Another night this other woman comes up to me in the hall with a goddam tonic bottle. You believe this? I goes, 'What the hell you think you're going to do with *that?*' She goes, 'Come on baby lady, let's see what you got under there.' So she starts to lift up my skirt and I push her away, only she laughs. Then she's coming at me again, only this time she's starting to take off her dress. No kidding. She ain't got anything on underneath. So here I am, fifteen years old, standing in this goddam corridor of this goddam jail with a sex maniac coming at me with a root beer bottle in her hand. And she ain't kidding either. I ain't about to yell for no one 'cause when they caught you messing around like that they'd put you both in solitary for four, maybe five, days. And when you've been in there like I was — they

put me in there the first time 'cause they heard I was going to try to escape after a show one night, which was a lie — you know you'll do anything, including getting raped, before you'll go back."

After telling Cottle lurid details of various homosexual encounters, Angela asked (1977:93), "So what else do you want to know about my days in the *ladies'* penitentiary?" And to show how resigned she eventually became to the whole state of affairs, there is the comment (1977:95), "I figured, they're giving me clean clothes, they're giving me food, I'm only getting raped once every couple of weeks, what I got to complain about?"

Although matters improved greatly after Angela was transferred to the juvenile institution, there remained an "overriding feeling of hopelessness" with a fair degree of certainty that "she was destined to return to this or some other comparable institution" (1977:93).

The Federal Juvenile Justice and Delinquency Prevention Act of 1974 (JJDP Act). The second major expression of concern about the institutionalization of juveniles was in the form of the JJDP Act of 1974. The chief sponsor of this act was Senator Birch Bayh, a strong proponent of human rights and welfare over his long political career. The act was far-reaching in its accomplishments; for example, it established the Office of Juvenile Justice and Delinquency Prevention in the Department of Justice, it authorized that office to make grants to states and local governments for the purpose of funding programs aimed at the reduction and control of delinquency, it created a center for evaluation and research by the name of the National Institute for Juvenile Justice and Delinquency Prevention, and it provided $350 million over a three-year period so that the preceding provisions could be carried out.

But most important for present purposes were the provisions in the act for preventing the placing of status offenders in locked facilities and requiring that delinquents be housed separately from incarcerated adults. Since Congress cannot dictate to the states in matters of criminal and juvenile justice under the federal system delineated in the U.S. Constitution, there was no way that compliance with those provisions could be mandated. So Congress used a carrot-and-stick approach made possible by its taxing and allocation powers — an approach used in such other areas as insistence on a maximum speed limit over all states and an attempt to set a minimum drinking age of twenty-one for alcoholic beverages. As mentioned earlier, Congress allocated a substantial amount of money for grants and other provisions of the JJDP Act. But, in order to receive funds, each state had to submit a plan to carry out the provisions of the act and related provisions in an earlier act (the Omnibus Crime Control and Safe Streets Act of 1968). And the state plan had to (Public Law 93-415, Title II Sec. 223[a])

   (12) provide within two years after submission of the plan that juveniles who are charged with or who have committed offenses that would not be criminal if committed by an adult, shall not be placed in juvenile detention or correctional facilities, but must be placed in shelter facilities;
   (13) provide that juveniles alleged to be or found to be delinquent shall not be detained or confined in any institution in which they have regular contact

with adult persons incarcerated because they have been convicted of a crime or are awaiting trial on criminal changes.

The effort to keep youngsters out of locked facilities is commonly called *deinstitutionalization* even though it may apply to detention facilities as well as correctional institutions. As important as the 1974 federal legislation was, it was not the initiator of the notion of deinstitutionalization of status offenders. For example, one year earlier, in 1973, the state of Maryland had forbidden the detention and institutionalization of status offenders (see Rubin, 1983). And in that year, the National Advisory Commission on Criminal Justice Standards recommended prohibiting courts from sending status offenders to institutions for delinquents.

Several important organizations have recommended going considerably beyond deinstitutionalizing status offenders by removing them from the jurisdiction of the juvenile court entirely. In its report of 1967, the Task Force on Juvenile Delinquency of the President's Commission considered the advantages and disadvantages of that type of action in some detail but decided on the milder recommendation (1967:27) that "serious consideration should be given complete elimination from the court's jurisdiction of conduct illegal only for a child."

But other organizations were far less cautious in unequivocally recommending that the juvenile court have no jurisdiction over status offenders. These organizations include the National Council on Crime and Delinquency, the Massachusetts Committee on Children and Youth, the Oklahoma State Chamber of Commerce, the American Legion's National Americanism and Children and Youth Division, the National Association of Counties, and the Association of Junior Leagues. Hickey (1977) has presented a full listing of organizations that took that position up to the year of his writing and a thorough presentation of the justifications. In brief, they follow: (1) status offenses call for the help of mental health and youth-serving agencies rather than the strong arm of the law, (2) the separation by many states of offending youths into delinquent and status offense categories (PINS, CHINS, etc.) has failed to produce the distinctively different treatments intended — as we have seen above, for example, there have been at least as many status offenders in some jails as serious delinquents, (3) contrary to the positions of many in law enforcement, a status offense may not reasonably be considered a prelude to later criminal behavior, and (4) often criminal law violations are plea-bargained down to status offenses and the process produces a disrespect for law.

Clearly, there were many forces in society that created an appropriate *Zeitgeist* for passage of legislation like the JJDP Act. But, because of various mediating forces, there was a softening of the provisions of the act over subsequent years. In 1977, Congress reauthorized the JJDP Act for three years at a considerably higher appropriation and extended from two to three years the time allowance for deinstitutionalizing status offenders. But more importantly, the amendments of the 1977 legislation allowed the administrator of the Office of Juvenile Justice and Delinquency Prevention to extend the deadline even beyond the three-year limit if there was "substantial compliance" on the part of a state. Further amendment came in 1980, when "substantial compliance" was defined in terms of "achievement of deinstitutionalization of not less than 75 percentum of such juveniles or through removal of such juveniles from secure correctional facilities and . . . through appropriate executive or legislative action, an unequivocal commitment to achieving full compliance within a reasonable time not exceeding two additional years" (Public Law 96-509). The 75 per cent removal stipulation in the amendment applied only to secure institutions and not to secure detention facilities. Moreover, the amendments of 1980 allowed juveniles who run away from court-ordered placements in shelter homes to be charged with contempt of court and detained as a result of that offense (which is a criminal-type, not a status, offense).

We turn now to the effects of the act and its amendments. A report in 1980 by Paul and Watt that summarized statutes relative to deinstitutionalization stated (1980:1):

> Since the Act has been in effect, 47 states have agreed to the outlined requirements, including the deinstitutionalization of status offenders, and received funds appropriated under the Act. Nebraska, Oklahoma, and Wyoming have never participated, while South Dakota, North Dakota, and Nevada voluntarily withdrew from the Act after initial participation. The reasons for nonparticipation often involve fundamental disagreements with the federal deinstitutionalization and separation [of children from adults] requirements. Some states view the financial incentive as insufficient contrasted with the expenditure of state funds necessary to achieve compliance with the Act.

But a closer look at the various statutes indicates that the preceding summary may be somewhat misleading. Even among the forty-four states that agreed to participate and never withdrew, there was wide disparity in the actual degree of deinstitutionalization. For example, only twenty-three states (as of 1980) had statutes prohibiting the committing of status offenders to secure institutions. Other states have had disagreements with various aspects of the deinstitutionalization requirement and had statutes that generally prohibit placing status offenders in secure facilities followed by language permitting secure detention or institutionalization under certain conditions. These exceptions most often included the following (Paul and Watt, 1980:3): "(1) runaways, (2) juveniles not amenable to treatment in an open facility, (3) juveniles who are a danger to themselves or others, and (4) second time alleged or adjudicated status offenders." A full ten of the forty-four states allowed status offenders to be detained in or committed to a secure facility without stated restrictions, and in a few others, there was a prohibition against sending a status offender to a state training school but not to a secure private facility.

Thus, one is not inclined to conclude that the JJDP Act of 1974 and its amendments had a comprehensive, unambiguous effect on state legislation even in the case of states that agreed to the requirements of the acts and received funding. On the other hand, Kobrin and Klein (1982; 1983) reported significant reductions in the actual detention and institutionalization of status offenders in an evaluation of deinstitutionalization at a number of sites where special programs received funding from the Office of Juvenile Justice and Delinquency Prevention. The average reduction in detention was 43 per cent, and the average reduction in institutionalization was 67 per cent. The investigators commented (1982:24, 25), "Taking these two sets of data together, it seems clear that a reduction in secure placement of status offenders did take place during the program period." But the level of deinstitutionalization never did come close to zero, and, in fact, five jurisdictions showed an actual increase in secure detention of status offenders.

The results of the Handler et al. (1982) study of deinstitutionalization in seven states are in agreement with those of Kobrin and Klein (1982; 1983), leading to the conclusion (1982:88), "the most basic goal of deinstitutionalization—that status offenders no longer be sent to the large red-brick institutions—has been substantially accomplished." Lerman (1980:282), on the other hand, was less certain of the accomplishments of deinstitutionalization when he cautioned that "a new youth-in-trouble institutional system" may have evolved in the form of private homes and shelters. As Schneider (1984:423) has observed, "The decline in status offender commitments to public correctional facilities after 1974 was accompanied by a marked increase in the number of these youths committed to private correctional institutions. When the private and public commitments are combined, the total number of youths designated as status offenders in correctional facilities reached 12,354 in 1977 —compared with a combined total of 9,613 in 1974." Dore, Young, and Pappenfort (1984) compared the results of the 1981 national survey of residential facilities for children with the results of the 1966 survey to assess the effects of deinstitutionalization (and similar emphases in mental health). Of a total of 4,814 residential facilities for youths with special needs in 1981, 1,642 were juvenile justice facilities. That represented almost a tripling from the 647 in 1966. The increase resulted for the most part from the larger number of private facilities (from 20 per cent of the total in 1966 to 37 per cent in 1981). Of most importance to the investigators was the striking reduction over the fifteen years in average size of facility, including those in juvenile justice. More than three fourths in 1981 had capacities for under fifty-one youths, and more than half had twenty or fewer residents.

It is important to note, however, that the figures given by Schneider (1984) and by Dore, Young, and Pappenfort (1984) are based on institutions and ignore the effect of deinstitutionalization on detention, where the confinement of status offenders was most obvious prior to the effects of the 1974 act.

In her summary of the effects of the deinstitutionalization process, Schneider (1984) pointed out that Utah experimented with removal of the jurisdiction of the juvenile court over runaways and truants (but not such other status offenders as incorrigibles and tobacco and alcohol users) between 1971 and 1975. But, as of the date of her report—1984—only two states (Washington and Maine) had laws that (1984:411) "the juvenile court cannot detain, petition, adjudicate, or place a youth on probation for the behaviors previously identified as status offenses." Services for youths are expected to be provided by community agencies on a voluntary basis.

However, several studies have shown that these services are often not available in states where there is court jurisdiction but no incarceration, as well as in the states where there is no court jurisdiction whatsoever over status offenders. The absence of needed services has been reported by Schneider, McKelvey, and Schram (1983) and by Handler et al. (1982), among others.

Finally, Bortner, Sunderland, and Winn (1985) examined the interaction between race and deinstitutionalization in a midwestern metropolitan county. Their data came from 32,000 referrals to the juvenile court over a two-year period prior to the state's compliance with the 1974 federal act (1973–1974) and a two-year period after compliance (1976–1977). They observed a slight trend toward lesser use of secure detention and greater informality, but overall there was little change in court operations or policy over the two time periods. Most startlingly, the rate of detention for black status offenders, particularly females, was actually greater during the latter period than during the former one.

In conclusion, it is clear that in general the placement of status offenders in secure facilities has decreased greatly since the first federal legislation in 1974 —but the process of secure placement for them has not ended. Moreover, it is not clear, first, how many such youths are now sent to private facilities, including shelters and group homes, instead of the public institutions, and, second, whether appropriate services are being provided for misbehaving children when courts lose jurisdiction or lose interest because of the removal of their punitive tool of incarceration.

Deinstitutionalization in Massachusetts. The third major expression of concern about the institutionalization of juveniles took the form of deinstitutionalization in Massachusetts. The deinstitutionalization in this section refers to a process whereby *all* offenders, even serious delinquents, were released from correctional institutions —and almost all of the institutions were subsequently closed, permanently. Detailed reviews of Massachusetts deinstitutionalization, its antecedents and aftermath, may be found in Bakal (1973), Serrill (1975a; 1975b; 1975c), Ohlin, Coates, and Miller (1974; 1975), Holden (1976), Ohlin, Miller, and Coates (1976), Coates, Miller, and Ohlin (1978), Wilson (1978), and Bakal and Polsky (1979).

The process leading to that radical deinstitutionalization started in the 1960s —as did many of the other processes that led to change in juvenile justice. Several groups of citizens, including that Massachusetts Committee on Children and Youth, the League of Women Voters, and the Massachusetts Society for the Prevention of Cruelty to Children, demanded reform of the state's juvenile correctional institutions. The groups charged that children were beaten and psychologically abused in the institutions, that solitary confinement was used extensively and brutally, and that unnecessary regimentation took such forms as shaving heads and marching in formation. Two of the institutions to which the reformers directed their attention, interestingly, were the Lyman School for Boys at Westboro, founded in 1846, and the Industrial School for Girls at Lancaster, founded in 1854. These were, as discussed earlier in this book, the first public correctional institutions in the United States for boys and girls, respectively.

Six major investigations of the institutions in the latter 1960s, including one by the U.S. Department of Health, Education, and Welfare (1966), generally confirmed the criticisms of the advocates for reform. But the Division of Youth Services (DYS), which administered the institutions, defended its methods, and the director of DYS was an articulate spokesman for the general philosophy of the institutions.

A reform-minded man became governor of Massachusetts in 1969 with outspoken support for the groups advocating change in juvenile institutions. He asked for the resignation of the director of DYS and set up a committee to find a qualified replacement. The committee selected Jerome Miller, a faculty member from the School of Social Work at Ohio State University. Before making the actual appointment, the governor strengthened Miller's position by making DYS an autonomous department and calling its head the commissioner rather than the director. The governor indicated his strong desire for major change in these words (Serrill, 1975c:30–31): "I had been to some of the state and county [training schools] and God, I was repulsed—to think that we were paying something like $10,000 a year just to keep a kid in a cage without any type of rehabilitation. It was just really horrible. And I figured that if I didn't do any other damn thing while I was governor, I was going to [change] that system."

Miller took on the job of commissioner with great gusto and issued a series of directives aimed at making the juvenile institutions more like therapeutic communities. One of his first directives was to allow the youths in institutions to wear their hair in any way they chose. Many others followed, including an order to permit youths to wear street clothes rather than institutional garb, an order that forbade physical abuse and harsh sanctions even in the institution that housed the most disturbed and rebellious youngsters (corporal punishment was not against the law in Massachusetts at the time), a directive that removed control of cigarette allocation from staff members, who used that control for reward and punishment, and a directive that discontinued the policy of silent marching in formation between activities.

Those relatively minor changes were followed by such major ones as creating programs for boys and girls in the same institution, establishing coed cottages, reducing considerably the average length of stay for youths in the institutions (from eight months to three months), and recruiting and placing loyal adherents to Miller's philosophy of institutionalization. There was initial grumbling by a staff that had grown accustomed to the status quo. That mild resistance turned to open rebellion as it became clear that Miller intended to change the operations of the institutions radically. The rebellion took such forms as heckling Miller at public meetings and propagandizing people with a stake in the system, such as judges, probation officers, police officials, and legislators.

In 1971, Miller decided that he would not be able to bring about the reform he intended because of staff opposition and because the controversy he created reduced considerably the time he could remain as commissioner. That led to the conclusion that the only way to change the system was to eliminate it. As reported in *Science* (Holden, 1976:447):

> He [Miller] is quoted in a 1973 issue of the Boston *Real Paper* as saying: "My goal was to tear down the system to the point where Heinrich Himmler and the SS couldn't put it back together again." Unable to fire political appointees who had gained Civil Service status, he simply pulled the rug out from under them by abolishing their fiefdoms. In less than 2 years, Miller closed down all six training schools, whose population only a few years before had been 800.

As reported earlier, the Lyman School for Boys in Westboro, Massachusetts, was the first public institution of its kind when it opened in 1846. According to Serrill (1975c:29), the closing of the Lyman School by Miller on January 17, 1972, "was a spectacular event, in which a caravan of cars and motorcycles descended on the institution, picked up thirty-nine remaining youngsters, and

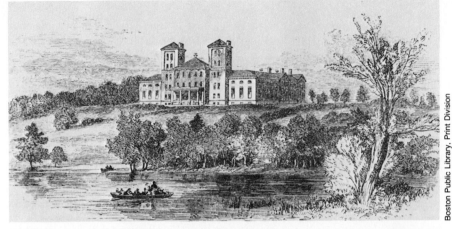

The Lyman School for Boys in Westboro, Massachusetts, as seen in 1860. It opened in 1846 as the first American reform school and was closed in 1972 as part of a move toward deinstitutionalization.

sped off to the University of Massachusetts at Amherst, where the youngsters stayed until homes were found for them."

Closing the institutions, of course, created the problem of finding other types of placement for the youths. A conference was organized at the University of Massachusetts to arrange for the transfer of a large number of youths to the community. In addition to formerly incarcerated youths and DYS staff members, college students from three colleges and universities in the area participated in the conference. The college students served as advocates for the youths while arrangements were being made for their placement. About two thirds were placed in community settings as a result of deliberations at the conference; about equal numbers of the remaining youths were placed in a private facility, ran away, or were not placed. The youths sent to the private facility were considered too disturbed or too dangerous to be set free. Interestingly, Ohlin, Coates, and Miller (1974:96) reported that staff members at Lyman were so aghast at the whole undertaking that they circulated "rumors of mass escapes, chaos, and widespread sexual misconduct at the Conference." The goal was to arouse the public so that there would be insistence that the youths be brought back to the institution. That effort was at least partially deflated when one university official commented that (1974:96) "the DYS youth had actually been less trouble to the university than a convention of the American Legion."

The number of youngsters who remained in secure facilities after Miller's deinstitutionalization was about fifty. And despite continuing opposition to the policy by such people as angry judges, legislators, and police officers, the number of youths in secure facilities ranged between about fifty and seventy in the era 1975–1978 (see Holden, 1976; Wilson, 1978). The remaining youths committed to DYS were sent to a large array of nonresidential programs, to group homes, to foster homes, to a large boarding school, and to "concept houses" modeled on drug-free programs for adults. To avoid the difficulties of terminating incompetent people under civil service in future arrangements, private contractors were used in all components on a "payment-for-service" basis.

Miller's expectation of a short tenure as commissioner of DYS was fulfilled. He resigned in 1972 to become director of the Department of Family and Children's Services in Illinois. He was fired by the governor of Illinois from that position in August 1974 and went to Pennsylvania as commissioner of the Office of Children and Youth, the state agency responsible for delinquents. That affairs did not go any better for Miller in Pennsylvania is shown in the following article from the *Philadelphia Inquirer* of July 12, 1976 (pages 1-B and 3-B):

> When Dr. Jerome G. Miller was put in charge of treatment for the state's juvenile offenders, he arrived with a firm commitment to replace the old, large lockups with private homes or small group facilities.
>
> Today, however, the swelling turmoil and debate caused by Miller's "deinstitutionalization" philosophy and his outspoken style threaten not only to wipe out his meager progress but to topple him as well.
>
> Since his appointment 14 months ago as Pennsylvania's Commissioner of Children and Youth, Miller, 44, has attracted the scorn of many of the state's juvenile judges and lately has become the target of a special Senate investigation.
>
> The hostility directed against Miller stems mainly from his decision to close to juveniles the State Correctional Institution at Camp Hill.

© Bill Powers, Frost Pub. Group, Inc.

A cell at the Camp Hill institution in Pennsylvania that Jerome Miller decided to close while he was the state commissioner of children and youth.

But his troubles also reflect the larger controversy in juvenile corrections circles over whether repeat youthful offenders need more or less institutional confinement.

And, indeed, Miller was fired from his job in Pennsylvania and moved on to become head of a nonprofit agency whose aim is correctional reform.

The Right to Treatment

A development within the field of mental health that has had profound implications for juvenile institutionalization is the right to treatment, a concept initially articulated by Birnbaum, a physician and attorney, in 1960. Clearly, the juvenile justice system could easily have expected this extrapolation given the many criticisms of institutionalization. Several states have specifications in their codes giving mentally disturbed people the right to treatment if they are committed to public hospitals. As an example, the code of the District of Columbia states that "a person hospitalized in a public hospital for a mental illness shall, during his hospitalization, be entitled to medical and psychiatric care and treatment" (D.C. Code, sec. 21-562, 1981).

That statement in the D.C. code led to an important court decision in 1966. A man by the name of Rouse was acquitted by reason of insanity on the criminal charge of carrying a deadly weapon, and was then committed to a mental institution. The misdemeanor offense implied a maximum sentence of one year, but Rouse remained hospitalized for three years. He filed a petition for release, contending that he did not receive the treatment that the D.C. law required during his three years at the mental hospital (which exceeded in length the maximum penalty for the misdemeanor offense). The ultimate decision by a federal appeals court (*Rouse v. Cameron,* 373 F. 2d 451, 1966) agreed with that contention but, perhaps more important, suggested that there may be a constitutional right to treatment based on due process requirements (Fourteenth Amendment) and the prohibition of cruel and unusual punishment (Eighth Amendment). A constitutional right, it should be pointed out, exists even though there is not a specification of that right in a code, as in the D.C. code above.

In 1972, another court decision extended the thrust of *Rouse v. Cameron.* A complaint by residents in Alabama hospitals for the mentally ill led a federal district court to hold that there indeed was a constitutional right to treatment for patients involuntarily committed through civil proceedings (*Wyatt v. Stickney,* 344 F. Supp. 373, 1972). And the decision was affirmed by an appeals court ruling. It decreed that civil commitment occurs without the procedural safeguards (due process requirements) of a criminal trial and that treatment provides the justification, or *quid pro quo,* for involuntary commitment. The court went even further in specifying three fundamental conditions for effective treatment: a humane physical and psychological environment, a qualified staff that is large enough to administer adequate treatment, and plans for treatment that are designed in accord with individual needs.

Summarizing subsequent developments, as well as future prospects, in the arena of the right to treatment in mental health, Beis (1984:150) has written:

The Supreme Court [of the United States] has never explicitly endorsed this *quid pro quo* theory. In fact, Chief Justice Burger rejected it in his separate opinion in *O'Connor v. Donaldson* [422 U.S. 563, 1975]. Nevertheless, many writers conclude that the theory remains forceful and vigorous. They point to the frequent use of the theory by federal courts, the absence of Supreme Court action striking down the theory, and the unanimity of favorable law review commentary.

Many courts have equated civil commitment without treatment to punishing persons for their disabilities. Punishment for mental disease is thought to be an infliction of cruel and unusual punishment. Even if treatment is provided, administering such treatment in inadequate facilities may constitute cruel and unusual punishment.

Historically, the philosophical basis for the juvenile court was *parens patriae* (as derived from equity or civil proceedings). The court was geared to help and rehabilitation rather than to punishment, and nonadversary processes were used without the usual due process standards. Accordingly, the juvenile proceeding was often conceptualized as civil rather than criminal. It is easy to see, therefore, how the arguments for the right to treatment in the case of mental health patients might be applied in the case of institutionalized juvenile offenders. In both cases, one sees involuntary commitment by civil proceeding, a goal of treatment rather than punishment, and the notion of a trade-off, or *quid pro quo,* between forfeiture of the due process requirements of a criminal trial and an informal proceeding aimed toward help and rehabilitation. (For a fuller explication of the similarities between civil proceedings in mental health and adjudicatory hearings in juvenile justice, and their implications for the right to treatment, see Renn, 1973.) The *quid pro quo* nature of the juvenile proceeding has, of course, been discussed throughout this century, but Ketcham, a juvenile court judge, most directly anticipated the later right-to-treatment arguments in his statement (1961:100):

> [The mutual compact between delinquent and the state] can be regarded as an agreement whereby the state, through the juvenile court, is permitted to intervene, under broadly defined conditions of delinquency or violations of the law, in the lives of families who have given up certain of their constitutional safeguards . . . such an intrusion of governmental supervision is premised on the assumption that the state will act in the best interests of the child and that its intervention will affirmatively enhance the child's welfare. Applying the contractual analogy, it follows that unless the state satisfactorily performs its obligations under the compact, the juvenile and his parents should have the right to consider the agreement broken and to repossess their full constitutional rights.

As discussed earlier in this chapter, Wooden (1976) reported on extremely cruel treatment at the Indiana Boys School in Plainfield. That cruelty led to a class action suit alleging violation of Eighth Amendment (prohibition of cruel and unusual punishment) and Fourteenth Amendment (requirement of due process to deprive a person of liberty) rights. The court agreed with the plaintiffs and ordered changes at the institution to eliminate the cruel practices. But, of more relevance to current considerations, the court, in a separate judgment, declared that the boys had a right to adequate rehabilitative treatment. The decisions were appealed to a federal circuit court.

The appeals court agreed with the district court (*Nelson v. Heyne,* 491 F. 2d at 358, 1974):

> The district court decided that both Indiana law and the federal Constitution secure for juvenile offenders a "right to treatment," and that the School failed to provide minimal rehabilitative treatment. Defendants contend that there exists no right to treatment under the Constitution or Indiana law, and that if there is the right, the Quay Classification System used at the School did not violate the right. We hold, with the district court, that juveniles have a right to rehabilitative treatment.
>
> The right to rehabilitative treatment for juvenile offenders has roots in the general social reform of the late nineteenth century, was nurtured by court decisions throughout the first half of this century, and has been established in state and federal courts in recent years.

The court went even further in stating that the right to treatment implied a minimum acceptable standard for *individualized* care and treatment.

Another case of significance in the right to treatment for incarcerated juveniles was originated by a class action suit on behalf of children committed to the custody of the Texas Youth Council (TYC). Wooden (1976:8, 9) had such comments as the following to illustrate the brutality in TYC facilities:

> "Crumb" or "sitting on lost privileges" is usually reserved for weekends. The student is forced to sit facing a wall or fence all day, forbidden to speak or fall asleep.

> at the Crockett School, female offenders are often placed in handcuffs and beaten.

> For the boys the most fearsome threat is the constant reminder of Mountain View, the maximum security facility down the road from Gatesville. With its high double fence topped with massive rolls of barbed wire and patrolled by armed guards in jeeps, the facility is imposing and menacing. The reputation is deadly.

> Here the guard administers blows to the child's bare back with the palm of his hand while the boy kneels with his head between the guard's legs. "Running in place" puts the youngster in the same position except the guard runs in place. The friction to the sides of the head causes burning and severe headaches.

The plaintiffs in the class action suit complained not only of abuses such as those described above but of tear gas, mace, and similar chemicals used to control crowds in many of the TYC facilities. The trial led to orders from a federal district court that proscribed the blatant abuses and set specific changes that were required for adequate care and treatment. In no uncertain terms, the court in *Morales v. Turman* (383 F. Supp. 53, 1974) declared a constitutional right to treatment that included a set of minimum standards given in detail, as the following examples illustrate (at 105):

> **4.** A psychological staff, to consist of psychologists holding either Master's degrees or Doctorates in psychology and experienced in work with adolescents, sufficient in number to meet the needs of the children.
> **5.** Provision of either individual or group psychotherapy for every child for whom it is indicated.

A ruling by an appeals court (*Morales v. Turman,* 562 F. 2d 993, 1977) acknowledged the appropriate use of the Eighth Amendment's prohibition of cruel and unusual punishment to correct the abuses in TYC facilities, but it denied any constitutional right to treatment. In the words of the decision (at 998): "The case law has not universally accepted a right to treatment for the mentally ill. . . . The argument for a right to treatment is even less strong as related to juvenile offenders." And the appeals court was particularly disdainful of the specific treatment requirements given by the trial judge.

This is where the issue of the right to treatment in juvenile justice stands at the moment. While several lower federal and state courts have continued to base decisions on the constitutional right to treatment (e.g., *Martarella v. Kelley,* 349 F. Supp. 575, 1972; *Pena v. New York State Division for Youth,* 419 F. Supp. 203, 1976; and *Morgan v. Sproat,* 432 F. Supp. 1130, 1977), no federal appeals court has acknowledged the constitutionally based right to treatment since 1974. While the U.S. Supreme Court has not ruled on the issue, the statements in *Donaldson v. O'Connor* (422 U.S. 563, 1975) do not indicate a great deal of sympathy in that court for right-to-treatment arguments.

One obvious and persisting result of the right-to-treatment cases has been court-ordered improvements in the care and handling of institutionalized juveniles. As mentioned in the several cases reviewed above, arguments of cruelty and abusiveness on the part of staff have been components of all suits. The assertion of a constitutionally based right to rehabilitative treatment, that is, has been accompanied by demands for the cessation of cruel and unusual punishment (as required by the Eighth Amendment). The validity of these demands has been acknowledged by appeals courts as well as trial courts; the result has been change, often court supervised, in the day-to-day treatment of the youngsters. For example, there were extensive improvements in the training schools operated by TYC after the *Morales* decision, even given the serious reservations by the appeals court about the right-to-treatment arguments. Those improvements included significant personnel changes, the discontinuance of abusive practices, and the elimination of clearly inadequate facilities.

It might not be unreasonable to argue for that as an optimum resolution, given the dependence of right-to-treatment arguments on a medical model for delinquency. Woody and Associates (1984:95) summarize the issue nicely:

> While guaranteeing institutionalized juveniles a right to treatment is one step to ensure a rehabilitative milieu, there are inherent problems in juvenile treatment that is based generally on a medical model. The deviant juvenile is considered to be someone who can be "cured" through proper treatment. In point of fact, no one has developed a reliable treatment to cure the "disease" of delinquency. Moreover, it is a dangerous assumption that any type of treatment will benefit "sick" delinquents more than allowing them to mature without institutional intervention.

Interestingly, Robinson (1980) has raised similar issues even in the realm of mental illness, where the very name implies the medical model. He bases his position on Thomas Szasz's contention that there is a "myth of mental illness" that has become the foundation for a gigantic psychiatric/psychological enterprise with multiple "therapies." In Robinson's words (1980:138), there are "grave doubts . . . about the value, the validity, and the very conceptual foundations of these therapies"; therefore, "To say . . . that the involuntary patient has a right to treatment may finally be translated to mean that he has the macabre right to be the involuntary subject of an aimless experiment."

Those positions define the controversy regarding a constitutionally based right to treatment for incarcerated juveniles. Whatever the ultimate directions taken by the courts on the issue, it seems clear that the right to treatment will be a viable basis for action in states where there is a code specifying that right. But a decision of the U.S. Supreme Court (104 S. Ct. 900, 1984) makes it likely that the use of state courts rather than federal courts will be required for such actions.

Parole

Whatever the conditions that led to the incarceration of a youth, and whatever the conditions and interactions of the incarceration, the youth will eventually be released from the institution. In the words of the Task Force on Corrections, President's Commission on Law Enforcement and Administration of Justice (1967:60):

> Whatever rehabilitation they [that is, offenders] have received, whatever deterrent effect their experience with incarceration has had, must upon release withstand the difficulties of readjustment to life in society and reintegration into employment, family, school, and the rest of community life. This is the time when most of the problems from which offenders were temporarily removed must be faced again and new problems arising from their status as ex-offenders must be confronted.

Release from an institution may be unconditional, as when a state code specifies the discharge of a youngster when a certain age is reached, or conditional, as when the youngster leaves the institution with a set of behavioral requirements that will be supervised by an agent of the state. In most cases of unconditional release and in all cases of conditional release, various services will be made available to the youngster in the attempt to achieve a smooth reintegration into society. Historically, the expression *release on parole* had been used to specify conditional release under supervision because of the similarities with parole in the adult prison system. But, as Betz (1959) found, in the area of juvenile justice, the word *parole* eventually became the equivalent in usage to such others as *discharge, aftercare, release, furlough,* and *placement.* She thought it desirable to have (1959:942) "a more fitting term," but in the absence of one decided to use *parole* as the equivalent of *release from a juvenile institution.*

Clearly emphasizing the service rather than the supervisorial aspects following release from an institution, the Task Force on Corrections (1967) pled for the use of the term *aftercare* rather than *parole.* The task force believed that the use of *aftercare* would (1967:149) "separate juvenile programs from the legalistic language and concepts of adult parole." But the plea does not seem to have been effective in view of the widespread use of the word *parole* at the present time.

Regardless of the terminology, there are certain noteworthy elements in the process that leads from residence in a juvenile institution to life in the community: the release decision, parole supervision and services, and conditions of parole.

The Release Decision

Using broad criteria, Forst, Fisher, and Coates (1985) classified five states as "determinate sentencing" jurisdictions and forty-five states plus the District of Columbia as "indeterminate sentencing" jurisdictions. Just under three fourths of the jurisdictions with indeterminate sentencing gave the release decision to their juvenile correctional agencies, and the others to their parole boards or to juvenile court judges.

Assuming that the time of release is not fixed by law, as when a maximum sentence is completed or a certain age is reached, the release decision is based on estimates of the youth's progress toward rehabilitation and the likelihood of successful return to the community. Although she did find certain general patterns in her survey of release practices in an array of training schools, Betz (1959:943) commented, "There are probably as many methods of determining when a child is ready for placement as there are training schools." In most cases, there is a minimum length of stay required for eligibility, which may be specified in a state code, but beyond that, some authorities use a formal credit system, some use a casework approach involving written evaluations, some base the decision primarily on completion of training or on completion of training in conjunction with other accomplishments, and some use an approach that considers the number and array of problems created by the youth in the institution. In addition, there is evaluation of such community factors as employment and educational possibilities, the home environment, and the attitudes of family members (or foster parents) and significant others. The use of community factors is illustrated in the following summary of the file of a youngster who was recommended for release from a juvenile institution (as presented in Boyd, 1983:309):

> Although facing serious economic situations, the Browns are a relatively stable family. . . . Jim is reported to be very sensitive to his problems — comes from a culturally deprived family who moved from a rural setting (to the city). The family was rejected by the community and Jim retaliated by drinking and becoming involved in delinquent associations. . . . a return home is not possible at this point, therefore, a foster home should be tried. . . . Jim has expressed some interest in auto mechanics and this avenue should be pursued . . . he needs a strong expressive individual he can identify with — is presently too dependent on others. [The foster home] is well-furnished and well-kept. . . . he will attend X school — has preregistered and has been given a tour of the school.

The body that determines when a youth is released from an institution is often referred to as the "juvenile parole releasing authority." That authority, according to the National Advisory Commission on Criminal Justice Standards and Goals (1973), has typically consisted of full-time staff members of juvenile correctional institutions. But in other states, the decision regarding parole has been the responsibility of the youth commission to which youths are committed by the juvenile or family court, a board constituted for the sole purpose of parole decisions (this may be the same board responsible for the parole of adults), or the court that made the commitment leading to the incarceration.

The following illustrates a state code where the juvenile parole releasing authority is the state's youth commission (North Carolina General Statutes, 1983, Art. 52):

§7A-654. PRERELEASE PLANNING

The Director of the Division of Youth Services shall be responsible for evaluation of the progress of each juvenile at least once every six months as long as the juvenile remains in the care of the Division. If the Director determines that a juvenile is ready for release, he shall initiate a prerelease planning process. The prerelease planning process shall be defined by rules and regulations of the Division of Youth Services, but shall include the following:

(1) Written notification to the judge who ordered commitment;
(2) A prerelease planning conference shall be held involving as many as possible of the following: the juvenile, his parents, court counselors who have supervised the juvenile on probation or will supervise him on aftercare, and staff of the facility that found the juvenile ready for release. The prerelease planning conference shall include personal contact and evaluation rather than telephonic notification.

§7A-655 CONDITIONAL RELEASE AND FINAL DISCHARGE

The Division of Youth Services shall release a juvenile either by conditional release or by final discharge. The decision as to which type of release is appropriate shall be made by the Director based on the needs of the juvenile and the best interests of the State under rules and regulations governing release which shall be promulgated by the Division of Youth Services, according to the following guidelines:

(1) Conditional release is appropriate for a juvenile needing supervision after leaving the institution. As part of the prerelease planning process, the terms of conditional release shall be set out in writing and a copy given to the juvenile, his parent, the committing court, and the court counselor who will provide aftercare supervision. The time that a juvenile spends on conditional release shall be credited toward his maximum period of commitment to the Division of Youth Services.
(2) Final discharge is appropriate when the juvenile does not require supervision, has completed a maximum commitment for his offense, or is 18 years of age.

An interesting case on the right to parole was decided by the Supreme Court of California in 1979 (*In re Owen E.*, 23 Cal. 3d 398). In 1974, Owen, who was seventeen years old, shot and killed his father after a family argument. He admitted the killing in the adjudicatory hearing and was committed to the California Youth Authority (CYA) in the dispositional hearing. For eighteen months, he participated fully in the institutional programs and was assumed to be making normal progress toward rehabilitation. He applied for parole, but it was denied by the CYA because (at 400) "he had not yet accepted responsibility for his actions resulting in the commitment and did not fully appreciate his obligations to society."

Shortly thereafter, an appeal to the juvenile court that committed Owen to the CYA led to an order that set aside the commitment and placed him on probation. The order of the juvenile court led to an appeal by the CYA and eventual decision by the state's highest court. That court decided in favor of the CYA, stating that the law did (at 406) "not authorize judicial intervention into the routine parole function of CYA." Once a commitment is made, the CYA (as the state's youth commission) becomes the sole juvenile parole releasing authority, which may not be circumvented by the vacating of a commitment order by a juvenile court.

Parole Supervision and Services

Aftercare supervision and services are usually the responsibility of an agent called a parole officer. The endeavor requires monitoring school attendance or work habits, making sure that the parolee does not engage in criminal behavior, approving leisure-time activities and the people with whom the parolee associates while engaged in these activities, monitoring time away from home and broad movement patterns, and so on.

In his book *Juveniles on Parole,* Arnold (1970:70) summarized the variations in approach of parole officers as follows:

> What parole officers actually do varies tremendously, just as different teachers, mechanics, and presidents vary in how well they do their jobs. One officer works sixteen hours per day in order to visit the homes and hangouts of all his parolees every month, whereas another confines his activities largely to his office, to which the parolees are expected to come (by mail if not in person) to report every month. Some officers are friendly; some are unfriendly. Some are very "concerned"; others seem a bit cynical. The most remarkable thing about these variations in work styles is that we do not really know which ones of them work "best."

Using the data from a study completed by the Pennsylvania Board of Parole, Arnold reported that parole officers spent about 70 per cent of their time in activities related to the supervision of their charges. About 30 per cent of the time spent in these activities involved personal contacts, about 4 per cent telephone contacts, about 24 per cent travel, about 24 per cent record keeping, and about 18 per cent miscellaneous work. The average time spent per month on each case was two hours, divided as follows: personal contact with parolee, fourteen minutes; personal contact with adviser or employer, thirteen minutes; telephone contacts, 6 minutes; collateral contacts, sixteen minutes.; travel, thirty-five minutes; record keeping, thirty-five minutes; and unsuccessful attempts at contact, one minute. According to Arnold (1970:71), "The key point in the above data is the small amount of time spent actually adjusting the environment of each parolee — 49 minutes per month even if we count all the time spent in contacts [14 + 13 + 6 + 16]."

Clearly, forty-nine minutes per month is not much time to spend in relevant contacts, especially when it is considered that a parole officer has the "two-sided endeavor — surveillance and treatment" (Arnold, 1970:39). Surveillance stems from the mission of parole officer as protector of society, and treatment or casework represents a continuation of the correctional efforts of the institution. Some have argued that it is impossible for a single person to act effectively both as police officer in surveillance and as a social caseworker. And matters are considerably complicated by a central function of the parole officer, which is to determine when to recommend the termination of parole, either by revocation of the parole or by discharge.

Given that state of affairs, it is perhaps not surprising that various evaluations have shown that parole is generally ineffective. In addition to the inherent
complexities in the role of parole officer, there have been arguments that parole
officers spend a disproportionate amount of time with parolees who cannot be
helped at all, and that the typical social casework approach of parole officers is
inappropriate. Arnold (1970:142), in fact, argues that a marked increase in
parole officers (with a concomitant decrease in caseload for each) might prove
ineffective because "several studies have suggested that individual casework
approaches . . . do not produce noticeable improvements in offenders'
behavior."

Conditions of Parole

When a youngster is released from an institution under parole, certain conditions are imposed that could lead to revocation of parole if not followed to the
satisfaction of the supervising officer. The conditions might include committing
no illegal offenses; having no contact with certain individuals or certain groups;
using no drugs and drinking no alcoholic beverages; maintaining a passing level
of performance in school; keeping a job or taking active steps toward making
one likely in the future; remaining in a specified geographical area; contacting
the parole officer on a regular basis; and returning home each night no later
than a certain hour.

Clearly there is some question as to how carefully these conditions can be
monitored by a parole officer who spends an average of forty-nine minutes in
relevant contacts per month, even though those contacts are usually supplemented by developed relationships with people like the police, school officials,
and employers, who will notify the officer or the parole agency if the parolee has
conspicuous adjustment problems.

The discretionary power of the parole authority to revoke parole, if the
conditions are not fulfilled to its satisfaction, have been limited by a decision of
the U.S. Supreme Court and related decisions by lower courts. In *Morrissey v.
Brewer* (408 U.S. 471, 1972), the Supreme Court determined that a parolee's
liberty was valuable and that its termination required an orderly process. The
Court makes it clear, however, that the requirement for an orderly process is
limited (at 480):

> We begin with the proposition that the revocation of parole is not part of a
> criminal prosecution and thus the full panoply of rights due a defendant in such a
> proceeding does not apply to parole revocations. . . . Parole arises after the end of
> the criminal prosecution, including imposition of sentence. Supervision is not
> directly by the court but by an administrative agency, which is sometimes an arm
> of the court and sometimes of the executive. Revocation deprives an individual, not
> of the absolute liberty to which every citizen is entitled, but only of the conditional
> liberty properly dependent on observance of special parole restrictions.

The standards for the required orderly process were specified as follows (at
488, 489):

> We cannot write a code of procedure; that is the responsibility of each State.
> Most States have done so by legislation, others by judicial decision usually on due

process grounds. Our task is limited to deciding the minimum requirements of due process. They include (a) written notice of the claimed violations of parole; (b) disclosure to the parolee of evidence against him; (c) opportunity to be heard in person and to present witnesses and documentary evidence; (d) the right to confront and cross-examine adverse witnesses (unless the hearing officer specifically finds good cause for not allowing confrontation); (e) a "neutral and detached" hearing body such as a traditional parole board, members of which need not be judicial officers or lawyers; and (f) a written statement by the factfinders as to the evidence relied on and reasons for revoking parole. We emphasize there is no thought to equate this second stage of parole revocation to a criminal prosecution in any sense. It is a narrow inquiry; the process should be flexible enough to consider evidence including letters, affidavits, and other material that would not be admissible in an adversary criminal trial.

In cases decided before *Morrissey v. Brewer,* several courts declared that youths were not entitled to special hearings when an authority revokes parole. For example, in *Loyd v. Youth Conservation Commission* (287 Minn. 12, 1970) the Supreme Court of Minnesota concluded that procedural formalities would handicap the controlling authority and perhaps create obstacles to the operation of the entire parole process. And in *Bernier v. State of Maine* (265 A. 2d 604, 1970), the Supreme Judicial Court of Maine concluded that a hearing is not constitutionally required prior to revocation of a youth's parole — a simple administrative ruling is all that is necessary.

But in *State v. MacQueen,* decided in 1979 (163 W. Va. 620) — that is, after *Morrissey* — the Supreme Court of Appeals of West Virginia stated (at 623):

> The nature of the interest of the juvenile parolee is not less valuable than that of an adult parolee. The termination of liberty afforded by parole must be accomplished through some orderly process.

But the court did rule against a request for the full due process protections of a criminal prosecution.

To strengthen the position of a need for procedural formalities prior to revocation of parole, many states now have a statement in their codes that specify that right.

In most states, a juvenile parolee may be recommended for discharge from parole at any time, although there is general reluctance to discharge a parolee before there is a minimum period of time to observe adjustment, usually one year.

Success and Failure in Parole

On the basis of several studies, Arnold (1970) has concluded that a youth is more likely to fail in parole if he or she is black rather than white, has been involved in crime for an extended period, has had substantial contact with the correctional system, and has committed predatory crimes (like burglary and forgery).

Chambers (1983) studied 239 youths released on parole in New York State. They had been convicted and sentenced by adult criminal courts as thirteen-, fourteen-, and fifteen-year-olds under that state's punitive legislation of 1978 (see Chapter 10). At the time of the investigation, the youths were between seventeen and nineteen years of age and 74 per cent black. In 12 per cent of the cases, parole was revoked and the youths returned to custody, but there was good adjustment to the community in 77 per cent of the cases, and marginal adjustment in the remaining 11 per cent. The cases where parole was revoked differed from those with good adjustments principally in the realm of productive activity — 47 per cent of the former were either employed or in an educational program, whereas only 14 per cent of the latter were so engaged. The investigator concluded that the probability of successful parole went up considerably when there was intensive prerelease preparation with active supervision during the first six months of parole that emphasized employment or an educational program.

Wiederanders (1983) interviewed 193 male parolees from the California Youth Authority. The youths had a high rate of arrests and confinements both before institutionalization in a Youth Authority facility and after release on parole. But almost one fourth of them avoided arrest over a two-year follow-up period, and an additional 34 per cent were arrested only for minor violations that did not lead to revocations of parole. While attitudes expressed during institutionalization were almost uniformly against the commission of more crimes, almost half admitted to criminal behavior during the early period of parole. A number of factors were useful in equations used to predict successful parole. These factors include having friends who are not delinquent, not belonging to a gang while institutionalized, having no problems with drugs or alcohol, living outside of the Los Angeles megalopolis, and spending a high proportion of time employed or in school while on parole.

Parole as conditional early release from a correctional institution has been attacked from both ends of the political spectrum. From the conservative direction, the process has been criticized as being too lenient and too costly for offenders who deserve to be punished. From the liberal direction, it has been pointed out that the evidence indicates that parole does not seem to lessen the amount of time served in an institution. In the words of the National Advisory Commission on Criminal Justice Standards and Goals (1973b:390), "one major criticism of present parole laws is that their administration tends to result in more severe penalties in a criminal justice system that already imposes extensive State control."

While the result has been considerable effort to reduce the use of parole for adults in recent years, that has not been the case in the juvenile area.

Summary

Detention refers to the process whereby youths are kept in secure and restrictive facilities prior to the determination of disposition by a court. They are so detained for an array of legal reasons that include protection of the youth and protection of the community, and an array of extralegal reasons that include a desire to punish the youth and fear of antagonizing the police by releasing him or her. *Institutionalization,* on the other hand, refers to the process whereby youths are kept in secure and restrictive facilities as the result of a dispositional decision by a juvenile court. The presumed purpose of institutionalization is rehabilitation.

Youths may be detained in a locked facility designed for juveniles — often called a juvenile hall — or in an adult jail. Institutionalization may be in a cottage, a facility that is a miniature penitentiary (a state training school), a jail or prison, a camp or ranch, or a private facility. In some states, youths are sent to reception and diagnostic centers for evaluation prior to institutional placement.

Since the purpose of detention is secure holding prior to the dispositional hearing, there is no emphasis on treatment. But the rehabilitative goal of institutionalization necessitates treatment and teaching programs of many types, including traditional and group psychotherapy, social therapy, and both vocational training and academic education.

Although there have been questions about the practices of detention and institutionalization since the earliest days of juvenile justice, the questioning has become more intense in recent decades because of a more compassionate social perspective regarding the downtrodden or underprivileged. Books, studies, and reports have pointed out the deplorable conditions and abusive practices in many facilities, the personal degradations felt by many child inmates, and the widespread use of adult jails for detention. It was argued by many that detention was used far more frequently than needed and that institutionalization all too often did not include sincere efforts to rehabilitate. Arguments that detention was overused included evidence that only a small proportion of detained youths were eventually institutionalized, that status offenders were locked up at least as frequently as serious offenders, and that the prediction of dangerous behavior (the threat to the community) was a very uncertain enterprise. Arguments that institutionalization frequently did not involve efforts to rehabilitate emphasized the abusive, self-serving behavior of staff members.

Three important paths toward change occurred during the past two decades. First, several class action court suits, some of which claimed a right to treatment for institutionalized children, led to court decisions that directed improvement in facilities, conditions, and day-to-day treatment of youths. Second, the federal government entered the picture in 1974 with its Juvenile Justice and Delinquency Prevention Act. The act had three principal components: it created a federal agency devoted to juvenile justice and delinquency prevention, it designated funds for programs aimed at reducing delinquency and rehabilitating offenders, and it provided financial incentives to the states to stop putting status offenders in locked facilities (detained or institutionalized) and placing young offenders of any type in facilities that held adult offenders. The process of keeping status offenders out of locked facilities is called the deinstitutionalization of status offenders. And third, the state of Massachusetts, in the early 1970s, deinstitutionalized all juvenile offenders; that is, all public institutions in the state were closed. Most of the former inmates were discharged to their communities, but a small number (about fifty) were sent to private facilities.

When a youth is released from an institution, he or she may be supervised for a period and provided various services to achieve smooth reintegration into society. The word *parole* emphasizes the supervisorial aspects and the word *aftercare* the service aspects of the process, but the two words (along with several others) are used interchangeably to refer to release from an institution and reentry into the community. When the release is conditional, a parole officer evaluates the youngster on a continuing basis and initiates a recommendation for discharge. A violation of the conditions of parole can lead to return to the institution for those on conditional release. Those on unconditional release, on the other hand, are not supervised and may not be returned to the institution for violation of parole but are usually provided services to aid their readjustment.

Endnote

1. A position given by Rubin (1985:128) is of interest in this context. He states, "Estimates of the number of children held in jails annually approximate 500,000. As many as 60 of these youths will not emerge alive from jail custody." The two sources given for the estimate of 500,000 are Sarri (1975:116) and Office of Juvenile Justice and Delinquency Prevention (1983:1). That represents, of course, a sizable discrepancy from the 120,000 given above. The difference seems to stem, at least in part, from what is included in the expression "adult jail." In some cases, "adult jail" apparently includes both city or county facilities and facilities used by police on a temporary basis prior to transporting people to the city/county facility. The report of the Children's Defense Fund (1976:3), for example, refers to staff visits to 449 jails in 126 counties and nine independent cities, yet a listing of "jails" visited in its Appendix A contains a very large number of police departments. In other cases, the police facility is called a "police lockup" to distinguish it from an adult jail. According to the report of the Office of Juvenile Justice and Delinquency Prevention (1980), the average length of stay for a juvenile in a police lockup is one day (as compared with an average of 4.8 days in adult jails, as distinguished from police lockups).

   That report points out that there are no accurate national data on the numbers of youths in police lockups and proceeds by a crude procedure of extrapolation (1980:26) to estimate that there are about as many juveniles in adult jails as in police lockups during a given year. Using the 120,000 figure as an estimate of juveniles in county facilities (narrow definition of adult jail), one comes up with an estimate of 240,000 juveniles in adult jails and police lockups during a year of the mid-1970s.

   Since the estimate of 500,000 given by Rubin came from reports published in 1975 and 1983, one cannot explain the discrepancy on the basis of a change in jailing practices over years.

References

Allinson, Richard. 1983. There Are No Juveniles in Pennsylvania Jails. *Corrections Magazine* 9, no. 3: 13–20.

Arnold, William R. 1970. *Juveniles on Parole: A Sociological Analysis.* New York: Random House.

Bakal, Yitzhak, ed. 1973. *Closing Correctional Institutions.* Lexington, Mass.: Lexington Books, D. C. Heath.

———, and Polsky, Howard W. 1979. *Reforming Corrections for Juvenile Offenders.* Lexington, Mass.: Lexington Books, D. C. Heath.

Bartollas, Clemens, and Miller, Stuart J. 1978. *The Juvenile Offender: Control, Correction, and Treatment.* Boston: Holbrook Press.

———, and Sieverdes, Christopher M. 1983. Institutional Games Played by Confined Juveniles. *Adolescence* 18: 609–618.

Beis, Edward B. 1984. *Mental Health and the Law.* Rockville, Md.: Aspen Systems Corp.

Betz, Elizabeth A. 1959. Release from Training Schools. In *The Problem of Delinquency,* edited by Sheldon Glueck, 941–947. Boston: Houghton Mifflin.

Birnbaum, M. 1960. The Right to Treatment. *American Bar Association Journal* 46: 499.

Blackburn, Donald G. 1959. Institutions for Juvenile Delinquents. In *The Problem of Delinquency,* edited by Sheldon Glueck, 687–694. Boston: Houghton Mifflin.

Bortner, M. A., Sunderland, Mary L., and Winn, Russ. 1985. Race and the Impact of Juvenile Deinstitutionalization. *Crime & Delinquency* 31: 35–46.

Boyd, Neil 1983. Juvenile Release Programs in British Columbia and Ontario: A Comparative Analysis. In *Current Issues in Juvenile Justice,* edited by Raymond R. Corrado, Marc LeBlanc, and Jean T. Trepanier, 603–614. Toronto: Butterworths.

Breed, Allen F. 1953. California Youth Authority Forestry Camp Program. *Federal Probation* 17: 37–43.

Bureau of Justice Statistics. 1986. *Children in Custody. Public Juvenile Facilities, 1985.* Washington, D.C.: U.S. Government Printing Office.

California Youth Authority. 1969. What is I-level? *California Youth Authority Quarterly* 22: 3–6.

Chambers, Ola R. 1983. *The Juvenile Offender: A Parole Profile.* Albany, N.Y.: Evaluation and Planning Unit, New York State Division of Parole.

Children's Bureau, U.S. Department of Health, Education, and Welfare. 1959. The Role and Contribution of the Training School. In *The Problem of Delinquency,* edited by Sheldon Glueck, 694–698. Boston: Houghton Mifflin.

Children's Defense Fund. 1976. *Children in Adult Jails.* Washington, D.C.: Washington Research Project.

Clear, Todd R., and Cole, George F. 1986. *American Corrections.* Monterey, Calif.: Brooks/Cole.

Coates, Robert B., Miller, Alden D., and Ohlin, Lloyd E. 1978. *Diversity in a Youth Correctional System. Handling Delinquents in Massachusetts.* Cambridge, Mass.: Ballinger.

Cottle, Thomas J. 1977. *Children in Jail: Seven Lessons in American Justice.* Boston: Beacon Press.

Cressey, Donald R. 1965. Prison Organizations. In *Handbook of Organizations,* edited by James G. March, 1023–1070. Chicago: Rand McNally.

Dore, Martha M., Young, Thomas M., and Pappenfort, Thomas M. 1984. Comparison of Basic Data for the National Survey of Residential Care Facilities: 1966–1982. *Child Welfare* 63: 485–495.

Duffee, David. 1980. *Correctional Management.* Englewood Cliffs, N.J.: Prentice-Hall.

Ferdinand, Theodore N. 1978. Female Delinquency and Warren's Typology of Personality Patterns. *Social Work Research and Abstracts* 10: 32–41.

Ferster, Elyce Z., and Courtless, Thomas C. 1972. Post-Disposition Treatment and Recidivism in the Juvenile Court: Towards Justice for All. *Journal of Family Law* 11: 683–708.

Forst, Martin L., Fisher, Bruce A., and Coates, Robert B. 1985. Indeterminate and Determinate Sentencing of Juvenile Delinquents: A National Survey of Approaches to Commitment and Release Decision-Making. *Juvenile and Family Court Journal* 36: 1–12.

Gendreau, Paul, and Ross, Robert R. 1983–1984. Correctional Treatment: Some Recommendations for Effective Intervention. *Juvenile and Family Court Journal* 34: 31–39.

Gerard, Ray. 1970. Institutional Innovations in Juvenile Corrections. *Federal Probation* 34: 38–40.

Goldfarb, Ronald. 1976. *Jails: The Ultimate Ghetto.* New York: Anchor Books.

Grant, J. Douglas, and Grant, Marguerite Q. 1959. A Group Dynamics Approach to the Treatment of Nonconformists in the Navy. *Annals of the American Academy of Political and Social Science* 322: 126–135.

Handler, Joel F., Sosin, Michael, Stookey, John A., and Zatz, Julie. 1982. Deinstitutionalization in Seven States: Principal Findings. In *Neither Angels Nor Thieves: Studies in Deinstitutionalization of Status Offenders,* edited by Joel F. Handler and Julie Zatz, 88–126. Washington, D.C.: National Academy Press.

Henderson, Charles R., ed. 1910. *Prison Reform and Criminal Law.* New York: Charities Publication Committee.

Hickey, William L. 1977. Status Offenses and the Juvenile Court. *Criminal Justice Abstracts* 9: 91–122.

Holden, Constance. 1976. Massachusetts Juvenile Justice: Deinstitutionalization on Trial. *Science* 192: 447–451.

Jesness, Carl F. 1967. Differential Treatment of Delinquents in Institutions. In *National Association of Training Schools and Juvenile Agencies, Proceedings: 63rd Annual Meeting,* edited by Jack C. Pulliam. Anaheim, Calif.

Ketcham, Orman W. 1961. The Unfilled Promise of the Juvenile Court. *Crime and Delinquency* 7: 97–110.

Keve, Paul W. 1984. *The Consequences of Prohibiting the Jailing of Juveniles.* Richmond: Virginia Commonwealth Univ. Prepared for the Chicago Resource Center.

Kobrin, Solomon, and Klein, Malcolm W. 1982. *National Evaluation of the Deinstitutionalization of Status Offender Programs: Executive Summary.* Washington, D.C.: U.S. Department of Justice, Office of Juvenile Justice and Delinquency Prevention.

——. 1983. *Community Treatment of Juvenile Offenders: The DSO Experiments.* Beverly Hills, Calif.: Sage.

Lerman, Paul. 1968. Evaluating Institutions for Delinquents. *Social Work* 13: 55–64.

——. 1975. *Community Treatment and Social Control. A Critical Analysis of Juvenile Correctional Policy.* Chicago: Univ. of Chicago Press.

——. 1980. Trends and Issues in the Deinstitutionalization of Youths in Trouble. *Crime & Delinquency* 26: 281–298.

Miller, Frank W., Dawson, Robert O., Dix, George E., and Parnas, Raymond I. 1985. *The Juvenile Justice Process.* 3rd ed. Mineola, N.Y.: Foundation Press.

Monahan, John. 1981. *Predicting Violent Behavior: An Assessment of Clinical Techniques.* Beverly Hills, Calif.: Sage.

National Advisory Commission on Criminal Justice Standards and Goals. 1973a. *Court.* Washington, D.C.: U.S. Government Printing Office.

——. 1973b. *Corrections.* Washington, D.C.: U.S. Government Printing Office.

Office of Juvenile Justice and Delinquency Prevention. 1980. *Juvenile Justice: Before and After the Onset of Delinquency.* Washington, D.C.: U.S. Department of Justice.

——. 1983. *It's Your Move: Juveniles in Adult Jails and Lockups.* Washington, D.C.: U.S. Department of Justice.

——. 1986. *Juvenile Detention and Correctional Facilities Census, 1985.* Ann Arbor, Mich.: Inter-university Consortium for Political and Social Research.

Ohlin, Lloyd E., Coates, Robert B., and Miller, Alden D. 1974. Radical Correctional Reform: A Case Study of the Massachusetts Youth Correctional System. *Harvard Educational Review* 44: 74–111.

——. 1975. Evaluating the Reform of Youth Corrections in Massachusetts. *Journal of Research in Crime and Delinquency* 12: 3–16.

Ohlin, Lloyd E., Miller, Alden D. and Coates, Robert B., eds. 1976. *Juvenile Correctional Reform in Massachusetts.* Washington, D.C.: U.S. Government Printing Office.

Paul, Warren N., and Watt, Helga S. 1980. *Deinstitutionalization of Status Offenders: A Compilation and Analysis of State Statutes.* Denver, Colo.: State Legislative Leaders Foundation.

Peterson, Donald R., and Quay, Herbert C. 1961. Personality Factors Related to Juvenile Delinquency. *Child Development* 32: 355–372.

Pleune, F. Gordon. 1959. Effects of State Training School Programs on Juvenile Delinquents. In *The Problem of Delinquency,* edited by Sheldon Glueck, 711–721. Boston: Houghton Mifflin.

Poulin, John E., Levitt, John L., Young, Thomas M., and Pappenfort, Donnell M. 1980. *Reports of the National Juvenile Justice Assessment Centers. Juveniles in Detention Centers and Jails: An Analysis of State Variations During the Mid 1970's.* Washington, D.C.: U.S. Government Printing Office.

President's Commission on Law Enforcement and Administration of Justice. (1967). *The Challenge of Crime in a Free Society.* Washington, D.C.: U.S. Government Printing Office.

Quay, Herbert C. 1964. Personality Dimensions in Delinquent Males as Inferred from the Factor Analysis of Behavior Ratings. *Journal of Research in Crime and Delinquency* 1: 33–37.

——, and Werry, John S. 1972. *Psychopathological Disorders of Childhood.* New York: Wiley.

Reichel, Philip L. 1985. Getting to Know You: Decision-Making in an Institution for Juveniles. *Juvenile and Family Court Journal* 36: 5–15.

Renn, Donna E. 1973. The Right to Treatment and the Juvenile. *Crime and Delinquency* 19: 477–484.

Robinson, Daniel N. 1980. *Psychology and Law: Can Justice Survive the Social Sciences?* New York: Oxford Univ. Press.

Rothman, David J. 1979. *Incarceration and Its Alternatives in 20th Century America.* Washington, D.C.: U.S. Government Printing Office.

Rubin, H. Ted. 1983. Status Offenses: The Law and the Law in Practice. In *Status Offenders: A Sourcebook,* edited by John P. Murray, 47–65. Boy's Town, Neb.: Boy's Town Print Shop.

——. 1985. *Juvenile Justice: Policy, Practice, Law.* 2nd ed. New York: Random House.

Sarri, Rosemary. 1974. *Under Lock and Key: Juveniles in Jails and Detention.* Ann Arbor, Mich.: Univer. of Michigan, National Assessment of Juvenile Corrections.

——. 1975. Juvenile Detention. In *New Directions in Juvenile Justice,* Proceedings of the Iowa Civil Liberties Union Bicentennial Symposium.

Schneider, Anne L. 1984. Deinstitutionalization of Status Offenders: The Impact on Recidivism and Secure Confinement. *Criminal Justice Abstracts* 16: 410–432.

Schneider, Anne L., McKelvey, Jill G., and Schram, Donna D. 1983. *Divestiture of Court Jurisdiction Over Status Offenses. The Assessment of Washington's Juvenile Code,* Vol. VII. Eugene, Oreg.: Institute of Policy Analysis.

Serrill, Michael S. 1975a. Juvenile Corrections in Massachusetts. *Corrections Magazine* 2, no. 2: 3–12.

——. 1975b. The Community Advancement Program. *Corrections Magazine* 2, no. 2: 13–20.

——. 1975c. Moving the Kids Out: A Unique Experiment. *Corrections Magazine* 2, no. 2: 29–40.

Smith, Charles P. 1980. *Relative Costs of Removal of Juveniles from Adult Jails or Lockups.* Sacramento, Calif.: National Juvenile Justice System Assessment Center, American Justice Institute.

——, Berkman, David J., and Sutton, John. 1980. *Reports of the National Juvenile Justice Assessment Centers. A Preliminary National Assessment of the Status Offender and the Juvenile Justice System: Role Conflicts, Constraints, and Information Gaps.* Washington, D.C.: National Institute for Juvenile Justice and Delinquency Prevention.

Special Study Committee on Criminal Justice Standards and Goals. 1975. *Juvenile Justice Standards and Goals.* Madison: Wisconsin Council on Criminal Justice.

Sorrentino, Joseph H. 1975. *The Concrete Cradle.* Los Angeles: Wollstonecraft.

Sullivan, Clyde E., Grant, Marguerite Q., and Grant, J. Douglas. 1957. The Development of Interpersonal Maturity: Applications to Delinquency. *Psychiatry* 20: 373–385.

Sumner, Helen. 1971. *Locking Them Up: The Study of Juvenile Detention Decisions in Selected California Counties.* New York: National Council on Crime and Delinquency.

Task Force on Corrections, President's Commission on Law Enforcement and Administration of Justice. 1967. *Task Force Report: Corrections.* Washington, D.C.: U.S. Government Printing Office.

Task Force on Juvenile Delinquency, President's Commission on Law Enforcement and Administration of Justice. 1967. *Task Force Report: Juvenile Delinquency and Youth Crimes.* Washington, D.C.: U.S. Government Printing Office.

Teeters, Negley K. 1950. Institutional Treatment of Juvenile Delinquents. *Nebraska Law Review* 29: 577–604.

U.S. Department of Health, Education, and Welfare, Welfare Administration, Children's Bureau. 1966. *A Study of the Division of Youth Services and Youth Service Board.* Washington, D.C.: U.S. Government Printing Office.

U.S. Department of Justice. 1979. *Children in Custody: A Report on the Juvenile Detention and Correctional Facility Census of 1975.* Washington, D.C.: U.S. Government Printing Office.

Warren, Marguerite Q. 1969. The Case for Differential Treatment of Delinquents. *Annals of the American Academy of Political and Social Science* 381: 47–59.

———. 1971. Classifications of Offenders as an Aid to Efficient Management and Effective Treatment. *Journal of Criminal Law, Criminology and Police Science* 62: 239–258.

Wiederanders, Mark R. 1983. *Success on Parole: The Influence of Self-Reported Attitudes, Experiences, and Background Characteristics on the Parole Behaviors of Youthful Offenders. Final Report.* Sacramento, Calif.: Department of the Youth Authority.

Wilson, Rob. 1978. Massachusetts: The Legacy of Jerome Miller. *Corrections Magazine* 4, no. 3: 12–18.

Winterdyk, M. A., and Griffiths, Curt. 1984. Wilderness Experience Programs: Reforming Delinquents or Beating Around the Bush? *Juvenile and Family Court Journal* 35: 35–44.

Wooden, Kenneth. 1976. *Weeping in the Playtime of Others: America's Incarcerated Children.* New York: McGraw-Hill.

Woody, Robert Henley, and Associates. 1984. *The Law and the Practice of Human Services.* San Francisco: Jossey-Bass.

CHAPTER 12

Treatment of Young Offenders in Other Countries

We have now examined how the American juvenile justice system operates. But how does the American system compare with those found in other countries? Juvenile delinquency exists in every nation in the world, and all nations have found ways to cope with young people who break the law. Their methods differ greatly, with some societies treating delinquency as primarily a legal problem; some, as a problem of social welfare; others, as a problem that must be handled with a combination of legal and welfare remedies. In this chapter, we will examine the major ways in which juvenile delinquency is dealt with around the world.

An International Overview

Juvenile Delinquency in Comparative Perspective

Although crimes are committed by juveniles in every country and society, the degree to which juvenile delinquency is considered a problem, as well as the magnitude of the problem, differs greatly. Statistics can only indicate the extent and significance of juvenile delinquency in different nations of the world. The varying ways in which nations keep track of criminal activities make it extremely difficult to use available statistics to compare levels of criminal activity —including juvenile delinquency— among different nations. Nevertheless, statistics do indicate that in some places, juveniles comprise a major portion of those who break the law; in others, only a fairly small proportion. In most Western industrial societies, about one fifth to one third of reported crimes are committed by juveniles; in the United States, as we saw in Chapter 1, juveniles account for about one fourth of such crimes. In Norway, the proportion is even higher; over half of the reported crimes were committed by juveniles in the years between 1979 and 1982, the most recent years for which statistics are readily available. Many Third World countries, by contrast, report that a very small proportion of crimes are committed by juveniles. In Nigeria, for example, juveniles are reported to have committed only about 8 per cent of the crimes; Niger and Senegal report that only about 7 to 8 per cent of crimes were committed by juveniles. Venezuela reports less than 4 per cent; the African nation of Malawi, a very low 2.5 per cent. In general, data are unavailable for communist societies (statistics from International Criminal Police Organization, 1984; 1985).

Again, such figures are not fully comparable. Patrick Edobor Igbinovia (1985) has discussed the African statistics, in particular, arguing that juvenile delinquency is underreported from most countries in Africa south of the Sahara. Still, the varying levels are suggestive and are not entirely artifacts of differences in reporting. Clayton A. Hartjen and S. Priyadarsini (1984), in an in-depth study of delinquency in one non-Western nation, India, have argued that such countries do, in fact, experience significantly lower rates of juvenile delinquency vis-à-vis adult criminality and that this has to do with the distinctive characters of such societies. It is worth looking briefly at Hartjen and Priyadarsini's study because it helps to illuminate not only the differences between nations regarding juvenile delinquency but also some of the issues we have discussed in earlier chapters here.

To see the significance of Hartjen and Priyadarsini's findings, it is important to recognize, first, that there is much in the Indian juvenile justice system that may be traced back to the days of British colonial rule. Juvenile law closely resembles that of both Britain and the United States. The only significant differences seem to be that probation is used much less frequently than in this country and that the juvenile courts tend to function pretty much as criminal courts. There is some variation in juvenile justice in India, since that nation, like our own, gives jurisdiction over juvenile offenders to the states. But the overall thrust of juvenile law in India has been quite similar to that of the United States.

This makes all the more striking the difference between the level of juvenile crime in India and that for the United States. As Hartjen and Priyadarsini (1984) show, the overall crime rate in India is much lower than in the United States — the murder rate is about one third of the American rate; robbery, about 2 per cent — and the proportion of juveniles reported in violation of Indian laws is also quite low. Juveniles were reportedly involved in only about 3.4 per cent of violations of the Indian Penal Code in 1974, the year on which Hartjen and Priyadarsini focused.

The authors offer several reasons why juvenile delinquency rates in a country like India should be so much lower than those in the United States and other Western industrial nations, even though the two juvenile justice systems are similar. In general, they argue that many of the conditions that American and other Western theorists have cited as causes of delinquency in our own society do not apply in Third World, largely agrarian societies such as India. In particular, they focus on the absence of what they call an "adolescent 'leisure class'" (1984:76) in Indian society, a group that, they argue, has much to do with delinquency in our own society.

According to Hartjen and Priyadarsini, the main forces in India serve to integrate young people into the larger society. Traditions of strong social and kinship ties remain strong. Economic necessity creates an important role for young, unskilled workers, for children and young people who must contribute to their families' survival. Indian young people, therefore, do not experience the kind of alienation found among the young in Western societies. Feeling a part of their community, they do not so readily turn to delinquency. The social integration of youth found in such a traditional society as India is, the authors argue, a major barrier to delinquency.

Students will not be surprised to learn that Hartjen and Priyadarsini find much of value in Hirschi's theory of social control (see Chapter 6), although they go beyond Hirschi to argue that the "stake in conformity" (1984:208) that tends to inhibit delinquency is influenced by the character of the society itself. As they argue, the socioeconomic characteristics of developing countries lead to high involvement with others, encouraging community-based social control and a high stake in conformity. The socioeconomic characteristics of developed societies, by contrast, lead to low involvement with others, encouraging a reliance on external sources of social control, e.g., the police and the courts. This leads people to feel that they have less of a stake in conformity since they feel that they themselves are not directly responsible for the health and stability of the society — hence, they argue, the higher rates of delinquency in Western, industrial nations.

There is much to support their argument. Hartjen and Priyadarsini themselves cite the cases of other Third World nations—and even of such non–Third World nations as Japan and Switzerland—where strong webs of social relations and obligations include young people, in support of their case. Igbinovia (1985), while arguing that delinquency figures for Africa underrepresent the level of juvenile crime, nevertheless recognizes that such crime is significantly less in sub-Saharan African countries than in Western industrial nations (and that the crimes tend to be minor crimes, also not the case in the West). He, too, notes the strength of family and tradition.

And, indeed, a recent study of delinquency in Japan by Hiroshi Wagatsuma and George A. De Vos (1984) gives independent support to such a case. Looking at a fairly poor Tokyo community, Wagatsuma and De Vos also cite low rates of both crime and delinquency and argue that a high degree of neighborhood integration and interaction—and cultural traditions that give great value to community ties—tended to militate against delinquency.

It is difficult to say whether changing historical, social, and economic conditions will produce higher levels of delinquency. L. Craig Parker (1986) has described an increase of delinquency in Japan. He has ascribed the increase to a range of factors; among them he has stressed the growth of individualism as an ideal in Japanese life and a corresponding decrease in the appreciation of traditional ties of family and community. Igbinovia (1985) cites African criminologists who make a similar argument. It remains to be seen whether this trend will continue and how widespread it will become.

Still, we can say with certainty that, as a problem, the significance of juvenile delinquency varies markedly from society to society. In some, the problem posed by juvenile delinquency is severe. In others, young people commit only a tiny portion of the criminal acts to which society must respond. As comparative research in this area proceeds, we shall learn much more about why such variation occurs.

Major Legal Approaches to Delinquency

Legal approaches to juvenile delinquency also vary greatly from country to country. Even the ages at which young people can be considered "delinquent" and the reasons for their being so considered vary considerably. In general, most nations recognize a minimum age below which a child is not considered to have sufficient capacity for distinguishing between right and wrong to be held liable for what would, in the case of someone above that age, be considered a delinquent act. Although there may be welfare measures available to society when such children get into trouble, their behavior is not to be dealt with as delinquency. No nation goes below seven for a minimum age, but many have set higher ages at which a young person is to be held sufficiently responsible for criminal or other acts to be adjudged delinquent. In Japan, for example, the age of legal responsibility is fourteen, as it is in Yugoslavia and Italy. In Sweden, the age is fifteen. Other nations are within this general range. Nigeria has set ten as the age of legal responsibility; Poland and France, thirteen. In Israel, the minimum age is nine by law but twelve by practice.

The age beyond which an offender is to be tried as an adult rather than treated as a juvenile also varies. In many countries, the maximum age for treatment as a child is eighteen, but in Japan and West Germany it is twenty-one. In Cuba, by contrast, the maximum age for such treatment is sixteen, having been lowered from eighteen in 1973 in response to a serious rise in the nation's delinquency rates for several years (Salas, 1979).

In other ways nations differ from each other in their handling of delinquency. In France, England, Sweden, and elsewhere, as in the United States, there is great concern for "status offenses" and for preventive work with those juveniles who are "at risk" as well as those who commit acts that would be considered "criminal" regardless of the offender's age. In such nations as Argentina or Yugoslavia, however, juveniles are governed by the same criminal code that governs adults. Although they are to be treated differently from adults by the criminal justice system, there are no status offenses for which juveniles may be detained and treated or tried.

General Tendencies in International Juvenile Justice

But, at the same time, there are also some general international trends that one may identify in looking at approaches to juvenile justice systems around the world. Although, as we shall see, these trends are far from universal, they do characterize the development of juvenile justice systems in many parts of the world.

One of these is the continuing spread of institutions and procedures designed specifically for juvenile offenders. Although such institutions have existed in some parts of the world, including the United States, since the nineteenth century, they have only recently entered other areas. Nevertheless, throughout this century there has appeared a steady interest in tailoring juvenile justice to the juvenile offender. As nations in the Third World have achieved their independence since World War II, they have established distinctive facilities and procedures for juvenile delinquents even as older nations have sought refinements to make their systems more responsive to what are believed to be the special characteristics of young offenders. In some cases, this has meant the creation of separate courts for juveniles, or even of alternative forms of adjudication, while in others it has meant the creation of special protections for juveniles within the larger criminal justice system. But, in any case, one can see the continuing development of special regard for juveniles throughout the world.

Another general trend internationally has been the raising of the minimum age at which a young person may be considered delinquent. English history alone shows how this changed in the twentieth century. The first English juvenile court law, passed in 1908, set seven as the minimum age at which a child could be adjudged delinquent — in keeping, as we saw in Chapter 7, with the common law tradition. In 1933, a new Children and Young Persons Act raised that age to eight, at the same time raising the age at which one may be tried as an adult from sixteen to seventeen years. In 1963, another Children and Young Persons Act raised the minimum age of liability to ten years (Midgley, 1975). Still more recently, the 1969 Children's and Young Persons Act raised the minimum age at which one could be adjudged delinquent to twelve (Gandy, 1977), an age still a bit lower than that recognized in such other European nations as France, Sweden, or Italy. This general tendency has been well in keeping with the corresponding tendency in the Western world to extend the length of dependency well into "adolescence."

Treatment: An International Aim. But perhaps the clearest and most significant general tendency, internationally, has been the widespread accept-ance of treatment rather than punishment as the appropriate response by society to juvenile crime. Virtually all juvenile justice systems include important rehabilitative emphases based on an assumption that state intervention into the socialization of the youngster during adolescence can produce a reformation in character. Moreover, this rehabilitative orientation has been greatly broadened to include not only the young offender but the larger social context in which he or she lives, with counseling and other services directed toward the family and the peer group as well.

Related to this, in several countries, has been an effort to create approaches to juvenile justice that are as comprehensive as possible, involving educational institutions, social workers, and even the police in the work of rehabilitation. In France, for example, a Juvenile Protection Unit organized within the Paris police in 1976 engages not only in the normal work of criminal investigation but also in preventive work, including investigations of family life and the counsel-ing of youngsters "at risk" along with their families (Juvenile Protection Unit, 1978). Placing all such efforts under the umbrella of juvenile reform is intended to provide a more nearly holistic approach to the treatment of the problems likely to produce delinquency.

Decriminalization. In addition, there has also been a general tendency to create juvenile justice systems that seek, as nearly as possible, to remove the young offender from anything like a criminal justice system. This has meant, in some places, the creation of alternatives to any form of courtroom procedure — even the procedures of a juvenile court. In Scotland, Sweden, Australia, and elsewhere, many cases are now heard by panels composed of lay people rather than by judges, with counseling and advising rather than adjudication being at least the expressed purpose of the hearing body. Moreover, there has also been, officially, a widespread adoption of policies stressing treatment in the commu-nity rather than institutionalization as the best sentence for the juvenile of-fender. Probation, supervision, or such less strict institutions as weekend at-tendance centers have been widely adopted as preferable alternatives to reform schools, youth prisons, and other institutions in which young offenders have been incarcerated.

We have already noted, in earlier chapters, the growing criticism of this tendency in the United States and the corresponding "hardening of the pro-cess" for juveniles. Similar criticism and a similar hardening of the process have occurred in other nations, too. In England, especially, there exists a large body of opinion opposed to what is considered to be the "decriminalization" of juvenile justice and supportive of an increasing legalism in court procedures as well as the frequent use of institutionalization and "punishment" for juvenile offenders. One may note a similar movement in Canada, embodied in a 1982 Young Offenders Act (Hackler, 1984; Chisholm, 1983).

In addition, the appearance of these developments in some societies may be more superficial than indicative of substance. Lemert (1986), for example, has traced the development of the Italian juvenile court system since its inception in the 1930s down to the present and has concluded (1986:539) "that the Italian juvenile court is more of a symbolic demonstration or a set of rituals than a vehicle of substantial justice." He stresses, among other factors, the low status of juvenile court judges and the inefficiency of the juvenile courts themselves. He sees roots for the failure of the juvenile courts in a conflict between a juvenile court ideal much like that of the United States, on the one hand, and such more traditional Italian values as familism and a rejection of public authority. Nevertheless, general tendencies identified here seem to be strong and widespread internationally.

For all these general tendencies, however, it is possible to identify several types of fairly distinctive approaches current in various countries at the present time. At one pole are those systems which, although they give an important role to treatment, nevertheless rely on what is essentially a criminal justice model for dealing with young offenders. At the other pole are those which seek to reject such a model in favor of an approach fully oriented toward counseling and social welfare. Somewhere in between are systems that seek to synthesize elements of each approach to one degree or another. The American system would be included in this group, but other nations are also making this kind of effort. In addition, one may identify distinctive juvenile justice systems in the Soviet Union or the People's Republic of China that, because of their official foundations in Marxism, take appropriately based approaches to the problems of juvenile delinquency. For the rest of this chapter, we will look in more depth at examples of each of these approaches to juvenile delinquency.

The Legalistic Approach

Argentina

Few if any nations in the world subject young offenders to the full force of the adult criminal justice system, but in some societies the treatment of juvenile delinquents is based, for the most part, on a criminal justice model. Although there are elements of social welfare and prevention in such systems, in keeping with more general international tendencies in the practice of juvenile justice, the identification of the "juvenile offender" as a youngster accused of committing a crime stands at the center of the juvenile justice system, as does a focus on questions of guilt or innocence. Such an approach may be found in several places — Yugoslavia or South Africa, for example — but for an in-depth look at such a system we will focus here primarily on the juvenile justice practices of Argentina.

The definition of delinquency in Argentina is, itself, a highly legalistic one: juvenile delinquents are those minors who commit acts that are defined as crimes for both juveniles and adults (David, 1977). Status offenses are not recognized in Argentina, so that children are not adjudicated by a juvenile court for acts for which adults would not be adjudicated (David and Scott, 1973). Children under sixteen are not held legally responsible for their acts, although they can be taken under the protection of the court and committed to an institution for the protection of minors if the court feels such a course to be appropriate. Young people sixteen to eighteen are responsible, but if they commit a crime that would result in a year or less in jail, they are not subject to the regular judicial process. If they commit a more serious crime, they go through regular court proceedings but receive penalties different from those reserved for adults. Young people from eighteen to twenty-two years old are subject to the full criminal judicial process; any penalties are, however, served in separate institutions designed to keep them away from older criminals (David, 1977).

Prosecution of the juvenile offender in Argentina takes place on two levels. On one, the handling of serious crimes such as robbery, theft, rape, or homicide is governed by the Argentina Penal Code. On the other is a range of minor offenses including those of drunkenness or disorderly conduct. Such offenses are covered by the "Codes of Contraventions," which define less serious acts and provide for alternatives to passing through a court-bound judicial process. For acts covered under the "Codes of Contraventions," the offender's case may be acted on by the municipal chief of police, who can pass a sentence of up to thirty days in jail. Such cases go before no court at all, whether involving a juvenile or an adult offender. Those cases going before the court — and Argentina lacks a specialized court system for minors — are, thus, violations of the penal code (David and Scott, 1973).

When a juvenile violates the penal code and is brought before the court by the police or by a complainant, the case is assigned a number, and a dossier called the *expediente* is begun almost immediately. The *expediente* contains all evidence, reports, documents, and other records relevant to the case. The *expediente* will serve as the basis on which the case is to be decided. Adult and juvenile cases alike are decided by a judge who examines the evidence on both sides as summarized in the *expediente*. Thus, such dossiers tend to be extraordinarily full, containing police reports, reports from social workers and psychiatrists, and other information that may have a bearing on the case (De Fleur, 1970). There are few public trials in Argentina, no juries, and no oral presentation of testimony. Thus, the role of the judge is extremely powerful, and the contents of an *expediente* extremely important (David, 1981).

The Argentine legal process, despite the reliance on such documents as reports from social workers, places great weight on police evidence and police testimony. When the police can establish the "legal truth" in a case, the judge will generally go along with the police presentation of a charge. In addition, there is no plea bargaining — reduction of a charge in return for a guilty plea from the accused — in the Argentine system. Changes in a charge generally result from problems in evidence or, occasionally, when an influential family is involved (David and Scott, 1973).

When a young offender is found guilty by the court, several dispositions are possible. As we have noted, children under sixteen, while avoiding any formal prosecution, may be committed to special institutions, as can those sixteen to eighteen years of age, though they can be subject to criminal proceedings. Such institutions have, however, been considered to be woefully inadequate (David, 1977), so that while such alternatives exist and have existed since 1919, many of those young offenders adjudged guilty of crimes are sent to jails that are separate from but essentially similar to those used for adults.

Thus, one sees in the Argentine example a good case of a highly legalistic approach to juvenile delinquency. Delinquency itself is defined in terms of the penal code, and the procedures for handling juvenile offenders are virtually identical to those prescribed for adults. Although, to be sure, Argentine law recognizes that young people of certain ages must be held more or less responsible for criminal acts and takes care to separate young from adult offenders, it is nevertheless the case that the juvenile offender is a young person adjudged guilty of a criminal act; this adjudication stands at the center of the Argentine juvenile justice system.

Other Legalistic Systems

Yugoslavia. Although the legalistic approach is not the favored one in the modern world, Argentina is not alone in taking such a stance toward juvenile crime. In Yugoslavia, for example, although one can identify strong welfare components, the approach to juvenile delinquency is essentially legalistic. Yugoslavia has a wide range of institutions intended to work for children's welfare and protection and for the prevention of delinquency. Young people up to fourteen years of age are referred to such agencies in instances of trouble. However, those from fourteen to eighteen who run afoul of the law are taken before what is essentially a criminal justice system. For minor offenses, the state provides a "petty offense judge." Hearing such cases as those involving traffic violations, the petty offense judge can order educational measures, fines, or short-term imprisonment for those found guilty (Selih, 1978). Juveniles from fourteen to eighteen accused of more serious crimes must go to a formal court.

For serious offenses, the case of a juvenile is in the hands of the public prosecutor, who, on receiving a police report, has the sole discretion of dismissing a case or presenting a charge to the court. Like Argentina, Yugoslavia has no separate courts for juveniles. There is a system of juvenile panels and special sections for juveniles as part of its regular court system, but the key difference between such sections and adult courts is in the effort to incorporate material from social welfare agencies into court proceedings. Before the court, procedures are much the same for the adults and juveniles alike. *Parens patriae* has never been accepted as a legal doctrine in Yugoslavia, so that the child has the same protections as adults in court, including — as in the United States since *Kent* and *Gault* — the right to have counsel present at all stages of the proceedings.

For those found guilty, several measures are possible. Reprimands are issued in some cases, as are orders for strict supervision by parents, a foster family, or a social welfare agency. In addition, the law provides for several kinds of reformatory institutions, and, in especially severe cases, for "juvenile imprisonment." Over the last ten years, it should be noted, strict supervision in one form or another has accounted for over half of the dispositions in Yugoslavian juvenile cases.

The Yugoslavian juvenile justice system clearly incorporates some elements of social welfare, but its thrust is nevertheless legalistic. There is no effort to remove a youngster accused of an offense from the procedures of the criminal justice system. Although treatment plays an important role in the dispositions available to a Yugoslav court, it is nevertheless the outcome of what is essentially a criminal proceeding. As in Argentina, a juvenile offender is above all a young person adjudged guilty of a criminal act, and the process of adjudication stands as the key to the system. Certainly, many of the developments in the American juvenile justice system over the last quarter century have moved it in the direction of legalism, at least those having to do with the operations and jurisdiction of the juvenile courts.

South Africa. Another system that retains clear ties to a criminal justice model is that of South Africa. There, too, a child charged with committing a criminal act is tried under the regular criminal law. The age of full criminal responsibility is seven years, and any child over that age accused of committing a crime will be brought to trial before a regularly constituted criminal court. Although children are tried in separate proceedings, and with the public excluded, in most respects the trial of a juvenile offender is identical to that of an adult. The court atmosphere is formal; the charges are read and the child is required to plead; evidence is presented and the child has the right to cross-examine witnesses; the child may be represented by counsel. Only if adjudged guilty do "principles of differentiation" enter into the proceedings. Usually in passing sentence the judicial officer is to take the reports of social welfare workers into account.

A variety of dispositions is available to a South African judge: reprimands, forms of probation and suspended sentencing, and reform schools, as well as fines and imprisonment, can be imposed on the young offender in South Africa. In addition, South African courts may impose corporal punishment, with whipping serving in recent years as the most common disposition in juvenile cases. Such whippings can be brutal. If in excess of four strokes, a whipping will often cause bleeding and scarring, and South African law allows up to ten "cuts" to be administered to young offenders. The average South African sentence is for six strokes. Whipping is used for juvenile offenders and adult criminals alike (Midgley, 1975).

Despite the attention that may be given to social welfare reports at the time of disposition, then, South Africa's system of juvenile justice bears extremely close ties to the larger criminal justice system. Indeed, it shows the least concern for "juvenile delinquency" as a distinctive problem of social and criminal justice and stresses, even more than the Argentinian and Yugoslav systems, the character of the young offender as a person adjudged guilty of a criminal act. Even in the disposition of cases, South African courts tend to focus on the punishment of crime rather than treatment as a response to delinquency.

In such systems as those of Argentina, Yugoslavia, and South Africa, then, juvenile delinquency is treated as, above all, a legal problem to be handled through the legal mechanisms of the criminal justice system. Although, again, considerations of child welfare are not absent from these systems, the tendency is, nevertheless, to focus on the criminal character of the juvenile delinquent. Legal procedures maintain this point of view. And, again, one can certainly see a tendency toward legalism in many recent American developments as well.

The Social Welfare Approach —————————————————

Scotland

One of the most significant efforts in recent years to move the handling of juvenile delinquency away from a criminal justice model has taken place in Scotland. The Scottish juvenile justice system itself may be traced back to 1908, with the creation of juvenile courts. This system subsequently underwent a number of reforms, each emphasizing prevention over punishment in the approach to problems of juvenile crime. The real push for reform came in 1961, however, with the appointment of a committee under the chairmanship of Lord Kilbrandon to consider Scottish provisions "relating to the treatment of juvenile delinquents and juveniles in need of care or protection or beyond parental control" (in G. Murray, 1976:3–4). The Kilbrandon Committee published a report in 1964 advocating that juvenile offenders under sixteen be taken out of the criminal justice system and that alternative procedures be set up for them. This report became the basis of a distinctive Scottish approach to juvenile justice, an approach established with the passage of the Social Work (Scotland) Act 1968.

The underlying philosophy of the Kilbrandon Report and of the resulting Scottish system was based on the central importance of treatment. The report itself recommended strongly against the use of criminal proceedings for young offenders since, it argued, "the 'crime-responsibility-punishment' concept militates against preventive action against *potential* delinquents . . . a stigma is attached in the public eye to the conviction of a crime . . . the standard of proof is high" and, thus, from the standpoint of due process, the state was prohibited from taking necessary preventive actions. Moreover, the report argued against a criminal justice approach because "punishment cannot be extended to any substantial degree beyond the individual offender . . . but treatment can be applied beyond the individual who committed the act to others" (in Morris, 1972: 693). The 1968 act embodied the Kilbrandon Committee's views —views supported, too, in a 1966 government "White Paper"—by establishing a "Children's Hearings" system in which juvenile offenses were to be heard by a panel of concerned citizens, relying heavily on reports from social workers and other professionals. This panel was empowered either to dismiss the case or to make a supervision order for the young offender. The act established the minimum age of legal responsibility at eight, and the hearing panels were given authority to treat all "in need of compulsory measures of care" under the age of sixteen, or those between sixteen and eighteen who were in such need and who were already under a supervision order (Martin, Fox, and Murray, 1981).

Moreover, the Scottish act identified several categories of children as "in need of compulsory measures of care." Obviously, the act was aimed toward those accused of violations of the criminal code, but also subject to the system were those out of parental control or who fell into bad company, those suffering from parental neglect, and truants. In addition, underscoring the protective character of the act, female children living in households in which incest had taken place or any children living in homes with someone who had been guilty of a crime could also be taken before a panel. Since the act was passed, by far the greatest number of youngsters have faced the system as a result of having committed offenses — 80 per cent in 1979, and the proportion has been fairly constant since the system was established — but the scope of the act was intended to be quite broad, and youngsters have been referred to the system for the entire range of causes recognized by the 1968 act.

The crucial figure in the operation of the Scottish Children's Hearings system is the individual known as the "reporter." In cases where a juvenile is charged with the commission of an offense, the police must take the case to the reporter, whose job it is to investigate the charges and to determine whether the accused is in need of care other than that which the parents can provide. The reporter may then decide to take no action, may refer the child to a voluntary supervision program, or may, if the child appears to be "in need of compulsory measures of care," refer the case to a children's hearing. Should the case go to a hearing, the reporter is responsible for organizing the hearing, seeing to it that all the necessary information is received by hearing panel members, and attending the hearing in order to provide whatever other information may be needed (Finlayson, 1976:48–50).

In general, for a case involving a criminal offense to go to hearing, the question of guilt must be established beforehand, but this is usually done by the child's own admission. If the child should plead innocence, then the reporter must also apply to the local sheriff (a judicial officer in Scotland, where the criminal court is called a "sheriff's court") for a finding, and, indeed, in such cases, the young offender can still receive a regular trial. Even in the event of such a trial, however, juvenile cases are commonly referred to a hearing for disposition.

Once a case goes to a hearing, it is presented to a panel of lay people, based on the reading of the reports and the hearing itself, to diagnose and treat the causes of problems in a juvenile offender.

Prior to the hearing, the members of the panel receive reports from social workers and from the school attended by the child. Panel members may also receive reports from psychiatrists, child guidance agencies, and other professionals. These reports comment on the child's family background, on previous experiences with such agencies, and on the child's school habits, and provide clinical assessments of the child (Hiddleston, 1976). The reports not only give the panel members necessary information on the young offender but serve as the basis for much of the discussion that will occupy the hearing.

The hearings do not take place in anything like a courtroom. They usually occur in a fairly informal setting and involve the three panel members and the child, along with parents and, often, a social worker. Legal aid is not available to children appearing before a hearing, but families are permitted to be accompanied by a friend or other representative. The hearings generally last under a half hour. Panels must observe certain procedures, including a plain statement of the charge, a consultation with the family in regard to disposition, and a discussion of the substance of the background reports given to the panel. Nevertheless, the hearing is to be characterized by informality and open discussion, as panel members work with the child and family in order to find the right treatment for the offender. Discussions tend to be fairly wide-ranging; the youngster is questioned not only about the offense but also about family life, school, hobbies, and future plans. Parents, too, may be questioned about their habits and behavior. Throughout, the dominant style of the panel members is supposed to be encouraging and sympathetic.

Several dispositions are available to a panel. It may decide simply to discharge the youngster on the ground that compulsory measures of care are not necessary; indeed, this is the decision in a great number of cases. It may order the child placed under supervision in the community, usually under the guidance of a social worker. Or it may commit the child to a "residential establishment" (Jones and Murray, 1978). In Scotland, such institutions include the "List D schools" — in essence, reform schools, residential assessment centers, and children's homes and hostels run by voluntary and religious organizations (K. Murray, 1976b). In keeping with the treatment focus of the Scottish system, however, institutionalization is the least frequently used of the possible dispositions available to the panel members (Jones and Murray, 1978).

There are clear conceptual ties between the Scottish system and the American juvenile court ideal as it began to emerge near the end of the last century. In its focus on treatment, in its effort to reach youngsters with problems as well as those accused of criminal offenses, and in its emphasis on informal procedures — even to the point of employing lay people rather than legal professionals to dispose of cases — the Scottish hearing system embodies much that proponents of juvenile courts hoped to create in the American juvenile justice system.

And like the American juvenile courts, the Scottish hearing system, in action, does not always measure up to its own ideals, at least not in the view of many critics. For instance, the 1968 act made no specific provision for the selection of panel members (K. Murray, 1976a), nor, for that matter, did it or the Kilbrandon Report seek to justify the use of lay people for the panels (May, 1977). The ideal has been to create panels that represent a cross section of the local population, but critics have argued that, in practice, panels tend to be fairly homogenous, drawn mainly from the middle class (Morris, 1972). Such panel members are not always sympathetic to lower-class offenders brought before them.

In addition, although panel members are supposed to be encouraging and friendly to young offenders — much like the ideal American juvenile court judge —transcripts and accounts of the hearings themselves show that, in Scotland as in America, this is not always the case. Panel members often confront young people angrily. Questioning can be sarcastic and abusive (Martin, Fox, and Murray, 1981).

But despite the extent to which Scottish Children's Hearings do not always take the form intended by the 1968 act, the social welfare focus of the system remains clear, and the Scottish system stands in sharp contrast with the criminal justice model examined earlier. Although, to be sure, children may still go to court — and, it should be noted, a hearing panel's disposition may be appealed by a youngster to a court of law — the main effort is to remove the young offender from the justice system altogether and to focus discussion and treatment on the child rather than the offense. This "decriminalization" of delinquency is a key to the social welfare approach to juvenile justice.

Other Social Welfare Approaches

Scandinavia. The lay hearing system is not unique to Scotland and was, in fact, pioneered in the Scandinavian countries. As early as the 1890s, Norway had established communal child welfare boards, composed of a medical doctor, a judge, and four elected members, to investigate juvenile matters (Sundeen, 1976). In Denmark, in 1905, "protection boards" composed of teachers, clergy and physicians were established for much the same purpose (Munch-Petersen, 1980). The Swedish system, based on child welfare boards, was established in 1902 (Nyquist, 1960), and these boards likewise consist of lay people chosen by the local government. Each board is served by a staff of social workers (Nyquist, 1978).

As in Scotland, the Scandinavian boards stress social and psychological questions and treatment over crime and punishment. Hearings are usually conducted with informality, and the boards deal not only with offenders but with those children who, for other reasons, are thought to be at risk. In Sweden, this means that the board deals with all delinquent and neglected youths under fifteen who get into difficulty (fifteen being the age of criminal responsibility) and with those from fifteen to seventeen whom the public prosecutor refers to the board rather than to a court for trial—as well as with some offenders from eighteen to twenty years old (Sundeen, 1976:115). In Denmark, the practice is much the same (Munch-Petersen, 1980:29). It should be noted, however, that when prosecutors do refer accused juveniles to court for trial—as happens, for example, in Denmark in about one half of all cases—the juvenile does go through the same adversarial legal proceedings as those confronting adults (Jensen, Mednick, and Van Dusen, 1984).

In the hearings themselves, the focus is mainly on welfare questions. In Sweden, the decision of whether a child shall appear before the board is in the hands of a social worker, who has considerable discretion in deciding whether to ignore an incident, simply to discuss it with the parents, or to take the child before the child welfare board. If the child goes before the board, panel members there, as in Scotland, not only discuss matters with the youngster but are supported by a report containing an array of social and psychological information (Sundeen, 1976). Thus, here too the effort is to "decriminalize" juvenile delinquency, in both approach and procedure.

South Australia. In the Australian state of South Australia, which has laid claim to having established the world's first juvenile court—in 1890 (Nichols, 1981)—a 1921 Juvenile Court Act established "Juvenile Aid Panels" to provide alternatives to court proceedings, especially for first offenders aged ten to sixteen (Sarri, 1978). A 1979 revision of the act renamed these "Children's Aid Panels" and gave them jurisdiction over young offenders from ten to eighteen. The panels consist of a police officer and a social worker and usually meet in the community welfare office of the district in which the youngster resides. Like panels in Scotland or the Scandinavian countries, the South Australian Children's Aid Panel seeks to uncover a range of factors that might have produced delinquent behavior in the child (Nichols, 1981:161). Juvenile courts remain in place, however, to hear serious offenses along with not-guilty pleas (Sarri and Bradley, 1980), and, although these courts also take cognizance of social and psychological factors, they remain legal bodies in which the young offender is encouraged to have legal representation (Nichols, 1981).

The systems we have seen in Scotland, Scandinavia, and South Australia represent efforts to establish not simply alternatives for juvenile offenders but alternatives to any system of juvenile justice, as such, by means of welfare-oriented and lay-run panels for addressing problems of juvenile misbehavior and crime. Adopting a treatment model almost exclusively, these systems make at least fitful attempts to "decriminalize" juvenile crime and, in line with general international tendencies, to draw heavily on community resources instead of institutions in seeking to keep juvenile crime under control.

Treatment and Punishment in Tension: England and Wales

The Evolution of English Juvenile Justice

Much of the background to the contemporary English system of juvenile justice is similar to that of the United States, which should not be surprising. After all, during the nineteenth century, there had been frequent contact between American and British reformers; ideas about the proper causes and treatment of juvenile delinquency were exchanged freely and were, as a result, markedly similar. Private reform schools were established in England as in the United States, and, as early as 1840, efforts were made to establish a juvenile court (Parsloe, 1978). The ideology of *parens patriae* was, of course, strong in English thought about the care of children. In addition, English law had provided for systems of probation beginning in the late nineteenth century, at about the same time as in the United States.

Finally, England established a distinctive system of juvenile justice at about the same time that such systems were being developed in the American states. This was done through the Children Act of 1908, establishing juvenile courts that were to be special sittings of magistrates' courts and were to handle all offenses committed by seven- to fifteen-year-old children (except those committed jointly with an adult). These courts had the power to deal, as well, with problems of neglected or destitute children. In addition, the act made provision for "juvenile-adults" from sixteen to twenty, who could be committed to special institutions, which came to be known as "Borstals," where they would receive some training and from which they would be subject to release under supervision (L. Fox, 1952:335).

Over the next half century, the 1908 Children Act was amended and refined. As we noted earlier, the Children and Young Persons Act of 1933 raised the minimum age at which a child was subject to juvenile court proceedings to eight and established a body of "approved schools," drawing together a body of older industrial schools and reformatories to treat youngsters from ten to seventeen. A Criminal Justice Act of 1948 further refined the English system by seeking to ensure that no children should be sent to prison. This act also provided for Attendance Centres, by means of which young offenders would receive "deprivation of leisure" without removal from home. The offender was forced to attend the center at hours not interfering with school or work, there to engage in a variety of activities. The 1948 act also provided for other institutions to hold young offenders over the age of fourteen.

As was also the case in the United States, however, major changes in the English system occurred in the 1960s. In 1963, a Children and Young Persons Act encouraged the diversion of young offenders from the juvenile courts and raised the age of responsibility from eight to ten. Later in the decade, in response to the urgings of social reformers, the government issued two "White Papers," each stressing decriminalization and treatment as opposed to criminal justice approaches in the handling of young offenders. Above all, these White Papers urged the increasing use of services other than incarceration for juvenile offenders and sought to put England in a distinctly welfare-oriented approach to juvenile justice. It is instructive to compare this development in English thinking with developments in the United States at the same time. If the encouragement of "decarceration" was in keeping with American concerns about the institutionalization of juvenile offenders, by stressing a welfare orientation, the White Papers moved the English system away from the due process concerns and the formalization of juvenile justice that also occurred in the United States during this time. This is significant, because the second of these White Papers, *Children in Trouble* (1968), directly influenced the passage of the Children and Young Persons Act of 1969, a major step in the development of the juvenile justice system in England.

The 1969 Children and Young Persons Act made several important changes in English juvenile justice. First, it further raised the minimum age from ten to twelve and provided that a child under twelve might be proceeded against only by "care" proceedings, with the commission of an offense being among those factors which could result in a "care" order (Gandy, 1977). The act required consultation between police and the local social service agencies (Parsloe, 1978) and officially encouraged "decarceration" as a response to juvenile offenses. Although possible dispositions still included fines (which were to be imposed upon the parent of a child under fourteen), orders to appear at an Attendance Centre, commission to a detention center or, for those over fifteen, to a Borstal, or various forms of supervision by probation (Cavenagh, 1981), as a part of the effort by proponents of the 1969 act to move more fully toward a welfare approach to delinquency, the act also encouraged the use of supervision with no penal sanctions instead of probation (using social workers instead of probation officers as supervisors); the absorption of approved schools and remand centers into a system of community houses; and the phasing out of attendance centers and detention centers, and of Borstals for offenders under seventeen. Although the juvenile courts remained intact, there was a clear move toward decriminalization and a welfare approach in the 1969 Children and Young Persons Act, which remains the basis of English juvenile justice.

The 1969 Children and Young Persons Act and English Juvenile Justice

Under the 1969 Act, English juvenile courts have both criminal and civil jurisdiction over children and young people under the age of seventeen. The court has original criminal jurisdiction over youngsters accused of all offenses except murder. The court has civil jurisdiction over care proceedings for a youngster whose "proper development is being avoidably prevented or neglected," whose health is endangered or who suffers from ill treatment, who "is exposed to moral danger," who "is beyond the control of his parent or guardian," or who "is not receiving efficient full-time education suitable to his age, ability and aptitude" (Parsloe, 1978:147–148).

As in the United States, the police play an important gatekeeping role in English juvenile justice under the 1969 act. They have primary responsibility for referring young people to the courts and considerable discretion in making such referrals. If possible, the police are expected to avoid sending a young person before the court through the use of what is called a "police caution" or through referral to an appropriate social welfare agency (see a related discussion in Chapter 9). It is also the responsibility of the police, in a criminal action, to investigate the charges as part of the determination of a young person's guilt or innocence. Finally, the police must decide, should they take a youngster before the juvenile court, which type of proceeding is to be conducted.

In the English juvenile justice system, two types of proceedings are held in the juvenile courts. One is a care proceeding, in which a young offender may be found in need of further supervision, usually within the community. The care proceeding is intended to identify the kind of supervision appropriate to the individual young person. The other is a criminal proceeding, which focuses on the question of guilt or innocence and, in the case of a finding of guilty, on determining the proper disposition. Young people accused of grave offenses, we should note, may be referred to the adult criminal courts. This is a requirement in cases of murder (Farrington, 1984).

In the juvenile court itself, the atmosphere is supposed to be less formal than that of the adult court. Procedures are supposed to be orderly; their benefit to the young person is supposed to be made clear (Cavenagh, 1981). Juveniles brought before the court may have legal representation and may apply for legal aid if they or their families cannot afford an attorney. For youngsters in danger of being institutionalized, there must also be a "social inquiry" report. This report, prepared by probation officers or social workers, is intended to give the court the background it needs in passing sentence on the youngster by giving a full picture of the young offender's family life, school record, social circumstances, and other relevant information (Farrington, 1984).

As we have already noted, one major purpose of the 1969 act was to encourage decarceration. The dispositions available to the court recognize this purpose, and the social inquiry report plays a major role in determining whether a youngster will receive one of the available forms of probation and supervision or will be sentenced to one of the several types of institutions in England devoted to young offenders. The English approach does not go as far as the Scottish or Scandinavian in basing juvenile justice primarily on welfare concerns. But the 1969 act clearly intended to give those concerns an important place in the juvenile justice system.

The Tension

But what makes the English system significant, comparatively, is the extent to which its recent history reveals the real tensions that can exist between welfare-oriented approaches and more punitive ones, and the extent to which that history shows how that "hardening of the process" we discussed in regard to American juvenile justice in earlier chapters has an international dimension, as well. Despite the aims of the 1969 act, the welfare approach to juvenile delinquency never wholly caught on in the English juvenile justice system. In part, this was because English thinking was split by many of the same concerns that one sees in the United States, particularly by the division between those who genuinely want welfare-oriented approaches and those who believe that only punitive approaches will help to resolve the problem posed for society by juvenile crime.

This division was clearly apparent in England at the time the 1969 act was passed. Members of the Conservative party in Parliament objected to the act precisely because of its welfare orientation, and they focused particularly on its decriminalization of juvenile offenses. They objected to the role given to social workers rather than legal professionals in the decision of cases; they objected to the act on the ground that the dispositions available to the juvenile courts in no case constituted what they considered "punishment." Available dispositions, they argued, were either pure welfare measures or what were, in essence, deferred fines (Thorpe, Smith, Green, and Paley, 1980).

Perhaps those Conservative MPs need not have worried, for despite the aims of the 1969 act, English juvenile justice did not go very far in the way of a social welfare approach. The Canadian scholar Gandy (1977:19) has written that "England represents a prime example of the futility of trying to use the juvenile court as a simultaneous extension of the community's social welfare services and the criminal justice system." Indeed, English juvenile courts have tried to balance the two approaches since the passage of the 1969 act. But, in their operations, the courts have also shown something less than enthusiasm for the act's more welfare-oriented provisions.

For one thing, it appears that some of the act's provisions were never implemented at all, including that which raised the age of legal responsibility (Muncie, 1984). For another, many students of delinquency in England agree that juvenile authorities have failed to use properly and fully the treatment emphases of the act. Norman Tutt, in a 1981 article, argued that, in fact, the welfare approach was never really tried in England. There was no massive intervention by social workers into the juvenile justice system; instead, there was actually a *decline* in the proportion of offenders receiving supervision by a social worker and an increase in the group receiving fines or attendance center orders, or even imprisonment, dispositions that the act had sought to bring to an end (Burney, 1985; Tutt, 1981: see also Gelsthorpe and Morris, 1983).

Ironically, according to some observers, the possibility that the act would actually increase the punitive character of the juvenile justice system was built into the act itself. One of its purposes in developing a welfare-oriented approach to delinquency was to give great powers of discretion to the police, the courts, and other officials in order to encourage the handling of cases in a very individual way. In many areas of England, however, officials have used such discretion to serve more conservative ends. Parker, Casburn, and Turnbull (1980) have made in-depth studies of the operations of individual English juvenile courts and have found jurisdictions in which "punitive" ideologies — rather than an orientation toward welfare — have dominated virtually every aspect of the system's operations, from the conduct of the hearing to the usual sentencing of young offenders to custodial institutions rather than to the ideal of treatment within the community.

The 1982 Criminal Justice Act

These tendencies in the operations of the 1969 Children and Young Persons Act were ultimately given legal sanction in the 1982 Criminal Justice Act. The 1982 act was the result of sentiments that had begun to build during the debate over its predecessor. These sentiments had gained influence throughout the decade of the 1970s, especially as the Conservative party gained strength in English politics. This led, increasingly, to a return to a criminal justice model for handling juvenile crime. A 1975 Children Act provided formally for legal representation for youngsters accused of crime (Muncie, 1984). And, in 1977, powers were returned to the courts that had been given to social workers by the original act (Tutt, 1981).

In a 1979 general election, the Conservative party took power in England on a "law-and-order" platform, and, in 1980, the government issued a White Paper entitled *Young Offenders* that set forth a more conservative approach to juvenile justice in England. Treatment was not rejected in the Conservative White Paper. Diversion was recommended, chiefly through the use of police cautions (see Chapter 9). Intermediate treatment programs were maintained — although here they were recommended as voluntary programs for troubled youngsters rather than as possible dispositions for offenders by the courts. At the same time, the White Paper proposed to retain and expand the detention center system (Morris and Giller, 1981). Indeed, the overall thrust of the 1980 White Paper was to return to a custodial approach: to create a juvenile justice system in which more youngsters accused of crimes would go to court and more of those found guilty would be institutionalized (1981:81–82; League Leader, 1981).

Much of what the 1980 White Paper recommended was written into law in 1982, in the Criminal Justice Act. In this act, as Muncie (1984) describes it, the state attempted to pursue goals of treatment and punishment at the same time. On the one hand, courts were given more discretionary power in sentencing, which appears to have encouraged the already existing trends toward custodial approaches. Along with this, the act "officially abandoned" parts of the 1969 act that had advocated phasing out custody for younger offenders. On the other hand, it provided for new, noncustodial dispositions, including the imposition of a curfew on the delinquent. It is not clear, according to Muncie, how such new, noncustodial measures are to take force. In any case, the increased use of custody, as favored in the 1980 White Paper, appears to be shaping the current direction of English juvenile justice.

The Conservative position represents what Tutt has described as the rediscovery of "the deliberately depraved delinquent." Identifying a "small minority" for whom treatment measures are likely to have no effect, the Conservatives in the White Paper favored a toughening up of the law to provide deterrent sentences rather than welfare measures for such offenders (Tutt, 1981:249). And in its general view of delinquents and delinquency, the White Paper took a much harder line than that found in English documents in previous years. Tutt notes, for example, that whereas the White Papers of the 1960s laid stress on the fact that juvenile offenders are also children, with connotations of immaturity and nonresponsibility, the 1980 document repeatedly refers to "juveniles," "juvenile crime," and "juvenile offending." In the earlier documents, the youngsters were children first and offenders second; now the order has been reversed, so that offending is to become the focus. And this view was to dominate English law and practice.

It is difficult to know at this writing how permanent the effect of this Conservative reaction will be for the English juvenile justice system, other than to strengthen tendencies already present for a legalistic approach and ones that emphasize punitive over welfare measures in dispositions. There are no clear data, interestingly, to confirm the relative effectiveness of one approach over the other (Farrington, 1984), so that the debate will necessarily have more to do with principles than with results. Nevertheless, we can see in the English example something of the difficulty in trying to achieve a balance between two approaches within a single system.

Treating Delinquency in Marxist States

The USSR

The magnitude of the delinquency problem in the Soviet Union is hard to know. No detailed national data exist on delinquency, and it is only in recent years that Soviet scholars and officials have begun to discuss the issue publicly. That there is a delinquency problem is, however, clear. As Juviler and Forschner (1978) have pointed out, recent years have also seen a widespread proliferation of agencies, educational programs, and delinquency prevention techniques that indicate that the Soviets themselves see a problem and are seeking ways of coming to terms with it.

Historically, the problem has been a serious one, especially as a product of the wars and revolutions of twentieth-century Russia. The revolution of 1917 and the subsequent civil war left many young Russians homeless and led to a dramatic rise in delinquency. Large groups of Russian youths, finding themselves in a disorganized society and without adequate adult supervision because of the death of one or both parents or the dislocations of their families, formed marauding bands, housing themselves in cellars and makeshift shelters near large urban centers. These *bezprizornye* (literally, "the neglected"), said to number more than half a million by 1921, proved intransigent because, authorities claimed, "they had been influenced by the picaresque life of the vagabond" — the self-indulgence, the excitement, the camaraderie of street gang life.

Today, with the Communist regime having been in place over seventy years, delinquency still remains a major Soviet problem. Much of it takes the form of offenses categorized under Soviet law as "hooliganism," acts that can include anything from disturbing the peace to harassing and beating up passersby, and may also include such disparate "offenses" as car theft and the expression of "unacceptable" opinions in a classroom (Zeldes, 1980). In the destruction and chaos wrought by World War II, many youngsters again became homeless and posed severe problems for the Soviet state. Since the 1950s, although Soviet society has remained fairly stable, delinquency has continued to be a difficult problem, although, again, its magnitude is hard to know (Connor, 1972a).

For the most part, juvenile status offenses seem to outweigh crimes as such, involving such acts as petty hooliganism and running away from home, children's homes, or reform schools. Thievery and group violence seem to dominate juvenile criminal activity, with about 75 per cent of juvenile stealing, robberies, and mayhem being committed by groups. These groups are, however, very different from the highly structured, relatively permanent American gangs. They seem to represent, rather, what has been described as a "spontaneous and temporary coming together for the purpose of some relatively specific act" (Juviler and Forschner, 1978:19).

Soviet Thought. As we noted in Chapter 6, the official explanation for delinquency in the Soviet Union, like that for all crime, derives from Marx and Lenin. According to this view, crime is the product of the exploitation of the masses; with the realization of socialist and, later, communist society, such exploitation will end, and the problem of crime will "wither away." Thus, as we have seen, Soviet criminologists argue that juvenile delinquency represents remnants of capitalism in Soviet society, with the delinquent being a "bearer of remnants of the past." They also cite the negative influence of Western literature and films on Soviet young people (Borodin, 1980). A newspaper notes that Russian adolescents insist on calling Moscow's Gorky Street *Brudvay*. Russian youths are said to engage in the same kind of "nihilistic revolt as that of their coevals in the west." The report observes (Geis, 1965):

> Party agitators exhort them. Komsomol bully squads rout them out of restaurants and cafes and send them home. Photographs of them are plastered on billboards under the heading: "Parasites, Get Out." They are shipped to virgin lands or to reconstruction sites in Siberia. But nothing that the party has been able to devise wins back the loyalty of the bored, nihilistic and disoriented generation.
>
> "This is our greatest defeat," a middle-aged party member conceded. "The young people have deserted the cause. I do not know how we are going to get them back." The number of internal rebels are great. They can be seen everywhere. They dance to western music. They wear western-style clothes. They act as much like westerners as they are able.

Delinquency, according to Soviet commentators, is an outgrowth of such continuing Western influence. "It is," Sakharov (1977:37) writes, "an abominable heritage of the past that ultimately will disappear totally."

Still, despite the power of the official explanation for delinquency as a remnant of capitalism, Soviet criminologists have also turned to explanations that have a more familiar ring to American readers. Like their Western counterparts, Soviet criminologists look to a plethora of social causes in seeking to account for the problem. The emotional and intellectual immaturity of adolescents, problems in the family, bad influences from adults, unemployment, and a lack of adequate recreational facilities are all cited by Soviet criminologists as reasons for delinquency. For the most part, modern Soviet modes of treating delinquency result from such views (Juviler and Forschner, 1978; Shichor, 1983; Zeldes, 1980).

Prevention. Prevention programs take several forms in the Soviet juvenile justice system. Much preventive work in the USSR involves educational programs designed to teach law and a consciousness of law to young people in Soviet schools. According to Wenk (1978:21), crime and delinquency are seen not simply as individual matters in the USSR but more as threats "to the proper functioning of the political processes which constitute communist government" because of the great stress on social interdependence in Soviet ideology. In addition, Soviet policy has sought to act against delinquency by stressing the strengthening of social stability and solidarity in order to increase "group conformity." In regard to juvenile delinquency, this has meant, as in many treatment-oriented juvenile justice systems, intervention into problematical family situations, or other areas where, by their actions, young people appear to be at risk (Yakovlev, 1979).

Much of the preventive work of this sort is carried on at the local level by Commissions for Juvenile Affairs. These commissions, composed of eight to twelve volunteer members, have broad responsibilities and powers. They are to detect and investigate cases of inadequate supervision of children and of problems of social adjustment; they exert control over the activities of educational and cultural institutions; they may curtail specific sources of negative influence. They can also invoke sanctions against parents who fail to supervise their children adequately. Additionally, all cases of lawbreaking by those under the age of criminal responsibility — and some for those above that age — are referred to the commissions. These commissions' preventive work has been complemented by the 1977 establishment of inspectorates on juvenile affairs, which operate to detect and safeguard those youngsters who lack proper supervision (Juviler and Forschner, 1978; Yakovlev, 1979).

Procedures of Juvenile Justice in the USSR

Soviet law does not provide for a separate system of juvenile courts to deal with young people accused of having committed crimes. The age at which one faces prosecution as an adult in the Soviet Union is sixteen, although for such serious crimes as homicide, intentional battery, rape, assault, malicious hooliganism, and others, the age is fourteen. Cases involving offenders below that age are, as we have noted, referred to Commissions for Juvenile Affairs for disposition, as are from 25 to 33 per cent of older youngsters up to eighteen whose cases may be transmitted to the commissions by the investigator, procurator (essentially, a prosecutor), or court. Such a recommendation may be made for a youngster under eighteen when the crime is of no great social danger or the possibility exists of correcting the young offender's behavior without applying the sanctions of the criminal law (Kelina, 1979). In such cases, the commissions may issue a public reprimand, may impose fines against either the young offender or his or her parents, or may order the separation of parents and children. In addition, young offenders may be sentenced to special technical schools intended especially for eleven- to fourteen-year-olds or to special vocational schools designed for those from fifteen to eighteen. These provide vocational and secondary education (Borodin, 1980; Juviler and Forschner, 1978).

Most youngsters above the age of criminal responsibility must go before the same courts that deal with adult cases, with criminal cases being heard at the level of the "People's Court," the lowest-level court in the Soviet judicial system. Juvenile cases must be heard with the participation of defense counsel and the young offender's parents or other representatives. In addition, in many cases it is obligatory that an expert in juvenile psychology participate in the hearing (Baturov and Reshetnikov, 1977). People's Court judges, who are popularly elected, receive training in law that includes work in the area of juvenile delinquency, and Juviler and Forschner (1978) have noted that since the 1950s, juvenile procedures have made increasing use of judges, prosecutors, and investigators who actually specialize in juvenile cases.

Should the young offender be found guilty, several dispositions are available to the judge of the People's Court. These include deprivation of freedom, deprivation of freedom conditionally (a suspended sentence), corrective works in the community (usually compulsory work at some job with a deduction of up to 20 per cent of one's earnings), and such other measures as a fine or "social censure" (Connor, 1972a). Soviet courts have, in general, favored short terms of deprivation of freedom for young offenders, with sentences averaging from eleven to twelve months (Minkovsky, 1976).

Punishment by deprivation of freedom is governed by the corrective labor law, the purpose of which, beyond punishment, is, in the words of one Soviet jurist, "to correct and reform offenders in the spirit of a conscientious attitude toward work, strict observance of the laws, and respect for the rules of socialist community life" (Shupilov, 1979:180). Juvenile offenders are sentenced to educational labor colonies that are intended to embody this principle. Inmates live in barracks, fenced off from the outside, and are expected to engage in socially useful work, which can include metal working, woodworking, and construction. They work for four to five hours a day and also receive compulsory vocational and general education. Those reaching age eighteen may be transferred to adult corrective labor colonies (Connor, 1972a:129–133; Shupilov, 1979:202), although Soviet criminologists and legal officials have recognized that this often produces the problems resulting from allowing young people to mix with older offenders (Connor, 1972b:385). The law provides for a maximum confinement of three years for juvenile offenders (Zeldes, 1980).

Juvenile Justice in Other Marxist States

The People's Republic of China. The juvenile justice systems of other Marxist states share basic assumptions and practices with the Soviet system, although they also reflect the needs and legal traditions of the specific societies they are intended to serve. In the People's Republic of China, which lacked a code of substantive or procedural criminal law until mid-1979 (Leng, 1982), the same sense of crime as a threat to the community as a whole is written into the law, and, as in the USSR, the age at which one faces treatment as an adult is sixteen, generally, with fourteen being the minimum age for more serious crimes. As in the USSR too, there are no separate juvenile courts, but the law provides that young offenders "shall receive a lesser punishment or a mitigated punishment" (Criminal Law of China, 1982:141–142). Neighborhood guidance teams, work-study schools, and reformatories are provided for young offenders in the People's Republic, although they may face adult punishments, as well, including fines and imprisonment (Jiuming, 1982). Chinese law provides that persons under eighteen at the time of the crime shall not receive the death penalty (Criminal Law of China, 1982), a provision also found in Soviet law (Kelina, 1979).

But perhaps the most significant feature of juvenile justice in the People's Republic of China is the importance of local, even neighborhood, "committees" to the system. An incident from mid-1985 is illustrative. In that year, after Hong Kong defeated the Chinese national soccer team in Peking, enraged youthful supporters of the Chinese hurled bottles at members of the visiting team, smashed at least a dozen buses, overturned cars, threw rocks and spat at foreigners, and injured thirty Chinese policemen. Westerners estimated that about 5,000 Chinese youths were involved in the outbreak. Government officials bemoaned the failure of the youths to adhere to the Maoist doctrine of "friendship first, competition second." Chinese newspapers described the rioters as "a small number of black sheep," while the police said that the riot was provoked by a core of "troublemakers" who had done similar things before (Burns, 1985).

In the weeks following the soccer game riot, members of the Chinese team apologized publicly, saying that their undisciplined behavior had set a poor example. "We have failed to live up to the expectations of the party and the masses of the entire country and let the people down," they wrote (China Gripped by Self-criticism, 1985). Foreign interpreters suggested that the riot seemed to represent "a cathartic outburst of pent-up frustration over recent price increases and other daily hardships" in Peking (1985). The 127 youths detained proved on investigation to be, rather than hooligans as first reported, university students and sons of party officials. Seven were eventually tried and given sentences ranging from six to thirty months in prison.

The public apology by the Chinese team members illustrates the results of the common method used in the country to resolve difficulties and disputes. China has more than 800,000 mediating committees, which serve in the place of the courts and bring neighborhood and workplace pressure upon a deviant to mend his or her ways and publicly to avow misbehavior, remorse, and future conformity. In a country in which "face" can be a particularly important aspect of social control, pressure from others can be much more effective than the impersonal court procedures that constitute the bulk of dispute resolutions in the United States.

Victor Li (1977), examining the Chinese system of social control, notes that the Chinese make strenuous efforts to keep laws simple and free of technicalities and that they have extensive public education about the nature of the legal system and its demands. He notes further (1977:145):

> small groups not only educate the public about law, but also play an important role in enforcement. They are extremely effective in bringing to light any member's deviations or incipient deviations from the accepted norms of thinking and behavior. Groups are formed of persons with close ties who must spend considerable time together. Thus, as a person's thinking begins to deviate, this is quickly observed by other members of the group during the course of study sessions or other activities. Similarly, one who steals would be unable to enjoy his newly found riches since the people around him would know or suspect how he had acquired them.

China has a system of social control that Westerners probably would regard as unduly intrusive upon privacy. Fragmentary reports indicate that the rates of crime and delinquency in that nation of more than one billion persons are probably lower than those in industrialized societies, as we have already discussed in regard to other developing nations. China also has what appears to be the toughest imposition of capital punishment by any nation in the world. An estimated 5,000 persons are executed there each year: what effect, if any, this has on ordinary crime, or whether the measure is primarily imposed on political offenders, is at the moment an unresolved question (see generally Tifft, 1985).

That allowance is made for juvenile offenders, however, is shown by a case in mid-1985 when the country's Supreme Court, in a rare public pronouncement, reported its review of a brutal rape-murder case. Fan Ming, eighteen, and Liu Xiloing, seventeen, had raped a seventeen-year-old girl and then killed her because they feared she would tell the authorities. They choked her into unconsciousness and then left her on the railroad tracks where she was run over by a train. The Supreme Court upheld the death penalty for both defendants, but ruled that Liu, because he was under eighteen, should be granted a two-year reprieve to show that he had rehabilitated himself. At the end of such a reprieve, Chinese courts generally lift a death sentence (Mann, 1985).

In recent years the Chinese have not only codified their criminal law but strengthened their law system generally and are enrolling thousands of young persons in law schools. For the first time since the Communist takeover in 1949, Supreme Court decisions are being made public. Nonetheless, China restricts the ability of defense lawyers to challenge evidence presented by the state, because criminal trials are not seen as adversary proceedings but as undertakings in which prosecutors and defense attorneys strive for agreement. The effects of these changes on the Chinese juvenile justice system remain to be seen.

Cuba. Juvenile delinquency in Cuba, another country governed by Marxist doctrine, was at first largely ignored by the regime because it was preoccupied with subduing counterrevolutionary forces, but Salas (1979) believes that introduction of Marxist rule into Cuba fractured traditional forms of social control and thereby led to an increase in delinquency. Large numbers of urban youth were mobilized for work in rural areas, material rewards were replaced by moral incentives to increase production, the role of the family was undercut, and religion came under attack. In 1967, minors had participated in 41 per cent of all crimes committed in Cuba; by 1971, the rate had increased to 50 per cent. As a result, in 1973 the government lowered the age at which an individual may face prosecution as an adult from eighteen to sixteen.

Little information has been released in recent years on the extent of delinquency in Cuba, but the adoption of particularly repressive antidelinquency legislation in 1977 would indicate that the behavior has become increasingly disturbing to the regime. School failure is believed to be a particularly significant source of delinquent acts. It is said that "the child who does not attend school has obviously had an improper upbringing and the school cannot counteract this upbringing if he does not attend" (Salas, 1979:20).

Like the USSR and China, Cuba has no separately constituted juvenile courts. Juvenile cases are handled—along with such other cases as those involving minor crimes, violations of the health code, personal quarrels, and so on—in "popular courts," staffed by part-time, lay judges who, upon taking office, receive some basic legal training. Such sanctions as public admonishments, an order for educational improvement, or incarceration — usually to a work camp, but possibly to one's own home — lie within the power of the Cuban popular courts.

Juvenile Justice in Marxist Societies. Juvenile justice systems vary greatly in Marxist nations. Specific systems probably have as much to do with legal traditions and local conditions as with any significant groundwork Marxism itself may provide. Nevertheless, Marxist societies do share in common a view that delinquency is not only criminal but also a threat to society as a whole. They take, that is, a view of delinquency that stresses its political character. As a result, the treatment of delinquency itself has political as well as social implications. And, in this view of delinquency, Marxist nations occupy a place of their own in the response of the world's nations to juvenile crime.

Summary

The character and significance of juvenile delinquency varies greatly throughout the world. In our own society and in other industrial nations, including the Soviet Union, delinquency is and has long been a serious social problem. In other nations, and particularly in the Third World, scholars have debated the degree to which juvenile delinquency may be seen as a serious problem. Although the way statistics are kept makes comparisons risky, the rate of juvenile crime seems to be remarkably low in those nations.

There may be several reasons for such differences in rates of juvenile crime, but the one most often cited has to do with the relative strength of traditional social and family institutions. Where these are strong, they may serve to inhibit delinquent behavior in youngsters. Where they are weak — or where, under the impact of urbanization and industrialization, they become weak — they can no longer serve to inhibit such behavior. Thus, juvenile delinquency becomes more significant. Social scientists have already noted such changes in parts of the world.

If one can find variations in the significance of delinquency, one can also find variations in approaches to juvenile justice in the nations of the world. This is not to say that there have been no general trends in juvenile justice internationally. There has been a general recognition of juvenile delinquency as a species of lawbreaking. There has been a general introduction of social welfare concerns. There has been a general tendency toward raising the age below which offenders are considered juveniles. And there has been a general move toward the use of probation, supervision, and other dispositions of juvenile cases that avoid incarceration. Still, major differences remain in the world's juvenile justice systems, and these allow us to categorize those systems in three rather broad groups.

Some nations such as Argentina and Yugoslavia take a strongly legalistic approach to juvenile justice. They focus their attention more or less exclusively on those youngsters who break the criminal laws of the nation rather than on "status offenders" or children "in danger." And they treat young offenders within the confines of the larger criminal justice system. They may provide for separate or closed hearings of juvenile offenders, or more lenient punishment, but in terms of focus and procedure, they treat young offenders as those who have broken the criminal law.

Other societies treat juvenile delinquency through approaches that are strongly based on concerns of social welfare. In such places as Scotland and in the Scandinavian countries, most young offenders are kept out of any proceedings resembling those of the criminal justice system. They are dealt with by panels of lay persons who are expected to put the welfare of the young person above the demands of criminal law and punishment. Although such systems are far from consistent in their adherence to the welfare approach, and although they do make provision for the institutionalization of young offenders, they nevertheless seek to move as far as possible toward the decriminalization of delinquency.

In England, there has been an attempt to combine the two approaches by maintaining several of the major aspects of a juvenile court system with strong criminal justice leanings but introducing into that system significant welfare components in regard to police practices, court procedure, and dispositions. The English system has not been everything its proponents hoped, and it has undergone great change since it received significant reshaping in 1969. It has also been inextricably tied to larger trends in English politics. There is some pessimism on the part of scholars, at least, about whether such a "mixed" system can ever really come into place.

Finally, we have looked at three examples of juvenile justice in Marxist nations. In the operations of their juvenile justice systems, there is no clear Marxist consensus. Nevertheless, all three have in common the desire to provide Marxist explanations for delinquency as a remnant of capitalism. All three share, as well, a strongly politicized view of delinquency as a form of social betrayal and have created responses to it on those grounds.

The American model for responding to juvenile justice must not, therefore, be thought of as the only way in which society may handle juvenile delinquency. Data on varying delinquency rates are so unreliable and so complicated by causal factors as to make it impossible to say which of the approaches we have examined may be the most effective at reducing the problem of delinquency in our own society or in other countries. But perhaps a consideration of alternatives will help to give us a fuller understanding of the institutions of American society as well.

References

Baturov, Genius G., and Reshetnikov, Felix M. 1977. Juvenile Delinquency Cases in Courts and Juvenile Commissions in the Soviet Union. *Juvenile Justice* 28:11–14.

Borodin, Stanislav V. 1980. The Soviet Union. In *Justice and Troubled Children Around the World,* edited by V. Lorne Stewart, 1:125–141. New York: New York Univ. Press.

Burney, Elizabeth, 1985. *Sentencing Young People: What Went Wrong with the Criminal Justice Act 1982.* Hants, England: Gower.

Burns, John F. 1985. Peking Council Meets over Soccer Riot. *New York Times* (May 21), 3.

Cavenagh, W. E. England and Wales. 1981. In *Justice and Troubled Children Around the World,* edited by V. Lorne Stewart, 2:35–66. New York: New York Univ. Press.

China Gripped by Self-criticism. 1985. *New York Times,* February 5, A7.

Chisholm, Barbara A. Canada. 1983. In *Justice and Troubled Children Around the World,* edited by V. Lorne Stewart, 5:1–20. New York: New York Univ. Press.

Connor, Walter D. 1972a. *Deviance in Soviet Society: Crime, Delinquency, and Alcoholism.* New York: Columbia Univ. Press.

———. 1972b. Soviet Criminal Correction System. *Law and Society Review* 6:367–391.

Criminal Law of the People's Republic of China, The, Adopted by the Second Meeting of the Fifth Session of the National People's Congress, July 1, 1979. 1982. *Journal of Criminal Law and Criminology* 73:138–170.

David, Pedro R. 1977. Juvenile Justice in Argentina. In *Youth Crime and Juvenile Justice: International Perspectives,* edited by Paul C. Friday and V. Lorne Stewart, 6–10. New York: Praeger.

———. 1981. Argentina. In *Justice and Troubled Children Around the World,* edited by V. Lorne Stewart, 2:1–34. New York: New York Univ. Press.

———, and Scott, Joseph W. 1973. A Cross-Cultural Comparison of Juvenile Offenders, Offenses, Due Processes, and Societies: The Cases of Toledo, Ohio, and Rosario, Argentina. *Criminology* 11:183–205.

De Fleur, Lois B. 1970. *Delinquency in Argentina: A Study of Cordoba's Youth.* Pullman: Washington State Univ. Press.

Farrington, David P. 1984. England and Wales. In *Western Systems of Juvenile Justice,* edited by Malcolm W. Klein, 71–95. Beverly Hills, Calif.: Sage.

Finlayson, Alan F. 1976. The Reporter. In *Children's Hearings,* edited by F. M. Martin and Kathleen Murray, 48–56. Edinburgh: Scottish Academic Press.

Fox, Lionel Wray. 1952. *The English Prison and Borstal Systems.* London: Routledge & Kegan Paul.

Gandy, John M. 1977. Juvenile Justice in England and Scotland. In *Youth Crime and Juvenile Justice: International Perspectives,* edited by Paul C. Friday and V. Lorne Stewart, 17–21. New York: Praeger.

Geis, Gilbert. 1965. *Juvenile Gangs.* Washington, D.C.: President's Committee on Juvenile Delinquency and Youth Crime.

Gelsthorpe, Loraine, and Morris, Allison. 1983. Attendance Centres: Policy and Practice. *Howard Journal of Penology and Crime Prevention* 22:101–118.

Hackler, James C. 1984. Canada. In *Western Systems of Juvenile Justice,* edited by Malcolm W. Klein, 39–69. Beverly Hills, Calif.: Sage.

Hartjen, Clayton A., and Priyadarsini, S. 1984. *Delinquency in India: A Comparative Analysis.* New Brunswick, N.J.: Rutgers Univ. Press.

Hiddleston, Vera. 1976. Reports for Children's Hearings. In *Children's Hearings,* edited by F. M. Martin and Kathleen Murray, 106–117. Edinburgh: Scottish Academic Press.

Igbinovia, Patrick Edobor. 1985. Perspectives on Juvenile Delinquency in Africa. *Journal of Juvenile Law* 9:12–35.

International Criminal Police Organization. 1984. International Crime Statistics for 1979 and 1980. St. Cloud, France: ICPO-Interpol General Secretariat.

———. 1985. International Crime Statistics for 1981–1982. St. Cloud, France: ICPO-Interpol General Secretariat.

Jensen, Kirsten, Mednick, Sarnoff A., and Van Dusen, Katherine. 1984. Denmark. In *Western Systems of Juvenile Justice,* edited by Malcolm W. Klein, 171–190. Beverly Hills, Calif.: Sage.

Jiuming, Wei. 1982. The People's Republic of China. In *Justice and Troubled Children Around the World,* edited by V. Lorne Stewart, 4:125–143. New York: New York Univ. Press.

Jones, Beti, and Murray, G. J. 1978. The Scottish Rejection of the Juvenile Courts. In

The Changing Faces of Juvenile Justice, edited by V. Lorne Stewart, 87–110. New York: New York Univ. Press.

Juvenile Protection Unit of the Paris Police Headquarters. 1978. *International Summaries: A Collection of Selected Translations in Law Enforcement and Criminal Justice* 1:99–109. Washington, D.C.: National Criminal Justice Reference Service, United States Department of Justice.

Juviler, Peter, and Forschner, Brian E. 1978. Juvenile Delinquency in the Soviet Union. *Prison Journal* 58 (Autumn/Winter):18–28.

Kelina, S. G. 1979. Substantive Criminal Law. In *The Criminal Justice System of the U.S.S.R.,* edited by M. Cherif Bassiouni and V. M. Savitski, 130–178. Springfield, Ill.: Thomas.

League Leader. 1981. *Howard Journal of Penology and Crime Prevention* 20:1–5.

Lemert, Edwin M. 1986. Juvenile Justice Italian Style. *Law and Society Review* 20:509–544.

Leng, Shao-Chuan. 1982. Criminal Justice in Post-Mao China: Some Preliminary Observations. *Journal of Criminal Law and Criminology* 73:204–237.

Li, Victor H. J. 1977. Law and Penology: Systems of Reform and Correction. In *Deviance and Control in Chinese Society,* edited by Amy A. Wilson, Sidney L. Greenblatt, and Richard H. Wilson, 140–150. New York: Praeger.

Mann, Jim. 1985. After 35 Years, High Court Goes Public in China. *Los Angeles Times* (May 28), 1, 19.

Martin, F. M., Fox, Sanford J., and Murray, Kathleen. 1981. *Children Out of Court.* Edinburgh: Scottish Academic Press.

May, David. 1977. Rhetoric and Reality: The Consequence of Unacknowledged Ambiguity in the Children's Panel System. *British Journal of Criminology* 17:209–227.

Midgley, James. 1975. *Children on Trial: A Study of Juvenile Justice.* Cape Town: National Institute for Crime Prevention and the Rehabilitation of Offenders.

Minkovsky, G. M. 1976. U.S.S.R.: Effectiveness of Treatment Measures and Problems of the Typology of Juvenile Delinquents. In *Juvenile Justice: An International Survey,* United Nations Social Defense Research Institute Publication No. 12 (Rome): 221–241.

Morris, Allison M. 1972. Children's Hearings in Scotland. *Criminal Law Review* November:693–701.

———, and Giller, Henri. 1981. Young Offenders: I. Law, Order and the Child-Care System. *Howard Journal of Penology and Crime Prevention* 20:81–89.

Muncie, John. 1984. *The Trouble with Kids Today: Youth and Crime in Post-War Britain.* London: Hutchinson.

Munch-Petersen, Erik. 1980. Denmark. In *Justice and Troubled Children Around the World,* edited by V. Lorne Stewart, 1:23–35. New York: New York Univ. Press.

Murray, George. 1976. Juvenile Justice Reform. In *Children's Hearings,* edited by F. M. Martin and Kathleen Murray, 3–18. Edinburgh: Scottish Academic Press.

Murray, Kathleen. 1976a. The Children's Panel. In *Children's Hearings,* edited by F. M. Martin and Kathleen Murray, 57–66. Edinburgh: Scottish Academic Press.

———. 1976b. Residential Provision. In *Children's Hearings,* edited by F. M. Martin and Kathleen Murray, 139–149. Edinburgh: Scottish Academic Press.

Nichols, Helen. 1981. South Australia. In *Justice and Troubled Children Around the World,* edited by V. Lorne Stewart, 3:141–174. New York: New York Univ. Press.

Nyquist, Ola. 1960. *Juvenile Justice: A Comparative Study with Special Reference to the Swedish Child Welfare Board and the California Juvenile Court System.* London: Macmillan.

———. 1978. The Swedish Approach to Juvenile Corrections. In *The Changing Faces of Juvenile Justice,* edited by V. Lorne Stewart, 135–147. New York: New York Univ. Press.

Parker, Howard, Casburn, Maggie, and Turnbull, David. 1980. The Production of Punitive Juvenile Justice. *British Journal of Criminology* 20:236–260.

Parker, L. Craig. 1986. *Parole and the Community Based Treatment of Offenders in Japan and the United States.* New Haven, Conn.: Univ. of New Haven Press.

Parsloe, Phyllida. 1978. *Juvenile Justice in Britain and the United States: The Balance of Needs and Rights.* London: Routledge and Kegan Paul.

Sakharov, A. R. 1977. On the Conception of the Causes of Crime in Socialist Society. *Soviet Law and Government* 15:37–54.

Salas, Luis. 1979. *Social Control and Deviance in Cuba.* New York: Praeger.

Sarri, Rosemary C. 1978. Information on Juvenile Aid Panels. Adelaide: Flinders Univ. of South Australia, School of Social Administration.

———, Bradley, Patrick W. 1980. Juvenile Aid Panels: An Alternative to Juvenile Court Processing in South Australia. *Crime & Delinquency* 26:42–62.

Selih, Alenka. 1978. Juvenile Justice in Yugoslavia. In *The Changing Faces of Juvenile Justice,* edited by V. Lorne Stewart, 111–134. New York: New York Univ. Press.

Shichor, David. 1983. Socialization: The Political Aspects of a Delinquency Explanation. *Sociological Spectrum* 3:85–100.

Shupilov, V. P. 1979. Execution of Sentences. In *The Criminal Justice System of the U.S.S.R.,* edited by M. Cherif Bassiouni and V. M. Savitski, 179–215. Springfield, Ill.: Thomas.

Sundeen, Richard A. 1976. Swedish Juvenile Justice and Welfare. *Journal of Criminal Justice* 4:109–121.

Thorpe, D. H., Smith, D., Green, C. J., and Paley, J. H. 1980. *Out of Care: The Community Support of Juvenile Offenders.* London: George Allen & Unwin.

Tifft, Larry L. 1985. Reflections on Capital Punishment and the 'Campaign Against Crime' in the People's Republic of China. *Justice Quarterly* 2:127–137.

Tutt, Norman. 1981. A Decade of Policy. *British Journal of Criminology* 21:246–256.

Wagatsuma, Hiroshi, and De Vos, George A. 1984. *Heritage of Endurance: Family Patterns and Delinquency in Urban Japan.* Berkeley, Calif.: Univ. of California Press.

Wenk, Ernst A. 1978. Delinquency Prevention Models in Schools. *Juvenile and Family Court Journal* 29, no. 3 (August):17–27.

Yakovlev, A. M. 1979. Criminological Foundation of the Criminal Process. In *The Criminal Justice System of the U.S.S.R.,* edited by M. Cherif Bassiouni and V. M. Savitski, 101–129. Springfield, Ill.: Thomas.

Zeldes, Ilya. 1980. Juvenile Delinquency in the U.S.S.R.: A Criminological Survey. *International Journal of Comparative and Applied Criminal Justice* 4:15–28.

PART **IV**

The Community

CHAPTER 13

The Community as a Resource in the Treatment of Delinquency

Culver Pictures, Inc.

At several points in the discussions of the preceding chapters we have seen examples where community agencies and processes were important ancillaries to the juvenile justice system. For example, in Chapter 9 it was pointed out that one alternative in police discretion is release of an arrested youth with referral to a community agency for appropriate treatment. As another example, in Chapter 10 the process of informal probation, in which a youngster is returned to his or her home rather than referred to court under various conditions that could include services from a community agency, was discussed. As a final example, in Chapter 11 we discussed the closing of custodial institutions for young offenders in Massachusetts during the early 1970s and the transfer of the former inmates to community facilities.

Indeed, that preference for informal, community-based treatment of young offenders was a significant aspect of the juvenile justice system from the time it came into existence in 1899. The act that established it specified that the newly created juvenile court should be biased toward probation and placement of a youth in his or her parental home or an equivalent family home (see Chapter 8). That preference was also part of the practice of Lindsey in Denver during those early years, and it remained, at least in theory, a central characteristic of juvenile court law and juvenile justice operations over subsequent years.

Diversion

Historical Development

According to Wallace and Brennan (1963), it became clear during the earliest years of the juvenile justice system that its operation included a bias for, perhaps an absolute need for, informal handling at levels before court appearance. There was discussion of the use of prehearing settlement of cases by probation officers as early as 1904, well before informal probation was part of juvenile law. In 1926, the National Probation Association acknowledged the desirability of such incorporation when it proposed a Standard Juvenile Court Law. As Wallace and Brennan (1963:444–445) have stated, justification of the act in terms of widespread practice was presented by the recommending committee of the National Probation Association as follows:

> The act follows the procedure [of handling cases informally] in many of the best juvenile courts by providing for a preliminary inquiry and investigation before a petition is filed. It proceeds upon the theory that it is better for as many cases as possible to be adjusted without a formal court hearing. The system of handling cases informally, usually through the probation department, is well recognized and in many courts half or more of the cases are adjusted in this way. This can be done without explicit statutory authority, the court having an inherent right to exercise discretion as to taking official jurisdiction, but the system has grown so widespread and is so generally recognized as beneficial that the committee believes it should be recognized in the law.

In the early 1930s, many police departments in larger cities developed programs for the informal handling of juvenile offenders. Lemert (1971:55–56) pointed out, "Some of the direct services police undertook for minors and their families [in those cities] were in the form of social investigations and casework-type treatment in which women police workers played an important role." The model for that type of program was the New York City Juvenile Aid Bureau, which was established in 1930, with a staff of police officers headed by an inspector. Closer to the approach of informal probation, and appropriately referred to as "police probation," was a development during the same era in which the police entered into informal agreements with violators and their parents that specified required behavior. That behavior might include mandatory visits to the police station, restitution for victims, no truancy, and study at home for a certain number of hours each day.

A noteworthy formalization of the process of informal approaches by the police to delinquency occurred when Passaic, New Jersey, established its Children's Bureau in 1937. There were four police officers assigned to the bureau who were expected "to turn any apprehended juvenile offenders over to the Children's Bureau" so that their problems could be analyzed and staff members assigned to guide readjustment (Boone, 1961:233). The staff at the bureau included two psychologists and a social worker. According to Boone (1961:235), "Every boy or girl reported for a law violation receives an individual psychological test and counseling from the psychologist. Parents are asked to accompany their youngsters so that they may have an opportunity to discuss any referral situation with the psychologist." Moreover, he pointed out (1961:255), "It is the social worker's responsibility to concern herself with the child's environment — his recreational activities, home life, church affiliations, camping experiences, and extracurricular activity."

The Recommendations of the President's Commission

In 1967, the very important report of the President's Commission on Law Enforcement and Administration of Justice led to profound changes in the pre-judicial handling of juveniles. Before presenting relevant features of the commission's report, it would seem of interest to point out that there were many prominent sociologists who, in their capacities as commission staff members and consultants, were influential in the specifics of its recommendations. Moreover, during the era of the mid-1960s, when the commission did its work, labeling theory was at a high point of acceptance in sociology (see Chapter 6).

The report of the commission summarized the state of affairs in the juvenile justice system as follows (1967:82):

> Informal and discretionary pre-judicial dispositions already are a formally recognized part of the process to a far greater extent in the juvenile than in the criminal justice system. The primacy of the rehabilitative goal in dealing with juveniles, the limited effectiveness of the formal processes of the juvenile justice system, the labeling inherent in adjudicating children delinquents, the inability of the formal system to reach the influences — family, school, labor market, recreational opportunities — that shape the life of a youngster, the limited disposition options available to the juvenile judge, the limitations of personnel and diagnostic and treatment facilities, the lack of community support — all of these factors give pre-judicial dispositions an especially important role with respect to juveniles.

Consequently, the informal and pre-judicial processes of adjustment compete in

importance with the formal ones and account for a majority of juvenile dispositions. They include discretionary judgments of the police officer to ignore conduct
or warn the child or refer him to other agencies; "station adjustment" by the police,
in which the child's release may be made conditional on his complying with
designated limitations on his conduct; the planned diversion of alleged delinquents
away from the court to resources within the school, clinic, or other community
facilities, by such groups as mental health, social, and school guidance agencies;
pre-judicial dispositions, at the intake stage of the court process, by probation
officers or sometimes judges exercising a broad screening function and selecting
among alternatives that include outright dismissal, referral to another community
agency for service, informal supervision by the probation staff, detention, and
filing a petition for further court action. In many courts the court intake process
itself disposes of the majority of cases.

But, the report (1967:82) went on to emphasize, "There are grave disadvantages and perils . . . in that vast continent of sublegal dispositions." Among
the disadvantages and perils it specified were the following: (1) The process
existed outside the guidance, control, and scrutiny of the formal processes that
protected constitutional rights. (2) The use of discretion was too often arbitrary,
based more on bureaucratic convenience than on a thorough evaluation of the
offender and careful consideration of available alternatives. (3) It was too easy
for illegal and discriminatory processes to intrude and for authority to be
abused by the prejudiced and overzealous.

On balance, however, the commission argued that informal pre-judicial handling was widely preferable to formal treatment and should be continued in a
modified form to control its various evils. The use of community approaches,
according to the report (1967:83), "avoids the stigma of being processed by an
official agency regarded by the public as an arm of crime control." It recommended the following changes to achieve that acceptable modified form: complete elimination of police probation; the uniform use of written standards, at
both police and probation levels, to guide decision making among alternative
dispositions for juvenile offenders; more in-service training for police and probation officers to further their understanding of the relationships among alternative dispositions, the needs of children, and the available community resources; and the elimination of the coercive features of informal probation.

Above all else, the commission recommended (1967:83), "Communities
should establish neighborhood youth-serving agencies — Youth Services
Bureaus — located if possible in comprehensive neighborhood community
centers and receiving juveniles (delinquent and nondelinquent) referred by the
police, the juvenile court, parents, schools, and other sources." It made clear
(1967:83) that the "bulk of the referrals could be expected to come from the
police and the juvenile court intake staff" in a process of diversion of appropriate youths away from the formal path in the justice system.

The Rapid Expansion of Diversion and the Reasons for That Expansion

The commission's position laid the foundation for the transformation of a
necessary and routine procedure in the pre-judicial handling of juveniles into a

national passion for an enterprise that became uniformly known as "diversion." Whereas, in the 1960s and earlier, the common practice was release and community referral, with more formal programs in some police and probation departments, by the mid-1970s there were hundreds of diversion programs, many of which called themselves Youth Services Bureaus or Youth Service Bureaus.

Many factors built on the foundation erected by the commission to create that result. Of primary importance were federal acts that generated the appropriation of moneys aimed at putting the recommendations of the commission into effect. The first such legislation occurred in 1968 in the forms of the Omnibus Crime Control and Safe Streets Act and the Juvenile Delinquency Prevention and Control Act. The federal funding generated by those acts went to various components of the justice system and to community agencies through the Law Enforcement Assistance Administration (LEAA) of the U.S. Department of Justice and the Youth Development and Delinquency Prevention Administration (YDDPA) of the U.S. Department of Health, Education, and Welfare. According to Gemignani (1972:3), when Congress amended the Juvenile Delinquency Prevention and Control Act in 1971, it agreed to an arrangement whereby "YDDPA should be the Federal focal point for prevention and rehabilitation activities *outside* of the juvenile justice system, and that LEAA should perform a similar function in relation to activities *within* the juvenile justice system."

But that attitude changed a few years later when, according to Altschuler and Lawrence (1981:4), "sentiment grew in Congress as elsewhere for a unified national program that gave the force of law to the concept of community-based programs and services as a means of preventing delinquency, and diverting youth from the juvenile justice system in general and from detention and correctional facilities in particular." That new attitude led to the Juvenile Justice and Delinquency Prevention Act (JJDP) of 1974—the act that was described in Chapter 11 in terms of its attempt to prevent the placement of status offenders in locked facilities by threats of the loss of federal funds. Its statement of purpose reflected the changed attitude as follows (Sec. 102 [b]): "It is therefore the further declared policy of Congress to provide the necessary resources, leadership, and coordination . . . to develop and conduct effective programs to prevent delinquency, to divert juveniles from the juvenile justice system and to provide critically needed alternatives to institutionalization."

The intent of Congress was reflected in the following Program Announcement, entitled "Diversion of Youth from the Juvenile Justice System," which was released by LEAA in April 1976. "Pursuant to the authority of the Omnibus Crime Control and Safe Streets Act of 1968, as amended, and the Juvenile Justice and Delinquency Prevention Act of 1974, the Law Enforcement Assistance Administration is giving major priority to the diversion of youth from the juvenile justice system through the use of Omnibus Crime Control discretionary funds." That was followed by the allocation of $10 million for the development of model diversion programs (see Dunford, Osgood, and Weichselbaum, 1982).

Guidance and additional incentives for the efforts were provided by two important monographs published early in the 1970s. The first, and clearly the more influential of the two, was entitled *Instead of Court: Diversion in Juvenile Justice*. It was written by Edwin Lemert, one of the consulting sociologists to the President's Commission. Lemert differentiated between "'primary' and 'secondary' labeling processes." In the monograph, Lemert discussed alternate models of diversion and provided the following perspective under "Conclusions" (1971:92): "Ideally, the diversion of minors from juvenile court will become a state of mind, an unquestioned moral position held by all child and youth welfare organizations, considered as a good in itself rather than a means to an end."

The second monograph, entitled *The Youth Service Bureau: A Key to Delinquency Prevention,* was written by Sherwood Norman and published in 1972 by the National Council on Crime and Delinquency, where Norman was a director. In the monograph, a Youth Service Bureau was defined as (1972:8) "a noncoercive, independent public agency established to divert children and youth from the justice system by (1) mobilizing community resources to solve youth problems, (2) strengthening existing youth resources and developing new ones, and (3) promoting positive programs to remedy delinquency-breeding conditions." The recommended mode of operation of the Youth Service Bureau was service brokerage, whereby referrals to it by the police and probation were evaluated and then referred to other agencies for required services. As stated in the monograph (1972:14), "The Youth Service Bureau is not itself a service agency so much as an agency for organizing the delivery of services to children and their families."

The National Effort: Boom, Evaluation and Reconsideration, Contraction

A number of factors contributed to the rapid and great expansion of diversion during the 1970s: the excitement of a new effort that offered hope of helping troubled youths without the attendant evils of the juvenile justice system, the possibilities of mobilizing community resources to combat a social evil that had eluded all previous attempts at control, the supporting arguments by leading theorists of crime and delinquency (see Cressey and McDermott, 1973, as well as Lemert, 1971), and, last but certainly not least, the lure of a substantial number of federal dollars. The extent of the boom is reflected in the opening sentence of a reader on diversion that was edited by Carter and Klein (1976:xi): "Seldom in the history of American criminal justice has a concept erupted on the scene and generated as much interest as that of diversion."

To illustrate the operation of early diversion programs that received federal funds (through LEAA), we turn to the Sacramento 601 Diversion Project and its successor, the Sacramento 602 Diversion Project, as reported by Baron and Feeney (1976). The first of these was directed at status offenders (as described in Section 601 of the California Welfare and Institutions Code), who constituted over one third of all cases referred to the juvenile court of Sacramento County in the early 1970s. During the period of project operation, diversion staff handled all status offenders referred to the Sacramento County Probation Department four days each week, and regular probation intake officers handled comparable referrals on the other three days. That created a control group as a comparison yardstick for purposes of evaluating the degree of success of the experimental or diversion group.

The diversion staff members, consisting of a supervisor and six probation officers, used crisis intervention and family crisis counseling as their modes of approach. Prior to the start of service delivery, they received considerable training in those modes of approach. According to Baron and Feeney (1976:5), the goal of the project was "to get the family to approach the situation not as a question of blame involving a child to be dealt with by some external agency, but rather as a situation involving the whole family and to which the whole family must seek to respond. The attempt [was] to loosen the family communication processes and to help the family achieve both the desire and the capability of dealing with the problem."

Evaluation of the results, which involved comparison of experimental and control cases, indicated considerable success. Only 3.7 per cent of the cases handled by project staff were referred to juvenile court, as compared with 19.8 per cent of those handled in the usual way by the intake officers; the project cases spent fewer nights in detention than control cases as a result of the initial referral and fewer nights in detention during a year of follow-up; and the project reduced recidivism by 14 per cent over all offenses and 40 per cent for felonies. Moreover, the success of the project was achieved at a considerably lower cost than that of usual probation operations.

Those results led to the second experimental program, the Sacramento 602 Diversion Project, in which youths referred for criminal-type behavior were accepted for diversion services (Section 602 of the California Welfare and Institutions Code deals with youths who violate criminal laws). The general procedure of the 601 Project was repeated for the new project, including special training of probation officers assigned to the program, the handling of a control group by regular intake staff, and the emphasis on family counseling. The evaluated accomplishments of the 602 Project were even more impressive than those of the 601 Project — there was a 99 per cent reduction in court petitions, overall recidivism was reduced by 40 per cent, and criminal recidivism was reduced by over 50 per cent. In 1974, the Sacramento approach was declared "exemplary" in a national evaluation by a division of LEAA, and that carried the implication that the project received endorsement as a model for other agencies throughout the country (only four other programs were so chosen initially).

Although the Sacramento project was indeed emulated widely, the proliferation of diversion programs involved a much broader diversity of approaches. Some programs were components of criminal and juvenile justice agencies, as was the case in Sacramento; others were components of social service agencies, public or private; and still others were independent, community-based operations. Some programs followed the brokerage format recommended by Norman (1972) and only made referrals to appropriate service-providing agencies, while others provided direct services to youths sent to them. Some programs accepted referrals only from the police, some only from probation, some from both police and probation, and some from a larger array of sources that included schools. Among the direct services provided by programs were family counseling, individual therapy, peer counseling, job development and job counseling, drug counseling, advocacy, educational counseling and tutorial assistance, placement in recreational and craft activities, and short-term shelter. Compendia of the diverse array of juvenile diversion programs may be found in O'Brien and Marcus (1976), Rutherford and McDermott (1976), Wright and Dixon (1977),

O'Brien (1977a), Shepherd and Rothenberger (1977), Altschuler and Lawrence (1981), and Rubin (1985).

Virtually all of the diversion programs were subjected to formal evaluations, because that was required of social programs receiving federal funding. The results were generally significantly less positive than those found in Sacramento, although successes that indeed supported the optimism generated by the Sacramento findings did occur. Reviews of many of those evaluations may be found in Palmer and Lewis (1980) and in Altschuler and Lawrence (1981). But perhaps the most significant evaluation was that reported by Dunford, Osgood, and Weichselbaum (1982). Their evaluation was directed at the programs funded by the $10 million allocated by LEAA in 1976. The goal (1982:1) "was to evaluate the concept of diversion rather than assist in short-range decisions." Their findings indicated that the programs met the criteria of diverting youths from the justice system and (1982:16) "were less coercive, less controlling, and more oriented to meeting clients' needs than comparable justice agencies." On the other hand, Dunford, Osgood, and Weichselbaum (1982:16) found, "A diversion disposition was no more successful in avoiding stigma, improving social adjustment, or reducing delinquent behavior than normal justice processing or outright release."

In addition to challenging evaluative results of that sort, a good deal of criticism of diversion began appearing in the sociological literature almost as early as the enterprise was launched. The criticism was based on both theoretical and operational arguments, including, interestingly, some derived from a labeling perspective. Schur (1973) set the tone for the criticism in his book *Radical Nonintervention,* in which he argued that society should be more tolerant of the diversity of youthful behaviors and attitudes and that children should be left alone by social agencies, including diversion programs, as much as possible. That position broadened to encompass several other features that formed a theme for the negative comments. First, it was argued that diversion staff members spend most of their energies on youngsters who would have been counseled and released by the police or by probation officers if the programs were not available — which produces not genuine diversion but, in terms widely adopted, "widening the net of social control" (see, e.g., Austin and Krisberg, 1981). Second, it was argued that there was just as much labeling by a diversion program as there would have been if a youth had moved onward in the justice system, and considerably more labeling than if the youth had simply been counseled and released without referral (which is, of course, an extension of Schur's, 1973, position; an interesting variant of it may be seen in Klein, 1976). Third, it was argued that diversionary activities violate the due process requirements of the U.S. Constitution in subjecting a youth to social control without proper procedural protections (for discussions of this issue, see O'Brien, 1977b, and Binder and Binder, 1982). And, finally, it was argued that there is discrimination in referrals to diversion programs — against lower-class youths, who "are being denied these services" although they "might benefit from diversion's family services" (Blomberg, 1977:10), and against females, who "are disproportionately involved in diversion programs" with the result that "diversion increases stigma and increases delinquency" among the females in a process of "hidden sexism" (Alder and Polk, 1982).

The Current Status of Diversion

The number of diversion programs for youths throughout the United States in the late 1980s is far smaller than the number in the mid-1970s. The evaluative results and the criticisms discussed above have contributed to the decline, but the major cause was the virtual total ending of federal funding (which was in itself affected by those evaluations and criticisms). The funding patterns in recent years and their effects on diversion are discussed by Rubin (1985:180) as follows:

> A number of youth services bureaus failed to survive more than a few years; others have continued eight years or longer. In general, they have not been readily embraced by local funding bodies, since they lack the political clout of the court and other more primary social services. However, bureaus in some communities have built useful political relationships and appear to be on a stable funding course. Some state legislatures appropriate funds for the state to contract with a bureau for its services.

But should diversion survive, given those negative evaluations and criticisms? The direction of an answer to that question lies in the distinction between "traditional diversion" and "new diversion" made by Rutherford and McDermott (1976) and reemphasized by Altschuler and Lawrence (1981). *Traditional diversion* refers to the discretionary processes of the police and probation where release of a youth from further processing is often accompanied by referral to a community agency. The American juvenile justice system could not operate effectively without that form of diversion. On the other hand, *new diversion* refers to the emphases that followed the President's Commission report in 1967, emphases that stressed formalized programmatic approaches to diversion. The expectation was that the new programs would coordinate available services, create new services, and encourage the police and probation to use those services instead of referral up the ladder of the justice system.

Traditional diversion, of course, will, indeed must, continue, but it should be modified by what has been learned over the years of the programmatic boom. It is important, too, for the formal diversion programs that remain with local funding, public or private, to adjust their modes and procedures of service delivery in accordance with the findings of the many evaluative reports, whether based on formal evaluation of operational data or on theoretical considerations. If these programs do not so adjust, it will be hard to imagine justifications for their survival. The major adjustments necessary are implied in the following summary of noted shortcomings (Binder and Geis, 1984:325):

> Many diversion programs, like many other human service programs, try to generate case loads. Sometimes, perhaps often, they involve themselves with youngsters who would likely be as well off if they were dispatched homeward after initial police contact. In addition, it seems unquestionable that diversion services are offered more in the affluent communities than in places where they might be more worthwhile by keeping minority youngsters from deeper involvement with the juvenile corrections system. Nor is there much doubt that the police are reluctant to refer "heavier" offenders to diversion agencies, though diversion might accom-

plish more positive results than eventuate from the traditional and more punitive dispositions.

Community-Based Programs and Group Homes _____

Overview

The most formal way in which community resources have been brought into play in the treatment of delinquency has been in the creation of programs, based within communities, which focus on using community ties and even community members as resources in the process of rehabilitation. Some of these programs might be called "group homes" in that they are based in residential facilities within the community in order to provide constant supervision and treatment to the young people referred to them. Others are nonresidential, representing efforts to divert troubled and delinquent young people from institutionalization. Some serve as settings not only for the treatment of delinquents but also for research on delinquency and rehabilitation measures.

There are many such programs in the United States. They are found in most states and in every major metropolitan area. They work in close cooperation with the juvenile courts: many receive the bulk of their referrals from the juvenile courts. Although some are privately owned and operated, and some are indeed profit-making ventures, many have been developed under the auspices of state and local government. As we shall see, the methods these programs use to treat delinquents vary greatly, and the question of their efficacy is far from decided.

Although much of the most significant development of community-based programs occurred in the 1960s and 1970s, it is not hard to see the roots of that development earlier in American history. Many of these programs, as we shall see, stress the importance of creating a homelike setting for delinquents in a manner not unlike that found among the advocates of the "cottage system" in the middle of the nineteenth century. Others have developed techniques to encourage self-government among their charges, reminiscent of the "junior republics" of the early twentieth century. And, indeed, they may be thought of within the larger historical framework of efforts to find alternatives to institutionalization for young offenders.

It is also possible to identify more obvious precedents for modern programs from earlier in this century. Certainly one such predecessor was El Retiro, a school for girls in Los Angeles. In 1920, El Retiro came under the leadership of Miriam Van Waters, an important early scholar in the study of delinquency and a major leader in the effort to reform the treatment of delinquents. Van Waters focused her efforts on the reintegration of young women in her care back into their communities. At El Retiro, she established procedures for self-government among the young women, created a "halfway" club for those released from El Retiro, and even started an alumnae group (Mennel, 1973).

One may also see a precedent for more recent community-based programs in the Chicago Area Project (CAP) of the 1930s. Although we had much to say about this project earlier, in Chapter 5, it is worth stressing now the importance of its community basis. The key assumption of the project's leaders was that

Views of rooms in community-based group homes.

delinquency occurred within a community setting and therefore could best be brought under control by the people in that setting; the project, of course, drew much of its support because of that community orientation (see Finestone, 1976).

The CAP also directly inspired later community-based programs. One may note, for example, the Hard to Reach Youth Project of the 1950s (Sorrentino, 1977). In this project, young indigenous leaders were employed on a part-time basis to work with gangs. These young men often took leadership roles within the gangs and served as liaisons between gang members and the community, as well as between gang members and the police.

These early precedents were fairly diverse in character, but all had in common the involvement of the community in the treatment of delinquents and, as well, the involvement of delinquents in the community as a basis for treatment. All sought to find viable alternatives to institutionalization as a response to delinquency.

A Summary of Goals and Intentions. And, indeed, despite the diversity of those early programs, as well as that of more recent efforts, it is possible to see a common thread of assumptions and purposes that tend to tie community-based programs together. These were clearly set forth by Irving Spergel in 1969, and his views remain operative today in regard to most if not all community-based programs. According to Spergel (1969:40), delinquency is seen to be "a function not only of economically and socially depriving systems but of a community committed to the wrong values." These wrong values are part of what he calls "a series of extraordinarily intricate, dynamic, yet intractable patterns of community breakdown," including divisiveness, stigmatization, and the failure of opportunities and services, among others he discusses. Community-based programs seek to counteract these problems by building social networks, providing training, and, above all, inculcating new values in young offenders. As Jensen and O'Connor-Clift have more recently written (1981:4): attachment to significant others, commitment to conventional lines of action, involvement in conventional activities and belief in the moral validity of norms and the law involve social bonds which can deter the juvenile from delinquent behavior. Their methods may vary, but that sort of assumption provides a common thread connecting all the major community-based programs for the treatment of delinquency. Thus, the attempt both to draw on the community and to create a new community for juveniles is the hallmark of community-based programs.

Significant Community-Based Programs and Group Homes

Although it is possible to identify many important community-based programs and group homes in the United States, several have taken on significance either because of their impact on their communities or because of the wider influence they have had on the treatment of delinquency. We shall survey the most important of them here.

Highfields. Among the first and most influential of the group homes with a strong community-based approach was that established at Highfields, New

Jersey, in 1950. It grew out of the thinking of F. Lovell Bixby and Lloyd W. McCorkle, who had worked together during World War II on military-related rehabilitation programs and who sought to apply what they had learned to creating new treatment programs for young offenders. The overall purpose of Highfields was summarized as follows (Weeks, 1958:viii):

> (1) the informal and intimate living for a short period in a small group of about twenty boys in a noncustodial residential center, (2) the experience of a regular routine of work under supervision, (3) evening sessions of guided group interaction (GGI) designed to give the boys insight into the motivations for their conduct and incentive to change their attitudes, (4) continuing group discussion outside these sessions during their leisure time.

By integrating the young offenders into a community of peers, McCorkle and Bixby sought to give them a chance for self-rehabilitation through participation in the life of the group.

These larger purposes guide the treatment philosophy at Highfields. The emphasis has been to create situations where boys are required to make their own choices about behavior while feeling secure enough to discuss those choices. Key interactions are not to be with staff members but, rather, with other boys.

The main assumption behind GGI is, as Whittaker has noted (1979:67), that "if the behavior of an individual delinquent is in fact maintained by a delinquent subculture, then effective rehabilitation should involve the peer group as an integral part of the treatment process." Thus, in GGI, the community of peers acts in ways that reinforce positive, prosocial values. At Highfields this has meant, above all, the use of group discussions in order to help the boys understand their own behavior and to learn to value alternatives to the ideas and values that tend to promote delinquency.

GGI provides the core of the Highfields experience. According to McCorkle, Elias, and Bixby (1958:79):

> The guided group interaction sessions permeate all phases of life at Highfields, whether it is work or play, fighting or arguing, eating or walking, and sometimes sleeping. On one occasion, a boy complained in a meeting that "A guy can get into trouble at Highfields even when he is sleeping." Before going to sleep he had talked a friend into throwing water at another boy. The next evening, when this incident was discussed by the group, he made his complaint. The pervasive impact of the group sessions is best illustrated by an expression that is commonly employed both in jest and in sincerity, that "everything a boy does can be a problem, you can't avoid problems around here. If you fool around, you got a fooling around problem, if you don't fool around, you got a being too quiet problem, what is a guy supposed to do anyway, you can't win."

Led by experienced staff, and meeting five nights per week, the GGI sessions are designed to make each Highfields resident look carefully at himself, his ideals, and his goals.

Highfields began under state auspices, and the delinquents going through the program are referred to it by the county's juvenile courts. They are to be between sixteen and seventeen years of age and to have no previous history of incarceration. Most referred to Highfields have been found to have committed offenses against property; others are guilty of offenses ranging from incorrigibility to traffic violations to vandalism to statutory rape (McCorkle, Elias, and Bixby, 1958). There are places for about twenty boys in the rural New Jersey home that serves as the Highfields residence.

There is a minimum of formal rules at Highfields, except that boys are not to leave the property unaccompanied by an adult. Days are full, beginning at six A.M. and not ending until after ten at night. Most of the boys work at a nearby state hospital forty hours a week, usually as farm laborers. This work itself is conceived to be part of the treatment program, teaching the boys responsibility. Evenings are taken up by GGI sessions.

Life at Highfields is not without conflict. The boys who are there have, after all, broken the law, and it is not surprising that most try to challenge the rules during their stay. In some cases, the "cottage parents" on the staff will assign extra work to be done during what are normally leisure hours. This may include digging garbage pits, scrubbing walls, or cutting the grass. In other cases, groups of the boys themselves will handle a problem youngster, in the context of GGI sessions.

Highfields has inspired a number of similar efforts using similar techniques. During the 1960s, the state of New Jersey established two other programs based on the Highfields model, but with some differences from it. In 1961, Essexfields was established to function very much like Highfields, but on a nonresidential basis. In 1965, the state began operation of Collegefields. This, too, was a nonresidential program, in Newark, but unlike either of the earlier programs, young offenders assigned to Collegefields spent their days pursuing educational activities rather than working. Nevertheless, all three used the techniques of GGI and sought to develop a community orientation that would militate against delinquency. As Collegefields' founders said, they sought to use the GGI approach to create a "culture of rehabilitation" (Allen et al., 1970).

Other states and cities, too, have drawn on the Highfields model. One may note, here, the Tarrant County Youth Center in Fort Worth, Texas, which uses both GGI techniques and a "homelike" setting to address delinquency (Cromwell and Townley, 1981). One may also note Dreyfous House in New Orleans (Slotnick, 1976), a facility opened in 1975 and deliberately modeled on Highfields. In addition, as we shall see, other methods developed for community-based treatment have drawn heavily on the assumptions and techniques of GGI.

The Provo Experiment. The Provo Experiment began in 1956 under the leadership of LaMar T. Empey, then of Brigham Young University in Utah. It was specifically designed to help habitual delinquents by giving them new values and a new approach to society. Empey and a collaborator, Jerome Rabow, spelled out the basis for their approach in a 1961 account of Provo (Empey and Rabow, 1961:683–684):

1. Delinquent behavior is primarily a group product and demands an approach to treatment far different from that which sees it as characteristic of a "sick" or "well-meaning" but "misguided" person.

2. An effective program must recognize the intrinsic nature of a delinquent's membership in a delinquent system and, therefore, must direct treatment to him as a part of that system.

3. Most delinquents are affectively and ideologically dedicated to the delinquent system. Before they can be made amenable to change, they must be made anxious about the ultimate utility of that system for them.

4. Delinquents must be forced to deal with the conflicts which the demands of conventional and delinquent systems place upon them. The resolution of such conflicts, either for or against further law violations, must ultimately involve a community decision. For that reason, a treatment program, in order to force realistic decision-making, can be most effective if it permits continued participation in the community as well as in the treatment process.

Empey and Rabow raised other issues, too, but as these first four points indicate, the experiment was built on the theoretical basis that delinquency comprises a subculture and uses treatment methods intended to induce habitual offenders to reject that subculture in favor of a set of values, beliefs, and ideals inimical to delinquent activities.

The Provo Experiment was addressed to habitual offenders fifteen to seventeen years of age. Highly disturbed and psychotic boys were not included in the experiment, and offenses ran (1961:675) "the usual gamut: vandalism, trouble in school, shoplifting, car theft, burglary, forgery, and so forth." No more than twenty boys at a time were assigned to the project — which depended on close contact with the juvenile court — and new boys could enter only when an older boy was released. The program was nonresidential, and the average length of attendance was somewhere between four and seven months.

Treatment took place in two phases. Phase I involved intensive treatment, focusing on the effort (1961:685) "to create a social system in which social structure, peer members, and authorities are oriented to the one task of instituting change." There was little formal structure in the Provo Experiment, a deliberate decision on the part of its creators. As Empey and Rabow suggested (1961:686):

> The absence of formal structure helps to do more than avoid artificial criteria for release. It has the positive effect of making boys more amenable to treatment. In the absence of formal structure they are uneasy and they are not quite sure of themselves. Thus, the lack of clear-cut definitions for behavior helps to accomplish three important things: (1) It produces anxiety and turns boys towards the group as a method of resolving their anxiety; (2) It leaves boys free to define situations for themselves: leaders begin to lead, followers begin to follow, and manipulators begin to manipulate. It is these types of behavior which must be seen and analyzed if change is to take place; (3) It binds neither authorities nor the peer group to prescribed courses of action. Each is free to do whatever is needed to suit the needs of particular boys, groups, or situations.

And, as at Highfields, peer organization was central to the course of treatment at Provo.

Provo encouraged peer groups in several ways. One was to omit deliberately any orientation for new boys involving staff. Youngsters were forced to learn the nature of the program from other boys. Another was through the use of guided group interaction, borrowed from the Highfields model. At Provo as at Highfields, GGI was intended to get the youngster to question his own motivations in becoming delinquent, to suggest alternatives, and to get him personally involved in his own reformation and in the reformation of others. It was to make him part of a reformation group, working together to bring about change. Not incidentally, such an effort is also directed toward ridding the young offender of an "us versus them" mentality by placing sanctions for misbehavior in the hands of the boys themselves rather than in those of some "outside" authority figures.

A second major aspect of the Provo Experiment was its emphasis on work. According to Empey and Rabow, too many delinquent boys also had bad attitudes toward work, believing that "only suckers work." In the Provo Experiment, boys were employed by the city to do public works. Those who refused to work could be sent back to the court and committed to the state reformatory. Others who refused to work on their city jobs—for which they were also paid—might be sent back to the experiment's center, Pinehills, and forced to work for nothing, usually scrubbing the floor, washing windows, mowing the lawn, or cutting weeds.

Phase II built on the experiences of Phase I and was designed to ease the transition of the Pinehills alumnus back into the community. After release from Phase I, the youngster continued to meet for discussions with his old Pinehills group, and the group was expected both to monitor his behavior and to provide a setting for the continuing discussion of problems. In addition, and continuing to reinforce good attitudes toward work and good work habits, every effort was made to find suitable employment for the boy and to make him a productive member of society.

The Provo Experiment was, in every sense, just that—an experiment. Though instituted with county support, it was chiefly the product of the efforts of concerned social scientists and lay people, interested in creating a setting in which to test innovative approaches to delinquency. Although we shall have more to say of the evaluation of the experiment later, the Provo Experiment was consciously intended to evaluate and originate techniques for changing the lives of its delinquent clients.

We should also note here that an early account of the Provo Experiment (Empey and Rabow, 1961) led to expressions of serious concerns about this and other projects discussed in this chapter. Whitney H. Gordon, writing in the *American Sociological Review,* suggested (1962:256):

> In many ways—some of them superficial and some of them not—the techniques used at Pinehills are reminiscent of those employed by the Communists in Korea on selected groups of American prisoners of war. One sees the leverage of the group being applied to the individual by way of public confessions, the demand for candor, the infinite patience and inscrutability of authority. There appears the "carrot and stick" technique along with the utilization of role disruption and social anxiety as motivating forces. Beyond that, one is reminded how systematically and thoroughly the integrity of psychological privacy is undermined.

Provo raised, Gordon argued, a classic case of the question of how much the ends justified the means used to achieve them.

Empey and Rabow (1962) acknowledged the validity of Gordon's concerns, while denying the validity of his analogy between Provo and communist "brainwashing" techniques. Nevertheless, as they and Gordon equally understood, the changing of values can involve ethical questions that many scholars and students alike continue to find unresolved.

Silverlake. The Silverlake Experiment, a California project that ran from 1964 to 1968, grew out of the Provo Experiment and was also under the leadership of Empey (Empey and Lubeck, 1971). There was much to tie the Silverlake Experiment to the earlier Provo Experiment, except that, run in cooperation with the California Boys' Republic, Silverlake was a residential program, using a former orphanage located in the Los Angeles area.

There were three main program components in the Silverlake Experiment. Like both Highfields and Provo, Silverlake made use of the techniques of guided group interaction in meetings held five evenings a week (boys were encouraged to go home on weekends). A second major program component was school attendance. According to Empey and Lubeck (1971), school was to serve as the primary institutional linkage for the program because of (1) the ever-increasing need for academic and vocational skills; (2) the fact that employment with any career potential is extremely difficult for a teenage adolescent to obtain without formal education; and (3) the importance of the school as the major societal institution for adolescents. This emphasis on education rather than work was one obvious difference between Silverlake and Provo. Indeed, such work experiences as did comprise the third major component of the Silverlake Experiment chiefly involved maintaining the house and grounds of the experiment's residential site.

Like the Provo Experiment, Silverlake took what was essentially a subcultural view of delinquency and sought to create what Empey and Lubeck (1971) referred to as a "program culture" to displace the old values and assumptions of delinquency. Silverlake also avoided too much formal structuring in order to place the key responsibility for order and behavior in the hands of the boys. And, again, Silverlake may best be thought of as an extension of the earlier Provo project, allowing Empey and his colleagues a new opportunity to test what had been learned from the earlier experiment in a new, slightly different setting.

Achievement Place. Achievement Place is a project that began in Kansas in 1967. Designed both for the treatment of "predelinquent" youths referred by the court and for continuing research on rehabilitation, Achievement Place is based, not on subcultural theory, but on approaches rooted in behavior modification, in using methods of positive and negative reinforcement directed mainly toward changing the behavior patterns of its subjects. From three to eight boys are treated at any one time in the old home that serves as the setting for Achievement Place. There they live under the supervision of a pair of house parents — called "teaching parents" — whose function it is to supervise, treat, and manage them.

The key assumptions behind a behavior modification approach to delinquency have been concisely summarized by Whittaker (1979:57–58) as follows:

1. A child's psychological nature is his behavior; directly observable and measurable actions constitute the sum and substance of personality. . . .
2. Behavior is largely controlled by the environment and, in the case of operant or active behavior, is either strengthened, maintained, or diminished by its immediate effects on the environment. Therefore, if the reinforcers for any given behavior can be identified and brought under control, the behavior itself can be similarly controlled.
3. The symptom of the troubled child is the entire problem; it is not simply an external manifestation of some underlying disease process, psychoneurosis, or character disorder. If the acting out of the delinquent, or the bizarre behavior of

the psychotic child, is stopped, then the basic problem of delinquency or psychosis has been solved.

Achievement Place embodies these assumptions in its approach to delinquent children.

The key distinguishing feature of Achievement Place is its use of what is called a "token economy" (Phillips et al., 1971). The tokens represent points that are earned for good behavior or lost for bad behavior. Points may be earned for such positively evaluated activities as keeping up with current events, cleaning one's room, a neat appearance, reading, doing housework, or keeping up with schoolwork. Points may be lost for such things as bad grades, aggressive or disobedient behavior, sloppiness, using poor grammar, or stealing, lying, or cheating (Phillips, 1968). Points are accumulated daily and weekly and may then be exchanged by the youngsters for various privileges — such as watching television, snacks, or even permission to leave Achievement Place — or even money. The goal is to use the incentives provided by the token economy to inculcate good behavior in those participating in the Achievement Place program.

For most of its existence, Achievement Place contrasted sharply with other programs we have been discussing in the degree of responsibility placed upon the staff. In keeping with the emphasis on behavior modification rather than on the development of an alternative culture, there was little concern for peer organization and networks. In the early 1970s, however, some measures of self-government were introduced into Achievement Place, within the framework of the token economy (Hoefler and Bornstein, 1975). This has involved, for one thing, the use of trials presided over by the boys themselves to deal with instances of misbehavior. It has also involved the institution of an elected "manager," whose job it is to assign tasks around the home, to supervise snacks and other activities, and to monitor social behavior. Initially, this was a position that could be purchased, at auction, using tokens. It was soon learned, however, that popular election was an arrangement much preferred by the boys themselves (Phillips et al., 1973).

Achievement Place has, like Highfields, led to other, similar projects. Notable among these is the Bringing It All Back Home Project, established in western North Carolina in late 1973 (Jones, Fields, and Timbers, n.d.). Here, too, principles of home-style, familylike living were combined with the techniques of the token economy in order to try to bring about behavioral changes.

House of Umoja. Unlike the projects we have been considering, the House of Umoja was not the product of any social-scientific enterprise but was, instead, the outgrowth of concern on the part of a private citizen, Sister Falaka Fattah. It opened in 1968 in West Philadelphia after Sister Fattah, a journalist living in the area, learned that her sixteen-year-old son, Robin, had become involved in gang activity. Deciding that the only way to deal with the problem was to confront the entire gang, Sister Fattah invited the gang to live with her and her family in their home, which she named the House of Umoja (*umoja* means "unity" in Swahili). Her idea was to create an extended family of which every gang member could feel a member and thus to give each a place in a supportive network. The agreement she made with the young men was a simple one: the gang members were to avoid any illegal activity. The Fattahs would help keep them out of jail and out of trouble (Leavy, 1982).

Since the initial days of the project, it has grown significantly. It has moved beyond the Fattah home to make use of other houses in the neighborhood that the Fattahs have acquired. There are close connections with the juvenile courts in Philadelphia; the courts may refer young offenders to the House of Umoja for care and treatment. The project itself has been credited with significantly reducing gang violence in Philadelphia.

The program to which young offenders must submit at the House of Umoja seeks to replicate a strong family life. Young men living in the house are required to rise at 6 A.M. and to participate in an early-morning conference on "goals for the day." They must perform regular assigned chores in the house and are also to attend school. Their schoolwork is closely monitored. They are not to use rough language. They must also attend a weekly review session — called the Adella — at which they may be assessed fines for infractions of rules or for displaying a bad attitude. In return, they receive not only Sister Fattah's efforts to create a familylike atmosphere but also a ten-dollar-a-week allowance — not to mention freedom from incarceration (Bolling, 1982).

The House of Umoja seeks to create a strong, prosocial peer group through the Adella, which meets every Friday evening. This meeting is intended to resolve conflicts within the community as well as to deal with individual problems. Any member of the household is entitled to lead the discussion. An individual found guilty of misbehavior is given the responsibility of setting his own punishment, subject to the group's approval. According to Woodson (1981:53), who has observed the house, although fines are common, "the most severe sanction is to tell others on the street that the youth is not a person of his word." Not unlike guided group interaction in terms of its use within the House of Umoja, the Adella has also been used to settle hostilities between rival gangs.

Again, the House of Umoja is not a venture of social scientists, and Sister Fattah sees its basis primarily in black nationalism. In trying to create an extended family, Sister Fattah deliberately chose what she saw as an African model for extended kinship — for a feeling of kinship, as she sees it, going beyond blood relationships. The very name *Umoja* refers to an ideal for unity among black people in order to inhibit the destructive and disruptive activities of gangs. But the reported success of her program has brought support and funding from a wide array of sources, including the Catholic Archdiocese, the Pew Memorial Trust, and the Commonwealth of Pennsylvania. Sister Fattah has also won a presidential commendation for demonstrating the possibilities of private community activities in combating social problems.

Elan. Located in Poland Spring, Maine, Elan was founded in 1971 by Joe Ricci, himself a former delinquent, in collaboration with Boston psychiatrist Gerald Davidson. A for-profit operation drawing youngsters from many states, Elan has also been quite controversial, especially for its treatment techniques. Like some of the other projects we have seen, Elan deals mainly with habitual offenders — about half privately referred and half referred by the state. It promises to effect a reform within eighteen months (Taft, 1979).

Like other programs we have seen, Elan relies heavily on peer pressure and community commitment to produce reform. Rules are tight; duties are difficult.

All youngsters must work within the community and are deliberately assigned jobs in their weakest areas (Taft, 1979:20) "to teach them to function under adversity and learn to accept failure." All begin within a hierarchical social structure as "workers" with the possibility of moving to such higher levels as that of foremen and "coordinators."

The regulation of behavior depends heavily on peer pressure. The residents watch each other and are responsible for calling down misbehavior, for verbally reprimanding those who misbehave through what is called a "haircut." A haircut may take several forms (Taft, 1979:21–22):

> Haircuts can involve just one person (a "blast") or a dozen (a "round robin") or two dozen (a "21-gun salute"). For graver offenses, there is a "charge" — "where the whole house lines up and gets their hostilities off at you," in one boy's words — or a "general meeting," the highest form of reprimand.

Other sanctions include the loss of privileges or even being forced to face public embarrassment. A "crybaby" was forced to wear a diaper and carry a bottle; others, to carry signs reading. "HELP! I am an emotionally crippled monster."

The most controversial aspects of Elan's history were reports surfacing in about 1975 focusing on the use of corporal punishment at Elan. A report from the Massachusetts Department of Youth Services cited the use of spanking at Elan and also reported that youngsters were forced to stand in a corner every day for weeks at a time. They also described a "boxing ring" where boys and girls accused of being bullies were forced to fight all comers until defeated. In 1979, Elan banned spanking; but some of the controversy remained (Taft, 1980).

There have been other controversies about Elan, including some focusing on its profit-making character. But its ties to the larger realm of community and group homes should be clear. Relying heavily on peer pressure and peer interactions, and on feelings of community commitment, Elan derives its approach from the kinds of delinquency theories that stress the need to inculcate new values as the major focus of reform.

VisionQuest. Founded in 1973 in Tucson, Arizona, by Robert Ledger Burton, VisionQuest, like Elan, is a private program enrolling young offenders from several states. Treatment at VisionQuest features a twelve- to eighteen-month program combining a range of experiences in order to change delinquent behavior. It includes extensive wilderness training involving hiking, mountain climbing, and boating. It also features a wagon train program, in which youngsters travel for hundreds of miles in horse- and mule-drawn wagons under primitive, pioneer conditions. It also uses what is called "attack" therapy, in which experienced counselors shout at and even physically restrain youngsters (Sweeney, 1982).

This program, like others we have discussed, tends to attract habitual offenders. Although drug addicts and those found to have committed "premeditated" violence are not accepted into VisionQuest, most youngsters in the program have spent time in institutions or other programs prior to coming to VisionQuest. Some are referred by the courts; a few, by their parents. The VisionQuest facility itself is open; there are no locked doors. But, as with other

Joe Kennedy/*Los Angeles Times*

Covered wagons carrying youths of the VisionQuest program near Needles, California.

programs, the emphasis is on commitment, and young people placed in Vision-Quest must pledge not to run away.

The wilderness training that serves as one component of the VisionQuest treatment is hard. Much of this training takes place in two primitive camps VisionQuest operates — one in New Mexico, the other in Pennsylvania. A stay at one of these camps includes three weeks of training, during which campers live in tipis, followed by a nineteen-day "quest" made of such trials as a "blind walk" (youngsters hike blindfolded), rock climbing, and a six-mile run. Three days of the quest are devoted to a "solo," in which each young person must seek a "vision," writing down his or her thoughts or reading something significant.

The wagon train has given the program the most publicity. This component of wilderness training was introduced in 1976, when a VisionQuest contingent joined the American Bicentennial Wagon Train. The change in the participants was so noticeable that the wagon train was made a permanent part of the VisionQuest treatment. The covered wagons move forward at a rate of seventeen miles a day, and participants are responsible for making and breaking camp each day and for keeping the train in motion. They must also learn to handle the teams of horses and mules that pull the wagons, and even to ride.

There are other facilities in the VisionQuest program. A former dude ranch in Arizona serves as a training facility for youngsters assigned to the wagon train. VisionQuest operates several residential treatment centers in the Tucson area.

There is also a "HomeQuest" program consisting of intensive counseling for problem youngsters and their parents, conducted while the youngster lives at home. Often the families included in this program are those of young people who have gone through other VisionQuest treatments.

But certainly the most controversial feature of VisionQuest has been its use of "attack" therapy. The confrontations this therapy involves occur if a youngster fails to perform his or her commitments, becomes disruptive or angry, or tries to run away. They may appear to be little more than shouting matches, as one staff member will shout at the youngster while both are surrounded by other staff members. But very often the confrontations involve what are called "physicals," in which senior staff grab young people and physically restrain them. As described by one sixteen-year-old (Sweeney, 1982:30):

> When they go to restrain you, they act pissed off too. . . . They surround you to make sure you don't hurt anyone. Then you're screaming and yelling and getting out frustrations and cussing them off the wall. Then they let you up off the ground, and you talk about things that are really bothering you. Usually things with your family.

Physicals are not supposed to include slapping, punching, or otherwise abusing a youngster.

The St. Louis Experiment. This program was conducted in St. Louis between 1970 and 1974. In some ways, according to its creators, the St. Louis Experiment elaborated on such earlier programs as that at Provo (Feldman, Caplinger, and Wodarski, 1983:37): "Like Empey and his colleagues, we believe that an adequate intervention program must make conventional and delinquent alternatives clear to youths, lead them to question the ultimate utility of delinquent alternatives, and help conventional alternatives assume more positive worth." Unlike other programs, however, the St. Louis Experiment stressed the importance of treating the young offender in the "open community." More than that, though also in keeping with a subcultural model for delinquency, the experiment did not simply use peer pressure but deliberately sought to provide the specific peer orientation of "prosocial" youngsters. In St. Louis, young offenders were assigned to regular youth groups at a suburban community center. One or two such youngsters would be placed in a group that otherwise consisted of six to twelve "prosocial" peers. This meant that group interactions primarily involved young people who had no behavioral problems rather than exclusively youngsters who all held to delinquent values and goals.

Youngsters were referred to the St. Louis Experiment from a variety of sources. The prosocial youths were those who normally participated in community center activities. Problem youngsters came from local mental health centers, juvenile courts, and residential treatment centers for children and youths, as well as from a special school district for learning-disabled and physically handicapped children. The group activities also varied. Youths took part in arts and crafts activities, athletics, hikes and trips, and group discussions. Groups received the guidance of trained experimenters and students, who served as group leaders. There was, then, much to tie the St. Louis Experiment in with other programs we have been examining, particularly in its theoretical bases. But its use of "prosocial" peers in the treatment process was a new element in community-based treatment strategies.

Ocean Tides. Ocean Tides is a residential treatment project for hard-core juvenile offenders located in a religious complex operated by the Christian Brothers, a teaching order of the Catholic church, in Rhode Island. There is a central site in a rural area overlooking Narragansett Bay and five group homes located in urban settings. Most youngsters referred to Ocean Tides spend about six months in the Narragansett site prior to being placed for a more extended period in one of the group homes, so that the latter serve as halfway houses for reintegrating the youngsters back into life in the community.

The Ocean Tides program is offered to boys between the ages of thirteen and seventeen who have been adjudicated to be juvenile delinquents by the family court. Status offenders are not referred to Ocean Tides; no specific act of delinquency renders a youngster ineligible for referral. Indeed, it has been suggested that "the individual profiles of the children in this program would have served to bar them from admission to the majority of voluntary treatment centers" (Lindner and Wagner, 1983:27).

Treatment at Ocean Tides consists of three main components: education, group living, and social services. The Narragansett center has its own school, which stresses self-motivation and achievement. The group living experience is intended to build a sense of community and includes daily peer-group counseling sessions. Confrontation is not, however, emphasized in these sessions. Instead, group leaders stress mutual support and self-help in peer relationships, even as they attempt to encourage youngsters to evaluate alternatives to delinquent values. Social service programs include programs not only for the children but also for the families of delinquents. Not only is counseling offered, but youngsters are encouraged to visit their homes on weekends to maintain and improve family relationships.

Misbehavior is said to be rare at Ocean Tides. The population is small—only about twenty-one boys at any one time—so that behavior is easily monitored. In general, there is an effort to fit punishment closely to the offense. A boy throwing food might be made to remain and clean up. One refusing to participate in recreational activities might be assigned extra workouts. Others might be denied privileges of watching television or a trip to the movies.

Youngsters assigned to one of the group homes receive treatment similar to that offered at the Narragansett site, although they attend local public schools rather than one affiliated with the program itself. The group homes are small, serving about seven boys, and are intended to provide a semblance of a strong family life in the urban environment from which most of the youngsters come. In 1979, Ocean Tides expanded to include a nonresidential diversion program as well.

The Effectiveness of Community-Based Programs and Group Homes

Up to this point, we have deliberately ignored specific questions of how effective these community-based programs and group homes are in treating delinquents. As we noted in describing several of these programs, many were set up with strong research components, which have allowed investigators to evaluate, continuously and over time, the effect they seemed to be having on the delinquent youngsters. Some have even been the setting for systematic experimentation. These programs provide the greatest insight into the effectiveness of community-based treatments, and we shall focus on the findings of investigators associated with such projects here. But we shall note that the question of effectiveness is of more than scientific interest, as in some places this question has taken on widespread social and political importance.

The Provo Experiment. The Provo Experiment has provided the occasion for some of the most significant findings in regard to community-based treatment methods. In a book published in 1972, Empey and Erickson were able to report conclusions based on over a decade's experience with the project, longer than most of the other projects we have examined (Empey and Erickson, 1972).

Empey and Erickson are cautious in stating their conclusions about the effectiveness of the Provo Experiment. They acknowledge its failures, but they also note indications of success (1972:222):

> The evidence also indicated that significant reductions were made, not only in the number of postintervention arrests, but in the number of offenders who were arrested. In every program, those delinquents who committed *fewer* offenses after intervention far exceeded the number who committed more offenses. Even though delinquency was not totally cut off, like water through a spigot, the overall flow was diminished considerably.

They go on to suggest that "incarceration was less effective than community intervention" in reducing the number of delinquent acts among youngsters treated in the two kinds of situations.

Through further analysis, Empey and Erickson sought to control for such variables as age and social class in trying to determine the impact of specific rehabilitation programs. They also looked toward other factors that might have made the program more successful, especially a better cultivation of networks with the outside community. But, on balance, they argued that the program was at least a modest success and a better method of handling delinquents than traditional methods of detention and incarceration.

This sort of cautious optimism is echoed in most other studies of community-based programs. McCorkle and his colleagues, evaluating the earlier program at Highfields—where the guided group interaction method was pioneered—concluded (1958:126):

> There is no reason to suppose that the primary goals or basic drives of either group were substantially changed. With the conventional reformatory group on the one hand, the goals remained distorted or unclear, the drives unrecognized or unaccepted. In contrast, among the Highfields group, there was movement toward a clearer view of primary goals and substantially increased acceptance of primary drives. The changes imputed to both the Highfields boys and the conventional reformatory group seemed clear in the sample studied. Moreover, they are congruent with what we know about reformatory life in general and with the letters written by the Highfields boys. Nevertheless, we cannot at this point wholly

exclude the possibility that these changes in this particular group are the result of the happy coincidence of a new and surprising method of treatment, applied by an ingenious, sympathetic, industrious management, to a group of delinquents whose capacity for rehabilitation was inherently high.

McCorkle and his group did not think this "happy coincidence" to have been the case, but they were not prepared to dismiss it out of hand.

This kind of guarded optimism is the norm in evaluating community-based projects. One may see it in regard to such programs as those at Provo, Highfields, and elsewhere which use one version or another of guided group interaction. Yehl and his associates (n.d.) have argued that one reason for this is that such programs lead to increased resident morale and to positive behavior changes in delinquents, although they question whether those programs result in any real interpersonal or intraphysic changes. They, too, judge the treatment to be a success.

One may also see cautious optimism in the evaluation of such "behavior modification" programs as the one at Achievement Place. Hoefler and Bornstein (1975) note that studies comparing Achievement Place boys with those from the Kansas Boys' School and boys on probation, all of whom had been released for at least one year, show that over half of those from the Boys' School and over half of those who had been on probation had been readjudicated by the court and sent to a state institution. In contrast, only 19 per cent of those who had been through Achievement Place had gone back before the court. They also note apparent differences in the school performances of boys in the respective groups. But Hoefler and Bornstein also argue that it is not entirely clear how much of the difference was due to the experience of the "token economy" and how much of whatever positive effect Achievement Place might have was due to other considerations such as status within the Achievement Place community.

Other critics, one should note, have questioned even the cautious optimism that we have seen. Murray and Cox, Jr. (1979), while accepting the validity of the findings of such experiments as those at Provo and Silverlake, have argued that data taken in Chicago in the mid-1970s do not conform the hypothesis that community-based programs are superior, and they urge that other factors may be at play in the kinds of differences other studies show. Pabon, while favorable toward such programs, has nonetheless concluded (1985:43): "Surveys of the results of large numbers of treatment projects have so far yielded little conclusive evidence that any of them work. The assumption that deinstitutionalization of juvenile offenders is more effective than incarceration is relatively untested." He describes arguments in behalf of most intervention strategies as "cherished assumptions." (See Chapter 16.)

Whittaker (1979), in the most comprehensive overview of such programs to date, has effectively summarized the strengths and weaknesses of major approaches to community-based programs. Among other points he makes about such behavior modification projects as Achievement Place, Whittaker (1979:64–65) cites twelve strengths:

1. Behavioral approaches provide a systematic and effective means for teaching alternative behavior to troubled children.
2. The behaviorists have helped immensely in specifying such important but

ill-defined treatment variables as relationship, role modeling, and teaching interaction.

3. The behavioral model is a communicable model—easily understood by line staff—which increases the probability of consistency in treatment between different staff members.

4. The behavorial approach has helped child care professionals focus on the specific behaviors that are causing the troubled child or his family difficulty and then devising equally specific strategies for dealing with them.

5. The behavioral approach does not assume an "illness model" of childhood disorders but, rather, focuses on specific steps that may be taken to "unlearn" old behaviors while adopting new ones.

6. The behavioral approach lends itself particularly well to comprehensive evaluation; goals are clearly specified in advance, and treatment procedures are explicit.

7. Individual behavioral programs are often difficult to establish—particularly for many of the complex interpersonal behaviors.

8. The organizational context is a critical intervening variable in determining the success or failure of a behavioral approach to child treatment. This is particularly true in residential settings.

9. Token economies apparently are subject to the same market forces as money economies and must be carefully monitored to avoid such things as inflation and recession.

10. Helping the child make the transition from the artificial environment of the behavioral treatment program to his home community is a difficult problem —particularly if control of environmental reinforcers is limited.

11. Behavioral programs are easily sabotaged—either unwittingly or purposefully—by staff members who may be unclear on or in disagreement with basic program objectives.

12. The early stereotype of behavior modification as "cold," "mechanical," and "Machiavellian" continues to exist in many communities and represents a problem of considerable magnitude for staff training and community acceptance.

Whittaker's tenth point, concerning the transition from the artificial environment of a treatment community to the less controllable reality of the outside world, has been of particular concern to those involved in the treatment of delinquents.

Concerning guided group interaction, the second major approach to community-based treatment, Whittaker offers a similar list of strengths and weaknesses. On the positive side, Whittaker (1979:70–71) states:

1. For those older adolescents whose delinquent behavior originates and is maintained in the peer group, GGI presents a potentially powerful technique for going to the heart of the delinquent subculture and orienting it in a positive direction.

2. With its daily meetings, peer confrontation, and focus on present problems, GGI significantly lowers the probability of the delinquent's being able to "con" his way through the treatment program.

3. In an institutional setting, GGI can link school, cottage, and community behavior in a way that helps to ensure improvement across systems. It is a positive approach that stresses "growth" rather than illness and is, in many respects, a true "self-help group."

4. GGI is less expensive than traditional training school programs when used in a community-based setting.
5. Group leaders do not require extensive graduate professional education and are often selected for training from the ranks of line child care staff.

On the negative side:

6. Some critics have argued that GGI is to a large extent based on personality rather than method. Some programs have centered around a single messianic leader, who brooks no compromise with the "rightness of the model." . . .
7. Relatively little has been written about the method itself. The literature is sparse, and few formalized training programs for group leaders exist. Thus, agencies desirous of trying out the model often find that they have to buy into a long-term consulting contract to receive the necessary staff training.
8. GGI is presented as a total approach to youth treatment, and its use as an adjunctive therapy has been discouraged in favor of an "all-or-nothing" approach. This would seem to render useless the notion of differential diagnosis and treatment for the youthful offender.
9. As a way of organizing a total therapeutic milieu, GGI leaves much to be desired. With so much power invested in the group leader and so much action taking place in the group meeting, other staff—notably child care workers—can begin to feel that they are little more than caretakers.
10. The data—as with most total-treatment approaches—are at this point unclear. The present literature is particularly limited in two important areas: For what type of youthful offender does GGI appear to be most effective? What organizational structures provide maximum enhancement for the GGI approach?
11. GGI is less effective with the younger troubled child, for whom the peer group is less powerful, and for psychotic children or severely emotionally disturbed children.

On balance, Whittaker (1979:69) writes, "the effectiveness of GGI remains open to question."

Community-Based Programs and Policy Concerns

Minnesota. With so much uncertainty among social scientists, it is not surprising that in several states serious policy questions have been raised about the use of community-based programs for the treatment of juvenile offenders. This occurred in Minnesota, for example, with the issuance of a 1977 report entitled "Residential Community Corrections Programs in Minnesota: Summary and Recommendations" by the Evaluation Unit of the Governor's Commission on Crime Prevention and Control (Minnesota Governor's Commission, 1977). The Evaluation Unit's report cited the number of clients referred to residential facilities who failed to complete the program of treatment and argued, based on a study of recidivism, that (1977:64) "once differences on background variables are taken into account, there are no statistically significant differences between juvenile residence clients and their respective parolee or probationer comparison groups"—that is to say, residential treatment, as such, seemed to be no more effective than traditional methods. Based on such findings, the unit recommended increased scrutiny on residential care programs and, more controversially, a halt to the funding of *new* residential community corrections facilities.

The unit's report was opposed by community corrections groups and by the Minnesota Department of Corrections. For this reason, the Governor's Commission itself refused to accept the report and sent the questions back for further study and investigation. Some of the issues raised against the report were essentially methodological, focusing on questions of data collection and analysis. Others involved substantive issues of interpretation, as proponents of community programs argued that the evidence showed that community-based programs did, in fact, reduce recidivism. But the key point here is that the results on both sides were far from conclusive, and this raised serious questions about the kind of support the state ought to give to community-based programs.

Massachusetts. In Massachusetts, these issues have been no less significant, in part because of state policies developed in the early 1970s aimed at "deinstitutionalizing" the treatment of juvenile delinquents. As discussed in Chapter 11, the process began in 1969, when Jerome Miller became commissioner of the Massachusetts Department of Youth Services. Shocked by the conditions of the state's institutions for juvenile offenders, Miller began first to reform those institutions and, later, to work toward their gradual phasing out. This resulted, by 1974, in the creation of a system of community-based programs responsible for the care and treatment of most of the state's delinquents. The transition was chaotic (see Coates, Miller, and Ohlin, 1978); there remained a mix of institutions and facilities in the state, but community-based programs are firmly rooted as the foundation of treatment for juvenile offenders in Massachusetts.

With the triumph of community-based programs, however, has also come a new awareness of their limitations. In Massachusetts, much of this awareness has focused on the serious offender, particularly the juvenile adjudged to have committed a violent offense. Although proponents of community-based treatment have maintained that such youngsters will be helped by community-based care, they have also had to confront society's demand for protection from the violent offender and society's demand that such offenders be separated from the community. The extent to which community-based treatment and secure confinement can be reconciled remains a difficult question, one that both proponents and opponents of community-based systems continue to confront (see Vogel and Thibault, 1981; Coates, 1981).

Summary

This chapter discussed the major modes of treatment of juvenile delinquency in the community: diversion and such special programs as those offering residential care. Since diversion implies the redirection of youths from a path up the justice system ladder from the police through probation to the court, it has necessarily been a component of juvenile justice since its earliest days. That is, police and probation officers have been encouraged to use counsel and release, often with referral to a community resource, since the earliest days of the juvenile court.

That informal process was given a bit more structure during the 1930s, when police departments in the larger cities adopted specialized programs for treatment in the community in place of upward referral. One of these programs was police probation, which was similar to informal supervision by probation, but without the codified status in the law that informal probation had by that time.

But it was not until the late 1960s that diversion moved from a routine component of justice system operations to a position that could evoke the following description by Carter and Klein (1976:xi): "Seldom in the history of American criminal justice has a concept erupted on the scene and generated as much interest as that of diversion." The direct stimulus for that eruption was the report of the President's Commission on Law Enforcement and Administration of Justice in 1967 and the considerable federal funding that the report generated. In its recommendation for the widespread adoption of Youth Services Bureaus to facilitate the diversionary process, the commission was influenced by labeling theory, which was then a theory of considerable importance in sociology. Handling youths informally in the community in place of movement up the justice ladder, it was argued, would avoid stigmatization. The Juvenile Justice and Delinquency Prevention Act of 1974 was important in furthering that aim of the commission, as it was in the deinstitutionalization of status offenders (Chapter 11). The sociological justifications for diversion were argued most eloquently by Lemert in 1971; he had also been influential as a consultant to the commission.

That boom in diversion programs lasted until the late 1970s, when the process of severe contraction started. The prime reason for that contraction was the almost complete termination of federal funding, which was motivated by many formal evaluations indicating that diversion was no more effective than routine operations of the justice system, by legal and theoretical objections to diversion raised by lawyers and sociologists (including labeling theorists who now saw diversion as a labeling process in its own right), and by a general change in the climate of the federal government in regard to support for local social programs. Important evaluations of diversion were those reported by Baron and Feeney (1976) for the Sacramento 601 and 602 projects and by Dunford, Osgood, and Weichselbaum (1982) for projects that received special federal funding—while the former found diversion to be a successful alternative, the latter found diversion effective neither in avoiding stigma nor in reducing recidivism. The arguments against diversion on labeling grounds were presented early and effectively by Schur (1973).

Although diversion programs based on the models envisioned by the President's Commission continue to exist in the late 1980s, they do so almost entirely on the basis of local funding.

Community-based treatment and rehabilitation programs and group homes also have something of an erratic history. As we have seen, there have been significant efforts over the last three decades to develop responses to juvenile delinquency that combine the same focus on community resources found in diversion programs with innovative, experimental techniques of treatment and, often, strong research components intended to evaluate the effectiveness of approaches. Sometimes privately funded, occasionally created under state auspices, these programs and homes have been the subject of both wide controversy and attention.

By far the greatest number of these homes rely for treatment on some form of guided group interaction (GGI). Pioneered at Highfields, in New Jersey, GGI combines peer pressure with counseling and mutual discussion of problems in an effort to make delinquents see for themselves the root causes of their behavior and to help them develop motivations for reformation and change. GGI, in one form or another, was not only used by Highfields but also served as the basis for treatment approaches in such varied programs as the Provo and Silverlake experiments and, with major variations, at the House of Umoja and Ocean Tides.

A second major approach, pioneered at Achievement Place in Kansas, is founded on the ideas of behavior modification. According to this approach, if one can develop rewards that lead to significant changes in behavior, then the delinquency will be overcome. At Achievement Place, this approach is maintained through what is called a "token economy," as youngsters learn to act in ways that maximize rewards to them within a closed system.

The controversies surrounding the efforts we have examined have grown, to some extent, out of the operations of individual programs. Privately run homes, in particular, have often given rise to scandals having to do mainly with treatment methods, including charges of violence and abuse directed toward their residents.

No less seriously, however, there have been pointed disputes about the effectiveness of both GGI and behavior modification as approaches to treatment. In particular, social scientists and others have questioned the extent to which either approach makes a difference in the lives of delinquents and have referred to the similar rates of recidivism between those who have gone through such programs and those who have gone through the more traditional paths of the juvenile justice system. As we have seen, even some creators of such community-based approaches have been fairly modest in assessing their success.

Whether such programs will continue to grow and develop remains, of course, to be seen. Certainly, as we have suggested, the legal implications of these programs, and the very practical issues they raise, especially in regard to serious offenders, are far from resolved.

References ─────────────────────────────

Alder, Christine, and Polk, Kenneth. 1982. Diversion and Hidden Sexism. *Australian and New Zealand Journal of Criminology* 15:100–108.

Allen, Robert F., Dubin, Harry N., Pilnick, Saul, and Youtz, Adella C. 1970. *Collegefields: From Delinquency to Freedom.* Seattle: Special Child Publications.

Altschuler, David M., and Lawrence, Janet S. 1981. *Reports of the National Juvenile Justice Assessment Centers: A Review of Selected Research and Program Evaluations on Police Diversion Programs.* Washington, D.C.: U.S. Department of Justice, National Institute for Juvenile Justice and Delinquency Prevention.

Austin, James, and Krisberg, Barry. 1981. Wider, Stronger, and Different Nets: The Dialectics of Criminal Justice Reform. *Journal of Research in Crime and Delinquency* 18:165–196.

Baron, Roger, and Feeney, Floyd. 1976. *Juvenile Diversion Through Family Counseling.* Washington, D.C.: U.S. Government Printing Office.

Binder, Arnold, and Binder, Virginia L. 1982. Juvenile Diversion and the Constitution. *Journal of Criminal Justice* 10:1–24.

Binder, Arnold, and Geis, Gilbert. 1984. *Ad Populum* Argumentation in Criminology: Juvenile Diversion as Rhetoric. *Crime & Delinquency* 30:309–333.

Blomberg, Thomas G. 1977. Diversion and Accelerated Social Control. *Journal of Criminal Law and Criminology* 68:274–282.

Bolling, Landrum R. 1982. Volunteerism: The President and Sister Fattah. *Saturday Evening Post* 254, no. 1:18–20, 88.

Boone, George C. 1961. The Passaic Children's Bureau. *Crime and Delinquency* 7:231–236.

Carter, Robert M., and Klein, Malcolm W., eds. 1976. *Back on the Street: The Diversion of Juvenile Offenders.* Englewood Cliffs, N.J.: Prentice-Hall.

Coates, Robert B. 1981. Deinstitutionalization and the Serious Juvenile Offender: Some Policy Considerations. *Crime & Delinquency* 27:477–486.

———, Miller, Alden D., and Ohlin, Lloyd E. 1978. *Diversity in a Youth Correctional System: Handling Delinquents in Massachusetts.* Cambridge, Mass.: Ballinger.

Cressey, Donald R., and McDermott, Robert A. 1973. *Diversion from the Juvenile Justice System.* Ann Arbor, Mich.: University of Michigan, National Assessment of Juvenile Corrections.

Cromwell, Paul F., Jr., and Townley, J. Michael. 1981. Tarrant County Youth Center: Innovations in Program and Funding. *Juvenile and Family Court Journal* 32, no. 1:51–57.

Dunford, Franklyn W., Osgood, D. Wayne, and Weichselbaum, Hart F. 1982. *National Evaluation of Diversion Projects: Executive Summary.* Washington, D.C.: U.S. Department of Justice, National Institute for Juvenile Justice and Delinquency Prevention.

Empey, LaMar T., and Erickson, Maynard L. 1972. *The Provo Experiment: Evaluating Community Control of Delinquency.* Lexington, Mass.: D. C. Heath.

Empey, LaMar T., and Lubeck, Steven G. 1971. *The Silverlake Experiment: Testing Delinquency Theory and Community Intervention.* Chicago: Aldine.

Empey, LaMar T., and Rabow, Jerome. 1961. The Provo Experiment in Delinquency Rehabilitation. *American Sociological Review* 26:679–695.

———. 1962. Reply to Whitney H. Gordon. *American Sociological Review* 27:256–258.

Feldman, Ronald A., Caplinger, Timothy E., and Wodarski, John S. 1983. *The St. Louis Conundrum: The Effective Treatment of Antisocial Youths.* Englewood Cliffs, N.J.: Prentice-Hall.

Finestone, Harold. 1976. *Victims of Change: Juvenile Delinquents in American Society.* Westport, Conn.: Greenwood Press.

Gemignani, Robert J. 1972. Youth Services Systems: Diverting Youth from the Juvenile Justice System. *Delinquency Prevention Reporter,* Youth Development and Delinquency Prevention Administration, U.S. Department of Health, Education, and Welfare (July–August), 1–7.

Gordon, Whitney H. 1962. Communist Rectification Programs and Delinquency Rehabilitation Programs: A Parallel? *American Sociological Review* 27:256.

Hoefler, Sharon A., and Bornstein, Philip H. 1975. Achievement Place: An Evaluative Review. *Criminal Justice and Behavior* 2:146–168.

Jensen, Eric L., and O'Connor-Clift, Patricia. 1981. Theoretical Foundations for the Design and Placement of Community-Based Treatment Facilities for Juveniles. *Juvenile and Family Court Journal* 32, no. 3:3–10.

Jones, Robert J., Fields, Saraveen, and Timbers, Gary D. n.d. A Consumer-Satisfaction Format for Evaluating Community-Based Treatment Programs for Juvenile Offenders. Ms.

Klein, Malcolm W. 1976. Issues and Realities in Police Diversion Programs. *Crime & Delinquency* 22:421-427.

Leavy, Walter. 1982. A Mother's Love Stops Gang Killings. *Ebony* 37, no. 5:59-64.

Lemert, Edwin M. 1971. *Instead of Court: Diversion in Juvenile Justice.* Washington, D.C.: U.S. Government Printing Office.

Lindner, Charles, and Wagner, Brother Robert. 1983. The Ocean Tides Experiment: Treatment of Serious Juvenile Offenders in an Open Residential Setting. *Federal Probation* 47, no. 1:26-32.

McCorkle, Lloyd W., Elias, Albert, and Bixby, F. Lovell. 1958. *The Highfields Story: An Experimental Treatment Project for Youthful Offenders.* New York: Henry Holt.

Mennel, Robert M. 1973. *Thorns and Thistles: Juvenile Delinquents in the United States, 1825-1940.* Hanover, N.H.: Univ. Press of New England.

Minnesota Governor's Commission on Crime Prevention and Control. 1977. Residential Community Corrections Programs in Minnesota: Summary and Recommendations. Governor's Commission on Crime Prevention and Control, State of Minnesota.

Murray, Charles A., and Cox, Louis A., Jr. 1979. *Beyond Probation: Juvenile Corrections and the Chronic Delinquent.* Beverly Hills, Calif.: Sage.

Norman, Sherwood. 1972. *The Youth Service Bureau: A Key to Delinquency Prevention.* Paramus, N.J.: National Council on Crime and Delinquency.

O'Brien, Kevin E. 1977a. *Juvenile Diversion. A Selected Bibliography.* 2nd ed. Washington, D.C.: U.S. Department of Justice, National Institute of Law Enforcement and Criminal Justice.

————. 1977b. Returned to the Streets: Legal Issues Raised by Juvenile Diversion Programs. *New England Journal on Prison Law* 1977:381-436.

————, and Marcus, Marvin. 1976. *Juvenile Diversion: A Selected Bibliography.* Washington, D.C.: U.S. Department of Justice, National Institute of Law Enforcement and Criminal Justice.

Pabon, Edward. 1985. A Neighborhood Correctional Program for Juvenile Offenders. *Juvenile and Family Court Journal* 36, no. 2:43-47.

Palmer, Ted, and Lewis, Roy V. 1980. *An Evaluation of Juvenile Diversion.* Cambridge, Mass.: Oelgeschlager, Gunn and Hain.

Phillips, Elery L. 1968. Achievement Place: Token Reinforcement Procedures in a Home-Style Rehabilitation Setting for "Predelinquent" Boys. *Journal of Applied Behavior Analysis* 1:213-223.

————, Phillips, Elaine A., Fixson, Dean L., and Wolf, Montrose M. 1971. Achievement Place: Modification of the Behaviors of Predelinquent Boys Within a Token Economy. *Journal of Applied Behavior Analysis* 4:45-59.

————, Phillips, Elaine A., Wolf, Montrose M., and Fixson, Dean L. 1973. Achievement Place: Development of the Elected Manager System. *Journal of Applied Behavior Analysis* 6:541-561.

President's Commission on Law Enforcement and Administration of Justice. 1967. *The Challenge of Crime in a Free Society: A Report.* Washington, D.C.: U.S. Government Printing Office.

Rubin, H. Ted. 1985. *Juvenile Justice: Policy, Practice, and Law.* 2nd ed. New York: Random House.

Rutherford, Andrew, and McDermott, Robert. 1976. *National Evaluation Program: Phase 1 Summary Report.* Washington, D.C.: U.S. Department of Justice, National Institute of Law Enforcement and Criminal Justice.

Schur, Edwin M. 1973. *Radical Nonintervention: Rethinking the Delinquency Problem.* Englewood Cliffs, N.J.: Prentice-Hall.

Shepherd, Jack R., and Rothenberger, Dale M. 1977. *Police-Juvenile Diversion: An Alternative to Prosecution.* East Lansing, Mich.: Community and Youth Services Unit, Michigan State Police.

Slotnick, Marcia. 1976. Community-Based Residential Treatment Facilities: The Case of Dreyfous House. New Orleans, La.: Mayor's Criminal Justice Coordinating Council.

Sorrentino, Anthony. 1977. *Organizing Against Crime: Redeveloping the Neighborhood.* New York: Human Sciences Press.

Spergel, Irving. 1969. *Community Problem Solving: The Delinquency Example.* Chicago: Univ. of Chicago Press.

Sweeney, Paul. 1982. VisionQuest's Rite of Passage. *Corrections Magazine* 8, no. 1:22–32.

Taft, Philip B., Jr. 1979. Elan: Does Its Bizarre Regimen Transform Troubled Youths, or Abuse Them? *Corrections Magazine* 5, no. 1:17–28.

———. 1980. Follow-up: Elan — and Joe Ricci — Are Prospering. *Corrections Magazine* 6, no. 1:48.

Vogel, Ronald E., and Thibault, Edward A. 1981. Deinstitutionalization's Throwaways: The Development of a Juvenile Prison in Massachusetts. *Crime & Delinquency* 27:468–476.

Wallace, J. A., and Brennan, M. M. 1963. Intake and the Family Court. *Buffalo Law Review* 12:442–451.

Weeks, H. Ashley. 1958. *Youthful Offenders at Highfields: An Evaluation of the Effects of the Short-Term Treatment of Delinquent Boys.* Ann Arbor, Mich.: Univ. of Michigan Press.

Whittaker, James K. 1979. *Caring for Troubled Children: Residential Treatment in a Community Context.* San Francisco: Jossey-Bass.

Woodson, Robert L. 1981. *A Summons to Life: Mediating Structures and the Prevention of Youth Crime.* Cambridge, Mass.: Ballinger.

Wright, William E., and Dixon, Michael C. 1977. Community Prevention and Treatment of Juvenile Delinquency: A Review of Evaluation Studies. *Journal of Research in Crime and Delinquency* 14:35–67.

Yehl, J. G., Ahlering, R. F., Anderson, P. D., Silvergleit, I. T., and Grush, J. E. n.d. Evaluating the Effectiveness of a Guided Group Interaction Program. Ms.

CHAPTER 14

Delinquency and Social Institutions: Family, School, and Religion

© Yvonne Freund

Major organized aspects of existence in contemporary societies — matters such as family life, education, and religion — inevitably come to be regarded as having a strong association with the presence or absence of delinquent behavior. These forces are presumed to be so prevalent and so significant that it is difficult to imagine that they do not in some manner precondition whether or not we obey or violate the law. The common assumption is that adherence to religious principles, success in school, and security and love within the embrace of the family all will contribute powerfully to satisfactory and law-abiding social adjustment. School failure, disruptive and hostile family conditions, and absence of adherence to religious views are all presumed to be associated with maladjustment and with juvenile delinquency.

In many ways, these ideas offer a shorthand summary of an actual truth: people with admirable adjustment in other major spheres of social life also tend to adjust to the demands of the laws bearing upon the behavior of juveniles. But in other ways, the conventional wisdom on these matters is too simplistic and far from scientifically satisfactory. For one thing, the concepts involved are very difficult to express in a clear-cut manner. What, for instance, constitutes a healthy family environment? Some families seem blissful, each member affectionate, helpful, respectful. Suddenly, the teenage son seizes a rifle and guns down half a dozen strangers in the city square. The newspapers report the episode with huge headlines: "Model Child Goes on Savage Rampage." Experts retrospectively detect that, perhaps, the family was "too perfect," that its members were play-acting, and their apparent love and decency was a cover for deep tension that beset them all, tension that they were unable to relieve in any directly expressive manner. In addition, of course, even if we can agree on what is a good family situation, it is obvious that such families produce a fair number of delinquents, even if the number falls below that for families deemed more disorganized.

The same difficulties and uncertainties prevail in regard to the relationship between education and religion, on the one hand, and juvenile delinquency, on the other. Adjudicated delinquents disproportionately tend to be Roman Catholics, but it would be irresponsible to say that this religion is more apt to turn youngsters into delinquents than others. Roman Catholics tend in large cities to have a large proportion of lower-class members, and it is the class position of youths rather than their religious affiliation that plays a dominant part in their misbehavior. Besides, of course, any religion contains a vast amount of orthodox and heterodox doctrine, and it is exceedingly difficult to determine which aspects of these teachings are being absorbed by the congregation in general or by any particular member of it. School too is a vastly complex institution. Teachers can be very different, what they teach varies, and the composition of their classes can have an important bearing on the class members. Simply assigning a pupil to another classroom can have striking effects on his or her performance and behavior.

It is intellectually careless, therefore, to suggest that there exists any simple relationship between the family, the school, or religion and delinquency. The relationship is very complicated — at times, indeed, other circumstances may overwhelm any effect that school, religion, or family may exert. It is our task in the present chapter, with the foregoing reservation carefully in mind, to explore

*"Still, did you ever stop to think where
you and I would be if it <u>weren't</u> for evil?"*

The problem of delinquency helps to sustain a network of
social, legal, and community services and organizations.

some of the intricacies of the connection between family, school, and education
and juvenile delinquency.

The Family

Many of us have a strong belief that family upbringing represents the single
most important factor in determining the kind of person we become. Certainly,

whether or not we drink or smoke, how we vote, our social attitudes, and many other aspects of our behavior can fairly easily be tied to the way in which our father and mother do those things. At the same time, all of us are keenly aware that a given family is apt to produce stunningly different kinds of children. Brothers and sisters who are just a year apart can be so different that people wonder if they really could be the offspring of the same parents. Indeed, a recent article (Plomin and Daniels, 1987) bears the title: "Why Are Children in the Same Family So Different from One Another?" Almost two dozen commentators on the article add their own interpretations. One writer observes, for instance, that it is not the family environment that matters but how the child perceives that environment, and that such perceptions can vary dramatically. Others note the importance of genes and fortuitous events on the shaping of different children in the same family, while one commentator points to the significance of "niche picking" by children — the establishment and acting out of *their* roles in the family.

Particularly intriguing has been the finding by Robins et al. (1985) that persons tend to recreate their past — that is, to remember it — in terms of their present. In this regard, we could expect delinquents to have memories of a much more disturbed upbringing than that recollected by their nondelinquent peers, a matter that bears importantly on the accuracy of studies based upon recall. Robins et al. (1985) also found that when memories required a value judgment —such as whether a parent was hard on the children, whether a mother hid or expressed her anger, or whether the father's drinking embarrassed the family— the level of agreement between siblings was no better than 29 per cent.

These are the kinds of considerations that make us wary of any flat statements about the direct relationship between family conditions and juvenile delinquency. There certainly is considerable research evidence to provide credence for the general view that a "healthy" family milieu will inhibit delinquency. This takes place primarily through the operation of two mechanisms. First, a guardian conscience is inculcated in the youngster. This conscience restricts participation in delinquent acts because it prelabels such acts as "wrong" and "shameful," and because the possessor of the condemning conscience knows that he or she will feel guilty during and after the delinquent episode and will be ashamed of having betrayed parents whose views are regarded as important and whose approval — even if they are deceased — means something. Second, alternative satisfactions are offered, which preclude the necessity to engage in delinquent acts in order to obtain thrills, goods, or other kinds of rewards. It is obvious that a child who has a decent allowance will feel less inclination to steal something that can be legally purchased, and that a child who gets a good deal of attention and affection will not have to shoplift to get merchandise to distribute to friends in order to gain desperately desired approval. But, again, we must be careful not to take such generalizations too literally. They depict tendencies and are not immutable truths, because many children with what by reasonable standards seem to be adequate financial resources nonetheless steal, and quite often steal things that they appear to have no use for whatsoever.

Other researchers maintain that birth order has an impact on delinquency, with the middle-born children most prone to lawbreaking. A possible explanation, they believe, is that the middle-born child is the most likely to be exposed to deviant behavior by siblings, since through its life the largest number of children at vulnerable ages are still in the home (Biles and Challinger, 1981). Fischer (1984) similarly argues that "infectious examples" within the family represent important delinquency precursors. But more important than this, he points out that a thorough review of the literature on the relationship between the structure of the family and delinquency pinpoints overcrowding as a vital negative factor. Family size, Fischer (1984) notes, remains implicated in delinquency when family income, socioeconomic status, parental criminality, and the composition of the family all are held constant. Overcrowding can aggravate tempers because of constant close contact, and the absence of physical space often means that nobody can readily escape and find privacy elsewhere when tensions build in a family. For a child, out-of-sight-out-of-mind may at times provide an escape from emotional confrontations.

We have in earlier chapters reviewed and critiqued formulas that flatly insist that certain structural features of the family are directly tied to subsequent delinquent activity. In particular, we have stressed that the characteristics — such as broken homes and inconstant discipline — have to be perceived and acted upon by the youngster before they can have any particular consequences. At the same time, it has to be emphasized that unsettled home conditions produce unsettled personal responses more often than calm, nurturant home situations. Research tends to find at least three consistent relationships between later difficulty with the law and the way a child is raised: first, the parents of delinquents are less warm and affectionate; second, they are inconsistent in their child-raising practices; and third, when they are themselves aggressive, they are more apt to raise aggressive children (Campbell and Shoham, 1969).

Two emotional elements of family life most likely to be regarded as crucial determinants of later law-abiding or delinquent behavior are its tenor, that is, the general atmosphere of the home, and the family interaction patterns (McCord, McCord, and Howard, 1961). In one study in which family styles were observed for a number of "normal" children and for families with delinquent children, it was found, for instance, that the delinquent often exercised more influence in the family than one or both parents (Hetherington, Stouwie, and Ridberg, 1971). The families of delinquents also had considerable difficulty resolving conflicts. In the normal families, though conflicts were common during problem-solving processes, a satisfactory solution ultimately was reached.

In a comprehensive review of the research literature exploring the relationship between family interactions and delinquency, Tolan, Cronwell, and Brasswell (1986) found the following five items characterizing the home life of delinquents:

1. The delinquents' families have more frequent parental disagreements and present conflicting directives to the children;
2. The delinquents' families show less differentiation between the influence of the parent and the child on family decisions, with families of delinquents exhibiting egalitarian or child-skewed power distributions;
3. The delinquents' families express less positive affect and more negative affect; or, more simply, they show less approval and are more critical of their children than nondelinquent families;

4. The delinquents' families misperceive a greater proportion of communications; and
5. The delinquents' families present a larger proportion of communications that indicate an unwillingness to compromise.

These items, of course, must stand as general guidelines rather than as hard-and-fast conclusions. For one thing, they are based on research that almost invariably takes place after a child has been adjudicated a delinquent or has caused difficulty in and for the family. Understandably, the young person's behavior and the behavior manifested toward the offender may well have changed, perhaps dramatically, after the delinquent's encounter with legal authorities. In addition, the categories represent generalizations, not categoric predictors; that is, any one family could well manifest each of the characteristics noted above and all of its children turn out to be nondelinquent. The items, research-based, stand as warning markers.

Studies that focus on family atmosphere and interaction patterns as precursors of delinquency lead to conclusions that therapeutic efforts ought to concentrate not on the delinquent in isolation but on the delinquent and his or her family members. A typical treatment program in this genre (Stratton, 1975) utilized a problem-solving orientation to discover what problems were disrupting the family. Then family members gathered together for therapy and expressed their feelings about such problems, and efforts were made to determine how the family had been dealing with them. The therapist attempted to lead the family as a unit to appreciate the inadequacy of its tactics and to try new methods.

A review of the literature on thirty-seven programs of family intervention with delinquents found that they employed a wide variety of approaches, depending on the therapeutic orientation of their leaders; nonetheless, Tolan, Cronwell, and Brasswell (1986:633) report, "Surprisingly, despite these limitations, results have consistently shown positive effects from family therapy with delinquents."

Child Abuse

In recent years, special attention has been directed toward the relationship between having been abused as a child and later engaging in delinquent acts. Newspaper stories and television treatments continally present sordid tales of the sexual molestation of children, especially at day care centers, and tell of the beatings that children suffer within their own families or from foster parents. The American Humane Association, which collects figures on child abuse, notes that the reported totals rose from 669,000 cases in 1976 to 1.9 million in 1985 (McQueen, 1987). Much dispute centers on proper methods of response to child abuse. Battering children physically and neglecting them seems indefensible, though there may be legitimate differences about what constitutes unduly harsh treatment and what might be regarded as legitimate chastisement. Much more controversy surrounds the sexual abuse of children. Some persons maintain that the hysteria that often accompanies reports of child sexual abuse can create more harm than the abuse itself (Nelson, 1984). Their argument is that for many young children the experience of sexual abuse, while it may be frightening, does not inherently seem as awful to the child as it does to adults. In addition, the need for the child to repeat the story to the authorities, often innumerable times, and, if there is a trial, to be confronted by an insinuating and hostile defense attorney, may be more damaging to the abused child than the act of sexual molestation or sexual abuse.

It is arguable whether there is more child abuse today than there was in earlier periods of our history, despite the huge increase in reported cases (Daro, 1987). The phenomenon of child abuse, though noted throughout history (Gordon, 1983; Solomon, 1972), was first effectively called to public attention in the early 1960s by a team of physicians (Kempe et al., 1962), who labeled such abuse "the battered child syndrome" and declared that it was a "clinical condition," that is, a situation falling within the realm of medical practitioners. That label, as Pelton (1985:51) notes, "was to prove crucial in helping to gain the attention of the wider medical profession to the problem, helping to publicize it and encouraging the state to take action." Pelton argues that the label was "emotive" but that it played down the legally and socially deviant aspects of child abuse by defining it as an illness. Subsequently, behavioral scientists have insisted that 90 per cent of child abuse can be explained by social circumstances (Straus, 1980).

The term *child abuse* blankets a considerable range of actions, including such matters as emotional abuse, medical neglect, willful malnourishment, and sexual victimization (Gelles, 1987). Five factors are believed to be particularly related to child abuse: (1) it involves a "cycle of violence"; that is, patterns of family violence tend to be transmitted from one generation to another, so that abused children themselves are apt to become abusing parents; (2) it predominates in families with low socioeconomic status; (3) it is related to life-styles manifesting social and structural stress — stress factors include unemployment, larger-than-average family size, a new baby, a handicapped family member, illness, death, or child care problems; (4) it is particularly found in families showing social isolation and absence of community ties, that is, families with few friends and few recreational outlets; and (6) it is related to the family structure, most notably arising in families in which there is little shared decision making (Gelles, 1987).

Although abusive parents may tend to produce children who as adults are abusive, it is not an inevitable outcome. Kaufman and Zigler (1987), for instance, examining a large sample of persons who had been abused as children, found that two thirds of those who were themselves physically abused, sexually abused, or extremely neglected made satisfactory, nonabusive parents. They write:

> In the past, unqualified acceptance of the intergenerational hypothesis has had many negative consequences. Adults who were maltreated have been told so many times that they will abuse their children that for some it has become a self-fulfilling prophecy. Many who have broken the cycle are left feeling like walking time bombs. In addition, persistent acceptance of this belief has impeded progress in understanding the etiology of abuse and led to misguided judicial and social policy interventions. The time has come for the intergenerational myth to be put aside. (Kaufman and Zigler, 1987:191)

Lewis and her colleagues (1979) point out that delinquent children experienced and witnessed violence within their own families more often than nondelinquents with the same social backgrounds. It often follows that when persons are in difficulty or attempting to establish some set of behavior patterns, they tend to rely upon adaptive (or maladaptive) responses that they encountered within their own homes. College students, for example, often are astonished when first meeting the parents of their friends or roommates to discover how very much the children and the parent behave alike; and this often is true despite the children's having insisted that they don't really get along well with their parents because they are "so different."

Sexual abuse of children, which usually evokes the greatest amount of public concern, has shown enormous increases in reported offenses, up from 7,559 cases in 1976 to 123,000 in 1985, according to American Humane Association figures. Scholars generally believe, in accord with Finkelhor (1987:234), that "most of the growth is probably accounted for by the intensification, through media exposure and professional education, of efforts at case detection." Typical of such reports was the recent revelation by Michael Reagan, forty-one-year-old son of the president, that he was repeatedly sexually molested as a seven-year-old by a day-camp leader who was a father figure to him. The president's response echoed that of many fathers: "I'm sorry. When he was a little boy, he didn't let us know at the time." Changes in the patterns of family life also may be contributing to the increase in child sexual abuse. More divorces, for instance, expose children to more stepfathers, men who generally have less protective attachment to them, and the greater number of families with both parents working has inevitably led to children having larger amounts of contact with strangers who serve as caretakers.

Self-report studies indicate that about 5 per cent of all American adults say that they have been sexually assaulted. Girls are twice as likely as boys to be sexually assaulted as children. The offenders generally are fathers or stepfathers (7–8 per cent); other family members, especially uncles and older brothers (16–42 per cent); and neighbors, family friends, child care workers, and other authorities (32–60 per cent). The ages from nine to twelve are the most vulnerable, while, depending on the research study, from 42 to 75 per cent of the incidents are single, nonrecurring events (Finkelhor, 1987).

Foster Home Placements

It is not an easy matter to take remedial action when families are severely flawed. There exist in the United States strong feelings that parents have the inalienable right to manage their children as they see fit, provided they do not employ clearly abusive practices. Courts are extremely reluctant to remove the children from their own homes, in part because experience often indicates that, however inadequate, children come to regard their own parents and their home as the best and the most comfortable situation and to be miserable when put elsewhere. In a classic autobiographical sketch of his career as a delinquent, Stanley in *The Jack-Roller* (Shaw, 1930) tells how he was placed with an extremely rich Chicago family but felt so ill-at-ease and unsure of himself that in short order he ran away, back to his apartment in the slums, where his stepmother constantly vilified him.

Judges today also are faced with a severe shortage of foster homes in which to put children whom they might want to remove from what they regard as peccant living conditions. For one thing, the large number of women now in the labor market has reduced severely the pool of persons available to serve as foster parents. Those homes being used for foster placements often are as awful or more awful than the places the children had been removed from. To illustrate, in Maryland a suit was filed in 1987 on behalf of 2,800 foster children in Baltimore charging that some as young as three years had been raped and that many had been medically neglected and otherwise mistreated in foster homes. In the District of Columbia in 1986, five foster children, three of them infants, were burned to death in a fire in their inner-city row house. The foster mother had left them in the care of a sixty-five-year-old alcoholic and former convict who was drunk when the fire broke out (McQueen, 1987).

Contributing to Delinquency

The original juvenile court statutes, which sought to be benevolent and compassionate toward young persons who had violated the law, turned punitive when they dealt with what they regarded as the contributory sins of the delinquents' parents. If children were no longer to be held criminally responsible for their lawbreaking behavior, then the source of that responsibility would have to be located elsewhere. Such an attitude led to the enactment of offenses that were called "contributing to delinquency." The first such law was passed in Colorado in 1903; at present forty-two states have "contributing to the delinquency of a minor" in their codes. The typical law forbids acts that "aid, abet, induce, cause, encourage or contribute" to delinquency (Garlock, 1983). Under "contributing" statutes it is not necessary in order to obtain a conviction for the youngster to have engaged in delinquent behavior, but only for the adult to have done something that seems to make it more likely that the young person will become a delinquent. Take, for example, the case of *State v. Gans* (151 N.E. 2d 709, *cert. denied,* 359 U.S. 945, 1959). The adoptive parents of an eleven-year-old girl had taken her from Ohio to West Virginia, where, with their connivance in misrepresenting her age, she was married in what apparently was a legal ceremony. On their return to Ohio, the parents were convicted of contributing to the girl's delinquency, with the prosecutor maintaining that what had been done "tended" to cause their daughter's delinquency. Similarly, in 1942, a father was convicted for contributing to delinquency for directing his child, for religious reasons, not to salute the flag. The child was expelled from school for this behavior (*State v. Davis,* 120 P. 2d 802, 1942). The Ohio appellate court, in a 5–2 decision, spelled out what it saw as the preventive nature of the contributing law and sustained the conviction of the parents of the married girl (151 N.E. 2d 293, 1957):

> It is apparent that the purpose of that clause is to prevent a delinquency before it occurs rather than to await such delinquency and then to punish the adult offender. The purpose of the clause is to avoid the undesirable result which might arise if an adult is permitted to pursue a course of conduct which tends to cause a child to become delinquent. . . . A disease is much easier to prevent than to cure.

The court overlooked the fact that many diseases are much easier to cure than to prevent. It concentrated on the imputation that because of her marriage, the eleven-year-old would probably become a school truant; therefore, encouraging the marriage encouraged the delinquent act of truanting, a fact, the court pointed out, even more deplorable because the girl had been a good student. But, even if the girl did attend school, the court decreed, "the more successful her marriage would be the more it could tend to cause her to act so as to adversely affect the morals of her classmates."

Contributing-to-delinquency statutes often tend to be employed when it is difficult to make a case that will stand up in court against an adult for behavior involving a juvenile. The evidence may be weak, or there may not have been credible witnesses. Contributing-to-delinquency statutes, in attempting to punish parents for the behavior of their youngsters, may placate public indignation, but they also are likely to further disturb an already fractured family relationship. Legal actions may alienate the child even more from the parents by causing the latter to increase their rejection or to seek revenge for the punishment they received because of the child. Such prosecution may also add infantile power to the child's delinquent repertoire by providing it with a weapon against the parent, the threat of additional court action. The possibility of punishment may also inhibit parental participation in juvenile court hearings and plans (Geis, 1963).

Overview

It seems apparent that there is some relationship between the experience that a child and adolescent has within the family and the behavior that the person exhibits in the extrafamily world. The precise ingredients that produce particular forms of outcome, however, are extremely difficult to specify. This is especially so because family life generally is so encompassing that it can be categorized only in very broad terms. Family A may be said to carry on in a hostile fashion, Family B in a loving manner. But Family A is not invariantly hostile; there are periods of reconciliation, moments of deep affection. Similarly, Family B would be very unusual if it did not experience moments of anger and frustration. In Family A, the children may become virtually immune to the atmosphere and may find comfort and warmth with relatives, such as grandparents. And in Family B, children accustomed to a cozy atmosphere may be devastated even by very brief periods of anger and be seriously scarred emotionally.

Johnstone (1980) suggests that three major problems have beset efforts to understand adequately the impact of the family upon the delinquent behavior of its young members: (1) a failure to clearly isolate how the major components of the family systems relate to delinquent behavior; (2) a failure to discriminate the types of youthful misbehavior influenced and not influenced by the family; and (3) a failure to study the family in the context of the wider community.

While it is difficult to pinpoint the precise relationship between any one form of family life and any one child in that family, certain patternings have been located by researchers. It is generally agreed that the structure of the family — whether it is broken or intact, for instance — plays a less significant role than the way that the family carries out its business. Earlier work that pinpointed broken families as precursors of delinquency is now largely discredited. Children from broken homes were adjudicated delinquent more often by the juvenile courts, it is now suggested, because judges did not have intact situations to which to return them (Johnstone, 1980:88).

In a recent comprehensive review of "all accessible reports on relevant research" on the relationship between the family and juvenile delinquency, Loeber and Stouthamer-Loeber (1986:30) report that certain factors appear to be the "most powerful" family conditions for predicting delinquency, while a second group is less powerful, and a third group weaker predictors. They claim that these factors hold similar importance for both girls and boys.

The most powerful category of factors includes lack of supervision, parental rejection, and a low level of parent-child involvement. In some environments, research indicates, extremely strict supervision may be more important in preventing delinquency than a warm and stable home. *Rejection* refers primarily to an absence of parents' appreciation of their children. The items of lesser predictive power were background variables, including the nature of the parents' marital relations and parental criminality. Least powerful were the factors of parental discipline, parental health, and parental absence.

The National Commission on the Causes and Prevention of Violence, after examining the complex relationship between the family and violent delinquent acts, could only conclude—as most persons do—that the family must be important in instilling values and attitudes that feed into such behavior, even if we cannot state with much precision how this occurs. The commission's recommendations on the family grow out of its belief that stable and loving family life somehow must be buttressed (Campbell and Shoham, 1969:188):

> Neither the government nor any other institution of society can make a husband and wife create a relationship of love among themselves and their children: they must do that on their own as individuals. But government can at least try to create the conditions under which stable families can thrive. It can make it possible for fathers to have jobs, and hence to have a self-respect that comes from being able to support a family. Government can act against hunger, disease, poor housing, and urban decay, thereby creating a humane environment in which humane personal relationships can develop. Schools can give hope to the young, and to the parents whose hope is in their children. Churches can awaken men and women to the moral and spiritual dimensions of family life.

This clarion call for social reform, issued only about two decades ago, demonstrates clearly the continuous flux in contemporary family life in America. No government body today would dare issue a statement calling only for jobs for fathers; it would have to attend to the demands of the women's movement for equal access to the workplace for women and for satisfactory day care facilities. In only a short period in the United States, the nature of family life for many persons has undergone dramatic changes. It will be some time yet, of course, before we will have dependable information on the manner in which the newly emergent family life-styles bear upon the phenomenon of juvenile delinquency, but it probably can be presumed that there will be no clear-cut, unarguable conclusions that what has happened to the traditional family has directly and unequivocally contributed to the rate and form of juvenile delinquency.

The School

We have already noted, in Chapter 9, that the school bears important relationships to juvenile delinquency in our society. Not the least of these relationships, as we noted there, lies in the role that the school has come to play in socializing children and youths, including serving, as a court of first resort, to adjust many situations that involve delinquency. Such situations are treated as disciplinary problems and corrected by the disciplinary procedures available within the school setting.

But the relationships between the schools and delinquency are considerably more complex than this and involve issues and concerns of which scholars and the public are only now becoming fully aware. Among these are an apparent increase in the frequency and intensity of delinquency *within* schools with which normal disciplinary procedures cannot adequately cope, the argument made by a number of influential scholars that the schools have actually helped to produce delinquency, and the special problems of delinquency involving students who are unable to "keep up" with the normal learning progress expected by the schools. We shall consider each of these issues.

Violence, Theft, and Intimidation in the Schools

The problem of delinquent behavior has long been a fact of life in schooling. Medieval schools and universities were plagued by disruptive acts. Throughout American history, our schools have had to confront disorder and violence, from the rebellious disorder of the nineteenth-century universities to such folk customs as "turning out" the teacher, often accomplished by force (see Chapter 7). However, since the 1970s, the problem of crime and violence in our schools, along with the daily occurrence of such other forms of delinquency as drug dealing and use, has come to seem especially significant. Particularly during the late 1970s and early 1980s, the popular press and other media focused attention on crime in the nation's schools, especially in the larger cities. *Newsweek* headlined such a story "City Schools in Crisis" (1977), indicating one widespread image of disorder in urban schools.

Concern about school crime has also been expressed by scholars. Rubel (1977) documented significant increases in school crimes in the years between about 1955 and 1975. These crimes included larceny, assaults on other students and on teachers, robbery, extortion, and arson. Rubel described perceptions on the part of both students and staff that schools were becoming unsafe places to be. McDermott (1979) similarly documented a high level of school crime in a survey of twenty-six cities, and although concluding that for the most part school crime generally was not serious crime, he highlighted its extensiveness.

Concern about school crime has also been expressed by various federal committees and agencies. During 1975, the Subcommittee to Investigate Delinquency of the United States Senate Committee on the Judiciary conducted an investigation of school violence and vandalism, publishing its findings in a report, the title of which summarized the conclusions — *Our Nation's Schools — A Report Card: "A" in School Violence and Vandalism* (1975). The subcommittee not only documented increases in the frequency and intensity of crimes in the schools but reported—despite the popular identification of school crime with the urban Northeast—that the problem was nationwide. And the subcommittee's report highlighted some particularly remarkable instances (1975:27):

> We did learn of a rather shocking example of such conduct involving elementary school youngsters that vividly demonstrates the seriousness of problems confronting the school community. In April 1973, three third grade pupils, in Winston-Salem, North Carolina, were charged with robbery for allegedly forcing two nine-year-old classmates to pay nearly $1,000 in extortion payments over an eight-month period. The three boys, two aged nine and one aged eleven, allegedly threatened their classmates with beatings or death if the money was not paid.

It is, perhaps, no wonder that the subcommittee questioned how much students could learn, or teachers teach, in such an environment.

This investigation was followed, in April, June, and September 1975, by a series of hearings conducted by the subcommittee on the subject of school violence and vandalism (U.S. Senate, 1976a; 1976b). Indiana Senator Birch Bayh (see Chapter 11), chair of the subcommittee, referred to the nation's schools, in an introduction to the hearings, as "combat zones" (1976a:2), and a series of witnesses—including scholars, school administrators, teachers, and students—corroborated Bayh's description. Particularly vivid was the testimony of one teacher who, contrary to the popular identification of school crime as an urban, minority problem, described the situation at her all-white rural Missouri school (176a:229):

> Since November 1974, approximately 8 months ago, the following events have taken place: (1) Approximately $6,000 in equipment and supplies has been stolen from the high school plant; (2) One teacher's car was stolen from his own driveway, driven several miles away and then burned; (3) Another teacher had the windows broken in both his home and his car; (4) Another teacher had four .22 rifle bullets shot into his car while it was parked at school at night; (5) One teacher was attacked and beaten by a male student during school hours in the high school; (6) Another teacher was attacked and stabbed in the hand by a female student with a knife which she had brought to school for that purpose. A janitor was also injured trying to help the teacher; and (7) An unloaded .22 pistol was confiscated from an 8th grader who had the bullets in his pocket.

The teacher concluded, "To say that events such as the ones I have just listed did upset normal educational routines in our district is an understatement" (1976a:229).

In 1978, another government study, *Violent Schools—Safe Schools,* published under the auspices of the U.S. National Institute of Education (NIE), further reported on the extensiveness of violence and vandalism in schools. This study by the NIE occurred in three phases. Phase I involved a mail survey of principals of 4,000 public elementary and secondary schools; Phase II, site visits to 642 public junior and senior high schools, including interviews of students and staff; Phase III, an in-depth exploration of 10 schools with histories of school crime and violence. Although the study reported some leveling off of school crime and violence after the early 1970s, and after a marked increase in such problems beginning in the late 1960s, it also concluded (1978:1, 3) that "the problem is as serious as it has ever been, the risks of violence for young adolescents in cities are greater at school than elsewhere, and around 6,700 schools are seriously affected by crime."

The NIE report also provided some striking statistics of school crime in the mid-1970s. For example, 11 per cent of high school students reported the theft at school of something worth more than a dollar in any given month. This represents, as the NIE report indicated, about 2.4 million incidents in a month. Moreover, 1.3 per cent of high school students — about 282,000 students — reported having been physically attacked in a typical month. About 12 per cent of teachers reported having suffered thefts. About 0.5 per cent reported physical attack in a typical month — a seemingly small proportion but representing around 5,200 teachers (1978:1, 3). No less striking were statistics of what the report called "other signs of trouble in schools" (1978:1, 4–5):

22% of all secondary students reported avoiding some restrooms at school because of fear.

16% reported avoiding three or more places at school for the same reason.

20% of the students said they were afraid of being hurt or bothered at school at least sometimes.

3% said they are afraid most of the time, representing around 600,000 secondary students.

4%, or around 800,000, stayed at home from school in the previous month because they were afraid.

12% of the secondary school teachers, representing some 120,000, said they were threatened with injury by students at school.

12% of teachers said they hesitated to confront misbehaving students because of fear.

Almost half (48%) of the teachers reported that some students had insulted them or made obscene gestures at them in the last month.

Such statistics made more impressive the dangerous situation that, according to the NIE report, characterized the nation's schools.

It is possible, as McDermott (1979) has stressed, to exaggerate the extent of crime in the nation's schools. All studies agree, for example, that most thefts are petty thefts and that few crimes of violence result in serious injury. Gottfredson and Gottfredson, in an extensive critique of the NIE study, have written (1985:4), "the main problems of disruption are day-to-day indignities suffered by school staff, not wholesale mayhem and plunder." And, indeed, as Smith (1984) has emphasized, there remains a need for more systematic record keeping on both the frequency and the intensity of such crime. Nevertheless, it appears that school crime has shown an increase within the past three decades and has become a visible part of the life of the schools.

Explanations of School Crime

How can we account for the widespread and increasing occurrence of school crime? Two major schools of thought have emerged, one of which views school crime as a symptom of more general changes in American society, the other of which looks for the causes of crime in the school itself. The most influential exponent of the former view is Toby (1980), who sees the origins of the increase in school crime in, above all, the increasing permissiveness of American society.

Drawing on the evidence provided by the NIE's 1978 study, Toby urged a focus on "social trends in American society that made it more difficult for public schools to control predatory, violent, or malicious student behavior" (1980:26). Among these trends Toby cited the existence of distinctive youth subcultures that alienated students from education, along with the continuing pressure to keep young people in school longer, including young people indifferent to education itself.

In addition, Toby called attention to the increasing regard for children's rights and "due process" in school discipline, which he believes ties the hands of school administrators and teachers alike in correcting problems of behavior on the part of students. He also noted the difficulty schools have in turning to the juvenile courts for assistance in dealing with behavior problems, particularly since *Gault* (see Chapter 8).

But Toby cast summary blame on "the erosion of the authority of the classroom teacher" (1980:30). According to Toby, the status of the teacher has significantly declined in our society, and with it the respect of students for teachers. Moreover, he argued, 1960s and 1970s critiques of American education — which condemned the schools and appeared to blame teachers for most of the problems — helped to erode both the status and the authority of the teacher in the classroom, making it difficult for teachers to maintain order. Stressing, as had the Senate subcommittee, the impossibility of education in schools where students and teachers worry more about their own safety than about learning, Toby argued for a strengthening of control on the part of schools over their students and for the relatively free use of expulsion in order to rid the schools of disruptive and violent young people.

Others shared Toby's view of the problem. Such professionals in education as John Ryor, president of the National Education Association, and Albert Shanker, president of the American Federation of Teachers, also cited the dangers of "the new permissivism" (Moorefield, 1977) and urged measures to tighten school discipline and increase school security. And, in fact, the decade of the 1970s, in particular, saw massive increases in school security, in the form of the creation of more damage-resistant physical plants and beefed-up school security forces. Indeed, according to Moorefield (1977), by the late 1970s, the Los Angeles school security force, to take one example, was the second largest police force in the United States.

In contrast to the views of Toby and of such figures as Ryor and Shanker are the ideas of those theorists who identify the causes of school violence and disorder in the nature of the schools themselves. Indeed, these ideas predate the work of Toby and other critics of permissiveness and had a particularly influential statement in Stinchcombe's *Rebellion in a High School* (1964). Stinchcombe investigated disruptiveness among high school students and concluded that, above all, disruptiveness in school was related to perceptions of the connection of school work to future possibilities in life. To summarize (1964:71):

1. Students' chances of success in the post–high school job market are determined by origin, ability, school attended, sex, and so forth.
2. The perceived value of school depends on the school's perceived connection

WHIPPED TO DEATH FOR MISSPELLING A WORD—FRIGHT-
FUL FATE OF A LAD AT SOUTH NEWMARKET, N. H.

A somewhat more extreme form of discipline than that
advocated by people calling for greater exercise of control by
schools.

with success. This perceived connection varies among social classes, ability
groups, sexes, races, and neighborhoods.

3. Perceived lack of connection of school work to occupational success produces
   rebellion.
4. Perception is roughly accurate on these questions, hence rebellion is concentrated in groups which actually have poor articulation of current work with
   future status.

Stinchcombe described school rebellion as a form of "expressive alienation"
(1964:5) whereby students who do not feel that successful academic performance will materially affect their chances for success in the larger society
display their frustrations with both the school and the society as a whole.
School disorder thus becomes a significant symptom of the failure of society to
overcome the structural inequalities of poverty, racism, and class
discrimination.

Stinchcombe's views have been widely accepted by those who have studied
school violence and vandalism. They were, for example, the dominant views in

testimony before the U.S. Senate subcommittee investigating juvenile delinquency in the schools (1976a; 1976b). Stinchcombe did intensive research to support his conclusions, and subsequent investigators have extended that research and elaborated still further on his conclusions. In particular, several scholars have argued that disruptiveness grows not only out of a perception of poor chances for success in life but also out of a need on the part of disruptive students to raise their own self-esteem in the school setting (Gold, 1978) or to find alternative rewards, even alternative sources of enjoyment (Csikszentmihaly and Larson, 1978) in a social context and an institutional setting that appears to offer little. These scholars have also specifically criticized solutions to school disorder predicated on increased rules and discipline since, as Glasser (1978) argues, those students most likely to engage in disruptive activities are those who have the least stake in school as such, seeing neither long-term benefits nor immediate rewards in education and school life. Only when school itself can be made to seem useful and involving can one expect to see any significant diminution in school disorder, including violence and vandalism.

Gottfredson and Gottfredson (1985) investigated many specifics of school organization and operation that appear to contribute to school disorder. These involve such very concrete features as relations with the larger community, school size, staffing, and funding, as well as the school "climate" (1985:105), including the kinds of attitudes that teachers and other staff members project toward students. They suggest that significant changes in the schools will do much to reduce problems of violence, vandalism, and disruption.

Corporal Punishment and the School

The issue of the use of physical punishment in the schools cuts to the heart of the debate about proper forms of discipline and the matter of permissiveness. Nine of the fifty states — New York, New Jersey, Massachusetts, Vermont, Rhode Island, New Hampshire, Maine, Hawaii, and California — explicitly ban corporal punishment in their schools. So do a number of large urban districts, such as St. Louis, Atlanta, New Orleans, and Minneapolis. But in many other schools, corporal punishment is common. In some places, it is required that there must be parental consent to paddling students and that the punishment be carried out in front of at least one witness.

Opponents of the practice insist that it is no different from child abuse. It is estimated that 20 per cent of the instances of such punishment produce bleeding, severe bruises, or other kinds of physical trauma that would characterize criminal child abuse. It is argued that such punishment merely fuels a cycle of violence among those who are exposed to it. In Winder, Georgia, in 1986, a thirteen-year-old who had been paddled two days before stabbed his elementary school principal to death. Georgia law stipulates that teachers who administer physical punishment to pupils "in good faith" and where the punishment is not "unduly severe" are to be exempt from criminal or civil actions against them for such acts.

Some school officials strongly defend the practice. They are apt to note that they were so disciplined as youngsters and adjusted perfectly well. The superintendent of a rural Georgia district also maintained: "We've been using it here since the schools began, and I don't know what we'd do without it. The only alternative is to send the unruly kids home, and they won't learn anything there" (Schmidt, 1987).

The School as a Cause of Delinquency: "Strain Theory"

These views of the causes of school violence and disorder are important because they fit into a larger context of discussion on the issue of juvenile delinquency and the schools, one provided by the argument that the schools themselves actually cause, or at least contribute to, juvenile delinquency. This argument is most consistent with the strain and anomie theories discussed in Chapter 5, in that it concludes that school serves for many young people as a source of frustration, and that the frustration they feel leads them into delinquent activity. This argument was offered as early as the mid-1940s in a pioneer study by William Kvaraceus (1945). After extensive research into the schools and the students in one community — Passaic, New Jersey — Kvaraceus concluded (1945:136) that the school is "an active agent in the genesis of aggressive behavior." As he summarized his findings (1945:156):

> In general, the school picture of the delinquent presents an unsatisfactory, unsuccessful, unhappy, and hence extremely frustrating situation which precedes or accompanies undesirable behavior. The delinquent group was found to differ significantly from the general school population in many of the factors studied. This was true of low marks, truancy, repetition or nonpromotion, school transfers, and schools attended.

Among those factors, Kvaraceus singled out school failure as especially important. As he understood the causal sequence leading to delinquency, repeated failure in school produces frustration in a young person, which, with significant frequency, leads to rebellion and delinquency. In a later study, Kvaraceus (1966) continued to view school failure as a significant cause of delinquency and described delinquency as an alternative means of achievement for many youngsters. Thus, one corrective he proposed was a concentration on the part of the schools in building egos rather than forcing young people into delinquency by failing them.

Kvaraceus's views were given support by some of the leading theorists whose work we have already discussed, particularly by such theorists as Cohen (1955) and Cloward and Ohlin (1960) (see Chapter 5). As Cohen argued, for example, schools "*reward* middle-class ambition and conformity to middle-class expectations" (1955:113). Because many lower-class and working-class young people do not conform to middle-class expectations and do not hold to middle-class ambitions, they are labeled failures in school and treated as such; hence, they are attracted to delinquency. Cloward and Ohlin, while they turn Cohen upside down and see delinquency as a matter of frustrated rather than deviant ambitions, nonetheless share the view of both Cohen and Kvaraceus that the school is a source of the difficulty. For them, education in American society is a means to mobility, except for those whose social origins "constitute a restraining influence" on what they can hope to achieve (1960:98). Because lower-class and working-class youths — and, more particularly, minority youngsters — are well aware of the structural barriers they must face, the experience of schooling becomes more a source of frustration than an avenue to success. It does more to produce than to correct delinquency.

Several other scholars have supported Kvaraceus and the positions of Cohen or Cloward and Ohlin. Moore (1961) sought to establish the link between frustrations caused by the school experience and a tendency toward delinquency in young people. Schafer and Polk (1967) presented data to indicate that school failure and school misconduct tend to *precede* delinquency, and they have argued that the school experience is a major cause of delinquency. They note, in particular, that school failure results in a loss of self-esteem and, hence, in a search for alternative sources of esteem through delinquent acts. They argue, too, that the perceived irrelevancy of education, particularly on the part of young people with low socioeconomic status, also produces delinquency. Schafer, Olexa, and Polk (1972) have emphasized the way in which "tracking" —grouping students according to past and expected levels of performance— may contribute to delinquency. Finally, Polk (1976) has documented a relationship between low school status and delinquency.

The School as a Factor in Delinquency: "Control Theory"

A second major approach to understanding the role of the school in delinquency as such is consistent with the control theory proposed by Hirschi (see Chapter 6). According to Hirschi (1969), the causes of delinquency are to be sought in the attachment of young people to the institutions of society, including the school. Examining a population of urban California delinquents, Hirschi found that they tended to show little attachment to the school, either in terms of the educational process or in terms of the social life that centered around it. Hindelang (1973) found the same lack of attachment on the part of a rural New York delinquent population—confirming Hirschi's findings.

It is possible to see important differences between strain and anomie theories, on the one hand, and control theory, on the other, in terms of their understanding of the relationship of schools to delinquency. Both, we should stress, identify a close connection between school failure and delinquency; both are based on findings that delinquents tend not to do very well in school. Kvaraceus, in his pioneer study, compared the school performances of delinquent boys with those of the general student population in Passaic. He found that 98.4 per cent of delinquents earned either minimum passing grades or failing grades in school, in a context where such grades accounted for only 36 per cent of the grades given citywide. Subsequent studies indicated similarly poor performance on the part of juvenile delinquents. Both theories also stress that delinquents do not like school. Kvaraceus (1945:151) noted that 67 per cent of delinquents in his study expressed such feelings. Hindelang (1973:478) reported that among his rural male population, 63 per cent who report liking school but only 45 per cent who report disliking school "report low delinquent involvement."

The difference in the theoretical approaches is less over such data as these— which are consistent with both—than over the nature of the link between the school and delinquency. Strain and anomie theories argue that school failure precedes delinquency and is part of a larger process whereby young people are led to seek alternative sources of satisfaction and self-esteem, one of which may be and often is delinquency. Control theory argues that the connection between

Peter Freed/*The New York Times*

School attendance is encouraged in a program initiated by Eugene Lang (at left, in second row) that guarantees a college education for students who finish high school.

school failure and delinquency is a product of the way in which both are symptoms of a general lack of attachment on the part of a young person to society, a lack of attachment that can be the product of a variety of social and, as we shall see subsequently in this chapter, individual sources.

Thornberry, Moore, and Christenson (1985) offered an interesting test of the two approaches by comparing the predictive capacity of each in regard to dropouts. They argued that if strain or anomie theory were correct, then dropping out of school should reduce frustrations and reduce subsequent criminal activity on the part of dropouts. If control theory were correct, they argued, then dropping out, as a symptom of alienation, should not reduce subsequent criminal activity; indeed, it should increase such activity, since one mechanism of social control, however minimal, would be removed from the lives of those leaving school. Their data indicated that, indeed, criminal activity did increase among dropouts—thus, they argued, giving support to control theory.

It is possible, however, to take issue with such findings, even with the test itself. For one thing, the dropout's confrontation with a society that has few rewards for those lacking basic educational skills is hardly likely to bring a reduction in frustrations, although it may bring new ones, and stronger ones. For another, it is not clear that the two types of theory are mutually exclusive, as the test described above seems to imply. Indeed, the results of school failure have been said by strain theorists to include a lack of attachment to the school as an educational and social institution, and they have seen this as an important factor in delinquency (e.g., Polk, 1976). The causes of that lack of attachment to school, identified by control theorists, can include early and repeated failure, among other things. Perhaps the most we can conclude, given current research, is that the link between poor school performance and delinquency is well established but that the explanation for that link remains problematic.

IQ and Delinquency

One effort to make that link clearer and less problematic has been in studies that draw connections between intelligence — as measured by IQ — and delinquency. We have already noted how early criminologists and more recent "constitutional" theorists have called attention to IQ as a factor in delinquency (Chapter 4). Sociologists, who have done the most work on schools and delinquency, have historically not given much attention to IQ as a factor, since it focuses on individual characteristics rather than on social forces. But Hirschi and Hindelang (1977) have attempted to revive an interest in IQ on the part of sociologists and have argued that, indeed, IQ does represent an important causative factor in delinquency. Citing scattered studies showing correlations between IQ and both self-reported and adjudicated delinquency, they argue that one possible role which IQ can play in causing delinquency is in terms of school performance. Young people with low IQs may do poorly in school, leading to the kinds of processes both strain theory and control theory describe — to failure or to an inability to form attachments to the school as an institutioñ.

Hirschi and Hindelang did no more than to suggest a relation and to urge further exploration of the issue. Menard and Morse (1984), who did carry out such further explorations, reached conclusions that led them to dispute the Hirschi and Hindelang "model" (1984:1347). Like Hirschi and Hindelang, they recognized that IQ, as a factor in social behavior, was mediated through the school experience. But rather than seeing it as a causative factor, Menard and Morse, in keeping with labeling theories (see Chapter 5), argued that delinquent behavior, to the extent that it had sources in negative attitudes toward school, grew out of the school's own response to poor school performance and low (measured) intelligence. Schools, they wrote, were quick to label low-IQ students as failures and, hence, to encourage the kinds of frustrations and needs that, according to strain theory, can lead to delinquency. The cause lay in the institution, not in the young person who did badly on IQ tests.

The issue is far from resolved. At the present state of investigation, there is little convincing evidence to prefer Hirschi and Hindelang over Menard and Morse, or vice versa. The debate does, however, point to one direction for studying specific areas of the link between poor school performance and juvenile delinquency.

Learning Disabilities and Juvenile Delinquency

A second area that has led to much research and to much debate is the apparent link, identified by some scholars, between learning disabilities (LD) and juvenile delinquency (JD). This link received significant discussion by Murray (1976), who identified both problems and possibilities in focusing on an LD/JD link. Murray (1976:21) defined LD such that it refers to those children of any age who demonstrate a *substantial deficiency in a particular aspect of academic achievement because of perceptual or perceptual-motor handicaps, regardless of etiology or other contributing factors.* . . . Operationally, we include as learning disabilities the perceptual and perceptual-motor handicaps which are often labeled dyslexia, aphasia, or hyperkinesis.

Murray then explored, through a review of the literature, the relationship of LD to JD.

According to Murray, two causal chains were generally hypothesized in the literature to identify a potential link between LD and JD. One has been labeled the "school failure" hypothesis and is consistent with similar hypotheses identifying the school itself as a causal factor in juvenile delinquency. According to the school failure hypothesis, as a result of the child's perceptual and attention problems, the products of LD, the child is perceived by adults, even during preschool years, as a discipline problem; moreover, the child is inherently handicapped in achieving academically. Thus, teachers and peers alike categorize the child as a failure, and, indeed, the child does do poorly in school, resulting ultimately in those frustrations or needs for alternative sources of self-esteem that, according to strain theory, can lead to delinquent behavior. LD thus serves as a causative factor in the more general process linking school failure to juvenile delinquency.

The second hypothesis that has been used to link LD with JD is the "susceptibility" hypothesis. According to this line of argument, LD not only consists in handicaps to learning but in other behaviors that are problematic — in a short attention span on the part of the LD child, in a general impulsiveness, in a poor ability to learn from experience. The result is, as Murray summarized the argument (1976:27), "decreased effectiveness of the usual social sanctions [and] rewards" and, thus, an "increased susceptibility to delinquent behavior." The susceptibility hypothesis is not far removed from control-theory-based explanations of links between poor school performance and delinquency, using LD to explain a general lack of attachment to dominant social institutions and values.

Reviewing the existing research on the LD/JD link, Murray found less than impressive evidence for either hypothesis. While he acknowledged that scattered studies showed a higher proportion of LD youngsters than non-LD youngsters among the delinquent population than would be expected from their representation in the general population, he found little evidence that directly confirmed the causal linkages the two hypotheses proposed. Studies purporting to support the school failure hypothesis tended to base their argument on the presence of the link, but with little real investigation of the process by which that link was supposed to be made — into the behavior of parents, teachers, or school administrators, for example. In examining studies purporting to support the susceptibility hypothesis, Murray noticed a failure to link the personality traits described for LD youngsters with a demonstration that those personality traits were also displayed by delinquents.

Murray's conclusions are important to quote (1976:65–66):

the existence of a causal relationship between learning disabilities and delinquency has not [been] established; *the evidence for a causal link is feeble.* . . . with few exceptions, *the quantitative work to date has been so poorly designed and presented that it cannot be used even for rough estimates of the strength of the link.* . . .
. . . *no study has yet been conducted which even claims to demonstrate that the*

average delinquent is more likely to suffer from learning disabilities than his nonde-
linquent counterpart.

Murray saw a pressing need for more and better research.

One other problem was identified by Murray in his review of the literature, and this was a definitional one. As he noted, one reason the evidence seemed so inconclusive was that different studies used different definitions of LD. Murray's own was fairly rigorous, focusing on such diagnosable handicaps as dyslexia and aphasia. Other studies before and after Murray's have relied on what might be called performance-based definitions of LD, as in the work of Dunivant (1982:3), who defines LD as "impairments of perceptual, thinking, and communicative processes which are manifested by a significant discrepancy between a child's expected achievement (based on intelligence test scores) and his or her actual achievement." The variability criticized by Murray continues to characterize LD studies, rendering problematic the conclusions they draw. This was made clear in a document released by the comptroller general of the United States (1977) shortly after Murray's study appeared. The report concluded, based on extensive studies of delinquents in Connecticut and Virginia, that some link exists between LD and delinquency. However, both the Department of Justice and the Department of Health, Education, and Welfare, in responses published as part of the report, argued that the state of existing research made any firm conclusions in regard to causal links between LD and JD inappropriate.

Continuing research does explore the possible link between LD and delinquency, identifying higher-than-expected frequencies of LD in delinquent populations and seeking to account for that fact. The comptroller general's report estimated that about 6 to 7 per cent of the general student population has primary learning problems but noted that 33 per cent of delinquents tested in the studies on which it was based were found to have such problems (1977:8, 25). Satterfield, Hoppe, and Schell (1982), in a study of one specific disability, attention deficit disorder (ADD), have shown that delinquency occurred at a higher rate among a population of adolescent boys with ADD than among a control population of normal boys. They reported (1982:796), "The percentage of ADD subjects arrested at least once for a serious offense in the lower, middle, and upper socioeconomic classes was 58 percent, 36 percent and 52 percent, compared with 11 percent, 9 percent, and 2 percent for the controls," a statistically significant difference for each class. Differences between classes were not significant.

Other studies have emphasized, however, the great complexity of any LD/JD link. Broder and Dunivant (1981) presented evidence to indicate that the significance of the link between LD and JD is, in fact, greater for young people of high socioeconomic status — young people for whom other social and structural frustrations would have less relevance. But they have also noted that when one compares self-reported delinquency figures with official delinquency figures the results are especially interesting. Such a comparison indicates that LD youngsters are not more likely to commit delinquent acts, based on self-report data, although they are more likely to be adjudicated delinquent by the juvenile courts.

This finding has led to the creation of a third hypothesis to explain an LD/JD link, the "different treatment" hypothesis (Zimmerman et al., 1981). According to this hypothesis, the significant factor in the LD/JD link is society's response to the youngster with learning disabilities. Although the exact mechanism remains open to investigation (Zimmerman et al., 1981), this hypothesis urges the investigator to focus primarily on the mechanisms by which society responds to juvenile offenders and to identify ways in which those with learning disabilities must face unequal treatment in the juvenile justice system itself. Thus, LD is not a cause of delinquency as such; but it is a factor in the classification of a youngster as delinquent.

The LD/JD link thus remains problematic. Certainly, it is too early to infer a causal relationship between learning disabilities and delinquency. Nevertheless, existing evidence and approaches have produced recommendations for paying closer attention to the possible role LD can play in delinquency. Thus, Reilly, Wheeler, and Etlinger (1985), after a study indicating that juvenile delinquent and LD groups tend to perform on a comparable level in school, urge that teachers of juvenile delinquents "should be well-trained in special education and should be familiar with the emotional manifestation of learning problems in order to work effectively with the population" (1985:207). Post (1981) has stressed the legal implications of an LD/JD link, urging that, where relevant, the diagnosis of a learning disability in a youngster brought before the juvenile court should serve as a defense (see also Winter, 1983).

Religion

"If One Is Truly Religious, One Cannot Be a Delinquent"

The notion that there is an inherent antithesis between religion and delinquency has been illustrated at various points in this book. For example, in Chapter 2, we saw that the Puritan minister Cotton Mather taught that the basic sinfulness and depravity of children could be controlled only through piety, including full subjugation to the will of God. And in Chapter 7, we saw that religious observances and prayers were important components in the routines of the houses of refuge during the nineteenth century — religion went along with discipline and orderliness in the overall effort to achieve rehabilitation and morality. Finally, in Chapters 9 and 13 we saw that a police officer might divert a youngster from the juvenile justice system by release accompanied by referral to a community agency that could be a local church.

Since religion is widely associated with such concepts as goodness, morality, concern for the rights and welfare of others, righteousness, and rewards in the hereafter for proper behavior in life, it is not surprising that many expect less delinquent behavior among the religious. Thus, the sociologist Father Joseph Fitzpatrick (1967:318) refers to a religious person as one who is self-disciplined and self-denying, who strives toward a certain form of perfection, and "who shuns thievery, crude forms of violence, destructiveness." He then states (1967:318):

> When the literature on delinquency speaks of religion as an important element
> in the prevention and control of delinquency, it generally has in mind this kind of

religious formation. This results in a person who has been formed to know God, recognize his dependence on Him, who seeks to do God's will. In our Western tradition, this would ordinarily issue in behavior in which one has a strong sense of personal worth, a clear purpose in life. He is one who respects his neighbor and lives as a peaceful citizen.

As the preceding discussion indicates, religion has been assumed as important in both the prevention of delinquency and the rehabilitation of delinquents. Hirschi and Stark (1969:202) point to the preventative aspect as follows: "Religious leaders traditionally blame 'rising crime and immorality' on a decline in religious conviction, and many argue that religious commitment is the *only* secure basis for moral behavior." An example of a firm statement of the general position that religion is the most effective path toward the formation of a morally good personality, and that the morally good personality, in turn, forms the basis for the avoidance of delinquency, may be found in the article by the priest John Coogan (1954). The corrective aspect of religion is emphasized by Hirschi and Stark (1969:202) in the following illustration: "From time to time judges advise juvenile offenders to attend church for periods of months or years. . . . the judge assumes that religious training and commitment produce moral character, he assumes such attendance may lead to repentance and reform." A sophisticated analysis of the ways religion may be used effectively in rehabilitation, accompanied by examples of religiously related programs, may be found in Fitzpatrick (1967).

The Early Years

Early tests of the assumed negative relationship between religion and delinquency took the form of comparing delinquents and nondelinquents on church attendance. For Healy and Bronner (1936) the comparison involved 105 delinquents and 105 nondelinquent controls who were siblings of the delinquents. They found that 43.8 per cent of the delinquents and 61.0 per cent of the controls attended church services or Sunday schools regularly; 11.4 per cent of the delinquents but only 7.6 of the nondelinquents did not attend church or Sunday school at all. For the Gluecks (1950), the comparison involved 500 delinquents and 500 matched nondelinquents. Their findings were similar to those of Healy and Bronner in that 39.3 per cent of the delinquents attended church regularly, as did 67.1 per cent of the nondelinquents.

But it is indeed hazardous to assume that results like the preceding provide convincing evidence of a relationship between religiousness and nondelinquency. Church attendance may indicate nothing more than conformity to social expectations, not any pattern of beliefs in the supernatural that defines religion. One would expect youngsters who show conformity in the area of church attendance to show it too in the absence of delinquent behavior. In addition to being influenced by general patterns of conformity, church attendance and similar religious activity are related to such social variables as class, ethnicity, denominational affiliation, and strength of family ties, as discussed in the introductory comments to this chapter. Fitzpatrick (1967:318) has nicely summarized the interpretive difficulty as follows:

It is well known now that these [measures of religious activity] are not reliable indexes of the influence of religion on behavior. What is needed are studies which discriminate between religion and variables such as class and cultural background; and studies which reveal the quality of a person's commitment to religion's belief and practice rather than a simple description of the faith he holds or the practice he pursues. Furthermore . . . studies [like those of Healy and Bronner and of Glueck and Glueck] fail to take into account the complicated relationship of religion to social control. Social control is only one function which religion may fulfill in a society and it is a very ambiguous one.

Studies Using the Self-report Technique

The General and Some Specific Effects of Religion on Delinquency. As discussed in Chapter 1, the method of self-report became widely used in the years following its systematic introduction by Short and Nye in 1957. In 1962, Middleton and Putney reported the results of a study of the relation between religion and morality using college students as subjects. Subjects were asked if they would be behaving within their own ethical principles if they engaged in certain violations of traditional "ascetic standards" (such as gambling and nonmarital sexual intercourse) and certain violations of accepted "social standards" (such as minor theft and striking a person in anger). They were also asked if they had actually engaged in any of those actions in the past three years. Three different measures of "religiosity" were used: the first to distinguish between "believers" who claimed belief in a personal God and "skeptics" who were atheists or agnostics, the second to differentiate those who attended church at least once every two weeks from those who did not, and the third to establish (1962:144) "intensity or importance of conviction as determined by agreement or disagreement with the statement, 'Religion is one of the most important things in my life.'"

Middleton and Putney found that believers were more likely than skeptics to regard violations of ascetic standards as wrong and to say that they were less likely to engage in them. The believers, however, were *not* more likely than skeptics to regard violations of social standards as wrong, nor were they less likely to engage in them. A similar picture emerged when the groups that differed on the variables of church attendance and religious intensity were compared on actions during the past three years in violation of ascetic and social standards. They inferred (1962:151), "There is thus no evidence that our results are a function of the particular measure of religiosity used."

When they compared only believers and skeptics who regarded given anti-ascetic actions as wrong, Middleton and Putney found that the believers were no more likely than the skeptics to refrain from violating those norms. That led to the conclusion (1962:151), "The greater tendency of the skeptics to violate ascetic norms is due simply to their greater tendency to reject these norms." To illustrate, skeptics were less likely to regard gambling and nonmarital sexual intercourse as wrong, but those skeptics who did regard them as wrong were as unlikely as believers to have gambled or engaged in nonmarital sexual intercourse during the past three years.

Their overall conclusion was (1962:151) "that the religious and nonreligious in our society share the same basic social values [that is, those relating to behavior that is harmful to society and generally considered delinquent] and are about equally likely to live up to them," although the two groups do differ on the standard of ascetic morality. There was no evidence, in short, that religion and religious sanctions were important in the control of delinquent behavior.

The study reported by Hirschi and Stark (1969) emphasized evaluation of the attempts by religion to control behavior by threats in the hereafter, as its title — "Hellfire and Delinquency" — indicates. They approached the task by measuring church attendance and relating it to measures of interpersonal morality, obedience to the law, and belief in the existence of an afterlife where there are spirits capable of punishing one for misbehavior during life on earth. The results showed that church attendance had no relationship with reluctance to exploit other people (interpersonal morality), a weak relationship to attitudes favorable to obedience to the law, and a strong relationship to belief in the existence of a supernatural, potentially punitive realm. Those results led to the statement (1969:209), "If religiosity does affect delinquency, its major path of influence must be through its effect on belief in the existence of other-worldly sanctions, for it is only here that differences by church attendance are in any way pronounced."

They evaluated the extent of delinquent behavior by the use of official records as well as by self-reporting. Comparing both official and self-report data to belief in the supernatural and to frequency of church attendance showed no relationship. In the words of Hirschi and Stark (1969:210), first, "Students who believe in the Devil and in a life after death are just as likely to commit delinquent acts as are students who do not believe in a supernatural world" (italics removed), and second (1969:211), "Students who attend church every week are as likely to have committed delinquent acts as students who attend church only rarely or not at all" (italics removed).

But, importantly, they did find a negative relationship between their measures of delinquency and the variables that were unrelated or weakly related to church attendance: first, the willingness to exploit other people to get ahead, and second, obedience to the law. The overall pattern of results led the investigators to conclude that law-abiding behavior results from social attachments (see the discussion of Hirschi's control theory in Chapter 6 and in the "School" section of this chapter) and that (1969:212, 213) "the church is irrelevant to delinquency because it fails to instill in its members love for their neighbors and because belief in the possibility of pleasure and pain in another world cannot now, and perhaps never could, compete with the pleasures and pains of everyday life."

Burkett and White (1974) followed up the research of Hirschi and Stark and appropriately entitled the resulting article "Hellfire and Delinquency: Another Look." They argued that Christian youths may indeed be inhibited from delinquent acts by the implication of biblical morality but that secular influences may be equally effective in keeping the nonreligious from delinquency. In their words (1974:456), "going to church and believing in God may help prevent delinquency, but so may participation in school athletics or Junior Achievement." That position, they decided, could be tested by focusing on the differential effectiveness of religious controls on victimless crimes, in particular the use of marijuana and alcohol by minors. The reasoning was as follows: while secular forces of control had eased their condemnation of such victimless crimes, that relaxation was not typical among Christian leaders. Consequently (1974:456), "If Christian faith is 'relevant' to delinquency, this fact should show up most clearly in the case of delinquent acts that are condemned by the churches but publicly condoned by influential secular spokesmen." The similarity of that reasoning to the conclusions of Middleton and Putney (1962) should be noted. What Burkett and White (1974) referred to as "victimless crimes" are very similar to the "violations of ascetic standards" of Middleton and Putney.

In their study, Burkett and White used the same three scales as Hirschi and Stark to measure interpersonal morality, obedience to law, and belief in supernatural forces that could sanction; and they used the self-report scale of Hirschi and Stark to measure delinquent involvement in larceny, vandalism, and assault. In addition, they asked subjects to report frequencies of church attendance and measured use of marijuana and alcohol in terms of the frequencies of reported use.

Their overall results were quite consistent with those of Hirschi and Stark, including the findings that church attendance was most closely related to belief in the supernatural (as compared with interpersonal morality and obedience to the law) and delinquency involvement was strongly and negatively related both to high interpersonal morality (unwillingness to exploit or take advantage of others) and to obedience to the law. "On the other hand," they reported (1974:459), "and in contrast to their [Hirschi and Stark's] conclusions, a very definite relationship exists between religious participation and the use of alcohol and marijuana." Thus, in accordance with the findings of Middleton and Putney (1962), church attendance (or religious participation) was not negatively related to criminal activities that are predatory but was negatively related to activities that are illegal (unlike others that are only immoral) but have no direct victims. That leads to their overall conclusion regarding religion and delinquency (1974:461), "the inability to find a clear relationship between religion and the commission of offenses against persons and property may not mean that the churches are failing to instill a love of neighbor. Rather it may mean that their efforts to produce law-abiding citizens are duplicated by a great many secular influences."

Denominational Effects. The importance of denominational salience in determining behavior was demonstrated by Albrecht, Chadwick, and Alcorn (1977), who used only teenage Mormons in their study. They found that religious variables (including church attendance) were better predictors of victimless deviance (like "drank beer" and "smoked marijuana") than of deviance involving victims (like "shoplifted" and "started fights"). That, of course, supports the position of Burkett and White (1974), but the effect seemed to be emphasized because of the strong prohibition against the use of tobacco, alcohol, and drugs in Mormon theology. While peer and family expectations seemed more important than religious variables in deviance involving victims, especially for boys, religious factors did make significant, independent contributions. In the words of Albrecht, Chadwick, and Alcorn (1977:273), "By combining three sets of factors — religion, peer behavior and family relationships — we have come up with some fairly strong equations [for predicting deviance, both with and without victims]." They concluded that religion was more important in understanding deviance than previously had been found in the literature of self-report studies.

Jensen and Erickson (1979) extended the denominational focus in a study using youths from three religious denominations—Roman Catholic, Protestant, and Mormon—and added size of community as another variable—the metropolitan area of Tucson, Arizona, versus three small towns in an adjacent county. In contrast to various earlier findings, Jensen and Erickson found differences over denominations in the reporting of delinquent offenses, and the differences did not seem to be due to differences in socioeconomic levels. But, more important, their results indicated that it was not (1979:164) "the victimless quality of drinking and marijuana use that accounts for their more persistent and relatively stronger association with measures of religiosity than most other offenses." Rather, it stemmed from the particular moral values of certain denominations which may or may not be widely held over all denominations. Jensen and Erickson (1979:169) summarize the point as follows: "In short, variations by offense may represent a complex blend both of properties of offenses and of the variable moral concerns of different denominations."

Finally, they found that delinquency was more likely to be related to denominational affiliation in the samples from the small towns. Indeed, they concluded (1979:167), "had our study included only metropolitan students, our observations concerning denominational differences would have been quite comparable to previous studies, all of which were based on metropolitan populations." Perhaps, they conjectured, religious affiliation is more relevant for social differentiation, more visible, and more important for social interactions and relationships in small towns than in larger cities.

The study of Rhodes and Reiss (1970) is worthy of note as a final example of research examining denominational effects, although its central analysis relied on official court records to evaluate delinquency; self-report data were used primarily to substantiate that the results coming from official data were not contaminated by such factors as discrimination in who is adjudicated. The self-report data, moreover, were not based on the usual type of self-report questionnaire, which involves a long list of offenses preceded by some such inquiry as "Have you ever ——?" or "Have you in the past three years ——?" Rather they were based on an individual's checking, on a broader questionnaire, if he or she does either or both of the following "pretty often": "break laws" and "swipe things." In addition, because of the special significance of educational norms for certain religious denominations, the investigators used school records to evaluate truancy. Both delinquency, based on court records, and truancy, based on school records, were expressed as prevalence rates.

Rhodes and Reiss measured several aspects of religion, including religious preference, personal church attendance, and parental church participation, and such deviance-related characteristics as socioeconomic status, age, and sex. They found that official delinquency was related to religious preference, personal church attendance, and parental church participation, even after adjustment for major social variables. The picture was a bit more complicated in the case of truancy, but it was clear that truancy was related to religious preference, even after adjustment. They concluded (1970:97):

The life chances of being a delinquent or truant . . . are probably not independent of fact or type of religious orientation or of individual and family participation in church activity. Jews and nonfundamentalists have the lowest delinquency rates. Subjects with no reported church connection have the highest rates. Contrary to the predicted pattern, male Baptists and Catholics have higher rates . . . than the fundamentalists.

Religion, the Community, and Social Control. Noting the stronger general effect of religion on delinquency found by Albrecht, Chadwick, and Alcorn (1977) among Mormons and by Higgins and Albrecht (1977) among tenth-graders in Atlanta, Georgia, Stark, Kent, and Doyle (1977) argued that religion was effective in containing delinquency only where religious commitment was the norm in the community. (That argument was contained in the broad discussion of religion and delinquency presented by Fitzpatrick in 1967 and could account for the differences found by Jensen and Erickson [1979] between metropolitan Tucson and and nearby small towns.) In their words (1982:7), "in social groups wherein a religious sanctioning system is the mode and is expressed in daily life, the propensity to deviate from the norms will be influenced substantially by the degree of one's commitment to the religious sanctioning system." On the other hand (1982:7), "where the religious sanctioning system is not pervasive, the effects of the individual's religious commitment will be muffled and curtailed. In such a setting, religion will not find everyday expression, but will tend to be a highly compartmentalized part of the lives of its adherents." And indeed their study of a national sample of sixteen-year-old boys supported that contention. They found a large negative relationship between religious commitment and delinquency in schools where religious students predominated (the South was most conspicuously represented in this group) and no relationship in the most highly secularized schools (which were on the West Coast, where the sample of Hirschi and Stark [1969] came from).

The results of a study by Elifson, Petersen, and Hadaway (1983) showed that religiosity and delinquency were negatively related over a wide variety of measures of both variables but that religion did not operate independently of the numerous other moral influences of society; it seemed to operate as a component in a social network. As they expressed the phenomenon (1983:521), "It appears that the relationship of religiosity to delinquency is so closely tied to the family and other influences that it has little influence that is statistically independent of other predictor variables." Their subjects, incidentally, were from suburban De Kalb County, which is in the metropolitan area of Atlanta, Georgia.

The particular influence of peer associations as part of the social network encompassing religion and delinquency was studied by Burkett and Warren (1987). Their sample of high school youths from a medium-sized city in the Pacific Northwest reported on extent of their marijuana use during the preceding year. They also measured the amount of involvement with other users of marijuana and the degree of religious commitment (which was based on frequency and personal importance of religious activities).

The data showed clearly that the effect of religion on one type of deviant behavior, marijuana use, was mediated through its influence on selection of peers. Burkett and Warren (1987:127) summarized the overall results as follows: "youth with lowered religious commitment are vulnerable to progressive and more exclusive involvement with other users, and with that they are increasingly likely to use marijuana. Religious youth, on the other hand, are likely to select as companions those who are similarly inclined both in attitude and behavior. . . . [and this process produces] an effective moral community which supports beliefs which inhibit the use of marijuana."

The Question of Deviance Amplification, or, Can Religion Lead to Increases in Delinquent Behavior? Fitzpatrick (1967) has presented several examples in which religious beliefs have led directly to deviant behavior. One such case involved deeply Christian Germans who resisted Nazi activities prior to World War II. They were considered criminals by the German people generally. In more recent years, religious people in the United States have helped immigrants who reported abuses in Latin American countries to enter and live illegally in the United States (sometimes, indeed, declaring their churches as sanctuaries), and religious leaders, up to the level of cardinal, in Third World countries have actively (and often at great personal risk) participated in efforts to overthrow corrupt totalitarian government. Both types of activity have been considered criminal.

Of course, those cases do not violate the sense most people have in regard to reporting religion as being antithetic to deviance or delinquency—they are understandable in terms of the clash between the humane principles underlying religious beliefs, on the one hand, and political realities and accompanying laws, on the other. But is it possible that religion can actually lead to increases in behavior that is criminal or delinquent in the traditional sense? That effect is widely referred to as "deviance amplification." Some support for deviance amplification by religion has come from the research of Middleton and Fay (1941) showing greater religiosity among delinquents than among nondelinquents and from studies indicating that stern prohibitions by some denominations on the use of alcohol and other drugs may lead to excessive usage when religious bonds are eliminated (see, e.g., Straus and Bacon, 1953; Jensen and Erickson, 1979, and the discussion of Mizruchi and Perucci, 1970).

Peek, Curry, and Chalfant (1985) examined the question of deviance amplification in a study of the effects of religiosity on delinquent behavior over time. Their data came from high school students interviewed at three time periods (as sophomores, juniors, and seniors). Religiosity was measured by a scale involving attitudes toward statements like "being devout in one's religious faith" and "always attending religious services regularly and faithfully." Delinquent behavior was measured by reports of students regarding the number of times they committed each of twenty-six delinquent acts. The specific acts were grouped into the following scales: serious delinquency, aggressive delinquency, theft-vandalism, school delinquency, family delinquency, and total delinquency. Supplementing the religiosity and delinquency measures, Peek et al. (1985) classified the students into one of three denominational groupings: Baptist/Methodist, Presbyterian/Lutheran/Episcopalian, and Roman Catholic.

When control variables (city size, socioeconomic status, family intactness, and others) were introduced, they found *positive* relationships between religiosity measured at the initial time period (sophomore level) and all scales of delinquency used at the last time period (senior level). Those positive correlations reached statistical significance for the serious, aggressive, theft-vandalism, and total delinquency scales. That pattern of results led to the following statement (Peek et al., 1985:126): "These positive associations suggest deviance amplification: higher levels of [early] religiosity have over time become associated with high levels of later delinquency." When Peek and his colleagues examined the relationships between initial religiosity and later delinquency separately by denominational grouping, they found the effect most conspicuous in the Baptist/Methodist group.

As a final test for deviance amplification, they compared youths who had remained low in religiosity over time with those who had shifted from high to low religiosity. Delinquency at the late reporting time for those who shifted from high to low religiosity was consistently higher than it was for those who remained at low religiosity, and the effect was greatest for the Baptists/Methodists. One explanation offered by Peek et al. (1985:128) to explain the phenomenon was, "[Youths whose religiosity has decreased] may attempt to compensate for their previous restraint from desirable conduct by stepping up their participation, especially before their last year of high school . . . ends." An alternate explanation depends upon possible effects of religion on the sequencing of delinquent behavior over various ages.

The Overall Picture at the Present Time

The immediate picture from the array of studies on religion and delinquency is one of seeming inconsistency and confusion. Indeed, the review of the literature on the effects of religion on deviance by Tittle and Welch (1983) emphasized the inconsistency of results and explained that pattern by pointing both to methodological errors and to an absence of theoretical focus in most studies. Yet there seems no question that our knowledge of the relationship between religion and delinquency has been considerably advanced since early studies showed such gross phenomena as differences in church attendance between delinquents and nondelinquents. Certain broad inferences seem possible at this time which can provide the foundations for future theoretical development. We will consider three of these.

First, one would be safe in inferring that religion, as practiced in the United States in all its diverse modes, does not produce broadly "good" boys and girls who do not violate criminal or status codes. Rather, it seems that religions have effects on the behaviors of their young followers primarily as components in the general array of forces aimed at socialization. The results of Elifson, Petersen, and Hadaway (1983) and Burkett and Warren (1987) most clearly show that religious beliefs and behaviors interact with family, peers, and other moral forces to produce social control of delinquency. Related to that is the conclusion by Stark, Kent, and Doyle (1982:22) "that it is not merely the religiousness of individuals, but also that of their social environments, that matters."

Second, it seems clear that religions are more selectively effective in controlling ascetic or victimless offenses than offenses where there are direct victims. That differential effectiveness results in part from the long tradition in Christianity of emphasis on personal asceticism or the need to control certain immediate physical needs, and the lesser flexibility of the churches than other sources of social control in responding to changes in cultural mores. The effect shows up most dramatically among Mormons, who most vigorously condemn the use of tobacco, alcohol, and drugs.

Finally, the evidence is convincing that there are denominational differences in the effects of religion on delinquency that are independent of such related variables as socioeconomic status and area of residence. These may be related to differential emphasis over denominations in particular prohibitions, to variations in the mode of interaction between denominations and other sources of social control, or to differences in the degree to which religious participation is translated into attitudinal commitment and, in turn, to control of unacceptable behavior.

In concluding this overall picture, a perspective presented by Fitzpatrick in 1967 is as valid after the subsequent accumulation of a substantial body of research results as it was then. He pointed out that the (1967:319) "role of religion in social control is neither simple nor consistent. . . . it operates effectively only when there is widespread consensus of the society about their values and norms of behavior." And then he emphasized (1967:320):

> it must be acknowledged that a religion, although it is often a major element in social control, does not appear to be necessary for social control. At the present time, in the United States and elsewhere, many of the most law-abiding citizens are people with no religious belief; and it is clear from delinquency records that many of the delinquents are religiously affiliated. In other words, other motivations than religious ones can insure conformity to social norms for people with no religious faith; and . . . the possession of religious faith, even though it be strong, is no assurance of social conformity.

Summary

We have stressed throughout this chapter the complex nature of the relationships between juvenile delinquency and such social arrangements as the family, the educational system, and religion. Delinquency itself may readily be pinpointed: a person in the requisite age span either has or has not engaged in the kinds of behavior prohibited by enactments of state legislatures. But within this condition there is an extremely wide range, in terms of such matters as the seriousness of the behavior and the number of different times it is carried out. Besides, of course, it is far from an easy matter to obtain a totally reliable measure of delinquency.

Such issues become much more complicated when we have to dissect institutions as variegated as the family, the school, and religion as they bear upon the commission of delinquency. The structure of what we call "the family" covers an extraordinarily wide range. Children are most often raised by what we call intact families, with mothers and fathers present, but the ages, personalities, occupations, values, attitudes, and background of these persons — not to mention how they relate to each other and to their child or children — vary enormously. Other children are raised by single parents, either father or mother, by grandparents, by older siblings, by foster parents, by remarried parents, or by parents living with others, either platonically or in sexual relationships.

Besides, these arrangements are constantly shifting in terms of their representativeness, and it can be one thing to be the only child of divorced parents among one's friends and another to be surrounded by a majority of youngsters who come from sundered family backgrounds. Today, also, one in five children is born out of wedlock, compared with one in ten in 1970 and one in twenty in 1960. Twenty-two per cent of children today live with one parent, compared with 12 per cent in 1970. Nearly two thirds of the children in school now go home to an empty house, because whoever cares for them is working. Today, only 48 per cent of married couples have children living with them now, compared to 57 per cent in 1970. These changing conditions give different meaning to what is, or should be, a family.

The population of persons under eighteen — the age bracket from which juvenile delinquents are typically drawn — peaked at 69 million in 1970 and had dropped to 64 million by 1987. It is expected to climb to 67 million in the late 1990s, then to fall back to the current level around 2010 and to remain there for the rest of the twenty-first century. Such demographic patterns are bound to have an important impact on the extent and the nature of juvenile delinquency.

Similar considerations apply to the school and to religion. They are immensely multifaceted phenomena, and, at best, we can only derive time-bound clues stated in broad terms about their significance in causing or inhibiting juvenile delinquency.

For some children, the family is a place to eat and sleep, with relationships with caretakers kept to a minimum. For them, peers are the most important component of their lives. For others, everything is learned, everything refracted, everything refined within a family setting. For some youngsters, school is a place to daydream, to mingle with friends, to establish a reputation, to engage in sports. For others, it is an intense learning experience. Religion has a profound impact on some youngsters; others can take it or leave it, and still others have little or no contact with formal religions. For those influenced, that influence will vary by denomination, and within denominations, by the kind of lesson absorbed, and by a host of other factors.

With these considerations firmly in mind, let us see what kinds of conclusions research has suggested about these intricate ties between these major social institutions and juvenile delinquency.

The Family. Research indicates clearly that the same family can produce very different kinds of children; there continues to be considerable debate about why this is so. Obviously, each child has a different place in the family organization, but a more powerful contribution may be made by the genetically formed attributes of the individuals. Particular emphasis has been placed in recent research on the fact that, despite the nature of the home environment, different children tend to perceive that environment quite differently and, therefore, to respond to it in individualistic ways.

Middle children seem to be most prone to become engaged in delinquency, and family size, particularly when associated with overcrowding, seems to play an important role in the genesis of illegal behavior. Overcrowding often means that a youngster cannot escape family tensions, which then escalate beyond control. In addition, families with inconsistent child-rearing practices, and those in which the parent or parents are themselves aggressive, have been found to be related to the production of delinquent children. These findings have led to recommendations that treatment for delinquent children ought to involve not only the youngster but the members of his or her family as well.

Child abuse, including sexual abuse, has become a prominent concern during recent years. Reported cases have increased dramatically for both behaviors, but our best belief is that such figures reflect a growing public sensitivity to the issue, though it may be that the infusion of greater numbers of outsiders into the raising of children, a function of an increasing divorce rate, may be tied to an escalation of the abuse of children. Medical practitioners and social scientists currently are engaged in something of a "turf" debate, concerned with the proper disciplinary explanations of child abuse. Physicians tend to see it as a medical problem, best handled within their practicing realm. Others regard child abuse as a function of social circumstances, not as a question of "illness" requiring medical attention.

Child abuse tends to be particularly prominent in families with low socioeconomic status, undoubtedly because of the greater tensions created by their lack of the wherewithal to confront life more gracefully. It also is tied to social isolation, and to the presence of similar patterns of abuse of parents by their own parents. This last item, however, is not conclusive, for research by Kaufman and Zigler (1987) indicates that two thirds of the persons who were themselves abused make satisfactory, nonabusive parents.

Girls are twice as likely as boys to be victims of sexual abuse, with the abuser most often neighbors, family friends, child care workers, and other authorities. The ages from nine to twelve are those in which the greatest amount of victimization occurs.

Efforts to ameliorate the negative impact of families upon their offspring have included foster home placements and the enactment of statutes outlawing what is called "contributing to the delinquency of a minor." Foster home placements are becoming less useful as more American women enter the labor market, often reducing seriously the quality of sites available. Children also often resist being placed away from their parents, regardless of how destructive their home environments appear to be.

Contributing-to-delinquency statutes place a criminal burden upon parents for the misdeeds of their children. Legal scholars, however, have criticized these laws because what they prohibit is said to be unconstitutionally vague and imprecise. In many states, it is not necessary for the youngster to have been adjudicated a delinquent for the parent to be convicted for "contributing," and the statute often appears to be employed when there is not sufficient evidence to gain a conviction on more traditional grounds.

The School. Controversy surrounds the precise role of the school in keeping youngsters from delinquent behavior or training them in law-abiding ways. For most youngsters, the school occupies a very considerable portion of their lives, six or seven hours a day for about 180 days a year, and for twelve years, if they continue through high school. Inevitably, such exposure is going to have a strong impact on most of those who undergo it. But that impact need not bear very directly on whether or not they engage in delinquent activities, however much it may condition their attitudes and values and the knowledge they gain about diverse matters.

The school itself as a crime setting often arouses public attention and concern. A recent federal report, for instance, insisted that "chaos in the classroom" was "an enemy to American education." It maintained that three million schoolchildren are victims of crime each month and that the cost of vandalism exceeded the expense of textbooks. President Reagan, in a radio broadcast, insisted that "the problem is so bad that almost eight percent of urban junior and senior high school students missed at least one day in the classroom per month because they are afraid to go to school." The president contended that campaigns against school crime were handicapped by court decisions, such as a New Jersey ruling that search of a student's locker was a violation of that student's rights.

Similarly, others, such as Toby (1980), have focused on permissiveness as a major force producing violence and crime in school buildings. In particular, Toby has bewailed the fact that there is constant pressure to keep young people in school for many years, even though they are indifferent to education while they are there.

Critics of the focus on school violence charge that the schools are being unfairly portrayed as "blackboard jungles" and that, instead of merely deploring the violence, the government should provide resources for better counseling, higher teacher salaries, and other measures to upgrade the educational environment. While parents rate discipline as the major problem of schools, teachers single out lack of parent interest as the biggest stumbling block to improved education. Particular emphasis has been placed, as well, on the fact that structural factors may play a part in disruptive school behavior: the schools are not relevant to the kinds of lives that many children are destined to lead, and they therefore have no stake in the curriculum.

Other theorists have insisted that the schools induce frustration and lowered self-esteem in many pupils. They believe that school failure pushes a youngster into seeking alternative ways to gain prestige and a sense of value, and that among the more appealing alternatives is a career in delinquency. Control theory, which differs in its stress on the causal connections, posits that the connection between school failure and delinquency is a product of the way in which both are symptoms of a lack of attachment by the youngster to various aspects of conforming social existence.

There also has been a focus on personal traits—such as IQ and learning disabilities—and school maladjustment leading to delinquency. In both instances, research seems to be suggestive but not conclusive on the importance of these conditions as precursors of delinquency.

Religion. From the earliest days of our colonial era it has been widely assumed that religious children are less likely to engage in delinquency than nonreligious children. The assumption implied not only that religion was important in the prevention of delinquency but that it could be used effectively in correcting the behavior of youths who have strayed into delinquency. That use was most dramatically in evidence in the houses of refuge of the early nineteenth century, and it remains part of the treatment structure imposed by many justice system personnel to the present day.

Research dating from thirty-five and more years ago, that of Healy and Bronner (1936) and the Gluecks (1950), for example, obtained results supporting that position in comparisons involving delinquents and nondelinquents. The delinquents attended church less regularly than did the nondelinquents.

Studies on the assumed negative relationship between religion and delinquency expanded greatly, and became considerably more complex, as the method of self-reported delinquency was becoming firmly established. In addition to church attendance, these studies used such indices as stated beliefs in God or an afterlife, degree of personal commitment to religion expressed attitudinally, and parental church attendance to measure a concept widely referred to as "religiosity."

The pace-setting research of Hirschi and Stark in 1969, using the self-report method, led to the conclusion that religion was irrelevant to delinquency, a position that no doubt shocked many with the historical beliefs sketched above. But other research softened the blow somewhat in findings that religion may be differentially effective in controlling "ascetic" or "victimless" offenses like gambling and the use of marijuana. That differential effectiveness, it was hypothesized by Burkett and White (1974), stems from the fact that religion is just one element in an array of factors that produce social control and has greatest impact in areas of deviance where other elements are less demanding.

Several studies have highlighted denominational differences in the control of delinquency. Although the evidence indicates that some denominations are more effective than others in that control on an overall basis, it does seem to be the case that there is considerable variation in moral concerns over denominations with the result of variable effectiveness over behaviors. To illustrate, Mormons have strong prohibitions against the use of alcohol and drugs, and, as a result, there is a particularly small amount of such behaviors as drinking beer and smoking marijuana among Mormon youths.

As research relating religion and the control of delinquency has increased in sophistication, it has become apparent that religion does not operate independently in the network of all moral influences in society. Other important components in that network with which it interacts include the degree of religious commitment in a community, the family, and peer associations.

There are many examples where religion has been the motivating force for humane efforts that defied authority, often seriously enough to be considered criminal. But can religion actually lead to increased delinquency — a process called "deviance amplification" — among youths? Some studies have shown that stern prohibitions of certain behaviors by various denominations can lead to an exacerbation of those behaviors when participation in those denominations has ceased. In addition, Peek, Curry, and Chalfant (1985) found *positive* relationships between religiosity and delinquent behavior when the religiosity was measured two years prior to the self-reported delinquency.

In general, the research evidence indicates that religion does not produce broadly "good" boys and girls but that behavior is controlled selectively in accord with the moral priorities of the separate denominations and their modes of interaction with other social processes.

References ────────────────────────────────

Albrecht, Stan L., Chadwick, Bruce A., and Alcorn, David S. 1977. Religiosity and Deviance: Application of an Attitude-Behavior Contingent Consistency Model. *Journal for the Scientific Study of Religion* 16:263–274.

Biles, David, and Challinger, Dennis. 1981. Family Size and Birth Order of Young Offenders. *International Journal of Offender Therapy and Comparative Criminology* 25:60–66.

Broder, Paul K., and Dunivant, Noel. 1981. *Change in Delinquent Behavior as a Function of Learning Disabilities.* Williamsburg, Va.: National Center for State Courts.

Burkett, Steven R., and Warren, Bruce O. 1987. Religiosity, Peer Associations, and Adolescent Marijuana Use: A Panel Study of Underlying Causal Structures. *Criminology* 25:109–134.

Burkett, Steven R., and White, Mervin. 1974. Hellfire and Delinquency: Another Look. *Journal for the Scientific Study of Religion* 13:455–462.

Campbell, James A., and Shoham, Shlomo. 1969. The Family and Violence. In *Law and Order Reconsidered,* vol. 10, edited by James A. Campbell, Joseph R. Sahid, and David P. Strang, 177–189. Washington, D.C.: National Commission on the Causes and Prevention of Violence.

City Schools in Crisis. 1977. *Newsweek* (September 12), 62–70.

Cloward, Richard A., and Ohlin, Lloyd E. 1960. *Delinquency and Opportunity: A Theory of Delinquent Gangs.* Glencoe, Ill.: Free Press.

Cohen, Albert K. 1955. *Delinquent Boys: The Culture of the Gang.* Glencoe, Ill.: Free Press.

Comptroller General of the United States. 1977. *Learning Disabilities: The Link Should Be Determined, but Schools Should Do More Now.* Washington, D.C.: U.S. Government Printing Office.

Coogan, John E. 1954. Religion as a Preventive of Delinquency. *Federal Probation* 18 (December):29–35.

Csikszentimihaly, Mihaly, and Larson, Reed. 1978. Intrinsic Rewards in School Crime. *Crime & Delinquency* 24:322–335.

Daro, Deborah. 1987. *Confronting Child Abuse.* New York: Free Press.

Dunivant, Noel. 1982. *The Relationship Between Learning Disabilities and Juvenile Delinquency.* Williamsburg, Va.: National Center for State Courts.

Elifson, Kirk W., Petersen, David M., and Hadaway, C. Kirk. 1983. Religiosity and Delinquency. A Contextual Analysis. *Criminology* 21:505–527.

Finkelhor, David. 1987. The Sexual Abuse of Children: Current Research Reviewed. *Psychiatric Annals* 17:233–237.

Fischer, Donald G. 1984. Family Size and Delinquency. *Perceptual and Motor Skills* 58:527–534.

Fitzpatrick, Joseph P. 1967. The Role of Religion in Programs for the Prevention and Correction of Crime and Delinquency. A consultant's paper in Report of Task Force on Juvenile Delinquency of the President's Commission on Law Enforcement and Administration of Justice, *Juvenile Delinquency and Youth Crime.* Washington, D.C.: U.S. Government Printing Office.

Garlock, Peter D. 1983. Contributing to the Delinquency of Minors. In *Encyclopedia of Crime and Justice,* vol. 1, edited by Sanford H. Kadish, 240–242. New York: Free Press.

Geis, Gilbert. 1963. Contributing to Delinquency. *St. Louis University Law Journal* 8:59–81.

Gelles, Richard. 1987. The Family and Its Role in the Abuse of Children. *Psychiatric Annals* 17:229–232.

Glasser, William. 1978. Disorders in Our Schools: Causes and Remedies. *Phi Delta Kappan* 59:331–333.

Glueck, Sheldon, and Glueck, Eleanor. 1950. *Unraveling Juvenile Delinquency.* Cambridge, Mass.: Harvard Univ. Press.

Gold, Martin. 1978. Scholastic Experiences, Self-Esteem, and Delinquent Behavior: A Theory for Alternative Schools. *Crime & Delinquency* 24:290–308.

Gordon, Linda. 1983. Child Abuse, Gender, and the Myth of Family Independence: Thoughts on the History of Family Violence and its Social Control. *New York University Review of Law and Social Change* 12:523–537.

Gottfredson, Gary D., and Gottfredson, Denise C. 1985. *Victimization in Schools.* New York: Plenum Press.

Healy, William, and Bronner, Augusta F. 1936. *New Light on Delinquency and Its Treatment.* New Haven, Conn.: Yale Univ. Press.

Hetherington, F. Mavis, Stouwie, Roger J., and Ridberg, Eugene H. 1971. Patterns of Family Interaction and Child-Rearing Attitudes Related to Three Dimensions of Juvenile Delinquency. *Journal of Abnormal Psychology* 78:160–176.

Higgins, Paul C., and Albrecht, Stan L. 1977. Hellfire and Delinquency Revisited. *Social Forces* 55:952–958.

Hindelang, Michael. 1973. Causes of Delinquency: A Partial Replication and Extension. *Social Problems* 20:471–487.

Hirschi, Travis. 1969. *Causes of Delinquency.* Berkeley, Calif.: Univ. of California Press.

———, and Hindelang, Michael J. 1977. Intelligence and Delinquency: A Revisionist Review. *American Sociological Review* 42:571–587.

———, and Stark, Rodney. 1969. Hellfire and Delinquency. *Social Problems* 17:202–213.

Jensen, Gary F., and Erickson, Maynard L. 1979. The Religious Factor and Delinquency: Another Look at the Hellfire Hypothesis. In *The Religious Dimension: New Directions in Quantitative Research,* edited by Robert Wuthnow, 157–177. New York: Academic Press.

Johnstone, J. W. C. 1980. Delinquency and the Changing American Family. In *Critical Issues in Juvenile Delinquency,* edited by David Shichor and Delos H. Kelly, 83–971. Lexington, Mass.: Lexington Books.

Kaufman, Joan, and Zigler, Edward. 1987. "Do Abused Children Become Abusing Parents?" *American Journal of Orthopsychiatry* 57:186–192.

Kempe, C. Henry, Silverman, Frederic, Steele, Brandt F., Droegemueller, William, and Silber, Henry K. 1962. The Battered Child Syndrome. *Journal of the American Medical Association* 181:17–24.

Kvaraceus, William C. 1945. *Juvenile Delinquency and the School.* Yonkers-on-Hudson, N.Y.: World Book Co.

———. 1966. *Anxious Youth: Dynamics of Delinquency.* Columbus, Ohio: Charles E. Merrill.

Lewis, Dorothy O., Shanok, S. S., Pincus, J. H., and Glasser, G. H. 1979. Violent Juvenile Delinquents: Psychiatric, Neurological, Psychological, and Abuse Factors. *Journal of the American Academy of Child Psychiatry* 18:307–319.

Loeber, Rolf, and Stouthamer-Loeber, Magda. 1986. Family Factors as Correlates and Predictors of Juvenile Court Problems and Delinquency. In *Crime and Justice,* vol. 7, edited by Michael Tonry and Norval Morris, 29–149. Chicago: Univ. of Chicago Press.

McCord, William, McCord, Joan, and Howard, Alan. 1961. Family Correlates of Aggression in Nondelinquent Male Children. *Journal of Abnormal and Social Psychology* 62:79–93.

McDermott, M. Joan. 1979. *Criminal Victimization in Urban Schools.* National Criminal Justice Information and Statistics Service Analytic Report SD-VAD-8. Washington, D.C.: U.S. Government Printing Office.

McQueen, Michael. 1987. Foster-Care System Is Strained as Reports of Child Abuse Mount. *Wall Street Journal* (June 15) 1, 17.

Menard, Scott, and Morse, Barbara J. 1984. A Structuralist Critique of the IQ-Delinquency Hypothesis: Theory and Evidence. *American Journal of Sociology* 89: 1347–1378.

Middleton, W., and Fay, P. 1941. Attitudes of Delinquent and Non-delinquent Girls toward Sunday Observance, the Bible and War. *Journal of Educational Psychology* 32:555–558.

Middleton, Russell, and Putney, Snell. 1962. Religion, Normative Standards, and Behavior. *Sociometry* 25:141–152.

Mizruchi, Ephraim H., and Perucci, Robert. 1970. Prescription, Proscription and Permissiveness: Aspects of Norms and Deviant Drinking Behavior. In *The Domesticated Drug: Drinking Among Collegians,* edited by George L. Maddox. New Haven, Conn.: College and Univ. Press.

Moore, Bernice Milburn. 1961. The Schools and the Problems of Juvenile Delinquency —Research Studies and Findings. *Crime and Delinquency* 7:201–212.

Moorefield, Story. 1977. North, South, East, and West Side Story. *American Education* 13, no. 1 (January–February):12–16.

Murray, Charles A. 1976. *The Link Between Learning Disabilities and Juvenile Delinquency: Current Theory and Knowledge.* Washington, D.C.: U.S. Government Printing Office.

Nelson, Barbara J. 1984. *Making an Issue of Child Abuse: Political Agenda Setting for Social Problems.* Chicago: Univ. of Chicago Press.

Peek, Charles W., Chalfant, H. Paul, and Milton, Edward V. 1979. Sinners in the Hands of an Angry God: Fundamentalist Fears About Drunken Driving. *Journal for the Scientific Study of Religion* 18:29–39.

Peek, Charles W., Curry, Evans W., and Chalfant, H. Paul. 1985. Religiosity and Delinquency Over Time: Deviance Deterrence and Deviance Amplification. *Social Science Quarterly* 66:120–131.

Pelton, Leroy H., ed. 1981. *The Social Context of Child Abuse and Neglect.* New York: Human Sciences Press.

Plomin, Robert, and Daniels, Denise. 1987. "Why Are Children in the Same Family So Different from One Another?" *Behavioral and Brain Sciences* 10:1–44.

Polk, Kenneth. 1976. Schools and the Delinquency Experience. In *Delinquency Prevention and the Schools: Emerging Perspectives,* edited by Ernst A. Wenk, 21–44. Beverly Hills, Calif.: Sage.

———, and Richmond, F. Lynn. 1972. Those Who Fail. In *Schools and Delinquency,* edited by Kenneth Polk and Walter E. Schafer, 56–69. Englewood Cliffs, N.J.: Prentice-Hall.

Post, Charles H. 1981. The Link Between Learning Disabilities and Juvenile Delinquency: Cause, Effect and "Present Solutions." *Juvenile and Family Court Journal* 32, no. 1 (February–March):58–68.

Reilly, Thomas F., Wheeler, Larry J., and Etlinger, Leonard E. 1985. Intelligence Versus Academic Achievement: A Comparison of Juvenile Delinquents and Special Education Classifications. *Criminal Justice and Behavior* 12:193–208.

Rhodes, Albert L., and Reiss, Albert J., Jr. 1970. The "Religious Factor" and Delinquent Behavior. *Journal of Research in Crime and Delinquency* 7:83–98.

Robins, Lee, Schoenberg, Sandra P., Holmes, Sandra J., Ratcliff, Kathryn S., Benham, Alexandra, and Works, Jan. 1985. Early Home Environment and Retrospective Recall: A Test for Concordance Between Siblings With and Without Psychiatric Disorders. *American Journal of Orthopsychiatry* 55:27–41.

Rubel, Robert J. 1977. *The Unruly School: Disorders, Disruptions, and Crimes.* Lexington, Mass.: D. C. Heath.

Satterfield, James H., Hoppe, Christiane M., and Schell, Anne M. 1982. A Prospective Study of Delinquency in 110 Adolescent Boys with Attention Deficit Disorder and 88 Normal Adolescent Boys. *American Journal of Psychiatry* 139:795–798.

Schafer, Walter E., and Polk, Kenneth. 1967. Delinquency and the Schools. In U.S. Task Force on Juvenile Delinquency, President's Commission on Law Enforcement and Administration of Justice, *Task Force Report: Juvenile Delinquency and Youth Crime,* 222–227. Washington, D.C.: U.S. Government Printing Office.

———, Olexa, Carol, and Polk, Kenneth. 1972. Programmed for Social Class: Tracking in High School. In *Schools and Delinquency,* edited by Kenneth Polk and Walter E. Schafer, 34–54. Englewood Cliffs, N.J.: Prentice-Hall.

Schmidt, William E. 1987. Spanking in School: Tradition Is Under Fire. *New York Times* (July 9) 1, 14.

Shaw, Clifford R. 1930. *The Jack-Roller: A Delinquent Boy's Own Story.* Chicago: Univ. of Chicago Press.

Short, James F., Jr., and Nye, F. Ivan. 1957. Reported Behavior as a Criterion of Deviant Behavior. *Social Problems* 5:207–213.

Smith, Valerie. 1984. Tracking School Crime. *American School and University* 57, no. 1 (September):54–59.

Solomon, Theodore. 1972. History and Demography of Child Abuse. *Pediatrics* 51:773–776.

Stark, Rodney, Kent, Lori, and Doyle, Daniel P. 1982. Religion and Delinquency: The Ecology of a "Lost" Relationship. *Journal of Research in Crime and Delinquency* 19:4–24.

Stinchcombe, Arthur L. 1964. *Rebellion in a High School.* Chicago: Quadrangle.

Stratton, John G. 1975. Effects of Crisis Intervention Counseling on Predelinquent and Misdemeanant Juvenile Offenders. *Juvenile Justice* 26 (November):7–18.

Straus, Murray A. 1980. A Social Perspective on Family Violence. In *Violence and the Family,* edited by Maurice R. Green, 7–31. Boulder, Colo.: Westview.

Straus, Robert, and Bacon, Selden D. 1953. *Drinking in College.* New Haven, Conn.: Yale Univ. Press.

Thornberry, Terence P., Moore, Melanie, and Christenson, R. L. 1985. The Effect of Dropping Out of High School on Subsequent Criminal Behavior. *Criminology* 23:3–18.

Tittle, Charles R., and Welch, Michael R. 1983. Religiosity and Deviance: Toward a Contingency Theory of Constraining Effects. *Social Forces* 61:53–80.

Toby, Jackson. 1980. Crime in American Public Schools. *The Public Interest* 58:18–42.

Tolan, Patrick H., Cronwell, Ronald E., and Brasswell, Michael. 1986. Family Therapy with Delinquents: A Critical Review of the Literature. *Family Process* 25:619–649.

United States National Institute of Education. 1978. *Violent Schools—Safe Schools: The Safe School Study Report to the Congress.* 3 vols. Washington, D.C.: U.S. Government Printing Office.

United States Senate. Committee on the Judiciary. Subcommittee to Investigate Juvenile Delinquency. 1975. *Our Nation's Schools—A Report Card: "A" in School Violence and Vandalism.* Washington, D.C.: U.S. Government Printing Office.

———. 1976a. *School Violence and Vandalism: The Nature, Extent, and Cost of Violence in Our Nation's Schools.* Washington, D.C.: U.S. Government Printing Office.

———. 1976b. *School Violence and Vandalism: Models and Strategies for Change.* Washington, D.C.: U.S. Government Printing Office.

Winter, Bill. 1983. Learning Disability: The Young Offender's Curse. *American Bar Association Journal* 69:427.

Zimmerman, Joel, Rich, William D., Keilitz, Ingo, and Broder, Paul K. 1981. Some Observations on the Link Between Learning Disabilities and Juvenile Delinquency. *Journal of Criminal Justice* 9:1–17.

Special Issues

Female Delinquency

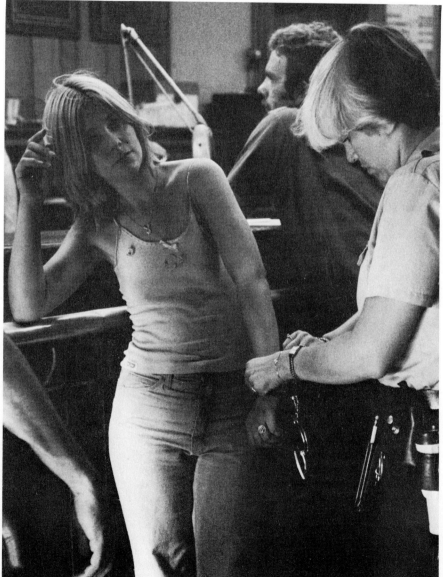

A chapter devoted specifically and only to female delinquency requires an introductory explanation. Advocates of women's rights have succeeded in recent times to a considerable extent in persuading the courts and legislative bodies that women must be treated in the same manner as men, that there are no significant differences between the sexes. Obviously, on the average, women are physically weaker than men (though, in a telling measure of strength, they live a good deal longer), and it is women, not men, who bear children. Nonetheless, advocates for women's rights argue that child rearing reasonably can be shared by men and women and that women ought to have available to them every opportunity to pursue jobs and careers, if they desire to do so. Wages for men and women should be equivalent and promotion unrelated to gender distinctions. Work leaves ought to be available to either the father or the mother or both when a child is born to a couple.

The Major Issues

If these premises are being translated into public policy, why, then, should a separate chapter in this text be devoted to the subject of female delinquency? The answer is that, as we saw in Chapter 1, there are very significant differences in the rate and kind of delinquent behavior committed by girls and young women in contrast to that of boys and young men. These differences undoubtedly to a great extent reflect the manner in which females are trained and the values they come to incorporate. But the distinctions are so striking and so fundamental to an analysis of delinquency that they demand special treatment.

F. Carter Smith/*The New York Times*

Inmates working in a garment factory at the Texas Department of Corrections, women's prison, Gatesville. In Texas, youths 15 years of age or older at the time of a felonious offense may be dealt with as adults.

It is possible that as full equality of the sexes is achieved, the pattern of female delinquency will come to look much more like that of males, both in terms of rates and in terms of the kind of acts committed. As Vedder and Somerville (1970:164) have noted, apparently with distaste: "Considering the direction our modern society is taking, it will not be unreasonable to expect more serious female delinquency . . . in the future." A recent detective mystery, written by a woman, tells of "five women in town and two in outlying villages complaining of obscene telephone calls." The extraordinary aspect of the matter, the author writes, "was that their caller also was a woman" (Rendell, 1977:175). Much debate takes place today on the effect of feminism on female crime, with some scholars saying that the liberation movement has caused some women to lose their traditional inhibitions about engaging in acts such as burglary and robbery (Noblit and Burcart, 1976). Others insist that there has been no significant increase of female participation in such "street" crimes, and second, that female criminal offenders are virtually the last group to be reached by the women's rights movement, which at this time is primarily a middle-class phenomenon (Mukherjee and Fitzgerald, 1981).

The only notable crime increases among women, it is maintained, are in larceny and in white-collar crimes. But these upswings are said to be largely insignificant in terms of any serious threat to society, with the larceny primarily being shoplifting, which traditionally has been a feminine crime, at least on the level of amateur endeavors, and the white-collar offenses, though counted as embezzlement, largely being nothing more sinister than checks written with insufficient funds behind them or on nonexistent accounts.

Some persons argue that it will be males who will most benefit by the women's rights movement: they will become more like women, and will in time demonstrate lower levels of aggression and other forms of predatory delinquency. Others insist that women, released from the bonds that have historically governed their behavior, will come to behave just as men do: they will kill, steal, and engage in serious white-collar crime much more often once they obtain the professional and corporate status that will offer chances for such kinds of lawbreaking. Finally, there are those who adhere to a third and, at least for the moment, seemingly more unlikely position: they maintain that the liberation of women from age-old restraints will give rise to a wave of much worse delinquent behavior than that of males, since females will go to extremes to try to prove their equality. Adherents of this position point to the common belief among workers in juvenile detention centers that facilities for girls pose much more serious control problems than facilities housing boys. They insist that girls don't play by the rules, that is, rules regarded by men as sensible and sporting. When upset, they claim, girls will throw hysterical tantrums (while boys more often will withdraw and contain their personal emotions), and when outraged, girls will fight "unfairly," scratching, biting, pulling hair, and otherwise employing "outrageous" tactics. The evidence for such a scenario is far from substantial, but the folklore of male-female differentials in delinquency detention units is widespread.

Another expression of the view that women are at least as vicious as men — but more skilled at camouflaging their meanness — can be found in the work of a prominent writer of detective fiction. Dorothy Sayers (1955) has a police inspector say: "When a woman is wicked and unscrupulous, she is the most ruthless criminal in the world—fifty times worse than a man, because she is always more single-minded about it." Sayers' protagonist, Peter Wimsey, answers: "They're not troubled with sentimentality, that's why. We poor mutts of men stuff ourselves up with the idea that they're romantic and emotional. All punk, my son" (1955:204). It is debatable, however, whether Sayers accepted this viewpoint or was satirizing male ideas.

Those taking this last position—that liberation will uncork terrible discharges of female delinquency—cite several notorious cases of recent decades in which women and girls participated in particularly gruesome crimes. Most memorable were a group of young women involved in the murder of Sharon Tate, a motion picture actress, and in a variety of other terrorist acts in southern California (Bugliosi and Gentry, 1974; Emmons, 1987; Gilmore and Kenner, 1971; Livsey, 1980). One of the women, Susan Atkins, asked if she had any regrets about the brutal killing, replied: "Remorse? What I did was right for me" (Holbrook, 1972:30). Similarly, Patricia Hearst was first kidnapped and later persuaded to join the so-called Symbionese Liberation Army (SLA) in at least one bank robbery (Baker and Brompton, 1974; Boulton, 1975; Reeves, 1976; Weed and Swanton, 1976). It is arguable, however, whether the acts of these women would have taken place without the very strong leadership of charismatic males, such as Charles Manson, who recruited and led the Tate murder group, though he himself did not participate in the killing.

Girls in Gangs

Though their offenses were much more heinous, the female lawbreakers in the Manson and SLA episodes were duplicating a common pattern found among young gang members in inner-city areas. Vedder and Somerville (1970:39) describe interaction between the sexes in gang activity in the following terms:

> The girls are often expected to submit to the sexual advances of the boy members. They sometimes assist boys in gang fights by concealing weapons such as knives and fingernail files. . . . They concealed these weapons in the then popular high pompadour arrangements of their hair. Girls have been used by boy gangs to waylay leaders of rival gangs—the traditional "decoy" technique. These seem to be the principal activities of even those girls who organized their own female gangs such as the "Shangrila-Debs," "Robinettes" and others.

Girl gangs are reported by Vedder and Somerville rarely to function without an affiliation with a male group, to which, it is said, they give "fierce loyalty" (1970:40). That members of girl gangs can be as hostile to authority as their male counterparts is vividly illustrated by the diatribe of Kitty Hanson (1964:125), who expresses a common conviction among gang members that adult censure drives them into deviancy:

> Wherever you look, wherever you turn, authority is there in the shape of parents, teachers, priests and policemen, social workers and truant officers—a great Greek chorus of do's and don'ts chanting about how you've goofed and where you've failed. And man, you can't stand that for long. After a while you've got to cut out or go nuts—or turn it all around and tell yourself that it's you who are right and the Greek chorus that is wrong. That's easy enough to do because half the time the chorus doesn't practice what it preaches anyway.

Comprehensive studies of female gangs are just beginning to appear and to provide a more three-dimensional view than when female gangs were examined only peripherally in studies focusing on male groups. Short and Strodtbeck (1965), for instance, commented on the social disabilities and physical unattractiveness of female gang members, but this was only a passing, impressionistic judgment made in a much wider context of their work with Chicago gangs.

In a detailed investigation of girl gangs in the East Los Angeles area during the 1960s, Bowker and Klein (1983) reported that each gang averaged from ten to fifteen active members and an equal number of inactives. The age range, fourteen to sixteen years, was more limited than that in male groups. There were no cases of female gangs unaffiliated with male groups. The girl gangs tended to be organized by siblings and girlfriends of male gang members and then to expand membership by recruiting their own friends (see also Giordano, 1978).

More recently, Campbell (1984) concentrated on the relationships among the girls themselves in three New York gangs and found that they can be viewed as "sisters in the gang instead of as molls." She pinpoints the intense camaraderie and the strong dependency that comes to exist between gang girls. Nonetheless, Campbell grants that over the years the fundamental gang role of females has not altered substantially. Girl gangs exist, she reports, as an adjunct to the male gang, and the range of possibilities open to their members is dictated and controlled by the boys. "Girls are told how to dress, are allowed to fight, and are encouraged to be good mothers and faithful wives. Their principal source of suffering and joy is their men," Campbell (1984:266) observes. The girls, she points out, may occasionally defy the men, often argue with them, and sometimes patronize them, but "the men remain indisputably in control" (1984:266).

Women and Hidden Crime: The Pollak Position

Particularly controversial regarding female crime and delinquency are the views first expressed in 1950 by Otto Pollak, who maintained that females actually commit as much crime as males but that their kind of crime is more surreptitious and sneaky and therefore is less readily detected. Pollak maintains, for instance, that women tend to use poison for murder, taking advantage of their control over meal preparation. Poisoning, especially in earlier times, when the Roman Catholic church banned autopsies, is a particularly difficult form of murder to detect. Similarly, Pollak believes that female dominance in nursing the sick offers fine opportunities, which have been taken, for doing away with weak and susceptible victims without being detected. Pollak also noted that, at the time he was writing, submitting to an abortion was a criminal offense, and that millions of women had done so, and not many had been prosecuted. Shoplifting too, he pointed out, shows a heavy preponderance of female offenders, especially young girls, and very few arrests. Shoplifting, he thought, might be traceable in part to particular cravings that sometimes appear with pregnancy and to intense advertising campaigns directed at women which seek "to create ever new temptations" (1950:131).

Pollak's position has not escaped unscathed. Leonard (1982), for example, points out that he offers no proof for many of his statements. She also observes that Pollak is claiming the existence of undetected crime, which, by its very nature, is largely unknown. Leonard also finds many of his assertions implausible. "The likelihood that women are poisoning untold numbers of sick husbands and children is ridiculous," she (1982:51) notes. "How could Pollak possibly know that such crimes are taking place?" Smart (1976) clothes her critique of Pollak in more generalized terms. His position, she (1976:52) says, "is indicative of a certain attitude towards women which infers that simple, biologically-based, causal factors can explain the motivation and reasoning of complex, culturally located and socially meaningful acts."

Killings of newborn children by women are also used by Pollak to try to demonstrate the point that females are as violent as men but that the realms in which they operate are more secretive. Studies indicate that about 90 per cent of the infanticide cases in England during the seventeenth century, when such killings were more common than today, were committed by women, a figure matching the rate of murder and manslaughter attributed to men (Hoffer and Hull, 1981:98; see also Piers, 1978; Rose, 1986).

That Pollak is off target, and that social (and consequent psychological) considerations are fundamental to an understanding of the striking variations in male and female delinquency, is brought home by the statement of Sutherland and Cressey (1970) that the ratio of male-female crime rates varies (1) from one nation to another, (2) with the social position of the sexes in different countries, (3) with the size of the community, (4) with age, (5) with area of residence, (6) with time, and (7) with degree of integration into the family. If gender alone dictated the difference, the variation in all cultures should not be as disparate as it is.

The Debate over Physiology and Delinquency ─────────────

Proponents of any position on the arguable relationship among gender, feminism, and delinquency have to grant that there are physiological distinctions between the sexes that dictate certain behavioral variations. There are ways in which this is obvious. Women cannot commit forcible rape, though it is notable that approximately 200 women are arrested each year in the United States as accessories in forcible rape cases: most often they cooperate with a male companion in employing a ruse or force (such as holding a weapon) to do in the victim. And women are understandably less likely to undertake crimes of violence that involve physical confrontations with male victims, such as unarmed muggings, because they are not likely to fare as well as men in such physical confrontations. They can, of course, pick on other women, youngsters, or the aged, but, if nothing else, this limits their possible involvement in the offense.

Biological differences, however, tend to be less pronounced in youngsters compared with older persons, though girls weigh less than boys at birth, and this differential grows until about the age of twenty, when there is a 20 per cent weight difference between the sexes. Girls have less muscle than boys, and by age twenty, they are 10 per cent shorter than males. Girls also are not as well coordinated as boys, with the exception of fine muscle coordination. As infants, girls sleep more and are less vigorous than boys (Sherman, 1971:8). All of these differences may play into the pattern of delinquency, some rather directly, others more subtly.

Two particular aspects of femaleness alleged to be related to juvenile delinquency merit attention. Hysteria is a condition, perhaps based in physiology but more likely psychological, that illustrates tactics used by medical science either to put a stigma on women, or, perhaps, reasonably to differentiate men and women. Premenstrual tension is a condition, perhaps based in hormonal action, that also pinpoints what may be both real and defined differences between young men and young women. The importance accorded to the premenstrual syndrome (PMS) varies considerably. It will be downplayed or perhaps ridiculed as having little, if any, significance by women seeking to counter views insisting that because of PMS women require special treatment (which may be a way of saying that they should be confined to lesser roles). Girls and women who are charged with serious criminal offenses, such as the murder of lovers or husbands, however, have increasingly relied upon a defense of premenstrual tension to obtain a verdict based on diminished responsibility. They were suffering so much stress and anxiety prior to their menstrual period, they maintain, that they were not adequately in control of their emotions or behavior and did not appreciate the awfulness of the crime they committed.

Hysteria

The origin of the term *hysteria* and the understanding in early medicine of the roots of the condition are instructive. The word comes from a Greek stem meaning "womb," and it was believed, incredibly, that hysteria was the result of a wandering of the womb from its proper place in the female body upward into the stomach or the throat. Hysterical women who could not speak properly, for example, were believed to be strangling from suffocation by the meandering womb. The condition was said to affect young girls and widows particularly. The explanation of physicians — perhaps predictably — was that the patient's womb was discontent because of neglect. What was required was regular sexual intercourse; then the womb would return to its place, particularly if the woman became pregnant (Lefkowitz, 1981; Vieth, 1965). In the absence of that resolution, doctors prescribed what, given the basis of their diagnosis, were obvious remedies. Noxious substances should be placed by the mouth and pleasant ones at the genitals. The abhorrent smells would drive the womb downward into the body, and the attractive ones would further impel it in the direction it ought to be moving. As Edward Jorden (1603: Chap. 7), a seventeenth-century physician, indicated: "Apply evil smells to the nostrils, and sweet smells beneath. Let the bodies be kept upright, straight laced, and the belly and throat held down with one's hand."

Hysteria continues in many medical circles to be regarded as a disorder notably apt to be located among girls. It is marked by conversion symptoms, where, for instance, a person cannot walk though there is no apparent trouble with the limbs, or suffers a wide variety of what are regarded as disabling physical symptoms, such as fainting spells (or, as they are more technically known, vasodepressor syncopes [Engel, 1962:149]). The standard definition of hysteria is that it is a condition characterized by the presence of "gross, often dramatic, somatic symptoms, unexplainable on an organic basis" (Alarcon,

1973:259). Many persons believe that when men experience precisely the same difficulties doctors are inclined to explain their problems in other diagnostic terms: they simply see hysteria where they expect it to be, and fail to notice it in situations where they don't anticipate its appearance. Others argue that women are trained by their parents and by social rules to react to difficulties in ways that have come to be defined as hysterical, while men respond to difficulties in other physical and psychological ways (Smith-Rosenberg, 1985).

Certainly, the phenomenal overrepresentation of young girls in two kinds of hysterical phenomena indicate that there is some real social or physical basis for the early caricature of the sexual roots of the phenomenon. In virtually all recorded episodes of mass hysteria it has been young girls who were most affected (Colligan, Pennebaker, and Murphy, 1982). In addition, young girls stand out — for some reason pairs of nine- and eleven-year-olds — in the most notorious accusations in the history of the human race of other women as witches. At Salem in 1692, where twenty-three persons ultimately were hanged for witchcraft, it was nine-year-old Betty Parris and her eleven-year-old cousin, Abigail Williams, who first uttered the accusations against the crones (and later some of the most respected matrons) of the village (Boyer and Nissenbaum, 1974:2). The girls claimed to see these women standing on the courtroom rafters and otherwise engaging in all sorts of bizarre activities. What the girls reported we now thoroughly understand were vicious falsehoods, though we still do not know whether they were prompted by nastiness (see Ewen, 1933:111; Hutchinson, 1718:6; Upham, 1867:4–5) or by hysterical fear (Beard, 1882; Caulfield, 1943; Hansen, 1969). In Lowestoft in England, nine-year-old Elizabeth Pacey and her eleven-year-old sister Deborah also led an ugly witchhunt that resulted in the hanging of two elderly women (Geis and Bunn, 1981), while the ages of the accusers in a notorious Spanish case at Pamplona in 1527 also were nine and eleven (Baroja, 1964). In the most famous witchcraft case in Scotland the accuser was Christian Shaw, the eleven-year-old daughter of a rural laird (Adam, 1978).

Premenstrual Syndrome

About one in seven women are believed to suffer from difficulties prior to their menstrual period severe enough to interfere with daily activities. It is arguable whether such difficulties are totally biologically determined or whether they represent a problem associated with contemporary civilization or present-day social attitudes. Some research workers believe that the cause of PMS lies in sluggish thyroid activity (or hypothyroidism). In 1986, a study of 300 women reported an "absolutely profound" correlation between PMS symptoms and thyroid difficulties, a condition cleared up by and large with the taking of thyroid pills (Brayshaw and Brayshaw, 1986).

The term *premenstrual syndrome* was first coined half a century ago by Frank (1931), a medical doctor, who said it was marked by breast swelling and tenderness; headaches; edema of the eyelids, cheeks, and extremities; abdominal discomfort; and "uncontrollable irritation and depression which manifests itself in manic or melancholic crises." Frank maintained that the number of suicides among women was highest during the time immediately prior to menstruation (see further Dawood, McGuire, and Demers, 1985; Osofsky and Blumenthal, 1985).

Many feminists challenge what they regard as the simplistic notions of Frank and his followers. They argue, for instance, that no acceptable experimental work has demonstrated the existence of such a syndrome, and they find it interesting that the norm against which the behavior of women is measured is one of passivity, amiability, and good-naturedness. In particular, they resent the tendency to write off behavior with deep and complicated origins as nothing more than the result of cyclical mood changes related to menstruation. Suicide, they point out, is not the consequence of a fluctuation in mood but the result of a large number of other circumstances, many of them considerably more significant than any possible cyclical mood shift, presuming that such a shift exists at all. A woman may be oppressed, overwhelmed, physically ill, or otherwise in severe trouble when she kills herself, and it is insensitive and stupid, some writers say, to override her fundamental difficulties with a banal physiological "explanation" (Laws, Hey, and Eagan, 1985). On the other hand, the same writers do not mean to dismiss the fact that some women do report physical and some emotional mood changes that seem to be related to their menstrual cycle. But it is pointed out that most cultures do not attend to such issues: Janiger, Riffenburgh, and Kersh (1972), after a search of anthropological records, found "many items pertaining to cultural myths, taboos and superstitions associated with menstruation, but no report of premenstrual distress as such."

Laws, Hey, and Eagan (1985) believe that PMS is as much a political as a medical issue. We could just as readily suggest that there is a condition known as the "pre-breakfast syndrome," they point out. This syndrome would be found among people who stagger out of bed, depressed at the dawn of a new day, feeling wobbly and uncertain, at least until they have some food and, perhaps, coffee to stimulate their circulation. Such a syndrome exists, but it is not notably important, just as the PMS syndrome may exist for some persons sometimes but has been accorded altogether too much significance because, these authors suggest, it allows a chauvinist to put down female behavior at times as uncontrollably erratic. Note, for instance, in regard to female delinquency, the opinion of Katharina Dalton (1982:719), a British medical doctor, and the most prominent supporter of the importance of PMS as an influence on behavior:

> Among PMS women, increased libido is occasionally noticed in the premenstruum. . . . All too often it is this nymphomanian urge in adolescents which is responsible for young girls running away from home, or custody, only to be found wandering in the park or following the boys. These girls can be helped, and their criminal career abruptly ended with hormone therapy.

The use of PMS as an excuse for criminal behavior was highlighted in the early 1980s in the British trial of Christine English, who killed her lover by driving her car over him after he threatened to end their affair following a quarrel about his drinking and his relations with other women. Dalton, according to a London newspaper, the *Sun* (November 11, 1981), as an expert medical witness, testified that English had been suffering from PMS for thirteen years:

"It would make her irritable, aggressive, impatient, and confused, with loss of self-control." The jury acquitted her.

What, all told, can we conclude from a review of material on hysteria and the premenstrual syndrome as these conditions (and other matters specifically tied to girls and women) relate to juvenile delinquency? The answer, at least for the moment, has to be, "Not much." It is very difficult to disassociate science from ideology. Certainly, the absurd notion of Hippocrates and his followers—a notion that survived for centuries—that hysteria was caused by the womb wandering soulfully about the body, seeking surcease, can be taken as prototypical of a view rooted in a dismissive if not hostile attitude toward women. The evidence is, perhaps, less certain with regard to PMS, but we are inclined, pending much better evidence, to regard research such as that by Pauline Slade (1984) as pointing in a persuasive direction. Slade had 118 student nurses report their mood and their physiological condition on a regular basis, with the subjects not knowing that this was a study of the relationship between their feelings and their menstrual cycle. She found cyclic changes related to menstruation in the physiological realm, but "psychological changes occurred randomly throughout the cycle" (1984:1). Slade points out that women who experience negative moods during the premenstrual period tend to associate such moods with PMS. When they experience precisely the same moods at other times, they tend to attach them to personal or environmental factors.

In essence, then, it is clear that the subject of female delinquency affords an especially good opportunity to examine issues of upbringing and biology and consequent illegal behavior. At this time, evidence connecting delinquency to biological aspects of gender is inconclusive, but the topic remains significant for further investigation.

The Double Standard

The investigation of relationships between gender and delinquency also provides a forum for opening up questions about what is called "the double standard." A suitable definition is supplied by Keith Thomas (1959:195), an eminent Oxford University social historian:

> Stated simply, it is the view that unchastity, in the sense of sexual relations before marriage or outside marriage, is for a man, if an offense, nonetheless a mild and pardonable one, but for a woman a matter of utmost gravity.

The justifications and rebuttals of the double standard throughout history are worth close attention because they tell us a great deal about the attitudes that condition the manner in which female delinquency is defined and treated today. Certainly of profound importance has been the irrefragable fact that sexual intercourse on the part of females might result in pregnancy. Without satisfactory birth control procedures (whether in the form of mechanical contraception methods, the use of pills, or attempts to calculate periods of nonfertility), whether or not a woman conceived after sexual intercourse often was little more than a lottery. And conception outside of wedlock in Anglo-Saxon societies posed frightening consequences, not the least of which was ostracism from those who deemed themselves "respectable." One writer (Graham, 1898:140) has portrayed vividly the consequences in Scotland of female sexual deviancy:

> Even more feared than the pillory was the punishment of having to appear in church every Sunday for a given number of weeks, usually twenty-six or fifty-two, to be harangued for half an hour in front of the congregation by the minister — for which, in some churches, offenders were fastened to the wall in iron collars, or jougs. This was the penalty for adulterers and fornicators . . . and was greatly feared. So much so, that it caused a sharp rise in the infanticide rate, for women who had illegitimately become pregnant preferred to risk the capital penalty for infanticide than admit the facts and suffer such extreme public humiliation.

The essential biological snare for women, of course, was that maternity was readily established; paternity, more doubtful and arguable. At least as important, unquestionably, has been the millennium-old tradition that women are and should remain "purer" than men. Sex consistently has been portrayed to women as "dirty" or, alternatively, as a treasure that a young woman can bestow upon the honored man of her choice. For men, on the contrary, sex has been regarded as an intense biological drive, demanding satisfaction, preferably through marriage or, failing that, through involvement with a declassé group of "available" females, who offer service for money or who are regarded as sexually wayward and therefore outside the mainstream of decent society.

Why the Double Standard?

Sociobiologists, who find functional attributes in social customs, insist that the double standard serves the purpose of allowing the fittest females — the healthiest, the prettiest, the smartest — to locate the most suitable fathers for their children, thereby constantly improving the gene pool of the race. If women were to be as sexually promiscuous as men, without abortion or birth control, they would be apt to be "trapped" into giving birth to children with less desirable fathers, genetically speaking. Therefore, women trade sexual access, the sociobiologists maintain, for the "best" male traits they can acquire for their offspring in the mating marketplace (Symons, 1979). The process presumably operates selectively like the condition in many animal groups where the strongest, most aggressive male collects and guards a harem of females and allows no other male to mate with any of them. Certainly, there is no arguing against the position that historically women have been trained to use sexual skills adroitly to acquire husbands, to tease and to promise but not to yield until the male has made a firm commitment to marriage.

Jeffery (1971) finds this pattern particularly pronounced in the middle class. "The middle-class girl," he notes, "knows how to play the sex game so as to avoid pregnancy, to get an abortion, or to get married. She exchanges sex favors for protection and security. The lower-class girl cannot use sex in the same manner" (1971:158).

The best explanation of the origin and perpetuation of the double standard probably lies in the unequal distribution of power among men and women throughout time in Western civilization. Men controlled the political economy, and it was very much to their advantage to enforce the position that, while they were to be accorded sexual license, women were to be restrained from such behavior. For one thing, such rules made more certain their assurance that they were the fathers of the children their wives bore. The emotional turmoil that can result from uncertainty about paternity has been vividly portrayed by the Swedish playwright August Strindberg in the drama *The Father* (1897). Another explanation for the double standard is offered by Thomas (1959:216) after an inventory of a number of hypotheses:

> it seems that . . . insistence on female chastity cannot be explained by reference to the fact of childbirth and elaborations thereon, but that the solution is more likely to be found in the desire of men for absolute property in women, a desire which cannot be satisfied if the man has reason to believe the woman has been possessed by another man, no matter how momentarily and no matter how slight the consequences.

Thomas grants that he is "well aware that this conclusion leaves many questions unanswered," but we are inclined to agree with him that his explanation fits most satisfactorily with the historical evidence.

What is absent from this explanation is an answer to the question of how men came to be able to enforce their wills and serve their own ends, that is, from where their power derives. The most common explanation is that women were willing to trade autonomy for the protection and support necessary to assure the safe nurturance of their offspring. Christina Larner (1985:84) offers a variant of such a position, suggesting that "all women threaten male hegemony with the exclusive power to give life; and the social order depends on women conforming to male ideas of female behavior." This rather cryptic interpretation implies that since women can destroy human life by failing to reproduce, men were driven to control them to ensure their own perpetuation. But the idea fails to establish why women might be less interested than men in reproduction, though an explanation could lie in the extreme dangers associated with childbearing in early times.

An intriguing alternative viewpoint is that of Sherfey (1966), who argues that women are not biologically adapted to a single spouse, monogamy, or the prolonged adolescence of contemporary society. She believes that the high sexual drive of women is the basis of masculine efforts to impose subordination upon women (1966:119, 120):

> It is conceivable that the *forceful* suppression of women's inordinate sexual demands was a prerequisite to the dawn of every modern civilization and almost every living culture. Primitive women's sexual drive was too strong, too susceptible to the fluctuating extremes of an impelling, aggressive eroticism to withstand the disciplined requirements of a settled family life — where many living children were necessary to a family's well-being and where paternity had become as important as maternity in maintaining family and property cohesion. . . . Not until these [sexual] drives were gradually brought under control by rigidly enforced social codes could family life become the stabilizing and creative crucible from which modern civilized man could emerge.

Contemporary Themes

Relationships between the sexes are presently in a striking state of transition, and the changes underway bear an important relationship to our understanding of female delinquency. At the moment, near the end of the 1980s, it seems impossible to foretell precisely how matters will develop. There does not appear to be any question that women will enter the work arena in increasing numbers, partly because they want to and partly because, for financial reasons, they feel that they must do so. Nor does there appear to be any doubt that women will succeed in opening up further opportunities to be treated equally with men, in terms of hiring policies, advancement, and compensation. Their case in this regard is too compelling not to prevail.

How men and women, and girls and boys, ultimately will come to relate to each other in various spheres—work, sex, play, and family, among others—seems much less certain. Working women, for instance, typically desire or demand that their husbands share equivalently in housework and child rearing, but it is a constant lament that they have been unable to get their mates to do so. In countries where women have been in the work force in large numbers for many years, such as Sweden and the Soviet Union, reports indicate that many men continue to be uncooperative in regard to sharing domestic chores with their wives (Voznesenkaya, 1986).

The solutions to a dilemma such as this are manifold, and diverse people obviously will choose individual ways of dealing with the problem if it faces them. Ultimately, perhaps, some common approach will emerge that will mark American relationships. Men ultimately can curtail their personal or work-related involvement and take on domestic pursuits. Females can assume what has already been dubbed the "superwoman" role and handle both work and family chores singlehandedly (Berg, 1986). Or women can leave the marketplace and return to home and hearth. Other options also exist: child-rearing and domestic responsibilities can be sublet to third parties, such as live-in servants and child care centers. Couples can opt to be childless, a pattern already significantly on the increase in the United States (Callan, 1986), or men and women can fashion life-styles that do not involve marriage or cohabitation. If homosexuality is on the increase (it may be so, or it may now be practiced less furtively), this too may be a result of an inability or unwillingness to adapt to newly emerging gender-role demands in the mainstream society. The impact of the newer relations between the sexes in the United States is indicated in recent Census Bureau statistics, which show that American women now are bearing too few children to maintain long-term national population growth. Population levels are primarily maintained by the continuing influx of immigrants.

Finally, of course, nobody can reasonably predict the results of current conditions in future generations. Children raised by families with both parents working may decide that they do not want their own children so brought up and may style different approaches to child rearing, or, alternatively, they may carry current trends further.

At the same time, sexual relations, the issue at the core of the double standard and the item lying at the heart of female delinquency, also are in a considerable state of flux. Undoubtedly, more young and unmarried women are engaging in sexual intercourse more frequently and with more partners than was true a few decades ago, though the growing fear of AIDS is likely to have a severely dampening effect on this trend. Some women now are as casual about sex as men traditionally have been, though most others are more restrained. Of those who are promiscuous, many after a while report feeling "used" and "exploited" —perhaps a carryover of their training in the belief that sex and love are not readily separable.

Is Unmarried Teenage Pregnancy Also Juvenile Delinquency?

As a result of changing attitudes about sexual relations, more girls and young women also are having children out of wedlock and raising them alone. This is a fundamental aspect of the relationship between female sexual delinquency and major currents in contemporary American life. The most rational (and perhaps the only possible) defense of continuing to regard sexual waywardness among girls as juvenile delinquency is that, unless it is curbed, the consequences for those who indulge in it can be extremely detrimental. Boys can walk away from a partner's pregnancy, perhaps nonchalantly, perhaps with some emotional damage, but it is rarely apt to interfere seriously with the course of their lives, unless they elect to have it do so. Girls, on the other hand, unless they choose to have an abortion, which may clash with personal or religious convictions, will often undergo dramatic changes in their lives when they become pregnant and bear a child. Society can say that its strong reaction to female delinquency represents an attempt to protect girls from an experience that they will wish they had not had, if not now then at least when they look back on it some years later. An obvious counterargument, of course, is that how people choose to run their lives is their own business and that if young girls care to indulge freely in sex and to have children out of wedlock that is their option. Those who counter this viewpoint generally rely on two responses: first, that the girls are too young to adequately know what is in their own best interests, and that minors always have been protected; and second, that unmarried girls who bear children very often end up on welfare roles, since they often are untrained to do satisfactorily remunerative work and cannot earn enough to support themselves and the child adequately. Therefore, they become a burden on the taxpayers, who, because of this, are entitled to try to protect themselves by seeking to penalize and prevent such behavior through defining it as illegal. If, on the other hand, these are not to be the consequences of "wayward" sexuality, then the rationale for treating it as a form of delinquency is undercut.

These cross-currents, it can be seen, are intimately connected to the phenomenon of female delinquency. In the following pages, we will portray some of the characteristics of that delinquency and will link these characteristics with the wider social changes discussed in the introductory pages of the present chapter.

The Extent and Nature of Female Delinquency ─────────

A brief review and extension of the discussion in Chapter 1 about differences in male and female delinquency would seem useful at this point. There is, of course, no dispute that males under the age of eighteen commit about 3 to 7 times more criminal offenses of the type that come to the attention of the authorities than do females (Wolfgang, 1979). Self-report studies, however, continually report much lower ratios, generally in the range of 1.2 to 1 to 2.5 to 1 (Canter, 1982; Hindelang, Hirschi, and Weis, 1981; Smith and Visher, 1980). Statistics indicate that boys are primarily involved in property offenses while girls' misbehavior is focused in sex and home-related misbehaviors.

A particularly comprehensive analysis by Canter (1982) of information acquired by the National Youth Survey on self-reported delinquency offers an inventory of the kinds of distinctions found between males and females. Interviewers spent about an hour with each of 1,725 adolescents, aged eleven to seventeen, paying them $5 for their participation in the survey. In none of the forty delinquent and seven drug behaviors were girls more frequently involved than boys. Statistically significant greater male participation was found for the following property offenses: damaging others' property, stealing a motor vehicle, stealing more than $50, evading payment, breaking into a building, and joyriding. For stealing less than $50 and buying stolen property, however, the difference, though showing higher male involvement, was much less sharp. As expected, boys also were more involved in the violent crimes of gang fighting, strong-arming students and others, and aggravated assaults. Boys, in addition, were 45 times more likely than girls to carry a hidden weapon. In all, boys were far more apt to be involved in serious offenses than girls.

The National Youth Survey also found more alcohol and heroin use among males but equivalent recourse by boys and girls to marijuana and other illegal drugs, a finding compatible with those of other researchers (Jessor and Jessor, 1977; Wechsler and McFadden, 1976). The study also confirmed the general belief among research scholars (Steffensmeier and Steffensmeier, 1980) that delinquency patterns did not alter much during the decade after the mid-1960s, the period during which the women's rights movement began to take hold.

A corollary study of self-reported delinquency was carried out by Hindelang (1971), who surveyed 820 students in a Catholic coeducational high school in Oakland, California. He found a larger degree of male involvement in promiscuous sex behavior, gambling, and theft of more expensive items. The ratios were smaller (though males almost always exceeded females) for cheating on school examinations; hit-and-run accidents; heroin use; drinking; using LSD, methedrine, or mescaline; using false ID; and sniffing glue.

As Hindelang (1971:526) notes, "Although the females report markedly less delinquent involvement, the pattern of female delinquency is strikingly similar to that of the males." It is, Hindelang suggests, "primarily the *frequency* of the activities and not the focal activities themselves which differentiates male and female delinquent involvement in the sample." Hindelang also noted that the delinquency patterns were "relatively versatile," that is, that one offense tends to go hand in hand with others.

Commenting on the results of Hindelang and a host of other research workers who conclude from self-report studies that males consistently are involved more completely and more often in virtually all delinquent activities, Jensen and Eve (1976), note that such results might be (but probably are not) incorrect. "It may be," they observe, "that girls are less willing to acknowledge delinquent acts than boys, and hence only 'appear' to be less delinquent." But they find little reason to adopt such a skeptical position; instead, they point out that the reasons for accepting the findings are very persuasive (1976:429):

> All we can say is that numerous investigations carried out at different points in time, in different regions of the nation, in a variety of different cities and sociodemographic groups, using a variety of alternative measures of delinquency (both official and unofficial) and divergent research techniques have consistently discovered a sex differential in delinquency. This may be more than can be said of any other statistical regularity in the study of delinquency and, in view of such consistency, it seems fairly safe to conclude that girls are "really" less involved in delinquency than are boys.

The double standard, as we have indicated, earmarks sexual waywardness by females as a matter with which juvenile authorities come to be concerned (Greene and Esselstyn, 1972). Several major delinquency types, including prostitution and running away, will be discussed here as illustrative of the double standard. This condition, "the casting of specific law violations into the broader categories of incorrigibility, running away, or sex delinquency," has been labeled by Smart (1976:22) the "sexualization of offenses." She notes that juvenile courts routinely impose pretrial physical examinations, often involving lengthy detention periods, upon girls and young women who are apprehended for delinquent behavior (see the related discussion in Chapter 11). These examinations seek to detect pregnancy and venereal infections, neither condition, of course, being a law violation (Chesney-Lind, 1973). That boys and girls who have committed delinquent acts often are sent to the same or similar institutions also reinforces the idea that sexual delinquency, in terms of punishment, is as serious as criminal behavior (Smart, 1976).

As noted in Chapter 10, in the years prior to the federal effort to deinstitutionalize status offenders, up to 70 per cent of incarcerated girls were placed in institutions for status offenses, compared to 23 per cent of boys. And once they were committed, juvenile status offenders were subject to court jurisdiction longer and held longer than male juvenile offenders (Mann, 1984). In many instances, girls are sent to institutions not because they are deemed in any way to be dangerous but because the authorities despair of finding a suitable placement for them. Within institutions either for status or criminal-type offenses, girls often are taught skills that, to the anger of feminist writers, reinforce traditional gender roles. As Rogers (1972:223) notes, for instance, in regard to the Long Lane School to which delinquent females in Connecticut are sent, "It still prepares women to re-enter the community as nineteenth century domestics." Similarly, Campbell (1984) deplores the efforts to reform girl gang members by teaching them "cosmetics, comportment, and etiquette" (see also Chesney-Lind, 1977; Moyer, 1985).

Runaways

The rationale for the strong focus on female runaways in the enforcement of the juvenile delinquency statutes is that such behavior is assumed to be a precursor of serious personal problems and more serious lawbreaking. The following three cases (Riback, 1971:313, 314) represent instances in which young girls were committed to correctional facilities under the New York statute, after a finding that they were "wayward minors," either because they were "morally depraved" or "in danger of becoming morally depraved."

Esther was living alone because her mother had been committed to a state mental hospital. Esther was expelled from school; the principal had charged her with "sexual promiscuity." She then was deemed a wayward minor and placed in a foster home. After her mother was released from the hospital, Esther wanted to return home, but her social worker refused to give her permission to do so. Esther ran away.

Marion had lived in foster homes since she was five years old. When she was seventeen, she bore an illegitimate child. Marion's social worker wanted Marion to give her child up for adoption, but when she refused to do so, she too was adjudicated a wayward minor. Previously Marion had run away from her foster home when she was not permitted to see the father of her child.

Dominica, the oldest of eight children, had had a confused family life. Her mother, an alcoholic, had been married four times. Her mother was found to be unfit, and all the children were placed in foster homes. Then Dominica ran away, and her mother requested that a warrant be put out for her arrest. Dominica was then allowed to stay at home, but she was placed under a curfew. She had no recollection of being placed on probation, but after she left home without permission (she was suspected of having attended a drug party), Dominica was charged with violating probation.

Running away is a not uncommon precursor of teenage prostitution. The girls (and, increasingly, boys as well) believe that they have no other means by which to support themselves. If they look for legitimate work, their employer or fellow workers are apt to detect that they are underage and report them to the authorities. Besides, they are not likely to have legitimate marketable skills. About 75,000 to 1 million American youths run away each year. There are two girl runaways for each male, a figure that perhaps reflects the tighter restraints imposed upon young girls by their parents. Runaway girls are said often to come from families with a "bewildering array of simultaneous problems" (Stewart and Zaenglein-Senger, 1984:432), with physical abuse a leading determinant of running away (Walker, 1975). Most of the runaways return or are returned to their homes within forty-eight hours after they depart, and about 10 per cent remain absent either permanently or for long periods of time. A few decades ago, as part of the flower-child or hippie movement, running away became something of an adolescent fashion. The meccas changed from time to time: from San Francisco in 1966–1967 (Cavan, 1972) to Boston the following year (Blum and Smith, 1972) and then to Boulder, Colorado (Weisberg, 1985:13).

Teenage Female Prostitution

Prostitution in the United States was estimated by Winick and Kinsie (1971) to gross more than a billion dollars annually and to involve between 100,000 and 500,000 women. Basing their conclusions on interviews with more than 2,000 prostitutes, the authors note that in contrast to the dramatic coloration they are given on stage, in films, and in novels, most prostitutes have relatively uninflected, rather drab personalities. In describing her work, a typical prostitute will say that it is "a little more boring" than her former job as a file clerk.

The suicide rate among prostitutes is seen by Winick and Kinsie as indicating

Arrest on suspicion of prostitution.

a high degree of alienation and unhappiness among its practitioners. Seventy-five per cent of a sample of call girls were said to have attempted suicide, and 15 per cent of all suicides brought to public hospitals are reported to be prostitutes. The median age of prostitutes is between twenty-five and forty, but there has been a dramatic increase in "baby pros," girls between the ages of twelve and sixteen (Bracey, 1979).

The family backgrounds of prostitutes, according to a study by Silbert and Pines (1982:476), seem to have been "surprisingly comfortable." James (1978:53), noting an increase in juvenile prostitutes from "affluent and overindulged" backgrounds, explains the relationship between the values the girls have learned at home and the lure of prostitution:

> Along with succumbing to intense pressure to be sexual and to measure self-worth in direct relationship with money-making ability, middle-class life yields other conditions that make prostitution alluring. . . . It appears that for them [middle-class prostitutes] it is basically entertaining to dress up with your friends and go down on the street and con, cajole, and be the aggressor. The extravagant sensation from the illegality, projected immorality, and danger of prostitution is a relief from the neutrality of suburbia. . . . It is just something to do—another high.

Silbert and Pines (1982) interviewed 200 current and former prostitutes in the San Francisco Bay Area, of whom 60 per cent were sixteen years of age and under, with "many" reported to be ten, eleven, and twelve. More than three out of five of the women and girls had been beaten—differentiated from being spanked—by at least one of their parents, with such beatings taking place once a month or more for 45 per cent of those who were hit. A similar percentage reported being victims of incest or sexual abuse when they were between the ages of three and sixteen, with ten the average age of first sexual victimization (Silbert and Pines, 1983). First intercourse took place at 13.5 years; for most of the girls it was not a good experience. As one noted: "I thought it would make someone like me, but it backfired" (1983:482). Before they began prostituting themselves for money, the girls on the average had had sexual intercourse with thirteen different men. Silbert and Pines (1982:488, 489) summarize their material in the following terms:

> The primary picture . . . of entrance into prostitution is one of juveniles running away from impossible situations at home, who are solicited for prostitution, and start working for a pimp because they have no other means of support due to their age, lack of education, and lack of necessary street sense to survive alone.

Paul Gebhard's (1969) study of prostitution, along with numerous others, concludes that few of the women are forced into the business. Only 4 per cent of the women Gebhard interviewed could be deemed to have gone into prostitution unwillingly. Even these, Gebhard notes, had alternatives. As he (1969:29) observes, "The female who says her husband or boyfriend forced her into prostitution is saying she chose prostitution rather than lose her mate and possibly experience a beating. Even the brothels would not want the problem of confining a captive beseeching her clients for rescue."

Most major cities have pockets of illegal prostitution; only in fifteen of Nevada's seventeen counties is the behavior legal. Typical of what occurs is the depiction of a San Francisco investigative committee:

> The range of prostitution in San Francisco is fantastic. Practitioners may be male or female; black, white, or oriental. They may be 14-year-olds hustling as part of a junior high school "syndicate" operation; they may be hippies supporting the [drug] habits of their "old man" (or their own habits); they may be moonlighting secretaries who sell their favors on a selective basis through legitimate dating services. Places of assignation run from rundown hotels to luxurious hilltop apartments. (San Francisco Committee on Crime, 1971:3)

Adolescent prostitutes tend to prefer older to younger customers, largely because they pose less threat and are easier to rob. They also are said to prefer Asian men and foreign sailors, because they believe these men treat them better than other customers (Weisberg, 1985).

Pimps and Prostitutes

Pimps often locate themselves inside metropolitan bus terminals, looking for the out-of-town runaway girl who arrives in an overwhelming city friendless and without money. Such girls make prime recruits for prostitution. Typically, the pimp will befriend the runaway, offer her shelter and comfort, and gradually turn her into his service as a streetwalker or call girl.

The process by which pimps persuade young girls to enter prostitution has been depicted by Milner and Milner (1972). Successful pimps possess acute street understanding of techniques that are used to deal with alienation. They deliberately isolate young girls from their previous associations and place them in an environment in which there are no contradictions of the life-style that the pimp is pushing. As a successful San Francisco pimp puts it:

> It's like going into the Army where they take you away from all your friends. You create a different environment. It's a brainwashing process: the whole thing is creativity. When you turn a chick out, you take away every set of values and morality she had previously and create a different environment. You give her different friends. You give her instead of squares or bookkeepers or secretaries, clerks, and so forth for friends, you give her professional hos [whores]. (Milner and Milner, 1972:95)

The Milners, trying to explain the willingness of young girls to remain in what objectively often appears to be a dismal and degrading existence, liken the situation of ghetto prostitution to that of lobsters in a basket. Fishermen, they point out, never cover lobster baskets, because "if one lobster tries to crawl out, the rest will pull him back in" (1972:129). Young prostitutes can avoid the indignities and the requirements of the nondeviant world by confining themselves to a milieu in which they can meet the demands, however self-defeating the life may be. In addition, the Milners and other writers stress that the excitement of street prostitution and the often intense devotion of the hustlers to their pimps serve to keep them on the streets as long as they can earn money.

Pimps afford protection, a sense of worth and love, and an opportunity to make a considerable amount of money (though few teenage prostitutes retain very much of their earnings). An interview with a runaway teenage prostitute in New York demonstrates the flavor of the relationship between the girl and her pimp, a relationship that most persons would find both perverse and puzzling. The questions posed in the following paragraphs are those of a writer asking to comprehend the phenomenon of teenage prostitution (Sereny, 1985:38).

> Did he ever beat her, as some of her later pimps had? "He never laid a hand on me, no. He looked after me — he was worried about me. He was concerned about me going on the streets." But it was he who *put* her there. "Yes," she said matter-of-factly, "that's his job."
> And she never got any indication that he felt there might be something wrong in sending a twelve-year-old girl out on the street? "He was concerned for me," she repeated, still steadfast in her loyalty to the thirty-two-year-old man who had started her in prostitution.
> Did she herself feel anything wrong with it? "At first, before I was doing it, of course I didn't know anything much about it; it was something I thought I wouldn't like to do. But then, after I got myself into it, it didn't seem so bad. It was kinda fun."

Upbeat evaluations of hustling such as the above typically turn sour after the youngsters have been working for a while. They usually learn that the pimps are using them unconscionably, feeding them a practiced line and exploiting them mercilessly. Most pimps work three or four different women — their "stable" — and are adroit at pretending that each is the particular favorite. While the charade lasts, it can keep the young prostitute at work. "I thought I was in love with him," says one teenager, who had since returned to home and school. "I didn't look at it as prostitution, you know. I looked at it as doing him a favor because he took care of me, and gave me so much attention and so much affection, you know. I'd do anything for him, you know" (Sereny, 1985:223).

This particular girl had become disillusioned when she learned that her pimp actually had sold her to a colleague and then skipped out on her. Sickness, particularly venereal diseases, beatings by customers, and numerous arrests can bring home forcefully the message that teenage prostitution is a dead-end enterprise. But some teenagers persist in the "life," as they call it, in part because they find discipline and routine intolerable. Sereny (1985:12) notes, for instance, that one youngster she was interviewing became bored within a few minutes: "Her concentration span on anything outside herself was close to zero."

Summary

Prostitution by teenage girls represents one of the more extreme aspects of female delinquency. It offers an important illustration of at least two fundamental points related to such delinquency: (1) that girls and young women participate to different degrees in different kinds of delinquent acts than boys and young men, acts that can be related to their biological makeup and social training; and (2) that society often responds in a very different manner to the delinquencies of young females than to those of young males.

The police, for instance, seem to be much less interested in trying to hassle and arrest teenage male prostitutes than they are in dealing with females (Weisberg, 1985). For one thing, police officers are squeamish about interacting with other men in ways that have sexual overtones, and most young male prostitutes traffic in homosexual services. For another, law enforcement personnel, reflecting social values, are less concerned with male sexuality than they are with female sexual waywardness.

At the same time, law enforcement personnel historically have not bothered to arrest and process the male customers of juvenile prostitutes, although some change in policy is becoming apparent now. In part, the reluctance stems from the perception of customers as engaging in an understandable transaction — at least, a transaction that the officers can readily comprehend and one with which they can empathize. In part also, the customer is needed to testify against the prostitute, though there is no reason why the situation could not be reversed, with the girl implicating her patron. Police sometimes try to enforce the law against pimps, under statutes proscribing living off the wages of a prostitute. But such efforts tend to be frustrated by the unwillingness of the teenage prostitutes to testify against the pimps, either out of fear or because of affection.

Female delinquency offers interesting insights into the changing relationships between men and women in the United States and abroad. Eased sexual controls, for instance, may ultimately lead to the diminution or the demise of teenage prostitution, as the demand for sex for pay lessens, though this does not seem to be a likely near-term prospect. Lethal communicable diseases, such as AIDS, will have a very strong impact on sexual permissiveness and prostitution. More arguable is the effect that the ethos of the women's rights movement will exert upon the extent and types of female delinquency. It seems likely that, in time, girls and young women will be less subject to legal restraints in regard to sexual involvement than they are at present. Whether at the same time females will begin to commit more of the kinds of delinquency now perpetrated by males, however, remains to be seen.

This chapter dwelled at some length on the uncertain manner in which gender roles are now undergoing reformulation in the United States and elsewhere and the likely effects of such changes on female law violations. At present, it does not appear that the women's rights movement is having a strong effect on forms of delinquency. In part, this is because girls and young women committing delinquent acts are not part of the mainstream of the feminist movement, nor do they participate to a significant extent in the role changes that the movement advocates. Biology certainly exerts considerable influence on different patterns of male and female delinquency, particularly the quality of strength. Girls and women traditionally have been penalized (or protected, depending upon your viewpoint) by the sexual double standard, which abhors sexual waywardness by women while blinking at the same behavior on the part of men. Delinquency statutes, backed by public opinion and concern with possible teenage pregnancy, reinforce the double standard by singling out girls for punishment when they violate sexual mores.

Perhaps the most intriguing aspect of the phenomenon of female delinquency, however, is the fact that girls and women commit so much less law-violative behavior than boys and men. Of all the correlates of delinquency and crime — matters such as age, sex, race, intelligence, ethnic background, social class — it is gender that stands out most prominently as the strongest predictor of illegal acts. Either what they are or what they learn obviously contributes profoundly to the way females behave in regard to the law. If men could be induced to behave in the same manner — by whatever tactics work with women —we would have gone a very long way toward a solution to the problem of delinquency. The truth of such an assertion, however, is undercut by the corollary truth that it appears quite unlikely that such a situation is apt to develop, at least within the foreseeable future.

References

Adam, Isabel. 1978. *Witch Hunt: The Great Scottish Witchcraft Trials of 1697.* London: Macmillan.

Alarcon, Renta D. 1973. Hysteria and the Hysterical Personality: How Come One Without the Other? *Psychiatric Quarterly* 41:258–275.

Baker, Marilyn, and Bromton, Sally. 1974. *Exclusive! The Inside Story of Patricia Hearst and the SLA.* New York: Macmillan.

Baroja, Julio Caro. 1964. *The World of Witches.* Translated by O. N. V. Glendinning. Chicago: Univ. of Chicago Press.

Beard, George M. 1882. *The Psychology of the Salem Witchcraft Excitement of 1692 and Its Practical Application to Our Time.* New York: G. P. Putnam's.

Berg, Barbara J. 1986. *The Crisis of the Working Mother: Conflict Between Family and Work.* New York: Summit Books.

Blum, Jeffrey D., and Smith, Judith E. 1972. *Nothing Left to Lose: Studies of Street People.* Boston: Beacon Press.

Boulton, David. 1975. *The Making of Tania Hearst.* London: New English Library.

Bowker, Lee H., and Klein, Malcolm W. 1983. The Etiology of Female Juvenile Delinquency and Gang Membership: A Test of Psychological and Social Structural Explanations. *Adolescence* 18:739–751.

Boyer, Paul, and Nissenbaum, Stephen. 1974. *Salem Possessed: The Social Origins of Witchcraft.* Cambridge, Mass.: Harvard Univ. Press.

Bracey, Dorothy H. 1979. *"Baby-Pros": Preliminary Profiles of Juvenile Prostitutes.* New York: John Jay Press.

Brayshaw, Nora D., and Brayshaw, David D. 1986. Thyroid Hypofunction in Premenstrual Syndrome. *New England Journal of Medicine* 315:1486–1487.

Bugliosi, Vincent, and Gentry, Curt. 1974. *Helter Skelter: The True Story of the Manson Murders.* New York: Norton.

Callan, Victor J. 1986. Single Women, Voluntary Childlessness and Perceptions About Life and Marriage. *Journal of Biosocial Science* 18:479–488.

Campbell, Anne. 1984. *The Girls in the Gang: A Report from New York City.* New York: Basil Blackwell.

Canter, Rachelle J. 1982. Sex Differences in Self-report Delinquency. *Criminology* 20:373–393.

Caulfield, Ernest. 1943. Pediatric Aspects of the Salem Witchcraft Tragedy. *American Journal of Diseases of Children* 65:788–802.

Cavan, Sherri. 1972. *Hippies of the Haight.* St. Louis: Critics Press.

Chesney-Lind, Meda. 1973. Judicial Enforcement of the Female Sex Role: The Family Court and the Female Delinquent. *Issues in Criminology* 8:51–69.

———. 1977. Judicial Paternalism and the Female Status Offender. *Crime & Delinquency* 23:121–130.

Colligan, Michael J., Pennebaker, James W., and Murphy, Lawrence R., eds. 1982. *Mass Psychogenic Illness: A Social Psychological Analysis.* Hillsdale, N.J.: Lawrence Erlbaum Associates.

Dalton, Katharina. 1982. What Is This Premenstrual Syndrome? *Journal of the Royal College of General Practitioners* 32:713–723.

Dawood, M. Yusoff, McGuire, John L., and Demers, Laurence M., eds. 1985. *Premenstrual Syndrome and Dysmenorrhea.* Baltimore, Md.: Urban and Schwarzenberg.

Emmons, Nuel. 1987. *Manson in His Own Words.* New York: Grove Press.

Engel, George L. 1962. *Fainting.* 2nd ed. Springfield, Ill.: Thomas.

Ewen, C. L'Estrange. 1933. *Witchcraft and Demonianism.* London: Heath Cranton.

Frank, Robert T. 1931. The Hormonal Causes of Premenstrual Tension. *Archives of Neurology and Psychiatry* 26:1053–1057.

Gebhard, Paul H. 1969. Misconceptions About Female Prostitutes. *Medical Aspects of Human Sexuality* 3:29–32.

Geis, Gilbert, and Bunn, Ivan. 1981. Sir Thomas Browne and Witchcraft: A Cautionary Tale for Contemporary Law and Psychiatry. *International Journal of Law and Psychiatry* 4:1–11.

Gilmore, John, and Kenner, Ron. 1971. *The Garbage People.* Los Angeles: Omega Press.

Giordano, Peggy G. 1978. Girls, Boys and Gangs: The Changing Social Context of Female Delinquency. *Journal of Criminal Law and Criminology* 69:126–132.

Graham, H. G. 1898. *The Social Life of Scotland in the 18th Century.* Edinburg: Nevis.

Greene, Nancy B., and Esselstyn, T. C. 1972. The Beyond Control Girl. *Juvenile Justice* 23 (November):13–19.

Hansen, Chadwick. 1969. *Witchcraft at Salem.* New York: George Braziller.

Hanson, Kitty. 1964. *Rebels in the Streets: The Story of New York's Girl Gangs.* Englewood Cliffs, N.J.: Prentice-Hall.

Hindelang, Michael J. 1971. Age, Sex, and the Versatility of Delinquent Involvement. *Social Problems* 18:522–535.

———, Hirschi, Travis, and Weis, Joseph G. 1981. *Measuring Delinquency.* Beverly Hills, Calif.: Sage.

Hoffer, Peter C., and Hull, N. H. E. 1981. *Murdering Mothers: Infanticide in England and New England, 1558–1803.* New York: New York Univ. Press.

Holbrook, David. 1972. *Sex and Dehumanisation in Art, Thought and Life in Our Time.* London: Pitman.

Hutchinson, Francis. 1718. *An Historical Essay Concerning Witchcraft.* London: Knaplock.

James, Jennifer. 1978. *Entrance into Juvenile Prostitution.* Washington, D.C.: National Institute of Mental Health.

Janiger, Oscar, Riffenburgh, Ralph, and Kersh, Ronald. 1972. Cross-Cultural Study of Premenstrual Symptoms. *Psychosomatics* 13:226–235.

Jeffery, C. Ray. 1971. *Crime Prevention Through Environmental Design.* Beverly Hills, Calif.: Sage.

Jensen, Gary F., and Eve, Raymond. 1976. Sex Differences in Delinquency: An Examination of Popular Sociological Explanations. *Criminology* 13:427–448.

Jessor, Richard, and Jessor, Shirley. 1977. *Problem Behavior and Psychosocial Development.* New York: Academic Press.

Jorden, Edward. 1603. *A Brief Discourse of a Disease Called the Suffocation of the Mother.* London: John Windet.

Larner, Christina. 1984. *Witchcraft and Religion: The Politics of Popular Belief.* Oxford: Basil Blackwell.

Laws, Sophie, Hey, Valerie, and Eagan, Andrea. 1985. *Seeing Red: The Politics of Premenstrual Tension.* London: Hutchinson.

Lefkowitz, Mary R. 1981. *Heroines and Hysterics.* London: Duckworth.

Leonard, Eileen B. 1982. *Women, Crime, and Society: A Critique of Theoretical Criminology.* New York: Longman.

Livsey, Clara G. 1980. *The Manson Women: A "Family" Portrait.* New York: Richard Marek.

Mann, Coramae Richey. 1984. *Female Crime and Delinquency.* University, Ala.: Univ. of Alabama Press.

Milner, Christina, and Milner, Richard. 1972. *Black Players: The Secret World of Black Pimps.* Boston: Little, Brown.

Moyer, Imogene L., ed. 1985. *The Changing Roles of Women in the Criminal Justice System: Offenders, Victims, and Professionals.* Prospect Heights, Ill.: Waveland Press.

Mukherjee, Satyanshu, and Fitzgerald, R. William. 1981. The Myth of Rising Female Crime. In *Women & Crime,* edited by Satyanshu Mukherjee and Jocelynne A. Scutt, 127–166. Sydney: Allen and Unwin.

Noblit, George W., and Burcart, Janie M. 1976. Women and Crime. *Social Science Quarterly* 56:650–657.

Osofsky, Howard J., and Blumenthal, Susan J. 1985. *Premenstrual Syndrome: Current Findings and Future Directions.* Washington, D.C.: American Psychiatric Press.

Piers, Maria W. 1978. *Infanticide.* New York: Norton.

Pollak, Otto. 1950. *The Criminality of Women.* Philadelphia: Univ. of Pennsylvania Press.

Reeves, Kenneth J. 1976. *The Trial of Patty Hearst.* San Francisco: Great Fidelity Press.

Rendell, Ruth. 1977. *Shake Hands Forever.* New York: Bantam Books.

Riback, Linda. 1971. Juvenile Delinquency Law: Juvenile Women and the Double Standard of Morality. *U.C.L.A. Law Review* 19:313–342.

Rogers, Kristine Olson. 1972. "For Her Own Protection . . .": Conditions of Incarceration for Female Juvenile Offenders in the State of Connecticut. *Law & Society Review* 7:223–246.

Rose, Lionel. 1986. *The Massacre of the Innocents: Infanticide in Britain, 1800–1939.* Boston: Routlege and Kegan Paul.

San Francisco Committee on Crime. June 3, 1971. *A Report on Non-Victim Crime in San Francisco. Part II: Sexual Conduct, Gambling, Prostitution.* San Francisco: San Francisco Committee on Crime.

Sayers, Dorothy. 1955. *Unnatural Death.* New York: Avon.

Sereny, Gitta. 1985. *The Invisible Children: Prostitution in America, West Germany, and Great Britain.* New York: Knopf.

Sherfey, Mary Jane. 1966. The Evolution and Nature of Female Sexuality in Relation to Psychoanalytic Theory. *Journal of the American Psychoanalytic Association* 14:28–128.

Sherman, Julia. 1971. *On the Psychology of Women: A Survey of Empirical Studies.* Springfield, Ill.: Thomas, 1974.

Short, James F., Jr., and Strodtbeck, Fred L. 1965. *Group Process and Gang Delinquency.* Chicago: Univ. of Chicago Press.

Silbert, Mimi and Pines, Ayala M. 1982. Entrance into Prostitution. *Youth & Society* 13:471–500.

———. 1983. Early Sexual Exploitation as an Influence on Prostitution. *Social Casework* 28:285–289.

Slade, Pauline. 1984. Premenstrual Emotional Changes in Normal Women: Fact or Fiction? *Journal of Psychosomatic Research* 28:1–7.

Smart, Carol. 1976. *Women, Crime, and Criminology: A Feminist Critique.* London: Routledge and Kegan Paul.

Smith, Douglas A., and Visher, Christy A. 1980. Sex and Involvement in Deviance/Crime: A Quantitative Review of the Empirical Literature. *American Sociological Review* 45:691–701.

Smith-Rosenberg, Carroll. 1985. The Hysterical Woman: Sex Roles and Role Conflict in Nineteenth-Century America. In *Disorderly Conduct: Visions of Gender in Victorian America,* edited by Carroll Smith-Rosenberg, 197–216. New York: Knopf.

Steffensmeier, Darrell J., Steffensmeier, Renee H. 1980. Trends in Female Delinquency. *Criminology* 18:62–65.

Stewart, Cyrus S., and Zaenglein Senger, Mary M. 1984. Female Delinquency, Family Problems, and Parental Interaction. *Social Casework* 65:428–432.

Sutherland, Edwin H., and Cressey, Donald R. 1970. *Principles of Criminology.* 8th ed. Philadelphia: Lippincott.

Symons, Donald. 1979. *The Evolution of Human Sexuality.* New York: Oxford Univ. Press.

Thomas, Keith. 1959. The Double Standard. *Journal of the History of Ideas* 20:195–216.

Upham, Charles W. 1867. *Salem Witchcraft.* Boston: Wiggin and Lunt.

Vedder, Clyde B., and Somerville, Dora B. 1970. *The Delinquent Girl.* Springfield, Ill.: Thomas.

Vieth, Ilza. 1965. *Hysteria: The History of a Disease.* Chicago: Univ. of Chicago Press.

Voznesenkaya, Julia. 1986. *The Women's Decameron.* Translated by W. B. Linton. New York: Atlantic Monthly Press.

Walker, Deborah K. 1975. *Runaway Youth: An Annotated Bibliography and Literature Overview.* Washington, D.C.: U.S. Department of Health, Education, and Welfare.

Wechsler, H., and McFadden, M. 1982. Sex Differences in Adolescent Alcohol and Drug Use. *Journal of Studies on Alcohol* 37:1291–1301.

Weed, Steven, and Swanton, Scott. 1976. *My Search for Patty Hearst.* New York: Crown.

Weisberg, D. Kelly. 1985. *Children of the Night: A Study of Adolescent Prostitution.* Lexington, Mass.: Lexington Books.

Winick, Charles, and Kinsie, Paul M. 1971. *The Lively Commerce: Prostitution in the United States.* Chicago: Quadrangle.

Wolfgang, Marvin E. 1979. Race and Sex Differences. In *Criminology of Deviant Women,* edited by Rita Simon and Freda Adler, 139–149. Boston: Houghton Mifflin.

CHAPTER 16

Violence, Drugs, and Status Offenses

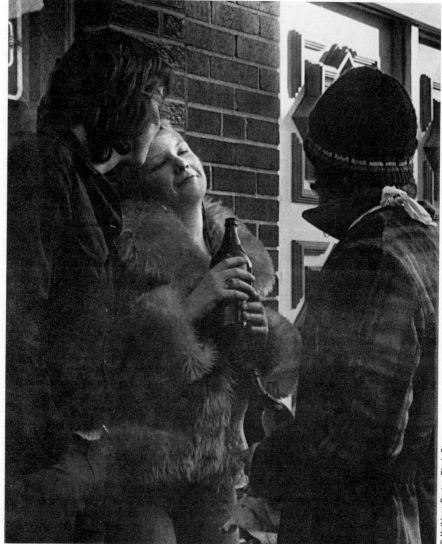

© Kathleen Foster, Black Star

Juvenile delinquency can be examined from a number of different perspectives. We have, in previous chapters, focused on a general statistical portrait of the extent and the nature of delinquency, discussed theoretical perspectives, and dealt with methods of control. In this chapter we single out for further concentration three particular kinds of juvenile behavior that pose significant issues for the philosophy and the operation of the juvenile justice system: violent offenders, juvenile drug offenders, and status offenders.

Violent Crimes by Juveniles

When an attorney reported the decision of the court in Fort Worth, Texas, to his ten-year-old client, telling him, "We lost," the boy placed his head in his hands and started crying *(New York Times,* February 3, 1987). Seeing the sad little boy, one would hardly have guessed that the decision was based on convincing evidence that he had severely beaten and stabbed a 101-year-old woman. Other instances of juvenile violence mentioned in that same *New York Times* article were a ten-year-old babysitter in California strangling the child who was in her care and a twelve-year-old youth in New York charged with twenty-seven felonies, including robbery, aggravated assault, and first-degree rape.

To show that those were not isolated events, highlighted by the newspaper because they generated journalistic interest, we turn to Table 1.1 (Chapter 1), which shows arrests in the United States for various Index (more serious) crimes in 1984. We will focus on the rates of arrest for violent crimes for youths between the ages of ten and seventeen, bearing in mind that youths ten to seventeen constituted about 12.6 per cent of the national population in that year. Those youths accounted for 24.8 per cent of the arrests for robbery, 14.9 per cent of the arrests for forcible rape, 13.5 per cent of the arrests for aggravated assault, and 8.3 per cent of the arrests for murder and nonnegligent manslaughter. Summing over categories shows that 16.6 per cent of all arrests for violent crime (as defined in the *Uniform Crime Reports, UCR),* were youths between ten and seventeen; that is, they accounted for almost 32 per cent more arrests for violent offenses than their numbers in the population would predict.

While the figure of 8.3 per cent in the case of murder and nonnegligent manslaughter is below the population percentage of 12.6 for youths, it is still an astonishingly large number considering the magnitude of the crime. The discrepancy between the general repugnance at the concept of one human criminally killing another human and the widespread feeling (perhaps hope is a better word) of the innocence of youth makes criminal killings by youths a topic of special interest.

"Kids Who Kill"

"Kids Who Kill" is the title of an article written by Sorrells in 1977. He studied thirty-one juveniles charged with homicide or attempted homicide,

A 14-year-old boy arrested in New York City for the murder of two teenagers.

using probation investigatory reports, police records, and mental health records. The following are sketches of two of the homicide incidents (1977:312, 313):

> Eddie, fifteen, had been in trouble quite a bit, mostly for a variety of thefts. He was attached to a particular girl, but they kept their relationship hidden from their parents and their peers. Learning that she was seeing another boy, he took his rifle to her house, called her to her bedroom window and confronted her. When she confirmed his suspicions, he shot and killed her, saying, "If I can't have you, nobody else is going to."
>
> Manny, seventeen, had been arrested twice for auto theft and once for being drunk in public. One afternoon, when he and some friends were getting "stoned" on beer, marijuana and PCP ("crystal"), someone said that one of the group had informed the police of some drug sales and suggested that he be taught a lesson. Manny and two others forced the alleged informer into a car and drove to an irrigation canal, where one of the other boys held the informer under water until he drowned.

The following are some of the demographic and personal characteristics of the thirty-one juveniles that Sorrells (1977) found: twenty-nine were males (one of the two females was a prostitute who beat one of her clients and left him to die); about two thirds lived in an urban community; slightly more than half were black (which corresponded with the racial composition of the area studied); six had never been arrested before, six had records of one or two prior offenses, and nineteen had records of three or more (up to twenty-six) prior offenses; sixteen had committed other offenses involving injuries; none were considered psychiatrically disturbed or legally insane; twenty-one of the families of the juveniles were characterized by such terms as violent, argumentative, or unstable, while only seven were described as "apparently healthy."

Sorrells (1977) concluded that the romantic depiction of violence on television and in movies was a prime motivator of murder by juveniles. Moreover, he pointed out (1977:319), "One youngster who had stabbed a man to death commented that he didn't expect his victim to writhe and gasp while dying—people don't die like that on TV. Thus, popular television not only promotes violence as the preferred mode of resolving conflict but also distorts the viewer's appreciation of what violence is truly like." He thought that the path to control of extreme juvenile violence was the counterbalancing of the influence of the media by family models promoting compassion, integrity, and nonviolence.

In the cases depicted above, Manny had participated in a murder as a member of a gang involved in drug sales, whereas Eddie murdered as an individual in a jealous rage. The question of differences between gang and nongang homicides motivated the research of Maxson, Gordon, and Klein (1985). They analyzed the data on file on more than 700 gang and nongang homicides in the two major law enforcement agencies of Los Angeles County (the Los Angeles Sheriff's Department and the Los Angeles Police Department). Homicides were included in the analysis with at least one suspect in the age range ten to thirty, so that only a segment of the population were juvenile delinquents.

Maxson, Gordon, and Klein found considerable differences between gang and nongang homicides, particularly (1985:220) "with respect to ethnicity, age, number of participants, and relationship between the participants, properties closely related to the *group* nature of the events." They learned, contrary to the expectation of many, that in the case of slayings involving rival gangs it was common for participants on both sides of the clashes to have had no prior personal contact. More in accordance with general expectations, they found greater involvement of automobiles in gang killings, the primacy of intraethnic relationships, and a preponderance of males and minority-group members in gang murders. Finally, gang suspects, as well as their victims, were considerably younger than the nongang suspects and victims.

The Violent Young Offender and the "Serious" Young Offender

While every violent young offender is a serious young offender, it would seem important at the outset of this discussion to differentiate between the two because of varying perspectives in the literature. Generally speaking, all of the *UCR* Index crimes that kill, hurt, or threaten the physical well-being of other people, namely, murder/nonnegligent manslaughter, forcible rape, robbery, and aggravated assault, are regarded as violent offenses. And, of course, a juvenile who commits one of those offenses is a violent young offender.

The definition of serious young offenders is not so easily handled. On the one hand, Mann (1976), in his report on *Intervening with Convicted Serious Juvenile Offenders,* accepted a working definition of a serious young offender as a youth who has committed any of the four violent crimes of the *Uniform Crime Reports* (given in the preceding paragraph) or arson. For him, that is, except for the addition of arson to the serious category, a serious young offender is a violent young offender as defined by the *UCR* criteria. Zimring (1977) similarly equates serious offending with violent offending, but much less specifically than Mann. To Zimring (1977:17), the proper focus for work dealing with the serious juvenile offender encompasses "the particular forms of adolescent criminal activity that involve serious threats to life or a sense of physical security of victims and potential victims of violent crime."

On the other hand, Smith and Alexander (1980:6) specify three criteria of relevance in their definition of seriousness: "violence or injury to *persons,* property loss or damage, *chronicity* or repetition of offenses." In their work, Smith and Alexander determined seriousness of offense on the basis of the Sellin-Wolfgang Seriousness Scale and then factored in chronicity to define the serious juvenile offender. In their words (1980:11, 12):

> A serious juvenile *offense* includes the following offenses (or ones of at least equal severity) as measured by the Sellin-Wolfgang Seriousness Scale:
>
> • homicide or voluntary manslaughter
> • forcible sexual intercourse
> • aggravated assault
> • armed robbery
> • burglary of an occupied residence
> • larceny/theft of more than $1,000
> • auto theft without recovery of the vehicle
> • arson of an occupied building
> • kidnapping
> • extortion
> • illegal sale of dangerous drugs
>
> A serious juvenile *offender* is one whose offense history includes adjudication for *five* or more serious offenses (on the Sellin-Wolfgang scale), or one who is adjudicated for *one* or more offenses whose severity is equal to homicide or forcible sexual intercourse as measured by the Sellin-Wolfgang scale.

The Sellin-Wolfgang Seriousness scale was presented in 1964 by Thorsten Sellin and Marvin Wolfgang as a method for assigning numerical values reflecting the degree of seriousness of delinquent acts. The score assigned to a given act depends on certain of its components (such as extent of injury to a victim and amount of loss in a theft) and the presence of aggravating factors (use of a weapon or verbal intimidation). The number assigned for seriousness, or total score, is a sum of separate weightings for crime components and aggravating factors. Several components may enter into a given sum because of more than one victim having been injured in the crime or because both physical harm and property loss occurred.

Using statistics from *UCR* and from the National Crime Survey (a means of assessing criminal victimization — see Chapter 1), Strasburg (1984) demonstrated that serious juvenile crime turned upward in the late 1950s, then increased notably between 1960 and 1975, with the increase showing up largely in violent crimes. It seemed to remain at a steady state, or even to decline slightly, over subsequent years. Strasburg pointed to the great discrepancy between the steady or downward trend and the increasing fear of the public about serious young offenders (and the resulting often punitive social responses as described in Chapter 10).

The close relationship among serious offenses, violent offenses, and the repeat offender was highlighted by Wolfgang (1977:173) in his statement, "The chronic offender continues to be the most important category with which the criminal justice system should deal in its concern about serious, particularly personal injury offenses." That statement evolved from a substantial body of research motivated primarily by the finding of a study by Wolfgang, Figlio, and Sellin (1972) that the bulk of crime is committed by a relatively small group of offenders (see Chapter 1). Their study involved a cohort of males, born in 1945, who lived in Philadelphia between the ages of ten and eighteen. Of the total of 9,945 boys in the sample, 3,475 were delinquents but only 627 boys were responsible for over 50 per cent of all offenses committed. There was, in short, a small group of chronic offenders who accounted for most of the crime. In later work, Wolfgang (1977) traced a sample of 975 subjects from the original cohort (that is, 10 per cent of the cohort) into adulthood, including 567 who were interviewed on such variables as education, occupational history, and "hidden" (or self-reported) offenses. He found that the likelihood of being an adult offender is almost four times as great for a man who was a juvenile offender as it was for a man who was not. In addition, he learned that the chronic young violator was not likely to continue offending into adulthood, and, most importantly, that there was a continued high seriousness of offenses by adults who were frequent, serious offenders as youths. Wolfgang (1977:173) summarized the picture as follows: "Serious offenses are committed frequently by a relatively small number of offenders: up to age thirty in a birth cohort. . . . Serious offenses, officially known and self-reported, committed by juveniles, have a higher probability of being committed by these same persons as adults."

Further evidence of the relationships among chronic offense patterns, seriousness, and violence may be found in Tracy, Wolfgang, and Figlio (1985). That report, which compared a 1958 cohort with the original 1945 cohort in Philadelphia, pointed out that chronic delinquents in the 1958 group committed more serious and more violent crimes than the 1945 group. Other cohort studies that contain corroborating results have been reported by Hamparian et al. (1978), Strasburg (1978), and Farrington (1979).

To conclude this section dealing with the serious young offender, a few comments are necessary on the current controversy regarding the best mode of treating them. In 1979, Murray and Cox compared the effectiveness of treatment of serious offenders (as broadly defined to include offense seriousness, not necessarily only violent offenses, and the number of prior offenses) in a community-based program with treatment in correctional institutions. The community-based approaches ranged from nonresidential treatment to inpatient psychiatric counseling. The investigators introduced a novel method of measuring treatment results, called the "suppression effect," using a comparison of postintervention and preintervention delinquency. The reason given for the measure is as follows (Murray and Cox, 1979:32): "The question is not whether delinquency is in any sense cured, but whether things get better. The reference point is not zero, but the preintervention state" (see Chapter 13).

The findings of the research were at considerable variance with the general deinstitutionalization mood of the 1970s and with the general expectations of many, perhaps most, social scientists (see the discussion of deinstitutionalization in Massachusetts in Chapter 11). The suppression effect for the delinquents sent to institutions was greater than the effect for those treated in the community. That is, the community-based programs did not do as well as institutionalization in reducing postrelease arrests (about 17 per cent less well). The investigators explained the results on the basis of the deterrent effect of incarceration (1979:176): "We suggest that recidivism was reduced for the simplest reason of all: Society credibly changed the short-term payoffs of delinquency. Society did what was necessary to get delinquents' attention, and gave them some good reasons why they should not do those things any more."

Objections to the work and conclusions of Murray and Cox (1979) started appearing even before the research was formally published. For example, in 1978, Gordon et al. argued that there were methodological flaws and that the suppression effect could be explained by the operation of a statistical artifact (see also McCleary et al., 1979). More recently, Lundman (1986) used data from the Silverlake Experiment and the Provo Experiment to question Murray and Cox's finding that institutionalization suppresses delinquency more than community-based programs and their explanation that fear of punishment is the basis for the suppression.

A note of caution is in order at this point in regard to the hazards involved in assuming that all institutionalized youths or all those referred to state correctional agencies for institutionalization are serious offenders or that chronic offenders are necessarily serious offenders. Miller (1977) — the same Miller who was responsible for deinstitutionalization in Massachusetts as described in Chapter 11 — has warned that many youths are sent to correctional institutions or agencies by courts for administrative convenience rather than because they have been serious offenders or in any way dangerous. He emphasized (1977:57), "What is really meant here [youths locked in secure settings presumably because of the seriousness of their offense patterns] is not a 'dangerous' or 'violent' juvenile, but rather a juvenile who is a 'pain in the ass' to the court or agencies; one who repeatedly engages in minor delinquencies and does not stay where he/she is told."

Characteristics of Violent Offenders and Their Acts

Hamparian et al. (1978) studied 1,138 people who were both in the cohort years 1956–1960 and had been arrested before the age of eighteen for at least one violent offense as classified by the Columbus (Ohio) Police department. Before discussing their results, it is notable that these investigators reanalyzed certain data from the earlier cohort study of Wolfgang, Figlio, and Sellin (1972) and found that (1978:6) "chronic offenders accounted for 61.0 percent of the violent crime committed by the whole cohort."

Males outnumbered females in the cohort by a ratio of six to one, and blacks were overrepresented by a ratio of four times their proportion in the county population. Nearly a third of the cohort lived in census tracts that contained only 7.8 per cent of the county's population, and their homes for the most part had incomes below the county median.

The 1,138 members of their cohort committed 1,504 violent offenses over a twelve-year period. The nature of the offenses varied from murder to fist fights that came to the attention of the police and became matters of official record. Under one third of the offenses could be classified as serious crimes against the person. Nearly all cohort members committed far more property than violent offenses but did become specialists in certain types of crime, while about one third of the cohort were chronic offenders in that they were arrested for five or more offenses. These were mostly for nonviolent offenses; moreover, there was no pattern of progression to more and more serious offenses. Indeed, Hamparian et al. (1978:128) reported, "If there is a substantial number of youths who are repetitively committing violent acts, their delinquencies have not come to the attention of the police." Columbus, in short, did not contain an urban jungle as seems to be the case in the larger cities of this country.

Finally, the investigators traced the criminal histories into adulthood of the twenty-two individuals with the worst records. They found (1978:131):

> seven have had no adult arrests in Ohio. Six have been arrested on minor charges but have not been incarcerated. Six were bound over to an adult court as juveniles, found guilty, and are now serving sentences — or, in one case, a life sentence — in prison. Their offenses included 3 aggravated murders, 2 aggravated robberies, and 1 forcible rape. Finally, 3 have been arrested as adults and are serving sentences for burglary, motor theft, and possession of burglary tools respectively.

In 1978, Strasburg presented the findings of a year-long study of juvenile violence in which he interviewed specialists in delinquency and juveniles with histories of violent offenses, and analyzed over 500 juvenile court records in New York City. He defined a "violent crime" as (1978:8) "any act of homicide, forcible rape, assault, or robbery, or any attempt at one of these acts" — that is, the Index crimes against the person were his violent acts. But he defined a subgroup of these as "serious violent crimes" in the following way (1978:8): "acts of homicide; forcible rape; robbery in which a weapon is used or the victim is injured; and assaults in which more than a minor injury is inflicted (i.e., the victim is at least treated by a physician). Attempted homicide and rape are included. Attempted robbery is included if a weapon is used or the victim is injured. Attempted assault is not included."

In accordance with the results of Hamparian et al. (1978), Strasburg found only a small number of delinquents who were chronically violent, although he did note that recidivists were responsible for a large majority of violent crimes. Consistent, too, with previous results were his findings that juvenile violence is predominantly a phenomenon of boys and minority youths (particularly black). But an interesting and subsidiary finding was that female delinquents who were brought to court were just about as likely as male delinquents to be charged with a violent crime, although the females were charged with fewer serious violent crimes than the males.

Four other results are particularly noteworthy. First, there was a weak negative relationship between socioeconomic status and juvenile violence, but no difference in patterns of violence between youngsters who did and those who did not come from families on welfare. Second, there was no evidence of severe psychological or emotional disturbance in the vast majority of cases. Third, there was no evidence of a pattern in the crimes of recidivists. And fourth, the number of offenses that a delinquent committed was of little use in predicting the occurrence of a violent or seriously violent offense in future behavior.

More recently, Hartstone and Hansen (1984) described 114 juvenile offenders who had been adjudicated for violent crimes. Some of their findings were that official and self-reported data indicated that there was no crime specialization and that the type of crime varied for an individual from occurrence to occurrence. Similar results had been reported by Hamparian et al. (1978) and Strasburg (1978); as in the earlier studies, too, there was no evidence of progression from nonviolent to more serious offenses. Although gang involvement was not a significant factor, friends of the offenders apparently participated in a wide range of delinquent activities. Homes of the offenders were characterized by low socioeconomic status, intrafamilial violence, and a considerable amount of criminal activity on the part of other family members. There was a high rate of delinquency on the part of the offenders — they had an average of 10.5 petitions filed in juvenile court and were adjudicated an average of 5.7 times.

Drug Use by Juveniles _____

Use of Drugs and Serious Criminal Acts

The conventional wisdom is that the use of illicit drugs increases substantially the likelihood of serious delinquency, particularly violent delinquency. In support of that position, Hartstone and Hansen (1984), in their study of adjudicated violent offenders, found that about 50 per cent of the offenders reported that drugs (including alcohol) contributed substantially toward producing their violent behaviors. Moreover, about 40 per cent noted using drugs immediately prior to committing the offense for which they had been adjudicated. Similarly, Smith and Alexander (1980:31) make the following statement on the basis of a pattern of research results: "a substantial amount of serious juvenile crime stems directly from substance abuse during adolescence."

On the other hand, a startlingly opposite conclusion was reached by Johnston, O'Malley, and Eveland (1978) after their longitudinal investigation of drug use and delinquency among males. They employed a five-point index of drug use starting with (1) no use of illicit drugs and (2) use of marijuana only, to (5) more than experimental use of such drugs as amphetamines, barbiturates, and cocaine or any use of heroin. Delinquency was measured by a self-report scale divided into two indices, one based on items covering "theft and vandalism," and the second on items covering "interpersonal aggression." They did find strong positive relationships between drug use and level of delinquency, but the effect was considerably greater for theft and vandalism than it was for interpersonal aggression. But, and this was the basis for their surprising conclu-

A mural on the side of a public school in New York City by artist Keith Waring.

sion, while the seriousness of drug use was directly related to the seriousness of earlier delinquency, changes in drug use and delinquency were not related. For given patterns of initial drug use, youths who increased their usage over five years did not show increases in delinquency, and general decreases in delinquency of similar magnitude were rated over several years for all drug groups (1 to 5). Those and other observations led Johnston, O'Malley, and Eveland (1978:155, 156) to conclude:

> nonaddictive use of illicit drugs does not seem to play much of a role in leading users to become the more delinquent people we know them to be on the average. The reverse kind of causation seems considerably more plausible, that is, that delinquency leads to drug use. For example, we think it quite possible that delinquents who, because of their delinquency, became part of a deviant peer group are more likely to become drug users because drug use is likely to be an approved behavior in such a peer group. . . . Both delinquency and drug use are deviant behaviors, and therefore both are more likely to be adopted by individuals who are deviance prone.

Despite the indications that delinquency led to drug use rather than the other way around, because of the small number of addicts in their sample, the investigators could not conclude that drug use does *not* lead to crime. They stated (1978:155), "Although our data would tend to suggest that the kind of person who progresses through drug use to heroin is likely to display substantially more criminal behavior than average, even before drug use, it seems quite likely to us that many addicts increase their levels of crime to support their habits."

In accord with the conclusions of Johnston, O'Malley, and Eveland (1978) is the developmental model for involvement in drug use that was proposed by Kandel et al. (1976), using the results of cross-sectional research and supported by the longitudinal data of Kandel, Kessler, and Margulies (1978). According to the model, recourse to alcohol follows a pattern of minor delinquency and exposure to close friends and parents who drink. The use of marijuana follows participation in minor delinquency and adoption of a set of beliefs and values conducive to marijuana use that are held by peers but opposed to parental standards on many dimensions. Finally, the use of other illicit drugs follows (Kandel, Kessler, and Margulies, 1978) "poor relationships with parents, and exposure to parents and peers who use a variety of legal, medical, and illegal drugs, by psychological distress, and by personal characteristics somewhat more deviant than those of the novice marijuana or hard-liquor user."

But Why Do Youths Become Drug Users?

In the discussion above, we saw, first, that there were indications that the use of illicit, nonaddictive drugs follows delinquent behavior (Johnston, O'Malley, and Eveland, 1978), and, second, that there are certain social and personal patterns that precede the use of hard liquor which differ somewhat from those that precede the use of marijuana and which, finally, differ somewhat from those that precede the use of illicit drugs other than marijuana — although the patterns involve minor delinquent activities in all cases. That picture has taken on greater specificity in Kandel's discussion of "predicting drug initiation in adolescence" in her chapter in the *Annual Review of Sociology* (1980). She analyzed the predictive items in three categories: sociodemographic factors, interpersonal attributes, and intrapersonal influences of parents and peers.

Sociodemographic Factors. The results of several studies indicate that sociodemographic factors are not influential, either in absolute or in relative terms, in accounting for the process of initiation into drug use. For example, Kandel, Kessler, and Margulies (1978) used the reports of secondary students in New York State to assess the effects on drug use of such demographic variables as sex, race, religion, family income, and father's education. There was no significant effect for any of these variables on the use of hard liquor, marijuana, or illicit drugs other than marijuana.

Interpersonal Factors. According to Kandel (1980:269), the most consistent and reproducible finding in drug research is the strong relationship between an individual's drug behavior and the concurrent use of his friends, either as perceived by the adolescent or as reported by the friends. She writes, "On no other characteristic except age and sex is the similarity within adolescent friendship paired as high as it is for marijuana use." Moreover, the use of drugs by peers, either perceived or reported, and the assumed tolerance for drug use among peers are important and consistent predictors of youthful initiation into the use of alcohol and illicit drugs of all sorts. The close association between peer acceptance of drugs and individual drug use seems to be based on peer networks that are drug-specific rather than on general drug subcultures of the type described by Cloward and Ohlin (see Chapter 5).

The importance of peer influences in initiating drug use led Norem-Hebeisen and Hedin (1981) to recommend peer-group strategies in its prevention. One such strategy is the "peer participation program," which has been described, along with several other strategies, by Resnick and Gibbs (1981). In a program of that sort, the youths participate in all the responsibilities of a real-life endeavor that is usually restricted to adults — as, for example, assessing school problems in a formal survey or developing approaches to youth employment and career development. The active participation in the endeavor, the day-to-day responsibilities, and the decision-making powers, according to Resnick and Gibbs (1981), interrupt any tendency toward initiating drug use.

Several studies have shown the importance of parental characteristics in the initiation of drug use, including parental attitudes toward and use of drugs and the nature and quality of parent-child interactions. To illustrate, Jessor and Jessor (1978) found, in a study of high school students, that there was more marijuana use as parental approval of the behavior was greater and there was less marijuana use the more a student perceived his or her relationship with parents as supportive.

For both parents and peers, behaviors are more important in the initiation of adolescent drug use (as well as in changes of other kinds in drug use) than values and beliefs. Kandel, Kessler, and Margulies (1978:95) suggest, accordingly, that "adolescent socialization may take place more through a modeling effect than through social reinforcement."

Intrapersonal Factors. Although there is considerable evidence that youthful users of marijuana and alcohol show patterns of deviance beyond the use of the drugs, and sets of attitudes and values that reflect lessened conformity to social expectations, there have been conflicting results regarding the role of personality and other intrapsychic factors in initiating drug use. Some investigators have found such characteristics as psychological distress, depression, alienation, and low self-esteem to precede the use of drugs, according to Kandel (1980), while others have not found those results. However, many studies have consistently shown a pattern of decreasing grades, more school and class absences, and declining academic motivation among high school students prior to the use of marijuana and alcohol.

Prevalence and Trends in Drug Use

Prevalence Data. In 1986, Johnston, O'Malley, and Bachman reported on the prevalence and trends in the use of drugs by high school students nationally. Their data were based on yearly surveys from 1975 to 1985, using samples of seniors in public and private secondary schools throughout the forty-eight continental states. Measurement of drug use and other variables were mostly determined by staff of the research project during normal class periods by use of questionnaires.

Table 16.1 contains the prevalence rates of drug use at the time of the most recent survey (1985). The data are based on the responses of about 16,000 seniors.

About 61 per cent of the students reported using illicit drugs at some time in their lives, although about one third of them (or 21 per cent of the total sample)

TABLE 16.1   Prevalence (Per Cent Ever Used) and Recency of Use of Sixteen Types of Drugs (1985) [Approx. N = 16,000]

	Ever Used	Past Month	Past Year, Not Past Month	Not Past Year	Never Used
Marijuana/Hashish	54.2	25.7	14.9	13.6	45.8
Inhalants	15.4	2.2	3.5	9.7	84.6
Amyl & Butyl Nitrites	7.9	1.6	2.4	3.9	92.1
Hallucinogens	10.3	2.5	3.8	4.0	89.7
LSD	7.5	1.6	2.8	3.1	92.5
PCP	4.9	1.6	1.3	2.0	95.1
Cocaine	17.3	6.7	6.4	4.2	82.7
Heroin	1.2	0.3	0.3	0.6	98.8
Other opiates	10.2	2.3	3.6	4.3	89.8
Stimulants Adjusted	26.2	6.8	9.0	10.4	73.8
Sedatives	11.8	2.4	3.4	6.0	88.2
Barbiturates	9.2	2.0	2.6	4.6	90.8
Methaqualone	6.7	1.0	1.8	3.9	93.3
Tranquilizers	11.9	2.1	4.0	5.8	88.1
Alcohol	92.2	65.9	19.7	6.6	7.8
Cigarettes	68.8	30.1	(38.7)*		31.2

*The combined total for the two columns is shown because the question asked did not discriminate between the two answer categories.

Source: Johnston, O'Malley, and Bachman (1986:25)

used only marijuana. That means four of every ten students reported using an illicit drug other than marijuana at some time. In the table, it is clear that marijuana was used far more frequently than any other drug (54 per cent lifetime use) and that the stimulants (amphetamines) were second (26 per cent). The remaining more frequently used drugs were used on a lifetime basis in the following order: cocaine (17 per cent), inhalants (15 per cent), sedatives (12 per cent), tranquilizers (12 per cent), and hallucinogens (10 per cent). The drugs that are slightly indented in the table, it should be noted, are types of the general class immediately above that listed at the left margin — thus, LSD and PSP are types of hallucinogens.

About 5 per cent of the seniors reported using marijuana and alcohol on a daily basis. The percentage of daily use was about .04 per cent for cocaine, inhalants, and stimulants and about .03 per cent for hallucinogens, PCP, and nitrites. These latter figures may seem trivially small, but they take on more significance when one considers the dangers of several of the drugs and that .04 per cent or .03 per cent of the population to which these results may be generalized are shockingly large numbers.

Table 16.2 shows lifetime prevalence for certain subgroups. The listing "College Plans" refers to responses by the seniors to a question asking if they expect to complete four years of college. The male rate exceeds the female rate for every drug except stimulants, tranquilizers (where the two rates are equal), and

TABLE 16.2 Lifetime Prevalence (by Per Cent) of Use of Sixteen Types of Drugs by Subgroups, Class of 1985

	Marijuana	Inhalants	Amyl/Butyl Nitrites	Hallucinogens	LSD	PCP	Cocaine	Heroin	Other Opiates	Stimulants (adjusted)	Sedatives	Barbiturates	Methaqualone	Tranquilizers	Alcohol	Cigarettes
All Seniors	54.2	15.4	7.9	10.3	7.5	4.9	17.3	1.2	10.2	26.2	11.8	9.2	6.7	11.9	92.2	68.8
Sex:																
Male	56.6	18.5	11.1	12.4	9.4	6.6	19.7	1.4	11.3	24.6	12.3	9.9	7.1	11.7	92.6	67.4
Female	51.5	12.4	4.9	8.0	5.6	3.1	14.8	0.8	9.1	27.6	11.0	8.3	6.0	11.7	91.9	69.7
College Plans:																
None or under 4 yrs	59.1	16.5	9.2	12.5	9.7	6.8	20.2	1.6	11.5	31.9	15.2	11.9	8.7	13.4	93.0	75.9
Complete 4 yrs	50.2	14.5	6.9	8.0	5.6	3.4	14.6	0.9	9.3	22.6	9.6	7.4	5.3	10.8	91.9	63.7
Region:																
Northeast	62.2	18.3	10.0	15.7	9.4	7.3	25.9	1.6	12.0	27.6	13.4	10.5	7.9	14.0	95.0	71.4
North Central	53.8	14.6	7.5	10.2	8.5	3.1	11.5	1.2	10.4	27.7	12.0	9.6	6.8	11.5	93.5	71.6
South	44.5	13.0	6.0	5.8	4.8	3.4	11.1	1.2	7.2	22.1	11.1	8.0	6.7	11.1	89.7	65.1
West	60.4	17.0	9.2	10.9	8.2	7.1	25.4	0.8	12.7	29.1	10.9	9.1	4.9	11.2	90.6	67.4
Population Density:																
Large SMSA*	59.2	14.9	8.8	13.9	8.1	6.2	24.1	1.4	9.8	25.8	12.3	9.8	7.0	11.9	93.5	70.2
Other SMSA*	54.6	15.6	8.7	9.6	8.0	4.3	16.2	1.2	11.0	26.2	12.0	8.9	7.2	11.7	91.4	67.8
Non-SMSA*	49.3	15.6	6.1	8.2	6.4	4.5	13.1	1.0	9.5	26.8	11.2	9.3	5.6	12.1	92.0	68.9

*Standard Metropolitan Statistical Area

Source: Johnston, O'Malley, and Bachman (1986:32)

cigarettes. Another clear pattern occurs under "College Plans" where high school seniors planning to complete four years of college show lower rates for all drugs than seniors not so planning. The picture in the other categories is less clear, but it does seem that there are lower prevalence rates for illicit drug use in the North Central Region, the South, and in nonmetropolitan areas (non-SMSAs).

Table 16.3 shows the percentages of seniors who reported using marijuana and other illicit drugs during the preceding year. While the differences are not large, the use of drugs was higher for males than females, lower for those expecting to complete four years of college than for those who do not, highest in the Northeast and West and lowest in the South, and positively related to population density.

Trend Data. Turning now to trends in the use of drugs by youths, Table 16.4 shows percentages of marijuana and other illicit drugs over the period 1975 to 1985. The rows preceded by "Revised Version" are necessary because of changes in the questionnaire that were introduced in 1982. It appeared to the investigators that a sharp increase in reported uses of amphetamines in 1980 and 1981 resulted from the inappropriate inclusion in the responses for diet and stay-awake pills that were widely advertised during the era with names that made them sound like amphetamines. New questions introduced in 1982 differentiated between controlled substances and these noncontrolled, over-the-counter pills. Both questionnaire approaches were used in the samples of 1982 and 1983, and then only the revised form was used beginning in 1984.

TABLE 16.3 Annual Prevalence (by Per Cent) of Sixteen Types of Drugs by Subgroups, Class of 1985

	Marijuana Only	All Illicit Drugs Except Marijuana
Sex:		
Male	48	28
Female	44	26
College Plans:		
None or under 4 years	50	32
Complete 4 years	43	24
Region:		
Northeast	53	33
North Central	46	26
South	37	21
West	53	33
Population Density:		
Large SMSA*	50	30
Other SMSA*	47	27
Non-SMSA*	43	26

*Standard Metropolitan Statistical Area

Source: compiled from figures presented in Johnston, O'Malley, and Bachman (1986).

The data of Table 16.4 are shown in the more interpretable (at a glance) graphic form in Figures 16.1, 16.2, and 16.3. In terms of annual use (Table 16.4 and Figure 16.2) the use of marijuana increased steadily from 1975 to 1978, remained at the high plateau for two years, and then decreased steadily to 1984. There was a slight increase in 1985. The trend picture shown in thirty-day prevalence rates (Table 16.4 and Figure 16.3) is very similar to that one. Between 1976 and 1982 there was a gradual, but steady increase in percentages who used illicit drugs other than marijuana on an annual basis. According to Johnston, O'Malley, and Bachman (1986), most of the earlier use (between 1976 and 1979) was due to the increasing popularity of cocaine among high school students. However, the rise between 1979 and 1982 was in part due to the respondents including over-the-counter stimulants in their responses for those years.

If the stimulants are excluded from the calculations, as indicated by the small markings (◀) next to each year's bar in Figures 16.1 to 16.3, the picture is one of decreasing use of illicit drugs other than marijuana after an extended period of virtual level use.

Using the results discussed above as well as data obtained from other surveys, Johnston, O'Malley, and Bachman (1986:19, 20) summarize their findings as follows:

> over the past five years there has been an appreciable decline in the use of a number of the *illicit drugs* among seniors. . . . However, in 1985 there occurred a halt in these favorable trends . . . as well as an increase in active *cocaine* use. There also appears to be some increase in the use of *opiates other than heroin.* . . .
>
> While the overall picture has improved considerably in the past five years, the amount of illicit as well as licit drug use among America's younger age groups is still striking when one takes into account the following facts:
> [about 61% of high school seniors have tried an *illicit* drug, including about 40%] who have tried some *illicit drug other than* (usually in addition to) marijuana. . . .
>
> One in twenty high school seniors in 1985 smoked *marijuana daily.* . . .
>
> About one in twenty seniors drinks *alcohol daily,* and some 37% have had *five or more drinks in a row* at least once in the prior two weeks. . . .
>
> Some 30% of seniors have smoked *cigarettes* in the month prior to the survey and 20% are daily smokers. In addition, many of the light smokers will convert to heavy smoking after high school. . . .
>
> Clearly this nation's high school students . . . still show a level of involvement with illicit drugs which is greater than can be found in any other industrialized nation in the world. Even by historical standards in this country, these rates still remain extremely high.

Theoretical Issues in Drug Use by Youths

In 1980, Kandel pointed out that the earlier sociological theories that were specifically aimed at accounting for drug use, such as Cloward and Ohlin's anomie theory, were generally ignored. She explained that phenomenon as follows (1980:250): "In drug research, the neglect may . . . reflect the fact that earlier drug theories were developed to account for heroin addiction, the most deviant of the forms of drug use, while current studies deal with a range of patterns in the normal noninstitutionalized population, where heroin addiction

TABLE 16.4 Trends in Lifetime, Annual, and Thirty-Day Prevalence in an Index of Illicit Drug Use

	Class of 1975 (9400)	Class of 1976 (15400)	Class of 1977 (17100)	Class of 1978 (17800)	Class of 1979 (15500)	Class of 1980 (15900)	Class of 1981 (17500)	Class of 1982 (17700)	Class of 1983 (16300)	Class of 1984 (15900)	Class of 1985 (16000)	'84–'85 change
Approx. N =												
Percent reporting use in lifetime												
Marijuana Only	19.0	22.9	25.8	27.6	27.7	26.7	22.8	20.8	19.7	—	—	
Revised Version	—	—	—	—	—	—	—	23.3	22.5	21.3	20.9	−0.4
Any Illicit Drug Other Than Marijuana*	36.2	35.4	35.8	36.5	37.4	38.7	42.8	45.0	44.4	—	—	
Revised Version	—	—	—	—	—	—	—	41.1	40.4	40.3	39.7	−0.6
Total: Any Illicit Drug Use	55.2	58.3	61.6	64.1	65.1	65.4	65.6	65.8	64.1	—	—	
Revised Version	—	—	—	—	—	—	—	64.4	62.9	61.6	60.6	−1.0
Percent reporting use in last twelve months												
Marijuana Only	18.8	22.7	25.1	26.7	26.0	22.7	18.1	17.0	16.6	—	—	
Revised Version	—	—	—	—	—	—	—	19.3	19.0	17.8	18.9	+1.1

												Change
Any Illicit Drug Other Than Marijuana*	26.2	25.4	26.0	27.1	28.2	30.4	34.0	33.8	32.5	—	—	
Revised Version	—	—	—	—	—	—	—	30.1	28.4	28.0	27.4	−0.6
Total: Any Illicit Drug Use	45.0	48.1	51.1	53.8	54.2	53.1	52.1	50.8	49.1	—	—	
Revised Version	—	—	—	—	—	—	—	49.4	47.4	45.8	46.3	+0.5

Percent reporting use in last 30 days

												Change
Marijuana Only	15.3	20.3	22.4	23.8	22.2	18.8	15.2	14.3	14.0	—	—	
Revised Version	—	—	—	—	—	—	—	15.5	15.1	14.1	14.8	+0.7
Any Illicit Drug Other Than Marijuana*	15.4	13.9	15.2	15.1	16.8	18.4	21.7	19.2	18.4	—	—	
Revised Version	—	—	—	—	—	—	—	17.0	15.4	15.1	14.9	−0.2
Total: Any Illicit Drug Use	30.7	34.2	37.6	38.9	38.9	37.2	36.9	33.5	32.4	—	—	
Revised Version	—	—	—	—	—	—	—	32.5	30.5	29.2	29.7	+0.5

Note: Data based on original and revised amphetamine questions. Revised questions about stimulant use were introduced in 1982 to exclude more completely the inappropriate reporting of nonprescription stimulants.

*Use of "other illicit drugs" includes any use of hallucinogens, cocaine, and heroin, or any use of other opiates, stimulants, sedatives, or tranquilizers not under a doctor's orders.

Source: Johnston, O'Malley, and Bachman (1986:47)

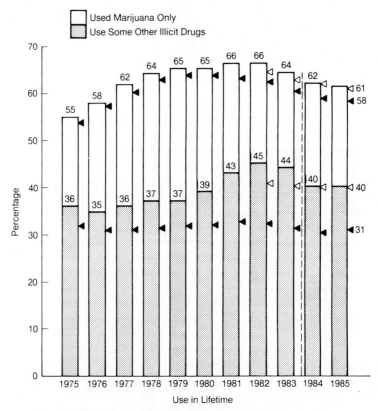

Figure 16.1 Trends in Lifetime Prevalence of an Illicit Drug Use Index (from Johnston, O'Malley, and Bachman, 1986:49)

Use of "some other illicit drugs" includes any use of hallucinogens, cocaine, and heroin, or any use which is not under a doctor's orders of other opiates, stimulants, sedatives, or tranquilizers.

◀ indicates the percentage which results if all stimulants are excluded from the definition of "illicit drugs." ◁ shows the percentage which results if only nonprescription stimulants are excluded.

The dashed vertical line indicates that after 1983 the shaded and open bars are defined by using the revised amphetamine questions.

is rare and where the interest is as much in normal development as in deviance per se." She presented four theoretical frameworks that more adequately reflected the knowledge, empirical and inferential, of the time: the theory of problem-behavior and deviance proneness, social learning theory, the theory of derogation as the antecedent of deviant behavior, and adolescent socialization theory.

The theory of problem-behavior and deviance proneness to explain drug use was developed by Jessor and Jessor (1977; 1978) out of a broader social-psychological theory initiated about ten years earlier. The theory postulates three domains: the personality system, the perceived environment system, and the behavior system. Characteristics of the personality and perceived environment systems and their interactions produce a state referred to as "problem-behavior proneness" that carries implications for a higher or lower probability of the occurrence of a problem behavior like drug use. The personality system can foster lower academic achievement and low self-esteem, and the perceived environment system can result in low parental support and high approval from friends for engaging in problem behavior, both increasing proneness to problem behavior.

There are two structures in the behavior system: a problem-behavior structure and a conventional-behavior structure. Groups of behaviors in each of these structures serve similar social-psychological functions in terms of the personality and environment systems and their interactions — for example, smoking marijuana and engaging in malicious property damage may serve to express repudiation of conventional norms.

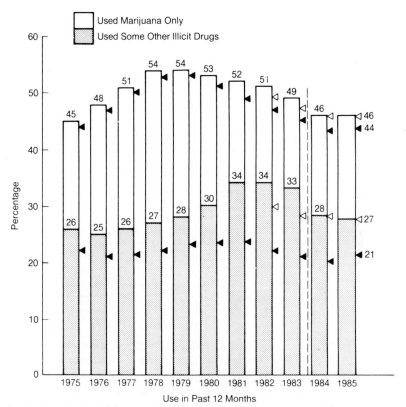

Use of "some other illicit drugs" includes any use of hallucinogens, cocaine, and heroin, or any use which is not under a doctor's orders of other opiates, stimulants, sedatives, or tranquilizers.

◀ indicates the percentage which results if all stimulants are excluded from the definition of "illicit drugs." ◁ shows the percentage which results if only non-prescription stimulants are excluded.

The dashed vertical line indicates that after 1983 the shaded and open bars are defined by using the revised amphetamine questions.

Figure 16.2 Trends in Annual Prevalence of an Illicit Drug Use Index (from Johnston, O'Malley, and Bachman, 1986:51)

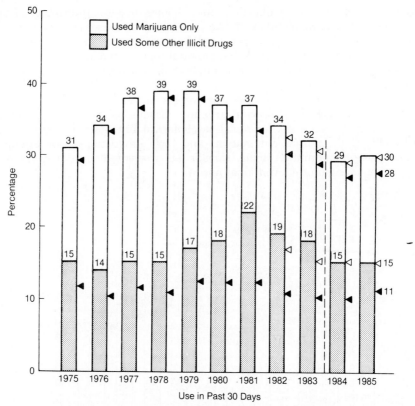

Use of "some other illicit drugs" includes any use of hallucinogens, cocaine, and heroin, or any use which is not under a doctor's orders of other opiates, stimulants, sedatives, or tranquilizers.

◀ indicates the percentage which results if all stimulants are excluded from the definition of "illicit drugs." ◁ shows the percentage which results if only non-prescription stimulants are excluded.

The dashed vertical line indicates that after 1983 the shaded and open bars are defined by using the revised amphetamine questions.

Figure 16.3 Trends in Thirty-Day Prevalence of an Illicit Drug Use Index (from Johnston, O'Malley, and Bachman, 1986:53).

Social learning theory, as presented by Akers (1977) and Akers et al. (1979), assumes that drug-using behavior, like all other behavior, is learned in interactions with significant groups of people by imitation, definitions of the behavior as good or bad, and the use of rewards and punishments for the drug use and alternative behaviors.

The theory of self-derogation as formulated by Kaplan (Kaplan, 1980; Kaplan, Martin, and Robbins, 1982) is based on the concept of a self-esteem motive. When a person encounters an experience in nondeviant membership groups of importance that is very ego-damaging, he or she may identify with a deviant subculture, such as drug-using peers, and participate in its activities in order to restore the damaged self-esteem. The restoration of self-esteem comes with the respect and approval generated in the deviant subculture. For example, failure in school may lead to a feeling of considerable self-derogation, which leads to the use of marijuana in the context of drug-using peers and a reduction in the negative self-image.

Finally, adolescent socialization theory amalgamates concepts from social learning theory and Hirschi's social control theory (see Chapter 6). The theory is described in Kandel, Kessler, and Margulies (1978) and Kandel (1980). According to the theory, drug use has a clear starting time and results from attempts to come to terms with social influences that are in conflict. The social influences of central importance are parents and peers. Since behaviors and values are determined by the sets of social relationships in which youths are involved, it becomes crucial to understand the entire network in order to understand the various processes of socialization.

In accordance with social learning theory, imitation and social learning are considered important processes that operate in the network. Adolescents are more likely to drink alcohol if their parents use hard liquor, and more likely to use marijuana if their peers use drugs. And adolescents are more likely to use drugs if that behavior meets with the approval of (is rewarded by) parents or peers who are important to them. In accordance with control theory, the quality of the bond between parents and adolescent may be effective in restraining him or her from using drugs.

In the process of recommending integration of these theoretical perspectives as a major research agenda, Kandel (1980:257) summed up the separate contributions as follows: "The Jessors provide a broad framework within which to organize the various levels of variables assumed to affect drug behavior; Kandel emphasizes the adolescent's social environment of peers and parents; Akers further specifies the mechanisms that explain how individuals are molded by environmental forces; and Kaplan stresses the influence of a central individual attribute, self-derogation."

Since that plea for integration, however, there has been more testing of separate theories than attempts at integrating them. The research of Akers and Cochran (1985), Dembo et al. (1986), and Marcos, Bahr, and Johnson (1986) provide excellent examples.

Akers and Cochran (1985) compared social learning theory, control theory, and anomie theory using survey data on adolescent drug use. Questionnaires obtained self-report information from students in grades 7 through 12 in three midwestern states. The degree of use of marijuana was measured by a six-point scale that had values from use every day or nearly every day to never used. The following are examples of variables used in the assessment of each theory: social learning—index of imitation, praise for not using marijuana, and reinforcement balance; control (social bonding)—maternal attachment, paternal attachment, value of education; anomie (strain)—educational aspirations, occupational aspirations, alienation.

According to the investigators, the research results provide unequivocal support for social learning. Their comments on the implications for the other two theories are as follows (1985:135):

> Social bonding theory also is supported by the findings, but only when the effects of social learning variables are not considered. When the bonding variables of belief, commitment, and attachment are placed in the same equation with social learning variables, their effects disappear while the social learning variables retain

their strength. Almost no support is found for anomie or strain theory as an explanation of adolescent marijuana use in this sample.

Dembo et al. (1986) compared control theory and social learning theory as explanatory forces for a group of junior high school students in New York City who were of either Puerto Rican or black heritage. Demographic and drug use information was obtained by questionnaire. The drugs surveyed were tobacco, alcohol, marijuana (including hashish), LSD and similar chemicals, depressants, narcotics, solvents, and stimulants. The analyses were confined to the first three of the drugs (tobacco, alcohol, marijuana) since under 6 per cent of the youths reported using any of the other drugs.

Critical comparison for the study involved the three variables: parental drug use, child drug use, and attachment to parents. Control theory, according to Dembo et al. (1986), leads one to expect that attachment to parents encourages conformity to general social values, including disapproval of the use of drugs by juveniles, and, therefore, that increasing attachment should lead to decreasing drug use regardless of the level of parental use of drugs. On the other hand, learning theory leads to the expectation that there is a negative relationship between attachment to parents and juvenile drug use when parents do not use drugs or use them at a low level, and that the relationship does not exist when parents use drugs at moderate or high levels. That expectation results primarily from the emphases on imitation and modeling in social learning theory. The results of the study were indeed in accordance with social learning theory — attachment to parents varied inversely with juvenile drug use when parental drug use was low or moderate, and there was no relationship between attachment and juvenile drug use when parental drug use was high.

Marcos, Bahr, and Johnson (1986), however, did find support for control theory when it was enhanced by such propositions from differential association theory as the one stipulating that behavior patterns are primarily derived from close personal associations. They found that the foremost influence on adolescent drug use was friendships with drug users. Second in importance in determining drug use was belief in conventional values. Parental and religious attachments, too, had effects on adolescent drug use, but the former operated indirectly in effecting that use.

Status Offenses

The term *status offense* in juvenile court law derives its meaning from the fact that the behaviors embraced within the category apply only to persons whose status within the society is that of a minor. Similar behavior on the part of adults is regarded as their own business; they are presumed to be old enough to suffer or to enjoy without state interference the consequences of what they choose to do so long as the behavior is not illegal. For them, with few exceptions, what is denoted as crime involves acts that hurt or deprive other people. For juvenile status offenders, the forbidden acts tend to be regarded as detrimental to the well-being of the juvenile, not other persons. (See Chapter 1.)

Juvenile status offenses have been separated into three types by Teitelbaum

A runaway youth is reunited with his mother at a police station.

(1983). First, there are behaviors that are proscribed because the person doing them is regarded under the age of discretion and in need of protection. This would include such things as use of tobacco. Then there are behaviors that are believed to be necessary for the proper upbringing of a young person and that person's training for assumption of a satisfactory social role. This group would include obedience to parents and guardians. Young persons who are brought to the attention of the authorities on the grounds of failure to adhere to parental discipline typically are labeled "incorrigible" or "unruly." Often, they will have attempted to escape from the home environment and will then come under the "runaway" heading. Finally, there are youngsters whose general adaptation is deemed unsatisfactory; they will be considered "wayward" or "growing up in idleness or crime."

There are, of course, no restrictions on persons over the age of eighteen using tobacco, regardless of the possible consequences for them and for those who depend upon them or upon whom they depend. Nor does, say, a twenty-seven-year-old woman or man need to heed the admonishments of her or his parents, regardless of how sound they might be or how disastrous their own course of conduct might seem to be. Equally well, any person can live as idly and parasitically as he or she chooses, if the person can figure out a way to manage it. Nor will the law interfere if a college student chooses to be habitually truant from his or her classes.

Disobedience to parents, one of the conditions that gives rise to a juvenile status offense, has been of serious social concern throughout the history of Western civilization. In Roman times, fathers exercised what, at least in precept, were totally dictatorial powers over their children. The Old Testament, Deuteronomy 21:18–21, leaves no question about how serious filial disobedience was considered in the religious community:

> If a man's son is stubborn and rebellious against the voice of his father and of his mother, refusing to listen to and to obey them when they discipline him, then his father and mother must lay hold of him and bring him to the gate of his city, to the elders of his town, and they shall say to the elders of his city, "This our son is stubborn and rebellious; he refuses to listen to us; he is a spendthrift and a drunkard." Then all the men of the city shall stone him to death. Thus you shall exterminate evil from you.

As discussed in Chapter 2, a similar rule was included in the statute book of colonial Massachusetts, though there is no record of its draconian penalty ever being invoked. Juvenile court laws, following tradition, incorporated the same kind of provisions, indiscriminately bracketing them with specific forms of crime, such as robbery and burglary, that were committed by juveniles. It is notable, as Teitelbaum (1983) points out, that little attention is paid to the nature of the dictates of parents that led to the "rebelliousness" of offspring: the disobedience might relate to serious kinds of infractions or it could involve petty disputes over use of cosmetics, curfew, friends and cleaning up one's room. Often nothing is said about whether the commands are reasonable or whether they represent arbitrary and tyrannical impositions on the child.

Not until the 1950s and 1960s was there any serious challenge to the concept of status offenders. The assumption was that the juvenile court was benign, always seeking the best interest of the young person before it, even if that young person didn't understand its concern or see the justice of its judgment. There also was an unchallenged belief that the behaviors classified as status offenses were strong signs of predelinquent behavior, that is, that they were satisfactory indicators of the likelihood that the young persons were well on their way to involvement in criminal behavior. It took some years for it to be appreciated that there might be, as Rubin (1960:514) noted, "situations . . . in which the child beyond control is sound and healthy, and the lack of control is due to attempt at excessive control, or to some ignorance or neurotic need on the part of the parent that the child may naturally resist."

Particular impetus for change was supplied by acceptance of labeling theory, which insisted that negative definitions of a youngster tended to reinforce wayward behavior, and that the most promising treatment was the most benevolent treatment. Such viewpoints underlay the Juvenile Justice and Delinquency Prevention Act of 1974, which made continued federal funding of state and local juvenile justice programs contingent upon the removal of juvenile status offenders from secure placements. Instead, they were to be dealt with in nonsecure institutions and treated within community-based programs. The response of the states to this mandate has been uneven, an issue discussed at considerable length in Chapter 11. A number of states also allow status offenders to be placed with delinquents in secure facilities if it is ruled that they are unamenable to treatment programs established for status offenders.

The act was opposed by many parents, police officers, probation officers, and juvenile court judges. This opposition led to various amendments, including permitting confinement of status offenders for up to twenty-four hours before and after adjudication and for incarceration for violations of valid court orders. Despite these concessions, a study (Costello and Worthington, 1981) found that several states had evolved a variety of other tactics to circumvent the spirit of the act. Courts will, for instance, use the power to declare a juvenile in contempt to change a status offender into a delinquent. In some states, as well, status offenders are being committed to secure mental health facilities. It also was found that status offenders were being declared delinquent by judges though the facts of the case supported only an allegation of a status offense. Finally, the investigators report that in some states semisecure facilities had been developed to hold status offenders.

The use of the contempt power by judges to deal with truants in ways other than those set forth by status offender laws is illustrated in a case recently brought before the appellate court in northern California (Hager, 1987). Michael G., a fifteen-year-old from Fresno, refused to go to school. A juvenile court judge ordered him to undergo counseling, perform work in a community service program, and "attend school regularly and not be tardy or absent." Michael, in the face of the order, continued to stay away from school. The judge cited him for contempt and ordered him to be confined for forty-eight hours — over the weekend — in Juvenile Hall, a secure facility forbidden by law for use with status offenders. The weekend period was chosen, the judge noted wryly, because "I certainly wouldn't want to place the court in the position of depriving the minor of the opportunity to attend school."

The order was suspended while the case was being appealed. Michael's attorneys argued that the use of the contempt power was a sham tactic for circumventing the intent of the legislature. The appellate judges, in their questions, appeared to agree with their lower court colleague. Said one, "If a judge sitting in juvenile court can't make an order stick, that's just wonderful for the kid's development, growth, and image of the law." They seemed to side with the prosecutor, who argued, "There comes a point where you have someone who's simply incorrigible. He did thumb his nose at the court. At that point, what's left?"

The dialogue between the court and the attorneys for both sides indicates in a capsule manner the fundamental issues in regard to status offenders: the intense desire to do something to have them behave in what is regarded as a satisfactory way and the unwillingness to allow the use of heavy-handed tactics in response to what is defined as rather mild deviation, deviation that seems to harm nobody very much except the violator.

Critics bewail these developments and continue to argue that the juvenile court should not be allowed to exercise any control over status offenders. They insist that status offense behavior, such as parental disobedience and truancy, is not precriminal. They believe that it is at worst immoral, and that it is "transitional deviance through which youths pass without further difficulty" (Teitelbaum, 1983:988). A longitudinal study of 2,003 juveniles appearing before the Wayne County Juvenile Court in Detroit provided some evidence in general support of this position. Felonies had been committed by 57.5 per cent of the sample and misdemeanors by 8.4 per cent, while 34.1 per cent was charged with status offenses. Overall, 42.8 per cent of the sample appeared before the court at least one additional time. The status offenders' problems, however, appeared to become less serious over time, while those of youths charged with a felony increased slightly in seriousness. The author reports that the status offenders' continuing behavior threatened society considerably less than the behavior by persons in the other groups. Less than half of the status offenders' subsequent offenses were criminal, whereas nine of ten of the repeat offenses for the felony and misdemeanor groups were for additional felonies and misdemeanors. The author interprets the findings as support either for less authoritative intervention with status offenders or for removing them entirely from the jurisdiction of the juvenile court (Kelley, 1983). Similarly, Rankin and Wells (1985), examining the results of self-reported delinquency in a national panel survey, indicate that patterns of juvenile misbehavior are more likely to be stable or constant over time than to increase in seriousness.

On the other side, most officials are persuaded that there are young persons in early difficulty who, if identified, can be helped and kept from more serious trouble. They are unwilling to abandon totally the interest of the state in what they regard as a benevolent mission. A particularly interesting attempt to retain the principle of intervention but to alter its focus is Iowa's Family in Need of Assistance law. It replaces the status offender category with a new provision, involving both parents and young persons, that allows the court to order both to participate in treatment programs.

Model Codes

Juvenile justice has been blessed by the attention of a number of sophisticated study groups that have sought to formulate what they regarded as "model codes." Such codes represent the distillation of the wisdom of their compilers, who survey existing practices throughout the nation, examine the empirical and theoretical writings on the issues, and then feed in their own expertise. The result typically is a proposed set of laws, accompanied by a review of the general subject they address and a comprehensive rationale for the approach endorsed.

In recent years, three major model juvenile justice codes have been promulgated. The standards issued by the Institute for Judicial Administration in collaboration with the American Bar Association (the IJA/ABA standards) are generally regarded as the most influential set. The IJA/ABA project was begun in 1971 and resulted, over the course of the next nine years, in the publication of twenty-three volumes dealing with different aspects of the system of juvenile justice.

The second set of standards is the work of the National Advisory Committee on Juvenile Justice and Delinquency Prevention and is usually referred to as the Task Force standards. The Task Force was established in 1974 and was made up of twenty-one persons appointed by the president to serve for four-year terms. It was required that one third of the Task Force members be under the age of twenty-six at the time of their appointment. The Task Force issued its standards in 1980.

The National Advisory Committee on Criminal Justice and Goals (or NAC), the third standard-setting group, was formed by the federal Law Enforcement

Assistance Administration in 1975 to prepare reports in areas such as organized crime and juvenile justice and delinquency prevention. The work of the subgroup of NAC dealing with juveniles was published in 1976.

What is noteworthy for our purposes is the fact that the three groups showed little disagreement in regard to virtually all of their recommendations — except for those concerning status offenses. The report of the Massachusetts Juvenile Code and Revision Project has aptly summarized the results of the work of the three standard-setting groups in the following terms:

> There is a surprising degree of conformity between the standards, which can be attributed in part to the "incestuous" character of their development (there is a significant degree of overlap in the personnel involved in the standards), in part to their relatively simultaneous creation, and in part to the leading influence of the IJA/ABA standards, from which the other two standards appear to have borrowed liberally. This conformity has resulted in very substantial areas of philosophical agreement, a number of areas of relatively technical disagreement, and one area of substantial philosophical disagreement. The area of substantial philosophical disagreement involves the question of the propriety of making noncriminal misbehavior (or "status offenses") cognizable in the juvenile court. (Schwartz, 1985:ii)

The essence of the disagreement on status offenses is that the IJA/ABA standards take the position that such offenses should not be subject to the jurisdiction of the juvenile courts. The other two groups — the NAC and the Task Force — maintain that status offenses should come under juvenile court jurisdiction.

The IJA/ABA report supports its view that noncriminal misbehavior should be excluded from family and juvenile court jurisdiction by arguing that these courts have been ineffective in dealing with noncriminal misbehavior and that other institutions, such as schools, would be more appropriate for handling them. The IJA/ABA standards also take the position that when a misbehaving juvenile is treated in the same coercive manner as a delinquent this makes the entire system seem unfair in the eyes of the misbehaving juvenile.

On the other side, the NAC denotes four types of behavior that it believes should remain under court scrutiny: (1) repeated unauthorized absences from school; (2) repeated unauthorized absences from home for more than twenty-four hours; (3) repeated disregard for or misuse of lawful parental authority; and (4) acts of delinquency committed by youths under the age of ten years. The Task Force endorses each of the four conditions set out by NAC and adds another: (5) repeated use of intoxicating beverages by juveniles. The NAC report notes that its recommendation was hotly contested within the committee itself but that it was concluded that until available services for misbehaving juveniles were more numerous and effective, it would be unwarranted to withdraw juvenile court jurisdiction. For both committees, "misuse of parental authority" — one of the behaviors proscribed — would allow the courts to invoke jurisdiction over the parents as well as their offspring. The courts also could be able to involve public agencies, such as the welfare system, in plans to handle misbehaving youths, all as part of an approach labeled "Families with Service Needs."

State Definitions of Status Offenders

Despite contrary recommendations of the prestigious IJA/ABA standard-setting group, a review of the laws in some of the larger jurisdictions (Schwartz, 1986) shows that many states, such as Florida, blur the distinction between noncriminally misbehaving and neglected children. The Florida code has a category called "dependent child," which it defines as including the following: (1) children abandoned, abused, or neglected by their parents or other custodians; (2) children placed with an agency for purposes of adoption; (3) children who are persistent runaways, who are habitually truant from school, and who habitually refuse to obey the reasonable and lawful commands of their parents or legal custodians; and (4) children of parents who have voluntarily placed them with a licensed agency, and whose parents have failed to comply with the requirements of a "performance agreement."

In a different approach, New Jersey law establishes the label of a "juvenile-family crisis" for status offenses. This category embraces the behavior, conduct, or condition of a juvenile, parent, or guardian, or other family member that presents or results in (1) a serious threat to the well-being and physical safety of a juvenile; (2) a serious conflict between a parent or guardian and a juvenile regarding rules of conduct, which has been manifested by either (a) repeated disregard of lawful parental authority by a juvenile or (b) repeated misuse of lawful parental authority by a parent or guardian; (3) unauthorized absences by a juvenile for more than twenty-four hours from his home; and (4) a pattern of repeated unauthorized absences by a juvenile from school.

An illustration of the more traditional juvenile court approach to status offenses — and to juveniles in general — can be found in the Ohio law, which defines an "unruly child" as one (1) who does not subject himself to the reasonable control of parents, teachers, guardians, or custodians by reason of being wayward or habitually disobedient; (2) who is a habitual truant from home or school; (3) who so deports himself as to injure or endanger the health or morals of himself or others; (4) who attempts to enter the marriage relationship in any state without the consent of his parents, custodian, legal guardian, or other legal authority; (5) who is found in a disreputable place, visits or patronizes a place prohibited by law, or associates with vagrant, vicious, immoral, criminal or notorious persons; (6) who engages in an occupation prohibited by law, or is in a situation dangerous to life or limb or injurious to the health or morals of himself or others; and (7) who has violated a law applicable only to a child. (See Chapter 1.)

A Case Study: Illinois

In Illinois, status offenders fall into a category called Minors Otherwise in Need of Supervision (MINS). The treatment of persons so classified was carefully studied by the Chicago Law Enforcement Study Group, a coalition of twenty-three Chicago community, social, and legal organizations, which engages in empirical research and the development of strategies and public education on criminal and juvenile justice issues. Members of the group spent hours in court observing the way MINS cases were handled and interviewed the major participants in these proceedings. The study group, among other things, deplored the confrontational nature of proceedings which involved parents and their children, noting:

> Because of the parent-versus-child format, participants in the MINS proceedings display emotional extremes more often than participants in other court proceedings. MINS Court one moment is filled with crying and screaming accusations and denials between parent and child and the next moment with no visible signs of emotion. Some days the parents and youths seem like robots in slow motion. Whatever the emotional level, the minor apparently stands alone—a sharp contrast to the delinquency or adult criminal courtrooms, where the defendant's family often gathers around him, regardless of his alleged offense, not necessarily condoning his actions but lending him emotional support and sympathy in his conflict with the powerful State. (Linn et al., 1979:42)

The observers also found (Linn et al., 1979:45) that the official response to status offenders appeared to vary "according to the intensity of parental outrage and the subjective views of morality held by the police officers who charge a youth and the judges who dispose of the case." They report cases being heard in which youngsters were in court ostensibly because "he only plays baseball all day," "she hangs out with bad kids," "she yells at her mother," and "he disobeys the rules of the house by refusing to take the clothes to the cleaners." Judges seemed to courtroom observers to be "resigned to being unable to ameliorate the problems presented to them." They are, Linn et al. (1979:129) say, "left with dispensing platitudes, not justice." Among its forty remedial recommendations, the study group suggested that persons involved in MINS proceedings should be informed of their rights and should have an attorney appointed to press their viewpoint in court. It was also stressed that MINS youths should not be reclassified as delinquents solely to permit them to be detained.

Summary

Violence

Using the data in the *Uniform Crime Reports* (*UCR*) for Index crimes against the person (murder, manslaughter, forcible rape, robbery, aggravated assault), it is clear that youths between ten and seventeen commit violent offenses at a rate considerably above their proportion in the population (and much further above the rate that one might expect if one factored in the presumed innocence of youth). While homicides by youths occur at a lower rate than the other violent offenses of the *UCR*, they are not insignificant in number. Many such homicides are committed as part of gang activities, but many others are individual matters that may be motivated by such reactions as rage and jealousy. Gang homicide is preponderantly an activity of male minority-group members and involves younger youths than in nongang homicides.

While a "violent" young offender is clearly a "serious" young offender, some definitions of the latter include as specifying criteria major property crimes and the repetitiveness of criminal activity. In order to evaluate the degree of serious-

ness of a given crime, an approach like the Sellin-Wolfgang Seriousness Scale
may be used.

The important work by Wolfgang, Figlio, and Sellin (1972) showed that
serious crimes, particularly of the violent type, were mostly committed by a
relatively small group of delinquents referred to as "chronic offenders." Later
research indicated, moreover, that the pattern continued into adulthood. Since
the menace persists, a critical question is: What should society do about correcting serious offending patterns? Research by Murray and Cox (1979) seemed
to indicate that putting the responsible youngsters in secure correctional institutions may not be a bad idea after all, but the position (and the supporting
research) remains controversial.

Research directed at the violent youngster has produced the first outlines of a
picture. First, the youngster who committed a violent crime is most likely a
male minority-group member who lives in a low socioeconomic area. Second,
young offenders are not specialists in that there are variations in type of crime
from occurrence to occurrence. Third, there is no pattern of progression from
nonviolent offenses to more and more seriously violent ones. Fourth, contrary
to many depictions on television and in movies, violent young offenders in
general do not seem to be psychotic or otherwise psychologically disturbed,
although they may come from homes where there is a good deal of internal
strife. And fifth, certain criminal tendencies of peers seem to encourage violent
behavior even when there is no gang involvement.

Drug Use

It is widely believed that violent and other serious juvenile crime stems
substantially from the use of illicit drugs. But the results of several studies
indicate that the belief is not in fact accurate, at least for drug use that does not
involve addiction. And even more interestingly, those results raise the opposite
possibility that drug use results from an earlier pattern of delinquency.

If one groups the factors that initiate drug use into sociodemographic, interpersonal, and intrapersonal categories, one finds that the interpersonal factors
predominate. Indeed, the most consistent finding in drug research is that of a
strong relationship between an individual's drug behavior and the use of drugs
by close friends. Important, too, in initiating drug use are such parental characteristics as attitudes toward drugs, personal use of drugs, and degree of support
for children.

Survey results indicated that about 61 per cent of high school seniors have
used illicit drugs at some time in their lives. Marijuana was the drug mostly
used, followed by the amphetamines. Moreover, about 5 per cent used alcohol or
marijuana daily. Those seniors who reported expectations to complete four
years of college used every type of drug at a lower rate than seniors who did not
report such expectations.

Although the use of illicit drugs by high school students showed a general
pattern of increase between 1975 and 1980, there was a consistent decrease
between 1980 and 1984 — but a halt in the decline occurred in 1985. Despite the
overall decline, almost 50 per cent of the seniors in 1985 reported using some
illicit drug annually.

The principal theories used to explain youthful drug phenomena are sociological, psychological, or balanced between psychological and sociological constructs. Derogation theory is primarily psychological; social control theory and anomie theory are primarily sociological; and problem-behavior proneness theory, learning theory, and adolescent socialization theory have a balanced array of psychological and sociological constructs.

Status Offenses

The issue of status offenses cuts to the heart of an important aspect of juvenile court philosophy. Little dispute focuses around the question of whether the state ought to be legally permitted to take some action against young persons who violate laws that also bear upon the behavior of adults. A fifteen-year-old who murders an innocent person, a seventeen-year-old who mugs a stranger on a city street, a sixteen-year-old who burglarizes a house — all presumably ought to suffer the consequences of their violation of the law. The essence of the philosophy of the juvenile court approach is that these young persons deserve a special kind of handling on the grounds that their inexperience and their potential make them especially likely to benefit from proper kinds of treatment. In recent years, it has been charged that this benevolent philosophy has allowed juveniles to be deprived of basic rights that belong to all citizens. But there is no strong opposition to the position that juveniles who commit criminal acts should be treated by the justice system.

The matter becomes considerably more complicated when it turns to status offenses and offenders. If the treatment afforded by the state is benign and helpful, it is argued, then why not employ it with those who show signs of being on their way to more serious trouble? Why not keep under court jurisdiction those runaways, truants, and disobedient children whom parents and authorities complain about? Why wait until they cause real difficulty, both for themselves and for others?

Arguments for a hands-off position, on the other hand, take a number of forms. There are those who challenge the view that the treatment afforded status offenders is either benign or helpful, though this accusation, if correct, is remediable; presumably, interventions *can* be helpful; all of us have been helped at some time by something that somebody did with us. It is argued, however, that the symbolic nature of being involved with the juvenile justice system carries a detrimental connotation; it pins a label of "bad" on a young person. Intervention, persons of this persuasion say, either ought to be avoided until the person has done something that would be illegal for an adult as well or ought, at best, to be carried out by agencies that do not carry the negative image of any kind of court system.

That the IJA/ABA standards recommending abolition of the current approach to status offenses have not found their way into more than a few juvenile court statutes indicates an uneasiness with abdicating judicial responsibility for young persons who manifest difficulties in adjusting to the demands of the larger social system. Part of the failure to enact IJA/ABA recommendations clearly can be explained in financial terms: nobody wants to assume the costs of handling status offenses if the courts abandon their role. Part is inertia: it is difficult to give up a system that has been in place so long. And a large part is uncertainty: many status offenders seem in real need of help or control, and authorities are fearful that if they lose any of the arsenal of tactics that they now can employ to deal with such persons significant difficulties might ensue. Undoubtedly, status offenses will disappear from juvenile court law only when other ways of handling what are seen as the personal and community problems associated with status offenders become widely available.

References

Akers, Ronald L. 1977. *Deviant Behavior: Social Learning Approach.* 2nd ed. Belmont, Calif.: Wadsworth.

———, and Cochran, John K. 1985. Adolescent Marijuana Use: A Test of Three Theories of Deviant Behavior. *Deviant Behavior* 6:323–346.

———, Krohn, Marvin D., Lanza-Kaduce, Lonn, and Radosevich, Marcia. 1979. Social Learning and Deviant Behavior: A Specific Test of a General Theory. *American Sociological Review* 44:635–655.

Arthur, Lindsay G. 1977. Status Offenders Need a Court of Last Resort. *Boston University Law Review* 57:631–644.

Costello, Jan C., and Worthington, Nancy L. 1981. Incarcerating Status Offenders — Attempts to Circumvent the Juvenile Justice and Delinquency Prevention Act. *Harvard Civil Rights Civil Liberties Law Review* 16:41–81.

Dembo, Richard, Grandon, Gary, La Voie, Lawrence, Schmeidler, James, and Burgos, William. 1986. Parents and Drugs Revisited: Some Further Evidence in Support of Social Learning Theory. *Criminology* 24:85–104.

Farrington, David P. 1979. Longitudinal Research on Crime and Delinquency. In *Crime and Justice: An Annual Review of Research,* vol. 1, edited by Norval Morris and Michael Tonry, 289–348. Chicago: Univ. of Chicago Press.

Gordon, Andrew C., McDowell, David, Maltz, Michael E., and McCleary, Richard. 1978. Evaluating a Delinquency Intervention Program: A Comment. *Criminal Justice Newsletter* 9:16.

Hager, Philip. 1987. Truants in Jail: Court's Ability to Enforce Contempt Rulings Debated. *Los Angeles Times* (July 14), 1–21.

Hamparian, Donna M., Schuster, Richard, Dinitz, Simon, and Conrad, John P. 1978. *The Violent Few: A Study of Dangerous Juvenile Offenders.* Lexington, Mass.: D. C. Heath, Lexington Books.

Hartstone, Eliot, and Hansen, Karen V. 1984. The Violent Juvenile Offender: An Empirical Portrait. In *Violent Juvenile Offenders: An Anthology,* edited by Robert A. Mathias, Paul DeMuro, and Richard S. Allinson, 83–112. San Francisco: National Council on Crime and Delinquency.

Jessor, Richard, and Jessor, Shirley L. 1977. *Problem Behavior and Psychosocial Development: A Longitudinal Study of Youth.* New York: Academic Press.

———. 1978. Theory Testing in Longitudinal Research on Marihuana Use. In *Longitudinal Research on Drug Use: Empirical Findings and Methodological Issues,* edited by Denise B. Kandel, 41–71. Washington, D.C.: Hemisphere Publishing.

Johnston, Lloyd D., O'Malley, Patrick M., and Bachman, Jerald C. 1986. *Drug Use Among American High School Students, College Students, and Other Young Adults: National Trends Through 1985.* Washington, D.C.: U.S. Government Printing Office.

Johnston, Lloyd D., O'Malley, Patrick M., and Eveland, Leslie K. 1978. Drugs and Delinquency: A Search for Causal Connections. In *Longitudinal Research on Drug Use: Empirical Findings and Methodological Issues,* edited by Denise B. Kandel, 137–156. Washington, D.C.: Hemisphere Publishing.

Kandel, Denise B. 1980. Drug and Drinking Behavior Among Youth. *Annual Review of Sociology* 6:235–285.

———, Kessler, Ronald C., and Margulies, Rebecca Z. 1978. *Longitudinal Research on Drug Use: Empirical Findings and Methodological Issues.* Washington, D.C.: Hemisphere Publishing.

———, Treiman, Donald, Faust, Richard, and Single, Eric. 1976. Adolescent Involvement in Legal and Illegal Drug Use: A Multiple Classification Analysis. *Social Forces* 55:438–458.

Kaplan, Howard B. 1980. *Deviant Behavior in Defense of Self.* New York: Academic Press.

———, Martin, Steven S., and Robbins, Cynthia. 1982. Application of a General Theory of Deviant Behavior: Self-derogation and Adolescent Drug Use. *Journal of Health and Social Behavior* 25:270–289.

Kelley, Thomas M. 1983. Status Offenders Can Be Different — A Comparative Study of Delinquent Careers. *Crime & Delinquency* 29:365–380.

Linn, Janice, Zalent, Kim, Geller, William A., and Meyer, Harris. 1979. *Minors in Need: A Study of Status Offenders at the Juvenile Court of Cook County.* Chicago: Chicago Law Enforcement Study Group.

Logan, Charles H., and Rausch, Sharla P. 1985. Why Deinstitutionalizing Status Offenders Is Pointless. *Crime & Delinquency* 31:501–517.

Lundman, Richard J. 1986. *Beyond Probation:* Assessing the Generalizability of the Delinquency Suppression Effect Measures Reported by Murray and Cox. *Crime & Delinquency* 32:134–147.

McCleary, Richard, Gordon, Andrew C., McDowall, David, and Maltz, Michael D. 1979. How a Regression Artifact Can Make Any Delinquency Intervention Program Look Effective. In *Evaluation Studies Review Annual,* vol. 4, edited by Lee Sechrest and Associates, 135–161. Beverly Hills, Calif.: Sage.

Mann, Dale. 1976. *Intervening with Convicted Serious Juvenile Offenders.* R-1930-DOJ. Santa Monica, Calif.: Rand Corporation.

Marcos, Anastasios C., Bahr, Stephen J., Johnson, Richard E. 1986. Test of a Bond/Association Theory of Adolescent Drug Use. *Social Forces* 65:135–161.

Maxson, Cheryl L., Gordon, Margaret A., and Klein, Malcolm W. 1985. Differences Between Gang and Nongang Homicides. *Criminology* 23:201–216.

Miller, Jerome B. 1977. Systems of Control and the Serious Juvenile Offender. *The Serious Juvenile Offender,* Proceedings of a National Symposium, September 19 and 20, 1977, Minneapolis, Minnesota. Washington, D.C.: Office of Juvenile Justice and Delinquency Prevention, U.S. Department of Justice.

Murray, Charles A., and Cox, Louis A., Jr. 1979. *Beyond Probation: Juvenile Corrections and the Chronic Delinquent.* Beverly Hills, Calif.: Sage.

Norem-Hebeisen, Ardyth, and Hedin, Diane P. 1981. Influences on Adolescent Problem Behavior: Causes, Connections, and Contents. In *Adolescent Peer Pressure: Theory, Correlates, and Program Implications for Drug Abuse Prevention.* Washington, D.C.: U.S. Government Printing Office.

Rankin, Joseph H., and Wells, L. Edward. 1985. From Status to Delinquent Offenses — Escalation? *Journal of Criminal Justice* 13:171–180.

Resnick, Henry S., and Gibbs, Jeanne. 1981. Types of Peer Program Approaches. In *Adolescent Peer Pressure: Theory, Correlates, and Program Implications for Drug Abuse Prevention.* Washington, D.C.: U.S. Government Printing Office.

Rubin, Sol I. 1960. Legal Definition of Offenses by Children and Youth. *University of Illinois Law Forum,* 1960:512–523.

Schwartz, Lawrence D. 1985. *Comparative Analysis of Model Standards on Juvenile Justice.* Boston: Juvenile Code Study and Revision Project.

———. 1986. *Comparative Analysis of the Juvenile Codes of Ten States.* Boston: Juvenile Code Study and Revision Project.

Sellin, Thorsten, and Wolfgang, Marvin E. 1964. *The Measurement of Delinquency.* New York: John Wiley.

Smith, Charles P., and Alexander, Paul S. 1980. *A National Assessment of Serious Juvenile Crime and the Juvenile Justice System: The Need for a Rational Response,* vol. I. Reports of the National Juvenile Justice Assessment Centers. Washington, D.C.: U.S. Government Printing Office.

Sorrells, James M. 1977. Kids Who Kill. *Crime & Delinquency* 23:312–330.

Stiller, Stuart, and Elder, Carol. 1974. PINS: A Concept in Need of Supervision. *American Criminal Law Review* 12:33–60.

Strasburg, Paul A. 1978. *Violent Delinquents.* New York: Monarch, Sovereign Books.

———. 1984. Recent National Trends in Serious Juvenile Crime. In *Violent Juvenile Offenders: An Anthology,* edited by Robert A. Mathias, Paul DeMuro, and Richard S. Allinson, San Francisco: National Council on Crime and Delinquency.

Teitelbaum, Lee E. 1983. Juvenile Status Offenders. In *Encyclopedia of Crime and Justice,* vol. 3, edited by Sanford H. Kadish, 983–991. New York: Free Press.

Tracy, Paul E., Wolfgang, Marvin E., and Figlio, Robert M. 1985. *Delinquency in Two Birth Cohorts.* Washington, D.C.: Office of Juvenile Justice and Delinquency Prevention, U.S. Department of Justice.

Wolfgang, Marvin E. 1977. From Boy to Man—From Delinquency to Crime. In *The Serious Juvenile Offender.* Proceedings of a National Symposium Held in Minneapolis, Minnesota on September 19 and 20, 1977. Washington, D.C.: Office of Juvenile Justice and Delinquency Prevention, U.S. Department of Justice.

———, Figlio, Robert M., and Sellin, Thorsten. 1972. *Delinquency in a Birth Cohort.* Chicago: Univ. of Chicago Press.

Zimring, Franklin E. 1977. The Serious Juvenile Offender: Notes on an Unknown Quantity. In *The Serious Juvenile Offender.* Proceedings of a National Symposium Held in Minneapolis, Minnesota on September 19 and 20, 1977. Washington, D.C.: Office of Juvenile Justice and Delinquency Prevention, U.S. Department of Justice.

CHAPTER 17

Future Directions

Courtesy British Tourist Agency

There have been dramatic changes during the past century in the manner in which juvenile misbehavior and lawbreaking are viewed and the way that they are handled. The inauguration of the juvenile court in Illinois almost ninety years ago represents a landmark in both social and legal policy. Juveniles formally were declared distinctive from adults in terms of how they were to be regarded by the criminal law. They were defined as eminently redeemable from youthful incursions into lawlessness. Other youthful tendencies defined as wayward, such as truancy and running away from home, also were placed into the precincts of the juvenile court. An elaborate and distinctive system of law enforcement, court processes, and treatment modalities sprang into existence. It is noteworthy that these developments, almost entirely home-grown in the United States, soon would be duplicated throughout a large part of the civilized world.

Since that time, there have been periods of disenchantment with the dream that inspired the development of specialized treatment for juveniles. Some have maintained that it was no more than a camouflage for self-interested persons determined to impose their own rigid moral principles upon those from a lower class. Others find the blueprint particularly appealing but believe that it failed to be realized in the manner anticipated, perhaps because youngsters got tougher as life in the cities and suburbs became more impersonal, acquisition and self-aggrandizement more pronounced, and respect for authority less prominent. Finally, some critics of the revolution in juvenile justice have found that, though preeeminently benevolent, the movement failed to take account of human frailties and neglected to provide youngsters with the panoply of constitutional safeguards guaranteed to adults. This viewpoint, which found favor to a considerable extent in a series of Supreme Court decisions that began about two decades ago, has itself generated criticism: there are those who believe juveniles are too well insulated, so that decent attempts to help them are thwarted by detrimental and hostile court proceedings.

Scholars investigating these social and legal developments have produced a variety of theoretical explanations of the causes of juvenile delinquency. These explanations have unquestionably become increasingly sophisticated during the past decades, particularly as the ideas are subjected to rigorous empirical testing. Other lines of scholarly work have focused on enunciating and, in particular, on testing different ways of dealing with juveniles, attempting to measure their efficacy as well as other kinds of consequences for the juvenile, those near to him or her, the juvenile justice system, and the society in general.

The present chapter sets forth some ideas about the problems and the likely directions that will prove important in the future of the study of juvenile delinquency. The first section considers possible theoretical insights, noting, among other things, the likely development of biochemical theories, the need for longitudinal research, and the importance of cross-cultural research. The following section concentrates on public attitudes toward racial differences and the views of adults about youths in forming the patterns of juvenile justice. In both of these areas, it appears, Americans hold ambivalent views, and it is not easy to discern which, if either, will dominate. Finally, the chapter examines law-based methods of responding to delinquency that appear to be gaining prominence, with particular attention to preventive detention, capital punishment, and restitution.

The Future of Theory

What turns are theories of delinquency likely to take in the next several decades? Forecasting is always a precarious enterprise, in large part because some things can happen that nobody, unless he or she has supernatural prescience, is likely to be able to anticipate. And these occurrences may have a profound impact on the manner in which we come to view things. A deep financial depression turns people's minds toward economic interpretations of human events and behavior; a war produces feelings of togetherness and patriotism as well as terrible fears of death and destruction. Theories of delinquency may well be responsive to such overall concerns.

Similarly, developments in scholarly work other than that dealing with delinquency can have an important impact on how we regard juvenile misbehavior. Remember, for instance, the role that Darwinian thought played in the formulations by Lombroso, who portrayed criminals as persons who had not come sufficiently far along the trail of human development, atavistic throwbacks to earlier hominoid forms. And recall, too, how the idea of young people, as a separable category of human beings, emerged only in recent centuries, whereas before such time, illegal acts by adolescents were regarded as only another form of crime. We could return to such a situation — history portrays innumerable cyclical patterns — or we could come to regard children as even more precious and worthy of particular attention.

The Chinese policy that restricts families to only one child ought to provide an interesting lesson in how government demographic policy, seen as essential for general well-being, bears upon other aspects of social life, including delinquency. Will a nation of only children become a nation of spoiled, self-indulgent, and delinquent brats? Or will the only child become so precious that he or she will receive extraordinary care and love and become a member of a nation of persons with high self-esteem and contentedness? Even if we ultimately can discern sharp changes in patterns of delinquency that seem to occur as a result of the strikingly radical Chinese population policy, can a theory be fashioned that will accurately capture general characteristics of the genesis of delinquency, or will (as is more likely) the formulation be applicable only to the specific geographical site?

Nuclear Threats, AIDS, and Demography

Those among us with morbid mindsets might well argue that trying to read the future is a pointless task because, without adequate control of nuclear power, there is not apt to be any future in the long term, that someone, somewhere, is going to detonate a bomb so destructive that human life will cease on this planet. Wits with a wry twist of mind might respond that such a situation would cure the problem of delinquency and eliminate the need for theories to explain it. But those wits might only be employing humor in a way that is common, to deflect attention from deep concerns which are so overwhelming that they cannot adequately be dealt with in direct fashion. Nonetheless, theories of the future may come to depend on the constant uncertainty of human existence at any given moment as an important element in the explanation of delinquency, especially self-indulgent, live-for-the-instant misbehavior. In wartime, certainly, there almost invariably is a great loosening of the normal rules, when "tomorrow we may die" becomes the prevailing way of looking at things.

It is not unlikely that spread of AIDS, for instance, could have a deep effect on family life-styles, reducing the rate of sexual intercourse among unmarried persons and keeping more families intact, with a concomitant impact upon the control of delinquency, especially status offenses involving young women arrested for promiscuous sex patterns. But if an inoculation against AIDS is discovered, these situations are much less apt to develop and their effect on delinquency will prove insignificant.

The U.S. Census Bureau indicates that by the year 2000, only slightly more than a decade from now, the world's population will reach 6.2 billion persons. This is an increase of 27 per cent over the 1985 figure. Countries such as Mexico will grow as much as 42 per cent. Similarly, the number of persons sixty-five years and older in the world will increase by 46 per cent (U.S. Bureau of the Census, 1986). These demographic conditions undoubtedly will have an important effect on the profile of juvenile delinquency and, very likely, upon explanations of delinquency as well.

Futurists—persons who professionally try to divine from what is now happening, examined against what has gone before, in order to predict what is likely to come—talk of such things as underwater prisons, where lawbreakers will be kept in escape-proof confinement, and imagine a coterie of scientific developments that will make some forms of delinquency—things such as auto theft and burglary—very difficult, if not impossible. But few persons doubt that there will be young deviants, persons who do not adjust to the demands of the larger society for conforming behavior, and who injure others and deprive them of things. What explanatory schemes, then, are likely to gain ascendance in trying to account for the behavior of such youngsters?

Biochemistry and Delinquency

It seems reasonable that biological explanations of extreme forms of human behavior, particularly those concerned with the functioning of the brain, will become more significant. This work ought to be able to determine, with more accuracy than it has to date, why certain persons are more excitable, less affected by socialization processes, less able to incorporate social learning, and, perhaps, even why they are less sensitive than their peers to the hurt they inflict upon others. It is likely that the most useful theoretical developments will come in regard to the realm of acts of violence, with an ever-expanding range of pharmaceutics becoming available to tone down behavior that is deemed unacceptable and potentially dangerous. It should be stressed, however, that the emphasis in these results will likely apply to the more extreme and outrageous forms of behavior.

The human brain, a three-and-a-half-pound lump of gray tissue with more than 100 billion nerve cells, or neurons, is sometimes said to be the last great unexplored "frontier" of the universe. The field of neuroscience, which brings together persons with backgrounds in physiology, anatomy, neurobiology, biochemistry, and computer science, has been developed only within the past two decades. We now know from various studies that brain chemicals are released in minute quantities by one neuron to mediate its communication with other neurons. The release of these chemical neurotransmitters is said to be the essence of brain function. Recently, Jon Franklin (1987), a Pulitzer Prize–winning science writer, has insisted that since the brain subserves all human thought and behavior, and since the brain functions by means of chemical neurotransmission, it is in this area that we will find the cure for certain forms of juvenile delinquency. Franklin (1987:114) maintains that "every human thought, hope, passion, yearning, and insight results from chemical interactions between [brain] transmitters and receptors." New technology, Franklin believes, will affect our family lives, as well as the educational, political, and criminal justice systems.

In the past decade, for instance, devices have been developed for the dynamic imaging of brain function in human beings. Franklin (1987) believes that such imaging, through the use of positron emission tomography or nuclear magnetic resonance, could be useful for diagnosing accused delinquents or adult criminals who plead insanity. Other persons (Jacobs, 1987) doubt that techniques with such an application will be possible in the near future.

Social Science Theories

The biochemical realm aside, theoretical developments focusing on the social configurations associated with juvenile delinquency seem, at this time, less likely to involve dramatic changes or breakthroughs. Undoubtedly, there will be further refinements of Hirschi's control theory and, eventually, a thoroughgoing revision of its postulates, particularly in terms of a more definite weighting of the importance of particular forms of control upon particular kinds of individuals. A promising avenue of research likely to be taken would be to formulate a control theory that could be tested upon adults to find out the kinds of attachments and commitments, and other forms of association, that bear upon their lawbreaking.

In addition, longitudinal studies seem likely to provide better information on the way in which youngsters move into delinquency, continue the behavior, or desist. Such longitudinal studies ought to begin at birth and carry on for at least thirty years. To conduct them would take the career-long dedication of a cadre of social and biological scientists, plus the availability of a vast amount of financial support. But it hardly seems arguable that such a comprehensive research investigation, properly done, would be worth infinitely more than the innumerable makeshift and short-term inquiries carried out with lesser funds, studies often done for no more pressing reason than to publish an article or two. Allowing scholars to put together their own research agendas has an enormous amount of appeal: they will often develop projects that no bureaucratic agency would conceive or otherwise support. But highly sophisticated, enormously complicated team research, triggered by the obvious need for such work, and adequately funded, is necessary if we are going to derive the information that will lead to better theoretical statements. The development of nuclear energy, based on a driving wartime need, and based on work that brought together virtually every skilled scientist in the allied world in cooperative effort, offers a blueprint for the kind of research work that could be undertaken in the field of juvenile delinquency to move its theoretical underpinnings significantly forward.

Whither Critical Theory?

The future of critical and Marxist theoretical work in the field of juvenile delinquency seems particulary uncertain. It is not unlikely that some linkage may be forged between the more traditional explanations of illegal behavior and the Marxist insight that takes into account the distribution of power in capitalistic states as well as in socialist and communist regimes. No nation has approached what could reasonably be called "a dictatorship of the proleteriat" (that is, rule by the working class), and considerable evidence suggests that when some persons from the working class seize power during and after a revolution their subsequent behavior, in many regards, is little different from that of any other totalitarian rulers, particularly in terms of attempts to suppress the opposition and to retain power. All social systems seem to develop some pattern of stratification, with some segments enjoying a good deal more of what there is to savor than others. It would require extraordinary powers of persuasion — or legerdemain — to endlessly persuade the have-nots that they have nothing to complain about, especially in today's world where they have ample opportunity to learn a good deal about their own and other social systems. If juvenile delinquency springs to a great extent from feelings of alienation and dispossession, perhaps some distillation of elements of both critical and traditional theory will be able to capture the essential ingredients of that process.

On Theoretical Prescience

It is obvious that there exists no certain formula for predicting the precise direction that the turn of theory about juvenile delinquency will take. At this very moment, some person, acting independently or as part of a research group, may be working out a set of postulations that will, when they are published, come to be regarded as particularly promising ideas about the understanding of juvenile delinquency. That theory might concentrate primarily on the delinquent event, seeking to establish regularities in the immediate circumstances that trigger lawbreaking. It could focus on attempting to determine what was different in seemingly similar situations that led at one time to uneventful action and at another to lawbreaking. That is, on Tuesday a youngster might walk past a jewelry store on a dark evening, glance indifferently at its window, and continue onward. Four days later, passing the same store, the same youngster stops, picks up a rock, breaks the window, scoops up some of its contents, and races away. What produced the different responses on the different days? Certainly none of the existing theories accounts for this kind of precise event; at best, they might explain why this particular youngster rather than another one ultimately stole the jewelry.

Theoretical promise for such an approach presumably would lie in recording with some precision as many facts as possible about the daily lives of a large number of young persons, some of whom will end up committing acts of delinquency, others of whom might not. This could include information about how they feel when they awaken each day, what they eat, which people they meet and what is said to them and what they say, and how they feel about the interaction, the weather, as well as what ideas or thoughts or fears or expectations occupy their minds. Regularities might be detected after scrupulous examination of such a mass of material. It might be found, for instance, that significantly more acts of delinquency occur within a day or so of an especially unnerving event. Or, perhaps, delinquency might prove to happen significantly more often when a person is bored — or has been bored for three or four days — in contrast to when the person is preoccupied or even is involved in anxiety-arousing experiences.

The ever-increasing ability of computers to store and to array massive amounts of information would prove extremely valuable for a theorist seeking to establish and support a theory focused directly on conditions immediately related to delinquent acts.

Configurational Analysis

Closely related to the foregoing theoretical focus would be another approach that could play an important role in future theoretical work regarding delinquency. This approach, which might be called configurational analysis, would seek to locate similarities in certain delinquent acts and then try to pinpoint a constellation of circumstances that play into the lawbreaking behavior.

The high incidence of car theft by juveniles in the United States, for example, could be said to be closely tied to a number of basic conditions. The very high rate of car ownership in the country, the common importance of a car as a status symbol (particularly for adolescents), the widespread knowledge of driving and elementary mechanics among American youth, the encouragement of tinkering with motors and gadgets as a feature of American mores, the availability of cars in downtown areas, the carelessness in safeguarding automobiles, and broad insurance coverage — plus, of course, many other things — feed into the large number of car thefts in America. Such a configurational explanation, of course, sidesteps attempts to locate more general theoretical patterns, but it does focus on attributes of types of delinquency that might be shown empirically to correlate with changes in rates of the behavior.

The fact that different models of cars are stolen in different ratios in the United States offers a clue to the genesis of the behavior — as well as its complexity and the difficulty of formulating theoretical principles that will provide understanding and predictive relatability. Recently, for instance, the National Highway Traffic Safety Administration concluded that the cars most likely to be stolen are those having high dollar value and great demand either as complete vehicles or for their parts. The administration did not, however, differentiate between cars stolen by juveniles and those taken by adults, who often are members of organized gangs that steal to order for customers. The car most likely to be stolen in 1985 was the Buick Riviera, a top-of-the-line specialty sedan. It had a theft rate for the year of just over 16 cars per 1,000 vehicles manufactured. Least likely to be stolen were the Renault Fuego, various Volvo models, and such General Motors mid-size cars as the Pontiac Phoenix, Chevrolet Cavalier, and Oldsmobile Firenza. An exception to the rule that expensive cars are particularly likely to be stolen was the Rolls-Royce. There were no reports of stolen Rolls-Royces for more than two years, presumably because the cars are readily identifiable and carefully protected.

Cross-Cultural Research

It has long been thought that empirical and theoretical work in regard to juvenile delinquency would gain considerable sophistication as scholars throughout the world began to coordinate their investigations. Several conditions had to emerge before this became a possibility. Jet travel became commonplace only in the early 1960s — hardly three decades ago — and the mass movement of persons from continent to continent is a very recent phenomenon. In addition, for first-class research to be carried out, there has to be a fair amount of understanding of the subtleties of different cultures and the nuances of their languages. Americans, who dominate the study of juvenile delinquency, tend to be very poor linguists — rarely bothering to learn other languages well, if at all — but the Anglicization of the world, with foreigners learning to speak English, has enhanced the cross-fertilization of ideas and theories about delinquency. Further, many foreign students are beginning to undertake graduate training in criminal justice and the behavioral sciences in the United States (in previous times, Germany and the United Kingdom tended to attract them). In America, they are indoctrinated with theoretical notions that they can try to apply at home and can refine in terms of conditions that prevail in their cultures.

Such work is only just beginning to bear some theoretical fruit, primarily in demonstrating that what seems true on the basis of work in the United States often does not stand up well when it is transported beyond the boundaries of America. Religion, for instance, is an extraordinarily powerful force in Islamic cultures, and to omit it in theoretical frameworks, as we often do in the United States, is to ignore a highly significant factor elsewhere. Similarly, education has very different meaning and impact as we move around the world from one nation to another. For Americans, the experience of Japan seems to offer particularly compelling theoretical challenges. Typically, scholars in the United States regard factors such as a high rate of urbanization, crowding, and industrialization as powerful correlates of delinquency. But all of these conditions prevail to a very high degree in Japan, yet that country demonstrates one of the lowest delinquency rates in the world (Ames, 1981).

Little systematic cross-cultural work has yet been undertaken to try to explore the international concomitants of delinquent activity, but such work undoubtedly represents one of the particularly important founts from which the theories of the future will be derived. Cross-cultural research is extremely complicated, but it offers the best opportunity to determine whether factors that are said to be influential in a particular nation in eliciting delinquency are of equivalent importance in a different milieu. Difficulties that must be overcome include language variations (Precourt, 1979). Some cultures attend with specific words aspects of social existence that others ignore. Rosch (1975:177), for instance, points out that "the human visual system can discriminate some 7,500,000 different colors, but the most color names reported in any language are 4,000 English names of which only 8 are used very commonly." Some societies, for instance, typically distinguish by use of specific words between grandparents: in Sweden, a child will refer to his father's mother as *farmor,* his mother's mother as *mormor.* In English, on the other hand, we merely talk of our "grandmother," with no real linguistic attempt to differentiate between the women in question. Perhaps this is because grandparents are not of particular importance in our society; perhaps failure to denominate them with exact terms reduced their importance. Some societies, of course, have what for us are almost unbelievably complicated discriminations to demark blood and other personal relationships. Whether such arrangements are related to family life and whether different kinds of family life, in different countries, have a bearing on delinquency, is the kind of matter that theories of the future may begin to address. It seems fair to observe today that juvenile delinquency theory has made magnificent strides in terms of its sophistication from the state it was in, say, before World War II, less than a human lifetime ago. At the moment, though, there is a considerable range of competing theoretical viewpoints. It is arguable whether any one of them will, with refinement, emerge as the dominant paradigm or whether the theory of the future will take off in a new direction.

The Future of Public Attitudes

Public attitudes toward delinquency and delinquents, at this writing, present powerful contradictions, and, to the extent that public attitudes are connected with broader concerns in American culture, these contradictions are not likely to be resolved in the near future. On the one hand, as we noted in Chapters 8 and 10, it is not difficult to find ways in which American approaches to delinquents are becoming more legalistic, indicative of a tendency to "recriminalize" delinquency, that is, to treat delinquency less as a social problem and more as criminal activity. On the other, there is also evidence that the image of the delinquent as a heroic rebel against a false, uncaring society (see Chapter 2) remains important in American thinking. These tendencies to condemn and to celebrate the delinquent exist together in American culture. But despite their apparently contradictory character, each has such deep cultural roots that neither is likely fully to overwhelm the other.

The significance of the view of juvenile delinquents as criminals is shown not only by movements toward recriminalization (as discussed in Chapter 10) in the juvenile justice system but also by the evidence of popular culture. Beginning in the mid-1980s, American popular magazines have run — in a manner reminiscent of the popular focus on delinquency in the 1950s (see Chapter 2) — an increasing number of stories dealing with the problem of criminal behavior on the part of young people. But although this revival of interest in delinquency may be similar on the surface to the decade of the 1950s, the stories published more recently have differed from earlier ones in that, rather than discussing problems of "youth rebellion," they have raised grave concerns about the growth of serious crime among young people. Thus, in late 1985, *Newsweek* ran a lengthy account of "Kids Who Kill" (1985). A year later, the same magazine published a similar discussion, reporting FBI statistics that "1,311 kids under 18 were arrested for murder nationwide last year" (Children Who

Kill, 1986:93), representing only a leveling off of what had been a steady increase in juvenile homicides over the preceding eight years. About one month later, *Time* presented its own account, "Kid Killers."

The general tone of such articles has been to stress both the troubling frequency of brutal crimes on the part of teenagers and the difficulty of accounting for the violent behavior. An article in the *Ladies' Home Journal* captured the prevailing mood in the role it gave to the comments of a University of California, Berkeley, scholar (Coplon, 1985:165): "The 'meanness quotient' is going up. . . . These kids are more vicious, nastier, and more pernicious." The *Journal*'s writer even reported that the authorities "reminisce about the 'good delinquent' of the fifties blackboard jungle who stuck to petty larceny and breaking and entering" (Coplon, 1985:166). Such stories have focused attention on the most frightening and most obviously criminal behavior among those labeled "delinquents" and, indeed, have almost inevitably included discussions of the need to recriminalize our conceptions of delinquency and our society's response to it. As the *Newsweek* article on "Children Who Kill" asked, "Should they be treated and punished as adults?" (1986:93).

The 1986 *Newsweek* article offered rather strong evidence that many people felt the answer to its question should be "yes." For one thing, as the article indicated, most states do permit transfer to adult courts of juveniles charged with murder and other serious crimes (see Chapter 10). In addition, the article reported a Justice Department recommendation that youths under fourteen convicted of homicide be held for at least seven years in a juvenile facility, with all those over fifteen receiving treatment as adults. The article also raised the issue of capital punishment for teenage killers, noting that twenty-six states permit the execution of juveniles.

The issue of capital punishment for juvenile delinquents became, in fact, a key criminal justice issue in the mid-1980s (see Chapter 7 and below) and, indeed, serves as an important clue to American attitudes toward delinquents. The issue came to the fore when, in September 1985, a fifteen-year-old Arkansas boy was sentenced to death by injection for the murder of two elderly women and their great-grandnephew *(Los Angeles Times,* September 21, 1985). Although the sentence was eventually reversed, the case attracted nationwide attention. The interest and concern raised by the case was heightened because, less than a week earlier, the attorney general of the United States had declared that states are justified in executing young people who, when below the age of eighteen, commit capital crimes *(Los Angeles Times,* September 17, 1985).

It is difficult to gauge how widely the attorney general's views are shared by Americans, but there is certainly evidence to indicate some support. A 1986 poll of its readers by one popular magazine is revealing. To the question, "Do you approve of capital punishment for capital crimes committed by a person under eighteen?", 70 per cent of respondents answered "yes," with such comments as, "If they're old enough to commit the crime, then they're old enough to suffer the consequences. I believe a lot of minors who commit crimes do so because they know they can 'get away with murder'" (This Is What You Thought, 1986:23). It is probably to the point to note that, responding to the question, "Do you believe rehabilitation can be effective for minors convicted of murder?", over half, 54 per cent, said no—one respondent asking, rhetorically, "How could anyone rehabilitate a murderer?" (This Is What You Thought, 1986:23). The results of this readers' poll were supported by another survey in which 65 per cent of respondents agreed that "teens who commit murder should get the death penalty" (Death Penalty for Teens, 1987:86). It is interesting that the latter poll was conducted by *Seventeen,* a magazine intended for teenage readers. Although such polls are far from systematic, and, thus, one can draw only limited conclusions from them, they may be said to indicate the widespread presence of rather hard attitudes toward delinquents on the part of a great many Americans.

Still, there remains other evidence of contrary trends in American thinking. No less than in the 1950s, American popular culture today uses delinquency as an expression of resistance to an indifferent or hostile adult-controlled world. We have already noted the "Brat Pack" movies (Chapter 2), which often include delinquent or near delinquent characters intended to evoke our sympathy or our delight. In a comedy such as *Ferris Bueller's Day Off* (1986), much of the main character's appeal comes from his disregard for the institutions and laws of society. His antics include truancy, car theft, and the destruction of property. Such a seminal film as *The Breakfast Club* features a delinquent figure whose resistance to society we are to sympathize with, even admire. Along these lines, one may note the popularity of a group like the Beastie Boys, whose record and video "You Gotta Fight for Your Right to Party" connote delinquency.

This is not to say, in the manner of Wertham (see Chapter 8), that there is much in American popular culture that lures young people into a life of crime. It is to say that the image of the delinquent as one who understandably, even bravely, resists the constraints of American society continues to capture the American imagination. Thus, evidence of sympathetic as well as hardened

The Breakfast Club depicts resistance to society as understandable, even admirable.

attitudes may be found among the public. And this is not to mention the extent
to which scholarly investigation tends to view the delinquent as a victim of
social forces beyond his or her control.

Again, these contrary views of delinquency are deeply embedded in American
society. If it is possible to say that each appears to have practical support — the
hard view from the genuine brutality of some juvenile crime, the more sympathetic from the real social and psychological victimization many delinquents
have suffered — it is also possible to say that each view receives strong reinforcement from attitudes and ideas that are, in themselves, quite independent of
delinquency.

Among the more important of these ideas and attitudes are those having to do
with race, particularly among white Americans. We have already discussed, in
Chapter 1 and elsewhere, studies that have seemed to link or that have sought
to explore links between race and delinquency, but we must here note the very
strong ties between race and criminality — including race and delinquency — at
the level of popular thought. Two episodes from late 1986 help to make the
nature of those ties clear. One was the controversy that erupted when Harry
Lee, sheriff of Jefferson Parish, near New Orleans, Louisiana, announced that
he had ordered his deputies to stop blacks seen in white neighborhoods in the
parish. "If there are some young blacks driving a car late at night in a predominantly white area," he said, "they will be stopped" *(New York Times,* December
23, 1986). A second episode was the debate brought on by a report that some
shopowners in Washington, D.C., were refusing to let black men into their
shops for fear of robbery or attack. No less revealing was a defense of the
shopowners on the grounds that "white assailants are rather hard to find in
urban America" (quoted in McKinney, 1986:26).

What are we to make of such accounts? One important thing to note about
them is the link they show in white *perceptions* of blacks — of black males,
especially. They tie skin color to at least the potential for criminal behavior. It
is important to emphasize here that if minority young people are disproportionately represented in the delinquent population, it is by no means the case that
most minority young people are delinquent. Indeed, many self-report figures
indicate little difference between minority youngsters and those from the white
American community (see Chapter 1). The notorious case of Bernhard Goetz,
who shot four young black men in a New York subway (see Chapter 3), exempli-
fies a presumption of black criminality based less on what black people are
really like than on powerful, racist stereotypes of blacks.

These stereotypes continue to be encouraged by the popular media. As
McKinney (1986) has noted, magazine accounts of crime and delinquency may
be framed and, especially, illustrated in ways that link crime and race. One may
see the use of such stereotypes in more subtle ways as well. In the popular movie
Outrageous Fortune (1987), one long episode is built around the encounter
between the film's two white heroines and a large black — and menacing — cab
driver. The episode works only because of white stereotypes of black Americans,
stereotypes that include perceptions of potential criminality. It is not difficult
to think of other similar examples.

We have been discussing white stereotypes of black Americans, but it should
not be thought that similar stereotypes have not been imposed on other minori-

ties, as well, including Mexican-Americans and, for much of the nineteenth and twentieth centuries, Chinese-Americans.

What is the role of such racial stereotyping in American attitudes toward delinquents and delinquency? Most obviously, the stereotypes help to encourage the harsher responses advocated by at least some white Americans toward juvenile crime. Since at least the late 1960s, when openly racist appeals began to lose the prominent place they had taken in American public life since at least the early 1800s, a rhetoric of "law and order" has often been used to cover what are essentially racist concerns. This may be the case in regard to attitudes toward delinquency as well. The "law-and-order" views of those who favor harsh treatment for juvenile offenders may be said to represent a way of expressing more deep-seated racial ideas and racial fears. This suggests that so long as racist ideas remain alive among white Americans — and there is little, at this writing, to suggest that they will not — hard attitudes toward juvenile delinquents will continue to find unspoken support from them.

Paradoxically, and parenthetically, we may note that the tie between race and delinquency also occurs, to at least some degree, in more sympathetic views of delinquents — in those which stress the character of delinquency as a kind of heroic rebellion. To be sure, this does not often include the presentation of minority delinquents as heroes — not, at least, in dominant American popular culture. But it is suggestive that many influential, youthful white rebels have combined images of delinquency with what they believe to be black cultural styles. One may easily think of Elvis Presley, from the 1950s, in these terms, or of such more recent figures in rock music as the Rolling Stones. The underlying conceptions are no less racist, for all their positive intent, and, again, help to indicate the underpinnings of widely expressed attitudes toward delinquency as such.

Individualism and Delinquency

No less important than race, however, in influencing attitudes toward delinquency is that complex set of ideas which is often labeled "American individualism." In fact, individualism itself can best be understood as a divided concept, characterized by contradiction and paradox. On the one hand, there is the individualism of what has been called the "Protestant ethic." This is an individualism that stresses hard work, personal sacrifice, and moral accountability. It has strong religious roots, growing out of that concentration on the direct relationship between the individual and God that dominated the thought of the Protestant Reformation of the 1500s and of America's English colonists. As it took more secular forms in early America, it came to place great emphasis on both economic achievement and personal virtue. But at its root has been, and remains, a belief that the ultimate responsibility for one's fate rests with the individual, and that it is the individual who must be held ultimately accountable for his or her place in the world. This individualism has informed the creation of American heroes from Benjamin Franklin to Lee Iacocca. Its corollary, in regard to crime and delinquency, is obvious. Should one turn to a life of crime, even as a youth, one must be prepared to accept blame for one's acts.

But there has also long been another strain to American individualism, a strain that might be labeled "expressive individualism." In this case, individualism is a matter of, above all, self-creation, of finding one's true self and of creating an identity out of that self. And the search for identity has often meant, as well, a need to resist the claims of others on one's definition of self. This form of individualism emerged in American culture at about the beginning of the nineteenth century and was consistent with that appreciation for human nature which, as we saw in Chapter 2, helped to produce changes in the concepts of childhood and youth. American expressive individualism has long tended toward a kind of anti-institutionalism, toward a tendency to view society and its institutions as sources for restraints against self-realization. One need only think of the recent great stress on "getting in touch with one's feelings" in the rhetoric of contemporary therapeutic movements to see an example from our own time of expressive individualism.

If the emphasis on the delinquent's accountability is part of an American individualism of personal responsibility, the view of the delinquent as hero has strong ties to expressive individualism and also has fairly deep roots. One may see these roots in, for example, the first widely noted delinquent hero, Huckleberry Finn, whose lawbreaking and whose flight from "civilization" grew out of his inability to locate an authentic self in the face of society's constraints. *Huckleberry Finn* was first published in the 1880s. It was not the first work to link delinquency with the search for self-realization, and it has not been the last. One may note, for example, the enormous popularity of Salinger's *Catcher in the Rye,* from the time of its publication in the 1950s to the present.

The above discussion suggests several things. One, again, is that American attitudes toward juvenile delinquency have to do with more than delinquency and delinquents as such, being tied to a set of attitudes that are deeply rooted and very general. Second, it suggests that contradictions in attitudes toward delinquency are part of larger contradictions in American culture. This is important, because impressions of recent events in American life indicate that, if anything, those contradictions are becoming deeper. The works of such cultural critics as Lasch (1979), Clecak (1983), and Bellah et al. (1985) point to evidence that Americans are becoming even more individualistic and that they are trying to understand more about themselves and their world within the framework of expressive individualism. Everything is understood, to put it somewhat simply, in terms of how it makes one feel about oneself. As Clecak (1983) points out, matters ranging from political action to nutrition to religious belief are approached in terms of a search for self-identity. Bellah and his colleagues (1985) show how even charitable community work is often based on motivations having to do with personal self-fulfillment. If these critics are right, then, given the bases of American attitudes toward delinquency, the future direction of those attitudes becomes a complex matter.

In point of fact, both condemnatory and sympathetic attitudes may be seen as acts of self-celebration. To the extent that we define ourselves by what we are not, the hard attitudes of those who, for example, favor capital punishment for young capital offenders become a way of celebrating their own virtue — their own moral superiority to the offender. The polls we have cited are important not only for what they allow the respondents to say about a public issue; they are significant for what they allow the respondents to say about themselves — not a matter to be dismissed lightly.

Thus, the apparently contrary attitudes we have earlier traced are becoming not so much contradictions as variants on the same general theme of self-expression and personal identity. So long as expressive individualism remains a major component of American life, it is foolish to think that one view will somehow win out over the other. Rather, one must suggest that both will remain significant, perhaps even attracting the same adherents. It is not difficult to believe, for example, that many of those who took a hard line for *Seventeen* liked Ferris Bueller, too. Thus, whatever apparent trends we may see in American attitudes toward delinquency — whether toward harsher or more sympathetic views — we should not expect any major changes in those attitudes in the foreseeable future.

Legal Perspectives ─────────────────────────────

As may be recalled from Chapters 8 and 10, the United States Supreme Court handed down a series of decisions during the period from 1966 to 1975 that had profound effects on juvenile justice. Particularly important were *In re Gault* (387 U.S. 1, 1967), *In re Winship* (397 U.S. 358, 1970), and *McKeiver v. Pennsylvania* (403 U.S. 528, 1971). The *Gault* decision changed the nature of adjudication in the juvenile court from a social welfare process to a legal process by requiring such minimum procedural safeguards as the right to counsel and the right to confront and cross-examine witnesses. In *Winship,* the Court ruled that proof of delinquency must be established "beyond a reasonable doubt" rather than by such lower standards employed in civil proceedings as "the preponderance of evidence." And in *McKeiver,* the Court ruled that a jury trial was not a constitutional requirement for juvenile proceedings. Similarly, the courts have never declared that juvenile proceedings must be open to the public, though the Sixth Amendment grants this right to adult defendants.

The significance of the U.S. Supreme Court decisions and their impact on subsequent developments have been summarized by Feld (1984:161) as follows:

> Together, *Gault, Winship,* and *McKeiver* precipitated a procedural revolution in the juvenile court system that has unintentionally but inevitably transformed its original Progressive conception. Progressive reformers envisioned the commission of an offense as essentially secondary to a determination of the "real needs" of a child — the child's social circumstances and environment. Intervention was premised on the need for rehabilitation and social uplift, not on the commission of an offense. Although *McKeiver* refused to extend the right to a jury trial to juveniles, *Gault* and *Winship* imported the adversarial model, the privilege against self-incrimination, attorneys, the criminal standard of proof, and the primacy of factual and legal guilt as a constitutional prerequisite to intervention. By emphasizing criminal procedural regularity in the determination of delinquency, the Supreme Court . . . thereby [was] effectively transforming juvenile proceedings into criminal prosecutions.

Since these decisions, the transformation of the juvenile court has continued through legislative, judicial, and administrative action. In addition to increased procedural formality, there have been major changes in other parts of the system.

Let us consider several of these major changes, both substantively and in terms of their implications for the future of juvenile justice.

Preventive Detention

Preventive detention is a form of pretrial detention where a person is kept in a locked facility because he or she is assumed to be dangerous to society if freed from custody. As discussed in Chapter 11, the U.S. Supreme Court recently held in *Schall v. Martin* (467 U.S. 253, 1984) that preventive detention was constitutionally valid for juveniles. The decision was written by Justice Rehnquist, who now is chief justice.

Martin Gregory, fourteen years of age, was arrested and charged with robbery, assault, and criminal possession of a weapon (a gun). Under a provision of New York law permitting pretrial detention if there is a serious risk that a child will commit a criminal act between arrest and the adjudicatory hearing, Martin was kept locked up. His detention lasted for a total of fifteen days, at the end of which the court found him guilty on all counts and then released him on probation, despite his alleged danger to the community. Subsequently, both a federal district court and a federal circuit court (a court of appeals) declared the New York preventive detention statute unconstitutional because the detention served as punishment without proof of guilt. The courts ordered the release of all youngsters so detained.

The Supreme Court disagreed with the lower court rulings and declared (467 U.S. at 256), "We conclude that preventive detention under the [New York Family Court Act] serves a legitimate state objective, and that the procedural protections afforded pretrial detainees by the New York statute satisfy the Due Process Clause of the Fourteenth Amendment to the United States Constitution."

According to Worrell (1985–1986:179), "The mainstay of the Court's decision in *Schall* was an argument that because most juveniles are in parental custody, and because society generally approves of this fact, preadjudicatory juveniles have less of an interest in freedom from state institutional restraint than do preadjudicatory adults." Worrell (1985–1986:179) noted that the Court explained, "if parental control falters, the State must play its part as *parens patriae.*"

The decision of the Court was severely criticized in law reviews (e.g., Feld, 1984; Worrell, 1985–1986) as well as in a dissenting opinion by Justice Marshall. These writers argued that preventive detention for juveniles denies equal protection as constitutionally required, and that it serves as punishment without adjudication. The case of Martin is a dramatic illustration of this point since he was released to the community after being found guilty upon adjudication, though he had been detained ostensibly for protection of the community. Critics also have maintained that the prediction of dangerous behavior is virtually impossible, and that detention results in stigmatization.

Both Feld (1984) and Lee (1984–1985) expect the *Schall* decision to lead to an increase in the use of detention for juveniles in coming years, a reverse in the direction generally advocated for dealing with juveniles (see Chapter 11). But perhaps more important are the implications in the decision for a return to a preference for *parens patriae* standards in the place of due process standards in judging the validity of procedures for handling youths in the juvenile justice system. Indeed, in his dissenting opinion, Justice Marshall noted that the majority decision was not in accord with the tradition established by *Gault* that freedom from physical restraint is a precious commodity that may be denied only with full constitutional protections. He argued that the whim of a judge should not be allowed to equate state custody with parental custody. Marshall argued (467 U.S. at 288): "If the 'liberty' protected by the Due Process Clause means anything, it means freedom from physical restraint."

Executing Juveniles

According to Streib (1983:613), "capital punishment of children is reemerging as an issue of great national importance, sufficient even to capture the attention of the United States Supreme Court and the American Bar Association." (See Chapter 7 for a history of this trend.) In addition to a return to reliance in the United States on capital punishment for adults, Streib attributes the reappearance to the trend to more trials for juveniles in criminal courts, either by waiver or by original jurisdiction (see the discussion of these processes in Chapter 10). He points out that of the 14,029 legal executions in American history up to 1983, 287 have been for crimes that were committed by youths below the age of eighteen. As surprising as it may seem, 192 of these uses of the death penalty took place after the inauguration of the juvenile justice system.

In the case of *Eddings v. Oklahoma* (455 U.S. 104, 1982), the U.S. Supreme Court vacated the death sentence of Monty Lee Eddings, who was sixteen when he killed a highway patrol officer. The reversal was based on a technical error in the proceedings before the trial court. It is important to note that four members of the Court (including Justice Rehnquist) stated in their dissenting opinion (455 U.S. at 128) that "the Court stops far short of suggesting that there is any constitutional proscription against imposition of the death penalty on a person under age 18 when the murder was committed." Moreover, Justice O'Connor, even though voting with the majority to reverse the sentence, presented these views:

> The Chief Justice may be correct in concluding that the Court's opinion reflects a decision by some Justices that they would not have imposed the death penalty in this case had they sat as the trial judge. . . . I, however, do not read the Court's opinion either as altering the constitutionality of the death penalty or as deciding the issue of whether the Constitution permits imposition of the death penalty on an individual who committed murder at age 16.

These comments, as well as others in the decision, led Streib (1983:634) to point out that "the Court seems poised on the brink of finding no constitutional prohibition to capital punishment for crimes committed by minors."

This view apparently is also that of lower courts because, following the *Eddings* decision, a federal court in *Prejean v. Blackburn* (570 F. Supp. 985, 1983) upheld the death penalty for a juvenile on the basis that death was a proper penalty in retribution for the severe crime he had committed. Moreover, Just (1985) has pointed out that several state courts have concluded that the Eighth Amendment's prohibition of cruel and unusual punishment does not preclude the execution of juveniles. Only one state court at the time of his survey had decided that a defendant's young age was enough of a mitigating factor to warrant commuting a death penalty to life imprisonment.

Nonetheless, some resistance to inflicting the death penalty on juveniles might be read in a mid-1987 opinion of the Arkansas state supreme court, which reversed the capital murder conviction of Ronald Ward, who, sentenced when he was fifteen years old, was believed to be the youngest inmate on death row in the United States. The reversal was based on the prosecutor's use of all of his peremptory challenges to strike black people from the jury. Ward is black; his three murder victims were white. The case was returned to the lower court for a new trial.

Restitution

According to Galaway (1979:57), "Restitution refers to a sanction imposed by an official of the criminal justice system in which an offender is required to make a service payment or a monetary payment or both to the victim of the crime, to the community, or to both." Although the notion that criminals should make payment of money or services to their victims or to relatives of the victims is an ancient one (see Laster, 1975), it has had a major reawakening in recent years as a result of several social forces centering primarily on concern for the victims of crime. This focus has been particularly strong in regard to domestically abused women and rape victims, who are supported by women's rights groups.

Beyond the emphasis on the rights of victims of criminal acts, there have been arguments that the restitution process is beneficial to the criminal, especially if it is used as part of diversion from the criminal justice system. The argument is made that most persons raised in our society inevitably feel guilt when they injure others or deprive them of something illegally. They may bluster and brag about their emotional indifference to the suffering that they have inflicted on their victims, but ordinarily they can sustain that posture only if they keep their distance from those they have injured or robbed. If they are made to confront the victim directly, to witness that person's anger, anxiety, and indignation, they will develop a more realistic assessment of the consequences of what they have done. Similarly, through restitution, they may be able to alleviate some of the sense of wrongfulness and aberrance that their behavior has created in them.

Programs based on such premises may bring together the victims and the juvenile offender to discuss a contract that will result in canceling out the offense if its terms are fulfilled. The victim could point out that an act of vandalism ruined property worth several hundred dollars and ask that the offender repay that amount. Or the victim may require transportation to the hospital or work on a house damaged by vandalism or burglary. Personalizing the crime erases one of the strongest defenses most of us have to wrongdoing, our inability to empathize fully with those who have suffered. Diversion programs can create a particularly satisfactory environment for restitutive programs because they allow monitoring of progress and can provide access to jobs or community service tasks that will allow the juvenile to work off what is negotiated as his debt to those against whom he offended.

Galaway (1977) notes that restitution undoubtedly has been used regularly, though informally, in juvenile justice since the system began. An illustration is the insistence by a police officer that a youth pay for damages done through malicious mischief to property as a condition of immediate release. The increased formal interest in restitution as a basis for concern with victims overlapped in time with the boom in juvenile diversion programs that were described in Chapter 14 and produced a synergistic effect, enhancing both of them greatly. Restitution has now become a component of the program of virtually every juvenile court, with or without formal codification in state law. Schneider et al. (1977) selected a sample from the courts on the mailing list of the National Council of Juvenile Courts and found that 109 of 114 had provisions for requiring monetary payments to victims, either directly or through court auspices.

The case of *Durst v. United States* (434 U.S. 542, 1978) illustrates the manner in which the courts have come to view restitution. The federal Youth Corrections Act of 1950 (since replaced by the Crime Control Act of 1984) allowed restitution to be imposed upon youths under the age of twenty-two. Rickey Lee Durst and another youngster were convicted of obstructing the mails, while three of their companions were convicted of stealing property worth less than $100. That the offense took place on a reservation brought it under federal jurisdiction. Attorneys for Durst argued that the $160 restitutive order, imposed on him as part of his sentence of probation, represented a fine and was inconsistent with the juvenile law. Fines, the attorneys maintained, were punitive and therefore incompatible with the rehabilitative ideal of the statute.

The Supreme Court stated flatly that Durst's argument was without merit. The Court agreed with a district court judge who had noted:

> [A] fine could be consistent . . . with the rehabilitative intent of the Act. By employing this alternative [a fine and probation], the sentencing judge could assure that the youthful offender would not receive the harsh treatment of incarceration, while assuring that the offender accepts responsibility for his transgression. The net result of such treatment would be an increased respect for the law and would, in many cases, stimulate the young person to mature into a good law-abiding citizen. *(Durst v. United States,* 434 U.S. at 548)

Restitution also is now being regarded as a useful tactic for alleviating overcrowded juvenile facilities. A *New York Times* editorial (July 7, 1987), for instance, notes that restitution was common in the Middle Ages, with the offender being ordered to do the victim's work, pay medical costs, or give the victim money. Then the state became more involved in criminal matters, and fines went to the king, not to the victim. "Yet," the editorial writer notes, "it remains a valid, even constructive way to make criminals responsible for crimes."

Skeptics have worried that difficulty might be encountered in enforcing restitution orders. In such cases, if the juvenile defaults and the judge then orders that he be placed in a secure facility, it might be argued that this move represents imprisonment for debt, an unacceptable practice. The prevailing legal argument, however, has been that the incarceration is punishment for the original offense, not for the default. In addition, it has been found that most courts report little difficulty in getting good compliance from juveniles in regard to restitution orders. The greatest compliance risk appears not to be in terms of payments being made but in getting a juvenile to obtain and hold a job in order to make monetary restitution.

Keve (1978) has noted that both affluent and indigent persons are appropriate subjects for restitutive penalties that involve them emotionally in the giving of time and effort to some restorative assistance for the victim or the community. He observes that, to be effective as a treatment, restitution should involve payments that represent an extra effort on the part of the offender, a sacrifice of time or of convenience. The restitution assignment, Keve points out, should be clearly defined, measurable, and achievable — but not too easy. The assignment should be meaningful, not just busy work or a token gesture. Finally, it is advocated that restitution assignments should be designed to produce rewards for offenders who complete them successfully. In some instances, Keve notes, juveniles have obtained work in order to meet restitutive assignments that ultimately turned into a satisfying career.

Three of the better-known juvenile restitution programs, those in Maryland, Seattle, and Las Vegas, have undergone relatively stringent evaluations (Rector, 1978). The Seattle program involves three "community accountability boards" that operate in particular sections of the city. Each board is charged with developing a restitution plan for youths. Evaluations indicate that the work of at least two of the three boards reduced juvenile recidivism in the relevant areas as compared with other parts of the city. The Seattle studies, however, were unable to distinguish the impact of restitution from the impact of other treatments received by youths in the programs.

The Maryland program involves an arbitration officer who negotiates a restitution agreement between the juvenile and the victim. Comparisons between this approach and the usual methods of handling juveniles showed no difference in recidivism. It did indicate that the victims tended to view the offender and the offender's family in a somewhat more negative perspective after the arbitration hearing, one of the possible negative outcomes of face-to-face meetings.

In Las Vegas, the evaluation concentrated on characteristics of youths most likely to make restitutive payments. It suggested that a positive self-image, parents who view the youth as essentially "good," and proper employment of the youth are the three most important factors in determining whether the young person will complete the restitution program. In Minnesota, a similar study had identified five factors important for successful restitution: older age, higher socioeconomic status, small amounts to pay, not having a probation officer as the intermediary for payment, and a payment period that corresponded to the full length of employment (Chesney, 1975).

In terms of restitution, as well as preventive detention and the use of capital punishment as a penalty for juveniles, it appears that the trend for the immediate future is for the courts to return to earlier protective doctrines under *parens patriae* and to defer to the judgments of the state legislatures. These trends reverse the intervening stress on due process for juveniles. Goetz (1985:1231–1232) has aptly summarized developments as they have unfolded before the United States Supreme Court:

the Court has not significantly increased children's rights. It has merely decided who can best control or protect the child: the parent or the state. Given the increasingly conservative tone of the decisions in the area of children's rights, the Court will likely continue to defer to the authority that can promise the best development of the child. While the concerns of the child will be recognized, the Court, in the end, will defer to the authority of either the parent or the state.

Ultimately, of course, the way that the law bearing upon juveniles develops will depend upon the balance of views in the membership of adjudicatory bodies such as the U.S. Supreme Court. That membership itself will, of course, reflect the ideology of the incumbent elected officials, as well as such fortuitous circumstances as the opportunity they have to appoint justices and to have them confirmed. It seems unlikely, at the same time, that basic changes will take place in regard to the due process requirements first imposed on the juvenile courts by the *Gault* decision.

References

Ames, W. L. 1981. *Police and Community in Japan.* Berkeley, Calif.: Univ. of California Press.

Bellah, Robert N., Madsen, Richard, Sullivan, William M., Swidler, Ann, and Tipton, Steven M. 1985. *Habits of the Heart: Individualism and Commitment in American Life.* New York: Harper.

Chesney, Steven L. 1975. The Assessment of Restitution in the Minnesota Probation Services. In *Restitution in Criminal Justice,* edited by Joe Hudson, 146–186. St. Paul: Minnesota Department of Corrections.

Children Who Kill. 1986. *Newsweek,* November 24:93–94.

Clecak, Peter. 1983. *America's Quest for the Ideal Self: Dissent and Fulfillment in the 60s and 70s.* New York: Oxford Univ. Press.

Coplon, Jeff. 1985. Young, Bad, and Dangerous. *Ladies' Home Journal* 102, no. 8 (August):165–168.

Death Penalty for Teens. 1987. *Seventeen* (January), 86.

Feld, Barry C. 1984. Criminalizing Juvenile Justice: Rules of Procedure for the Juvenile Court. *Minnesota Law Review* 69:141–276.

Franklin, Jon. 1987. *Molecules of the Mind: The Brave New Science of Molecular Psychology.* New York: Atheneum.

Galaway, Burt. 1977. The Use of Restitution. *Crime & Delinquency* 23:57–67.

———. 1979. Differences in Victim Compensation and Restitution. *Social Work* (January), 57–58.

Goetz, John D. 1985. Children's Rights Under the Burger Court: Concerns for the Child but Deference to Authority. *Notre Dame Law Review* 60:1214–1232.

Jacobs, Barry. 1987. Love as a Neurotransmission. *New York Times Book Review* (February 8), 15.

Just, Rona L. 1985. Executing Youthful Offenders: The Unanswered Question in *Eddings v. Oklahoma. Fordham Urban Law Journal* 13:471–510.

Keve, Paul. 1978. Therapeutic Uses of Restitution. In *Offender Restitution in Theory and Practice,* edited by Burt Galaway and Joe Hudson, 59–64. Lexington, Mass.: Lexington Books.

Kid Killers. 1986. *Time* (December 22), 33.

Kids Who Kill. 1985. *Newsweek* (December 2), 55.

Lasch, Christopher. 1979. *The Culture of Narcissism: American Life in an Age of Diminishing Expectations.* New York: Warner.

Laster, Richard E. 1975. Criminal Restitution: A Survey of Its Past History and an Analysis of Its Present Usefulness. In *Considering the Victim: Readings in Restitution and Victim Compensation,* edited by Joe Hudson and Burt Galaway, 311–331. Springfield, Ill.: Thomas.

Lee, Deborah A. 1984–1985. The Constitutionality of Juvenile Preventive Detention: *Schall v. Martin*—Who Is Preventive Detention Protecting? *New England Law Review* 20:341–374.

McKinney, Gwen. 1986. Post Under Protest. *Black Enterprise* 17, no. 1 (December):26.

Precourt, Walter E. 1979. Ideological Bias: A Data Quality Control Factor for Cross-Cultural Research. *Behavioral Science Research* 14:115–131.

Rector, John M. 1978. *Restitution by Juvenile Offenders: An Alternative to Incarceration.* Washington, D.C.: Law Enforcement Assistance Administration, U.S. Department of Justice.

Rosch, Eleanor. 1975. Universals and Culture Specifics in Human Categorization. In *Cross-Cultural Perspectives on Learning,* edited by R. W. Brislin, S. Bochner, and W. J. Lonner, 177–206. New York: Sage.

Schneider, Peter R., Schneider, Anne L., Reiter, Paul D., and Cleary, Colleen M. 1977. *Restitution Requirements for Juvenile Offenders: A Survey of the Practices in American Juvenile Courts.* Eugene, Ore.: Institute of Policy Analysis.

Streib, Victor L. 1983. Death Penalty for Children: The American Experience with Capital Punishment for Crimes Committed While Under Age Eighteen. *Oklahoma Law Review* 36:613–641.

This Is What You Thought. 1986. *Glamour* (August), 23.

U.S. Bureau of the Census. 1986. *World Population Profile, 1985.* Washington, D.C.: U.S. Government Printing Office.

Worrell, Claudia. 1985–1986. Pretrial Detention of Juveniles: Denial of Equal Protection Masked by the *Parens Patriae* Doctrine. *Yale Law Journal* 95:174–193.

Author Index

Subject Index